After the Globe, Before the World

This book explores the implications of claims that the most challenging political problems of our time express an urgent need to reimagine where, and therefore what, we take politics to be. It does so by examining the relationship between modern forms of politics (centred simultaneously within individual subjects, sovereign states and an international system of states) and the (natural, God-given or premodern) world that has been excluded in order to construct modern forms of political subjectivity and sovereign authority.

It argues that the ever-present possibility of a world outside the international both sustains the structuring of relations between inclusion and exclusion within the modern internationalized political order, and generates desires for escape from this order to a politics encompassing a singular humanity, cosmopolis, globe or planet that are doomed to disappointment. On this basis, the book develops a critique of prevailing traditions of both political theory and theories of international relations. It especially examines what it might now mean to think about sovereignties, subjectivities, boundaries, borders and limits without automatically reproducing forms of inclusion and exclusion, or universality and particularity, expressed in the converging but ultimately contradictory relationship between international relations and world politics.

R.B.J. Walker is Professor of Political Science and Director of the Program in Cultural, Social and Political Thought at the University of Victoria, Canada. He is the author or editor of nine previous books and editor of the journals *Alternatives: Global, Local, Political* and *International Political Sociology*.

GLOBAL HORIZONS

Series Editors

Richard Falk, Princeton University, USA and R.B.J. Walker, University of Victoria, Canada

We live in a moment that urgently calls for a reframing, reconceptualizing, and reconstituting of the political, cultural and social practices that underpin the enterprises of international relations.

While contemporary developments in international relations are focused upon highly detailed and technical matters, they also demand an engagement with the broader questions of history, ethics, culture and human subjectivity.

GLOBAL HORIZONS is dedicated to examining these broader questions.

After the Globe, Before the World

R.B.J. Walker

Routledge
Taylor & Francis Group

LONDON AND NEW YORK

First published 2010
by Routledge
2 Park Square, Milton Park, Abingdon, Oxon, OX14 4RN

Simultaneously published in the USA and Canada
by Routledge
270 Madison Avenue, New York, NY 10016

Routledge is an imprint of the Taylor & Francis Group, an informa business

Typeset in Times New Roman by
Taylor & Francis Books
Printed and bound in Great Britain by
CPI Antony Rowe, Chippenham, Wiltshire

British Library Cataloguing in Publication Data
A catalogue record for this book is available from the British Library

Library of Congress Cataloging in Publication Data
Walker, R. B. J.
After the globe, before the world / R.B.J. Walker.
   p. cm. – (Global horizons)
Includes bibliographical references.
 1. International relations–Philosophy. I. Title.
JZ1305.W355 2009
327.101–dc22
                                        2009009372

ISBN10: 0-415-77902-2 (hbk)
ISBN10: 0-415-77903-0 (pbk)
ISBN10: 0-203-87124-3 (ebk)

ISBN13: 978-0-415-77902-9 (hbk)
ISBN13: 978-0-415-77903-6 (pbk)
ISBN13: 978-0-203-87124-9 (ebk)

Contents

Acknowledgements

It has taken a long time for me to be able to feel comfortable both with the orchestration of the many variations that are at play within the primary argument I try to set out in this book as well as with the purchase of the basic argument on the evidence about historical and structural dynamics that I have come to judge, rightly or wrongly, as most pressing. In the process, I have been privileged not only to have discussed many of my concerns with a lot of brilliant scholars, but also to have been able to work on, teach or present aspects of the analysis in many different institutions in different parts of "the world." I am especially indebted to the people who have been so hospitable in the Australian National University, the University of Jyväskylä, University of Tromso, Pontifica Universidade Catolica do Rio de Janeiro, Centre for the Study of Developing Societies, Delhi, Centre d'etudes et de recherches inter- nationales, Paris and Keele University. At the University of Victoria, I have been fortunate to have worked with one of the best political theory commu- nities to be found anywhere, and not least with a steady stream of graduate students who have established themselves as innovative scholars across diverse fields of research.

I have tried to acknowledge in the text itself many of the sources that have shaped my substantive argument. Many other people have been subjected to specific parts of the text as I made adjustments, erased details, curtailed detours and attempted to preserve some semblance of theoretical coherence without assuming much familiarity on the part of my audience with the spe- cific and often arcane languages so many theorists now use in order to resist falling back on the discursive routines they seek to challenge. The most important thing I have learnt in the process is that it is often both very difficult and very important to say things that are perfectly obvious.

For specific interventions, sometimes long and detailed, sometimes short and sharp, I am especially indebted to Jens Bartelson, Jen Bagelman, Didier Bigo, Philippe Bonditti, Evelyn Cobley, Costas Constantinou, Simon Dalby, Costas Douzinas, Mark Franke, Kevin Frost, Bulent Gokay, Elspeth Guild, Sakari Hänninen, David Held, Cristine Helliwell, Barry Hindess, John Horton, Jef Huysmans, Vivienne Jabri, Russell Kerr, Maria Koblanck, Friedrich Kra- tochwil, Sankaran Krishna, Arthur Kroker, Hans Lindahl, Andrew Linklater,

Warren Magnusson, Nizar Messari, Andrew Neal, Joao Nogueira, Nick Onuf, Anne Orford, Kari Palonen, Noel Parker, Mustapha Pasha, Raia Prokhovnik, Mark Salter, Michael Shapiro, Sabina Singh, Angharad Closs Stephens, hidemi Suganami, Delacey Tedesco, Anastasia Tsoukala, Jim Tully and Haipeng Zhou. None of these, of course, should be blamed for the many times I have chosen to ignore their very good advice.

My greatest debts, however, are to those who have shaped and stretched the daily life of my own imagination: to Kara Shaw; and to my children Johanna, Caitlin and Rhys.

1   Prelude

In this book, I seek to resist the effects of a rich and diverse array of discourses expressing claims about a need for, and evidence of, an historical and structural transformation from forms of political life articulated through the presumed authority of the modern sovereign state and the system of such states to something more universal: claims, most specifically, about the need to move *from* a politics of "the international" *to* a politics of "the world." I do so because I see scarcely any chance of thinking more imaginatively about our future political possibilities as long as these discourses continue to sustain desires for other ways of acting politically while simultaneously insisting that these other possibilities are entirely impossible, in principle as well as in practice.

It is not that I am unimpressed by various empirical claims about historical trends and structural transformations, or even by some of the visionary aspirations that are said to warrant such a move. I am nevertheless sceptical about widespread attempts to force evidence about and ambitions for historical and structural change into this particular account of what it *must* mean to make claims about a beginning, an ending and an intervening spatio-temporal trajectory. I am especially suspicious of the routines through which the terms "international politics" and "world politics" are assumed to be either interchangable or diametrically opposed – to be *either* synonyms *or* antonyms – in ways that mobilize both affirmations and denials of a specific philosophy of history, specific accounts of the necessary relation between spatiality and temporality, and specific accounts of where and what political life must be and who it must be for.

The book is thus constructed as an exploration of what it means to distinguish between an international politics and a politics of the world and, once this distinction is enacted as an array of constitutive contradictions, to frame claims about political possibilities and impossibilities – about freedoms, necessities, equalities, securities and sovereign authorities – that work by mobilizing accounts of political temporality promising to take us from one form of politics to the other while insisting, for very good reasons, that the promise can never be kept; while insisting, that is, that modern political life must be sustained within very precise spatiotemporal limits that are never only internal, never enacted only within the practices of modern subjectivity. In my view, it has become much too easy to assume that the distinction between a politics of the international and a presumed politics of the world (a distinction that I take to be a necessary, even if insufficient, condition of the possibility of specifically modern forms of political life articulated through relations and antagonisms between individualized subjects, sovereign states and a system of sovereign states) can be superseded, transcended or erased by imagining some sort of move from the one to the other.

A move from one political condition to another is now very easily envisaged as a journey from one space to another, one time to another, or perhaps even one spatiotemporality to another. This way of thinking about political possibilities may seem entirely straightforward, so to speak, even scarcely worth thinking about. Nevertheless, it is only possible to imagine this particular journey if we systematically refuse to think about what is at stake in the initial distinction, as well as in the metaphors of travel this distinction has enabled. For there is no doubt that both the distinction and the metaphors are far more troublesome than they usually appear; and quite obviously so to anyone attuned to the multiple conflicts over basic principles attending the articulation of modern forms of political life grounded in claims about liberty, equality, security and the bounded authority of territorialized sovereign jurisdictions. At some point, literally, the envisaged journey from an international politics to a world politics must cut, or must fail to cut, across the distinction between one condition and the other. Boundaries must loom ominously. Sites, moments and practices of contradiction must be politicized and/or depoliticized.

This is not to say anything that has not been known to many traditions of critical political analysis for several centuries, not least because what we now think of as critical analysis was partly generated by seventeenth- and eighteenth-century European reflections about various manifestations of this problem, usually in relation to distinctions between secular and sacred, immanence and transcendence, or the finitude of human existence and some infinite world beyond. Familiarity in some quarters, however, has done little to constrain the popularity of discourses promising to solve the problems of modern political life through a shift from an international politics to a world politics, nor to inhibit the conscription of various forms of critical analysis into the ranks of those recommending such a shift. In my judgement, and despite their influence on many impressive scholarly traditions, the effects of the point, or moment, of intersection between a seemingly benign conceptual distinction and a proposed temporal trajectory cutting across this distinction, along with the vast topological field of political possibilities and impossibilities that it both expresses and enables, demands intensive and urgent scrutiny.

My overall argument, to put it briefly, is that anyone seeking to reimagine the possibilities of political life under contemporary conditions would be wise to resist ambitions expressed as a move from a politics of the international to a politics of the world, and to pay far greater attention to what goes on at the boundaries, borders and limits of a politics orchestrated *within* the international that simultaneously imagines the possibility and impossibility of a move *across* the boundaries, borders and limits distinguishing itself from some world beyond. The point, that is to say, is precisely the point, together with the lines which flow from it in order both to discriminate and to connect: to include, to exclude, to both include and exclude so as to constitute a complex array of inclusions and exclusions, and to affirm both the possibility and the impossibility of some world beyond this array of inclusions and exclusions.

I cannot pretend that this will be an easy argument to make; on the contrary. It will require resistence not only to the currently popular but (as I will argue) conceptually fragile literatures that remain content to keep directing us down the road to some future politics of the world, but also to various literatures that may be fully aware that pervasive metaphors of travel from one spatiotemporality to another work to keep us where we are and what we are supposed to be, but nevertheless underestimate the importance of thinking about the ins and outs of a politics orchestrated within and beyond the spatiotemporal boundaries of an international order. In both contexts, I will insist that the boundaries of a politics of the international are at least as complex as the boundaries of a politics preoccupied with either individual subjects or sovereign states, and that it is to the boundaries of the politics of the international that we should look in order to understand the conditions under which modern claims to sovereignty and subjectivity have been sustained, and under which conditions these claims might be rearticulated.

While the argument will run in many different directions so as to break open patterns of analysis that have congealed into narratives about a move from an international politics to a politics of the world, it is one that I believe captures a broad consensus among many currents of critical scholarship concerned not only with claims about daunting transformations in political life, but also with the interplay between the limits of our capacity to understand these transformations and our understanding of what it means to be political within and between certain kinds of limits, borders and other sorts of boundary practices. With the partial but telling exception of some literatures about political economies, political ecologies, postcolonial situations, urbanizations, and so on, most of these traditions tend to frame their analyses in relation to practices of statehood or individual subjectivity rather than of the modern system of states. In my view, this is a profound mistake, even though I understand well enough why many scholars might be reluctant to engage with the literatures about the modern system of states that have emerged since the mid-twentieth century within the specific Anglo-American disciplines of political science and international relations. The boundaries, borders and limits expressed in the distinction between a politics of the international and a politics of the world – in the line transected by a line of temporal possibility and impossibility – suggests that we might want to be much less sanguine about our capacity to understand the workings of the boundaries, borders and limits of contemporary political life anywhere, but especially in relation to what we call the international, to what we might want to call the world, and to the collective voices that presume to speak about a politics of the international, a politics of the world, or a politics of states and subjects that simply assumes, without ever thinking about, a constitutive antagonism between a modern system of states and some other world beyond.

The broad array of discourses that concern me here rest, in part, on the assumption that a politics of the international generates problems resulting from patterns of particularism, pluralism and fragmentation (usually expressed through references to state sovereignty, nationalism and systemic anarchy) that must be solved by substituting patterns of commonality and universality (usually expressed in claims about humanity, reason, the planet or even the cosmos). Ultimate causalities might be identified in relation to other (usually "economic" or "social") forces, but unless politics is simply reduced to such forces, their crucial political expression is usually identified as a lack of unity and a consequent surfeit of conflict and violence; although it is difficult to avoid some residual sense that an order characterized by disunity somehow manages to hang together as a system, as a structure, as a process or even as just an ever-present possibility of war. These discourses also rest, and more profoundly, on the assumption that the kinds of commonalities and universalities that can be imagined as solutions to problems generated by the politics of the international must eventually add up to a politics of the world as such.

For all their popularity, both assumptions are impossible to sustain. The politics of the international already express an extensive and powerful account of the proper relationship *between* a particular form of particularism/ pluralism in the sovereign nation-state and a particular form of commonality/ universality in the international system of sovereign nation-states. Consequently, problems arising from a politics of the international cannot be attributed to particularism or to pluralism alone. Moreover, the historical construction of a relationship between sovereign nation-states and an international system of such states rests quite famously on the rift between the political world of modern "man" and any other world as such, so that any attempt to speak about a politics of the world necessarily confronts both the achievements and limits of specifically modern forms of subjectivity and all the ontological, epistemological and axiological difficulties they imply; and they certainly imply a very impressive range of difficulties. Thus in the first place, claims about a move away from the politics of the international tend to counterpose principles of particularism/pluralism and universality/commonality that are already expressed as a complementary and mutually productive but also antagonistic relationship; and in the second place they tend to presume that all the standard problems that have characterized the modern ambition for distanciation from an objective world beyond itself can be overcome through an idealization of the world that must be the principled objective of our political ambitions.

What I want to do in this book, then, is to understand, in order to resist, some of the practices through which narratives about the need to move from a politics of the international to a politics of the world have come to have such widespread resonance, even though they are so fundamentally at odds with our received understandings of a form of political life constituted through relations and antagonisms between claims to particularity/plurality and claims to commonality/universality: understandings that have been shaped especially by prior accounts of the early-modern European rupture between man and world, man and God, and modern man from any other kind of man. Modern political life already affirms powerful assumptions about what it *must* mean to move beyond or to articulate claims about possibilities and impossibilities within. These assumptions might be traced, among many vast fields of scholarly speculation, to the canonical thinkers of classical Greece, to Christian accounts of time and eternity or immanence and transcendence, or, my preference here, to the convergence of both Greek and Christian inheritances with the geometries and topologies animating early-modern European attempts to articulate principles of sovereign authorization and its spatiotemporal delimitation. Whatever nuances might be read into competing historical resources in this respect, claims about historical and structural transformation are always in danger of endlessly reproducing very specific accounts of space, time and authority that are already at work in the politics of the international, even while affirming transformations promising to leave the international somewhere behind.

To put it succinctly, but also to draw attention both to the difficulties of succinct formulation and to the way I will keep circling back to some persistent themes in what follows, there can be no simple beginning, middle or end to an analysis that seeks to engage with this particular account of beginnings, endings and a normalized but always problematic middle ground inscribed somewhere in between. This is so whether the middle ground between beginnings and endings is understood as a territorialized space marked by clear geographical borders, by an historicized time marking a linear trajectory into a promising but impossible future, or as a sharp and intensely over-coded boundary marking the point at which promise and ambition meet claims of impossibility and limitation: the point at which the ambition to escape from a condition of linear extensions and projections must return to the original condition of beginning, end and middle. As I will keep insisting in various contexts, there can be no simple move beyond a structuring of here and beyond, no easy alternative to what is already constructed as a politics of similarities and alternatives, nor, to invoke the language that has recently marked the welcome return of sustained though still constrained analyses of claims about state sovereignty, no obvious exception to a politics organized as a contradictory structuring of norms and exceptions.

The possibility of sustaining more imaginative accounts of any future political possibilities, of who might be able to create them, and of the conditions under which they might be created rests very largely, I will argue, on much greater scepticism towards the accounts of beginnings, endings and spatio-temporal trajectories expressed in prevailing narratives about a move from a politics of the international to a politics of the world. If alternatives to a politics of the international are to be identified or desired (and I am prepared to admit that this may be a very big conditionality in both cases), then they will have to be understood as alternatives to all those claims about what alternatives *must* be that are generated and reproduced in a politics of the modern international. A range of quite daunting questions is at stake in this respect: questions about what it means to make claims about the world; questions about the spatiotemporalities that are presumed to be somehow both within and in motion towards that world; and questions about the conceptions of authority that are at work in distinctions between the international and the world, in demands for a move from one to the other, and in prevailing assumptions about what it means to say anything intelligible at all about the world or the spatiotemporal articulations of political life within it.

Even from this brief formulation, it should be clear that much depends on how it has become possible to draw the lines of discrimination marking boundaries, borders and limits, in time quite as much as in space, and on how we have been encouraged to think about boundaries, borders and limits as if they were indeed just simple lines distinguishing here from there, now from then, normal from exceptional, possible from impossible or intelligible from unintelligible. The journey that is proposed as a move from a politics of the international to a politics of the world may be easily understandable as a simple line drawn from one condition to another, but this line especially, with its capacity to mobilize claims about spatiotemporalities that must be at work in contemporary political life, ought to make us think much more carefully about how complex practices of drawing lines have come to be treated as such a simple matter.

Indeed, one of the two sustained predictions that I venture in this book is that the character and quality of any novel form of political life, and the credibility of scholarly attempts to evaluate such novelty, will depend on the degree to which boundaries, borders and limits are understood as complex sites and moments of political engagement rather than as lines that merely distinguish one form of politics here or now, and another form of politics there or then. Many readers may think that this is an easy prediction to make, especially given the recent proliferation of literatures on boundaries, borders and limits. I would certainly agree. Even so, in the present analysis I am less concerned to show how this particular prediction might be sustained than to explore the consequences of thinking that our political futures do indeed rest less on either what we have come to experience as the politics of the international or on what some have promised as a politics of the world, than on an increasingly complex politicization, depoliticization and thus politicization of boundaries, borders and limits, not least those distinguishing a politics of the international and a politics that somehow exceeds the international.

Consequently, while I am sometimes drawn to some of their superficial attractions, the underlying force of my analysis is directed primarily against a broad range of attempts to articulate forms of political aspiration that are assumed to be more "ethical" or "emancipatory" on the grounds that they claim to be able speak a language of greater universality, and thus to be more open to the world: on the grounds, that is, that they are able to take us across the line that both enables what we have become as modern subjects, as citizens of sovereign states, and as participants in the politics of the international but which also defines an impossible aspiration for what we might become in some other framing of what it means to engage in a world that is somehow political. It would be much more productive, I want to suggest, to think more carefully about that line, about the way particular accounts of drawing that line work to shape where, when and what we think we are and might yet be, and about how we might yet be able to enact and respond to the drawing of lines in some other way.

I take much of my inspiration for this analysis from a wide variety of research projects in which I have participated with many different people over a considerable period: projects on orientalist practices in internationalist readings of "culture," on the co-constitutive relationship between concepts of space and epistemological dualism in early-modern science, on the rearticulations of concepts of temporal contingency from Machiavelli to Hegel, on various kinds of social movement seeking to reshape our understandings of local and global, on the ontological assumptions expressed in various claims about "the political," on experiences of Partition in South Asia, on convergences between international and postcolonial theorizations of the co-optation of dissent, and on changing relations between liberty and security in Europe after declarations of a supposed war on terror, among others. However, I have tried to abstract these particular sources of inspiration into a general form that might have broader application in judgements about political principles, even at the cost of seeming to be remote from any specific situations.

I have also taken inspiration from the writings of two exemplary early-modern European thinkers, Thomas Hobbes and Immanuel Kant. I do so in ways that are at considerable odds with the appropriation of these two figures in many claims about both a politics of the international and a politics of the world, and in a way that expresses both some annoyance at the continuing capacity of these thinkers to define the possibilities, limits and spatiotemporal topologies of our contemporary political imagination, but also some admiration for their capacity to undermine the canonical accounts of political possibility and impossibility in which they have been enshrined. To the extent that I draw on more contemporary writers, and especially on various historians of scientific reason, the early work of Michel Foucault, and many different people writing about postcolonial situations and the genealogies and topologies of modernity, it is less because they have somehow moved beyond (to some condition of some postmodernity, for example, as the kind of popularization that induces trivialization has sought to suggest) than because they have worked so hard to increase our awareness of how the modern world came to be shaped through multiple desires to move beyond predicated upon claims about a prior movement beyond whatever had supposedly come before. Whether understood as the rift between natural time and human time, the time of modern history and the times of "peoples without history," or the condition of mere time and the condition of some transcendental eternity, problems arising from the spatial arrangements of the politics of the international cannot be understood without a much more serious engagement with the politics of spatiotemporality through which figures like Hobbes and Kant participated in ruthless authorizations of inclusions and exclusions enabling modern forms of politics orchestrated as a multidimensional structuring of inclusions and exclusions; or with the degree to which they understood the tenuous authority on which these authorizations were enacted.

Where we are generally encouraged to assume that the most important lines of demarcation and conflict in modern political life are those inscribed spatially between the territorial jurisdictions of sovereign states in a system of such states, I will suggest that these depend on and continue to affirm an array of prior temporal discriminations that already define a ground for spatial discriminations; and I use the productive ambivalence expressed by the word "discrimination" to try to introduce what is at stake in a broad array of contemporary literatures about what it means to draw the line in order to constitute boundaries, borders and limits, both temporally and spatially. Again to resort to the deceptively succinct, any attempt to imagine some form of political life that might offer a desirable alternative to the politics of the international will have to pay attention less to the lines of discrimination demarcating jurisdictions on a spatialized geopolitical terrain than to lines of discrimination expressing a specific philosophy of time and historicity distinguishing the world of the modern international from any other world while simultaneously encouraging visions of escape into a politics of the world. Or, a little more bluntly, given that the politics of the international affirms an account of a political temporality before it expresses an account of political spatiality (an account of a political temporality that is nevertheless produced through assumptions about the achievements of a political spatiality in ways that find exemplary expressions in Hobbes' account of a social contract and Kant's gamble on the potential maturity of modern man), no useful attempt to imagine alternatives to a politics of the international can afford to embark on a quest for future possibilities without some understanding of the relationship between the narratives of origin enabling a politics of the international and the narratives of an escape from a politics of the international that would have us heading back to the world that modernity is so proud of having left behind.

It is certainly no accident, I suggest, that one of the most pervasive moves in contemporary political analysis involves an almost automatic resort to the terminology of "levels" arrayed on a scale of higher and lower: a terminology that affirms much of what we call common sense yet is uncannily reminiscent of the hierarchical world of the "great chain of being" against which modern forms of political life struggled so hard in order to affirm the possibilities and limits of modern freedoms, equalities, securities, and especially the forms of sovereign authorization expressed by the modern state. For all its attractions, the uncritical resort to this terminology, not least as the most pervasive way of organizing the analysis of international relations as an Anglo-American academic discipline since the mid-twentieth century, must be understood as a symptom of, and not a solution to, a much more profound set of problems arising from claims about the possibilities of modern sovereignties and subjectivities and the limits these must generate – as Kant especially already understood much more clearly than many of his contemporary followers.

Claims about the need for a move from an international politics to a world politics will be familiar, to the point of cliché, to anyone who has engaged with literatures on globalization, modernization, cosmopolitanism, human rights, humanitarian intervention, new forms of empire, a generalized exceptionalism, a planetary ecology, global governance, and other similar themes. The specificities invoked by such claims vary enormously, both in empirical content and in normative ambition. The general sense of the direction of political change, by contrast, is broadly shared. There are many disagreements about whether such a move is in progress or not, as well as about whether this version of progression, or simply Progress, is in fact possible or not, or desirable or not. These are nevertheless disagreements that invite assignments of a yes or a no to a reading of historical possibility that is firmly entrenched in the contemporary political imagination as a primary ground on which we might be positive or negative, progressive or reactionary, open to alternatives or locked into the necessities and ambitions of a fragmented but structurally determined array of sovereign states.

Various readers of this book will be attuned to different problems, literatures and scholarly traditions, but will no doubt be familiar enough with the highly generalized formal patterns I seek to engage here, and with their capacity to shape debate about what is most important and what is of only minor significance in thinking about the political opportunities before us, as well as about who these opportunities might be for. I have tried to construct my analysis of the effects of claims about such a move in a way that speaks to a diverse array of intellectual traditions while focusing most intently on those sites, moments and practices through which the confrontation between claims about historical change and claims about the structural continuities of a modern system of sovereign states has been prone to the sharpest affirmations of a yes or a no. I have especially tried to write in a way that focuses attention on what is at stake in claims about the place and time of the politics of the international in relation to claims about a potential politics of the world, but without buying into the presumption that the specific academic discipline of international relations has some privileged status in telling us what these stakes may be. As in many other cases, this is a discipline that works as an expression of a broader problem (and as a still useful source of leverage against even more parochial forms of political analysis) but which remains ill-prepared to think about its own relation to that problem.

Whatever one makes of the foibles of this specific discipline, of its framing as a field of "political science," or its obvious ties to the concerns of a small handful of influential states, problems posed by the structuring of modern political life within an international system (or as I prefer – so as to avoid the easy conflation of state and nation – within a modern system of states) are crucial. All too many attempts to think about future political possibilities remain preoccupied either with sovereign states that are presumed to be isolated from other states or with modern individual subjects caught between desires for autonomy and desires for collectivity; these more or less exhaust the ambitions of contemporary liberal political theory, for example, ambitions that I take to be in rather urgent need of sustained disruption. Other categories might be invoked also, not least those of class, race and gender; and other disciplines may offer opportunities for getting at some of my concerns in related ways, perhaps anthropology, political economy, political sociology, geography and postcolonial studies most especially. Nevertheless, it is in relation to claims about an international that both enable and delimit what it has come to mean to engage in specifically political forms of analysis that it has become most obvious that any claim to a politics of the world must clash with claims to universality arising from one specific set of claims about what that world is, how it is to be known, and how human beings ought to act within it.

Moreover, as a structure of inclusions and exclusions, the modern international must itself have a constitutive outside; much like the modern subject and the sovereign state. It is, of course, "the world" that must be identified somewhere and sometime beyond this politics of the modern international, even though some very specific even if massively influential versions of this world have also been brought into the politics of the modern international, in ways that must make any claim that we need to think about a move from the politics of the international to a politics of the world seem very puzzling indeed.

This relationship between the modern system of states and the world drives both the substance and the form of my analysis. In some respects, it may seem utterly absurd or at least practically irrelevant to speak about anything being outside the modern system of states. In other respects, it may be perfectly obvious that much of contemporary political life exceeds the bounds of this particular framing of where and what political life *must* be. The interplay of the absurd and the obvious marking a line of identity and difference between a politics of the international and a politics of the world, I will suggest, offers at least a modest purchase on what needs to be engaged in narratives about what it must mean to move beyond, or to be able to identify alternatives, or to claim ownership of the lights showing the way to a brighter future simply by moving from the one to the other. As the line between the politics of the international and the politics of the world appears to be more obviously complex, the line promising to take us from one to the other will become more obviously troubling, despite its extensive grip on the contemporary political imagination; or at least on the political imagination that continues to believe that the interplay of a politics of the international and a politics of the world understood as either synonym or antonym affirms its own claim to universality, and continuing legitimacy.

I am not among those who believe that the modern sovereign state acting in a world of international relations remains the best or even the least worst option before us, but nothing I say will suggest that states are insignificant or incapable of important achievements, despite the lamentable effects of neoliberal celebrations of unbridled market rationality over the past few decades. In this context, I think the most challenging questions before us concern the changing relationship between the practices of states and both the practices and problem of sovereignty. The experiences of the sovereign state do not exhaust our historical experiences of the practices of sovereignty, and I suspect that they will not exhaust our experiences of sovereignty in the future. At the same time, I am also strongly persuaded by a variety of claims about, at a minimum, the need for some understanding of ourselves as living within a singular biosphere on a fragile planet subject to intensifying and often vicious forms of capitalist modernization. I am well aware of the persuasive force of many claims about "our" commonalities, "our" shared vulnerabilities and "our" collective capacities. Nevertheless, I am entirely unpersuaded that the grand discourses about historical time, territorial space or political authority that are at work in the metaphor of a journey from international relations to world politics help us either to understand the dynamics that are widely understood as putting into question both the sovereign state and the structure of a system of sovereign states that both enables and is enabled by the sovereign state, or to think very creatively about forms of political life (and thus capacities to identify some other understandings of who "we" are as political agents) that are being shaped by these dynamics.

To counter the effects of the clichés about historical time, territorial space and political authority that are packed into the apparently benign and intensely seductive promise of a move from international relations to world politics, I seek to encourage greater attention to boundaries, borders and limits as complex sites, moments and practices of political engagement. The claim that we need to pay greater attention to boundaries has itself become a cliché across many scholarly disciplines. It is nevertheless one that offers far more opportunities for thinking about the political possibilities before us than the overwhelming array of narratives that would have us shifting across boundaries, borders and limits distinguishing an international from a world politics without seriously engaging with what it means to articulate, or cross, a boundary, border or limit, or even to draw a line. I especially want to explore what it might mean to take a broad range of analyses of boundaries, borders and limits as important contributions to a political, rather than, say, a legal, sociological, cultural, ethical, geographical or technological project.

All the clichés I engage here express powerful historical achievements, and claims that work both as principle and practice. They find expression in

popular culture, legitimations of public policy and specific strategies of scholarly enquiry, especially among those who fancy themselves to be unconcerned
with theories or abstract principles. They speak to the way we have come to
imagine the possibilities and impossibilities of liberty and equality within and
under necessity; and to the way we are encouraged to think about some other
possibilities in relation to some other necessities. They find expression in
everyday conversations among people with no formal training in conceptual
or political analysis and in the most esoteric conversations among people who
think long and hard about ontologies, epistemologies, axiologies and authorizations of political authority; which is why I try to avoid formulating often
difficult questions of principle in specific technical philosophical languages
while also insisting on the constitutive force of questions about principle in
people's daily lives.

For all their potential complexity, these clichés find expression in what can
seem to be a simple practice of drawing a line: of drawing a line marking a
journey from here to there or from past to future, of drawing a line at the
boundary of political jurisdictions, and of drawing the lines originating and
ending at the points at which lines must intersect, in space and time. Whatever else may be said about the possibilities of other ways of thinking about
future political possibilities, there can be no other such possibilities without
attending to the multiple ways in which the drawing of lines as boundaries,
borders and limits has long been a more complicated and contested affair
than we might imagine from the categories and theoretical controversies
sustaining so much contemporary political analysis.

One of the difficulties of writing about this kind of material is that so much
of the existing literature is concerned with an entirely false problem: that of
escaping from the dreaded claim to "political realism" that is so pervasive
both in the construction of Anglo-American accounts of international relations and in popular understandings of what it means to engage in political
life. As I have argued extensively elsewhere and will continue to insist here,
the (multiple and contradictory) claim to political realism is a consequence of
a prior set of idealizations, not least of the sovereign nation-state and of its
necessary relation both to the system of states and to the world. Setting up a
discipline of international relations on the assumption that political realism
has the status of the dominant intellectual tradition has encouraged claims
that we need to contemplate idealizations that might allow us to get away
from political realism; hence the famous opposition between realism and
various forms of utopianism in the Cold War era and the elaboration of various appeals to cosmopolitanism more recently. Again the dead-end signs are
clearly in view right next to the starting line. What must be put first, in my
view, are the idealizations and substantivizations (especially of sovereignty,
state, nation, subjectivity, history, reason, territory, law, liberty, equality,
security, *polis* and cosmos) that have already come to be treated as real, as the
necessary starting point for analysis, and as the normative ground on which
to think about the legitimation of violence at the boundaries, borders and

limits of modern political life, thereby encouraging further idealizations that can work only to legitimize a prior array of reified ideals.

One of the more profound effects of treating claims about political realism as a starting point for analysis has been a tendency to treat "ethics" as the appropriate ground on which to initiate the contemplation of future possibilities, a move that has all too often worked as a sustained evasion of what I take to be more explicitly political questions about the authorization of what ought to be considered to be ethical, or the point at which claims to ethical possibility must come to an end: at which exceptions must be made, and made legitimately. Between them, claims about political realism and supposedly more progressive claims about ethics have commandeered most of the discursive opportunities available for engaging with claims about a politics of the international or a politics of the world, often aided and abetted by disturbingly doctrinaire claims about methodological necessities that express little understanding of either the contested character of epistemological virtue or its complex relations with prior ontological and political commitments.

It is not that there is nothing to commend among at least some of the literatures claiming to be either politically realistic or ethically inspirational, especially those that find some way of refusing the overdetermining rhetorics counterposing the realistic to the normative. Nevertheless, both sorts of literatures have a bad habit of ignoring or crudely oversimplifying questions about what it means to claim political authority, and more specifically, what it means to make a claim to the forms of authority expressed by the modern sovereign state, and to knowledge about the forms of authority expressed by the modern sovereign state. Various traditions of political realism are right to emphasize the importance of state sovereignty, but have given up almost entirely on trying to understand how a claim to sovereign authority works. Various traditions of ethical analysis are also right to emphasize the inadequacies of claims to state sovereignty, but have similarly given up on trying to understand what it might mean to make a claim to political authority while happily relying on tacit assumptions about the proper form that political authority must take. Neither seems able to contemplate the possibility that the problem of sovereignty might be more extensive and more troubling than might be expected from the way in which we have come to believe that claims to the sovereignty of states acting within a system of sovereign states must be the only answer to the problem of sovereignty we will ever need, or from which we need to escape as fast as possible. This seems to me to be an especially serious mistake, and leads me to the second sustained prediction I venture in this book: that sovereignty will come to be understood as an intensely complex and urgent problem involving the authorization and delimitation of authority, and not as the name given to the also intensely complex answers to problems involving the authorization and delimitation of authority affirmed by the structural contradictions between the modern subject, the modern sovereign state and the modern system of sovereign states.

Again, this seems a fairly easy prediction to make, especially given the emergence of so many literatures seeking to "provincialize" European and North American accounts of what it means to be modern, but it is one that is sharply at odds with narratives about sovereignty as either here forever, or on its way out and up the road to some politics of the world. The *problem* of sovereignty seems unlikely to go away, even if the structural form of an internationalized political order remains resilient. Much of the form of my analysis thus seeks to draw attention to the extensive work that needs to be done in order to take challenges to prevailing forms of state sovereignty with the seriousness, but also playfulness, they require, and not with the usual stories about sovereignty forever, sovereignty farewell, or sovereignty up the levels of a new hierarchical order.

In my judgement, then, sovereignty will come to be an increasingly per-plexing problem, not a condition to be confirmed as either present or absent; and political life will increasingly be articulated in relation to the boundaries, borders and limits that we have become used to treating as mere demarcations between places where politics is supposed to happen. This is especially what we might expect if we pay attention not to the accounts of what must happen according to the narratives of here and there, now and then, presence and absence, internal and external, or norm and alternative/exception, that work to affirm the authority of the sovereign state and system of sovereign states, but to the ways in which that authority came to be authorized as a complex structuring of points/moments (of origin, of centralized authority and of ending), lines (as boundaries of sociocultural cohesion, as borders of secured identity, as limits of legal authority and as trajectories of future possibility) and planes (of political space, place and territory, of scalar levels and struc-tural ruptures) all framed against a world that is ultimately excluded but also included on specifically modern terms. When a topology of points, lines and planes is unable to sustain authorizations of origins, limits, and thus what must come in between or go beyond, we must expect a repoliticization of what it means to authorize authority, of what it means to declare an end or limit, and what it means to claim some necessary middle ground in between points differentiating here from there, now from then, and us from them. Thus while I have become increasingly agnostic about the plausibility of the many literatures seeking to persuade us about what now constitute the most important causal dynamics driving contemporary political life, I am increas-ingly persuaded that the spatiotemporal imagery through which we have made sense of the relations between origins and limits, and thus the location and character of political life in relation to the claims of the sovereign state acting within a system of sovereign states, can only be a deceptive guide to the possibilities before us now.

The basic argument expressed here was worked out some decades ago while exploring three very big debates about modern forms of scientific reason. My engagement with each of them has left clear traces in the present analysis. One concerned challenges (associated with Galileo Galilei and René

Descartes in particular) to prevailing ontological, theological and political traditions in early-modern Europe, and especially with the connection between specific concepts of space and specific forms of epistemology that eventually found their most important philosophical expression with Kant. Along with an even longer interest in philosophies of musical form, this largely explains my tendency to read modern political theory in fairly topological and mathematical terms, as well as a nagging feeling that I really ought to pay more attention to many other figures, perhaps Jean-Jacques Rousseau most especially. One concerned the sense of crisis generated by the historicization of reason in late nineteenth- and early twentieth-century Europe, and the implications of various challenges to the great synthesis forged by Isaac Newton for claims about subjectivity and objectivity in the social sciences: the kinds of debate that gradually centred on Max Weber's awkward relation to claims about modern rationality, claims that have since echoed in various stories about the "dialectic of enlightenment" as well as in some very peculiar claims about "postmodern relativism." This largely accounts for both my general impatience with attempts to impose methodological orthodoxies on analyses of political authority and my framing of sovereignty as a problem of authorization and delimitation. One concerned the possibility of comparative philosophy and political analysis in the face of Weberian accounts of a breakthrough to modernity and the profoundly orientalist character of so many portrayals of other forms of rationality. This is what still guides my concern with histories of modernity and the transposition of practices of alterity in time into practices of alterity, and exceptionalism, in space, and back again.

These literatures about the grounds of modern scientific reason probably seem to have very little to say about international relations. Nevertheless, it would be very difficult to make much sense of either Kant or Weber (the two figures I take to be indisputably at the heart of the most persistent accounts of what it means to speak about political life within a modern system of states) without some sense of their background in this respect. In fact, my guiding instinct in constructing the argument in the way I have is that questions about the limits of the international are already foreshadowed in early-modern accounts of the unbridgeable gap between man and world affirmed by Galileo and Descartes, largely assumed in Hobbes' monistic critique of Descartes, and subsequently reaffirmed in very different ways by Kant and Weber. The result is a reading of "the international" as a crucial expression of the limits of modernity; but, I hasten to stress, it is only one reading of what it means to invoke an international politics, and only one reading of what is at stake in making claims about modernity and its limits.

I start the analysis with an attempt to resist the familiar privileging of the individual, the state or the system of states as the unquestioned starting point of political analysis. I do so partly by considering what is at stake in various uncertainties about the relationship between the location and character of contemporary political life, and partly by considering what is at stake when the constitutive uncertainty as to whether the individual, the state or the system of states has ontological, structural, historical or ethical priority is usurped by the methodological and doctrinal certainties that have been at work in many forms of contemporary political analysis. My underlying ambition in this respect is to draw attention to the contradictory, antagonistic, aporetic or radically undecidable character of the most consequential principles enabling modern political life, especially in relation to prevailing accounts of state sovereignty and its limits, as well as to what it might mean to recover some sense of the contradictions and contingencies of contemporary politics from forms of political analysis that are content to simply begin, and thus end, with either the individual, the state or the system of states.

Having started this way, I necessarily resist developing a predictable and easily summarizable sequence of arguments towards a precise conclusion. If beginnings are increasingly difficult to take for granted, as I will argue in various contexts, then endings and firm conclusions must also become more troublesome, as will the political spatiotemporalities that are assumed to come in between contingent beginnings and endings. The form of my analysis is thus constructed so as to disrupt expectations of an easy linearity, in ways that correspond to the substance of my preoccupation with complex relationships between beginnings and endings, boundaries, borders and limits, and with the authorization of authorities that might authorize beginnings, endings, boundaries, borders and limits; my preoccupation, that is, with how we might now understand what it means to be political under conditions of considerable uncertainty. Some themes occur and reoccur in different variations, voicings, counterpoints, echoes, reverberations, rhythms and orchestrations, as I try both to mimic the density of repetitive discourses affirming a specific logic of possibility and impossibility, and to identify some of the key conceptual arenas that must be engaged if problems of sovereignty and politicizations of the boundaries, borders and limits of political life are indeed as important for thinking about our collective futures as I have come to think they are. I hope I have ended up not so very far away from where I begin: just a degree or so away from, rather than at the opposite end of, the spectrum of possibilities affirmed by modern accounts of sovereignty, subjectivity, inclusions and exclusions expressed in a system of states that can never become a politics of the world.

Both the overall organization of the analysis and many of my specific formulations derive from my sense that it is currently much more difficult to ask productive questions about political possibilities than it is to offer plausible answers; plausible, that is, because more or less predictable. There is no shortage of people offering predictable answers to the problems of contemporary political life. We are in much shorter supply of clear judgements about the grounds, or principles, on which particular answers ought to be taken most seriously, and in even shorter supply of clear judgements about what kinds of question we ought to be posing in order for any answers to be considered useful. Principles matter, in both senses of this term, not least when so many contemporary scholarly practices work to persuade us, contrary to everything we are supposed to know about modern sovereignties and their spatiotemporal and legal delimitation, that principles are both immaterial and already settled.

I thus try quite hard in this book not to offer easy answers, apart from my highly generalized predictions about boundaries and sovereignties. I am not offering policy advice, though my general formulations have been shaped by some often intense preoccupations with very practical problems. I am especially not offering support for any of the trivialized "perspectives," "paradigms," or "isms" that are currently on offer in many current textbooks and curricula. I am trying to think through why one might come to judge some sorts of question and some ways of posing such questions to be worth sustained scholarly engagement. This is why the analysis proceeds fairly slowly and indirectly across fields of scholarship in which it has become much too easy to assume that the questions being posed are both obvious and straightforward, and that the appropriate answers will eventually appear given sufficient hard work, methodological rigour and ethical commitment. The procedures I use to do so rely less on claims about novelty that might challenge established conventions in some (empirical, normative) way, than on an engagement with the very different understandings of common sense that are already at play in contemporary narratives about novelty and convention.

Some readers will prefer a much faster and more direct route in order to see which flags I eventually plant among the usual array of doctrinal commitments. For them I can only apologize for my obstinate refusal to think that there is a quick and easy procedure for identifying the ground on which one might now plant flags, as well as my deep suspicion that demands for quick and easy answers to questions about what it might mean to engage in political life in ways that somehow exceed the possibilities and impossibilities of a modern system of sovereign states have already caused sufficient damage. Some may nevertheless find it much quicker to think for themselves about some of the questions I seek to open up here: questions about what is at stake in the way the terms international relations and world politics work as both synonyms and antonyms; about what it might now mean to engage in political practices that make some claim to "the world" without relying on the comforting notion that the borders, boundaries and limits of a modern system of states are either here forever or are about to disappear; about the many ways in which the regulative ideal of a simple line distinguishing here from there and now from then is at odds not only with the boundaries, borders and limits of contemporary political practice, but also with the borders, boundaries and limits of a politics enabled within a modern system of states in relation to which many analysts seek to write our possible futures as a narrative of escape; about the costs of scholarly practices that mobilize profoundly naive accounts of the way things are that encourage an array of normative aspirations that are already inscribed in and work to reproduce the normative aspirations expressed in naive accounts of the way things are; about what remains troubling when scholarly assumptions prevailing in some parts of a modern system of states are taken to be the universal ground for analysing the relation between universality and particularity expressed either in a modern system of states or in any alternative to it; about the consequences of deploying terms like democracy, peace, cosmopolitanism or liberalism in order to engage hopes for a better future without also engaging with the conditions under which and limits within which hope or despair, better or worse, and past, present and future are already determined to be possible or impossible within a precise scalar order affirming what it must mean to be both a human and political being; and about how relatively minor and in some respects quite conventional differences of emphasis in the ways we engage sovereignties and boundaries may make a greater difference than claims about grand alternatives and differences predicated on the simplistic accounts of sovereignty and boundaries still enabling many scholarly categories, debates and claims to authority.

I do eventually end up reiterating a sequence of claims that are introduced as the analysis moves along: about the need to appreciate the complex yet elegant ways in which modern forms of sovereignty and boundary work only because they cannot possibly work as the conventional accounts predicated on a specific topology of point, line and plane say they must; about the need to engage with the structural and historical conditions through which a specific array of inclusions and exclusions has enabled an international order constituted as a scalar order of inclusions and exclusions; about the need to think about practices that work within boundary conditions that are invariably treated as mere lines distinguishing the included from the excluded; about the need to understand the specific spatiotemporal articulation of this always at least doubled array of inclusions and exclusions; and about the need to abandon presumptions of or hopes for something we have learnt to call the political, and think instead about practices of politicization and depoliticization that must always respond to the contingencies of human existence. While I am aware that such claims may seem abstract and remote, I am persuaded that they speak to the principles of authorization and the authorization of principles that must be engaged in one way or another by any attempt to reimagine our political possibilities and impossibilities, or to reimagine who we are as political actors able to reimagine our possibilities and impossibilities as political actors.

2 Political, international, theoretical

Location, location, location

International/world

The most challenging political problems of our time express an urgent need to reimagine where, and therefore what, we take politics to be. At least, this is the daunting conclusion I take to be affirmed in many recent literatures seeking to decipher the political implications of contemporary events, structural transformations and historical trajectories.

We are especially asked to be more sensitive to the limits of our inherited political traditions in relation to sharply contested claims about globalizations, localizations, technological innovations, differentiating identities, increasing inequalities, accelerating urbanizations, undue reverence for the undemocratic authority of capitalist markets, and novel forms of global governance, regional integration, terrorizing intransigence and imperial righteousness. Moreover, many of these specific claims express a more generalized awareness of shared vulnerabilities on a not-so-lonely planet. They typically generate demands for some kind of fairness and sustainability rather than rampant development; as if there could be some other way of organizing political life than on terms given by modern accounts of capitalist universalization unravelling in linear history. They often bring appeals to forms of authority that are somehow "higher" than those expressed through secular institutions of state and law; as if there could be some higher authority than that expressed in the law, or laws, affirming the liberty, equality and security of modern subjects living within the modern sovereign state and system of sovereign states.

Such claims especially provoke worries about forms of political life shaped by the assumed distinction between the citizen of a specific state and citizens of other states, and between man and world: shaped, that is, by assumptions about the separation of the modern individualized citizen-subject from the world that has become its object; about the separation of such citizen-subjects within specific sovereign states from other citizen-subjects in other sovereign states; and thus about the extraordinarily dynamic – modernizing – forms of political order that have shaped and been shaped by this modern citizen who is simultaneously subject to the authority of specific sovereign states and of the system of states that enables any specific sovereign state to exercise authority. Consequently, they also provoke worries about a renewed willingness to tolerate mass violence in defence not only of the sovereignty of particular – national, territorial – states in which modern citizen-subjects are supposed to thrive, but also in defence of the civilization of modernity[1] that finds its most important political expression through claims about the sovereignty of particular states; and thus also through claims about the modern individualized subject who is enabled to live in a modern and modernizing world that is understood to be coextensive with the system of sovereign states – that is, with what we have come to call both *international relations* and *world politics*.

We are, moreover, supposed to know more or less what we are talking about when we deploy such terms, even in such dense sequences, with their grand references to states, citizens, subjects, subjectivities, sovereignties and nations – usually in the plural – and nature, modernity, modernization, the states system, the international and the world – usually in the singular. We know them most readily, however, and know how to think about the relations between their plurality and their singularity, when we are able to locate them with some precision, usually in a specific spatial frame, and with clear procedures for specifying their spatial differentiation. To suggest that precision is increasingly elusive, or that differentiations are less clear than might be expected, is to become aware that the most basic categories through which we claim to make sense of modern political life feel disconcertingly sloppy, even less persuasive than any historical record might lead us to expect. To speak about globalizations, localizations, cosmopolitanisms, imperialisms, regionalisms, urbanizations and all the rest, is to risk suspicions that the prevailing understandings of how we relate pluralities and singularities has become very uncertain, and thus to wonder about how we have come to make distinctions and connections between singularity and plurality, identity and difference, universality and specificity, citizen and citizen, citizen and human or subject and world. To insist that, given what we now claim to know about the intensification of shared experiences and vulnerabilities, the proper term really ought to be *world* politics, a politics that encompasses the entire world – wherever and whatever that is taken to be – is to sense that the place of an international in any politics that lays claim to the world has become very uncertain, in ways that provoke profound questions about what it now means to advance claims about community, subjectivity, modernity and political authority.

We are supposed to know what we are talking about when we use all these terms because we are supposed to have little trouble knowing, with considerable precision, both where the place of the international is supposed to be in the world and also where it is not. Both forms of precision are crucial, but are often understood to be mutually exclusive.

On the one hand, the term international relations can be used as an easy synonym for world politics. Either term can then be used to describe the broadest context within which modern political life has been enabled, the context of the world as such, or more accurately, of the world as it is known to modern political life. Many attractions lie in this direction. How else are we to avoid the petty nationalisms and parochialisms insisting that political life occurs within particular states encompassing particular societies and specific cultures, especially given the way some of those states, societies and cultures have a disconcerting capacity to act as if the world is indeed articulated entirely within their own boundaries, jurisdictions and imaginations? Shifting from international relations to world politics implies shifting from the obviously local to something more enlightened and cosmopolitan, something vaguely planetary, something both more worldly and more mature. Indeed, it might be asked, who could now resist such a shift, except the most small-minded, ethnocentric, reactionary and wilfully ignorant nationalist?

On the other hand, the term international relations can be used to describe exactly the opposite of world politics, as the antonym affirming the absence and even impossibility of any politics that might encompass the entire world as it is known to modern political life. In this sense, the term expresses fragmentation rather than unity, a pluralistic differentiation of a world of modern sovereign states rather than the commonality of modern states encompassing the world as a whole. Small-mindedness, ethnocentricism, conservatism and wilful ignorance, it turns out, can be understood precisely as the greatest glories of modern political life, at least when celebrated in claims about freedom, autonomy and self-determination. And who would want to claim otherwise, at least without admitting to an unworldly streak of utopian gullibility? Who would want to deny that the most pressing political problems of our time arise from the fractured, pluralistic and perhaps even anarchistic structure of international relations that can never permit a politics of the world because the freedoms, equalities and securities of modern political life are celebrated within particularistic sovereign states and in relation to the citizens of such states, rather than to the citizens of some wider and more inclusive world?

To treat international relations and world politics as synonyms is to invite a seductive leap into discourses of universality and universalization. To treat them as antonyms is to invite an equally seductive leap into discourses of specificity and plurality. Both seductions rest on an even more profound desire to believe that, taken together, these very specific discourses of universality and plurality might eventually add up to a politics of the entire world. In either case, we are at least supposed to know what the relationship is, or must be, or might be. It is because we are supposed to know this that we can be pessimistic or optimistic, realistic or naive, reactionary or progressive, parochial or enlightened, dogmatic or critical. Accept this assumption, and it is difficult to come to any other conclusion, as has been said many times before in other contexts: not least by Thomas Hobbes in his exemplary seventeenth-century European account of the assumptions that must be made in order to imagine forms of political life subject to the authority of the modern sovereign state.[2] Accept this assumption, and we can only reproduce the pattern of affirmation and negation enabled by Hobbes' claim that there can be no authority above, below or beyond that of the modern sovereign state. Accept this assumption, I especially want to insist here, and we can only reproduce the logic of affirmation and negation enabled at the edge of the modern system of sovereign states that claims to be, but never can be, coextensive with the world. Read as both synonym *and* antonym, the relation between an international politics and a world politics affirms both the ambitions and limits – the possibility and impossibility – of specifically modern forms of politics: forms of politics that aspire to be universal, to engage the entire world, yet that must always eventually acknowledge, tacitly or explicitly, that the entire world is forever beyond reach.

In my view, the most important implication that can be drawn from many diverse and contradictory literatures on contemporary political life is that the assumption that international relations is either a synonym or antonym for world politics must be placed in very serious question. Both synonym and antonym are increasingly problematic, but their antagonistic and mutually constitutive relationship as twin expressions of what it means to speak of the possibilities and limits of a modern politics is even more troubling.[3] Many of the most challenging difficulties now engaging the analysis of contemporary political life arise not from the familiar routines through which international relations and world politics are considered to be synonyms or antonyms, but from the multiple ways in which the world – again, wherever and whatever that is taken to be – so obviously exceeds the grasp of a politics expressed as possibility or impossibility within or beyond the modern world of international relations.

This, I will insist, is not just a problem for institutionalized forms of international relations theory understood as a specific academic discipline in specifically Anglo-American contexts. It is also a problem for all other forms of political analysis and practice that work on the basis of assumptions expressed with consummate clarity in modern Anglo-American theories of international relations. Such theories have a much greater significance for thinking about the possibilities and limits of modern politics than might be guessed by examining the often stunningly trivialized debates that have been so characteristic of this specific discipline, and even more so than might be guessed from traditions of political theory and analysis that ignore but nevertheless assume international relations as the broader context shaping their overwhelmingly statist preoccupations.[4] For my purposes here, theories of international relations are especially instructive as expressions of modern accounts of the possibilities and limits of modern political life because they so persistently affirm assumptions about where, and therefore what, political life *must* be. They especially tell us about what it means to imagine political necessities and possibilities on the assumption that the world cannot exceed the claims to authority, and to authoritative knowledge, expressed at the limits of the international: at the limits, that is, where and when the international meets the world as either synonym or antonym; or, better, as both synonym and antonym.

In effect, modern political life expresses a claim that the world is co-extensive with the international, and must be contained *within* the international. This is part, and a widely neglected part, of what it means to refer to modernity as a culture of subjectivity,[5] and to modern politics as a practice centred on the possibilities and limits of freedom and equality *within* secure sovereign states. This claim has always been dubious, not least in ways that we might now express briefly by using terms such as colonialism and ecology, or by reflecting on the philosophies of history embedded in our standardized narratives about secularization or international law. It is nevertheless a claim that works as an extensive and almost incontestable wisdom. After all, it might be said, how can there be anything outside the international? Where in the world could this possibly be? How can we imagine forms of political life that exceed these horizons? The short answer is that it is simply not possible to envisage any such place within the modern political imagination – except as a condition of the very possibility of having a modern political imagination, as a constitutive outside enabling forms of political life organized as a spatial structure of insides and outsides. In principle, at least, modern political life cannot exist outside the modern international, even though this is exactly where some might insist that a lot of political life does indeed find its place; or, more precisely, where a lot of political life finds its place both inside and outside the modern structures of international relations, on boundaries that do not quite work as the categories of modern political analysis suggest they ought to work.

For all their many problems, modern Anglo-American theories of international relations remain interesting because they express so much apparently incontestable wisdom about the possibilities and limits of modern politics. They do so in ways that remain enormously persuasive, structurally, empirically and normatively, for reasons that require considerable explanation. Consequently, such theories also tell us a lot about what is at stake in claims that our most challenging political problems express an urgent need to reimagine where, and therefore what, politics is taken to be. The term international relations – the term we now use to refer to political practices organized within a structure of sovereign states expressing claims to specific (territorial) parts of the world – does indeed work in some sense as a synonym for world politics: for a politics of the world as the world is understood through the resources of a specific culture of modernity that nevertheless works by recognizing that its own relationship to any world has always been a profound problem. It also works very effectively as an antonym for world politics, affirming that modern political life expresses claims to freedom, autonomy and self-determination, and celebrating the distinction between human subjectivity and the world that is at the heart of the most profound uncertainties expressed by claims to modernity. The prevailing discourses of modern political life largely work within the limits expressed by the possibility of treating international relations as either synonym or antonym for world politics.[6] These limits are increasingly up for renegotiation, on many different grounds, in many different contexts, and in many different ways.

Consequently, to claim that the most pressing political problems of our time express an urgent need to reimagine where, and therefore what, we take politics to be is to demand greater clarity about how both antonym and synonym work to sustain claims about politics and world, given that modern politics ultimately rests on a constitutive claim about the distinction between man and world as the condition under which it became possible to imagine modern forms of political possibility and impossibility. On the face of it, there is something very odd (a matter, I will argue, of antagonistic, contradictory and mutually constitutive relations that have come to be expressed as simplistic and depoliticized dualisms) about the constant demand that we shift from international relations to world politics on the basis of assumptions shaping a modern culture that both celebrates and agonises over its supposed freedom from its own constitutive outsides: its freedom, especially, from what we have come to call nature, from what we have come to call theology and/or metaphysics, and from any other ways of being human except that affirmed by the potential autonomy of modern citizen-subjects. The slide from international relations to world politics, I want to argue, is much, much too seductive for a culture whose greatest ambitions have been cast as forms of resistance to any dogmatic claims to any simple world as such; resistance expressed in its most exemplary form by Immanuel Kant, who has nevertheless been treated as the brightest beacon guiding our way from international relations to world politics. Then again, it might also be said, and as I will say both with and against Kant, dogmatism has by no means become a scarce commodity in the analysis of modern political necessities and possibilities.

The list of challenges to established political conventions is undoubtedly long. It offers ample potential for scholarly squabbles and public debates about sequencing and priorities. It certainly exceeds the analytical competence of established disciplinary traditions of scholarship, not least because established scholarly disciplines are already overcommitted to specific sequences and priorities. It feeds multiple disputes about the interpretation of information and the specific ontological, epistemological and axiological commitments these interpretations should stimulate. Specific claims sometimes lead to sophisticated conceptual and empirical innovation; though they also lead to disputes about the grounds on which conceptual and empirical sophistication might now be judged. Sometimes such claims generate wild speculation, righteous indignation, and desperate affirmations of entrenched theoretical traditions; though they also intensify suspicions that the grounds on which we have come to think about both tradition and radical possibility are now precisely what is being called into question.

Most significantly, claims about specific trends and problems generate further claims about the limitations of established forms of political authority, especially about the always uncertain relationship between various practices of power and the territorially located institutions and procedures through which deployments of, and responses to, power are understood to be legitimate. Whether in relation to narratives about new or intensified trends and dangers, or to contestations over basic principles that have long been taken for granted, claims that we need to be more imaginative in our ability to work together (as the political animals of the *polis,* as Aristotle would put it, as participants in some community as we tend to put it now) increasingly run up against the multiple ways in which our authoritative expressions of political engagement are firmly located in a particular somewhere: within and between the spatial boundaries of modern states.[7] To imagine some other way of being political, it is often assumed, is also to imagine future possibilities without the benefit of those boundaries, those lines of both discrimination and relation that have shaped our most basic assumptions about what it means to be modern political subjects capable of responding to specific challenges or to more general structural and historical transformations. This is what gives such disconcerting force to claims that we need to reimagine where and what political life might be.

To articulate suspicions that political life often fails to take place where it is supposed to take place is to generate multiple questions about how to engage with whatever politics is supposed to be from those places within which it is supposed to occur. To contemplate the implications of various claims about the speed, acceleration and temporal contingency of contemporary political practices is to generate questions about how such practices can be contained and organized within the spatial boundaries of a particular somewhere. To claim that the boundaries of the modern state and the modern system of states are being displaced is to provoke uncertainty about where we are or what we might be as political subjects. To suspect that contemporary political life exceeds the instrumental and/or imaginative capacities of modern subjects conceiving themselves to be citizens of a particular somewhere is to raise doubts about our capacity to think about the prospects for liberty, equality, security and democracy, and thus about how we might still claim to be both members of a particular community and participants in some more broadly defined community, perhaps even one encompassing the entirety of humankind. To contemplate the possibilities of resistance or emancipation in relation to claims about the failings of the modern state, or to envisage plans for updating the United Nations so as to meet demands for fairer and more effective forms of governance, or to make claims about the significance of social movements that are somehow new, a civil society that is somehow global, or forms of violence that require still more violence, is to come up against many well defined boundaries, whether understood as physical borders or as other, less tangible forms of limitation: limits in space, limits in time, and limits in our capacity to imagine where and what we are in space and in time. Most disturbingly, to try to respond to claims that the problems of our age are worldwide in scope, involving complex economic, ecological and cultural processes that exceed the grasp of established political authorities, is to generate profound doubts about our capacity to engage with a world that has already been excluded as the necessary condition under which modern political authority has been constituted in the formalized spaces of abstractly sovereign jurisdictions.

Consequently, it is now scarcely possible to engage with contemporary political life without some sense that we risk speaking in terms that have lost much of their grip not only upon important empirical events but even more so upon the theoretical principles through which we are encouraged to make sense of and respond to empirical events. While many specific problems or trends attract pragmatic responses requiring little attention to conceptual coherence or to grandiose notions of spatiotemporality, once these responses impinge on established principles of political authority, responsibility, liberty, equality, security and democracy – upon the principles through which we have come to understand the possibilities and limits of a politics of modern subjects enabled within and between modern sovereign states – the spatiotemporal organization of what counts as a coherent and acceptable form of political life quickly become of great controversy.

In the meantime, ambitious one-liners are thrown around as once merely speculative concepts are puffed up for the talk shows, the best-seller lists, the quick sound-bites and the executive summaries. Claims about globalization, postmodernity, a conflict of civilizations, a coming anarchy, a third way, a risk society, a tipping point or a new empire blind us in a momentary glare, and then fade as complexities impinge and contingencies are brought to order. The stories we are told about contemporary transformations vary enormously. Anyone who claims to know how to offer a reasoned scholarly judgement about what they add up to is certainly tempting the fates. Nevertheless, in my judgement it is difficult to avoid the conclusion that our capacity to know how to engage with political possibilities because we know where those possibilities are to be engaged is in serious trouble. Much of this trouble arises in those contexts that we call the international: that strange and very puzzling place in which we are encouraged to imagine ourselves engaged in a politics that encompasses, or might one day encompass, the entire world; as if a politics both enabled by and sustaining the ambitions of specifically modern subjects could ever encompass the entire world from which such subjects have been separated as the necessary but impossible condition under which they can celebrate their liberties, equalities and securities.

Here today, gone tomorrow

For many commentators, the solution to the multiple challenges of our age is disarmingly simple: get rid of boundaries entirely, whether as physical borders or limits of principle. We are all supposed to be human after all; or at least we are all more or less modern; or participants in the great capitalist world economy; or just part of a complex but ultimately singular ecology. Boundaries, they say, are an anachronism. Their tidy delineations of earthly space pale into insignificance when viewed from beyond the horizons of our planetary atmosphere. Don't live in the past. Don't be parochial. Don't be chauvinistic. Be realistic. We must learn to live without them. For others, this solution is so hopelessly naive, even dangerous, as to warrant an equally simple claim that the boundaries of the modern state are here to stay. Be realistic, they also say. Boundaries are absolutely necessary for sustaining our statist achievements, even though these achievements may demand hard compromises between the necessities of security and the possibilities of liberty, or between peace at home and war abroad. In this view, the divisions and exclusions of the modern statist imagination still offer sufficient ground, literally, for thinking about our collective futures. We know what we must do because we know where we can do it, and where we can articulate responsibilities and mechanisms for doing so.

The interplay of these two familiar narratives has generated many comforting clichés about the sovereign state and doctrines of political realism, on the one hand, and about globalization and the need for more normative forms of theorization, on the other. Both narratives express obvious and often stunning oversimplifications, especially in relation to what it might mean to make claims to a political reality, to a theory of history or to a sovereign authority. They are nevertheless constantly reiterated in popular rhetoric, public policy, and the scholarly literature that is the more explicit focus of my attention here. They express familiar accounts of what it means to engage with necessities and possibilities in modern political life, of what counts as realistic, aspirational or simply naive: of how we *should* understand our limits as political beings in space and in time, and of how we *might* imagine ourselves as some other kind of political being in some other space and some other time. They frame the broad possibilities articulated in debates about the legitimacy of violence in responses to violence, about claims to rights that apply to every human being, about military interventions challenging principles of self-determination, about obligations that come with citizenship, about novel forms and technologies of governance and governmentality, about the role and limits of law.

Sometimes these clichés appear to be overruled by more complex and sophisticated narratives. Claims that we are caught up in processes that are both globalizing and localizing might be mooted in this respect. So, too, might claims that while boundaries may be dissipating in processes we classify as economic (like trade and financial flows), they are becoming increasingly elaborate in processes we classify as social (like the movements of certain kinds of people). Attempts to show how it is possible to "disaggregate" or "unbundle" various functions and sites of state sovereignty as an institution so as to examine contradictory tendencies among different functions and sites suggest a similar tendency. Indeed, it is difficult to see how it is possible to make any sense of political life anywhere without starting from some such observation about the contradictory dynamics observable across many boundaries. Yet such narratives only serve to highlight some of what is at stake in resisting claims about the eternal presence or impending absence of boundaries. To start to disaggregate or unbundle practices of state sovereignty is to pose questions about how far such disaggregation might be taken, or what happens in the process to distinctions between internal and external, or between power and authority. To point to contradictory trends between "the economic" and "the social" is to pose questions about complex practices through which the sovereign state has long mediated between flows of capital and social orders, as well as about the work that has to be done to affirm any clear-cut distinction between an economic and a social or between power and authority. To postulate contradictory dynamics of both globalization and localization, or universalization and pluralization, is to engage questions about how the boundaries of modern political life work precisely to affirm a specific (territorial) spatiotemporal articulation of the relation between global and local, or universal and particular. Such questions are undoubtedly important; indeed, they speak to much of what is at stake in claims about the need to reimagine where and what political life might be. They are nevertheless easily swamped, or kept within the boundaries of established accounts of where and what politics must be in a world of sovereign states, by clichéd narratives that affirm ever-present or imminently absent boundaries.

These clichés have been especially familiar in literatures canvassing the prospects for a grand historical shift from forms of political life predicated on the existence of modern sovereign states in a system of such states to forms that are somehow more integrated, or global, or cosmopolitan: a shift from forms of international politics shaped by a system of sovereign states to a somehow more authentically world politics,[8] or the inevitable absence of such a shift in a system of sovereign states destined to remain eternally the same.[9]

In fact, clichés about the presence and absence of boundaries enable what has probably become the most pervasive array of contemporary narratives about future political possibilities: those envisaging a transition *from* a world of fragmentation and conflict *to* a world of greater integration and harmony. These narratives remain influential, across all ideological and scholarly horizons, even though the world of modern politics is organized through complex relationships *between* principles of fragmentation and integration, *between* principles of unity *within* diversity and diversity *within* unity. Despite the enormous weight of literatures that seek to persuade us that our political futures depend on our capacity to abandon a world of particularities and pluralities in favour of a world of commonalities and universalities, just about the only prediction about our political futures that can be made with any degree of confidence is that such a journey is not an option.

This is not because, as the other conventional story goes, we will always live in a world of sovereign states coexisting in a system of sovereign states. It is because it is so absurd to start thinking about future political possibilities as if modern political life has ever been understandable in relation to the presence or absence of a sovereign state abstracted either from the system of sovereign states or from the specific conditions under which both the sovereign state and the system of sovereign states have been enabled to establish their place in the world. This place has long been profoundly problematic, in many respects. It has been problematic not least because this place works as, among other things, a claim to be able to know what it means to be able to speak about a world in which modern political subjects can take their place as subjects, as citizens and as members of a common humanity expressed within modern subjectivities, within modern sovereign states and within the modern system of sovereign states. To express ambitions for internalization, for subjectivity, for what modern political life has envisaged variously as freedom, liberty, autonomy and self-determination, is to assume a correlative ambition for externalization and the necessity for exclusion of the world, or worlds, left outside, or left behind.

The modern subject, the modern sovereign state and the modern system of sovereign states express a very specific accommodation between conflicting principles of political order, an accommodation depending on the articulation of clear boundaries both in territory and in law. In general terms, this is a fairly straightforward and perhaps entirely uncontroversial argument. Indeed, it is so uncontroversial that it is rarely stated. Its implications are nevertheless anything but straightforward, partly because modern political discourse and analysis is largely organized precisely so as to avoid recognizing let alone responding to them.[10] If modern political life has indeed been structured as a *relation* between principles of unity and principles of diversity (a complex relation that is expressed, at a minimum, as a claim to individual subjectivity, as a claim to state sovereignty, as an always unsettled relationship between the claims of individual subjectivity and the claims of state sovereignty, as a systemic condition of the very possibility of any claim to state sovereignty, as an always problematic relation between the sovereign authority of the state and the authority of the system of states, and as an even more problematic relation between the world of modern politics enabled within the sovereign state and system of states and any other world or worlds beyond), then it is difficult to see how other ways of thinking about politics can be imagined simply through the subordination or erasure of one set of principles by the other. Again at a very minimum, it is the *relation* between principles of unity and diversity that needs some more creative attention. It requires attention not least in terms of the boundaries in territory and in law that have enabled the structuring of a complex relation between principles of unity and principles of diversity within the modern subject, the modern sovereign state and the modern system of sovereign states.

In my view, the degree to which clichés about the presence and absence of boundaries have come to enable so many narratives about a political future that must move from fragmentation to integration, from an international politics to a world politics, betrays an elementary and even wilful failure to understand what has been at stake in the specifically modern understanding of the unity within diversity and diversity within unity expressed in the modern sovereign state and the modern system of sovereign states, and thus what has been involved in the emergence of modernity as a culture of subjects and subjectivities. Such narratives betray not only a failure of political imagination, but an even more basic failure of political analysis. In effect, as I will suggest in a variety of ways, they express a confusion of problem with solution, offering a progressive theory of history as a way out of a problem that is already constituted through a progressive theory of history.

Put differently, the challenges of contemporary political life cannot usefully be posed in terms of the dangers of an anarchy, whether supposedly natural or international: the dangers that are usually deployed to scare people into thinking the way forward must involve an historical shift towards universality and cosmopolitanism, or to persuade them that globalization involves a progressive shift towards an enlightened reason. On the contrary, the more pressing problem is to come to terms with the forms of universality, cosmopolitanism and globalization that have already produced and enabled (and have in turn already been produced and enabled by) a specific account of the necessary relation between universality and particularity within the modern subject, the modern sovereign state and the modern system of sovereign states.

If contemporary political life is in difficulty in large part because of the multidimensional inadequacies of the sovereign state and system of sovereign states, as, in very broad terms, I certainly think is the case, then any more creative political imagination must resist not only the forms of diversity and fragmentation expressed by the sovereign state and system of sovereign states, but also the forms of universality and integration that already enable the forms of diversity and fragmentation that are usually said to be so problematic. Put more heretically, and in terms of the thoroughly misleading categories that have structured theories of international relations since mid-twentieth-century writers such as E.H. Carr and Hans J. Morgenthau enabled profound political and theoretical antagonisms to be converted into sloppily dualistic choices between caricatured extremes,[11] doctrines of political realism may be a problem, but the doctrines of political idealism that have produced doctrines of political realism are even more of a problem. Put rather less heretically, all too many valiant and well meaning attempts to think otherwise about contemporary political possibilities have been lured into dualistic choices between realisms and idealisms, politics and ethics, necessities and freedoms or differences and universalities of the kind that force an impossible politics of choice between one and the other, while simultaneously mobilizing a theory of history that will take us from one to the other.

Such dualisms mask much more important problems. As one might readily gather from any of the canonical theorists who are nevertheless so often and so flagrantly cited as authoritative sources of unchallengeable caricature in claims about the international, modern politics is a politics of freedom *within* and *under* necessity, a politics that expresses ethical principles, and ethical principles that express political commitments: a politics of antagonisms between claims to differentiation and universalization that cannot simply be cut into two. Relations rule, contradictions prevail. Seductive narratives that rest on an affirmation of dualistic choices can only end in grand illusions and eventual disappointments.[12] Consequently, if it is necessary to reimagine where and what political life might now become, it is first of all necessary to appreciate the discursive force of claims about a universalizing philosophy of history that have both affirmed the necessity of a politics of modern subjects enacted within sovereign states enabled by a system of sovereign states while insisting on a proper trajectory of escape that might finally avoid all the dangers and insecurities of life within the sovereign state and system of sovereign states.

Lines: boundaries, borders, limits

Despite what I take to be the obvious inadequacy of clichés about the presence and absence of boundaries, and associated narratives about a future politics scripted along a path that might take us from fragmentation to integration, it is a far from simple matter to resist them; any more than it is a simple matter to resist other forms of the polarized opposition between presence and absence that has been so pervasive in what we usually call the modern world. After all, boundaries distinguish here from there, and us from them, sometimes very sharply: when push comes to shove; when security trumps liberty; when liberty trumps equality; when friend defines enemy; when citizenship comes before humanity; when an exception proves the rule; when authority dissolves before brute force; when violence must be deployed yet again. The sharp logic of affirmation and negation that has come to be associated with our most exemplary accounts of what modern political boundaries do, at least under extreme, or marginal, or exceptional conditions, is also to be found in our most popular accounts of what such boundaries are, and of whether they will continue to work as they are supposed to work.

The trouble with these particular clichés is that they have very deep roots in the normative, metaphysical and theological aspirations of modern political life, as one might expect when dealing with claims about the modern state, its sovereignties, its subjectivities, its systemic conditions of possibility, and its limits in space, in time, and in law. They are always liable to be activated in moments of stress, of crisis, of emergency; at times when their crass over-simplifications, their polarized appeal to both a radical conservatism and an apocalyptic revolutionism works so as to mobilize acquiescence in the necessity of drawing lines, or of their erasure. The imaginary of the thin line that divides our political presences and absences in spatial terms is reproduced in a political imaginary that poses a sharp temporal choice between the lasting presence or imminent absence of thin lines. The boundaries that divide our spaces on the ground also enable our political imagination in time.

Conversely, our ability to understand ourselves as modern subjects, acting in the temporal trajectory we have come to treat as the inevitable ground of modern freedoms, also maps our political imagination in space. Consequently, it has come to seem that the future, perhaps even more than the past, is a foreign country, and like many foreigners in the modern world, it is subject to a sharp logic of affirmation and negation.[13] The boundaries of the modern state and system of states thus have enormous reach into the regulative ambitions of modernity, and into the constitution of modernity as a way of being in the world that is simultaneously adrift from any other world.[14]

Although they can be easily dismissed precisely as mere clichés that no self-respecting scholar would take seriously, discourses affirming that the modern state and modern system of states are either eternal or ephemeral express the enormous force of a culture that has learnt to depend on, and yet systematically minimize, the importance of very specific forms of boundary: of, in principle, straight, thin lines that nevertheless curve into circuits of enclosure, keeping the modern subject, modern state and modern system of states intact and secure from those others that are nevertheless necessary for their very existence. The reimagination of contemporary political life especially depends on a willingness to think about boundaries less as sites at which very little happens except the separation of one political community, or state, or condition, from another, than as very active sites, moments and practices that work to produce very specific political possibilities of necessity and possibility on either side. In effect, where modern politics, and modern political analysis, have become extremely adept at thinking about the opportunities open on either side of a boundary, the extraordinary complexity, productivity and spatiotemporal specificity of boundaries goes largely unnoticed. Like skin on flesh, boundaries are easily rendered as superficiality.[15]

Perhaps this is a consequence of the way we look out of two eyes, scarcely noticing our nose in between. After all, modernity is often said to be a highly visual culture, one that is prone to be enchanted by its achievements in representing the world in flat spaces while believing that straight lines around the edges guarantee authenticity of representation; and prone, also, to believe that visual clarity leads to better knowledge, and better politics.[16] Perhaps it results from a sense that boundary zones are a little wild and dangerous; that it is wiser to send out the specialists with the appropriately toxic equipment, and hope they do not contaminate the rest of us. More likely it is a consequence of historical and structural processes whose stories will never be fully told, although we certainly know enough about the complex relation between politics and claims about nature, between the claims of an earthly secularism and a transcendental theology grounded, so to speak, somewhere above our heads, and between politics and the claims of a modern, secularized, nominalized and rationalized law, to discount any residual sense that boundaries are simply given, etched upon the world and waiting to be obeyed.

In some senses we have already been told too many times that we live on boundary lines rather than on either side of them, in ways that have turned names like Michel Foucault, Jacques Derrida and Gilles Deleuze into crucial sites of interrogation about what it means to speak about boundaries, borders and limits, but also into bland labels in an indiscriminate marketplace of ideas that work to affirm the natural necessity of specific boundaries, borders and limits. We have been bombarded with arcane discussions of how selves are constituted through specific delineations of others, of what it means to translate from one language to another, and of how spatial metaphors of inclusion and exclusion generate entire metaphysical architectures, complete with foundations, constructions and limitations, among many other lines of analysis about lines. This keeps the theorists amused and off the streets. We have been bombarded even more persistently with news affirming the increasingly bewildering complexity of contemporary boundaries. Think, for example, of the various practices that were once kept under some sort of control by terms such as culture, or economy, or technology, or ecology, or the categories recently mobilized by claims about globalization, Europe, empire, or a war on terror, and the sort of precise boundaries we associate with the modern state and states system are liable to seem, again literally, out of place. To think politically, however, is still very largely to take those lines very seriously indeed, as the continuing grip of clichés about their eternal presence or imminent absence suggests with underappreciated force.

Contrary to the clichés that work as twin sirens waiting to shipwreck any attempt to think more creatively about our political futures, the intuition that I seek to elaborate and interrogate is that it will be necessary both to be much more aware of how a specific framing of boundaries works so easily to reproduce a discourse of political limits that keeps us more or less where, and thus how, we are, and to think much more intensively about the complexity and productivity of contemporary boundaries, and especially about how they work simultaneously as sites of politicization and depoliticization. Like much else in the analysis that follows, this is perhaps merely to state the obvious: obvious, that is, in some contexts though certainly not in others.

Many contemporary literatures affirm that most of the hard political questions of our time converge on difficulties in the ways we think about boundaries as expressions of political possibility in space and time, but also that the relationship between politics and boundaries is becoming ever more elusive, especially in terms of claims about nature, claims about law, and, most frequently, claims about the strange phenomenon, and phenomena, we call humanity. Yet the more fluent we become in describing practices that seem to elude the kinds of boundary we associate with the modern state and system of states in cultural, sociological or economic terms, the less we seem to be able to think with much clarity about their implications for established principles of modern political life.[17] The more we are asked to forget about the kinds of boundary we associate with the modern state and modern states system, the more difficult it is to imagine how we might go about doing things politically at all, and consequently, the more easily we are persuaded that all roads must lead back to the modern sovereign state as the beginning, middle and end of all political possibilities.[18]

Hence my concern, in what follows, with various ways of thinking about how the modern political imagination came to affirm a specific structure of separations and relations as the primary condition under which it is possible to engage in what we now call politics. After all, this structure of thin lines did not appear out of thin air, despite the impression created so effectively by various thinkers struggling to respond to the difficulties of authorizing authority in post-medieval Europe. The boundaries through which modern accounts of political possibility came to be constituted are by no means natural, though they did help shape what we have come to call nature. Nor have modern accounts of political possibility ever managed to find a way of speaking about humanity without excluding rather a lot of human beings. Hence, also, my concern with how this structure of separations and relations produces a characteristic discourse about the necessary limits of modern political life; that is, about the necessity of a particular account of necessity and possibility.

These limits express and reproduce a constitutive account of territorial separation in formal bounded space. They affirm the conditions under which we might understand change and transformation in general and the possibilities of thinking about boundaries, about lines of both distinction and connection, in some other way. They also affirm the conditions under which we might try to make sense of how modern politics came to work in relation to a specific structure of separations and relations: the conditions, that is, under which it can be assumed that modern history *must* have been what it has indeed become. Modern forms of political life now appear to us to be most problematic in terms of boundaries enacted as forms of spatiality, but it seems unlikely that any engagement with spatially articulated boundaries will get very far, so to speak, without coming to terms with the temporal boundaries once articulated in early-modern Europe so as to distinguish European modernity from all its others: temporal boundaries that have enabled modern political life to be imagined as a temporal possibility enacted within spatially defined necessities.[19]

My hope is that this analysis might encourage a more sustained appreciation of various ways in which contemporary boundaries, and political possibilities, are much more perplexing than we might expect from all those discourses that insist that boundaries are only marginal, merely thin lines of separation, and that they must be either here to stay or about to disappear. Our political futures, and the most interesting forms of political analysis, will necessarily become more and more obsessed with boundaries, borders and limits, though not only of the kind we recognize from our experience of the modern state and states system, nor of the kind that can be reduced to a descriptive geography, an explanatory sociology or a deterministic economy; and certainly not of the kind that can be erased through an historical shift from a fragmented politics of international relations to a universalizing politics of the world.

Discrimination/relation

The clichés of presence and absence animating so much contemporary political life, like the boundaries whose presence or absence is at stake, affirm a very specific understanding of political possibility and impossibility: of the necessary correlation between the boundaries of the modern state and states system in formal territorial space (usually understood in terms of territorial borders) and the boundaries of the modern state and states system in law (usually understood in terms of limits of principle). While the boundaries of modern political life are multiple, expressible in all the familiar categories of polity, society, culture, economy, security and liberty, they appear as singularity, as converging or superimposed on the same spatially and legally defined ground. It is this apparent singularity that is often taken to mark the primary distinction between modernity and the overlapping jurisdictions of the medieval Europe, and to have been the distinguishing achievement of the modern state as the expression of both sovereign authority and national community.

In highly generalized terms, the regulative ambitions of modern political life as they were articulated by early modern figures such as Hobbes and Kant, and reaffirmed especially by figures such as Weber and Schmitt in the early decades of the twentieth century, involved a capacity to distinguish between the legal and the illegal, the normal and the exceptional, the mature freedom and the immature despotism, and the monopoly of legitimate authority here and the monopoly of legitimate authority there in relation to the spatial jurisdiction of the sovereign state. In my judgement, the crucial sites of complication in contemporary political life arise from multiple scepticisms about the correlation between such boundaries. Overdetermining clichés about the presence or absence of boundaries not only obscure much of the empirical complexity of contemporary political boundaries, but also undermine whatever capacities we have to respond to the challenges this complexity poses for the most basic principles through which contemporary political life has become organized and legitimized.

It is not that the empirical or material presence of modern states has ever been as simple or elegant as representations within a cartography of thin lines would suggest; on the contrary. The primary force of claims that the state is the central reality of modern political life is less about any physical existence or material reality than about the presumed normative necessity of shaping and containing modern subjects within boundaries that are simultaneously spatial and legal; in Schmitt's disturbingly minimalist formulation, a matter of a sovereign capacity to decide exceptions under the law of particular states.[20] It is always tempting to dismiss this understanding as an outmoded relic of a world gone by; but give in to temptation, and the clichés are ready and waiting for yet another round of presence and absence, another replay of the hopes and dangers involved in imagining an exception to what has come to be considered the norm. While it is not difficult to make a case that many of the regulative ambitions of modern politics are in trouble, it is not easy to come to terms with what it means to think about more imaginative alternatives once the boundaries expressing the limits (and thus origins) of modern political possibility (and thus of political necessity) are judged to be problematic. What is at stake here is not the availability of evidence that boundaries are rather more complicated than they are supposed to be, but what it might mean to speak about political life at all, given forms of complexity that are at odds with principles of inclusion and exclusion articulated in relation to clear thin lines at the edges of the modern state and system of states.

Even to start thinking about what is involved in making claims about a need to reimagine where and what we take politics to be, then, is to become immersed very quickly in large questions about boundaries, especially boundaries expressing and expressed as spatial borders and limits of principle. In the first instance, it is to confront a powerful discourse that would have us assume that boundaries are hardly worth thinking about: that they are either in place or they are not. This is an assumption that always becomes troubling once attention is focused on precisely what is being distinguished or separated from what, and how it is distinguished. To think of the limits of the body, the self or a tangle of friends, or to think about what lies beyond life on earth, is to start engaging with questions that are not so easily answered in such absolutist terms. Examine skin under a microscope, and it is not so easy to say exactly where the molecular body begins or ends. Consider the relation of mother and child or the dynamics of capitalist consumption, and the narratives of modern individualism seem utterly shallow. Wonder at the intermingling of human lives almost anywhere, and the delineation of friends and enemies across the boundaries of the modern state seems more than slightly ridiculous, or the effect of extraordinary violence. Nevertheless, modern political life has thrived on the creation of very sharp boundaries, lines that always express both limits and beginnings and work not only to distinguish and separate modern selves and states from other selves and other states, but also the world of modernity itself from all other worlds. Differences and antagonisms have thrived in many settings, but the highly structured patterns of differentiation and always potential antagonism expressed at the constitutive and regulative limits of modern politics are quite striking, both for the aspirations they express and for the dangers they invite.

Whatever story we tell about the emergence of specifically modern forms of social order and political possibility, it is difficult to avoid engaging with the ways in which any of the achievements of modernity we might care to celebrate, especially those that are expressed in the name of some universality, come at the huge cost of sharp boundaries between "man" and "nature," between "secular man" and some transcendental deity, and between "modern man" and any other way of being human. The celebration of the "freedom" of "man" from "nature," for example, is the central narrative of the emergence of modern science and philosophy out of various qualitative, essentialist, theocratic and "enchanted" forms of life. In this narrative, Descartes is remembered for his radical dualism of *res cogitans* and *res extensa,* and Galileo for his at least equally fateful distinction between the natural world of primary qualities and mathematical objectivity and the human world of secondary qualities and a subjective knowledge that can never be certain of its grasp on the world.[21] The crucial figure in this story, however, is undoubtedly Kant and his double insistence that the world itself can never be known, but that we might nevertheless bring the universality of human reason to bear on whatever phenomenal evidence of the world we might be able to identify.[22] Kant is at once an expression of the scepticism that came with an account of a modern subjectivity conscious of its separation from any world of objects, and an expression of the hope that the universality of human reason offers a way of overcoming all, or at least most, or perhaps only just a few such scepticisms.[23]

In a parallel narrative, the canonical figures of early-modern European political theory are remembered for their accounts of how modern man is cut off not only from some natural world and divine authority, but also from other men, caught up in the antagonisms of modern individualism, left celebrating the possibilities of modern freedom while lamenting the orders, enchantments and authorities that had been left behind, not least the sense of a common humanity, and natural law, that had been given up in favour of the promised freedoms of particular earthly communities under positive law. Again, Kant has become an expression of the achievement of modern accounts of subjectivity as a cause for both celebration and concern, as the most articulate analyst of what it would take to dare to "think for oneself"[24] as an autonomous subject and yet think within the parameters of a universal reason, and a universalizing history,[25] that might eventually drive all such subjects, despite themselves, down the difficult (even impossible) road towards a "perpetual peace."[26]

Despite the constitutive role of sharply delineated boundaries at the spatial edges of the modern state, both the possibility and the authority of modern states rest on the plausibility of the claim that the kind of politics enabled within their boundaries can be reconciled with some wider world. In this sense, claims of connection are just as important for an understanding of modern politics as claims to separation. Kant expresses the regulative ambition of modern political life in this respect, just as he names the regulative ambitions we still express through claims about modern reason.

The kind of universality that Kant could imagine in the form of a reason (perhaps ultimately transcendental in the sense of being backed by theological guarantees as well as the extraordinary capacities of mathematics and Newtonian science, perhaps immanently grounded in a gamble on the potential capacities of enlightened man to transcend the contingency of mere sensation) capable of guiding all "mature" modern subjects towards autonomy, had already lost much of its intellectual plausibility by the end of the nineteenth century. The constitutive categories of space and time to which Kant, like Newton, had ascribed such certainty turned out to be just one more contingent, even if tenacious, phase in the complex genealogy of modern claims to know the world with certainty. Nevertheless, the aspiration for connection has hardly disappeared. Various traditions of natural law, quasi-Kantian accounts of human rationality, as well as many empirical claims about the *de facto* subsumption of statist separations into the globalizing logic of a capitalist market, all struggle to show how the boundaries we associate with modernity in general, and a modern politics centred on the state in particular, must be overcome in the name of some other universality.

Understood in this sense, modernity expresses a celebration of separation, of freedom from and freedom within, but also laments its distanciation from the world in which this autonomy is to be achieved. For many philosophical traditions, this lament has led to various attempts to recover something like a Kantian conception of universal reason, an appeal to logic, or method, or mathematics, in order to preserve claims about science and scholarship from the threat of scepticism that must arise from a radical rupture between a knowing subject and an object that is to be known.[27] For political traditions, this has involved problematic relations between individualized subjects and the sovereign state, between particular sovereign states and the system of such states, and between the world of modern politics enacted within the modern state and system of states and the world, or worlds, against which the world of modern politics has been distinguished as a realm of freedoms, autonomies, and separations: a realm within which the absence of universality, and the necessities that come with the possibilities of freedom, imply the always potential legitimacy of violence on a massive scale.

States are particular. States are human creations. States celebrate the supremacy of their own authority. Yet their claim to authority also rests on a claim to be able to reconcile their particularity, secular authority and autonomy both with some common humanity beyond their particular jurisdictions, and with some physical place, habitat or nature underlying their formal, legal, institutional and social capacities to rule. In mundane terms, no modern political regime will easily forgo the opportunity to claim that the forms of life it expresses and enables are at once particular and universal; both national and international, as we say in the prevailing categories. The possibility of deploying either value, and prioritizing one or the other depending on circumstances, has been crucial to the resilience of modern statist forms of authority. Conversely, the need to affirm one value at the clear and absolute expense of the other has been a sure sign that this resilience is in trouble. Nevertheless, while a claim to be able to reconcile competing claims to universality and particularity within the state and states system works as a regulative ambition of modern political life, it is a claim that has long been difficult to sustain, as even the briefest acquaintance with the histories and contestations expressed in our canonical traditions of political thought will attest.

On the one hand, modern states are said to have emerged precisely as a challenge to forms of authority grounded in appeals to the prior authority of the world as such, whether understood in relation to the productions of an ultimate and infinite divinity, the mediations of Aristotelian and Thomist philosophy and natural law, or the immutable laws of physical existence championed by post-Galilean science. Cut adrift from the world of nature, indeed constituting nature as both radically and ambivalently other, modern political life has remained torn between an affirmation of its own secular sovereign authority and a need to affirm this authority as somehow grounded in something more substantial: as natural justice rather than nominal law, perhaps, or as rooted in some essentially ethical humanity or ancient histor-ical/biological lineage rather than some merely abstract citizenship or con-stitution. Much contemporary political debate has been animated by revivals of old debates between natural law and positive law that hark back to an era when claims about the autonomous secular authority of states were a strange novelty, when modernity found expression as an obsessive problematization of all foundations, or by related claims about the need to abandon politics in favour of the guiding hand of a universal reason that is more in touch with a deeper and somehow more essential understanding of the world, or even by forthright refusals of all secular authority in the name of some explicitly transcendental theology.

On the other hand, modern states are also understood to have emerged as a challenge to any authority articulated in relation to some wider world of human beings. They sought to affirm their absolute and universalizing authority within particular territorial spaces, an affirmation that nevertheless forced them to come to terms with their parochial presence in a wider world that was at once enabling and threatening. The prevailing narrative here has been what we have come to know as the theory of international relations, though some might prefer to privilege narratives about colonial subordination as a way of understanding how the universalizing particularities of modern states have been reconciled both with each other and with that broader humanity supposedly encompassed by the totality of modern states coexisting in the modern system of states. Whichever narrative is adopted, however, and however much the structures of international relations and colonialism are understood to be deeply problematic, the possibility of affirming a plurality of places within which particular universalities might be pursued has offered the most alluring way of avoiding a collapse into a singular universality, a unitary order, a singular imperium against which the modern state and system of states offered, and perhaps still offers, the possibility of political autonomy and freedom.

Systems of states are quite rare in human experience, even though the modern system of states is often taken to be as universal as modernity itself.[28] The freedom promised by the modern system of states, in contrast with the hierarchical and imperial orders from which it is usually understood to have emerged in early-modern Europe, expresses deeply troubling ambivalences

about the degree to which it rests on the celebration of a profound separation – from nature, from divinity, from others, from the always potential infinity of the world – or on some kind of connection, or reconnection, with
some kind of primordial or constitutable universality that allows us to
negotiate our freedoms under some sort of law. The modern sovereign state
and system of sovereign states are the primary sites at which this ambivalence
has been most forcefully expressed in political terms, though it is an ambivalence that is broadly recognizable as part of the characteristic status of
modern man, the modern subject whose separation from its others, from its
very conditions of possibility, is both glorious and traumatic.

Within the modern state and modern system of states, this generic condition of modern subjectivity is played out on terms given by a specific understanding of territorial space, a space that is never quite the same as the world
it is intended to represent, and which orchestrates the modern dilemmas of
separation and connection by securing the limits of political possibility in an
array of spatially defined boundaries. The modern state and states system
affirm an order that is at once terrestrial and territorial. Although terrestrial,
they express a freedom from the authority of any prepolitical nature.
Although territorial, they express an account of terrestrial organization that is
thoroughly abstract. Although they celebrate separation, separation has often
seemed intolerable, indeed terrifying.

As heirs to the classical *polis* and to the kind of secular sovereign state and
national society imagined by the early-modern Europeans, and supposedly
universalized as the natural home of political life everywhere within the
system of states, *within* the world of international relations, we have become
used to knowing who and what we are on the basis of assumptions about
where we come from. We live in time, wishing to be remembered for our
achievements here on Earth, rather than to be saved for all eternity, as
Machiavelli famously insisted; I am a citizen of here, and you are a citizen of
there; we here are friends, while you over there are our enemies, or at least in
need of a bit of civilization and development; "here I stand, I can do no
other," as Weber put it at the end of the First World War when recasting
Martin Luther's protestant individualism, among other formative traditions,
into a paradigm of modern man struggling to affirm both liberal and
nationalist understandings of the modern state, and offering us an awful
vision of twentieth-century international relations as an unlimited field of
inevitable violence.[29] Such assumptions still inform a common sense that is
difficult to challenge, not least because they do help us to make some sense of
what we take contemporary political life to be. Our experiences with the *polis*,
the state and the nation have indeed been foundational, as the metaphor goes;
a metaphor that invites speculation about the founding of foundations and
fears that our most trusted foundations might be no more than sticks buried
in quicksand, claims about necessity that rest only upon genealogies of contingency, mere names bearing no necessary relationship to whatever names
are supposed to name.[30]

At the same time, such assumptions do not quite tally with much of what we are now told about the spatiotemporal rearticulations of political practice and possibility. Frank Ankerschmit's widely quoted observation that "politics now seems to be everywhere ... but what is everywhere is in practice nowhere"[31] captures a broad sense of spatial disorientation that has been reproduced in many popular claims about disappearing boundaries and temporal flows. Since the end of the Cold War especially, but in relation to dynamics that can be traced back many centuries through intellectual traditions associated with the likes of Karl Marx and Adam Smith as well as Weber, we have been warned that processes and flows are likely to overwhelm any form of political life organized within clearly demarcated territories. Geographers, ecologists, urban sociologists, cultural theorists and even the few remaining critical economists have all warned us not to confuse place with space, or space with the geometrical points, lines and surfaces of Euclidean geometry.[32] Consequently, many literatures have begun to consider how we might think about politics without clinging to the imagery of the contained community, of the situated particularity within which our classical traditions have affirmed the possibility of acting politically.

Many of these literatures express broad theoretical ambitions, and have an eye on the identification of grand historical trends and transformations. Sometimes these are framed explicitly in relation to claims about the fate of the modern state. Sometimes they are framed more broadly in relation to the prospects for the kinds of progressive or enlightened political ideologies that became synonymous with what we are still inclined to call the modern world. At the same time, other literatures invoke less the rarefied readings of the histories and principles of a generically modern politics than the demand to know what is to be done, here and now, practically and precisely, about this problem or that crisis, given that so many aspects of contemporary political life seem to exceed the capacities of established institutions of power and authority.

The state, it has been fashionable to insist, is in trouble yet again, so we would be wise to resist the desire to answer all questions about political possibility through statist claims about the freedoms and necessities of life as a modern citizen. If statist accounts of what it means to be a citizen within a specific somewhere are compromised, the familiar argument goes, then many of the great questions about who we are and how we should act together must press more urgently against a received wisdom that prefers to believe that all the hard questions about political possibilities were already settled a long time ago, whether in classical Greece, in early-modern Europe, in our traditions of revolution and democracy, in our aspirations for liberty and equality, or in our ideals of individual and collective self-determination. Whatever one makes of such claims, it is clear that received wisdom still has the distinct advantage of knowing where we should be looking for politics, and of what we are likely to find were we to get there. Conversely, without this advantage, claims about the local, the global, the imperial, the cosmopolitan or the planetary tend to be exceptionally vague when it comes to specifying where and how our political life might now be enabled.

Grounded in a particular spatial understanding of the place of political activity, the contemporary political imagination may find it easy to contemplate the possibility that the state may not be the be-all and end-all of contemporary politics, but much more difficult to think about a politics that may be somewhere and something else. Ankerschmit's allusion to a politics that is simultaneously everywhere and nowhere is surely to be taken as a hyperbolic provocation that says much more about our sense of puzzlement than about our ability to say very much about what it might mean to have a politics in such strange locations. Better, perhaps, to remain guided by the wisdom of a Plato or an Aristotle, who between them managed to establish such an extraordinary duopoly on what it must mean to engage in political life precisely because they could so clearly imagine where politics must be found and thus what it might be.[33] More likely, as much of the contemporary literature on the fate of the state seems to imply, such wisdom is likely to be increasingly insufficient, or is at least in need of some valiant reworking so as to respond to spatiotemporalities other than those we might recognize from our imagination of the *polis*, the state or the nation.

Likewise, modernity seems to be not quite the condition under which we now live, assuming that we ever did, and also assuming that we know who is being identified when talking about a we that is somehow modern.[34] The kinds of aspiration for a more progressive form of collective existence that gave such energy to the great political doctrines of liberalism and socialism that crystallized in the nineteenth century are now widely judged to have lost a great deal of their momentum, even if many people are still willing to say that these doctrines remain the best we have and retain enormous unfulfilled potential. If modern accounts of what it means to stake a claim to knowledge and being are indeed losing their capacity to convince, or if the practices through which conviction is achieved seem to hang at least as much on the deployment of mass violence and the forceful attenuation of capacities for self-determination as on the natural progress of self-realization fondly imagined by the great eighteenth-century philosophers of Enlightenment, then there is less and less reason to expect that questions about where and what political life must be will find much satisfactory resolution in conventionalized claims about what it means to be modern.

It is very easy to get carried away with such thoughts. Clichés about the demise of the modern state or our entry into some postmodern condition are precisely clichés, often bringing considerable absurdity and confusion in their wake. Their value is doubtless symptomatic rather than analytic.[35] The state has always been in trouble. No particular state has ever achieved the tranquil condition of being that is so easily conveyed by the abstract noun. Notions of an abstract modernity similarly obscure enormous differences in the ways people live and the intermingling of multiple modernities that exceed any single theorization, as well as passionately contested disputes about what modernity is supposed to be. Nevertheless, even as clichés they express a widespread sense that many of the most basic principles that inform our conventional understanding of what it is possible to be as political creatures offer increasingly awkward grounds on which to make judgements about contemporary events and historical and structural possibilities. At the same time, the twofold logic that animates these clichés, and invites us to think of the state or modernity as either present or absent, as here or there, as eternally bound within or about to abandon its boundary conditions, also tells us a lot about the seductive quality of all those discourses that are so willing to tell us what the alternative to the modern political imagination must be: to tell us, that is, what it must mean to imagine forms of political life other than those that already depend on such well defined accounts of the limits of political and human possibility, and of the dire consequences that must follow once those limits are breached.

Subject, sovereign, international

Whether principled or pragmatic, the literatures now urging greater political imagination arise from many different places. They appeal to different kinds of evidence and argumentation. They often conflict in the principles they choose to privilege and in their readings of the histories, structures and experiences they choose to foreground. Some move towards this conclusion explicitly. Others show sufficient signs of frustration and anger to sustain my sense that they, too, would concur with the judgement that political life does not and cannot work very well in the places and forms in which we are told it must occur.

In working through the implications of this judgement, I am not explicitly concerned with any specific causal or explanatory analysis of why claims about the need to reimagine where and what political life is may be persuasive, although I draw upon a wide range of claims that are suggestive in this respect. I am concerned with what it might mean to take such claims as a ground[36] on which to work through some sort of diagnostic[37] of contemporary political practices: as a very tenuous ground that might nevertheless prove to be more productive in some contexts than the assumption that we already know what politics is and where it is to be found.

This concern arises, in part, from my judgement that we are currently confronted neither by any lack of empirical information about what is going on in contemporary political life nor by any paucity of claims about how that information should be interpreted. On the contrary, we are often overwhelmed by too much information, but also underwhelmed by scholarly traditions competing to interpret too many uneven and contradictory trends, often on the basis of overinflated claims about our capacity to decipher the causal secrets of the modern world and an underappreciation both of the clichéd character of the theoretical categories through which we are asked to make sense of empirical data, and of what it means to challenge the principles of modern sovereignty and subjectivity that are at work in these categories.[38] As I will suggest, attempts to make sense of contemporary political life within categories that rely on sharp dualisms between internal and external, on the erasure of such dualisms through declarations of flat planes of comparison, on their reproduction through hierarchical "levels of analysis," or on their temporal resolution through a theory of modernization that must always reproduce its originary sovereign delineations of inclusion and exclusion, are especially liable to both affirm and confirm normative assumptions about what contemporary political life should be like, rather than to offer any sense of what is empirically interesting about political life now.[39] Information may not be scarce, competing theoretical traditions may not be shy about trumpeting their virtues, but the spatiotemporal grounds on which we are expected to make judgements about claims to knowledge about contemporary political life have become notoriously contested and uncertain.

This is especially the case in relation to those grandiose discourses that once coalesced around either structuralist accounts of spatial extension or historicist accounts of temporal process that found both their enabling assumptions and their most caricatured forms in claims about an international "anarchy" and socio-economic "development", respectively. These accounts, once the indispensable narratives of Cold War social science, are now more easily understood less as reputable scholarly accounts of contemporary spatiotemporalities, structural processes or historical trajectories than as discursive practices of legitimation working to reproduce specific, and usually specifically liberal, accounts of how we ought to understand contemporary political life. Even so, while it may be fashionable to think of the frozen spatialities and modernizing teleologies of the Cold War era as relics of a world we can now hardly remember, they built upon accounts of spatiality and temporality that have a much longer heritage, and that continue to have an enormous influence on the ways in which we still think about political possibilities.

In part, this concern also arises from my sense that the contemporary difficulty of interpreting empirical, causal, structural and historical trends in scholarly terms is closely related to many difficulties confronting people struggling to make sense of what it might now mean to act politically in the world. Both the practices of knowing what we take the world to be, and the practices through which we seek to engage that world in ways we take to be somehow political, express common worries not only about the grounds on which specific judgements might be made, but also about the grounds, or their absence, for making judgements about judgement. It remains easy enough, for example, to lament the covert conservatisms enabled by pseudo-objectivisms in many academic disciplines, but there is also a widespread sense that too many accounts of political activism, resistance, and so on also rest upon fragile and nostalgic understandings of knowledge, power, authority and identity informed by quite conventional accounts of the origins and limits of modern political life.

My concern with what it might mean to engage with claims about where and what we understand politics to be under contemporary conditions is broadly shared across many literatures and situations. It expresses some of what is currently at stake in competing claims about the possibilities of political critique and in demands for scholarly strategies that are somehow more interdisciplinary, more sensitive to human diversities, while also being more cosmopolitan, and much more responsive to contemporary forms of mass violence, sociocultural exclusion, economistic (ir)rationality and ecological degradation. My concern will be especially unsurprising to anyone who has already concluded that there is much more to modern claims about sovereignty and subjectivity – the primary sites at which we have come to think about judgements about judgement, the formal procedures through which substantive and causal claims are authorized, the delineation of boundaries, the orchestration of spatiotemporalities and the relation between the world of modern politics and its separation/connection with some other world beyond – than might be guessed by looking at most literatures on international relations, world politics, globalization, modernization, development, and other fields of scholarship seeking to make sense of a politics that is somehow at play in what we call the world. Indeed, that there is much more at stake in claims about sovereignty than anyone might have gathered from an engagement with the methodologies of political analysis that came to be most pervasive in the second half of the twentieth century has become part of an emerging consensus across large and increasingly influential scholarly communities. Perhaps it is now scarcely possible to stake a claim to scholarly credibility without paying at least lip-service to the need to do rather more than assert that sovereignty *is*, that sovereign states simply are the foundation, the beginning and the end, of political analysis; at least, this certainly ought to be the case.

Even so, the highly contested status of contemporary claims about a politics that is somehow in and of the world, especially in the spatiotemporal form in which they have come to be expressed in the complex practices and sites that are now named as international relations, world politics, globalization, modernization or development, suggest that the problematization of sovereignty still offers considerable scope for critical political analysis, both in general terms and in relation to many very different practices and sites. Diagnoses of the relationship between the practices of modern sovereignty and our capacity to generate more imaginative accounts of political possibility still require a lot more unpacking, to use a perhaps quite feeble metaphor that nevertheless engages both the substantive concerns with forms of containment I want to examine, and the procedures through which I intend to examine them. As a practice that has worked so effectively to organize political life within clearly delineated strategies of containment, specifically modern accounts of sovereignty remain remarkably well wound up in dense little packages stored in the archives of modern political consciousness and reproduced in the procedures through which we struggle to come to terms with what sovereignty involves. A little more unpacking, unravelling, magnification and decompression, as well as much less loyalty to the containment strategies of specific disciplinary literatures, still offers some scope for understanding not only how modern forms of sovereignty work so as to affirm a relationship between where political life is and thus what it must be, but also what it must mean, and must not mean, to imagine politics in some other place, in some other way and as some other possibility for whatever kind of political subjectivity we are capable of imagining ourselves to be now.

The need for greater political imagination about our possible futures arises especially in relation to what I take to be specifically modern accounts of the spatiotemporal limits of political possibility enacted within and between the necessities and freedoms expressed through those bounded territorialities, institutions and practices we have come to know as the modern sovereign state acting within a structure of sovereign states. The double (and, by implication, triple and quadruple) foci of this excessively but necessarily long formulation are at the core of the specific argument I want to pursue. Much of the difficulty of reimagining where and what we take politics to be arises from the various ways in which both the state, and the distinction between any particular state and the states system that is the primary condition of the possibility of any particular state, already affirm a powerful repertoire of imaginings, visions, utopias, alternatives and other necessary possibilities for being otherwise. This repertoire builds on the deepest hopes and fears of cultures shaped by powerful philosophies of universal reason, on promises of transcendence in many forms, and perhaps especially on claims about freedom; freedom, that is, under certain conditions and within specific limits. It has sustained much of what we have come to think of as progress and emancipation. It is not a repertoire that can be summarily dismissed, any more than claims about sovereignty or practices of boundary construction are likely to disappear from political life, or any more than the inheritances we associate with Plato and Aristotle are likely to fade away politely as a consequence of the ambitions of so much contemporary critical theorizing.[40]

Suspicions now abound, however, that established accounts of what it must mean to think about other, and somehow better, forms of political life have become far too seductive in many contexts; that they express hopes and fears arising from particular histories and cultures, hopes and fears that are not entirely consistent with, or may even intensify, the challenges most likely to engage us now. These suspicions arise especially in relation to an increasingly pervasive, but only vaguely definable, sense that neither the modern state nor the modern system of states is able to monopolize the forms of political life that are now at play in what we so easily (and, as I hope will already be apparent from some of the density in the way have begun to set up the problem I want to address, much too easily) call the world.

Modern forms of political life project a possible perfectability in the organization of human life within the state that coexists with other states within a system of states that is assumed to be coextensive with a wider humanity.

Again, this is a longish formulation, and also necessarily so. Like many of the similarly longish formulations that follow, it is intended to draw attention to the multiple sites, moments and practices at which modern politics works: sites, moments and practices that we are more used to dealing with in their singularity than in their doubled, tripled and sometimes quadrupled forms. In terms that take account of the primary social and cultural aspirations that are widely assumed to have provided the substantive form, and regulative ambition, of modern political identities, modern political thinkers have tended to imagine a possible perfectability of human life within those nations that exist within those states that coexist with other states containing nations in a potentially peaceful, but also always potentially conflictual, relationship.

That is to say, modern politics has come to be, among other things, an international politics. This is so even though many of the most characteristic features of modern politics long pre-date the kind of structural formations we now call the international.[41] It is predicated on the assumption that all of humanity, all the peoples of the world, can be brought *within* the jurisdiction of some modern sovereign state that can itself find its proper place within the community of modern nations, within what is now often called the multilateral world of the international, so that the modern individualized political subject can find its home, its space for freedom under the necessity of law; although under which law is itself necessarily a matter of great contention. Or perhaps the logic works the other way around, so that we should say that modern politics has become, among other things, an individualist or subjectivist politics. It is predicated on the assumption that people must be understood as individuals, each in principle free and equal, and thus in need of a state to ensure their continued well-being, and some kind of arrangement between states to ensure the continued capacity of states to secure their modern subjects. Or perhaps it has become a statist politics, predicated on the assumption that it is the state that produces both its subjects and the system that somehow enables its own existence. Or perhaps, and as I will try to affirm in a variety of ways, the structural logics linking the international and the individual through the claims of the modern sovereign state are rather more multidimensional, co-constitutive and uneven than these familiar monological options – the "levels of analysis" that are so often affirmed as the necessary starting point for any analysis of modern political life,[42] the universality-within-particularity and community-within-unity affirmed by all our familiar narratives about individual autonomy and national integrity – tend to suggest.

At the very least, it is necessary to insist that an analysis of modern politics that chooses to isolate the modern subject, the modern state or the modern system of states as separate objects of analysis is going to produce a rather myopic academy. It will be an academy that will find it especially difficult to appreciate much of the explicitly contradictory character of modern politics. It will lose interest in the intrinsically problematic character of those principles that are most widely assumed to be foundational for modern political life, not least in relation to the ambiguous location of the claim to popular sovereignty, the claim to state sovereignty, and the claim to the principle, so loosely formulated as to have no simple name, not even that of international law, which insists that even sovereign states must not act in such a way as to disable the system of states that enables both the sovereign state and its sub-jects.[43] It will also lose interest in the ways in which modern politics responds to historically specific problems and becomes complacent about the degree to which modern forms of political life have been able to articulate historically foundational, but also historically contingent, answers: answers that, many literatures tell us, no longer respond very well to the kinds of question that are being posed in many contexts now. It will become especially complacent about the extent to which the contingent and often highly tentative relation-ship that has been established between the modern states system, the modern state and the modern subject over the past half a millennium or so is still sustainable, even as a regulative principle guiding our understanding of what political life ought to be about. All too much of contemporary political ana-lysis, it is fair to say, does indeed remain quite complacent in this respect, even when it lays claim to a concern with change and transformation.

Modern forms of politics have never been easy. States have rarely been able to exercise anything like a monopoly on power or authority within their claimed jurisdictions, and the possibility of realizing any such ideal has inspired horror as well as desire. The distribution of claims to nationhood converges very awkwardly with the distribution of claims to statehood. Aspirations for, say, democracy, the rule of law or social security within statist jurisdictions have brought many impressive achievements, but the gap between aspiration and practice is disconcertingly wide everywhere. Coexistence has all too often been a matter of conflict and mass violence, rather than of peace. Other practices of power and authority have been able to challenge statist understandings of what power and authority must involve, not least in rela-tion to claims about the generation of value in a globalizing capitalist market economy. Most significantly for my purposes here, the international, the organization of the modern system of (nation-)states, has never been coex-tensive with the world, a term that becomes ever more elusive even as our sense that it is the world, and not merely the international, that ought to be where and what our political futures ought to be about. Whatever the sources of difficulty in any future politics, however, we will have to get used to thinking about the limits of thinking about the limits of a modern politics in ways that invoke claims about the world when it is precisely the world that was excluded/included – that is, excluded and then included on different terms – so as to constitute a modern world of politics as a structure of inclusions and exclusions within the modern state and states system.[44]

Some forms of common sense may tell us that of course we live in the world, in the singular. There certainly seem to be overwhelming reasons for suspecting that we are all living very precariously in a single biosphere, and that much of this precariousness can be attributed to a singular and uni-versalizing but disconcertingly complex process we call capitalism. There may also be many sophisticated rationales for thinking and acting in more universal or cosmopolitan terms. It remains the case, however, that far from providing a firm ground from which to engage this common sense, or a single biosphere, or universal reason, modern political life is explicitly committed to its differentiation from the world it seeks to inhabit. Ridiculous this may be in some senses, as I often think, and as many of those whose struggles to envisage more imaginative forms of political life I most appreciate also think. Nevertheless, given the stakes of insisting that we are all in this, whatever it is, together, it would be disingenuous to assume that one can simply shift from modern reason, or Western reason, or European reason, or any other particular account of reason that works by insisting that subject is split from object, man is split from nature, and its own accounts of reason are split from any other account of reason, so as to lay claim to a politics that can speak to any world in the singular. Plausible stories about the unifying capacities of capitalist development, international disorder or planetary catastrophe are no excuse for the widespread failure to engage critically with the constitutive exclusions that have enabled modern political life to thrive on a specific account of necessity and possibility orchestrated through a particular pattern of inclusions and exclusions; nor for the assumption that this particular pattern of inclusions and exclusions provides the only ground on which to think now about necessities and possibilities in relation to claims about some common world.

The capacity of the modern political imagination to think about other ways of enabling political life hinges in very large measure on a capacity to assume that the patterns of inclusion and exclusion that have shaped a modern politics of inclusion/exclusion, centred, but also decentred, on the modern subject, state and states system, can be either perfected or transcended: that the boundaries of modern political life can indeed work to resolve all the contradictions of human existence or else disappear as we go further down the road of a universalizing history. In the meantime, it suggests, we have to put up with the imperfections of our immanent earthly existence. We are familiar enough with these apparent imperfections as still more people are bombed out of existence or dismissed from the realms of the properly human, and retain a strong sense that they might indeed be made less imperfect, or even transcended, but only in a future that is never quite within reach. However, the limits of this reading of political possibility, and of the so-called realities that have been identified in relation to it, are also becoming somewhat clearer.

The diagnostic that follows seeks to respond to various contexts in which this reading is indeed beginning to lose its analytical force. Paradoxically, this will involve a rather intransigent focus on the ways in which certain accounts of perfectability and transcendence, of the possibility of some other alternative, already regulate a political world of modern subjects, states and states system. Know thyself, as the familiar injunction goes. Resist the pretence that one can leave oneself so as to find the other – other traditions, other cultures, other worlds, other pasts, other futures – without finding that self already there, already ready and willing to engage with those others on one's own terms. This, too, has been a familiar injunction since at least the time of Kant, though less so in those literatures that are so impatient to insist that there must be some way out of here, some relatively obvious way of finding some other kind of politics that is somehow more in touch with contemporary trends, some simple way of imagining that we are already someone else. In brief, what needs to be engaged is not only the explicit relation between assumptions about where political life must occur and what specific claims about what political life must involve, but also an array of usually tacit assumptions about what it must mean to engage in a politics of escape.

Such a concern will involve identifying and cataloguing many familiar things, if only to show how easy and how dangerous it is to treat the sovereignty of the modern state as an unproblematic ground on which to think about alternatives to the politics of modern sovereign states. For it is in relation to sovereignty that we can most sharply engage many of the constituent practices that tell us what it *must* mean to make claims about the imaginary and the realistic, the possible and the impossible, the spatiotemporal conditionalities at work in what we call the world, and thus the freedoms that must or must not be enabled in what we understand to be the world of modern politics.

In this context, I share much of the judgement offered by Jean-Luc Nancy, one of many contemporary thinkers who have paid close attention to the workings of modern sovereignty in philosophical terms indebted to the now familiar disruptive influences of Nietzsche, Freud, Husserl and Heidegger, among others: "But this is certain: there is nothing on the horizon except for an unheard-of inconceivable task – or war. All thinking that still wants to conceive an 'order,' a 'world,' a 'communication,' a 'peace' is absolutely naive – when it is not simply hypocritical. To appropriate one's own time has always been unheard of. But everyone can clearly see that it is time: the disaster of sovereignty is sufficiently spread out, and sufficiently common, to steal anyone's innocence."[45] I would only want to add that to see the practices of modern sovereignty as a disaster should not lead us to stop thinking critically about sovereignty as a problem, one that does not have to be dealt with on terms given by specifically modern forms of state sovereignty. In this context, I am especially concerned to suggest that there is a lot more to modern claims about sovereignty than one might guess from all those textbooks on international relations that are so preoccupied with stories about state sovereignty as the only form of sovereignty there has ever been or might possibly be. To insist that modern forms of state sovereignty represent the only form or practice of sovereignty that has been, or can be, imagined offers a convenient way of defending the intellectual division of labour expressed in modern academic disciplines, but it is an insistence that can only be sustained within the comfortable myopias of such disciplinary divisions.

The *problem* of sovereignty, I will suggest, remains with us, perhaps in dramatically new forms.[46] Nevertheless, the specifically modern articulation of space, time and political identity that has enabled an historically con-tingent account of what sovereignty must be to work as a ground of all poli-tical authority – as the site of constitutive distinctions both between authorities and between legitimate and illegitimate authority – is arguably losing *its* authority, and on many grounds. In whatever way we might now manage to respond to the problem of sovereignty, it will not be by assuming that there is a necessary correspondence between a capacity to distinguish between legitimate and illegitimate authorities, and a capacity to distinguish between a territorial space of domestic jurisdiction and an external world beyond. I see no reason to conclude that we are moving to a political order without boundaries, borders and limits, without states or without sover-eignties, nor to one in which boundaries, states and sovereignties affirm the idealizations of the modern sovereign territorial state that have enabled our modern accounts of political possibility to attain the status of a hegemonic common sense. On the other hand, the disjunction between the continuing problem of sovereignty and the contemporary rearticulation of the spatio-temporal conditions under which modern forms of sovereignty have found expression in states, territories, nations and subjectivities is certainly opening out a range of problems that will challenge the ingenuity of established traditions of critical political analysis for some time to come.[47]

Again, Nancy has already identified some of what is at stake in this respect, in a manner that speaks to a broad range of attempts to think more imagi-natively about the limits of modern accounts of limits: "There doubtless remains to be invented an affirmation of separation which is an affirmation of relation ... which is what the State denies, refuses, or represses. ... The affir-mation of relation would have to be a *political* affirmation, in a sense that remains for us to discover."[48] Here I would only want to make what I think are two crucial and related points.

First, as I have already suggested, it is not only the modern sovereign state that has made it so easy to affirm separations and so difficult to affirm a politics of relations, but also the modern system of sovereign states. As many conventionalized readings of the historical emergence of an international politics have long affirmed, but as many other conventionalized readings have insisted to the contrary, the relation between sovereign states and the system of sovereign states should already suggest that the affirmation of separation and denial of relation has not been as easy as it may seem from accounts of political possibility that focus on the sovereign state alone, and especially on the way the sovereign state has been framed through the radically nationalist understandings of power politics that have come down to us from the early decades of the twentieth century. In this context, I especially want to play out some quite conventional understandings of the coproduction of the sovereign state and the system of sovereign states against the nationalisms and dualisms that became so influential in the construction of a specific discipline of inter-national relations in the second half of the twentieth century; and especially to resist the currently popular statist account of sovereign exceptionalism associated with Schmitt by insisting on the importance of the doubled forms of exceptionalism that were once identified with an opposition between Schmitt and Hans Kelsen, both figures expressing characteristically Kantian possibilities.

Second, and consequently, while I agree with Nancy and many others that patterns of denial, refusal and repression are very common in modern accounts of boundaries, borders and limits, it is a mistake to assume that modern affirmations of separation are not also affirmations of certain kinds of relation. On the contrary, as Nancy and many others have shown in various philosophical and literary contexts, considerable work is involved in the authorization of modern lines of discrimination, and much of this work can be understood as occurring on and within lines of discrimination that only appear to be clear lines of separation. This is especially apparent not only if we think about the supposed separation between the practices of the sovereign state and the practices of the system of sovereign states, but also if we think about how boundaries, borders and limits must express both inner and outer edges, enabling forms of political action both within and between sites at which it can be made to seem as if very little happens at all. The modern political imagination is profoundly indebted to specific spatiotemporal topologies of inclusion and exclusion regulated by idealized accounts of lines that seem to do no more than distinguish presence from absence, here from there, and now from then. Nevertheless, while such lines do indeed work as a regulative ideal – the ideal often affirmed as reality – they must also be understood as very intense sites at which considerable work must be done so as to affirm and enact the reality of the ideal, whether as principle, institution or material and forceful presence. In this context, I especially want to draw attention to the work that is done both within lines and between lines: within lines that may seem to have zero width, in the manner of Euclid's exemplary postulates, but which nevertheless host the most intense practices of sovereign authorization that are simultaneously internal and external; and between lines that may seem to be infinitesimally close, but which nevertheless express unbridgeable chasms and generate irreconcilable differences.

Thus while affirming Nancy's identification of what I take to be an increasingly popular sense that we confront both conceptual and practical challenges in thinking about boundaries, borders and limits as considerably more complex than the abstract lines of separation reproduced in so many modern cultural practices, I want to work through some key sites in which such complexity provokes new challenges to the limits of modern political possibility and impossibility expressed in claims about the modern system of sovereign states – about the political world of the modern international that is enabled by a principled and always doubled separation between the world of modernity and any other world – but also to do so while paying attention to the work that is already done on, within and through the boundaries, borders and limits that we usually understand as mere lines of separation.

Before that, however, I want to say more about what is at stake in thinking about political possibilities and impossibilities in this manner. I will do so, in the following chapter, by working through a range of overlapping ways in which it is possible to read many familiar narratives about the spatially located character of modern politics as simultaneously a politics of escape. This will provide a broad contextualization of what I think is involved in the increasingly puzzling character of the problem of sovereignty, and in the rearticulation of political possibilities and impossibilities at the boundaries, borders and limits within and beyond which we have claimed to be acting within the world while celebrating our freedom, as moderns, from any such condition.

3 The politics of escape

Times, spaces, politics

National / international

Of all the possible ways of beginning a discussion of contemporary political possibilities and necessities, I have so far shaped my framing of the problem I want to address so as to insist that modern political life is formally organized in relation to the claims and capacities of the sovereign state *and* the system of sovereign states: to both, though ambivalently, in ways that produce both fundamental conflicts, in principle and in practice, and multiple negotiations, reconciliations and accommodations of conflicting principles and practices. It is not organized in relation to either the sovereign state or the system of sovereign states. Or perhaps it is better to say that it is not organized in relation to either one or the other, except when modern political life is in some kind of crisis, when it is subject to exceptional conditions. Or perhaps it is even better to say that it is not organized in relation to either one or the other, even when exceptional conditions prevail, given that exceptional conditions in this case only affirm the rule that modern political life is formally organized in relation to the claims of both the sovereign state and the system of sovereign states. Slight variations in formulation open up immense conceptual arenas in this respect: arenas that are usually understood in relation to the most extreme conditions of war and the most abstract questions about when and where modern political life begins and ends, and thus to the way the boundaries, borders and limits of political life are supposed to work. There are doubtless many rhetorical advantages to be gained from posing simple existential choices between the sovereign state and the system of states, as there are in posing similar choices between individual and society, liberty and equality, liberty and security, knowledge and power, democracy and authoritarianism, or friend and enemy. Nevertheless, rhetorical advantage is an uneasy criterion of analytical coherence.

There is also some degree of empirical plausibility in the familiar claim that the modern system of states has only a weak and largely prescriptive expression in international law and enforcement capacity, and may thus be treated as a minor factor in situations shaped by state power, especially when the most powerful states really start throwing their weight around. Even so, modern political life cannot be understood through the discursive isolation of the state from the system of states, no matter how important or powerful any particular state might be, how weak the claims of international law may be, or how useful it might be to examine the modern system of states as an analytically discrete structural formation. Any attempt to do so wilfully effaces the contradictory character of modern politics and encourages silence about the most difficult sites, moments and practices of antagonism that must be negotiated, through resort to violence if necessary, and which must be engaged in any attempt to understand conflicts of principle and claims to sovereign authority. Weakness does not automatically translate into irrelevance. Greater power does not always imply greater authority. Self-assertion is no guarantee of political autonomy. Boundaries, borders and limits do not necessarily have only marginal significance. It may well be the case that statist parochialism remains a powerful political commitment, but it can never be an excusable scholarly strategy.[1]

Similarly, as modern political subjects, we are subject to the claims of necessity and possibility made by both the modern state and the modern system of states; by both the national and the international, as we are now able to say having learnt, through many ecstasies and many agonies, to conflate concepts of statist sovereignty with concepts of statist nationality. Sometimes these claims are reasonably consistent. Lines are then drawn loosely. Upbeat accounts of an enlightened internationalism prevail, precisely on the assumption that we are enabled to be both national and international – both different and yet similar, both citizen in particular and human in general – within the modern sovereign state that is enabled by the modern system of states. This is the stance advanced in the official rhetorics of states everywhere. Sometimes these claims are radically incompatible, in ways that have produced enduring and still active sites of controversy and conflict. Lines are then drawn sharply. Difficult decisions are taken. Exceptions are declared. Violence is deemed legitimate and the hard men take over. Nevertheless, while we may sometimes believe that the aspirations expressed as citizens of particular states are not so different from the aspirations expressed by the citizens of most or even all other states – aspirations we might thus consider to be not only international, but even a universal expression of a common humanity – sometimes our commitments as citizens of particular states override our commitments to anyone or anything else.

In times of war, especially, the claims of any particular state are liable to trump any other claim, to justify the priority of the obligations of citizenship over any obligations to some broader humanity, indeed to legitimize practices of inhumanity (even if under the rubric of just war), to trample over claims about freedom with claims about security, to privilege friend over enemy, and to celebrate one's own modern self both over all others and over all other forms of subjectivity. Limits are acknowledged, even celebrated. Violence erupts, and is deemed legitimate, necessary, the only possible option available for the defence of that modern self that nevertheless claims to be part of a broader humanity in whose name violence may become even more inhumane. Hypocrisies sprout like weeds in spring.

In times of peace, also, the claims of any particular state to a right of self-determination express the degree to which modern political life is predicated on the possibility of freedoms for particular communities, particular peoples, particular territorialized spaces, not on claims made on behalf of a politically undifferentiated humanity. National chauvinism rules, in peace quite as much as in war, although in peace claims about the compatibility of chauvinism with some sort of humanity can find plausible rhetorical ground. Limits are assumed, but scarcely acknowledged. Hypocrisies are cultivated, and bred into alluring displays of virtue. Scholarly parochialism is thereby vindicated. The political theorists can then endlessly cultivate their discourses of solipsism, and discuss principles of justice, rights or freedoms as if the singular state expresses a singular universe of politics and no-one needs to think about the systemic conditions under which a political theory can begin with claims about political life in a singular state, especially a singular state that has a hegemonic place in the structuring of a system of states.

Nevertheless, in practice as well as in principle, no state can survive without the system of states that enables any particular state to exist, to be recognized as existing, to claim sovereignty, to nurture nations, to foster parochial scholarly traditions, to privilege its own cultures, laws, interests and security over almost any other claim. As modern political subjects, we are always subject to the claims of both the modern sovereign state and the modern system of states, to obligations understood in terms of a particular understanding of citizenship and a particular understanding of humanity, but also as always potentially subject to demands that one of these sources of obligation be privileged over the other. Despite endless assertions to the contrary, modern political life is not orchestrated through a grand choice between claims to a generalized humanity and particularized citizenships, but through a double claim to both humanity and citizenship: a double claim that can hold sway only up until certain limits are broached and a privileging of one over the other becomes unavoidable: until responsibility is taken for drawing a line of radical discrimination.

Consequently, while difficult questions may be asked about the possibilities of political life either within the state or within the system of states, even more difficult, and prior, questions keep reappearing about the doubled form of modern political life expressed through our participation in both the state and the states system. Which has greater, or as it is usually and tellingly said, higher authority: the statist claim to sovereignty within its own territory and legal jurisdiction; or the system of states that is the necessary (sovereign) condition under which any state may make a sovereign claim? What is the authentic identity of that political being who is subject to the authority of both the state and states system, who aspires to the identity both of state citizen and human being? What is to be done, by whom, and on what grounds for judgement, when the antagonisms built into the organization of the modern state and system of states generates intolerable levels of violence, whether as overt wars between states or the militarization of human existence in general; or when the organization of political life can no longer rely on the presence of a system of states to enable the claims of sovereign states that express the possibilities, limits and costs of modern freedoms?

Such questions come in many forms. They find expression in many of the paradigmatic texts of modern European political thought. They were already foreshadowed in Machiavelli's recognition of the struggle between a political ethics and some other sort of ethics that must accompany aspirations for republican freedoms.[2] They animate at least some accounts of a tradition of international relations theory, especially those which pay attention to the broader cultural or legal context shaping the specific conditions under which modern accounts of freedom under/within necessity came to be expressed in relation to claims about secular sovereignties.[3] They remain pervasive in just about every contemporary debate about the legitimacy of violence, the promises and threats of globalization and empire, and the fate of the kind of political aspirations for freedom, justice, democracy and all the rest that hinge on the possibility, even necessity, of finding ways of reconciling all claims about citizenship and humanity within the modern sovereign state and system of states. They are difficult questions because they point to sites, moments and practices of radical undecidability, of aporias as some philosophers like to say, between claims that both presuppose and enable each other.[4] As modern political subjects, we are split creatures, both aspiring citizens and aspiring humans, subject to the ultimate authority of both the state and the system of states, celebrants of the securities and freedoms that have been achieved within and between the boundaries of the modern state, and witness to the enormous violence that has been unleashed as a consequence.

Most of what currently counts both as political theory, as the exploration of the principles through which what we have come to call the political that has been enabled within states, as well as the theory of the politics or relations that have been enabled between states, works on the assumption that all claims about citizenship and humanity have indeed been reconciled, at least in principle. Curiously, but in view of the argument I have begun to lay out so far, I hope unsurprisingly, this is an assumption that looks suspiciously like some popular versions of Kant's supposedly utopian aspiration for a perpetual peace. We are all modern people, but each state expresses a particular way of being a modern people, at least as far as the formal claims of the sovereign state and states system are concerned. All relations of universality and particularity may then be worked out *within* any particular sovereign state that supposedly enables the reconciliation of universality and particularity within states, or *within* the system of states that supposedly enables the reconciliation of universality and particularity between states.

Perhaps this is a reasonable assumption. It is affirmed by everyday discourse and by the Charter of the United Nations, by maps, passports and statistics, by violent struggles for national self-determination and by the Olympic Games and World Cup, though not the World Series. Whatever accounts might be offered of the historical processes through which the modern state and system of states came to frame the possibilities and necessities of modern political life, it is this assumption that has become our reigning account of who we are, who we must be, and who we must become as modern political subjects. It expresses the normative ideal of modern free and equal subjects enabled by free and equal sovereign states enabled by a system of sovereign states that expresses the political condition under which we are enabled to be modern human beings capable of acting in the modern world.

It might be comforting to assume that we live within political arrangements that have come to resemble the great Kant's ambition for an earthly perfection, and quite a few respectable people have certainly become a little carried away with the possibilities this implies. Nevertheless, Kant himself was entirely sceptical about the very possibility of this ideal coming to fruition. He was also precisely a thinker of antagonisms, limits and aporias of the kind to be found at the edges of potentially autonomous subjectivities; someone, it might be said, who would be quite bemused by the way his speculative account of a regulative ideal that could never be reached has become the assumed, even if not quite perfected, condition of modern political life that can be taken for granted as the way political life must be: in fact is, and must continue to become.

Many other scepticisms about this assumption have also been advanced. This is partly because it expresses an ideal that has scarcely been achieved by many human beings struggling to act in the modern world. It is partly because the promise of harmony expressed in the ideal implies the necessity of violence between those sovereign states that have not yet learnt how to coexist in a proper internationalism – the consequence drawn by those political realists who nevertheless cling to their (sometimes quasi-Kantian, sometimes explicitly nationalist) ideal of sovereign states and nations. It is partly because it expresses a particular account of what it means to be a human being capable of acting in the world: an account that may well work as an idealization of how we might reconcile universality and particularity but nevertheless expresses a culturally and historically particular way of framing questions about universality and particularity, not least in relation to what it means to be human or to make claims about the world.

It is in this context that we can understand what is at stake in the way so many forms of analysis make the elementary mistake of supposing that a problem framed as a radical dualism can be solved by an appeal to a monism defined as a shift from one half of the dualism to the other. This is not because, in their own terms, either political theory or theories of international are incapable of considerable sophistication; very much to the contrary. It is because the very existence of modern political theory and theories of international relations as distinct traditions of analysis reproduces a dualistic framing of what must be understood as mutually constitutive and always potentially aporetic relations between claims made by sovereign states and claims made by the system of sovereign states that enable the very existence of any sovereign state. When the most difficult questions posed by the structuring of modern political life occur right where the contradictory claims of the sovereign state and the system of sovereign states is always likely to become aporetic, the most influential traditions of political and international theory encourage us either to stay where and what we are on either side of the line between the sovereign state or the system of sovereign states, or to imagine a great leap from one to the other so as to eradicate the dangers of particularism and pluralism and move on to the potentialities of a more universalistically conceived humanity.

It is in this context also that we can understand what is at stake in the way the primary contradictions of modern political life appear to be set out spatially, on the territorial ground of the sovereign state here inside and the system of territorialized states there outside, and yet we are constantly invited to solve the problems arising from such contradictions through an appeal to temporality, through the processes of an emancipatory history, through a narrative that runs from here to there in time rather than in space. The temptation to drive the great bus of linear history through an aporia, a dead-end street, a point at which it is no longer possible to both eat and keep one's cake, is especially strong in this context given the force of claims about the emancipatory possibilities of a universalizing history that emerged, in the eighteenth and nineteenth centuries, after the basic principles of political life in the modern state and system of states had come to be framed against the prevailing hierarchies of premodern, medieval, feudal, imperial or theocratic order. It works especially well as a claim about the potentialities of temporal processes that might be enabled within the state, perhaps within every state. Yet it does not and cannot work in relation to a form of political life that is already organized as a relationship between particularity and universality: as a particular relation between universality and particularity orchestrated both within the state and within the system of states, and as an ultimately irresolvable antagonism between the claims of state and the claims of the system of states. Consequently, while the bus of linear history may offer a cheap ride, it can only travel around a short circuit: the endless ride from "political realism" to "political idealism" and back again, in the international relations camp, or the also endless extrapolation of some particular account of "justice" or "rights" within a particular state to some international or global setting and back again in the camp of those who assume that this is sufficient in order to engage in what we call "political" theory.

This is a ride we are especially invited to take again and again in stories about the development of a discipline of international relations shaped by shattered illusions and tragic wisdom after the war that was supposed to end all wars.[5] Enacting a discourse of perpetual oscillation, these stories nevertheless work as a very effective myth of creation. Enacting a myth of creation, they work so as to affirm both a norm of progress and increasing freedom, and a norm of endless repetition: the norm of a supposedly normative political theory, and the norm of a supposedly realistic international relations. Linear accounts of historical progress offer to take us from the particularities of the state to some more universally conceived existence, but also from the fragmented particularities of the states system to some more universally conceived existence. In both cases we start from some sort of particularity and move to some sort of universality. Yet this move is possible only if the relationship between the modern state and the modern states system is systematically ignored, if the constitutive contradictions of modern political life are wished away: if the achievements as well as disasters of a form of political life predicated on the possibilities of a universality-within-particularity and a particularity-within-universality are sabotaged by claims about the necessity for political realism in an international anarchy, or about the cataclysms that must befall us if necessity is ignored in favour of some other ambition. If the discipline of international relations offers the clearest expression of how an endless discourse of repetitions works when an appeal to linear progress in time fails to solve contradictions expressed in a territorialized space, however, modern political theory is scarcely capable of recognizing the ground to which it is so firmly attached when it expresses a part, and only a part, of what it might mean to engage with the necessities and possibilities of modern political life.

Consequently, to claim that the most challenging political problems of our time express an urgent need to reimagine where and what we take politics to be must involve, in the first instance, a refusal of the familiar short circuits of linear history and some re-engagement with the constitutive contradictions of modern political life in the modern state and system of states, and with the conditions under which the journey across an aporia has become both so attractive and yet so impossible. Not least, this implies greater sensitivity to the ways in which the apparently spatial forms of modern political life, forms that invite specific accounts of temporality as a way "out" of the contradictions between an inside and an outside they express, already enact those accounts of temporality as the very condition of being modern.

"Accept my assumptions … "

Neither the modern state nor the system of states appears to us simply as an object of political analysis. Neither is outside our capacities as hunters and gatherers of knowledge about our status as modern political subjects, and subjectivities. They appear, rather, as political practices that, among other things, produce and sustain many pervasive discourses about who we are as political subjects and how we should be analysing what we do when we understand ourselves to be acting politically. Our ability to know and engage with the modern state and system of states is enabled by our own conditionalities and achievements as subjects of the modern state and system of states. This is so whether we focus on a politics explicitly predicated on the state, internally or externally, or on a politics that is claimed to be somehow different from that which we have come to know in relation to the modern state and system of states. Any claim to a political science that pretends otherwise is always destined for dogmatism rather than for some kind of critical knowledge. Any claim to a normative vision of escape from the modern state and system of states will be caught within accounts of what it means to be a visionary, to effect an escape, to imagine the possibilities of being otherwise that are already produced by modern accounts of political necessity, possibility and subjectivity.

In this respect we have all too often confirmed Hobbes' bold seventeenth-century prediction that as long as we come to accept the assumptions he laid before us, as he became aware of the broad contours of the emerging world of modern subjectivities and knowledge practices, and the opportunities they offered for a way out of the specific conflicts over legitimate authority in an English society experiencing multiple instabilities and challenges to a decaying order, we can come to no other conclusions than his. In very large measure, we have indeed come to accept Hobbes' most basic assumptions about what it must mean to engage in political life, even when contesting them in the name of, say, the essential dignity of man prior to any political order, Lockean accounts of consent and popular sovereignty, Kantian visions of peace and progress, or a belief that all such mouldering European men are simply outmoded expressions of another age. We are all caught up in processes of "seeing like a state,"[6] and of reproducing assumptions about what the state must be in claims about what the state in fact is, what it does, what it promises, and what must happen if we try to do without it. Even so, while Hobbes managed to articulate assumptions that have congealed into many of the constitutive practices of modern politics, these assumptions were never cast in stone. Hobbes' preferred medium was law, a medium much less resistant to erosion, indeed one always in danger of being ripped and overwritten. Hobbes knew better than most that things fall apart, to invoke Chinua Achebe's more contemporary sensibility.[7]

Hobbes sets out his snappy, and in the context of his day, quite extraordinary account of how we ought to think about the world as a condition of even imagining an appropriate form of political order. It is now quite difficult to appreciate what he and other early-modern European thinkers achieved by telling us what it must mean to speak of space and time, language and cosmos, sense and nonsense, or human and humanity before launching into their stories about a state of nature, the social contract and the proper production of secure liberty under sovereign law: stories about where and when one needs to start thinking about political possibilities, and where and when these possibilities will necessarily come to an end. There is certainly quite as much at stake in what Hobbes achieves in his demolition of any other way of being, not least his dismissal of all those claims about Being taught in "all the Universities of Christendome, grounded upon certain Texts of Aristotle"[8] and his account of what it means to think and speak coherently, as in anything he says about human nature, the anarchical paranoia of modern man, or life after the social contract. Hobbes, after all, is widely regarded as the most articulate and precise theorist of modern sovereignty, of the practice of founding, of authorizing some spatiotemporal ground on which practices of power might be expressed as claims to authority, not least against and yet within a cultural context thriving on competing accounts of inclusion and exclusion.[9] Hobbes' own practices of founding still retain a widespread aura of natural necessity. They tell us a lot about the ways in which the discourses of the modern state and states system reproduce many of Hobbes' most magical spatiotemporal gestures so as to ensure that there can, and must, be no alternative to it, or them. They also tell us a lot about the ways in which our discourses of political analysis have come to be so comfortable treating his account of sovereign authority as a solid ground from which to launch their own claims to authoritative knowledge about power and authority.

Hobbes has become a name for many things. He expresses the achievements of huge structural and historical forces. He builds on traditions that take us back to those multiple and mongrel worlds we identify with the classical ages of Greeks and Christians. He is but one link to those also multiple and mongrel claims about, say, enlightenment, liberty, democracy and emancipation that fix our sense of political possibilities in relation to the parochial, even if universalizing, histories of one small part of the world. More than most other canonical political thinkers, he has been put quite firmly in his place as a man of a particular time struggling with particular problems within very specific horizons of intelligibility. Still, Hobbes remains arguably the most brilliant theorist of the modern political imagination, the one who tells us about the most basic necessities of seeing like a state as well as about the relationship between modern practices of authorization in general and the authorizing practices of the modern state in particular. It is both with and against Hobbes' ability to affirm many of the conditions under which we have been able to imagine modern political life, both as actuality and as possibility, that it is perhaps most necessary to work in order to recover some sense of what it might mean to imagine political life on some other terms; on terms, that is, that are not already given as the necessary but impossible other that already enables the modern state, the modern system of states, and the modern political subject that is precisely not other.

The contemporary limitations of the kind of political imagination we can see appearing in the texts of people like Hobbes, or of writers like Kant, who share very similar premises despite all those secondary commentaries and textbooks that keep polarizing the differences between them,[10] are especially visible in recent attempts to understand the volatile dynamics that are claimed to be disrupting our prevailing political institutions and expectations. Symptomatically, claims about temporality, historical change and structural transformation increasingly appear as problems that are irresolvable through the structuring of similarities and differences in territorial space. It has become more and more difficult to imagine political possibilities that are somehow novel, or alternative, or better, or otherwise, within a spatially privileged account of where and what politics must be. Nevertheless, it is not obvious how we can even begin to imagine a political life that is not contained within the modern state and modern states system. Our understanding of *politics* is not easily disentangled from the legacies of the *polis*, despite the multiple ways in which two and a half millennia of human histories, and a few centuries of especially dynamic "modernization," have altered just about every condition that once enabled a few cities thriving near the Mediterranean Sea to organize themselves in ways still informing some of the constitutive ambitions of modern states.

Hobbes' guiding instinct was to transform all opportunities for temporal contingency into the possibility of spatial order, the order he understood especially in geometrical terms inherited from Euclid. These were the very convenient terms that permitted universalist claims about topological form within limits defined as points at either end of a line: the limits distinguishing realms of measurable finitude from any possible infinity towards which divisible lines might otherwise project.[11] This was an instinct that conventionally marks him off from Machiavelli's prior attempt to articulate the possibility of a politics in time.[12] It is an instinct that also identifies him as someone who had an uncanny sense of what a world of modern subjects – a world of spatially delineated selves distributed in spaces separated from other spaces – would have to look like. For many commentators, Hobbes' instincts seem to be increasingly at odds with the temporalities of our times, with our sense that the networks, flows, and accelerations we see all around us must surely challenge the structures of spatial inclusion and exclusion we associate with the Hobbesian state. Indeed, in some respects it is Machiavelli's instincts that seem more immediately in touch with our temporalities, more in accordance with our increasingly pervasive sense that the world of politics will not stand still.

It is not that we now have to emulate Machiavelli's struggle to find ways of thinking and acting politically in a world of overdetermining theological universals, of imagining a world of humans acting in time, of creating something new in time in a world governed by ideals of an already perfected and God-given eternity. Among many other things, not least the many competing versions of human possibility animating creative renewal in Renaissance Italy, Machiavelli had to work against the claims of an omniscient deity, to stake a claim about the possibilities of *human* freedom, about the capacity of human beings to create something of value for themselves by themselves. In the process, he attracted as dark a reputation as one can imagine for one of the founding heroes of what we are now so pleased to call a humanism. We, by contrast, have only to reimagine the possibilities of political life in a world of overdetermining claims about the stateing of the world and the worlding of the state. It should not be that difficult. After all, our long, even if often desperate, celebration of humanism has indeed helped us to be able to imagine a palpable humanity, to understand ourselves as already part of some collectivity that is far more extensive than the ambitious Italian republics or the sovereign states that Hobbes and Kant saw developing further north a few centuries later.

Yet for all its celebrity, humanity is a name we assign to a possible world we hardly know how to speak about in political terms, unless we do indeed wish to claim that the modern state and the modern system of states are sufficient to allow us to speak about a politics of humanity: the claim advanced by voices of official political reason everywhere. According to this view, the international simply is the world. International relations is just a synonym for world politics. Or at least, as the story goes, once the entire planet is finally covered with the right kind of states, all participating in the right kind of states system, we will have finally transformed our world into a properly international experience for everyone. Nevertheless, it takes a fair degree of historical amnesia to be able to assume that the international is, or will eventually be, co-extensive with the world or with humanity. Both the state and the states system were constituted by abrupt, not to say violent struggles to set themselves off from the world and from any claim to humanity as such. These demarcations were precisely what set thinkers like Machiavelli, Hobbes and Kant into motion; into their various attempts to articulate worlds of political possibility that were separated from yet somehow still connected to some other world, whether of Nature, Man, God or those worlds against which self-affirming moderns had come to know themselves through crusades, conquests, colonizations, perplexities and wonder.

Many responses to contemporary political life seem to affirm a wish that we might somehow go back to an age before Machiavelli used his little dagger to help rip apart the world of political possibilities on earth from the world of theological universals that might obtain in heaven. Fortunately, we have the advantage over Machiavelli of knowing that the theological universals against which he worked to (re)-establish a possibility of political freedoms in particular places, and in relation to which the modern state and modern states system have worked out a specific account of the possible ways of organizing relations between universality and particularity, was merely a parochial account of creation and its effects. To work within claims about universality and particularity that were put into circulation in that specific arena is not going to offer a particularly easy way into thinking about what the human or the world might mean politically under contemporary conditions.

Claims about change, both about the spatiotemporality of human existence in general and about the spatiotemporal transformation of spatiotemporally specific forms of social life, have now become an indispensable part of any plausible account of what we do when we take ourselves to be acting politically.[13] Indeed, some theorists insist that modernity must be understood precisely as an era in which the world came to move with a vengeance, to embrace temporality, to invent History, to resist all spatial fixings and containerizations. Such accounts tend to pay special attention to the articulation of the sense of historicity that came to be expressed in Europe sometime in the late eighteenth or early nineteenth century, perhaps between the exemplary later texts of Kant and Hegel's more elaborately dialectical teleology. Such accounts tend to be especially impressed by the constructive/destructive dynamics of capitalist modernization understood as a singular even if contradictory process, and typically lead to claims about a contemporary collapse of the historical project sketched by the Kantians and Hegelians, and the emergence of new forms of spatiality, often on a global scale.[14]

Without doubting that we are now being asked to make sense of novel and confusing spatial practices, however, I am more persuaded by readings of modernity as an era in which the possibilities of temporality and change expressed by the Kantians and Hegelians were already enabled by the articulation of a spatiotemporally specific account of spatiotemporal foundations of the kind we find in Hobbes. Modern accounts of sovereignty may express borders in space, but they rest on borders in time, especially, as Fasolt has argued so provocatively, on the distinction between past and present that enables modern articulations of a claim to freedom in space and in time.[15]

While it may be difficult enough to make sense of emerging forms of spatiality, it is now even more difficult to make sense of temporality without resorting to the straight-line trajectories, the point-to-point teleologies, through which the modern world learnt to put order into time, and even to put time in its proper place. This place, and this order, was the modern state and modern system of states, raising questions about the relationship between this spatiotemporal order and its others, not least the order that is usually assumed to be prior to that of the modern state and states system, and about the point at which one gave way to the other, and even the possibility of knowing one from the other. Fasolt's provocation is precisely to identify a radical incommensurability and unintelligibility between early-modern defenders of claims to state sovereignty and defenders of a decaying empire. This poses problems for those who seek to make claims about historical knowledge that can indeed penetrate through the horizons of historical orders, but also draws attention to the relationship between the limits of history in specifying a ground of origin for the modern state and system of states, and the limits of the modern state and system of states as orders seeking to authorize the spatiotemporal grounds enabling modern forms of political life. It draws attention, that is, to a broad range of complex practices – in both sites and moments of action, mutual production, recursivity, liminality, connection, contradiction, and delimitation – at work both in the temporal accounts of the origins and futures of modern political life and in the spatial accounts of those borders that delimit and enable a structure of sovereign states and system of sovereign states.[16]

Whether read through accounts of modernity as a privileging of spatiality or of temporality, however, it is fairly clear that many contemporary accounts of change are sharply at odds with the expectations affirmed by the discourses of and about the modern state and system of states. Theorizations of change may not seem like such a huge problem for, say, the sociologists or historians, but they pose a rather profound problem for theorists of political life – and thus for sociologists, historians and everyone else who relies on accounts of society, community and subjectivity worked out in relation to the modern state. Everything else may be changing, transforming, differentiating, be in the process of becoming other than it has come to be, but the modern state and modern system of states, so many accounts of modern politics insist, or simply assume, goes on forever. Or at least, once perfected everywhere, the state and states system will be able to organize the world of politics so as to bring necessities and freedoms in line with a structure of inclusions/exclusions and universalities/particularities, a structure that enables the modern state to be the home of modern subjects and modern nations living under civilized modes of conduct governed through democratic institutions regulated by the rule of law in ways that minimize antagonisms with other states. Or, in yet another variation of the same basic theme, the eternal or perfectible state/ states system is just about to collapse in favour of some counter-narrative about their imminent disappearance, whether as utopian vision, apocalyptic nightmare, pragmatic evolution to new and higher forms of governance, a final realization of cosmopolitan reason, or the final collapse/relapse of states and states system into yet another imperial domination.

Many of these accounts of change suggest considerable conceptual trouble. The modern state may well be here for the foreseeable future, as some self-proclaimed political realists still insist; but this tells us very little about what states are likely to be, or what they will do, or how they will relate to a variety of other institutions and practices that so many take to be constitutive aspects of the political realities of our time. The modern state may well offer opportunities for improvement in many respects and in many places; but the ambition to realize a more perfect world of autonomous-though-interdependent democracies may well come to look a little imperfect when patterns of power and the construction of authoritative practices and institutions fail to emulate the territorial map of states that states insist we see when we look at the world in their terms. More likely, as more Machiavellian sensibilities might suggest, the narrative that tells us that the state and system of states is what there is and must be in the world, and indeed is coextensive with the world as such, is going to seem increasingly implausible, to lack the authority that might enable the reproduction of authority. But, the chorus shouts, more out of habit than expectation, what could be the alternative? Habitual questions invite habitual answers, and these are not difficult to identify in the now vast discourses that seek to interpret the changing context in which we now try to make sense of our political inheritances and our future possibilities.

The modern political imagination, enabled by the possibility of controlling and taming the contingencies of temporal existence within the spatial orders of the modern sovereign and territorial state, and thus the possibility of enabling the unfolding of modern times/histories within their protected spaces, has long struggled to resolve the consequent tension between the demands of spatial containment and the temporal dynamics released by just about everything else we have come to think of as specifically modern. Much of what now passes for a political realism derives from a normative claim that the modern state *must* somehow contain and control all the dynamic forces of the modern world, whether as capitalisms, industrializations or mass mobilizations. Much of what passes for a claim to political emancipation derives from a reading of history as the eventual withering away of the state and the realization of some other, more inclusive form of political community, whether in quick revolutionary time or slow evolutionary or functional time. Much of the sclerotic character of contemporary political analysis builds on the construction of an army of stereotypes on either side of this apparently endless debate between spatial continuities and temporal transformations.

These stereotypes have been assembled into the rhetorical strategies of a political realism (and thus a political liberalism) that slip and slide from claims about temporal contingency to claims about spatial and structural necessity, and many scholars are still prepared to use these strategies as an uncontentious ground for knowledge rather than as a rather extraordinary work of political art.[17] They have now become especially visible in many contemporary claims and counterclaims about globalization and the challenges that the many different processes conflated under this term pose to the capacities, authorities and boundaries of modern states, whether as territorialities, institutions or practices. They are equally visible in debates about the fate of modernity and the shifting relations of spatiality and temporality that have been identified under the equally dubious name of the postmodern. They are at the heart of competing claims about an internationalizing/globalizing political economy and the specific mechanisms of productions, technologies, distributions and exchanges that may, or may not, be disrupting the practices and institutions that have been enabled by and reproduce the spatiotemporal forms of the modern state and states system. They animate attempts to make sense of claims about changing relations between global and local, colonizer and colonized, national, multicultural and cosmopolitan citizenships, conflicts among civilizations, humanitarian responses to judgements about state failure, incipient imperialisms and other signs of struggle over who it is that ought to be thought of as a proper subject of politics if the conventional story about our privileged being as autonomous subject-citizens of sovereign states is indeed as threadbare as many now claim it now is, or should be.

Suspicions

Framed in this way, claims about the need to reimagine where and what we take politics to be immediately resonate with three groups of familiar and tightly interwoven suspicions about the sustainability of specifically modern accounts of political life: suspicions about the dangers of depoliticization; suspicions about the dangers of too much politicization; and suspicions about the dangers marked by the boundaries of the modern state and states system. Each of these suspicions has been aired in many different contexts and expressed in many different ways since the broad contours of modern political life began to take on some clarity over the course of the European seventeenth century. Each expresses aspects of the ambivalences, antagonisms and contradictions enabled by the secular dualisms affirmed by the modern sovereign-state, by the modern system of states, and by the modern subject that enables and is enabled by the modern state and system of states. Much of the contemporary force of calls to reimagine political life builds on the degree to which established ways of responding to these long-standing suspicions have lost much of their plausibility and legitimacy in many contexts. In all three cases, politics has come to be posed as an increasingly difficult *problem*, rather than as already or still-to-be-achieved principles and practices everyone can or should take for granted. While politics is, in principle, always intrinsically difficult to identify with great clarity, not least because the very act of identifying what it is can itself be identified as an important and historically contingent political practice, an increasingly conscious aspect of contemporary political practice has involved insistent and diverse challenges to the principles informing our sense of what counts as a properly political practice.

In some senses, all three suspicions can be traced back to what are widely taken to be foundational moments and texts of the most influential traditions of modern politics. This is why thinkers such as Machiavelli, Hobbes and Kant still allow for some critical purchase on contemporary dilemmas, despite the degree to which they have been so effectively codified into apparently unchallengeable accounts of what political life must involve.[18] In other senses, these suspicions have become especially acute as a consequence of a broad range of contemporary dynamics that are said to be destabilizing established ways of responding to the ambivalences, antagonisms and contradictions enabled by the modern state, states system and subject. This is why even the most creative re-engagements with canonical texts and traditions seem so inadequate, flimsy and overextended in the face of emerging situations, dangers and opportunities.

There have been suspicions, first, about the adequacy of prevailing accounts of the proper relation between politics and other apparently discrete aspects of human existence, and thus about the tendency towards depoliticization that, paradoxically, has been such an important characteristic of modern politics. Many of the great controversies, and achievements, of modern politics have been energized by attempts to distinguish between the political and the theological, the ethical, the social, the civil or the economic. Moreover, many of the most difficult problems of modern politics have turned on distinctions *within* what is usually taken to be modern political discourse between the political and the administrative, and, most contentiously, between a sovereign capacity to make political decisions and a democratic capacity to express or represent some sort of sovereign (or national) political community in whose name these decisions are taken.[19]

Sometimes there has been a fear that politics threatens to subsume everything else. This fear has driven various attempts to liberate the economic, or the ethical, or the private, or the civil from a specifically, and carefully delimited, sphere of political action, which is often reduced in turn to a matter of electoral contestation. Sometimes there has been a converse fear that politics is being surrendered to something else: to the private conscience of an individual, to the commercial logic of a competitive market, or to a rationalizing logic of instrumental efficiency. While often framed as a matter of public and private liberties, or of a tension between states and markets, these fears express an ambivalence about politics that is itself constitutive of how modern politics has been enabled in relation to the secular authority of the state rather than to the ultimately theocratic authority of church and/or empire. Having been constituted in relation to the secular state, politics has been articulated as both a promise and a threat: as a promise of secular achievement, of collective freedoms, of peace under law, of maturity and enlightenment, of national greatness; but also as a threat to other (pre-political) values, other freedoms, other claims to goodness, truth and beauty. In large measure, modern politics has responded to this ambiguous potential through various attempts to distinguish between complementary spheres: state and church; state and civil society; politics and government; public and private; politics and ethics; politics and economy; and so on. Specific forms of political practice have likewise sought credibility by seeking to balance these competing spheres of what was nevertheless ultimately understood as political life. Liberalism in general, and the welfare state and various forms of social democracy in particular, have been most explicitly framed as the best possible way of accommodating the competing demands of the split worlds of modern politics, the best way of finding an imagined middle ground between a tota-lizing politics and a radical depoliticization of politics in the name of some other kind of subjectivity and some other kind of authority. This ideal may have been articulated in relation to some very specific parts of the world, but has now come to be the regulative imaginary many deem to be appropriate for all people and all peoples everywhere.

Under contemporary conditions marked by the apparently inexorable demands of capitalism and/or modernization, and thus in ways that have been examined in terms largely laid out by nineteenth- and early twentieth-century writers such as Marx and Weber, among many others, the fear that politics has indeed been subsumed into or replaced by something else has seemed increasingly persuasive. Thus there have been persistent though often muted attempts, from both right and left, to resist the mere administration of things, the colonization of the life world, or the reduction of democratic practices to instrumentalities of representation and market rationality, and to canvass the possibilities of a revived sense of political community, some more authenti-cally political understanding of political life. For some, the classical *polis* has offered a standard against which modern political life could be found want-ing. More frequently, the unfulfilled, or betrayed, potentialities of the modern state have been of greater concern. These potentialities have been conceived in many different ways: as claims about nationalism, socialism, liberalism or republicanism, but, since the days of the American and French revolutions, almost always in relation to claims about democracy and democratization. In response, however, it has often been said that the *polis* or eighteenth-century notions of civil society can now name only the possibility of a conservative nostalgia unable to face up to the demands, the simple instrumental necessities, of a liberal capitalist modernity. Democracy can name only a technique of governance, not an expression or an enabling of the governed. Politics, far from being the condition of being human, as Aristotle had once claimed and various strains of nationalism, socialism, liberalism and republicanism have sought to reaffirm, is in danger of being snuffed out by the very processes that once seemed to promise political fulfilment.

In the contemporary context, the urge to avoid questions about politics, and to appeal instead to the ultimate authority of, for example, an ill-defined ethical community of humankind, an equally ill-defined rationality of a global market economy predicated on the valuation of property rather than the valuation of a sovereign political community, and/or technocratically driven forms of governance and representation, not to say crude military force unleashed in the name of democracy, has become a central feature of contemporary political debate.[20] It has again put into question many received assumptions about what we take politics to be and how we might, or might not, distinguish it from the ethical, the economic, or indeed from anything else, and how we might now judge claims about democracy in relation to claims about political authority. It is in this context, especially, that we can understand much of the contemporary obsession with renewing the less cynical promises of democracy in so many places, and the hope that through some new – participatory, agonistic, transnational – forms of democratization, all the great ambitions of a modern politics – ambitions for liberty, for equality, for justice, for security – might finally break the grip of instrumental reason, capitalist commodification and the injustices they ferment and reproduce.[21] Such ambitions have brought many achievements, and thus many calls to continue with the struggle. They have also brought many bitter disappointments.

Second, and conversely, there have been suspicions that modern politics is susceptible not only to various processes of depoliticization, as various aspects of human life are in some respects freed from an explicitly political arena, but also to the capacity of the modern state to arrogate all aspects of human life to itself in the name of a monopoly on authority, not least the authority to deploy violence. This suspicion was already widely aired among those who sought to articulate the possibilities of politics within a modern state in early-modern Europe, generating all those difficult questions about how the sovereignty of a state might be reconciled with the sovereignty of the people. Hobbes is often counterposed to John Locke in this respect, and the contradictions brilliantly identified by Rousseau can be read in relation to the historicist dialectics even more brilliantly systematized, and constrained, by Hegel. These and other readings have become central to the canonical accounts of the central problems posed by the great shift to the modern state as the proper home for a properly political life.

The consequence, however, can also be read in relation to all those historical struggles in which states have effectively minimized the sovereignty of the people in the name of their own supremacy, whether for the long-term good of the people, or for the short-term demands of some state of emergency. The danger of the modern state, we know all too well, is the potential for "totalitarianism," "authoritarianism," "fascism," or what has often, and disturbingly, been in danger of amounting to much the same thing, the monopolistic claim to a state sovereignty sundered from, but articulated in the name of, a popular sovereignty, and capable of effacing all claims to diversity in the name of its own collective unity. It is in this context that we can again understand much of the contemporary impetus behind claims about democratization, or even claims about the potentialities of a market rationality; but also the sense that the claims of sovereign states to be able to provide the conditions under which democratization might be possible are fundamentally at odds with the administrative and disciplinary apparatus, and in the final, or not so final, instance, the physical force and resort to war, they deem necessary for the constitution of a properly democratic politics.

Perhaps the most important constitutive gamble of modern politics, in fact, has been that the sovereign state would nurture rather than devour its citizens. Contemporary references to the "security dilemma" now tend to be dominated by analogies between the structurally driven competition among states coexisting in a system of states and Hobbes' account of a world of free and equal (modern, liberal) individuals in an abstract "state of nature," but Hobbes' major contribution in this respect may well be his commentary on the ways in which the sovereignty he insists must be constituted so as to protect free and equal individuals is not exactly guaranteed to live up to its promise. States are a source of insecurity precisely because of the way they promise to provide security. The subject of security, as I have put it elsewhere, is precisely the modern subject that must be secured.[22] States encourage claims about freedoms within their territory because to be within a territory is to be under law, under necessity and always subject to the exception that enables the rule. Again, many are sufficiently privileged to take a gamble of trusting in the freedoms and securities promised by the modern state, but it is also a gamble that very many people have lost, and lost very badly.

There have been suspicions, third, about the capacity of the modern state to fulfil its promise to provide a home for modern politics, even when struggles to sustain powerful institutions and practices of popular sovereignty have been relatively effective. These suspicions can also be traced back a long way. They are expressed in a broad range of claims about the increasingly problematic status of conceptions of the political *within* the modern state, given various suspicions about the plausibility of any sharp distinction *between* the internal spaces of the modern state and the spaces of the international, of the modern system of states, beyond. Difficulties arise here not in relation to the ambivalences and tensions between politics and something else, or to the capacity of states to impose their understanding of collective necessities on everyone and everything, but to the capacity of states to demarcate a clear limit to their capacities and jurisdictions, especially in relation to the claims of the system of sovereign states, and the claims of that system to express rights and needs that might be attributed to humanity in general.

It is this third group of suspicions that has come to be of most pressing concern in contemporary political life, though they implicate and complicate the other two sorts of suspicion in various ways.[23] They also explain much of the contemporary impetus both to reimagine where and what we take politics to be, as well as to wish that politics would somehow go away, or to suspect that politics is indeed already in the process of coming to an end. If we are to make any sense of what is at stake in contemporary calls to reimagine the political imagination, it is now necessary to pay a lot more attention to what happens on the line that effects an apparently sharp distinction between two distinct spaces: the domestic spaces of the territorial state, and the foreign spaces of the modern system of states, each with their own accounts of temporal and political possibility – a line that also assumes a capacity to draw further lines between the modern subject and other subjects/sovereigns and between the modern system of states and the wider world beyond. The doubles and triples of modern political life are easily multiplied.[24]

To take this line for granted is precisely not to affirm a set of realities that simply exist in the world, and which, fortunately or tragically, resist any attempt to imagine something different. It is to affirm an ensemble of historical and abstractly formulated but massively embodied accounts of what it *must* mean to divide the world, to discriminate between that which is included and that which is excluded, that which is friend and that which is enemy, that which is society and that which is anarchy, that which is normal and that which is exceptional: accounts that must be affirmed – authorized, legitimized – as the only condition under which worldly realities and political possibilities can properly be engaged. What counts for reality and necessity in modern political life, and thus what works to both enable and constrain the modern political imagination, has to be understood in the first instance as an enactment of an historically specific imagination of political possibility, an imagination that knows how to draw the line:[25] that knows both how to discriminate and how to authorize the discriminations that are enacted by sovereign acts of discrimination.

This enactment literally and figuratively centres on the practices of the modern state and its subjects; on all their potentialities and all their dangers. It especially centres on the discriminations and authorizations enacted and expressed in the practices and institutions of modern state sovereignty, practices which simultaneously draw the line in territorial space and differentiate between legitimate and illegitimate practices within the space they delimit. It is in relation to the sovereign practices of the modern state that we are supposed to understand what it means to draw the line: to distinguish between what is legal and illegal, possible and impossible, realistic and utopian, the properly political and the merely economic, civil or private internally and the also merely international, or perhaps theological, externally. The most important decisions about modern political life – about which and what kinds of people get to be counted among the included, about what has to be done to secure the inclusion, about what ought to be done once these inclusions are secured and normalized, about who gets to decide when previously accepted decisions are to be redecided or suspended, about who gets to decide who gets to make, and make binding, judgements about these and all other decisions – are made in relation to this line, this border that is so much more than a physical demarcation on earthly topography. It is the sense that this line has become a little problematic in some contexts and radically uncertain in others that has undermined so many convictions not only about what it now means to engage in political life, but also of what it would mean to struggle for something better, for something more democratic, for something recognizably political in an age in which suspicions about what now counts for politics have become quite intense.

To draw attention to contemporary suspicions about the distinction between the state and the system of states, the properly political and the merely international, however, is to run into extensive analytical difficulties. Not least, the modern disciplines of knowledge that seek to engage with modern politics and its imaginative possibilities are already carefully situated on either side of the line that distinguishes the political from the international. Moreover, they are themselves largely constituted through the assumption that this line *must* be drawn. They tend to observe both its discriminations and its authorizations as a natural condition rather than as an historical achievement, an ongoing practice, and an ongoing problem. In effect, they assume what they are now increasingly asked to examine. Many contemporary attempts to reimagine political imagination likewise seek to do so from either side of this line and, unsurprisingly, tend to both reproduce and reauthorize the line they seek to evade, transcend or simply ignore.

Although the line between the political and the international is widely judged to be increasingly problematic, and although questions about political life supposedly settled in relation to it are now asked with renewed urgency, it is a line that cannot be evaded, transcended or ignored. As a constitutive limit of modern politics in territorial space, it is also a constitutive limit of both modern political practice and the modern political imagination. As a demarcation, however, it is also the site of a mutual production, and much of what is interesting about it concerns the very active and diverse practices of mutual production that are enabled once the demarcation has been made. Many of these practices hinge on the ways in which the demarcation of an outside that affirms an inside produces a powerful sense of what it must mean to escape the inside: of what it means to escape from the modern achievement of a spatially delimited political community always seeking to go beyond what has already been achieved in time. Consequently, if modern political life is in need of reimagination, attempts to do so on terms uncritically assuming a stance on either side of the line that sets the limits of the modern political imagination will necessarily run into irresolvable difficulties.

While in some senses these difficulties are entirely familiar, they are often very difficult to see or act upon with any clarity. Because it has become much easier to become preoccupied with what goes on within the apparently distinctive realms that are generated by the line between the internal and the external, the intense practices that produce this line come to seem entirely unproblematic, or easy to erase. Consequently, we keep returning to the need to draw the line where it is supposed to be drawn, to read necessities and possibilities in terms demanded by this historically entrenched, but also historically contingent, delineation of necessities and possibilities. To think about the possibilities of some other political imagination is to become familiar with various narratives of escape that keep returning to where they started: to the line that both affirms what we must be as citizens of modern sovereign states, and offers us vistas of a wider – more international, more cosmopolitan, more humane – world that seems to be always unattainable. This line was once inscribed in the firm belief that it carried, or might carry, all the guarantees of universal reason, the possibilities of reconciling all contingencies within the necessities of state, the possibilities of inscribing a proper political home within the territorial spaces of a secular world freed, more or less, from the threats of religious warfare, stifling empires and all those peoples who were somehow both outside and inside the world of modern man. This was perhaps the belief that ultimately made the gamble on the political possibilities of the modern state so attractive. It has nevertheless been quite some time since these inscriptions of necessity and contingency have been recognized as yet another historical contingency.

Citizen, human, horizontal, vertical

Many readers will doubtless remain unpersuaded by the claim that the most challenging political problems of our time express an urgent need to reimagine where and what we take politics to be, often with very good reason. Scepticism about claims to novelty is always to be recommended. So, too, is scepticism about claims that all is well with established political principles, institutions and practices. Indeed, an insistence on both forms of scepticism, and thus about prevailing narratives of stasis and change, or structure and historicity, is now probably a necessary condition for thinking about our political futures in more imaginative ways.[26] However, there is sufficient consensus among diverse analytical perspectives about the limits, in several senses, of modern politics to warrant a more sustained discussion of what might be at stake in confronting these limits in discussions about a wide range of contemporary political challenges. While I am prepared to be sceptical towards many claims about how contemporary political life is being transformed by economies, technologies, movements and all the rest, there seems to me to be little doubt that the sharp distinction between the internal and external spaces of modern politics, or (crucially, what is not quite the same thing) between politics within states and international relations between states, is now extraordinarily difficult to sustain. It is difficult to sustain both in claims about empirical realities and in claims about legitimate authority: claims that are not always (indeed, are never) easy to keep apart.

That the distinction between the national and the international is in trouble as well as the source of many troubles may to some extent be gauged from the many scholars, journalists and even politicians who keep telling us so. They have told us so most recently in relation to claims about globalized production, free trade, humanitarian or pre-emptive intervention, the common fate of a planetary ecology, the need for an alliance against the proliferating barbarians, and so on. It has even become very easy for some people to speak of the world, or humanity, as a whole, as if either the world or humanity is an entirely unproblematic political category.[27] Some simply suggest that politics is politics is politics, no matter what the context, internally or externally, historically or geographically. Others suspect that an erasure of a sharp distinction between the political and the international may be the very condition of the possibility of a new politics, an emancipatory politics, a politics of cosmopolitans and citizens of the world. For them, the limits of modern statist political communities are precisely just historically contingent limitations on the possibility of becoming properly human. In these directions lie the great appeal of much of our ingrained common sense, and our sense of ourselves as capable of something new, and something better.

Yet what, from some points of view, may now be entirely obvious is also deeply perplexing. Modern accounts of what it means to be engaged in politics, of what it means to act politically, depend on historically rooted accounts of the limits of modern politics, limits that have been expressed most forcefully as the spatial limits of the modern state. These limits distinguish the modern state both from the world understood as some kind of planetary totality (thereby dividing not simply the internal from the external, but the properly political from the merely international) as well as from the world understood as that nature against which the modern state has been constructed as an historical, cultural and human artefact ultimately, even if reluctantly, at odds with any laws of nature. Modern accounts of political life rest on a very specific somewhere, on the specific political community within the modern state that is secure enough, and free enough, to permit humans to become properly human rather than abstract individuals without a home, without freedom, without responsibility, without a meaningful life, or even simply without life. The limits of modern statist political communities express the very conditions under which we have organized ourselves as properly modern subjects, as people capable of acting collectively, democratically and rationally to ensure our very capacity to act as agents aspiring to something better. Thereby lies the appeal of another common sense.

This double common sense is not easy to negotiate. It is not only the case that the distinction between the political and the international articulates our prevailing modern account of the limits of modern politics – limits that can be read negatively as limits and also positively as the very condition of the possibility of being both political and human – but also enables our prevailing accounts of what it means to do better, to do something dramatically new, to have a more just, more inclusive, more peaceful, more humane form of political life, indeed, and increasingly, to have a life at all.

In some contexts, this double commonsense presents little problem. What counts for politics within one specific state is easily equated with what must count as politics in all other states, in the world as such. This is especially the prerogative of the hegemonic: the hegemonic both in the sense of the great powers capable of imposing themselves upon all other states, thereby pushing at the limits of the distinction between a system of states that is the setting of modern politics and some other world for which we have tended to reserve the name (and the epithet) of empire; and the hegemonic in the sense of a capacity to engender a common sense that naturalizes all contradictions in routines and institutions that are scarcely noticed. In other contexts, however, any hegemon's obliviousness to the particularity of its claims to commonsense is precisely a violation of the basic codes of the modern states system: hegemons, yes, the conventions insist, if necessary to ensure systemic order, but hegemonic states rather than a potential empire threatening the very structure of a states system; and commonsense, of course, as long as it is a sense common to particular classes/societies/nations/states, rather than an uncommonsense imposed on all.

Nevertheless, these commonsenses sometimes collide. The commonsense of a common humanity that might be expressed in diverse societies or a common interest in sustaining the systemic rules that allow for diversity in unity sometimes collides with a commonsense rooted in the particularistic grounding of specific communities capable of properly political action. The collision is all too familiar. The claim to humanity or a common interest is seductive enough until questions are asked about whose account of a common humanity is being assumed, and who is being excluded from the account that prevails. The claim to the citizenship of specific states, with all its privileges, rights, and patriotic duties, is also seductive. But which comes first? Who draws the line? Who, or what, decides? How does this decision come to be taken, and come to have some degree of legitimacy?

A lot thus hangs on claims about the contemporary status of the distinction between the political and the international. It is in relation to this line that familiar contradictions of the modern states system are organized so as to permit not only the possibility of a proper politics within the confines of the sovereign state, but also the possibility of a broad range of different accounts of what that proper politics must be like within a structure that both expresses and organizes relations between states: that is, within a structure that privileges the diversity of political communities over all but the most basic – merely systemic,[28] or rule-governed,[29] or in some sense social,[30] or even in some sense sovereign but in any case necessary – arrangements required to prevent everything collapsing from a states system, with hegemons if necessary, into empire.[31] Again, the line is expressed in relation to the claims of the modern sovereign state. And again, the modern sovereign state is not something that simply is, that is simply inscribed on the face of the earth, but the site at which a lot of work is done to ensure that all the forces, and contradictions, of a modern system of states are resolved, whether at moments of crisis or in the unexceptional demands of everyday life. The line between the political and the international may look rather thin and narrow, even scarcely visible on the page or on the ground, but one would not be able to give much of an account of its capacity to constitute the world of modern politics from its size, physical presence or cartographic representation.

Consequently, a lot also hangs on the ways in which it has become so easy to treat the distinction between the political and the international as one that must either be affirmed as natural, necessary and simply realistic, or denied so as to articulate the possibility of some other politics; or, conversely, to articulate the possibility of the globalizing curse threatening to make politics as we know it impossible. The apparently simple logic of affirmation and negation imitates the apparently sharp distinction between politics and international relations. Both logics offer a range of seductive accounts of what it might mean to imagine some other kind of political imagination, accounts that are now deeply inscribed in categories, debates and disciplinary routines.[32] Thus, while it may be useful to be sceptical about conventional accounts of both continuity and change, it may be even more useful to reserve the most intense scepticisms for claims about freedoms and necessities that rest upon these seductions, the seductions of the fine lines of modernity that inscribe both the necessities and the possibilities of reconciling all the multiple contradictions of the modern political imagination.

Despite all the proclamations about the impending demise of the modern state, the modern political imagination still affirms a statist account of where and what politics must be, even when confronted with claims about the possibility of some other kind of politics. It especially depends on assuming a specific account of what it means to live in a world of states that claim to be sovereign, whether in space or in time. This account speaks not only to the character of the modern state, but also to the state of being modern, as well as to the legitimacy of modern accounts of what it means to be modern, or otherwise. The ease with which the options before us are said to involve either the continuing presence or imminent absence of the modern sovereign state as the site of legitimate authority expresses, again in many different senses, the profound limits of a modern political imagination that does not really know what to do about its own limitations.[33]

Calls for some new kind of politics are themselves not especially novel. Thinkers from the Renaissance, the Enlightenment, the age of Progress, the age of revolutions, or even the 1960s might all be invoked in this respect, all bringing with them not only different accounts of a specifically modern, or perhaps Western historical perspective, but also different accounts of what it means to have a perspective in time and aspirations for some other possibility in some other time.[34]

Claims about democracy, especially, have long been haunted not only by a sense of incompleteness in practice in the face of recalcitrant elitisms, class antagonisms and media manipulations, but of an incompleteness in principle. "We" *the* people always turn out to be "we" *a* people, one group among many competing groups of peoples, a particular aspiring to, or masquerading as, a universal, or a particular aspiring to a universal but subject to some other particular masquerading as a universal. This incompleteness in principle, this framing of universality and particularity as a structure of inclusion and exclusion, presence and absence, expresses a constitutive rift between a possible politics within a spatially demarcated community, whether understood as *polis*, state or nation, and an impossible politics among such communities. It also expresses a characteristic account of how novelty, change and temporality must be understood within and between the bounded spaces of such communities.

In very broad terms, then, modern political discourses, that is, claims about political possibility that depend on, among other things, the existence, determinations and freedoms of modern territorial states in a system of such states, offer two primary ways of resolving all questions about the proper relationship between universality and particularity, similarity and difference. Either universality is framed as the system, structure, society or community of sovereign states and particularity is expressed through the cultural, national or autonomous characteristics and practices of sovereign states: in short, one system, many states. Or the universal is framed as humanity as such, whether actual or potential, and particularity is expressed either in relation to specific collectivities of humans – cultures, societies, nations – or in relation to the modern individual; in short, one humanity, many peoples/people. These two possibilities generate the consequent possibility of framing claims about particularity/difference in relation either to the collectivities constituting the system of states or to the individual subjects who constitute such collectivities, and the parallel possibility of framing claims about universality as the totality of humans understood as modern individuals, the totality of peoples constituting the system of states (or "community of nations"), or some more abstract notion of humanity understood in terms of, say, reason, ethics or biological species.

The legitimacy of the modern state derives in large part from the claim that (unlike, most significantly, religions, sciences, economies or emperors), it is able to reconcile the multiple contradictions that are generated by these two possibilities. It does so by insisting that it can both enable (make secure and liberate) its individual/collective citizens to act in ways appropriate to some universalizable understanding of humanity in general, and that it can itself act in accordance with the rules necessary to sustain the universal system/community of modern sovereign states: in short, by insisting that it can reconcile the claim to citizenship within states with the claim to humanity/international community within a wider world; or rather, that it can effect such a reconciliation under certain conditions and within certain limits.

As a normative ideal, at least, modern states seek both to particularize the universalizing (though spatiotemporally parochial) demands of an international order that in some sense expresses a claim about humanity as such, and to universalize the particular, idiosyncratic and self-interested demands of its national citizenry. This normative ideal may be a thoroughly misleading guide to the historical complexity of the structures and practices of both modern sovereign states and the modern states system. It especially fosters the pretence that all states are in fact equal and autonomous members of a system/society of sovereign states unaffected by the dynamics of a globalizing capitalism or the legacies of various colonizations and imperialisms; and that the structure of the modern system of states is somehow coextensive with the political life of the totality of humans living on a single planet. Even as an ideal celebrating the promises of freedom and autonomy, it has long been understood that such promises also involve immense dangers, especially those involving the apparent necessity of wars between states, claims about the necessity of state violence in the limitation of domestic freedoms/autonomies, and the limited capacity of states to respond to the volatile dynamics of economic and ecological systems. It does, however, capture the broad conceptual context in which to understand the full force both of the claim of the modern state to exercise a monopoly of legitimate force within its territory[35] and the aspiration, paradigmatically expressed in the Charter of the United Nations, that we are indeed all (though ambivalently) people/peoples of a single international/global community.[36] Moreover, as a highly idealized but regulative account of the universality and particularity of modern politics, and of the possibility of reconciling all universalities and particularities as the ground on which modern politics is in fact possible, it works as a crucial constitutive practice of both modern politics and modern political analysis.

Not surprisingly, contemporary attempts to imagine some new kind of politics are forced to confront the basic contradiction between claims to humanity and claims to citizenship that enables our prevailing accounts of where and what political life must be. In large part, however, this confrontation has tended to occur on terms already set by the original contradiction, usually by insisting that the problem of modern politics is a matter of excessive pluralism, fragmentation or difference.[37] The possibility of change is thus characteristically understood either as a process of perfecting the claim of the modern international order to balance the competing claims of unity and diversity among equal and self-determining states (a possibility often associated with Kant's speculations about a world of peaceful republics), or as a shift from particularity to universality, from nationalism to cosmopolitanism, from nationalist and self-interested conflict to world order and global peace (a view often associated with Kant's commitment to the priority of a universalizing reason realizable either within autonomous individuals or in some overarching authority).

Both responses make sense, indeed have immense discursive force, as long as we assume that all contradictions between universality and diversity can indeed be resolved through the structure of spatial inclusion/exclusion expressed by the modern state, the modern states system, and the traditions of analysis that take this structure as an incontestable given. Kant's ambivalent articulation of this assumption remains a crucial guide to the modern political imagination in this respect. It permits the articulation of claims about humanity, ethical universality, or the world as such to be made in either international or somehow more global terms; but it also permits counterclaims about the dangers of transgressing the sovereigntist limits of internationalism or confusing global aspiration with imperialist ruthlessness.[38] For better and/or for worse, this assumption, which guides our prevailing sense of what it means to be progressive quite as much as what it means to engage in necessary violence at the limits of modern political life, is increasingly contestable, and, in my view, increasingly dangerous.

Whether in relation to claims about colonialism, development and hegemony in an international arena, or claims about inequalities and exclusions within states, there is a widely shared sense that established democratic aspirations are now confronting ever greater challenges. These challenges are usually identified with apparently novel circumstances, especially in relation to the unaccountable and hegemonic, or disorganized and incompetent, forms of governance and governmentality that express an emerging or mutating global order of some (perhaps postnationalist, perhaps postmodern, but probably not postcapitalist) kind. It is not especially difficult to conclude, as many well-placed commentators regularly do, that there is a vast and increasing gulf between the opportunities for democratic practices nurtured within the political communities of modern states and decisions taken in relation to, say, global trading systems and capital flows, missile defence systems, security against multiple forms of terror, the corporate monopolization of energy systems, or the genetic and chemical restructuring of food production. Some bemoan a "democratic deficit." Some try to reshape existing institutions to new conditions. Some deploy massive military force. Some take to the streets. In the meantime, leaders of the most powerful institutions are driven to reproduce narratives either of business as usual or of an unprecedented crisis that demands an immediate return to what is claimed to be business as usual. A necessary scepticism is thereby turned into a worrying cynicism and sense of powerlessness; or worse, the political mediation of all contradictions between universality and particularity is subverted by religious/ethical discourses about the saved and the damned, and the pluralistic structures of a states system are subverted by the univocal demands of unilateralism and empire. We have not been short of self-righteous political actors willing to deploy extraordinary violence in order to make things even worse.

Still, there remains a broad consensus in many places that the most challenging political problems of our time cannot be addressed in isolation or through unilateral action. We have become increasingly sensitive to the relational character of political existence, and the limitations of a political imagination, and a conceptual vocabulary, that privileges separations and thus distinct substances, identities and jurisdictions. As nineteenth-century figures such as Karl Marx and John Stuart Mill had already suggested, in their very different and still both helpful and unhelpful ways, it is difficult to engage in any plausible political analysis by assuming that politics is sharply distinct from, say, economics, culture or ethics.[39] Conversely, it is also difficult to come to terms with modern politics without some sense of how such distinctions have been produced and reproduced, with enormous consequences, until they have come to seem entirely natural and necessary. Similarly, it is now impossible to avoid the daily barrage of claims about the need to engage with the relational quality of human affairs, whether in terms of environmental or military dangers, the dynamics of production, trade and finance, or the infinitely contestable discourses about globalization. These claims are often sharply at odds with the organization of modern politics as precisely a system of separations.

While the history of modern politics can, in large part, be read as a complex sequence of, and even more complex relations among, specific and increasingly refined separations – as sacred and secular authority went their (never quite) separate ways, as the mechanisms and valuations of a capitalist market economy came to challenge the authority of state institutions, and as the spheres of ethics, privacy, property and civil society became increasingly "freed" from the jurisdictions of state authority – the basic structures of modern politics were in a crucial sense already constituted by practices of profound separation. One of these was expressed vertically. Hierarchical authority under God was subverted, but in some senses also reinscribed, by the modern secular authority articulated as the sovereignty of states. Many others were horizontal, most notably the separations between sovereign states (the concern of what we now call international relations theory), between proto-sovereign/national subjects/individuals (the concern of modern political theory and its derivatives), and between those deemed capable of a properly modern sovereignty/subjectivity and those who were not (the concern of the anthropologists, historians of empire, ideologists of development, theorists of postcolonialism and struggles around claims to indigeneity).

The horizontal and vertical dimensions of this fundamental restructuring of human organization in early modern Europe were intimately related. Again, in very broad but perhaps suggestive terms, the great chasm of principle that had been constructed in a vertical plane between heaven and earth, or time and eternity, was flattened onto a horizontal plane between the new secular–sacred beings of the modern world: sovereign territorial states and free, equal and potentially autonomous individuals. Practices of spatial extension gradually came to have priority over practices of hierarchy. The claims of both the "higher" and the "lower" were conflated into the same homogeneous space mid-way between the heights and depths of cosmic expectation. The political authority of the secular territorial state gradually achieved priority *over* the authority of religious claims to transcendence. Empires were brought down. Cities were subordinated. The flattening was never complete, and the hierarchical dimension was never erased; no account of the "realities" of modern politics can get very far without dealing with the complex constructions of higher and lower, and their relation with constructions of inner and outer, expressed especially in such murky concepts as class and great power hegemony and in their antagonistic relation with concepts of nation and sovereign inequality. Moreover, not everyone was as convinced as Machiavelli that the freedom of one's secular home is more important than the salvation of one's soul. The central tensions between claims to freedom/autonomy and claims to equality, between claims to citizenship and claims to humanity, and between universalizing standards of justice and particularist accounts of reason of state, point to some of the more obvious effects and controversies generated by this shift. The canonical sequence of modern political theory since at least the days of Hobbes and Locke records the most influential ways in which these tensions have been articulated, and to some extent resolved, in response to both large-scale social forces and particular interests and struggles.

Moreover, there is some irony, to say the least, in the way the flat spacings of modernity – the representational aesthetics, the cartographical projections, the territorial jurisdictions, the Cartesian ontologies, the Hobbesian sovereignties, the Lockean properties, the Kantian autonomies, the electoral representations – emerged simultaneously with an increasing recognition of the curvatures and connections of a shared geophysical habitat. The political significance of Gerhard Mercator's ability to represent a three-dimensional globe on a two-dimensional map by using a logarithmic scale so as to enable straight-line navigation on a compass bearing remains underappreciated in this respect.[40] It is an irony that says much about the paradoxes and contradictions through which modernity was constituted both as a problem and a project. It is also an irony that says much about a modern political imagination struggling to come to terms with contemporary claims about humanity, the globe, the planet: with what we bravely call the world.

The shift to a new politics of modern subjectivities was long, complicated and violent, doubtless understandable as a subtle modulation of prevailing concepts quite as readily as any sharp shift from old to new. It is still open to endless, and perhaps intensifying, historical speculation. To read the claims of modern politics on terms given by the regulative claims of the modern sovereign state, as I have been doing here, is certainly to underestimate the historicity and contingency of causalities and events that the claims of state sovereignty systematically efface,[41] not least because these claims work very hard to privilege the priority of spatial differentiation over temporal contingency. It is also to overemphasize readings of modernity that privilege Cartesian accounts of subjectivity and minimize, say, the profound rewriting of Cartesian assumptions effected by later writers such as Kant and Fichte, and the traditions of German idealism. In very general terms, however, one way of thinking about the widespread sense that the most challenging political problems of our time express an urgent need to reimagine where and what we take politics to be is to focus on the incongruity between the multiple claims about relationality that enable so much contemporary political analysis and debate, and the deeply entrenched and institutionalized recourse to the sharp separations through which modern politics, a politics of spatially demarcated inclusions and exclusions, of hopes for universality *within* the particular and for pluralisms *within* the universal, took shape against prevailing hierarchies so long, or perhaps not so long, ago.

At least, this is the broad line of approach I have been seeking to outline in a preliminary way, though without wishing to claim that this is the only, or even best, kind of approach that might be taken to such a complex and contested field of claims and counterclaims. In keeping with a long list of thinkers who have sought to resist the tendency to reify or naturalize a world of separated substances and containerized communities as the condition under which the world might be known and ordered, I want to underline the need to engage with the limits of the modern political imagination in relational and processual terms. Again, this is certainly not a novel endeavour.[42] It is, however, one that is at odds with the concepts and practices that tell us where and what politics must be in relation to the modern sovereign state, and what it must be to imagine politics on some other terms.

This incongruity is apparent in many different settings, but perhaps nowhere as clearly as in contemporary claims about international relations and world politics: terms that draw attention to the central contradictions of modern political life as a practice of universalities and particularities in space and in time, drawn to, but always aware of, the impossibility of any simple equation of modernity and world. We are constantly tempted to think we must move from fragmentation to unity, from *polis* to cosmopolis, from international relations to world politics. This temptation is already set up by a discourse that works as a specific articulation of the relation between fragmentation and unity, of international relations and world politics, of the state within which we can become simultaneously citizen and human. Frame one's story as a need to move from one option to the other, and we know exactly where it is going to end up, and how the critical commentaries will sweep us back in exactly the opposite direction. To resist this discourse, to try to move in both directions at once, for example, to reimagine the relationship between unity and diversity without clear distinctions between what we are here and what we are then, or between what we are now and what we must have been then, is to do disconcerting things to modern accounts of who we are as modern subjects living within sovereign states and somehow coexisting within a system of states on what appears to be a singular and not entirely happy planet. It is in this context, I believe, that both the limits of modern accounts of political life and the significance of processes that elude either physical or juridical containment are both most obvious and most pressing.

Political situations

Aristotle may have been right to insist that we are all political beings, even if one rejects Aristotle's family-man account of what it means to be a political being, or is sceptical of the specific distinction between the political and the nonpolitical that enables his conception of the political. Latter-day Aristotelians are certainly right to insist that much of what we are now encouraged to call politics, whether in the name of institutions of representation or the determining logic of rational choice in the capitalist market, has been profoundly depoliticized. Politics is not reducible to the administration of things, nor to a rational calculus of individual self-interest, no matter how important these have become as characteristic features of modern politics. As a host of thinkers from at least Max Weber onwards have insisted, the rationalization of modern capitalism and the hegemony of utilitarianism only make it more difficult, and more important, to identify what politics is and where it now occurs.[43]

Still, Aristotle's world is increasingly unfamiliar to us. It is not something one can automatically fall back on in order to challenge the dogmas of contemporary rationalisms, although this has been a powerful tendency in much of the recent critical literature. Whether reworked as a theory of states, of republics or of renascent civil societies, and whether reclaimed by followers of Jean-Jacques Rousseau, Karl Marx or Leo Strauss, Aristotle now often names a nostalgia for worlds we think we knew, worlds that still grant a certain coherence and plausibility to our sense of knowing what we mean when we talk about politics.

Most of us do indeed still think we know what we are talking about when we speak about politics. Even now, for example, remarkably few political theorists have qualms about replaying the old categories again and again, like organ grinders in the street. In some ways, in fact, political theorists may be among the least prepared to respond to claims that we need to reimagine the political. Political theorists, after all, are in large measure engaged in getting us to understand, and perhaps challenge, the historical and philosophical assumptions embedded in traditions and institutions we take for granted, already a difficult enough task given the largely ahistorical and uncritical character of so much modern political analysis. While many of them have demanded that we should reimagine what we take to be political, rather than imagine yet another variation on what we all already take the political to be, it is quite difficult to identify more than a handful who have showed some inclination to think politically in ways that are somehow "beyond" the territorial confines of the singular state. They may be concerned to get us to look at, and think critically about, the almost invisible conceptual waters in which we swim, but even they are not keen to look for long at the even less visible bowls that keep those waters in place. After all, what could possibly lie "outside" those bowls, those scarcely thinkable assumptions that enable us to enunciate principles of reason and right conduct? What, to be more specific, could possibly lie "outside" those basic principles of state sovereignty that inform our most basic accounts of what states are and what they do?

Aristotle invoked the *polis*. We invoke the state. Without the inheritance of the *polis* or the achievements of the state we would certainly not speak about politics the way we do now. We might still refer to crude indices of power and utility, but the most difficult puzzles of politics, we also know, rest less on logics of power and utility than on the possibilities of legitimate authority. Indeed, notions of power and utility that shun all concerns with legitimation risk intellectual incoherence as well as empirical irrelevance. It is in relation to questions about the authority of the modern state that the difficulties of speaking about and reimagining the possibilities of politics have become most perplexing. While we think we know what we are talking about when we speak about politics, we are also in the process of losing much of our capacity to speak about politics, precisely because we so readily assume that all questions about legitimacy, about the authorization of authority, are sufficiently answered by reference to the achievements of the sovereign state and system of states, by the place where politics is supposed to be.

Politics, we know, has something to do with powers and politicians, with governance and constitutions, with economies, identities and violence. It is not always a pretty sight. We know it when we see it, however, precisely because we assume it has a site, a location within which it occurs, or beyond which it can occur only in the most attenuated and debased forms, whether in the space between states or in that even more distant space that was once laid out so clearly beyond modernity and its system of states. For it is absolutely crucial to the modern political imagination that its attempts to reconcile our claims to citizenship in particular states with our claims to humanity conceived in some more universalistic terms are rooted in a claim about the primacy of spatial location. Moreover, this claim about the primacy of location is expressed in terms of an historically specific understanding of the character of spatiality and location, and of several distinct though related accounts of the character of our spatial inclusions and exclusions.

Political life came to be rearticulated in early-modern Europe against the prevailing hierarchies of feudalism, empire and theology, and in relation to the spatial terrain of the modern state, to the *polis* reborn, or reimagined, in an age of modernizing capitalism and global imperialism. This was the context in which modernity worked out its conceptions of sovereignty, identity, community, subjectivity, obligation, property and interest. These were the achievements that permitted subsequent generations to develop practices of nationalism, liberalism, socialism, democracy and the rest. These practices and concepts rested ultimately on a sharp spatial differentiation between life within a territorial jurisdiction and life outside and between such jurisdictions. While it is possible to refer to other historical situations in which spatial differentiations were important, the modern experience of spatial differentiation stands out precisely for the sharpness of its lines of demarcation.[44] A similar sharpness has characterized modern forms of aesthetic representation ever since the invention of three-dimensional perspective in Renaissance Italy. It was central to the transitions from Ptolemaic conceptions of the cyclical movement of heavenly spheres to the infinite universe charted by Galileo and his followers.[45] And just as the practices of early-modern science and culture tended to privilege a metaphysics of straight lines and infinite spaces, so also the practices of early modern politics affirmed the need for new forms of authority within the territorial spaces of the modern state. A Machiavelli writing in the Renaissance had to struggle even to give a name to this new site of political action. By contrast, a Hobbes writing in the mid-seventeenth century, and in thrall to the new sciences of Galileo and company, could lay out an entire political universe as if a modern sense of spatiality were the only one that could be imagined, at least as long as one were a man of reason, that privileged being who had learnt to read the world according to the necessities of Euclidean geometry.[46]

The man of reason lived inside. And inside, both circumscribed and inscribed as modern subjects and having internalized a claim to sovereign authority, men of reason could constitute the kind of order that would keep all threats to that order at bay; or at least under law, under a sovereign authority that was simultaneously inside a territorial space, outside the individuals who constituted it, above those individuals as their collective embodiment, and on the edge of that embodiment: the edge that faced both out to the state of war, and in to the order it constituted as legitimate. Having constituted an "inside," modern politics is always shadowed by those "outsides" that make that "inside" possible. There is the outside of interstate relations, that space of absent authorities, pragmatic accommodations, and inevitable wars. Here, the possibility of reconciling citizenship and humanity is given the name of peace and security; or, rather, the security of states is the name given to the primary reason why peace must be an impossible ambition. There is the outside of all those who were gradually, and usually violently, brought into the orbit of modern politics through practices of imperialism and colonialism, the outside of the European system of insides and outsides, that time of absent maturities, though an outside that had long contributed to those civilizing practices that were quickly domesticated inside. In this context, the possibility of reconciling citizenship and humanity is given the name of development and modernization, the temporal corollary of the spaces of international relations. And there is also the outside of all those inside who are excluded from full participation within the jurisdiction of sovereign authority. In this context, the possibility of reconciling citizenship and humanity is typically articulated under the names of equality, democracy, nationalism, multiculturalism and the rest.

The relations between the sovereign authority of the modern state and these constitutive outsides is, to say the least, complicated. It is difficult to imagine any plausible explanation of any consequential moment of modern politics that has not involved the interplay between and among these various outsides and the claim to sovereign authority or subjective conscience inside. Yet, in keeping with the spatial delineation of straight lines, and the sharp depiction of inclusions and exclusions that was so much a part of the way the early-modern Europeans learnt to deal with their new worlds, we still think about politics as if it were a simple matter to step outside: to leave the cosy world of political theory and go slumming with the hard men of interstate politics; to

leave the world of modernity, or the West, or the North, and work for alternative forms of development among the colonized, the Third World, the
South; or to leave the established order of the state and work at the "grassroots,"
locally, in civil society, in the private sphere, among the disenfranchised and
the socially, culturally and economically excluded. Nevertheless, despite the
conventions of state sovereignty, or the United Nations Charter, or the coloured
maps of political jurisdictions, stepping out is no simple matter at all. And the
notion that the great hope of reconciling citizenship and humanity lies with
conventional accounts of peace and security, development and modernization, or democratic and nationalist equalities, strains mightily in the face of
everyday experience.

Knowing where we are, we still persuade ourselves that pressing problems
of public policy can be dealt with by this or that authority here or there,
representing this or that political community. This is our automatic reflex, not
least because it accords with our everyday experience of being spatially located, our historical experience of a world of spatial separations, and our aesthetic experience of spatial representations. This conception of politics seems
as natural as the framed landscape on the wall, and as sensible as the fence
around the neighbour's garden.

Then we read the business pages and strategic analysts. We marvel at the flows
of trade and capital, the intermeshing and leveraged margins of the financial
markets, the flexible locations of production, the circulations of information,
the Groups of Seven, Eight or Twenty, the mysteries of the European Community, NAFTA or "Asia," the strange trades in illicit commodities, the
awesome gadgets of the military planners and the hypermodern networks of
the righteous prepared to unleash still more violence. We try to decipher who
makes what decisions where, and under what conditions; or why more is not
done about the massive debt burdens that shrivel the lives of the world's
poorest peoples; or how the virtuosities of capitalist markets can shrivel as
quickly as the sunlight moves across the lines of longitude. We find scholars
talking about human security, global ecologies, energy systems, or distinctions
between an international and a global political economy. We find international
lawyers speaking as though states are not the only subjects of international
law. We find interdependencies and neocolonialisms, functional regimes, resur-
gent religious and ethnic communities and overlapping citizenships. We find local
activists acting globally, global cities fusing transnational or transversal cultural identities, and claims about humanitarian intervention conflicting ever
more unsatisfactorily with the claims about domestic jurisdiction. Our pre-
valent maps are elegant, highly detailed, and generally sufficient to forestall
vertigo among the more privileged, but the dragons of the unknown world
are no longer just decorous motifs on the margin. In fact, they increasingly
suggest that it is becoming as futile to look for politics where it is supposed to
be as it is to look for the sources of lasting authority down the barrel of a gun.

The most challenging political problems of our time thus arise not only
from the need to reimagine what we mean by politics while being aware that

the modern political imagination already offers us a rich repertoire of alternatives that are already part of its most familiar narratives about what we must become. They also arise from the need to come to terms with the ways in which we know what we must always be because we have come to have and to naturalize a specific form of situated politics.

In this context, the key difficulty broached by claims about globalization is that the modern political imagination has always expressed considerable ambivalence as to whether our political situation is grounded in the territorial (though politically constituted and not simply natural) spaces of particular states, or in some apparently more abstract realm, in some world in which we can be more at home with our humanity. For in the modern political imagination, humanity can only have an abstract home, or at most be a tenant in the only home we moderns have, the modern sovereign state enabled within a system of sovereign states and in which we are citizens first and humans only as a consequence of our citizenships, and only then as long as push has not quite come to shove.

From this home, and negotiating this ambivalence, we can supposedly venture to those outsides which bring such embarrassments to the modern political imagination. Inside the state, women, children, minorities, aboriginals and deviants have fulfilled the role of internal outsiders, as the enemy within or the object of domestication and subjectification. Outside the state, wars between states express the necessary limits of sovereign authority: Carl Schmitt's clear expression of a capacity to decide the exception to politics as usual; Carl von Clausewitz's continuation of politics by other means.[47] Outside the modern world and its system of states, patterns of colonization show what must be done, or cannot be done, to bring everyone – every Other – into a common humanity, even at the cost of universalizing a system of modern states that depends on a radical distinction, indeed separation, between any common humanity and the citizenship of particular states.[48]

But what could it now mean to go "outside" while assuming that all divisions of nation, class, race and gender, of political communities here and there, are as sharply edged as the seventh paragraph of Article 2 of the United Nations Charter still insists? What could it mean to imagine a politics outside a politics which is already constituted precisely as a distinction between insides and outsides?[49] What could it mean to have a politics in which distinctions between the normal and the exceptional are not authorized by some sovereign authority capable of judging that which is here and that which is there, that which is the same and that which is different, that which is political and that which is merely private, or ethical, or subjective? What could it mean to engage in a politics open to possibilities in time, to the contingencies of human existence, without succumbing to illusions that all temporalities and all contingencies can and must be contained on a ground of spatial necessity? What could it mean to speak of universalities without succumbing to the claim that they are already enshrined in the normative ambitions of societies capable of dismissing all difference, all others, all particularities as signs of immaturity and a failure to speak the proper languages of modernity?

Some foreign ministers, customs officers and tabloid newspapers might still believe in the magical powers of straight lines, and many of us no doubt wish the magic was still working in many situations. Straight lines are nevertheless elusive phenomena, even if our most basic categories of modern politics rest upon a gamble that they can contain all the flux and unpredictabilities of social interaction. Again, the very attempt to imagine alternatives to a modern political imagination seems to lead directly into the languages and imaginative options resting upon the very assumptions that seem to be in question. More disconcerting still, claims about the need to reimagine the political run into not only accounts of spatial presence and temporal possibility reaffirming what politics has already come to be, but also multiple contentions about what it even means to refer to a world in relation to which we might somehow be political.

Binocular politics

To put my observations so far in a rather blunter form, the most significant difficulty with all those literatures cheerfully predicting the demise of the state, or solemnly asserting its continuing centrality, or blithely insisting that we have somehow left the world of sovereignty and sovereigns behind and can simply get on with refining our liberal achievements in a more pluralistic, ethical or conversational manner, is that they hardly begin to get at the enormous implications of their claims. They may mobilize functional explanations and rich descriptions of various kinds, often very suggestively. They may articulate more open and pluralistic accounts of reciprocity and mutual recognition of ever more fractured subjectivities, and push a little bit further on the potentials of liberalism as we have known it. When confronted with questions about authority, about legitimacy, about politics, however, they have surprisingly little to say, and a strong tendency to assume that something very much like a statist account of a singular political community can be taken for granted as the condition under which we must be thinking about our political futures. The framing of questions about universality and diversity, especially, tends to refer back to the ground of the singular state rather than to the system or society of states within which the categories of universality and particularity were enabled in a discourse of domesticity, or else to assume that a claim to universality is itself sufficient to provide an alternative to the statist/internationalist framing of the relationship between universality and particularity.[50] Three sorts of reasons for this are especially obvious, though still worth noting.

First, some involve the kinds of questions and procedures privileged by the modern social sciences, for which questions about legitimate authority have come to be interesting only if translatable into a utilitarian calculus of allocation. Modern social science may have many virtues, but despite the influence of traditions fermented by Max Weber and others, a sustained engagement with questions about political authority is rarely one of them. On the contrary, modern social science has itself been much more concerned to shore up its own authority through various claims about epistemology, method, or economic rationality precisely so as to distinguish itself from the dangerous worlds of political contestation as well as to advance claims within the institutionalized political economy of academic life. The consequence is considerable expertise on matters of technique and utilitarian calculation, and a remarkable combination of innocence and dogmatism when it comes to questions about the authorization, and suspension, of authority. In this direction lie all those debates about the effects of positivistic accounts of the logic of scientific explanation, the peculiarities of specifically American forms of academic life, and the hope that social science might somehow manage to transcend political dispute. For all the light and heat that has been generated by such debates, however, it remains the case that questions about legitimate authority, or the relationship between power and knowledge, have received relatively little attention, except insofar as they have been pushed into the specialized realms of the theoretical, the radical, the literary, the poststructural, or even the European. Yet a social science that is not centrally concerned with questions about legitimate authority, we might say, is a strange sort of legacy to bequeath to future generations, and it is not hard to predict that future generations will have to push such questions more firmly back onto the agenda of whatever form of social science is going to be of any use to them as anything other than instrumentalized and governmentalized objects.

Second, some involve the deeply entrenched traditions of specific disciplines. The most interesting case here is probably the kind of Anglo-American political science that has reified a specific reading of the modern state within four key "subfields" of enquiry: a comparative politics organized on a ground of an assumed universality, or theory of development, that permits comparison; an international relations organized on a ground of diversity expressed as fragmentation or anarchy; a domestic politics organized on a ground of particularity, nationalism and specificity/parochialism; and, crucially, a political theory organized to permit either a canonical (normative, historical) tradition rooted in claims about a particularistic *polis* or an ahistorical (socioscientific) claim about the empirical/rational behaviour of people as such. Again, this heavily statist classification of the proper subject of politics makes perfect sense in many contexts, and is rarely encountered in such a clear-cut form, but its effects are not subtle, especially on hiring practices, curriculum development, publication strategies, relations with other disciplines and, most of all, the treatment of what many might think of as some of the central concerns of political analysis – the state, power, authority, sovereignty, ideology, citizenship, and so on – as rather specialized and fragmented concerns.

While modern forms of political theory, for example, may also have many virtues, they depend very largely on drawing a veil over the background conditions that permit a focused concern with questions about freedom and justice within a bounded political community. Both the method and the extraordinary influence over several decades of John Rawls' *Theory of Justice* has been paradigmatic in this respect, and its capacity to depoliticize the practices of political theory has been especially unsubtle. Whatever the specific merits of his work, Rawls has come to name a broad understanding of what it means to do political theory in which many of the most basic questions about politics have been more or less evacuated, leaving only an abstract field of reason to be occupied by claimants to a philosophy or an ethics innocent of all notions of power, authority, social forces or legitimate violence, let alone of a world of differences beyond any particular state.[51]

The broader pattern in this respect is characterized with admirable, though perhaps unintentional, clarity in a survey by Andrew Vincent of the various tendencies constituting "the nature of political theory" in the twentieth century.[52] Vincent argues, I think persuasively, that the problem of establishing foundations for political judgement is a primary unifying theme across otherwise deeply divided traditions. Despite the comprehensiveness and care of the survey, however, Vincent identifies very little concern with sovereignty as a practice of authorizing authority, which one might expect to be at the core of any political theory exercised by the absence of foundations in a secular world; nor with any traditions of thinking about the system of states or international relations that might have something to say about the foundations of political life within any particular state; nor indeed with what it means to identify the character of modern political theory in terms of the "nature" from which modern political life has been constitutively distinguished. All three absences can be interpolated into many of the literatures that are discussed in the book – in relation to the "philosophy" of language and essentially contested concepts, to nationalist and other conceptions of community, to the limits of pluralism, to the obsession with "justice," and to why so many political theorists thought they could declare all existing traditions to be dead in order to get on with their rationalist calculations, their pristine histories or their apolitical philosophies – in ways that would give even greater momentum to Vincent's already incisive scepticism.

Perhaps even more curiously, theories of international relations have come to be vulnerable to claims about the need for some sort of universal method of the kind that is assumed to be appropriate for the comparative analysis of political practices in relation to which assumptions about a ground for comparison are assumed to be unproblematic. The whole point of a theory of international relations, it might be said, is that it expresses the difficulty of establishing any common ground except for the most basic rules of the international system necessary to enable sovereign states to coexist as expressions of radical difference. Understood as a system, as an expression of a single structural logic, the states system can indeed be read as an expression of similarities, of a common ground amenable to a common method. Understood as part of an always problematic relationship between claims to similarity and claims to difference, however, international relations must be read as a site at which any claim to a singular method must always be problematic also, unless claims to commonality emanating from particular, and hegemonic, particularities are taken to have a licence to decide the necessary relation between commonality and particularity.[53]

Moreover, while the four subfields of political science work very effectively to affirm the central significance of the modern state, the state is often more readily visible as a tacit assumption than as an explicit focus for enquiry, to the extent that we are subject to regular demands that the state be "brought back in"[54]. As I will argue extensively below, this is even more the case with the principle, institution and practice of state sovereignty.

Many other things also become more or less invisible as a consequence of this way of organizing knowledge about political life. This is especially so, to name briefly only six widely acknowledged arenas of contemporary debate, for: political economy (except insofar as it is assumed that the sovereignty of capital is subordinate to or containable within the sovereignty of the state); political sociology (except insofar as it is predicated on an assumed correlation between society, nation and state); gender (except insofar as a specifically gendered account of political subjectivity, the infamous modern man, is inscribed as an abstract universality); environment (except insofar as it is treated as an assumed ground both on which and against which modern political life has come to be framed as both natural and historical); cities (except insofar as they can be placed with the lower and local administrative capacities of the state; and for the great diversity of human experiences and ways of being human (except insofar as difference can be affirmed as the object of democratic pluralism within a statist monism, of comparison among similarly statist communities affirming a specific understanding of similarity and difference, or a teleology of political development as modernization).

In all these cases, the structure of the discipline works to produce a problem of how to add that which has already been excluded by including it in a way that affirms the normative ambition of the modern state and system of states. Not surprisingly, they remain marginal additions to an established understanding of what the study of political life must be about, and the analysis of political life is left struggling to reconcile its inherited sense of what politics must be about with proliferating claims about what is now politically interesting. It may be that disciplinary discipline is not always as strict as the professional codes demand, but the reproduction of disciplinary expectations has undoubtedly been effective for a long time. On the other hand, it would be difficult to argue that the specific discipline of political science now holds any convincing monopoly on ways of understanding contemporary political life. Like many other disciplines, it has largely lost the sense that its ostensible object of enquiry is a problem rather than a given, a site of problems and problematic principles rather than of expertise and a technical fix.

Third, some simply involve the limits of a modern political vocabulary that allows such fluency in speaking about politics as long as we know that it is safely contained within the modern state, but quickly falters when political life becomes less univocal. It is in this context that, to take examples that I have in mind throughout this discussion, we might understand the broad significance of contemporary claims about how struggles around a politics of "difference" exceed the ambitions of liberal pluralism; or how struggles around "cultures" and "ethnicities" exceed the ambitions of modern nationalism; or how "movements" that are identified as merely "social" exceed the place set out for them as minor or local components of something that is altogether more politically authoritative. It is in this context, also, that we might understand what is at stake in the use of seemingly natural concepts of "society" and "community" to effect a claim that univocality has indeed been achieved, despite all evidence to the contrary.[55]

I do not think anyone is able to offer more than very tentative and humble responses to the kinds of question about political possibilities that might emerge out of various scepticisms about the claims of the modern sovereign state and states system. I certainly think that simple stories about both the continuing presence of sovereign states and their imminent demise work so as to make it difficult even to ask questions about politics under contemporary conditions. Moreover, there is always a politics to the ways we identify what we call politics, not least to how we identify some *thing* to which the name can be assigned. Simple stories about the eternal presence or impending disappearance of modern sovereign states work especially effectively to enable many practices of depoliticization in contemporary political life, not least when critiques of contemporary statist practices and appeals to something more human, global, ethical or environmentally sensitive converge in claims about some more progressive or emancipatory alternative.

In one of his typically provocative interventions, Gilles Deleuze once asked "Did we kill God when we put man in his place and kept the most important thing, which is the place?"[56] The continuing force of claims about the eternal presence or impending disappearance of the modern state and system of states suggests that Deleuze may have been right to suspect that, while modern accounts of politics may claim to have freed themselves from divine authority, they have still clung tenaciously to a metaphysics of place, or perhaps it should be a metaphysics of a particular conception of spatiotemporality. It is not entirely clear to me (nor, I think, to Deleuze himself) that the separation of secular and sacred has ever been as clear cut as the formulation of this particular question might be read as suggesting. Nevertheless, modern accounts of the sovereignty of states do affirm a place, understood as a specific form of spatiotemporality, as the ground on which modern humans can construct a secular alternative to an authority that transcends merely human ambition.

It is this affirmation, which has very deep roots in both Greek and Christian traditions, that now seems to be under very sustained questioning. Much of this questioning, however, encourages either a ritualistic affirmation of the way things are (because this is where and what they are supposed to be) or an apocalyptic proclamation that everything is changing, that politics is everywhere and nowhere, that empire has replaced the states system, that humanity has replaced citizenship, that we have, or must have, a politics of the world. I doubt that the future of political life will be so simple; or that we can find some sensible middle ground between the extremes that are laid out for us in this way. Indeed, I would say that profound dilemmas must always haunt claims to some tolerable ground between intolerable extremes, and that the extremes of possibility and impossibility affirmed by the modern state and modern system of states are certainly becoming ever more difficult to live with.

Many forms of critical theory, at least since Kant, have been aware of versions of this characteristic dilemma of modern political thought, and the cooptation of dissent it has enabled. Affirm subjectivism rather than objectivism, and sustain the premise of a modern world of subjects and objects. Affirm a Romantic passion for particularities rather than Enlightenment demands for universal reason, and sustain the premise of a modern opposition between one and many. Affirm universalistic accounts of human rights and enable states to insist that they are the proper site within which we become humans having rights, even if this means making a few adjustments in the workings of the interstate system as the worldwide expression of that humanity that is divided into different humanities. Contemporary accounts of the fate of the sovereignty of modern states work in much the same way. They tell us what it must mean to affirm an alternative, to make an exception to an assumed norm, to find a way of transcending an assumed immanence. This is an affirmation that must always return to the same starting point, the starting point affirmed by theories of international relation by recourse to those wildly promiscuous discourses about political realism. The sovereignty of modern states is very much a matter of affirming specific starting points, which in turn imply specific endpoints and specific limitations, which in turn affirm specific possibilities for what comes in between, or what might come after. Sovereignty has become a problem in all these respects.

Over the past decade or two, many forms of contemporary critical analysis have consequently begun to focus on how modern sovereignty works, and has been enabled to work, as a political practice that enables other political practices. Much of this analysis has been historically or genealogically oriented. Some has drawn on more philosophically oriented analyses of modern forms of subjectivity. In the following section, I draw on both while being more explicitly concerned with how modern sovereignty works both by expressing and producing a characteristically modern framing of spatiotemporal relations and political identities.[57] This framing produces a characteristically modern way of responding to the spatiotemporal paradoxes – not the simple givenness – of modern sovereignty. If one wants to resist the cycle of repetitions that ensues from the discourses about the eternal presence or impending absence of sovereign states, it is necessary to think about how those discourses are produced by a specific framing of spatiotemporal relations, and how spatiotemporal relations may be changing under contemporary conditions.

One key issue here is that, as may be familiar from many contexts, we do not live in a world in which space is easy to distinguish from time. As may be obvious in many contexts also, the entire art of distinguishing between things, peoples, identities and places is not quite as straightforward as it has sometimes seemed. Where the modern political imagination rests very largely on a capacity to draw the line – a metaphor I use partly in the hope that it draws attention to some suggestive resonances among aesthetic, legal, metaphysical, theological, geographical and political discourses – the contemporary political imagination is going to have to develop other ways of thinking about lines, not least as lines of connection and temporary networks of relations among much more fluid and temporary subjectivities. We moderns certainly know how to draw lines where the discourses of the modern state tell us to draw them, with violence if necessary. We are much less adept at thinking about the ways in which other lines are being drawn and redrawn in contemporary political life, or about how we might seek to draw and redraw them more creatively.

It is thus to the politics of drawing lines, to the authorization of discriminations and exceptions, and thus to the relationship between sovereignties and boundary conditions, that I turn next. In the first instance this will lead me to engage with themes that found especially incisive expression in European debates about sovereignty in the 1920s but which, though still familiar in some sense, not least because they have been explored in many critical accounts of modern subjectivity, have been kept at bay by heavily conventionalized accounts of the sovereign state and system of states. On this basis, I will then consider Hobbes as a theorist of origins (and thus limits), Kant as a theorist of limits (and thus origins), and the way attempts to find some sort of escape from the accounts of origins and limits articulated by Hobbes and Kant have led not only to claims about the necessity of specific forms of normalized middle ground, but also to desires to solve all problems of human finitude expressed by the modern subject, sovereign state and system of sovereign states through a return to the scales of hierarchical order from which modernity is usually understood as one of the greatest of great escapes. I will then in the final chapter, return, twice, to the relationship between the problem of sovereignty and the spatiotemporal articulation of boundaries enabling or disabling our capacity to reimagine where, and thus what, we take politics to be.

4 Sovereignties, origins, limits

Discriminations/authorizations/exceptions

Politics/discrimination

To claim that the most challenging political problems of our time express a
need to reimagine where and what we take politics to be, even to claim that
imagination has anything of consequence to do with political life at all, is to
invite suspicions about the marginalization of more significant, or at least
more tangible, matters. Any such claim is liable to become caught within
rhetorics distinguishing the serious from the trivial, the urgent policy from the
distant abstraction: liable to be construed as a callous disregard for the politics of the moment, even as an irresponsible disinterest in matters of life and
death for thousands of people.

Some things, we know, are important. Others are less so. How we know which
is which, and who is this "we" that is able to get away with its claim to know,
are always matters of considerable dispute, again sometimes over trivialities,
but sometimes over the most basic assumptions that allow for distinctions
between the trivial and the serious. The slaughter of some 3000 people in New
York in September 2001 was widely judged to be much more important than
the killing of far greater numbers of people in many other acts of political
violence elsewhere. At a considerable greater level of conceptual intensity, claims
about certain kinds of freedom have come to be judged more important than
claims about equality, or fraternity, at least when it has to be acknowledged
that these are not always, and perhaps never, compatible values given the
dynamics and contradictions of modern capitalist societies, or of the modern
state. Somewhere in between the competing claims of modern liberalism and
evaluations of one spectacular event, we recognize that some things have
come to be framed as matters of national interest, as necessarily exempt from
the usual expectations of democratic scrutiny, while others have not. Of more
specific interest for the argument I seek to elaborate here, some claims about
security are consigned to the military, others to the police, the intelligence
agencies, the social workers, the insurance companies, the central banks, or even
the courts of human rights. As I have especially sought to stress in relation to

the contradictory structures of a modern internationalized political order, and thus to the specific conditions under which we have been able to imagine the possibilities and impossibilities of liberty, equality and security within the modern world, we are all supposedly subject to competing claims to citizenship and humanity, and are sometimes forced into difficult choices between them, even while both claims are sometimes at odds with the multiple and differentiated capacities of people and peoples as either political agents or human beings.

Start thinking about the way we distinguish between the serious and the trivial, that is to say, and it is not difficult to become lost in many of the most intractable dilemmas of contemporary political life. Generalizations may be abstracted, but specificities are necessarily affirmed. Universalities may be proclaimed, but exclusions are never far away. Judgements are enacted, and subsequently contested. Some things become important, so we discriminate, privilege, forget, obey. Even to start writing about such things is to become uncomfortably sensitive to the limits of grammar, vocabulary, tense and voice, and to the close but complex relationship between authorial authority and the authorization of political possibilities and impossibilities.

The ability to discriminate (and thus to categorize, to make comparisons and evaluations on the basis of judgements about what is similar or different) is constitutive of all human endeavours, not least of the practices through which humans seek to distinguish themselves from non-humans; to distinguish themselves not least from the natural, the divine and the barbaric or primitive, even to distinguish ordinary realms of human experience from possibilities of enlightenment and transcendence in which discriminations might somehow fall away. Many discriminations have ensued before this book came to be where it is now, especially given the comparative attractions of other books, other engagements, other articulations of time, space and value. There are always other things to do. Many fairly elaborate and contestable discriminations have been made in earlier parts of this book so that I can now try to shape my analysis through comments on the authorization of discriminations, thereby diverting attention from many other possible considerations, those that might more readily entice political economists, historians, philosophers, sociologists or geographers, all of whom would no doubt have very different things to say about the problems I seek to identify here. Many discriminations have been made, over a long period and through massively contested practices, to enable claims about the capacities of modern reason to be able to discriminate universally, even neutrally and peacefully. Many discriminations have been subverted so as to permit modern forms of discrimination to claim the status of neutrality, even universality, the only possible ground for judgement. Discriminations often seem so easy, the automatic acts of everyday existence that allow us to get up, eat, talk to the neighbours, get a job, get a life, or not. Yet to examine any specific discrimination is usually enough to remind us of the multiplicities and densities of human judgement, of the peculiarity of distinctions we take for granted, and of our reliance on, but also our unease about, absolute declarations of a yes and a no.[1]

Indeed, it is impossible to imagine a politics, or a credible political analysis, unconcerned with the conditions under which we are able to deploy discriminations and make judgements about discriminations, whether in specific situations or in relation to who or what is empowered to discriminate and act as an authority to judge, and under what conditions. The creative leap from hierarchical accounts of status to the horizontal jurisdictions of state by way of Renaissance accounts of *lo stato*, and thus our standard narratives about the transition from medieval to modern forms of political order in Europe, is especially instructive in this respect, but other stories about other ways of being political might also be told to similar effect. Conversely, it is equally impossible to imagine forms of political life, or analysis, that do not work so as to obscure the conditions under which some things have been declared to be serious, or real, as legitimately at the centre, or bottom, or top of things, and others have been dispatched to some other place, some other status or some other jurisdiction. This is why it is often so difficult to engage with what has come to seem obvious, even though it ought to be entirely obvious that modern political life builds upon an insistence that practices of discrimination are not just given in the nature of things.

As Hobbes was prone to say about desire, the need for discrimination may be universal (indeed prior to desire, especially to Hobbes' characteristically masculine understanding of desire), but specific forms of discrimination affirm the diversity of human experience. While there are many popular attempts to celebrate modernity as simply a culture of universality, whether actual or potential, these are very difficult to reconcile with most standard (though also contestable) narratives about the historical emergence of very specific ways of distinguishing universality from particularity, subjectivity from objectivity, and the construction of subjectivities within borders and limits; and not least with the construction of such subjectivities along a scale that runs, in principle, from the bounded individual to the bounded sovereign state to the bounded system of sovereign states to the world as such.

One way of thinking about what might be at stake in claims about the contemporary need for greater political imagination is to engage with the often-noted incongruity between the multiple trivializations of everyday politics – spectacles of bread and circuses recast for technologies of mass consumption and instant replay, cynicisms about the corruptions of professional politicians and overburdened institutions – and the seriousness of historical and structural transformations demanding collective responses that seem beyond the comprehension, capacity or even ambition of many existing authorities and their constituencies. The apparent ease with which many familiar but historically and culturally contingent discriminations are made and insinuated into the practices of everyday life and institutions is a crucial expression of what must be engaged so as to respond to many of the practical dilemmas of contemporary political life. They must be engaged especially in relation to claims about sovereignty, though not only in relation to claims about the sovereignty of the modern state that we have come to assume as the ultimate political expression, and judge, of what is most serious and what is most trivial.

Consequently, what I want to do in this chapter, by re-engaging with various ways of drawing lines that I have sought to destabilize in the discussion so far, is to open up a range of difficulties that arise once questions about sovereignty come to be understood in terms not of routinized claims about the eternal presence or impending absence of sovereign states in a system of sovereign states, but of the way in which claims about state sovereignty enact some very specific forms of discrimination that make it very difficult to engage with sovereignty except through endlessly repeated narratives about presence and absence. In part, my argument will reaffirm the way in which sovereignty has been examined in the context of specific traditions of epistemology,[2] but I also want to get at the relationship between sovereignty and the ontological and specifically spatiotemporal assumptions that have enabled modern forms of both sovereignty and epistemology to work as paradigmatic forms of authorizing authority.

Most specifically, I want to get at what might be involved in understanding the international structure of modern political life less as an expression of spatial distinctions between competing sovereignties, than as an expression of claims about temporality and history enabling constitutive discriminations between those who belong within the world of the modern international and those who do not. Where the standard narratives about the sovereignty of the modern state play out a paradigmatically spatialized narrative about the structuring of universalities within the particularities of modern subjectivities, I will continue to argue that this narrative expresses a prior understanding of temporality and historicity: an understanding that reproduces an account of the possibilities of boundaries, borders and limits articulated in a scarcely contestable, but nevertheless widely ridiculed myth about the origins of modern international order. To engage with the discriminating practices of modern political life, I will suggest, is to understand at least some of what is at stake in claims about what counts as authoritative knowledge about modern political authority, and what it means to distinguish between norm and exception in the interplay of competing sovereignties. Most significantly, it is to appreciate the enormous work that is now done to ensure any difficulties arising from the conceptual tension expressed in the synonym/antonym between international relations and some politics of the world are constantly effaced by references to the 1648 Treaty of Westphalia as the admittedly mythical origin of modern political possibilities and impossibilities.

Put simply, where the conventions of modern political analysis are most easily understood on the basis of spatialized discriminations between the internal and the external, that is, in terms of the boundaries, borders and limits of modern subjectivity, any critical engagement with such assumptions must also engage with two other forms of discrimination: one organized as a vertical distinction between higher and lower (especially in the context of the ways in which modernity has come to be understood as a concerted assault on forms of authority flowing from higher to lower); and one articulated temporally between before and after. Where so many accounts of what it might mean to imagine some other form of political imagination play out variations on the need to shift from a world of particularities to a world of universalities, I want to insist not only on the absurdity of ambitions for universality as a solution to problems generated by a very specific framing of the necessary relation between universality and particularity, but also on the need to pay much greater attention to the ways in which modern political life has been able to distinguish between universality and particularity within very specific and often very troubling limits. These limits work, in part, in the spatial practices of bordering, most troublingly when borders become the site at which all universalist aspirations become subject to exceptional conditions, as they do. They also work in the temporal practices of founding, most troublingly when myths of origin become sites at which universalist aspirations for a particular array of universalities within particularities are constructed as the exception to all prior forms of human experience, as the special case that is in principle apart from, but nevertheless claims to be coextensive with, the world as such. Many discriminations may indeed be utterly banal, but others are certainly not, though the grounds on which I, or anyone else, am able to make judgements about the difference remain eminently contestable.

Sovereignty/knowledge

As far as most contemporary forms of political analysis are concerned, sovereignty is quite obviously a shorthand for state sovereignty. State sovereignty, in turn, is assumed to work as the primary ground on which we moderns have been enabled to make and to give authority to discriminations that have enabled modern political life to develop as it has. Sovereignty is state sovereignty, and state sovereignty is the starting point of modern politics, despite a lingering and sometimes even pressing awareness of complex histories and competing authorities. Those attuned to various anthropological, historical, philosophical or theological literatures will be aware of the many parochialisms embedded in such assumptions.[3] Nevertheless, to speak about sovereignty now is very largely to assume that sovereignty is something that arrived in Europe along with the modern state some time in the sixteenth or seventeenth century, and which has been more or less present ever since. The arrival is conventionally marked by the writings of Jean Bodin in its earlier phases, and by Hobbes' later and considerably more extensive account written in the language of a recognizably modern science and philosophy.[4] Continuing presence is marked, though ambiguously, by international law, the United Nations Charter, the pronouncements of state governments, and symptomatically, even if paradoxically, by narratives about its continuing presence or imminent absence.

In whatever way we may come to understand the practices of sovereignty in less parochial terms, or in relation to the specific authorizations of religious authority and Roman law that provided many of the key resources enabling the articulation of specifically modern forms of state sovereignty,[5] it is difficult to imagine an analysis of the sovereignty of modern states that does not try to come to terms with the authorization of specifically spatial forms of discrimination as the authoritative ground on which all discriminations can be authorized in time and space. Modern forms of sovereignty express and reproduce very specific ways of drawing the line, both literally and metaphorically. They do so both through claims to physical territory and through institutional expressions of (legal) principle. Boundaries are articulated as both borders and limits, as lines upon physical terrain and lines inscribed as limits of principle, jurisdiction and identity. Limits in space, place and territory express limits in law, and limits in law express limits in power, authority, community, responsibility and liberty. There is perhaps little to be said that is new or even surprising in this respect.[6] This is, as some analysts have been prone to say, simply how it is, or, more accurately, how it is supposed to be. This is the normative ground on which we have been encouraged to discriminate between necessity and possibility, the universal and the particular, the normal and the exceptional, the friend and the enemy, and to resort to claims about security as the most pressing expression of what it means to articulate a political order within the spatial limits of the modern state and system of states. What remains of continuing interest, however, is the degree to which the once surprising has somehow become so unsurprising, to the extent that the very attempt to remember and re-engage with what was once so odd has come to be framed as somehow novel, sometimes exciting, sometimes frightening.

Political life has not always depended on the specific forms of discrimination that have been enacted through the practices of the modern sovereign state and system of states. These discriminations are certainly neither natural nor universal, though they have been naturalized in culture and in law, and universalized as the regulative ambition of a modern international order: naturalized and universalized, that is, in historically and culturally specific forms. Contemporary rhetorics of seriousness and triviality build on specific forms of discrimination and authorization – of judgement – that echo the discriminations, authorizations and practices of judgement – ways of drawing lines – that are expressed in the claims of modern sovereign states. These lines usually appear to be very thin, subject to precise – Euclidean – definition, as well as to be entirely passive, mere markers of essentialized differences. They may even find expression only at a specific moment of judgement and decision: a moment that nevertheless constitutes a centre, a fulcrum of authority, a monopoly, a norm, a semblance of political eternity. To think about what might be involved in challenging the claims and practices of sovereignty now is thus necessarily to engage with the very specific forms of discrimination and authorization that have come to seem so natural as the primary ground for modern political life that any other way of thinking about sovereignty, or politics, seems scarcely credible, except as the absence of whatever the claims of state sovereignty insist *must* be present.

The recognition that this ground was precisely not natural was a very large part of the problem that people like Hobbes were forced to confront in the mid-seventeenth century, in the midst of local turmoils expressing wider contestations about the grounds on which political authority might be authorized, especially given the uncertain status of the relation between language and world following the nominalist challenge to prevailing Aristotelian and Thomist realisms. On the other hand, it is now often difficult to remember that clear and sharp distinctions in space and time, and thus the Cartesian selves and Kantian subjectivities that the prevailing narratives of modern individualism (or, rather, of the "dividualism" of the modern self divided from the world) insist we must be, enabled many of the achievements of the emerging culture enabling people like Hobbes to challenge the authority of other practices of discrimination, other modes of authorization, and other grounds for political judgement.

Among other things, to focus on practices of discrimination is necessarily to take a sceptical stance towards influential forms of modern social science which still insist that proper scholarship must privilege epistemological and methodological criteria of scholarly enquiry. These demands have a long and complex history, involving not only the broad cultural force of a secularizing science, but also the specific, and in many respects very idiosyncratic, dynamics of American scholarship in the Cold War era. Whatever one makes of the credibility of such demands in general epistemological terms, it is especially in relation to claims about sovereignty that modern social science has had so very little to say, though it has not shied away from playing a part in the reproduction of clichés about eternal presence and imminent absence produced by the specific spatiotemporal forms of modern sovereign states. While it is certainly a mistake to underestimate the importance of epistemological and methodological criteria for scholarly enquiry, and especially of their contemporary complexity and contested status, to engage with claims about sovereignty is to recognize that it is an even greater mistake to underestimate the importance of the conditions under which specific authorizations of discriminations enable or disable epistemological and methodological resources. Modern social sciences, like modern sovereign states, make claims to authority on the basis of authorizations of discriminations, and discriminations among authorizations. The claim to know authoritatively and the claim to have political authority have much in common, as any of the usual list of great political thinkers from any era will insist in one way or another.

Much of the obsessive and repetitive quality of so many claims about modern social science, it would be fair to say, betrays a systematic failure to recognize the degree to which the modern forms of epistemology around which debates about appropriate method have come to oscillate were largely shaped as a problem – as an attempt to make sense of an historically specific account of the relation between knower and known – as a consequence of the radical distinction between subject and object effected by Galileo, Descartes and the other founding fathers of explicitly modern traditions of science and philosophy. This was a distinction imagined both as a (Euclidean, perspectival) line of sight from subject to object, and a line separating subject from object: the line on which Galileo reconstructed a classical distinction between the primary qualities knowable by a mathematical science and the secondary qualities of subjective human experience. In effect, the shift to a secularizing modernity brought its own cross: not one on a hill inviting an upward gaze and heavenly transcendence, but one on a flat space inviting movement along and across lines of latitude and longitude.

The standard narratives rightly refer to this process in terms of the emergence of characteristically dualistic formulations of mind or matter, word or thing, man or world, and so on. Nevertheless, in the context of claims about specifically modern forms of sovereign authority, especially, the relations between such terms took on fairly complicated forms. In addition to the processes through which the modern knowing subject came to be distinguished from the world that is to be known, it is also necessary to engage with the ways in which the perspectival line (of vision, representation, and so on) connecting subject and world implied a line cutting across all possible connections between subject and world and rendering them as mutually exclusive spheres. It is in this context that we can understand the longstanding interplay of claims that the relation of modern subject to world involves some sort of continuity, duality or complementarity (nurture *and* nature, for example, or citizen *and* human) with claims about the radical distinction, dualism, mutual antagonism or monistic reduction of one to the other. The problem that arises here concerns precisely where, and how, any form of continuity that might be construed between subject and world is to be disrupted so as to enable any claim to the freedom or autonomy of the individual subject, or the sovereign state, or the system of sovereign states.

On the one hand, modern forms of epistemology have sought to overcome the dangers of radical scepticism implied in any sharp distinction between subject from world, or knower and known. On the other hand, the very possibility of a modern subject capable of knowing and being in the world implied an ambition for precisely such a sharp distinction. Between these two possibilities arose many of the difficult problems still attending the construction of boundaries of the individual subject, of the state containing collectivities of individual subjects, and of the system of states containing multiple collectivities of individual subjects. In particular, we can understand how the boundaries of modern political life have come to be framed as clear and distinct lines of discrimination, but also as sites at which sharp discriminations might somehow give way to patterns of connection: a possibility, I will gradually suggest, that finds expression not only in the characteristic grids of cartographic representation, but also in assumptions about scale (and thus the lingering force of hierarchical accounts of higher and lower) and about the relationship between normalized curves of distribution and their limits (and thus the rather more than lingering force of claims about the necessary practices of exception enabling the spatiotemporal articulation of modern political life).

However else we come to understand the emergence of modern forms of politics, especially in relation to the claim to the secular authority of the sovereign state as the mediator between the individualized subject and the collectivity of people/peoples in the system of states, the rearticulation of vertical (theological, feudal, imperial) forms of authority *within* horizontal and spatially/territorially circumscribed formations was clearly the source of immense difficulties in early-modern Europe, in practice, but especially in principle. Assumptions of qualitative hierarchy gradually gave way to principles and practices of spatial differentiation: to subjectivization, objectification, territorialization and perspectival representation. Subject came to know object, but also to know that such knowledge was inherently unstable, prone to empiricisms and rationalisms, to realisms and idealisms, to the radical dogmatisms and scepticisms that drove Kant to try to hold the modern world together within the limits of human finitude: to hold it together, that is, within the gap that had opened up between two distinctions – between the distinction between an immanent earthly temporality and a transcendental heavenly eternity, on the one hand, and the distinction between a presumed (unknowable, noumenal) world and human perception of the (phenomenal, experiential) appearance of the world, on the other.[7] Between these distinctions, within the lines defining the modern world as neither theologically subservient nor epistemologically naive, the line from subject to object, or from man to world, could be bisected by another line, expressible as both physical border and limit of principle, marking the limits of their autonomy and of their knowability. This cross, in turn, enabled a grid on which to locate anything and anyone, to map presence and absence, to plot movement in space, to draw the line as both relation and as separation. All the great puzzles posed by the relationship between earthly immanence and heavenly transcendence could then be reformulated as puzzles about the relationship between the immanent possibilities/impossibilities of life within the sovereign jurisdiction of the territorial state, and the possibilities/impossibilities of relations with other, foreign, spatiotemporally different worlds beyond.

It is thus no accident that the most theologically charged moments of modern political life, those in which the problematic relationship between the right to give/take life assumed by the sovereign state imitates the right to give/take life once attributed to some transcendental deity, occur right at the edges of territorial authority, in the declaration of war between states, in the moment where God is always on one side or the other, in the moment when sacrifice is somehow deemed sacred, necessary, an act of and for freedom. Discourses about the limits of political possibility in horizontal space, in war, still echo in discourses about the limits of earthly existence in the face of transcendent divinity; as do discourses about the temporal road up and away from the limits of possibility articulated in horizontal space.

The Aristotelians never quite knew where they were in this great shift from hierarchy to horizontality, from quality to quantity, from natural law to the law of the secular sovereign; from limits populated by angels, perhaps, to limits populated by soldiers and customs officers. Nevertheless, the great heroes of early modern knowledge soon began to know their way around and to lay out the conditions under which modern subjects could be enamoured of both their subjectivity and their objective knowledge of a world that remained precisely object, separate, and, in Weber's terms, disenchanted. This is what allowed Hobbes to map the grids of the modern state and, in principle, the world beyond, in much the same spirit as Mercator had mapped the newly discovered world on his globes and projections in the previous century. Nevertheless, it is to Hobbes' lasting credit that he never forgot that the heroes of modern knowledge had articulated an account of knowledge precisely as a problem, and that it was no easy matter to replace accounts of authority grounded in claims about divinity with accounts grounded in claims about the separation of man from world.

It has been Hobbes' peculiar fate to have been converted into the archetypal political realist among theorists of international relations, the figure who tells a story about sovereignty as the way it is, and thus a site at which to mobilize claims about the natural and universal character of a world of sovereign states acting in a system of states. This conversion tells us a lot more about how a story about the necessary origins of modern sovereignty was constructed from the vantage point of twentieth-century preoccupations with modernizing nation-states than it does about Hobbes' capacity to imagine an emerging world of abstract authorities two-and-a-half centuries earlier. Indeed, it was only in the twentieth century that Hobbes came to be thought of as someone who had something to say about international relations at all.[8]

Unlike Hobbes, however, we have had some difficulty remembering that the sovereignty of the modern state is a problem, not a simple fact of life. While historically contingent, in ways that have attracted many famous stories about the shift to modernity and the rise of the West, the fateful moves to which Hobbes was responding have long been naturalized in many places as the only way of framing questions about knowledge, and thus as the proper ground on which to construct endless debates about the priorities of objectivity and subjectivity. The story of their inscription as a core achievement of early-modern Europe is now so integral to the prevailing narratives of modernity as to warrant only a passing mention, or a silent assumption, of an apparently natural break between ancient and modern, theology and philosophy, superstition and reason.[9] Consequently, it is now difficult to comprehend what was at stake in, for example, the way Hobbes' greatest text opens with an analysis of the physiology of sensation and its relation to human reason. Still, we have not entirely forgotten that this newly differentiated world of modern subjects and objects, of consciousness and the world outside consciousness, replaced or reconstructed other discriminations that had also come to seem unchallengeable. It has itself been challenged, in some places, and on many grounds, ever since.

For most contemporary philosophical traditions, in fact, the framing of the problem of knowledge in these terms has itself come to seem to be a bit of a problem, one that becomes especially troubling given the practices through which humans construct and reconstruct their subjectivities and objectify historical contingencies into social orders, institutions and authorities. Consequently, a great many debates about modern social science have hinged on a familiar incongruity: between the historically contested character of the distinction between self-affirming subjects and self-less objects that affirmed both the promise and the problematic character of a modernity supposedly freed from the discriminations of an Aristotelian/Thomistic cosmos; and the continuing appeal to modern epistemological claims to objectivity/subjectivity that seem to resist any sense that the modern construction of subjectivity and objectivity is indeed an historical achievement, and an ongoing problem, rather than a simple given.

This incongruity has now been a central feature of social and political analysis for at least a century. It is one of the constitutive sites around which modern social sciences have become institutionalized around a series of debates about causal explanation and hermeneutic understanding, structure and agency, the physical sciences and the humanities, and so on.[10] From one direction, accounts of subjectivity have been elaborated and re-elaborated so as to undermine almost any clear distinction between the self-identical man celebrated by Descartes or Kant and the world, or nature, or society beyond. From the other, this distinction has been asserted and re-elaborated as the primary condition under which prevailing notions of individual responsibility, conscience, rational action and legitimate science might be sustained. This was already part of the broad context out of which specific (Anglo-American) accounts of a positivistic empiricism and a utilitarian and economistic rationalism came to turn serious problems of knowledge into the powerful but very narrowly focused strategies of legitimate enquiry that flourished in the second half of the twentieth century.

Debates about legitimate knowledge in the modern social sciences have thereby come to rest not only on a capacity to discriminate among competing knowledge claims, but also on a distinction between subject and object that has enabled modern knowers to know what a knowledge claim is and how it might come to have some kind of credibility. In some quarters, this prior and historically contingent discrimination, and the accounts of knowledge it enables, has come to seem entirely unproblematic. The task of social science can then be treated more as a matter of methodological technique than of contested epistemological, ontological or axiological principles. In others, subjectivity remains a problem, objectivity remains a problem, and both the distinction and relation between subjectivity and objectivity remain a problem. For some scholars, in fact it matters little what kind of creature it is that is making claims to knowledge. This may well be a stance with which most mathematicians or astrophysicists, for example, are entirely comfortable; after all, merely human subjectivity can seem utterly trivial in such contexts. Nevertheless, when it comes to making knowledge claims about historically constituted practices, including the practices of mathematics and astrophysics, there are obvious dangers in ignoring the extent to which modern forms of knowledge are very tightly bound up with what it means to be a human subject: to be a knower making claims about what it means to know the world that, in turn, affirm what it means for a knower to be somehow part of the world that is supposedly known. Modern forms of knowledge, of the kind that have come to receive precise specification in relation to the claims of modern social science, are thoroughly implicated in the kinds of subjectivity produced by modern societies that know what they are precisely because they have made such a fateful series of discriminations between man and world, the natural world of apparent determinations and the social world of human possibilities. The claims to authority that are expressed in the principles, practices and institutions of the modern state both express and reproduce these discriminations, and in effect invite us to assume that these are the only discriminations that can be made.

This is why the core debates about method in the social sciences are so rarely about method alone, but work as surrogates for disputes about onto-logical and political commitments, about the discriminations and authoriza-tions of discriminations that are taken for granted by specific authorizations of what is to count as legitimate knowledge and sovereign authority. This is also why any attempt to pose questions about authorization as precisely a question have so often produced demands that epistemology be the only ground for scholarly encounter and controversy. Claims about epistemological relativism can then be deployed to affirm authority against anyone puzzled about the conditions under which such authority is considered to be author-itative, and any sense that knowledge is to be understood as a problem is erased in favour of sovereign proclamations about what the proper grounds for knowledge must be, or how the field of scholarship should be divided up into a carefully controlled array of methodological approaches or perspec-tives. In effect, epistemologies struggling with a problematic relationship between knower and known have often been deployed as a way of solving problems arising from an even more troubling relationship between the modern human subject and the world from which that subject has been dis-tinguished as the site and objective of a properly human freedom. This is a move that may work in many settings, but not when claims about author-itative knowledge are brought to bear on practices of sovereign authorization.

In any case, and much more prosaically, much of what social scientists do on a daily basis involves the development and reproduction of systems of classification, the codification of discriminations in typologies, models, hypotheses and depictions of what counts as evidence, much more than it does those practices of data-gathering and explanation that receive so much more critical scrutiny and ideological endorsement in socio-scientific judge-ments about scholarly judgements of subjectivity and objectivity.[11] Phenom-ena to be studied are divided up and arranged for analysis. Theoretical perspectives are set out as if on a supermarket shelf, with little sense of the ontological and epistemological commitments that are affirmed by a (usually neo-Kantian) discourse of perspectives. Without these discriminations, the textbook trade would collapse. Introductory classes would be too hard to teach. Scholars would have difficulty focusing on the task at hand and distinguishing between the important and the marginal, the workable and the red herring, the publishable and the frivolous, the authoritative and the fraudulent, the comfortable and the unsettling. Policy-makers would not know what advice to trust, what principles to affirm or challenge, or what stories to tell themselves about their own integrity.

After all, as Hobbes would certainly affirm, one does have to start somewhere. Why worry about practices of discrimination when most starting points are so obvious, so long-established and so generalized as to be uncontentious? The world is divided into countries, for example, so why not start a comparative analysis of politics by comparing the different political systems in these separate countries? The world has its geographical regions, so why not distinguish between the politics of the North and the South, with their contrasting stages of development, their varying commitments to democracy, and their somehow more and less civilized civilizations?[12] The world is made up of men and women, so why not discriminate between the public and private spheres in which these men and women live? People/peoples engage in economic, social, biological, political, aesthetic, philosophical and military activities, so why not organize the disciplines of scholarship accordingly? Nature is not nurture, so why not simply emulate the practices of the physical sciences, or of the humanities? Here are our friends and there are our enemies, so why not do good to those who live here and do ill to those who live there? We are at war with terrorists, so why should we bother with procedures devised to protect the rights of common criminals? The medieval schoolmen all spoke about superstitious nonsense, so why not start with more sensible and more rational modern assumptions, exactly in the spirit of good old Hobbes? There should be no need to go on. None of these categories is as clear-cut as they appear in the rhetorics in which they are deployed. Starting points are never as obvious or uncontested as they are made to seem. Enormous energies must be deployed to make them seem natural and uncontested, as Hobbes himself certainly knew much better than most.

The modern social sciences begin with discriminations and classifications that are both readily obvious and yet also obviously historically contingent and contested in the very practices that the social sciences nevertheless seek to explain. These discriminations are at play both in the construction of modern accounts of what it means to make a claim about knowledge of any kind – of the modern framing of what it must mean to enact knowledge as a problematic relationship between knowing subjects and a world beyond subjectivity that might be objectively known – and in the construction and reconstruction of those subjectivities and objectivities that are constituted in ways that might be known. To the extent that the social sciences seek to affirm grounds for judgement that are somehow beyond judgements about the discriminations and classification that enable their claims to knowledge, they inevitably reify the most conventional answers to questions that are right at the heart of modern conceptions of politics while simultaneously seeking to take themselves beyond politics. In general terms, and always allowing for significant exceptions, the stronger the generalized appeal to some kind of methodological and disciplinary orthodoxy, the weaker the acknowledgement of the contingency of (and political claims at stake in the discriminations and classifications enabling) the knowledge being claimed.

On the other hand, if no discriminations, then no judgements, no knowledge, and no politics. If no modern subjects in a world of objects, then no knowledge as understood in the canonical categories of modern epistemology; and no modern politics either. Hence various controversies about the status of modern subjectivities and the consequent fears about relativism, nihilism, an uncontainable proliferation of identities and agencies, and an abandonment of any ground on which to articulate a progressive politics; but also about what it means to qualify as a human being, a political agent, or someone with some scholarly authority to speak about human beings and their political agencies. Hence, also, all the memories of other contexts in which the prevailing discriminations of the age have been unceremoniously castigated as a wretched basis on which to think about either knowledge or politics. Plato's dismissal of the authority of (oral, poetic, complacent) tradition and Hobbes' withering contempt for "ignorance" and "frequency of insignificant speech" among the medieval schoolmen have been paradigmatic but certainly not unusual in this respect.

Discriminations enable our accounts of the good, the true and the beautiful, the saved and the damned, the primitive and the modern, the natural and the social, as well as the legitimacy of the incarceration, the execution, the torture, the intervention, the declaration of war. The capacity to discriminate is not only always necessary, a condition of the most mundane as well as the most sophisticated social practices, but in some sense always dangerous. It is never as easy as we might wish to differentiate between discriminations in the art gallery, book shop or laboratory and discriminations of superiority and inferiority or inclusion and exclusion in the street, the household, the immigration counter, the prison yard or the ministry of defence. Moreover, and as we are liable to be reminded whenever claims are mobilized about terrorists, illegal immigrants or the need to suspend some law, it is certainly not wise to assume that classification strategies ever stand still, or that they are deployed by rational agents rather than open and rapidly shifting fields of administrative procedure, technological innovation and statistical calculation. A politics of divide and rule may be universal, but also is always changing, not least in framings of here and there, higher and lower, now and then, included and excluded.

Most significantly, discriminations enable accounts of origins and limits, of the beginnings of things and the spatiotemporalities of their continuous or discontinuous occurrence. Enabling myths of origin, founding claims about foundation, shaping practices of temporal sequence and spatial differentiation, discriminations not only impose orders but generate events, put processes in motion, and drive theologians, philosophers, scientists, artists and political theorists to struggle with what it might mean to create something new, something somehow free from the determinations of the old. In the beginning was the *logos*, as one especially influential narrative of genesis insists. *Cogito, ergo sum*, as Descartes put it when helping to set the discourses of modernity into motion by imagining a line of geometrical extension free from representational form as the ground of all representation. Once upon a time in the state of nature, as it is said in all those discourses of modernization that have come to ground their strategies of legitimation as a spatiotemporal discrimination between us and them.

It is in the context of what we have come to call politics that the necessities and dangers of discrimination, as well as the need for sustained scrutiny of the conditions under which certain discriminations enact a ground, a starting point, for public judgements, are supposedly most intense. This is why it has been so difficult for philosophers, scientists or theologians, let alone social scientists, to sustain claims to be able to discriminate authoritatively in ways that are somehow beyond the reach of politics. It is also why it is so difficult to avoid the conclusion that even the attempt to distinguish between the political and the philosophical, or the scientific, or the theological, is itself such an important practice of political life. Not surprisingly, many if not most of the important developments in contemporary social and political analysis now express a judgement that discrimination (both in relation to the construction of analytical categories and concepts, and in the practices generating social and political distinctions) must become increasingly contested, whether in relation to claims about globalization, imperialism, postmodernity, identity politics, orientalism, postcolonialism, post-Newtonian science, post-something-or-other philosophy, or religious rejections of a supposedly secular modernity.

Discriminations/exceptions

Modern politics – that is, the kind of politics we associate with the forms of statist political community in a system of statist communities shaped in post-Renaissance Europe – is explicitly constructed as a very precise and intricately articulated system of discriminations. It works especially on the basis of constitutive distinctions between legitimacy and illegitimacy, rulers and unruly, insiders and outsiders. Among many other things, it is, or has come to be, a practice that tells us what politics is, or is not, and thus a practice that has to be understood in terms of how it has come to be defined rather than of stipulative definitions of what it is. As such, modern politics enacts systems of discriminations that in turn enable sequences of subsequent discriminations, including those which tell us when we should and should not discriminate, or under what conditions we might consider ourselves to be discriminating,[13] or when we should and should not challenge the discriminations that make all subsequent discriminations possible.

Here one might want to privilege Locke's fateful distinction between "the world that God gave to man in common" and the right to private property, as well as the subsequent reworking of this theme in Marx's theory of value on the one hand, and the marginalist school of market economics on the other.[14] Or one might prefer to privilege the struggles between sacred and secular authority that continue despite the stakes supposedly buried in God's long-dead ghost; or between public and private ethics despite the stubborn elusiveness of any clear distinction between public and private. Or perhaps one might begin to unravel the reified dualisms of male and female, the West and the rest, the human and the animal, and so on, through which characteristically modern accounts of political identity and subjectivity have been enacted, legitimized, and sometimes subverted.[15] Or we might think about how the specific discriminations of modern politics once enacted novel ways of making discriminations: a challenge to a world which could envisage Plato carving nature at the joints, or Saint Thomas filling in the gap between time and eternity articulated by Saint Augustine; or an affirmation of the need to impose names and definitions on a phenomenal world that does not conveniently disclose itself through a name. Or we might brave the texts of a Martin Heidegger so as to witness the struggles involved in resisting Aristotle's classification of the Being of beings and thus the temporal limits within which human beings come to be;[16] or the texts of those analytical philosophers who thrive on an aversion to all questions about Being and an obsession with the need to eradicate linguistic confusion through the articulation of clear conceptual and logical distinctions.[17] Or we might engage with the various critical techniques through which even the most successful discriminations between one homogeneous concept and another are shown to express heterogeneous and contingent relations with other concepts and systems of concepts that contradict any pretence to homogeneity, necessity and decidability.[18] Or, looking away from but not entirely abandoning such apparently abstract discussions, we might simply reflect in horror upon the specific technologies and cruelties through which people have been kept apart by the border patrols, the barbed wire, the grotesque walls, the gates to the prisons, or the airlifts to the camps, or come to wonder about their relation to our strange modern world of passports, visas, biometrical identifications and segregated citizenships.

All these established entries to the politics of modern discriminations and the discriminations of modern politics are undoubtedly important for attempts to reimagine political possibilities and impossibilities. They both enable and are enabled by specific and highly variable political practices.[19] The capacity to make a difference, to act in such a way that differences are made, is crucial to the mysteries of political power. Conversely, the capacity to act on the basis of differences made (on the basis of discriminations enacted between the legitimate and the illegitimate, and between the properly political and everything else) is crucial to the mysteries of political authority.[20] This is in part why the mysteries of authority can be neither simply reduced to, or easily distinguished from, the mysteries of power. It is also in part why the relation between the technologies and administrations of governmentality and both the capacity to mobilize and the legitimation of those technologies and administrations has become one of the most densely opaque themes of contemporary political analysis. Not even the lonely can evade classification. Even silences evoke sonorities, harmonies and rhythms.

Thinking about modern practices of discrimination can take us in many directions and engagements with many different forms of analysis across many scholarly disciplines and traditions, as well as with analyses of how those disciplines and traditions have been constituted and reproduced. In whichever direction we go, however, we are likely to become aware very quickly that modern political life constantly affirms a demand for some sovereign power/authority to distinguish that which is properly political and that which is not, or, to follow the early Schmitt's summation, or reduction, of part of our Hobbesian legacy in this respect, that which is the general rule and that which is the exception to the general rule.[21] For all that accounts of political power might be informed by the capacity of states to make a difference, to mobilize physical force and administer the differences made, and for all that accounts of legitimate authority might be informed by claims about the ethical, cultural or democratic sources of legitimation, modern politics ultimately rests upon a claim that the capacity to act, and to claim to act legitimately, rests with some sovereign, conceived largely as a constitutional, and constitutive, abstraction.

The scholarly conventions generally tell us that it was Hobbes who most clearly articulated the distinction between the political and the nonpolitical as an achievement of modern sovereignty; a sovereignty, that is, expressed not in the body of any particular being with a direct connection with some higher authority, but in the abstract and apparently secular embodiment of a particular ensemble of beings, of modern subjects.[22] It is this which marks Hobbes as the most important textual expression of the convergence between specifically modern forms of discrimination and the practices of modern political authority, and which partly ensures his centrality to contemporary attempts to come to terms with the limits of modern politics. Hobbes' account of sovereignty rested, in turn, on all the new distinctions and discriminations shaping the emergence of modern cultural formations, not least those expressing (again to resort to a shorthand version of a long, complex and contested story) Galilean, neo-Platonist, nominalist and other challenges to the prevailing essentialisms and Thomisms of the age. It rested especially on a prior distinction between what could and could not be said in properly rational or scientific discourse, and on some distinctive accounts of what it means to engage in such rational and scientific discourse.[23] It is in Hobbes, especially, that we can see the meshing of our distinctions between both the political and the nonpolitical, and the rational and the nonrational. It is in Hobbes that we can see our most basic assumptions about what is properly political being shaped by new discriminations in space and time, by new accounts of here and there, then and now, form and content, as well as by new accounts of who it is that can be properly political given these new discriminations. On this basis, Hobbes articulates our primary modern archetype of how our "natural" rights and moral obligations can be reconciled with our "civic" rights and duties as modern political subjects in an ahistorical but foundational moment of collective rationality: a transition from a "nature" that is projected from an idealized present simultaneously to an out there and a back then, and then shifted back to a here and now that defines both our being and our perfectability in a political community. All it takes is that patented mixture of Fear, Desire, Hope and the Reason that "suggesteth convenient Articles of Peace, upon which men may be drawn to agreement."[24]

Schmitt's less widely known yet broadly pervasive early-twentieth-century claim that "sovereign is he who decides on the state of exception" comes immediately in the opening sentence of his *Political Theology*, published in1922.[25] This is a claim that captures some of Hobbes' understanding of what it means to authorize discriminations, to affirm a capacity to distinguish between the legal and the extra-legal and to make this distinction under sovereign law. As with Hobbes, also, Schmitt's understanding of sovereignty emerged as a response to a period of immense turmoil, in his case one marked both by a devastating war and left-wing revolution of the kind experienced in Soviet Russia and widely expected in Weimar Germany. This was an era that produced many key texts that continued to inform intense discussions about sovereignty throughout the 1920s and 1930s, discussions that seemed to vanish with the increasing influence of Anglo-American forms of social science and analytical philosophy in the second half of the century.

Unsurprisingly, perhaps, many of the discussions from that era have begun to find many contemporary echoes as questions about sovereign authority have more obviously exceeded the grasp of empirical social science and analytical philosophy, in relation to both the claims of the modern state and the claims of modern scholarship. Ours, too, has become an age of apocalyptic warnings and attempts to shore up the sovereignty of territorial states in the face of dynamics of capitalist modernization that are widely sensed as spinning out of control. While much is to be gained by re-engaging with how Hobbes thought about the authorization of authority in a world of early modern subjectivities, much is also to be gained by re-engaging with the ways in which the sovereignty of modern states that Hobbes had framed in constitutional terms came to be reframed in relation to the modernizing and nationalizing forces that were understood to be so deeply problematic at the time Schmitt laid out his elegant, incisive and still deeply troubling definition. The double resonance of Schmitt's way of rendering the relationship between unity and diversity in a moment of decision at the edge of the modern nation-state both with the exemplary founding texts of early-modern politics and with the paradigmatic failures of modern politics between the First and Second World Wars – in both cases in relation to attempts to articulate political possibilities in terms of the potentialities and limits of modern accounts of rationality and subjectivity – gives us some sense of what is at stake in challenging the grounds on which we now make distinctions.[26]

Schmitt, a conservative Weimar jurist who later came to have strong Nazi connections, remains one of the great embarrassments as well as one of the great enigmas of modern political thought. Still, the elegant economy and residual ambivalence of his understanding of sovereignty as a capacity to decide exceptions is especially difficult to shake off if one wants to cling to the account of modern subjectivity whose limits, and conditions of possibility, he both assumes and affirms. This is a desire expressed most passionately by modern forms of liberalism. Indeed, modern liberalism makes little sense as a political doctrine without some understanding of its constitutive struggles to come to terms with the contradiction between an aspiration for universality and an affirmation of statist forms of community. The modern liberal subject is first of all a modern subject, and the modern liberal state is first of all a modern state. The many achievements of those liberalisms that have sought to reconcile the contradictions between modern states and modern subjects through principles and procedures of consent, representation, democratization, privatization, pluralization, toleration and so on are always liable to unravel when universalizing ambition is confronted with claims about national solidarities, interests and securities.

This is the possibility that became visible in Weber's struggles to envisage new concepts of subjectivity and responsibility that somehow remained both liberal and nationalist under conditions of a contradictory modernization,[27] and became most explicit in Schmitt's account of a sovereign exceptionalism: an account that effectively calls for the destruction of most of the defining features of liberalism as the price of saving the modern state and the modern subject. Against a fairly broad array of what he took to be distinctly worrying options, especially the revolutionary and even apocalyptic possibilities articulated in the name of a revolutionary class (of the kind expressed in Gyorgy Lukacs' recovery of the Hegelian dimensions of Marx),[28] messianic religion (of the kind that permeates some of Walter Benjamin's earlier writings),[29] or violence itself (as in the then influential writings of George Sorel),[30] Schmitt sought to affirm a capacity to make a final decision under the law of a specific state so as to constitute the unity of a specific people. Against progressive pluralists, corporatists and democrats (like Harold Laski and G.D.H. Cole), he affirmed the priority of what we even now call national unity, the unity that would come to be expressed in claims about the national interest, national security and all the rest. In terms that hark back to the early-modern era, Schmitt affirmed an absolute priority of citizens over humanity, though his conception of citizenship is a rude rebuke to the aspirations for democratic participation that we are now supposed to treat as specifically liberal achievements. As defenders of claims about national security have insisted ever since, a sovereign capacity to decide when liberties must be curtailed, the rule of law must be derogated, and democratic accountabilities must be suspended is the primary condition under which liberties might be enabled, the rule of law might be enacted, and democratic accountabilities might be extended.

Schmitt's formulation of sovereignty as a capacity to decide upon an exception to the rule constitutes the sharpest expression of the way in which the sovereignty of modern states works in relation to the line, the boundary, the spatial differentiation of a particular unity within and a world of others without. Although the formulation harks back at least to Plato's fateful contrast between Greek and non-Greek in the fifth book of *The Republic* and the schemes of comparison and valuation worked out in Aristotle's *Politics*, it is expressed with all the sharpness expected by a post-Kantian and especially post-Hegelian culture. Like many of the historical sources with which the formulation might be associated, however, it also expresses some uncertainty about whether that line is to be understood as a matter of absolute inclusion and exclusion, as suggested in his subsequent formulation of politics as a matter of friend–enemy relations,[31] or as the site of a mutually productive relationality, as suggested in his account of the way the exception is made by an act of sovereign decision that is both inside and outside the norm it affirms in the act of decision: as he puts it in a way that harks back to Hobbes' account of the sovereign who is both within and beyond the law, "(t)he exception is more interesting than the regular case. The latter proves nothing; the exception proves everything. The exception does not only confirm the rule; the rule as such lives off the exception alone."[32]

The difference between these two formulations of a constitutive difference seems to me to be especially significant. The existentialist or dualistic account of friend against enemy has certainly been influential in sustaining radically nationalist conceptions of political realism and state interests of the kind popularized by Morgenthau, but the formulation of a reciprocal relation between norm and exception is much less easily dismissed. Nevertheless, even when understood as a relation rather than an existential opposition, Schmitt's statism must be placed in its proper international context. After all, with a monadic relation between norm and exception, declarations of exception are quickly going to turn into a normal condition. Much more interesting and still difficult problems arise when the relationship between norm and exception in any particular state is understood both as a self-constituting process and as always doubled, as caught up in the co-constitutive relationship of the limits of both the sovereign state and the sovereign system of states. Indeed, what is quite striking about so much contemporary debate about new forms of exceptionalism in the wake of the end of Cold War, the "war on terror," and the unilateral ambitions of recent US administrations more generally is that it remains so tied to a monolithically statist account of modern politics, and is so willing to ignore the international conditions under which even the most Schmittean states can affirm their preferred forms of solipsism.

Given the historical differences in the contexts to which they were responding, any simple juxtaposition of Hobbes and Schmitt is guaranteed to conceal as much as it might reveal. Their worlds are separated by the impact of, to note only the most obvious, a rationalizing capitalism, the American and French Revolutions, various forms of liberal constitutionalism and more or less virulent forms of nationalism. Schmitt speaks to an age in which the (racial) homogeneity of national populations and sharp distinctions between them could be more or less assumed, at least in Europe, in a way that Hobbes could not easily envisage. In terms introduced by Michel Foucault,[33] Hobbes was engaged in a now classically legalistic form of sovereign politics, whereas Schmitt affirmed a form of biopolitics, the production, reproduction and disciplining of populations, the world of nationalisms and mass societies: the mobilizations that had already scared the life out of Carl von Clausewitz when contemplating the military innovations of Napoleon, and sent Weber off to find politicians capable of reconciling an ethic of ultimate ends with an ethic of responsibility. In effect, Schmitt simply affirmed ultimate ends, those of the state, the nation, the unity, above all liberal, pluralist and democratic differences. Schmitt's political theology invokes not a possible return from secular to sacred, but a secular leader who could command a population with something like religious authority, the capacity to mobilize populations for a properly political life. In any case, Schmitt's appropriation of Hobbes, like his implicit appeal both to Machiavelli and to Roman accounts of emergency powers, says more about his interest in resisting leftist movements for mass democracy in the emerging Weimar Republic, and about his preoccupation with experiences of democracy and dictatorship in Soviet Russia, than to an engagement with the ambiguities of classical texts. Hobbes' Euclidean lines may have been sharp enough, at least as expressions of emerging principle. Schmitt's lines, the expression of a moment of sovereign decision, articulated an account of the limits of modern politics that reminds us all too effectively of a century of wholesale slaughter orchestrated in the name of the historically instantiated sovereign nation state. Yet in both cases, what remains interesting about the way each works with these lines is that what is made to seem like a clear-cut distinction between one pre-existing existence, situation or status on either side works only because of a prior account of processes in which distinctions are anything but clear-cut.

Schmitt's explicit formulations were largely forgotten once very specific forms of social science began to be treated as the only legitimate way of making claims to knowledge about political life. If fundamental discussions about sovereignty require digging up the intellectual history of European fascism, better to let sleeping dogs lie still and pretend that the close connection between a rationalizing modernity and mass violence identified by Weber, Schmitt and so many others has been dealt with, not least by all those positivistic notions of scientific knowledge that were also shaped by counterrevolutionary ambitions[34] and by the achievements of Anglo-American forms of modernization.[35] Even so, various responses to Schmitt have played themselves out in many contexts and continue to shape contemporary debate. Leo Strauss was led to appeal to pre-Thomist forms of classical (Platonist, Aristotelean and Stoic) wisdom, and to affirm their aristocratic pretensions as a way out of the inevitable nihilisms of modernity.[36] Hannah Arendt was tempted by an idealized American revolutionary tradition as a way of recalling the promise of classical notions of public space. Sharing Schmitt's distaste for the internationalizing state as a revolutionary threat, Friedrich Hayek went looking for a different kind of statist intervention in the name of a free market economy, in a manner that has percolated through many contemporary claims about the benefits of a globalizing capitalist market that may still require authoritarian political institutions.[37]

Most significantly for the general line of argument I am working through here, the debates that developed in the 1920s and 1930s in relation to the claim to state sovereignty came to be structured very largely around an opposition between Schmitt and Hans Kelsen's neo-Kantian conception of (international) law.[38] In effect, where Schmitt pushed the claim to the sovereignty of a particular state to its most extreme limits, Kelsen insisted on the sovereignty of the states system that is the possibility condition for the sovereignty of any particular state.[39] The general ambition articulated by Kelsen is recognizable in the antipathy towards Schmitt, and Weber that one finds in the more recently influential texts of Jürgen Habermas. It is perhaps instructive, however, that Habermas's neo-Kantian (and in key respects, I will suggest below, not very Kantian) universalism has been strikingly innocent about the politics of international relations, and about the deeply contradictory character of a form of political life that can be polarized around the options affirmed by Schmitt and Kelsen; the singular sovereign under national law or the unity of singular sovereigns under universal law.

Most, though not all, commentaries on Schmitt have been concerned, like Habermas, with the reactionary potentials offered by his critique of the liberal and pluralistic forms of constitutionalism that, Schmitt believed, necessarily dissolve politics into just one form of association among others and reduce the state to a mere instrumentality, an administration of things: the dissolution and reduction of politics to the supposed banalities and mediocrities of the modern world. He is certainly not easy to take seriously as a significant site on which to think about more imaginative forms of political life, even though significant attempts have been made to turn his critique in the direction of hopes for a more radically pluralistic and agonistic democratic practice or a civil society freed from the rigid constraints of prevailing forms of liberal representation.[40]

Like Hobbes, Schmitt poses very hard questions. Just as one might prefer to engage with Locke rather than Hobbes because he works through a range of what many people find to be more positive stories about how one should act once political society has been established, albeit on the basis of strong (and highly contentious, not to say odious) colonial and religious commitments, so one might prefer to engage with more positive stories about social democracy and the rest than with questions about the limits of political authority: hence the attraction of those veils through which Rawlsian forms of political discourse abandon just about everything a Schmitt would think of as political. For the most part, we might say, contemporary democratic theory has rightly resisted Schmitt's anti-democratic reduction of political life within modern societies to a moment of sovereign decisionism. We might even say that Schmitt's abstract formulation gives expression to the worst possible way of thinking about modern political possibilities. Still, Rawls did not rely on those veils without reason. There comes a point where questions about limits, about origins, boundaries and exceptions, come back into sharp focus. For all that most political theorists have tried to ignore him, or to urge contempt for his ugly authoritarianism, Schmitt's account of sovereignty as a capacity to decide exceptions has in fact remained at the heart of modern conceptions of political life: the heart, that is, of those discourses which seek to defend the borders within which the political theorists can afford to draw their veils; the discourses we know as the theory of international relations, at least in their more nationalist forms.

Insofar as they are concerned with historical experiences, theorists of international relations are fond of invoking Hobbes and the emergence of a recognizably modern system of states in early modern Europe as the basic ground on which to think about the primary structural conditions they seek to understand. As a discipline, however, the analysis of international relations has been much more profoundly shaped by the experiences of two eras in particular: by the era before and after the First World War, the era to which Weber and Schmitt were responding; and by the era of post-Second World War American hegemony in which Weber and Schmitt, and all that they represented as expressions of a dangerous nationalism and even fascism, were quickly forgotten, or suppressed, or recast as the language of the hard men equipped to deal with dirty work at the border. Since the mid-twentieth century, Schmitt has been consigned to specialist duties alongside neo-Weberian readings of a tragic modernity, given a special place among that distinctive breed of political analysts who pride themselves on their ability to cope with the extremes of modern politics, with the state of emergency, the reason of state, the state of war and the declaration of national necessity.[41] Theories of international relations may be framed most frequently, though quite dubiously, through analogies with Hobbes' account of a state of nature, but the underlying force of modern claims about the demands of national security are much more intensely informed by Schmittean claims about a need to suspend the norms of democratic life in the face of the necessities of state and the state of emergency: claims that also get at rather more profound aspects of Hobbes' analysis than do attempts to equate Hobbes' account of a state of nature with the logic of a states system, and to equate both with a specific account of rational action in a competitive market. Strikingly, however, Schmitt has been consigned to specialist duties in the context not of a paradigmatic model of a modernizing nationalism, but of the paragon of a universalizing but ultimately profoundly nationalistic liberalism, in the theory of international relations as a specifically American social science.

The quite radical possibility articulated in Schmitt's account of sovereignty is that war will determine the substance of politics: that the exception explains everything. This possibility arises not only in relation to the identification of an enemy outside, but also to the identification of an enemy within. The line between friend and enemy is very tight, and the toleration for difference is very small. For Schmitt himself, this possibility seems to be set out explicitly so as to prevent the loss of politics within borders through the universalization of some broader humanity, whether through an onslaught by a revolutionary proletariat or through slower slippages towards liberal humanism. Nevertheless, and while it may be slightly reassuring to note that Schmitt's formulations arose from a now largely marginalized right-wing reactionary, it is not difficult to see how the basic logic has an appeal for all modern states seeking to affirm their autonomy, their sovereignty, their freedom, their community, their nation. In terms of a related theoretical language, it is also not difficult to see how modern forms of politics within sovereign states have been constituted through an assumed trade-off between the claims of security and the claims of liberty.

As Hobbes affirms, we live within sovereign states that enable freedom under necessity, liberty under obligations. It is a trade-off that, to revert back to Schmittean terms, requires exceptions to be made. The political theorists and moralists have it easy, it might be said. All they have to do is think up universal norms: thou shalt not kill; do unto others as you would have them do unto you. For the theorist of international relations, killing is precisely the absolutely necessary thing to do, in exceptional circumstances, in war, in the name of national necessity, when the line is as thin as it can possibly be, reducible to a mere moment of decision necessary to secure those freedoms, to secure the statist world of modern subjects. Except that what can be cast in familiar shades of darkest black and brilliant white when framed in relation to solipsistic nation-states becomes an altogether more complicated affair when framed in relation to a system of states that is the condition of the possibility of any particular state, where and when Schmitt meets Kelsen, and nationalism meets internationalism in complex practices of mutual constitution.

Exceptions/authorizations

Both Hobbesian and Schmittean traditions have encouraged us to assume that the voice of modern sovereign authority will always be most insistent in its delineations of the spatiotemporal limits of what is permissible: that which is legal and that which is not, that which is in and that which is out, that which is us and that which is other, that which is pressing and that which is trivial; that which is properly political and that which is merely civil, or cultural, or social, or economic, or biological, or private. Consequently, someone has to do the dirty work of modern political analysis, to face up to the extremes, the worst-case scenarios, the limit conditions. Someone has to see the world in simple blacks and whites, in the immature terms that make any good liberal cringe, precisely so as to insist that the limits of the modern sovereign state are the place where maturity comes to a stop, where modern politics makes its pact with the legitimation of mass violence. The theorists of international relations did not fully emerge as the most appropriate candidates for this role until the mid-twentieth century, even though the role itself might, or even must, be projected back onto some vaguely imagined dawn of modernity. Nevertheless, in the shift from early-twentieth-century German theories of the modern state to an American science of international relations, Schmitt's sharp reminder that the logic of a sovereign exceptionalism is always liable to trump the achievements of liberal constitutionalism found many echoes in claims about the need to suspend the conventions and hopes of a modern liberal society in the face of impending threats and insecurities. Seventeenth-century notions about "reason of state" and early twentieth-century accounts of a radical nationalism thereby found new life in Cold War discourses about "national security" and technologies of mass annihilation.

While Schmitt's formula may be most obviously alive in the spatial discourses of international insecurities, however, it also has broader relevance for the ways in which attempts to envisage forms of democracy anywhere that exceed the spatial limits of a particular somewhere are liable to run up against the limits of a sovereign decision to include or exclude, to normalize or exceptionalize, in the name of the state that is the prior condition of the *demos*. While theorists of international relations encourage accounts of a sovereign exceptionalism articulated in terms of threats from an outside, they also express accounts of a sovereign exceptionalism articulated as a need to secure a population of citizen subjects inside.[42] In both contexts, questions about the conditions under which norms are to be suspended remain far more difficult than questions about the values and practices that should constitute a norm; although many committed liberals and democrats still find it fairly easy to decide that mass violence and war is indeed the necessary cost of making the world safe for their own democratic states,[43] or quietly to assume radically nationalist accounts of universality and difference in order to canvass the possibilities of greater plurality within.[44]

The more conventional theorists of international relations are often criticized for having a narrow and staunchly conservative, even militaristic view of political life: for having an unsavoury fondness for the heroic and aristocratic anti-liberalism associated with Schmitt himself. The criticism is often overdrawn, but would nevertheless be a reasonable conclusion to come to after a brief engagement with some of the literatures on security policy in the Cold War era. Moreover, even when framed in more progressive socio-scientific terms, precisely as a discipline that has supposedly overcome its associations with the decisionism of the *machtstaat*, international relations has remained a discipline apart, one not widely celebrated for its critical acumen or theoretical innovation.[45] Nevertheless, as the designated students of the limit condition (of the security policy, the national interest, and the necessary violence of the state of emergency), theorists of international relations have at least had the merit of insisting that modern politics is indeed supposed to be (and not simply is) a matter of making the most difficult distinctions, of discriminating between friends and enemies, between the normal and the exceptional, between the realistic and the merely aspirational, between the demands of state sovereignty and the demands of a sovereign system of sovereign states: between, to shift into a somewhat different but still Schmittean register, *la politique* and *le politique, die Politik* and *das Politische,* polity and policy. In focusing on the necessity of limit conditions, on a sovereign capacity to discriminate between the political norm and the necessary exception to that norm, on the fundamental difference between politics as usual and the extrapolitical (or hyper-political) world of secret agents, security analysts, the machinery of war, and, in Clausewitz's terms, politics by other means,[46] they also point to the constitutive role of the sovereign act of discrimination in our most cherished and normalized accounts of where and what political life must be. In demarcating the borders on which exceptions are declared, they express the constitutive hypocrisies that have emerged in a world of multiple sovereignties, each asserting its own universality in particularity.

As Giorgio Agamben has observed in his recently influential but, I think, seriously flawed commentary on the paradoxical practices of sovereign authority, these accounts are already enabled by a paradigmatic distinction (which he associates, to my mind not very convincingly, with Aristotle), between a politically qualified life and the simple fact of living, whereby "bare life has the peculiar privilege of being that whose exclusion founds the city of men."[47] This distinction is paradigmatic in that modern political analysis and debate hangs on our ability to ignore, or to naturalize, the political practices through which specific accounts of what politics is and what it is not, and where politics is and where it is not, are established as a given, as an unchallengeable foundation. For Agamben, this heritage of exclusions, not least the Roman distinction between those who are worthy of sacrifice and those who are not, lives on in "the camp," in the proliferation of zones of incarceration in which people are treated as something other than human. These, for Agamben, express a new and more apocalyptic world in which exceptions are becoming generalized, escaping from the singular and contained sovereignties that Schmitt insisted must be the only alternative to the revolutionary apocalypse he so feared in the early 1920s.[48]

Partly with, but largely against, Agamben's preoccupation with the constitutive significance of Aristotle, one might want to insist that some of the most crucial acts of exclusion enabling modern political life were already expressed in Plato's *Republic*. They are expressed most explicitly in relation to the exclusion of non-Greeks, and non-citizens. They are expressed perhaps most fatefully at the very beginning of the text in the dismissal of traditional forms of authority required before he can even begin to pose questions about justice in the city: goodnight Cephalus, goodbye old world, welcome to the new discourses about justice in the world that rest upon the exclusion of other worlds. They are expressed also in the condemnation of those musics and poetics that encourage metaphorical slippages of meaning and sap the wholesome virility of those who must know their proper, just place in the social order.[49] Accept these three rather significant exclusions, and the way is open for the construction of a polite conversation about the conditions under which a just city might be founded; open, that is to say, to the construction of a constitutive account of the grounds of conversation as an opposition between a not quite definable account of universal justice and a very precise account of its defining nemesis, the relativism or conflation of truth and power articulated by Thrasymachus. Whatever one makes of the inscrutabilities of this particular text, these exclusions have certainly played a crucial role in the mobilization of Plato's *Republic* in general, and the figure of Thrasymachus in particular, so as to frame relations between both universality/particularity and knowledge/power in ways that are still expressed in promiscuous claims about "relativism" in contemporary political debate.[50]

Such classical sources are clearly not the only sites at which engagement with the relation between the authorization of discriminations and a politics of exception leads to a politics of origins and foundings. It would also be useful to meditate on the resonances, and differences, between the forms of exclusion and exceptionalism expressed in such paradigmatic moments of the classical founding of our modern accounts of political possibility with much more wide-ranging notions of banishment, heresy, transgression and sacrifice across many cultures, especially insofar as the exclusion serves to affirm patterns of inclusion and the exception serves to constitute the norm.[51] A seriously comparative politics, we might say, would need to compare the different practices of inclusion/exclusion that have enabled us to deploy specific practices of political comparison. Questions about whether to start thinking about politics on terms set by Aristotle, Plato, the classical inheritance more generally, or some other place and some other time entirely, lead to the obvious (but often conveniently forgotten) ways in which to begin – to found – is to include and exclude, and to include/exclude in very specific ways. The discriminating practices of modern politics themselves depend on discriminating practices that have ceased to be contentious, at least much of the time and in a great many, but certainly not all, places.

This is why, for example, it is often necessary to read the discriminating practices of modern politics in realms that effectively have been depoliticized as merely cultural, aesthetic or ethical,[52] or as merely a matter of competition among already established actors conforming to the already agreed rules of representation or market rationality. This is also why, despite its aura of late- or postmodern immediacy, and the widespread attempt to turn engagements with problems into codified perspectives, so much contemporary European critical analysis is so concerned to excavate those moments of founding that have sedimented into the unquestionable and even invisible assumptions of our languages, institutions and everyday life. As a broad range of contemporary literatures have suggested, both in very general terms and in relation to more specific concerns, this is also why to countenance the prospect of any other political imagination is to engage precisely with the limits of the modern political imagination, and the practices through which they are constructed as part of a very precise system of discriminations. These limits are unlikely to be trivial in their consequences no matter how distant they may seem to be from the immediate bustle of governance and policy.

More specifically, and whatever might be said about the prior significance of Aristotle, Plato, and other classical figures who have attracted most of the attention of so many critical philosophers, figures like Hobbes and post-Hobbesians like Kant remain important sites of contemporary political enquiry. This is not because they tell us anything useful about human nature or moral reason, the inevitabilities of international conflict or the teleologies of some imagined democratic peace, as many influential invocations of these thinkers continue to suggest. Still less is it because they articulate some eternal opposition between supposedly realist and idealist accounts of the options before us, as so many have insisted as a way of forestalling discussion of their constitutive clichés. Far from being paradigmatic opponents in an apparently timeless debate about the necessities and possibilities of political life, both Hobbes and Kant inform our modern sense of what it means to discriminate, of how we have agreed to distinguish the real from the ideal, the natural from the cultural, the legitimate from the illegitimate, the freedom from the necessity. They tell us, in a phrase, what it must mean to draw the line, and what it means to draw the line under specifically modern conditions. They also speak, when interrogated more critically, to the difficulty, perhaps even the impossibility, of drawing those lines, both physical and figurative, that so many people prefer to treat as natural and inevitable.

We can still grasp the spatiotemporal framing of here and there, before and after, that Hobbes mobilizes in his story of the founding of modern sovereignty in large part because this framing has been conveniently recast in more historical and sociological modes by Kant, Hegel, Weber, Schmitt and all the other canonical theorists of the modern state as the spatiotemporal container of modern politics. Still, this framing, even as amended, seems disconcertingly at odds with the spatiotemporal contexts in which we now live. We can also still see firm declarations of a state of exception, the suspension of established laws and procedures, of democracies, laws and rights, in the name of some new extremity, some new state of emergency, some new danger that legitimizes the sovereign decision to kill, to torture, to incarcerate, to invade. The spirit of Carl Schmitt's exceptionalism has by no means been eradicated from contemporary political life. Yet this state of exception does not always correspond easily to the limits of the sovereign state in a system of other sovereign states. The limits of modern politics are not easily kept where they are supposed to be. We have shifted rather quickly from the monstrous edifice of the Berlin Wall, perhaps the paradigm of a securitized territoriality, to a war on terrorism and forms of securitization potentially enactable anywhere (but not everywhere), even though territorial divisions are sometimes affirmed ever more forcefully, and versions of Partition, that paradigmatically modern solution to the ills of the supposedly premodern, have not yet lost their attraction everywhere.

In my view, this is what is ultimately at stake in all those contemporary claims about how sovereignty is being challenged, transcended or erased by emerging economies and technologies, by new sites of governance, new forms of cultural identity and human rights, by various claims about a democratic deficit, a global civil society, a cosmopolitan humanity, planetary ecologies, transnational social movements, and so on. While it has now become conventional to think of sovereignty merely as an attribute of states that are somehow either enduring or fading away, modern forms of sovereignty also express a much more generalized – and increasingly problematic – understanding of how we should discriminate, how we should make judgements based on certain kinds of discrimination: how we must choose between the inclusion and the exclusion, the legitimate and the illegitimate, the possible and the impossible, the normal and the exceptional, and what must have been excluded spatially and temporally in order to construct a politics of inclusion and exclusion within a modern international order. It is one thing to indulge in the familiar debates over whether states are here to stay or on their way out. It is quite another to engage with the fate of sovereignty as an expression of specifically modern accounts of what it means to discriminate, and to judge that we are all indeed citizens and/or humans – except ...

The law of twofold frenzy revisited

To draw attention to the fragility of modern forms of discrimination, then, is certainly not to endorse recently popular claims that boundaries are disappearing or that we have no grounds on which to make distinctions between the same and the different, the included and the excluded, the legitimate or the illegitimate. On the contrary, many of our difficulties may well arise from the proliferation both of boundaries and of grounds for judgement, and thus from our inability to think about pluralism and differentiation in ways that are not overdetermined by the canonical modern accounts of universality and plurality, or similarity and difference. Many more of our difficulties may arise from the disjunction between the practices through which new boundaries are being established and the practices through which discriminations and judgements are being authorized through established structures and institutions. Modern forms of discrimination are clearly not universal, temporally or spatially, even though they have enabled accounts of political community, in space and in time, that have found extensive expression in the structures and practices of the modern state and modern states system; and still enable a constant stream of claims about the need to think about universal aspirations and political emancipations as if these forms of discrimination between universality and particularity in space and in time can guide us towards some other politics.

Many analysts clearly feel that something significant is going on with the forms of inclusion and exclusion through which modern subjects have been constituted. It has now become fashionable in some contexts to think of boundaries as fluid and porous rather than fixed and immutable, as increasingly differentiated and disaggregated and understandable through some dialectics of recognition, whether neo-Hegelian or otherwise. Many would argue that it is more helpful to think of lines of connection and networks of relations than of sharp discriminations between the included and the excluded, or the political and the anarchic/private, that still enable our most influential understandings of future possibilities and legitimize the most extraordinary forms of violence.[53] Discriminations are always a problem, it might be said, and the specific forms of discrimination that have enabled and been enabled by modern claims to sovereignty have long been a problem, but if we are to engage with claims that modern forms of sovereignty are under sustained challenge, then we might be wise to pay rather more attention to the specific forms of discrimination that have enabled, and been enabled by, modern claims to the sovereignty of states.

Consequently, the claim that the most challenging political problems of our time express an urgent need to reimagine where and what we take politics to be should not be taken to denigrate more specific or more immediately practical problems. Rather, it should draw attention not only to the practices through which we have become used to discriminating between the serious and the trivial, but also to the practices through which modern politics both express and enable very specific discriminations: discriminations enabling both social practices and institutions and the claims to knowledge through which these practices and institutions are explained, understood, legitimized, reproduced and called into question. Still less, therefore, should this claim be read as some genteel idealism untainted by the concrete demands of everyday existence, or as some merely normative or utopian evasion of the necessities of realistic and responsible policy. Again on the contrary, it must lead to questions about how it has become so easy for such a claim to be construed as a disembodied theorization, especially one that can be judged from some presumed ground of concrete immediacy and responsibility.

In the conventions of our age, in the discriminations enacted by modern politics, to insist on the need to reimagine what we mean by politics is to be framed either as a meddler in mere abstractions (the kind of idealist known by the negation of some presupposed materialism) or as a peddler of merely normative prescriptions (as the kind of idealist known by the negation of some presupposed reality). Yet it is precisely our assumptions about responsibility and the material or realistic ground from which we are able to make judgements about the crucial and the trivial, to frame that which is real and realistic by contrast with that which is neither, that now seem to be in question in many contexts. This doubt, converging from many different and often mutually antagonistic directions, is at work in many demands that we must now reimagine what we mean by politics.

It may be the case that many sophisticated theorists have offered to take us away from all those crude, if elegant, distinctions that came to frame the understandings of man and nature that Descartes, Galileo, Hobbes and so on managed to crystallize out of themes already worked out by the classical Greek philosophers and the Christian theologians. They have offered complaint after complaint about all those great dualistic category schemes launched, or at least recast and refined, in early-modern Europe, and especially of a dualism of ideas and matter or body and consciousness, that still largely structure how we think and act in relation to the world, whatever and wherever that world is taken to be. Hegelians have worked through their dialectics. A host of provocative twentieth-century thinkers have shown how these dualisms are just so many language games that seduce us into category mistakes, logocentricisms, and naturalizations of assumptions and logics that are both historically and culturally parochial. Much of modern thought, sometimes quite as much as its supposedly postmodern variants, can even be understood as a concerted assault upon what Henri Bergson once called "the law of twofold frenzy,"[54] the modern dualistic categories that encourage us to think in terms of ideas as immaterial forces, of man as somehow split off from nature, of normative aspiration as somehow different from the world as we really find it, of a serious and responsible politics in one place and a nonpolitics of frivolity and irresponsibility in another.

For all the sophistications of the philosophers, however, and for all the self-criticism through which modern thinkers have tried to respond to the contradictions that arose once the early-modern Europeans articulated their accounts of modern man, that universal being who was both a part of and yet apart from that natural world that made him possible, our accounts of politics are still largely enabled by distinctions between ideas and material forces, between normative idealists and pragmatic realists, or between what in some recent jargons is called "constructivism" and something that is supposedly unconstructed (perhaps natural, perhaps essential, perhaps given in the religious tablets, the ethicist's *a priori*, the scientific reduction or the arbitrary reification) that seem singularly resistant to critique from almost any direction. Our radicalisms, we are sometimes prepared to admit, have had a disconcerting tendency to reproduce, or to be appropriated by, the forms of life they sought to replace. Our accounts of difference have had a strange habit of mimicking our accounts of the same. And those who have managed to articulate an incisive understanding of how this tendency works in relation to philosophical or literary practices are often as baffled as anyone else as to how it works in the practices of states, or economies, or societies.

Whether in relation to the established rhetorics through which idealisms must always be trumped by realisms and materialisms, or to rhetorics that insist on the priority of the immediate danger and the practical policy, to claim that the most challenging political problems of our time express a need to reimagine what we mean by politics is to be at play in realms that are easily characterized, variously, as the "abstract," the "theoretical," and, by projection against an assumed reality of the present, "the future." It is, in the political practices of our time, to court the metaphysical and utopian. It is, supposedly, to avoid both the unpleasant necessities championed by those who think they understand the structural logics of our era – most audaciously, perhaps, those understandings of natural necessity championed by utilitarian theorists of "rational choice" among individuals, "neo-realist" struggles among states, or calculators of future "risk" through projections from an idealized present. It is to avoid the evidence of the empirical data championed by those who think they understand how legitimate knowledge is to be obtained, despite all evidence about the promiscuity of evidence.

The primary difficulty posed by rhetorics of structural/natural necessity and empirical knowledge, however, is that they are claims to authority of precisely the same kind as the claims to authority that constitute modern forms of politics. They work so as to legitimize a very specific account of what politics must be, and do so by convincing us that this account is indeed what we now find, and must find empirically in the world in which we live. Many episodes of contemporary scholarly debate about how one should study politics resemble nothing so much as a parody of Schmittean sovereigns struggling to decide the limits of what is scholarly, scientific, rational or professional, and what is exceptional or even pathological.[55] The parody takes particularly troubling forms when, in textbook after textbook, Hobbes is still deployed not so as to enable an engagement with modern practices of authorization, about the possibility of political life as a problem, but for simply asserting an account of the way the world is, whether as a state of nature, a state of war, or a cosy club of rational economists.

Institutionally specific debates about legitimate method can seem terminally uninteresting to anyone not immediately caught up in their disciplinary effects, but the kinds of methodological dispute that have plagued the analysis of international relations have much broader and more significant resonances. They are of particular importance for any engagement with those increasingly vast literatures, now considerably exceeding the institutionalized resources of international relations theory, that seek to tell us about all the evidence affirming either the continuing importance or the imminent demise of the modern state. For there is something rather odd – a not quite forgotten sense of paradox, tautology and contradiction – about the practice of trying to make authoritative judgements about the fate of states claiming the mantle of sovereignty when sovereignty is itself our paradigmatic account of what is involved in making judgements and claiming authority.

Modern politics has indeed come to be understood as a matter of authority, or better, a process of authorization. It has also often not been understood even as it functions as a practice of authorization, not least by various attempts to inscribe politics within universalizing stories about struggles for power, authoritative allocations of values, who does what to whom, and so on, as if mere definition trumps all other forms of authorization. Modern politics is concerned not only with what authorities can do about this problem or that problem, but, first and foremost, with what counts as authorization, and with the conditions under which what counts as authorization is itself authoritative; or not. What is so often framed as the realistic and the responsible, as a matter of urgent policy or governance, is very often simply an evasion of politics in this sense, a practice of depoliticization. We are encouraged to treat the conditions under which we accept claims to authority as somehow natural, as given in the nature of things or in the universality of reason, in the unspoken assumption or the dogmatic assertion.

We are especially encouraged to treat as foundational conceptions of sovereignty and subjectivity, as these were shaped in the massive upheavals of early-modern Europe, and subsequently reshaped in struggles over states, nations, classes, democracies, sciences, colonies and genders. As some of the early-modern thinkers knew rather better than most of their successors, however, if these concepts are somehow foundational, they were also historical inventions, conventions through which political necessities were conjured out of strange stories about a state of nature and brilliant reinterpretations of the place, or non-place, of God in the affairs of man. The strength, and pathos, of recent lamentations about the collapse of foundational moral principles or the retreat from Enlightenment concepts of emancipative rationality is a very good indicator of how persuasive these early-modern inventions and conventions have since become.

Modern accounts of politics have been responding to claims about a disappearing God and nominalist accounts of language for a long time; indeed, it is difficult to see why anyone would ever make such a fuss about people like Machiavelli and Hobbes, among many others, if this were not the case. Much of the stridency of recent debates is much more usefully understood as a reminder of this longer heritage than of a claim that we have begun to move towards some (postmodern) era in which "foundations" have suddenly disappeared. Recently popular claims about disappearing foundations (derived from Richard Rorty)[56] or some similar claim about an "incredulity towards metanarratives" (derived from the rather more provocative work of Jean-François Lyotard)[57] have been mixed and matched with fast-and-loose conflations of claims about scepticism, pluralism, relationality, nihilism and relativism. As such, they have done much to undermine sustained engagements with the implications of all those philosophies of language and subjectivity that have been corralled, with some force, under the sign of the poststructural. Read in relation to the traditions of modern political thought, especially, the kinds of claims that have entered into so much debate about appropriate forms of knowledge in the social sciences border on the absurd. No serious analysis of political life can afford to forget that founding is a problem, even if much of political life, and political analysis, can be understood as the deployment of practices that enable us to forget that founding is always a problem.[58]

Part of the difficulty here is that claims about a loss of foundations have been constructed primarily in relation to discourses of "philosophy" and "ethics," discourses that are enabled by, but systematically forgetful of, the discriminations of modern politics, and yet also enable us to deploy the discriminations of modern politics. Thus Machiavelli retains his image as the bad boy of modern politics, the figure who struck his dagger through the heart of Europe to clarify the rift between virtue and *virtu*. Within the confines of the modern state, Machiavelli's problem may have been partly resolved through all kinds of convergence between public and private under the singular authority of an earthly sovereign that may, or may not, express the demands of both virtue and *virtu*. Still, Machiavelli's problem has never gone away. It has simply been swept to the edges of the modern state, to the externalities of international relations, to the designations of national states of emergency, to the ultimate elevation of national freedom and national security over the demands of what we so easily call humanity. The narratives depicting an abstract struggle between politics and ethics that have become so familiar, and so prominent in contemporary public debate over humanitarianism, responses to indiscriminate violence, and so on, rest largely on a systematic forgetting of the historical conditions under which the possibilities of a relationship between something called politics and something called ethics was once set up as an impossible antagonism in relation to the specific claims of the modern secular political community.

Claims about ethics have indeed become rather easy; at least this seems to be the characteristic stance of many contemporary liberalisms. Claims about when claims about ethics are to be suspended are much more difficult, though always easy enough when outrages are identified to justify the suspension. The problem may be framed in relation to Machiavelli's celebration of republican virtuosities, Hobbes' quick flip from prepolitical amorality to a civil society under the law, Kantian hopes for a more historical progression towards cosmopolitan reason, Hegel's proud two-step to the rational but particular state, Weber's more tragic two-step to the irrational-because-rational particular state, or the lightning flash of Schmitt's sovereign decisionism illuminating the abyss on the edge of all self-righteous political communities. In whatever version, the problematic relation between a political ethics and some other sort of ethics is precisely part of the condition under which modern states were constituted as the agents capable of reconciling all contradictions between *virtu* and virtue, historical freedoms and transcendental/universal/structural necessities, within a particular community. The abstract attempt to apply ethics to politics, truth to power, or universality to particularity simply conjures away the very specific ways in which these apparent opposites are already mutually constitutive of the modern state.

What is perhaps more novel, and perhaps offers some grounds for optimism despite all the odds, is the increasingly concerted refusal to accept that we have no choice but to believe the clever stories about man and nature or sovereignty and subjectivity concocted by the early-modern Europeans or else face the hellfire of ethical and cultural relativism and power politics. Claims about the necessity of these stories, and claims that the only alternatives to them are chaos, nihilism or some anarchical state of nature, are the two sides of the well-worn coinage of modern politics, the alternatives of desire and impossibility, of utopia and cynicism, of the norm and the exception, that make it so difficult to reimagine what we mean by politics on any other terms because these are precisely the terms on which modern politics has been possible at all. Machiavelli's dagger has been constantly resharpened even as its bloody effects have been repeatedly denied, at least until the next outbreak of threatening enemies, states of emergency and straightfaced hypocrisies comes along. International relations still trumps political theory, even while the universalizing ambitions that drive modern political theory enable international relations as the limit of modern political possibility. The state of exception still trumps the norm, even while the norm tells us about the impossibility of political life in a state of exception.

Origins/limits: outside the international

Then, there, now, here

As the preceding sequence of overlapping encounters with just a few of the troublesome edges at the spatial and legal limits of modern political life is intended to suggest, the most mysterious aspects of modern theories of political life concern when, and where, they start. Starting is always a mystery. To decide when and where something starts, to authorize a discrimination between old and new, is also to affirm what that something is; how it might live, grow, develop, become path-dependent; and whether, where and when it might end. Founding, as Machiavelli and Hobbes understood especially well, is always going to be a political problem. The interrogation of beginnings will always have us scrambling among ontologies, theologies and mythologies, seeking to return to parts that can never be fully reached and moments that can never be fully recovered, frantically covering up our fears of the unknown, imagining what it must have been, where it must have been, when it must have been. Think birth, biography or archaeology; or geologies, black holes and big bangs. Think the sacrifice, or the gift. Think photographs of a present that is always past; or yet another blank sheet of paper. Think time, and quickly move on to something less stressful. Think causalities and responsibilities; and think time yet again. Stare into space. Contemplate the abyss. Give up. Move on. Start again. And again.

More to the point here, think states with their temporally specific claims to permanence, and their grounding norms that have no ground. Think nations with their inventions of originary traditions, their fantasies of fathers and authenticities. Think constitutions, formal or informal, and the swarms of lawyers required to keep their groundless grounds in proper shape, to negotiate the terrain between that which is within and that which is without the law, and to reshape this terrain into a mere line, or decision, between what is within and what is without. In contemporary social, cultural and political theory it is perhaps Heidegger's *Being and Time* that has been the most consistent textual site through which we are invited to contemplate modern or

Western accounts of origins, to try to re-engage with the (pre-Socratic) sources of those forms of metaphysics we somehow now need to go "beyond."[59] Yet while even Heidegger's name may be sufficient in some places to suggest that the mysteries of origin are indeed profound, the claim that origins are always a mystery is hardly news anywhere. So, no, we can never really go home again. And, yes, timing is everything. A political science predicated on stasis has never stood a chance.

Modern theories of international relations have been especially shy, but also interestingly ambivalent, about where and when they start. They have been shy to the extent that some of our most extensive meditations on the problem of founding, not least those by Machiavelli and Hobbes, have themselves become foundational sites, names to convince us that reality starts then and there and continues here and now. They have been interestingly ambivalent to the extent that the accounts of international history that have been constructed to affirm a narrative about a modern logic of history as development do not quite tally with the histories that might be told about the internationalization of the world. Whether shy or ambivalent, however, modern theories of international relations express pervasive, though not universal, accounts of our times and our histories, our spaces, our identities, our possibilities and our limits. These accounts take us not to the texts of Plato and Aristotle, to which we are usually drawn in thinking about the foundational moments of the modern state, but precisely to the standard stories about early-modern European political thought expressed, at least in the Anglo-American world, in references to Machiavelli, Hobbes and Kant.

The conventions expressed in most accounts of international relations especially affirm the 1648 Treaty of Westphalia as the key moment in a long transition from pre-modern, or imperial, or theologically guaranteed conditions to the modern world of secular and territorial sovereign states. The precise historical significance of what has since become a primary part of the founding mythology of modern politics is open to protracted debate. Most would readily admit to relying on a convention, not on a claim that can be taken seriously as history, though the convention works well enough as a constitutive ground of modern histories.[60] As convention, however, it marks a supposedly decisive shift, in principle even if not in practice, from premodern religious hierarchies and wars of absolutist principle to modern secular rationalities and wars of pragmatic accommodation within a system of internalities and externalities. As such it can be read as one of the key moments in the authorization of a distinction between modern and non-modern worlds, between a politics of hierarchical subordinations and a politics of horizontal freedoms and equalities: the moments of a great exceptionalism in time that founds a system of exceptionalisms in space; and an articulation of exceptionalisms in space that, in turn, affirm an exceptionalism in time. Under modern conditions, in sharp contrast to whatever came before, there must be neither empire, in the singular, nor religious wars. Secular, self-interested behaviour must rule, and we must then hope that self-interested behaviour will somehow mutate over time from passions to interests and from egoistic solipsism to reciprocity and cooperation so as to reach an autonomy, a self-determination, that expresses our inherent universality-in-particularity and particularity-in-universality in a world strung out in horizontal space. So much is no doubt rather more than is to be expected from a relatively obscure treaty, but it is clearly the expectation that is expressed from the retrospective identification of this treaty as the founding moment of an internationalized modernity.

Despite their primary trade in claims about spatial extension, the theorists of international relations invariably read this moment temporally. They read it as a shift, sometimes short and sharp and sometimes long and muddled, into the relatively civilized (and highly idealized) realm of international relations and mutual respect, as a Kant might hope; a realm that is nevertheless susceptible (realistically speaking, in the idealized manner affirmed partly by Hobbes and partly by Schmitt) to a condition of war between friends and enemies. With their temporal moment firmly established, they can then revert to their trade in spatial extentions and disjunctions, to their idealizations of a domesticated civility and their cold calculations of realistic expectation in a system of territorially differentiated states. They can then worry about, or (given the prevailing division of intellectual labour) ignore, the precise relationship between the practices of states each affirming their territorially delimited claim to sovereignty and the systemic structures and practices that make these claims possible; a contradictory relationship to be examined both as a matter of historical experience and of overarching (legal, ethical, civilizational) principle.

Not the least difficulty with claims about 1648 as a founding moment, however, is that it leaves much of the world unaccounted for: as still unfounded; as lingering back in time, before the European achievement of secular freedoms and the wars they engender and yet somehow present within a world of modern states; as somehow outside while also inside the world of the modern international. The Treaty of Westphalia marks not only a foundational moment in which a properly modern world became possible as a condition of international relations, but also as a moment at which another world was ordained in opposition to it; a world, in part, deemed bereft of civilization and thus legitimately subject to colonial exploitation, though perhaps, eventually, over time, worthy of the opportunity to become mature, developed and a subject of a properly modern, spatial, international society.[61] So, no empires and no wars of religion; but also no premoderns, no barbarians. Modernity may be an amorphous thing, so hard to pin down with any precision, but we know it when we see it crystallize with conventionalized precision in a famous treaty that concluded 30 years of especially vicious religious wars.

Predictably enough, perhaps even reasonably enough, theories of international relations, or even of modern political life more generally, have tended to keep their attention focused much more on the world that, according to this convention, came to be included as a system of inclusions and exclusions, rather than on the exclusions that enabled modernity to constitute a world of modern subjects living within states coexisting within a system of states. 1648 marks a beginning, some kind of material origin or achievement, one that is somehow more effective as a statement of where and what we are than the complicated texts of obstreperous intellectuals like Machiavelli or Hobbes. It permits the construction of properly historical narratives about how modernity finally crossed a clear threshold, shifted from medieval hierarchies and messy theologies to a properly modern world. It marks the kind of breakthrough moment that might be compared with the contribution of specific Protestant sects to a breakthrough to modern capitalism that led Weber to produce such a powerful, and deeply contradictory, account of the logic of modernity as a modernizing process.[62] Indeed, Westphalia has become a name that theorists of international relations are still prone to give to an historical epoch, one that, like modernity itself, may or may not be coming to an end. Whatever historians make of the specific significance or otherwise of this treaty, it has become important precisely because so many narratives about it have worked to efface more complex histories, and to legitimize a claim about the origins of modernity that resonate with so many other accounts of what must be excluded so as to affirm modern accounts of the achievements and costs of modern inclusions and exclusions.

A standard and, in many ways, still very interesting text in this respect is the collection of essays edited by Hedley Bull and Adam Watson under the telling title of *The Expansion of International Society*, one of the core texts of the English School of international relations theory.[63] This had the notable virtue of being one of the relatively few international relations texts published in the Cold War era – or even since – to express some sensitivity to the parochial European roots of a universalizing/globalizing political order.[64] Yet both its title and overall organization express a familiar and problematic narrative about the unidirectionality of modernity. Judgements bred through colonial experiences are rarely very far away. The world is understood to have been brought inside modernity through the universalization of the modern states system as a consequence of "the domination of one of the several regional international systems that existed in the fifteenth century over the others, and over the less-developed parts of the world as well – a domination that united the whole world into a single economic, strategic, and political system for the first time."[65] The analysis unfolds through a narrative about "the entry of non-European states into international society," "the challenge to Western dominance," and on to "the new international society"; that is, to "the international order that has emerged from the ebb tide of European dominance."[66] Finally, the story goes, the world has literally been brought into modernity, at least as far as the world is organized within the forms of the modern state and states system. Consequently, the analysis concludes, "It is a cardinal fact about our present world, and one that affords some hope for the preservation of international order within it, that the international society which was forged in Europe in the same centuries in which Europe extended its sway over the rest of the globe, has not disappeared now that Europe's sway has ended, but has been embraced by the non-European majority of states and peoples as the basis of their own approach to international relations. If there are dangers that the new majority of states, as they seek to reform international society to take account of their own interests, might strain its rules and institutions to breaking point, so are there dangers that the European or Western minority might fail to see that it is only by adjustments to change that the international society they created can remain viable."[67]

This conclusion neatly summarizes an influential understanding not only of international relations, but also of the kind of balanced, reasonable, perhaps liberal, perhaps even deeply Kantian understanding of the kind of political life that has become possible towards the end of a process of modernization.[68] It is an account that acknowledges much of the violence and domination through which this process has been pursued. It issues warnings both to the currently hegemonic states as well as to the radical nationalists; in the all-pervasive categories of the day, to both the First World and the Third World, to the world of the already developed and the world of the still developing. It is reasonably conservative in its concern to ensure the kind of "order" that is a necessary ground for "justice."[69] It is also reasonably progressive in its ambition for a properly "universal international society."[70] It articulates a view of modern political life that was broadly echoed in almost any public discourse that aspired to be sensibly internationalist in the final decades of the twentieth century. Nevertheless, and for all that it might be praised as an analysis that is prepared to look beyond the usual Euro-American ethnocentricisms, and thus might be treated as a foil to the more overtly solipsistic character of "the American science of international relations," it is an analysis that ultimately shares many of the underlying assumptions that one finds in such paradigmatic celebrations of an imperiously unilinear view of history expressed in Walt Rostow's *Stages of Economic Growth*, one of the core texts of Cold War triumphalism.[71] International relations as a system of political possibilities in space is affirmed by an account of the political possibilities of modernization in time.[72] Thus speaks the well grounded and judiciously centred modern subject that can issue reasoned warnings to conservatives and radicals alike.

Nevertheless, 1648 is hardly the only date that might be invoked as a more or less useful originary foundation. Many of the essays in *The Expansion of International Society* already suggest a much more complex field of historical scholarship. The explosion of various literatures on world histories offers ample scope for those who wish to tell alternative stories.[73] Even if we stay with moments of great symbolic resonance, we might easily imagine stories of origins that privilege the emergence of a globalizing economic system and an emerging sense of the interrelatedness of the world some centuries before Westphalia.[74] Or the moments of collision when various Europeans went on their crusades or expelled the unbelievers, or when Columbus and Vasco da Gama went on their voyages.[75] Or the moments of negotiation and renegotiation through which Europe rewrote its self-understanding as a seat of Enlightenment,[76] not least in relation to the revalorization of China from an (imperial) civilization to be emulated to the barbarian (because imperial) that ought to be opposed by modern enlightened states.[77] Or the moments in which the abstract potentials promised by claims about secular sovereign states were elaborated through the mobilization of populations, of nations, of a biopolitics: the dynamics that would situate Clausewitz rather than Hobbes as the founding thinker of international relations;[78] or privilege the French Revolution and nationalism rather than the English civil war and the juridical state as key moments in the origins of modern politics, and lead Michel Foucault to meditate on the relation between Hobbes and Clausewitz as a way of coming to terms with what is at stake in Schmittean forms of exceptionalism.[79] Appeals to histories, genealogies and temporal contingencies have an unsettling effect; much safer, so much more secure for the modern subject, to stick with the conventions.

Here, now, there, then

Uncertainties about international/world history have their parallel in uncertainties about the choice of canonical texts through which the claims of various theories of international relations are grounded in basic assumptions about the world and its spatiotemporal origins. Hobbes' *Leviathan* is perhaps still the most widely cited of these, not least because it was published at a time that permits a straightforward conflation with those stories that privilege the Treaty of Westphalia as an originary ground. Moreover, although there are many good reasons not to start thinking about international relations by engaging with Hobbes, one of the better reasons to do so is that he starts from such an interesting place and time: not with 1648 or thereabouts, but with an abstract account of a here and now. On this basis, he proceeds to construct even more interesting places: a there and, especially, a then. *Leviathan* is, in many respects, a paradigmatically ahistorical text, though the historians must always insist on a need to put this ahistoricism in some kind of historical context. Nevertheless, in its construction of a here, a now, a there, and a then, it does speak to some of the practices through which the gap between the international and the world has been bridged in the modern political imagination, both temporally and spatially, despite all the ways in which the claims of the international have served to exclude the claims of much of the world.

Specifically, while it is really quite difficult to read Hobbes as a theorist of international relations, he can usefully be read as helping to articulate and enable a space in which the international might eventually occur by postulating a time, and then a place (the state of nature), as a regulative – though negative and, crucially, impossible – ideal beyond any realm in which an international might be conceived. Just as the modern subject and the modern state have their constitutive outsides, so too does the modern international.

Hobbes has been one of the most effective writers constructing an account of how this outside must work so as to produce a modern world of (multiple) insides and outsides. He articulates an account of origins that marks a constitutive exclusion enabling our dominant narratives about how we have come to live in a world of inclusions and exclusions. If Hobbes does indeed have something to say about international relations despite the relatively little he did, or even could, say about such a phenomenon, it is because he offers us such a powerful account of how sovereignty came to be what it must be. It is an account that tells us what it *must* mean to have a politics in space and in time, and to have to come to terms with the limits of that politics, both in space and in time. It is an account that still offers considerable purchase on what remains at stake in Schmitt's early twentieth-century account of state sovereignty as a capacity to decide exceptions, and how that account builds upon very specific authorizations of what it must mean to discriminate authoritatively.

Most conventions of modern politics tend to assume that the modern system of states has no boundary even while the primary dynamics of that system express the consequences of a life of modern subjects living within states with very precise boundaries. International relations, it is easy to assume, is as large as it gets. The professionals who engage with it attract reputations for dealing with the big stuff, with grand strategies, with the most consequential of historical and structural forces. This is not merely a matter of scale or disciplinary hubris. It is a judgement about history and geography, about where and who we are in space and time. The expansion of international society has come to an end, more or less. Everything and everyone has now been brought inside a system of insides and outsides. We have all become modern, except, perhaps, for a few small pockets of resistance still to be overcome in one way or another, by carrot and/or by stick, by corporations and/or by military belligerence. Or perhaps we have not all yet become modern enough, and there are too many wild and dangerous places, too much anarchy in Africa, too many failed states, too few compliant democracies in sites of strategic importance, too many other civilizations that are not yet properly civilized, too much of the wrong kind of monotheism; in which case the stick may be more effective than the carrot. For the most part, however, the extent to which we have come to think of the international as coextensive with the world as such has made any notion that the international has an outside of any kind seem a little odd; it is perhaps easier to think that the next stop is the Moon or the cosmic void. The modern state is the inside, the international is the outside; hence community and anarchy in their never-ending two-step. Where else is there? What else could there possibly be?

It is in this context that Schmitt postulates an account of sovereignty as a capacity to decide an exception to the norms of the modern territorial state. It is in this respect that he can be read as a nationalist echo of Hobbes' account of the capacities of a sovereign authority. It is in Schmitt that we find the account of how a specifically modern account of discrimination and authorization works to produce an account of the relation between norm and exception at the territorial boundaries of the sovereign state. With Hobbes, however, we can also see the makings of another distinction between norm and exception, one not articulated at the boundaries of the state, or framed as a reactionary critique of liberal accounts of a constitutional democracy, in the manner of Schmitt, but articulated at the boundaries of the modern system of sovereign states. In Hobbes, it is possible to see that the international also has, indeed must have, a constitutive outside. Like his account of sovereignty itself, this outside is written as an abstraction, though it is an abstraction that, again like his account of sovereignty, is always available for embodiment in the changing practices of a universal/particular political life. It works in the world to affirm the possibilities and impossibilities of the modern world precisely because it is abstract. Anyone can be outside, just as anyone can be sovereign; in both cases, substance matters less than form, although form itself works as a specific content, as various critics of, say, statist nationalisms, Kantian ethics, Adam Smith's political economy and Hobbes' account of masculine desire have long rightly insisted. It thus offers an instructive way of thinking about modern accounts of origins and foundations, and of what is at stake in the deployment of the Treaty of Westphalia as the origin of modern international relations, in narratives about the expansion of international society, and in the suspicion, articulated by Fasolt, that the temporal limits expressed in the transition from a world of pope and empire to a world of statist sovereigns has a lot to do with how we think about the spatial limits of a politics organized within and between sovereign states enabled by, and enabling, a system of sovereign states.

Hobbes makes four key moves in this respect, all of them well known, but also normalized and made to seem entirely uncontentious in various claims about where we have come from, how things started, and how life must be under the authority of the modern sovereign state. All four moves raise questions about the ways in which Hobbes has come to be framed as the quintessential political realist telling us about how things are, and shift him onto the terrain of the explicitly normative, the theorist who tells us most effectively how things must be under modern conditions. Hobbes builds on many prior strands or arguments in this respect,[80] but is now the figure through whom the contemporary force of such prior stands is most easily appreciated.

First, there is an assertion of an ontological universalism, the atomistic materialism that he offers as a replacement for the Thomism, ontological realism, or essentialism that he saw as the unfortunate curriculum of all the universities in Christiandom. This new ontological universalism entailed an epistemological universalism, a scientific method, the what seems, retrospectively, to be a rather messy combination of empiricism and rationalism predicated on a nominalist account of language. Hobbes was thereby able to constitute a ground on which to authorize a particular site of authority, and thus a particular community capable of embodying, expressing and acting in accordance with ontological/epistemological universals. This is the move he makes so quickly, and with such a sharp sense of humour, in the first few chapters of *Leviathan*, which now seem so innocuous, or merely "philosophical," as to be scarcely of any political interest whatsoever, despite the way they lay out so much of the basic ground on which modern politics is to be conducted. A particular account of Being, of being in the world, and of knowing about both Being and being in the world, is affirmed. All others are dismissed. Nice work if one can get away with it; as he so often has.

Second, there is the assertion of a universalist political ontology invoking claims about free and equal individuals; claims, that is, about that troublesome category we have come to know as modern man. It is worth noting the radicalism of this assertion, of Hobbes' willingness to take for granted a category that challenged both classical Aristotelian accounts of the collective character of human beings as political animals and Thomistic accounts of the natural hierarchy of all beings organized under God, and thus of the natural ordering of justice, and privilege.[81] It is also worth stressing that this is a modern and in some senses paradigmatically "liberal" account of human beings, not, despite all references to a state of nature, of some premodernity. Moreover, the universalism of this political ontology already seems to assume particularizing limits, a set of constraints that generate, or perhaps intensify, competition among these free and equal individuals: one of many examples of a reading of the presence of universality-within-particularity that is the hallmark of modern subjectivities.

Third, there is the projection of this universalist (though particular) political ontology in both temporal and spatial directions. The projection invokes a negative reading of this ontology in both cases.

Temporally, there is a projection backwards so as to constitute an account of a prior age, and condition of humankind: the so-called state of nature, part of that wider invention of a natural world necessary to affirm that ours is a world of culture, of positive rather than natural law, of an authority grounded in the authorizations of modern man rather than of a divine authorization expressed through nature.[82] Spatially, the peoples of North America are identified as specific examples of peoples still living close to, but not quite in, their natural state. There is a crucial degree of fuzziness in Hobbes' account of both cases; a fuzziness that must be ascribed not to Hobbes in particular, but to the more general logic within which Hobbes was struggling to imagine new political worlds.[83]

Spatially, Hobbes does not describe the peoples of North America as absolute negations of modern man; they are, he suggests, organized in families, driven by lust. Indeed, by contrast with later writers who are usually seen as more "liberal" and "progressive," notably Locke and Kant, Hobbes offers a rather benign picture of these spatially distant others. Temporally, and perhaps more importantly, he does not claim to be able to identify any empirical origin of man; he says that "it was never generally so, over all the world," and that "there had never been any time, wherein particular men were in a condition of warre one against another." Rather, he seems to be more interested in offering a logical version of a foundation myth, a logically constructed narrative about what the human past must have been, given the universal account of modern man he asserts to be existing in the present; a hypothetical narrative that would enable him to make a claim about "what manner of life there would be."[84] Hobbes' more empirical sensitivities always seem to be in some tension with his attraction to a more rigorous logic, a logic that nevertheless enables his depiction of an extreme condition of the life of (modern, protoliberal) man as "enemy to every man."[85] The possibilities of modern freedom and equality are transformed into the impossibilities of a past condition of anarchy, the condition that is so famously nasty, brutish and short.

Moreover, this logic of negation in time affirms a logic of negation in space. We thus have in Hobbes one of the key sites at which to observe the workings of a discourse about temporal foundations that also works as a discourse of spatial alterity, about the construction of relations with spatially distant others. Both are framed in relation to assumptions about a spatial and temporal presence, the presence he has already so sharply distinguished, by definition, from any other possibility of Being and being in the world.

Finally, Hobbes' subsequent move follows naturally, so to speak, though not so easily, from this move of negation. Having projected the present into a realm of temporal and spatial distance, he could specify the route back to the present both as a narrative about the origins of the present and as a story about how the impossibility of life in a state of nature could be transformed into a story about the possibility of life under sovereign authority. Here we see the familiar shift from mere freedom to liberty "according to the proper signification,"[86] from natural freedom to liberty under the law. Here we also see the fairly obvious difficulties posed by the logical structure of the more stringent moments of Hobbes' argument: if the contract were indeed possible, then the conditions prevailing in the state of nature would be insufficient to render the contract necessary; and if conditions were indeed so bad, then, short of some kind of special intervention (the judicious mixture of fear and reason that he is forced to invoke as a kind of socio-psychological solution to an abstract puzzle),[87] the contract would be impossible. Furthermore, here we also see the line from before to after, and by analogy, from there to here, that is traversed instantaneously, as a matter of hypothetical principle. Time is effectively reduced to a magical instant, thereby generating characteristic questions about the possibility of acting in time and history. Space is understood to be potentially infinite but is self-defined as finite, thereby generating questions about action at the limit. Both sets of questions are answered through a universalizing myth, open to both spatial and temporal formulations, about how modern subjectivities *must* have decided to become citizen-subjects rather than mere humans.

This is the moment of Hobbes' hypothetical decisionism, the invocation of a decision that must have been made in order to achieve the condition of normality of modern subjects. In Schmittean terms, this might be understood as the exception that is produced by negation of a claimed norm that then produces the norm in a new (positive) form. That is, one might read Hobbes here in relation not only to Schmitt's notion that "sovereign is he who decides the exception," but also to his claim that "(t)he exception does not only confirm the rule; the rule as such lives off the exception alone."[88] Schmitt thinks about this in relation to the modern territorial nation-state that he had come to take more or less for granted. Hobbes thinks about this in relation to a sovereign state that he saw as the only solution to problems he came to portray as the spatiotemporal negation of a claim about the being, freedom and equality of modern man, the desiring machine.

It is a well known but underappreciated story.[89] Universality is asserted, initially in general philosophical terms, then in terms of a philosophical anthropology; spatiotemporal difference is affirmed by negation; difference is returned to universality within the particularity of sovereign authority, leaving the residual categories of spatial and temporal difference available to be given substantive content in various – spatial and temporal – discourses of the outside. In general terms we see a powerful version of the great modern gamble that the sovereign capacity to discriminate between legitimate and illegitimate, between norm and exception, is congruent with a capacity to discriminate between a spatial realm of inclusion and a spatial realm of exclusion: the monopoly of authority in a particular territory as we have come to know it in Weber's formulation, the formulation that still expresses much of the commonsense of modern politics. The logic through which Hobbes projected a state of nature back in time and away in space is brought back so as to delineate a here and now that defines the conditions of political possibility within a singular, though universal, community. The condition of an impossible past, the projected negation of the present as the point of origin from which the present must have developed, returns as the point of sovereign authority to define all conditions of necessity and freedom. The condition of an impossible past projected spatially onto the peoples of America is brought back so as to define a spatial difference between a temporal presence here and a temporal absence – a backwardness – there. A decision is made that the (presumably) universal capacity to generate a collective decision to enter into political society must be a decision to produce a particular society of some people rather than a universal society of all rational beings.

Politics can then proceed within, inside the sovereign state. International relations can also proceed just this side of the border with the absolute negation of the world of modern subjects: as a condition of at least some order just this side of an anarchy conceived as the absolute negation of a specific account of order. The exception to the norm can be invoked in both cases. Schmitt later came to name the exception expressed in relation to a state that had become synonymous with a national population, a naming we have learnt to associate with the nastiest excesses of state power in the twentieth century. Hobbes lays out a ground on which exceptions are made possible in the name of the modern world in general. In effect, fearing the consequences of a civil war in England, he ordains the possibility of a civil war within a broader modernity, the world of the modern international.

Hobbes is primarily a theorist of the modern state. He says relatively little about what we have come to call international relations. Nevertheless, as a theorist of the modern state he does leave space, and time, for what we call the international. He cannot quite see his way back to the vanishing point on which his perspective on the world depends. The peoples of North America, he also admits, do not really seem as mutually paranoid as his logical imaginary would suggest. Still, it is the absolute negation of the present that sets up the framing of others as located somewhere between the past as absolute negation of the present, and the present as the positive affirmation of the creatures that Hobbes identifies as properly human, as somewhere on the road to a universalizing modernity. In this account, there is a world beyond even those who are known to be unmodern, a world against which the relationship between the identifiably nonmodern and the modern might be known, a regulative dystopia, the realism produced by and legitimizing the idealism.

In its extreme logical form, and in keeping with his fondness for Euclidean geometry and for the reframing of problems of finitude and infinity enabled by broader currents of neo-Platonist conceptions of knowledge, and the multiple legacies of Christian accounts of the perfection that is God and the imperfection that is life on earth, Hobbes offers a spatial account of temporality, an ahistorical calculus of freedom and necessity effected in a momentary switch from one condition to another. In its more relaxed empirical form, he offers instead the possibility of a story of a necessary shift over time – a necessary process of maturing in more Kantian terms, a necessary movement through History in Hegelian terms, the possibility of transforming passions into interests in more broadly liberal–utilitarian terms – rather than the abstract and instantaneous calculation that he claims must have happened at the moment of contract.

In either case, the spatialized temporal line that is constructed from an imagined point of origin back to the present is itself susceptible to spatial differentiation; to the distinction between the world of the here and now and the world that exists at the spatial and temporal limit of the here and now. Consequently, the line from then to now, and from here to there, is readily bisectable by the line that discriminates between here and there, now and then; the line marked especially on the territorial boundaries of sovereign states, and the line marked in readings of an origin of modern international relations in 1648.

The world of modern dualisms, we might remember, is always susceptible to a separation into competing monisms, and to the lure of the sensible middle ground. It is in relation to the world of politics, we might also remember, that discriminations are most obviously dangerous. Construct a dualism of past and present, or self and other, along a line that flies from an absolute present to an absolute past, or to an absolute other, and it is always likely to be bisected by the sharpest and most arbitrary of discriminations. Schmitt marks the point of convergence on the cross of political modernity with a moment of awesome decision as an exception affirms the norm. Hobbes marks the point of convergence on the cross of political modernity in which the world of modern subjects is distinguished from all other worlds, and modern accounts of discrimination in space become interchangeable with discriminations in time.

Modern political life does indeed affirm very sharp discriminations. Hobbes relied on an emerging intellectual culture that was much taken with the points, lines and planes of geometrical reason, and with an emerging world of secular authorities struggling with the legacy of authorities emanating from an apparently transcendent and infinite world beyond human knowing. Euclidean lines have zero width. Hobbesian sovereigns are constituted in a single instant. Hobbesian sovereign authorizations are absolute. Schmitt was responding to an altogether more massively contested world of discriminations, of conflicts between reason and unreason driven by the inexorable dynamics of modernization, quite as much as one of conflicts between sovereign nation-states after the war to end all wars. The most powerful response to Schmitt, the assertion, by figures like Kelsen, that sovereign states are themselves subject to the (exceptionalizing) authority of (international) law, and thus the framing of modern political life as an aporetic relation between claims of sovereign states and the claims of a system of sovereign states, nevertheless works well within the spatiotemporal horizons laid out in Hobbes' narrative about founding. The kind of arbitrary "groundnorm" on which Kelsen relies in order to assert the authority of some overarching law carries all the hubris of a modern world that nevertheless understands the ultimately contingent status of any modern subject making claims to universal law. Together, Hobbes, Schmitt and Kelsen capture the expression of the authorization of modern political authority in a structure of sovereign exceptionalisms; the exceptionalism that Schmitt, building on Hobbes, situates at the edge of the sovereign state, the exceptionalism that Hobbes constructs at the outer edges of that modernity we are all invited to come inside as the condition of a secured and properly political subjectivity; and the exceptionalism that both enables the system of states to recognize, admit or expel any of its constituent states, at least in principle, and encourages all the uncertainties about the universalizing claims about law, and modernity, that have nonetheless been the standard operating procedure for contesting the claims of sovereign states.

A broad acceptance of such exceptionalisms, at least when the going gets rough, when arbitrary foundations must be affirmed, when realities and normative necessities must be confronted, has become the condition under which modern political life has come to be considered both possible and desirable. This is not an acceptance that is often shouted from the tree tops. It goes against the grain of every account of progress and emancipatory possibility that has emerged since Hobbes put pen to paper. It speaks to the political realism that expresses the necessary limit of the idealization of a world of modern subjects and modern sovereign states in a modern system of states affirming an internalization of a process of modernization. It also speaks to the strange way in which modern discourses of emancipation are so ready and willing to agree to yet another round of violence when someone declares that just one more exception is called for, here and now.

Thus one can find in Hobbes not a convenient story about an international state of nature that can be used at will as a site at which to conflate multiple stories about human proclivities and structural necessities, but an embryonic account of the spatiotemporal world within which international relations must occur. It is a story that retains just as strong a grip on the modern imagination as does Johan Sebastian Bach's well tempered clavier, or old Mercator's lines of latitude and longitude: lines and harmonies that similarly enable us to fix our claims of orientation in a particular point, and chart our progress to anywhere else among the melodies of modernity.

In principle, this world came in four parts, with three zones of inclusion and exclusion. The doubles and triples of modern political life that came to be expressed in the framing of modern universals/particulars on a spatial terrain of separations depended on a fourth possibility, or regulative impossibility, the spatiotemporal zone of absolute negation that came to be seen as the point of origin of all modern possibilities/impossibilities. There is the modern individual subject, free, equal but now under the sovereign law. There is the modern sovereign state, constituted by modern subjects within a spatially delimited territory, but with authority over them and able to speak in their name. There is the modern system/society of states, each free but unequal and thus in a position of mutual jealousies and wars and "with their weapons pointing out" but not, as Hobbes insists, in a state of nature and therefore more or less tolerable. And there is the world beyond the system of states, a world that Hobbes could not actually find anywhere, and could not explicitly articulate in relation to a system of states that did not in any case yet exist; just as the place in which I have come to live was then "undiscovered" and so could not receive its proper delineation on old Mercator's maps. This was a world constructed in a Hobbesian but also more widely shared imagination as the possibility condition for constructing a modern statist imagination: as the outside of a modern world of insides and outsides, and which can always and anywhere be invoked as the point both of absolute origin and absolute limit of the here and now.

Thus one great fracture zone of modern politics is the one between the modern individual and the modern state, the zone that, within those states that consider themselves to be paradigmatically modern, has given rise to claims about state and civil society, public and private, state and popular sovereignty, state and nation, and thus about the practices of democracy and their possible corruption into a radical pluralism akin to Hobbes' account of anarchy, or a radical authoritarianism akin to Schmitt's decisionistic nationalism. A second great fracture zone is the one between the modern state and the modern system of states, the zone that has given rise to claims about state sovereignty and international society, the legitimacy of wars, and the final resort to a state of exception declared either by the sovereign state or the system of sovereign states. A third great fracture zone has been between those who are included in modernity and/or the modern state system, and those who are not. This fracture zone is the one that modern political analysis has been most reluctant to acknowledge or examine, but in modern political life is always open to the possibility of a state of exception articulated much more broadly than on the edges of the modern state.

The standard way of dealing with the fourth part of the modern world, and the third zone of fracture, has been the one sketched in Hobbes' story about the authorization of modern authority, the one reproduced in those apparently reasonable stories about the expansion of international society. It has involved reading a process of temporal development as a necessary process of internalization. Hobbes brings a particular group of universal beings into a particular community, bringing universal reason to fruition within the particular state. Kant, with whom I will engage shortly, subsequently seeks to internalize universal reason within each individual subject. Hobbes says very little about how different states might be brought within some sort of system/ society, but this ambition preoccupies most of what has since come to be known as the theory of international relations. Kant sets up the possibility, or impossibility, of the internalization of universal reason within mature republics as the regulative ambition for peace, but with a much clearer sense of how the spatiotemporal point of Hobbesian decisionism enables lines to be drawn from big to small but not beyond the finitude of human subjectivities, big or small.

On this basis, the great progressive hopes of internationalism in the twentieth century expressed ambitions for bringing the entire world into the international: national self-determination; the ending of formal colonialism; the construction of "universal" institutions embracing "we" the people/peoples of the United Nations; and so on. These hopes tended to be expressed less in theorizations of the international than of theorizations of temporal trajectories of modernization as a process of achieving the forms of humanity that Hobbes sketched, three-and-a-half centuries ago, as a process of returning to the present from the past that he had already constructed by absolute negation. The entire world, it was easily made to seem, had been brought into modernity, all states had achieved sovereignty and the world is the international; just as the state is natural, territory is the earth, and modern man really is a part of the world from which he was so famously cut apart in all the great foundation stories of the modern subject.

Outside the insider's outside

Hobbes' famous narrative both depends on and produces an outside, but it is an outside that is internal to a specific account of insides and outsides; just as what we call "nature" has been produced within a specific account of culture and nature. In this sense, the outsides of modernity are always doubled, as Kant would later affirm, but as most accounts of modern politics have sought to forget.[90] Hobbes starts with the here and now. He constructs a then and a there, on his, and our, own terms. He never quite finds them. They remain out of reach, phenomenal but knowable through the categories imposed upon them, as Kant would later say. Nevertheless, he knows they must be where they are supposed to be so as to guarantee the passage back to the here and now under radically transformed conditions: political conditions produced by an array of political practices that may be read just as a story in Hobbes' heavy text or as a complex array of forces that have enabled the production of something like an expansion of international society. In either case, there are no other others, at least according to the claims of modern sovereignty and the modern theory of international relations. There are no others except those that the discourses of modern sovereignty will know as the negations of the modern self and its potential organization within a universalizing system of particularities, the modern system of states that is the home of the modern political subject. Samuel Huntington may have thought he was describing a conflict between civilizations, but he, too, was also voicing a particular, and even more thuggish, way of thinking about a civil war.[91]

The obvious temptation is to insist that of course there are others; other cultures, other traditions, other ways of being in the world than those given by the tightly solipsistic discourses of modern sovereignty. Well yes, and no. Other cultures: yes, we know them well enough as nations, and thus through conflicts between competitive national "values," or the possibility of a solidarity among nations. Other religions, other civilizations, other histories, other ways of being: certainly, just put their substantive claims under the formal authority of sovereign states and modern system of states to ensure that all these other identities, all these other claims to Being and being in the world don't get out of hand; are ultimately subordinated not to the epistemological and hermeneutical negotiations of the historian or anthropologist, but to some authority that knows where, when and how to draw the line. Other ways of knowing: fine, just make sure we know their status in relation to modern authorizations of authority. Stop being so caught up in the tight and narrow discourses about sovereignty; open up to others; recognize alterity as the condition under which any selves, including the self-identical modern self, are possible; forget about the arrogances of modern reason: well, possibly. Just be prepared to make an exception when necessities arise, and remember that exceptions are both necessary to legitimize the rule, and will require the suspension of what is taken to be the norm. Complex zones of inclusion and exclusion, and of understandings and negotiations across the divide, can be reduced to no less complex but very thin lines and decisionistic moments at the drop of a sovereign declaration. Be prepared for violence; and not only at the territorial edges of the modern state.

The other obvious, and contrary, temptation is to insist that while all this may be a problem for those societies that have indeed come to be fully included within the world of modern international relations, and who can afford to think about sovereign states in relation to the rule of law, it is only of marginal relevance for those societies that are not. Again, yes and no. The grand narrative about modernization has not yet achieved – and in principle cannot achieve – the status of a requiem for an end of history. Societies struggling to put a sovereign state together, perhaps under something like a rule of law rather than a rule of simple military force, are in a somewhat different position than those who can afford to read world history from a supposedly sovereign centre. Yet while some societies may consider themselves to be among the excluded, as somehow outside the system of insides and outsides that has come to be understood as a process of progressive inclusion, any state that claims sovereignty is already caught up within the structures of inclusions and exclusions that have worked to affirm a world of constitutive exclusions. If that structure is experiencing stress anywhere, it is going to be experiencing stress everywhere, though with variations that are unlikely to be explained in terms of a silky movement along the road to modernization.

There are no simple lines, no zones of zero width, between insides and outsides, even when exceptions are declared, when particular discriminations are authorized so as to enable suspensions of some norm, when the abject but constitutive outside that haunts or mirrors the sovereign voice of normality and authority inside is rendered mute. The outside is always somehow inside, and the inside is somehow outside, whether in diagnoses of life supposedly within modernity, or in diagnoses of life between modernity or that which is supposedly outside. Limits simply cannot work politically if they are hermetically sealed. Beginnings are always mysterious. Limits are mysterious also, and perhaps rarely more so than when we try to draw a line between those worlds that define the world in terms of sharp spatiotemporal lines of inclusion and exclusion, and those that do not quite see the point, or the possibility, of doing so.

The Schmittean exception still explains some of what is at stake in the claims of a modern state fixed in its proper space in a system of sovereign spaces, even though contemporary practices of exceptionalism work in ways that make Schmitt's extremism seem very simple-minded, an altogether too theological rendition of socially, economically and technologically driven processes enabling exceptions to be made in the routines of ordinary, normalized, everyday life. Hobbes' production of a world of modern exceptions gives us a much wider, and in many respects more worrying, account of what is at stake in affirming the limits within which we need to engage with a sovereign capacity to decide exceptions. Lines are still being drawn, sometimes in ways and in situations some might judge to be tolerable, even sustainable, but sometimes in ways and in situations some might judge to be intolerable. The Schmittean legacy may now be somewhat easier to come to terms with in that so many of us have learnt to tolerate judgements about the tolerable and intolerable and to authorize discriminations between norm and exception in relation to the territorial limits of a sovereignty that has at least some potential to be popular, democratic, legitimate under law. It has not been possible to entirely erase a sense that there has been no clear line between democracy and dictatorship in our experiences with the modern sovereign state, even while the sovereignty of the modern state remains the regulative ambition of societies everywhere, whether already supposedly modern and democratic or still modernizing and thus supposedly more prone to dictatorships.

To destabilize those territorial limits, and the constitutive accounts of the origin of modern political space and modern political modern time, of the necessary spatiotemporality of the modern, is to rip the problem of sovereignty, the problem of origins and limits, away from the regulative account of what sovereignty must be that we find in people like Hobbes, in our dominant narratives about Westphalia and the expansion of international society and in the Charter of the United Nations. Since the mid-twentieth century, a lot of political analysis has tried to stop thinking about sovereignty, afraid of what it might have to confront in Schmittean accounts of a statist exceptionalism. Leave it all to the specialists in international relations. Affirm that it all started in 1648 and repeat the mantras of political realism. Look to Kant and Rawls for advice about something a little more becoming. Yet Schmitt affirms a world of dangers that arise when the borders of all sovereign authorizations converge on the borders of the territorial state in a system of states that can claim to be coextensive with the limits of the world. It is a world of dangers that is simply the obverse of our world of hopes for freedom, equality and something resembling a Kantian account of autonomy within the modern state. There may be many good reasons to suspect that we might yet find better ways of harmonizing the contradictions that arise when we aspire to a sovereignty that limits our claims to freedom and equality within spatial boundaries of the modern sovereign state acting within a system of sovereign states. Nevertheless, there may also be many good reasons to suspect that this is not our present situation; or even to suspect that Kant offers much less encouragement about the possibility of resolving contradictions than we are often told.

The fracture zones of modern political life have become strangely mobile. Discriminations are increasingly a problem. Authorizations are increasingly a problem. Exceptionalisms are increasingly a problem. Boundaries, borders and limits are increasingly a problem. Consequently, sovereignties are increasingly a problem. Perhaps this signals something better, perhaps it signals something worse; although from whose point of view we might assess judgements about changing forms of political judgement is not entirely clear. International relations used to be a site at which one could more or less ignore the problematic status of modern political judgement and assume that sovereignty simply is. It is becoming the site at which modern political judgements are coming to be most persistently problematic, at which modern accounts of sovereignty seem to respond less and less persuasively to questions about discrimination, authorization and a capacity to define the limits of political possibility. The assumption that modern sovereignty offers a monopoly of authority on what it means to respond to the problem of sovereignty is increasingly contested. The age in which political theorists could make do with a few veils to create an aura of cosy domesticity has gone the way of the Berlin Wall. On the other hand, the problem of sovereignty is becoming increasingly perplexing even while we experience all kinds of practices through which we are told what the proper answer to this problem must be; and what the proper way of imaging alternatives to this answer must be also.

In the following section, I pursue such dilemmas by switching from the trajectory that has so far taken me from discriminations, authorizations and exceptionalisms to the politics of founding expressed in the exemplary narratives of Thomas Hobbes to the equally exemplary framing of a politics of past, present and future expressed in the writings of Immanuel Kant. I want to do so partly to insist that it is with Kant, rather than with Hobbes, that it is necessary to engage in order to come to terms with the relationship between the problem of sovereignty and the international character of modern political life. More significantly, I want to explore two complementary trajectories along which we are constantly invited to imagine other ways of imagining political possibilities and impossibilities.

First, I want to replay my comments on the production of the line distinguishing past and present expressed in Hobbes' account of a social contract in relation to the way Kant produces a politics of possibility and impossibility within the aporetic limits of modern subjectivity. Perhaps more than any other canonical thinker, Kant expresses a very sharp understanding of what is at stake in claims about the historical necessity of a reconciliation of political necessity and impossibility within a modern subjectivity that is necessarily cut adrift from the world: from theological authority, from any natural order, and from any form of humanity that is not yet mature enough to participate in the world of modern subjectivities. In my view, Kant is far more usefully understood as a theorist of the impossibility of international relations than he is as the avatar of either national self-determination or supranational cosmopolitanisms, the two versions of Kant that have oscillated back and forth within literatures on international relations and world politics since the early twentieth century. It is in Kant that the difficulty of imagining forms of political life that celebrate a politics of free, equal and autonomous subjects who are simultaneously part of an international, a cosmopolis or a world politics is most sharply articulated. Kant is to be celebrated for his resistance to most of the standard Kantian stereotypes in this respect, while also to be resisted for his own complicity in authorizing intolerable discriminations affirming the maturity of modern subjects as a ground on which to judge any other ways of being human. I then, and secondly, want to draw attention to what is at stake in the chorus of claims that the only alternative to contemporary dilemmas arising from the horizontal articulation of modern politics is to appeal to some sort of hierarchical authority: a move that Kant understood to be profoundly at odds with the most basic aspirations for freedom and equality within a politics of modern subjectivities.

In relation to both trajectories, I want to push at what it might mean to say that boundaries, borders and limits, and thus sovereignties, are increasingly a problem, both in the sense that they are troublesome in concrete situations and in the sense that they express uncertainties about the most basic assumptions about political principle. Before that, however, some comments about a strange and almost forgotten age, the Cold War: an age in which political ideologies may have been massively contested, to the point of nuclear extermination, but debate about sovereignty as the basic principle of modern political life was almost as dead as a doornail.

5 Split finitudes, seductive hierarchies

Kantian impossibilities

Cold sovereigns, doubled histories

For much of the second half of the twentieth century, from the early 1950s to
the late 1980s, concepts of sovereignty made surprisingly few explicit appearances in scholarly discussions of political life, at least in those societies in
which sovereignty could be assumed as an already achieved condition. Clichés
about presence and absence prevailed. The origins of an internationalized
modernity, and thus the trajectories of a modernizing internationalism, had
sedimented into place. Radically ahistorical accounts of systemic logic could
become the exemplary ambition of a properly scientific theory of international
relations. Contradictions could be converted with little protest into dualistic
articulations of a here and a there, of a national and an international, of an
east, west, north and south, of friends, enemies and transitions from undeve-
loped to developed. In retrospect, at least, the discursive categories that
helped to shape and legitimize political trajectories and events expressed
spatiotemporal clarity, which in turn enabled considerable analytical confidence. In this context, the twin discourses of (normative, liberal) political
theory and (realist, illiberal but not non-liberal) theories of international
relations were able to assume, but rarely discuss, sovereignty as their shared
condition of possibility. Sovereignty, it seemed, was no longer an interesting
problem, scarcely even an essentially contested concept, merely a more or less
achieved condition to be celebrated or endured.

This is not to say that questions about sovereignty were entirely neglected,[1]
or to doubt that scrupulous investigations of particular literatures might still
reveal a more disruptive field of scholarship. Most political discourses of the
Cold War era encouraged homogenizing stereotypes that quickly settled into
comfortably narrow ruts, but revisionist investigation may well tell a much
more interesting story at some point. Even less is it to say that the effects of a
specific understanding of sovereignty were in any way diminished. The more-
or-less character of the condition still offered some scope for engagement and
debate. International and constitutional lawyers offered technical commentaries

on its application in specific circumstances, in ways that were sometimes of great consequence in those specific circumstances, though rarely discussed in relation to the way an increasingly professionalized discipline might engage with the limits and possibilities of political life.[2] There also remained a strong sense in some places that questions about sovereignty remained provocative in attempts to engage with the dangers of authoritarian and totalitarian states, especially in the context of the always uncertain relationship between state sovereignty and popular sovereignty.

Questions about sovereignty were especially prominent in debates about "change," about histories, futures and temporalities: debates largely organized through claims about the temporal presence and absence of spatially articulated sovereign states and their spatialized boundaries. The more that sovereignty was discussed in this context, however, the more a specific account of what sovereignty must be was reproduced in accounts of possible alternatives. In some contexts, literatures on the development of international organizations and European integration generated evolutionary and functionalist narratives about a world of sovereignties that should be, or was being, left behind. In others, questions about sovereignty were posed in relation to processes of formal decolonization, primarily in relation to claims about self-determination.[3] Such claims were explicitly understood as the completion of the project of political modernization shaped in sixteenth- and seventeenth-century Europe, the project already supposedly achieved in those societies that could consequently afford to believe that sovereignty was no longer a problem and might now be abandoned in pursuit of something more progressive. International society, it seemed, had expanded almost as far as it could go. Modernity had been internalized, again more or less, even if its full potential might still be unfulfilled (as Habermas was inclined to say when it had become clear that such complacencies were becoming more difficult to sustain after the structural formations of the Cold War era had begun to realign), critiques of modern reason had become briefly fashionable once again, and claims about globalization were able to congeal into an alternative discourse about necessities and possibilities.[4]

Although usually understood in highly spatialized terms, as the articulation of political authority in structural formations articulated in horizontal territorial space, the degree to which explicit discussions of sovereignty in the era of Cold War were largely focused on the analysis of some sort of "integration," on the one hand, and of "developing societies," on the other, gave powerful expression to the procedures through which modern claims to sovereignty work as a politics of spatiotemporality, not of a spatiality alone. As accounts of beginnings and endings in space, they also articulated accounts of beginnings and endings in time. More accurately, precisely as accounts of beginnings and endings in time, claims about sovereignty were able to work as accounts of beginnings and endings in space; although, as Hobbes' crystalline rendition affirmed, the specific account of beginnings and endings in time that enabled a modern statist account of the origins and limits of sovereign authority in space was already authorized by a specific account of the already assumed, but not yet achieved, spatiotemporal presence of modern free and equal subjects.

Symptomatically, accounts of a beginning, whether in 1648 or in a tradition of political realism receding into yet another not quite infinite past, sustained accounts of an eternal spatial present, the famous international anarchy, or international state of nature, although the specific character of nuclear weapons was also widely taken to imply radical transformation quite as much as radical continuity.[5] Deal with the problems of this eternal present first, it was conventional to insist, and we can deal with the possibilities of historical transformation later. This was nevertheless an insistence that rested on a tacit claim that the possibilities of historical transformation had already been dealt with through the more gradual linear trajectory of modernization that had brought, or was still bringing, the entire world into the structural logics of modern subjectivity, modern states and the modern system of states. Explicit engagements with sovereignty may have been surprisingly rare, but the effects of a specific understanding of sovereignty were always palpable; just as the parallel declaration of the death of political theory had the palpable effect of enabling the sovereign declaration of a new age of political theory from which obsolete traditions could be excised in favour of more precise, more technical, more mature conceits.[6]

Modern theories of international relations, like political theories of the modern state, explicitly privilege accounts of a political spatiality, whether through claims about an international anarchy or assumptions about the territorial state. Such accounts also work as a starting point, as an account of temporal origin, and thus as a powerful philosophy of history, though one that is summarily erased whenever claims about an international anarchy or the givenness of the territorial state are deployed as the obvious ground of political analysis and structural explanation. The spatiotemporality that Hobbes set out as a negation of the eternal present of the modern free and equal political subject expresses a broader pattern in this respect. Discriminating between its own self-authorizing subjectivities and its others in space and time, the modern world expresses characteristic but contradictory claims about its own intrinsic character, both as a culture of free and equal subjectivities and as a culture of innovation and change. Modernity is generally characterized in terms of both unchanging forms of subjectivity, actual or potential, and an obsession with change and transformation. Novelty is cultivated, but is largely understood as the realization of the potential that is already inscribed in its origins. Hobbes may have saved some of his rudest remarks for the decaying cultures of Aristotelian essentialism, but Aristotelian traditions of teleology ultimately came through the experience with considerable vigour.

Quite stunningly, Hobbes simply affirmed an account of the free and equal subject as what there is in the world of a modern humanity; and we still strive to work out how it is possible to be both free and equal subjects at the same time in the same place. We do so largely in relation to an account of history as a process of universalization and modernization, or in the Kantian terms that have shaped how we have come to think about universalization and modernization, as a process of maturization, of development understood as the realization of a teleology that is already given as the deontological promise of a modern subjectivity articulated against premodern essentialisms.[7] Once modern subjectivities are distinguished from all their others in time and in space, they generate their own characteristic ways of reconciling the contradictory demands of time and space. Insofar as modernity has affirmed a particular account of what it means to be a human being, the account of a free and equal subjectivity that Hobbes simply takes for granted despite the prevailing hierarchical essentialisms of his day, temporality has come to be understood as a process working *within* the invariant forms of an already present subject, whether understood as a particular individual subject, a particular sovereign state or a particular system of sovereign states. As I have tried to suggest in the discussion so far, this understanding must eventually confront two great difficulties.

On the one hand, it articulates a series of puzzles about how to reconcile universality and particularity or plurality in space and time on the basis of a prior exclusion of all other ways of thinking about universals, particulars, space and time. Consequently, any attempt to mobilize a temporality that might take us from particularity and plurality to some kind of universality will always be subject to critique, on the grounds not that universalism threatens pluralism through some kind of imperial domination, but that the very specific account of the relation between universal and particular expressed in this ambition is itself particular, even if hegemonic and indeed domineering. In this sense, for example, Kant was a parochial European, and whatever one may think of the substantive virtues of his account of reason and ethics, it is not obvious that he can be used as the basis for any attempt to rethink a politics of universals and particularities without some attention to his constitutive parochialism.[8]

On the other hand, and even accepting that Kant may have been right to affirm a constitutive distinction between a modern world of potentially autonomous subjectivities, and thus the philosophy of history expressed in his starting point, it is not so easy to see how this process might work, whether simultaneously or sequentially, through a particular subject, a particular state and a particular system of states given the *aporetic* relation between these three sites of both structure and agency, and also given the internal, subjectivizing character of a process that must always assume a constitutive externality. It is this second difficulty that I want to explore a little further here.

In this respect, and again in very broad terms, we might recognize in Kant's ambitions echoes of (stereotypically) Pre-Socratic accounts of (Parmenidean) permanence and (Heraclitean) change, Christian (Augustinian and Thomist) oppositions between time and eternity, and both Platonist aspirations for unchanging form and Aristotelian aspirations for change within and towards such forms. Or at least, we might recognize these echos in the accounts of the history of modern philosophy that has come to be formalized through the categories used by post-Kantian philosophers to make sense of the relationship between the modern world and all other possibilities. Machiavelli might then be read as a characteristic expression of the difficulty of thinking about temporal possibilities in a world largely persuaded by the impossibility of change in something already perfectly constructed through divine authorization. By (conventional) contrast, Hobbes works out a narrative about the potential permanence of the modern sovereign state precisely by affirming a very sharp change, indeed an instantaneous yet logically impossible rupture, between the here-and-now and the there-and-past that he imagines as the necessary condition under which modern subjects can authorize themselves as subject subjects. Furthermore, where Hobbes might be read as a characteristic expression of the search for an unchanging order once a rupture between modernity and all its others is affirmed, Kant might be read as working out a narrative about how change might, perhaps must, unfold as a universalizing but also particularizing – subjectivizing – history that will always return to an affirmation of the form of the modern subject, the form that is both origin and destination, both condition of possibility and regulative ideal of modern political life. Or at least, again, this is at the heart of our canonical stories about the ultimate grounds on which modern political life might be constituted as the realization of human freedom understood as the one acceptable starting point of rational speculation.[9]

These stories may or may not be narrated in richer and causally more persuasive terms once the Hegelians, Marxists, utilitarians and others engage with them in the nineteenth and twentieth centuries, but they nevertheless reproduce early-modern claims about the necessary (though contingent) origin of human possibilities in a rupture between man and world, between a secular immanence and a theological transcendence, and between modern ways of being human and all other possibilities: claims about a spatial present that generates problems of freedom and necessity in time that must be distinguished temporally from all other times in ways that demand a spatial ground from which to contemplate all subsequent temporal possibilities.

While Kant's *Critique of Pure Reason* is easily pushed into the box marked "philosophy" or even "science" and kept well away from the box marked "politics," especially in recent literatures associating Kant with claims about cosmopolitanism, democratic peace and so on, it nevertheless offers a powerful expression of modern political ambitions in this respect: ambitions that are framed within a theological and topological understanding of necessities, freedoms and limits that is not very far removed from Hobbes' account of the relations between the modern present and its spatiotemporal others.[10] In effect, the straight lines that a Mercator could deploy to control a new world of discoveries and movements in an increasingly problematic planetary spatiality could also be deployed to control an increasingly problematic planetary temporality, although Kant was perhaps drawn more to images of a three-dimensional globe than to a two-dimensional chart. Machiavelli's earlier attempt to articulate a politics of temporal judgement, of knowing when and how to act in order to create and sustain political possibilities in a world of temporal energies and contingencies, had come to seem far too difficult and/ or dangerous. Republican conceptions of liberty faded as liberalism turned towards more constrained alternatives. By the late eighteenth century, conceptions of temporality had been fundamentally reshaped, largely in terms expressed by Hobbes and Kant: reshaped, that is, so as to affirm a magical moment of founding, and thus a temporal discrimination between modernity and its others, a discrimination that permits the authorization of a spatialized sovereignty/subjectivity that can nevertheless never entirely erase the magic, arbitrariness, and logical impossibility of its own foundations.

In the era of Cold War, the effects of this move were conveniently laid out in perfectly spatialized terms. Under such conditions, it might be said, whatever could be articulated as cliché would be articulated as cliché, and the categories expressed in Anglo-American theories of international relations offered exceptionally rich pickings for collectors of clichés. In one part of the world, where East confronted West, all questions about political necessity and possibility were laid out on a ground of international relations: of balances of power, strategies of deterrence and diplomatic manoeuvres between states in a system of states largely organized by hegemonic powers and their allies. In another part of the world, where West or North confronted South, all questions about political necessity and possibility were laid out on a ground of political development, whether as an ambition for self-determination and/or as a structure of neocolonialism. An even briefer shorthand referred to First World and Third World, although the presumption of numerical sequence was exactly the reverse of the presumption of temporal sequence. The theory of history expressed in narratives about political development was itself an expression of the temporal distinction between modernity and its others that has worked as a foundational claim about beginnings and endings grounding modern political life within the spatial forms of the modern state and system of states. Expressed in temporal terms, it was the South that was assumed to have come first, to have been closer to the origins of human existence, to the forms that the modern world of international relations had somehow escaped through their greater maturity, a maturity that was nevertheless associated with a willingness to exterminate everyone and everything in nuclear confrontation. In that context, the stronger the assumption that the ideal of a modern self-determining subjectivity had been reached – the assumption that governed all that was most complacent and self-righteous about the claims to knowledge prevailing in Cold War social science – the less need there seemed to be for engaging with the constitutive foundations on which that ideal had come to be established. Conversely, the stronger the assumption that the process of modernization was only just beginning, the more need there seemed to be for constituting the properly sovereign conditions under which self-determining subjectivities could unfold as they should. Conceived as either the beginning or end of a teleology of both subjectivization and universalization, sovereignty could be assumed to be either silently in place, as space, or noisily in transit: under development, in a state of becoming rather than in the being of an established state. Conceived as the mid-point at which both universality and particularity and global and local could be reconciled with universal/particular subjects arrayed from small to large, as well as the mid-point of a past and a future each receding into some murky but necessary distance, sovereignty could only be what it must be as the single yet multiple centre of a world that might change, but can never move.

This is why questions about sovereignty seemed of interest only to the dull and pedantic, especially to those earnest types who were troubled by such apparently marginal phenomena as law, colonialism, international and regional institutions; or what was usually called "the normative," the search for "values" that might ground a political order in which sovereignty has somehow disappeared.[11] New foundations had been laid down by victors in war, hegemonies in wealth and the freezing of centres and limits in great power confrontation and a teleology of development. Memories of Schmittean and Kelsenian provocations could gradually fade away. Modernization theory could affirm the necessary internalization of modernity within all mature subjectivities, while systematically erasing any sense of the contradictory dynamics of modernity and modernization that were so crucial for Weber and which could still be discerned in the Americanized *machtpolitik* popularized through Morgenthau's discipline-defining text. Stories about the eternal verities of political life could then map out a quick and dirty template for teaching, theorizing and advice to elites in the specialized ministries. Any attempt to ask basic questions about the necessities and possibilities of modern political life could then be swamped by proclamations of the choice between realism and idealism, a dualistic choice that worked precisely to efface any sense of the contradictory character of modern politics, and especially of the *aporetic* relationship between sovereign states and the system of sovereign states that makes any sovereign state possible. If this "great debate" proved insufficient to establish complacency, there was always the possibility of switching to rhetorical declarations of epistemological and methodological rectitude as the appropriate ground on which to authorize scholarly possibilities.

Even when sovereignty did become an explicit concern, the term referred almost exclusively to the claims of modern states. State sovereignty was easily equated, in turn, with something identified as the modern nation-state. After all, the convergence of sovereignty, state and nation, and thus the collation of all boundaries and all limits at the same place and same time at the territorial border, was understood to be the great normative ambition of modern politics seemingly affirmed by the French Revolution, and reaffirmed by Weber, Lenin, Schmitt and Woodrow Wilson, as well as by various struggles for national self-determination after the war that was supposed to end all wars. It was subsequently reaffirmed again by convictions about state-led development and the correlation between state authority and the functional requisites of capital accumulation, as well as by the more general idea that the spatial formations of the modern state could be the primary agent enabling the unfolding of the potentialities of modernity in time. The differences between the juridical abstractions of a Hobbes and the more explicitly nationalistic formulations of Weber and Schmitt were thus easily ignored as the state came to be framed as an ahistorical category subject to the eternal laws of a political realism that was, some said, already perfectly understood by classical Greek historians like Thucydides, or commentators on China in the era of warring states.

For who needs to worry about history when history itself tells us that history is irrelevant? Who needs a philosophy of history or a politics of temporality when politics itself can be understood as a theology of eternity? Who needs to think about anything very much, given that Hobbes has already told us about the spatialities, temporalities, identities, liberties and necessities that must be at work in a modern world that has distinguished itself from all other possible worlds? Invoke the spectre of an international anarchy whenever the concept of sovereignty is mentioned, and we can all go back to sleep. Read anarchy as a logic of rational choice in a market society or a distribution between predetermined limits that might be brought into balance, and we can forget about politics entirely and get on with our objectifying duties as social scientists unconcerned with awkward questions about knowledge and power. Read histories as a linear History, and we all know what is to be done in order to bring the entire world into the world of modernity, to complete the expansion of international society, to fulfil the promises of an enlightened and egalitarian autonomy for all. Substitute a theology of eternity for a politics of temporality, and the textbook trade can tell endless stories about the merry-go-round of idealism and realism, or about the need to find some sensible middle ground somewhere in between. Try to suggest that all these clichés are really quite annoying, masking all sorts of questions about the practices of discrimination and sovereign authorization, and the disciplinary sovereigns can release their barrage of predictable rhetoric affirming the natural necessity of the origins and limits of their own sovereign authority.[12]

With the claim to state sovereignty having been suitably eternalized and naturalized, frozen into the spatiotemporal ground of all political possibilities and impossibilities, the question of whether the sovereign nation-state was here forever, or about to depart this earth in a steady journey to some other kind of politics, could also seem perfectly natural, and become a constant background to discussions of possible and impossible futures. Exactly what kind of journey this might be was rarely clear, but it was always doubled. It expressed both a theory of history as a trajectory taken in the past, and a theory of history as a trajectory to be taken in the future, both trajectories expressing, like Hobbes' account of spatiotemporal distance, assumptions about where and what we are in the present.

On the one hand, this question affirmed a narrative about the bringing of the world into the international, about the expansion of international society, about a historical teleology of entry into modernity within a sovereign nation-state among other sovereign nation-states. This is the narrative that finds its exemplary expression in Kant's comments about the capacity of sovereign states to maximize the potential for both political freedom and international peace in a "federation of free states,"[13] or at least in some pervasive interpretations of what Kant *must* have meant by such comments. On the other, it affirmed a narrative about the continuation of that journey as a loss of state sovereignty and of all parochial nationalisms, although the final destination, whether as a functionally integrated Europe, a United Nations that might somehow escape its status as a merely international organization beholden to its members,[14] or the Habermasian vision of a cosmopolitan law that "goes over the heads of the collective subjects of international law to give legal status to the individual subjects and justifies their unmediated membership in the association of free and equal world citizens"[15] often looked suspiciously like a sovereign state on a larger scale and with a higher authority.[16] This is the narrative that finds its exemplary expression in Kant's comments about the need for some sort of centralized "international state" that "would necessarily continue to grow until it embraced all the peoples of the earth,"[17] or at least, again, that finds its expression in some interpretations of what Kant *must* have meant in his opaque commentary on political possibilities and necessities.

Kant is indeed the crucial figure in this respect, though not because he can be pinned down with any precision, whether as realist or idealist, internationalist or cosmopolitan. Again this may be obvious enough to an extensive community of specialist commentators, but scarcely at all to the enormous literatures that have sought to identify Kant with edifying answers to hard questions about the limits of modern political possibility. Kant's political writings, like many of his more technically philosophical texts, articulate uncertainties and ambivalences that express his lasting impact as a framer of questions rather than as a source of clear-cut answers. Nevertheless, all too many commentaries on his political writings, it would be fair to say, especially as these are read through the pamphlet on "Perpetual Peace" that is usually singled out as his primary contribution to theories of international relations, tend to give one-sided accounts of him as affirming the priority either of state sovereignty or of some supranational authority. This is a tendency that imposes far too much interpretive certainty on a site of considerable and still instructive imprecision. The ambivalence and imprecision that is expressed in this specific text still has an extraordinarily powerful resonance; even though Cold War complacencies about the status of sovereignty and modernity as more or less achieved conditions have been thoroughly shattered, and the narratives of spatiotemporality that are captured in Kant's formulation of the conditions under which a perpetual peace is even thinkable as the necessary but impossible freedom of the modern subject have lost much of their plausibility in many contexts.

Put in slightly different terms, many of the complacencies of the Cold War era, exemplified above all by the unproblematic treatment of claims about sovereignty and the consequent reduction of all political possibilities to a dualistic choice between realism and idealism, expressed a profoundly uncritical reproduction of options framed by the thinker most associated with the possibilities of critique, and thus with what it means to overcome dogmatism and aspire to enlightenment. As a matter of textual interpretation, there is something instructively odd about the way Kant has been appropriated as a thinker affirming one side or the other of the dualisms he is so famous for posing, despite all the well known difficulties of putting this particular splitting of the world back together again, and in spite of all the instabilities that have been traced so meticulously by so many commentators. As one recent inheritor of such commentaries has put it, we confront Kant trouble,[18] far-reaching instabilities that place persistent question marks against any attempt to use Kant as a fixed position in an essentialized matrix like those naming Kant as source or ambition of a tradition of international relations theory. As a matter of contemporary critical possibility, also, there is something odd and perhaps even more instructive about the way the spatiotemporal options Kant seems to lay out so as to think about the possibilities and limits of a new world of autonomous subjectivities still mesmerize so many of those seeking to imagine political possibilities on some other terms.

Having been slipped into the role of the archetypal idealist, Kant has been put to work as a convenient synonym for ethics. Having been slipped into the role of the archetypal normative theorist, the possibility of critique has been put to work as a stance to be taken from some transcendental ground. Having been framed as the far end of a line starting with someone like Hobbes, he has been used to further the cause of all those who believe that the line itself marks the proper trajectory for some other political imagination. Kant, that is, appears as a promise of solutions, despite vast libraries of commentary in which Kant appears as a key moment in the formulation of problems. Consequently, and at least in relation to claims about the international, Kant appears as someone who can be used to draw attention to the impossibility of the many contradictory positions that have been articulated in his name so as to recover at least some sense of what is involved in claims about the system of states or the international; but also as someone whose own formulation of the problem of the international is itself in need of much sharper critique precisely for what he takes for granted (or, more generously, risks taking for granted in his bold hypothesis about the capacities of mere human reason) as the point of origin from which to imagine the realization of the project of human freedom.

The stakes involved here are not trivial. Kant is the figure who is broadly understood to have articulated the strongest ambitions of modern politics: ambitions for the reconciliation of claims to universality and claims to diversity *within* the modern subject: ambitions not just for the mere survival of modern free and equal subjects as subjects of the Hobbesian sovereign, but the potential realization of modern subjects as self-conscious subjectivities and citizens. This is where the differences between these two thinkers of modern political subjectivities becomes most consequential. Moreover, this is not an ambition that may be given up lightly, even if it is a parochial ambition that rests on a narrative about spatiotemporal origins authorizing a very sharp discrimination between modernity and all its others: a discrimination that is always likely to legitimize the declaration of exceptions at the spatiotemporal limit. Far from being an easy source of ethics, a high ground from which to judge the inadequacies of the present, or the visionary willing us to move from conflictual pluralism to harmonious universalism, Kant invites attention to trajectories that take us both to Schmitt and to Kelsen: to the limits of the sovereign state and to the limits of the system of sovereign states. He invites attention also, if perhaps less willingly, to the account of human freedom he articulates within multiple but contradictory sites of subjectivity: to the hypothesis, ambition and starting point enabling both of these trajectories to become so seductive, at least until the limits of subjectivity are broached where individual meets state, state meets the system of states, and the system of states meets claims to some other world beyond.

At least quite as much as Hobbes, Kant seems to have been keenly aware of the limits of the ambitions he formulated so powerfully. In ways that might remind us of many of the difficulties of interpreting Plato's constitutive imagination of the just city, it is not always easy to distinguish the positive vision from the satirical critique. Moreover, as he said himself, he sought, like Copernicus, a point from which to calculate the being and becoming of the world, taking advantage of the recently invented modern subject rather than the sun in order to do so, while still retaining some sense that other advantages lay elsewhere. What can be read as Kantian certainties can also be read as Kantian contingencies, as conjectures and hypotheses requiring sustained critical interrogation. Moreover, in some respects Kant offers only the merest sketch of what later could be delineated in resolute banality. Kant was writing, it might be said, in a context in which the antagonisms between the sovereign state and the system of sovereign states were not as insistent or intense as they later became in an age of nationalisms, and was thus merely offering sketchy intimations of what must happen at the *aporetic* limits where self-righteous nationalisms meet their international conditions of possibility. This was also a context in which he could still readily imagine ways of resolving contradictions through an appeal to something obviously higher, something more universal, something closer to God. Nevertheless, he seems to have clearly understood that such an appeal would necessarily undermine the very possibility of reconciling claims to universality and claims to diversity *within* the modern subject. Get too close to God and the possibilities of modern politics as a project of human freedom necessarily shrivel. Get too far away from God and the possibility of affirming the universality that might be brought into the particularities of modern subjectivities and citizens becomes a troubling business, at least in a culture for which claims that God had lost his grip, or even expired, generated anxieties that still reverberate.

Kant was attuned to such now familiar problems, and to the limits of political possibility they implied for any attempt to think either outside or above the sovereign spaces within which universality might be brought inside the particularities of modern subjectivity and citizenship. Indeed, Kant's conventional place in the canons of modern thought rests precisely on his vaunted resistance both to the rationalisms that appealed to higher – eternal, transcendental, mathematically or theologically given – truths about the world, and to the empiricisms that some had claimed give access to the world through unmediated sight and sensation. Refusing the impossible extremes of some transcendental ideal and some equally unreachable world beyond mere sensation, Kant navigates the huge terrain lying between the limits at which the immanent world of human finitude fails to meet the transcendental world of cosmic and theological infinities and the limits at which the experience and appearance of phenomena fail to meet the noumenal world that is beyond epistemological reach of the merely human knower.[19]

The sharp line between subject and object that marks Descartes' entry into the modern canon of founding fathers is thereby turned into a much more complex affair, into an entire world of modernity at work within a line of apparently zero width, albeit a world that is regulated by other sharp lines on either edge: lines inscribed just this side of an unknowable realm that might well extend out, or up, or back as far as infinity; the lines within which Kant seeks to work out the possibilities and impossibilities of human finitude. These are the lines that mark the site of intense technical debates about, on the one hand, the status of the *a priori* categories of experience and their grounding, or lack of grounding, in some transcendental metaphysics, and, on the other, the plausibility of claims that categories deployed by secular human subjects might sustain credible forms of knowledge about mere phenomena. Much of the critical force of Kant's double suspicion about these limits of finite human knowledge has subsequently become severely compromised: on the one hand, by various attempts to ignore Humean and Kantian objections to the naivety of unmediated empiricism, to insist that phenomena give direct access to noumena and that sense impressions reveal some real and unmediated world; but on the other, and perhaps more significantly, by the tendency to reduce "metaphysics" to a more easily dismissible "religion" so as to defuse the problematic *relation* between immanence and transcendence that drives so many of Kant's own formulations.[20] Both moves thereby enable a trail of commentaries struggling to push him over one side of the line or the other.

This desire to push Kant over one side or another of a line is undoubtedly the central characteristic of treatments of Kant in contemporary debates about the fate of the sovereign state and the system of sovereign states.[21] It is a pattern that is even encouraged by Kant himself, partly because he changes his mind,[22] partly because he tends to respond to different audiences with different messages, partly because he often shifts focus from one site of political agency to another, but also because the options Kant lays out, both for "progress" in time and for "peace" in space, seem to force engagement with the limits of the modern political imagination and with both the desire for transcendence and the impossibility of its realization that are both expressed and mobilized at these limits. Ultimately, this is why even though Kant may offer an incisive account of the *problem* of international relations, and, consequently, an effective antidote to much that has been offered in the guise of Kantian theories of international relations and cosmopolitan reason, Kant also names many of the conditions under which it has become so difficult to imagine any other political imagination.[23] Accept *these* assumptions, and go around in circles; or take the next bus heading straight for the edge, or over the top.

Kant against Kant

Read as a prototypical modern liberal, as the literature I seek to engage seems to demand, though in ways that I think say more about contemporary liberalisms than about Kant's texts, Kant seeks to affirm a set of familiar claims about the liberty and equality of the modern subject. These claims are made with greatest force in terms of an injunction to think for oneself: an account of liberty under the double but not easily reconciled necessity of both universal reason and the sovereign state; and an account of equality within a community of mature, modern subjects differentiated from other, immature subjects.[24] The grand ambition is for autonomy, the account of freedom that Kant introduces as a capacity of properly self-ruling subjectivities rather of merely obedient subjects of the sovereign.

Such autonomy, like all freedoms and all liberties, is possible only under certain conditions, in this case conditions enabling universal reason to be brought into the modern subject, into subjectivity, with law as the external expression of inner moral freedom;[25] although in this case the subject is already instantiated as the site within which universal reason resides as the *telos* of human freedom. It is possible to think for oneself as long as one thinks rationally, in a mature way; that is, in a way that is already mobilized within the potentials of an *a priori* account of what human freedom must be.

Such conditions can be imagined in relation to a universality that is assumed to be transcendent: the position sometimes attributed to a Kant, who somehow remains committed to an older tradition of rationalism, or, more generally, to the shift to Protestant accounts of individual conscience, or to the popular view that Isaac Newton had conveniently laid out in secular terms the God-given laws of worldly order. They can also be imagined in relation to a universalizing potentiality that is understood in immanent terms, in recognition that if Newton did indeed speak the language of God, it was only in a historically contingent dialect: the position conventionally attributed to the much more provocative Kant, who gives the capacity to deploy the categories of reason to an imminent and finite humanity, as well as to the various families of neo-Kantianism that have subsequently celebrated the constitutive, but never quite guaranteed, universalities inherent in deductive logic, principles of simplicity and elegance, the relative disinterest of an intellectual class, or a commitment to procedural principles and communicative competence. This is the hydra-headed Kant, who animates so many debates that appear to be concerned with epistemology and method but ultimately concern far more serious questions about what it means to claim knowledge in terms of the potentially autonomous modern subject, to whom Kant risked attributing constitutive capacities for rational ways of knowing.

The relation between these two broad readings of Kant marks the line of absolute discrimination between the immanent and transcendent, between the theological and the political, between claims to universality that are available to modern man as modern man and claims to universality that are available only to that unmodern man who has direct access to some higher reason. Or, better, it marks the line that is itself constituted through the mutual production of immanence and transcendence, secular and sacred, temporal and eternal, the line that invites rhetorical appeals to something beyond merely human knowledge in order to shore up knowledge that is, after all, merely human. This far more interesting – and credible – Kant lays his bets with the rational capacities of the merely human, perhaps making him a little closer to Machiavelli than might be comfortable, close enough in any case to drive many who crave secure universalities to try to avoid the traumas of political contingency by climbing up into the rafters of ethics and law, and risk cavorting with theology and metaphysics. This is the Kant who also has to confront the problem of founding, of risking claims about the teleological necessity of freedom unfolding within potentially autonomous subjectivities, of instantiating categorical conditions of human knowledge just inside the line distinguishing immanence from transcendence, and of initiating the trajectory that might take us from potentiality to an actuality that must also end up just this side of the line distinguishing immanence from transcendence. Kant's regulative ideal of founding is no less constitutive of his regulative ideal of moral and thus political ambition than is Hobbes' exemplary narrative about the spatiotemporal negation of a brave new world of free and equal individuals.[26]

In more explicitly political terms, Kant thinks about the ambition for autonomy in relation to the possibility of perfecting the potentialities implicit in the organization of modern political life within a sovereign state that is somehow situated in a world of other sovereign states.[27] Seeking the universal *within* the particular, he already assumes a domestic community within which to envisage a modern subject with sufficient courage to use its own understanding. Yet it is far from clear how, or where, any particular sovereign state is situated in relation to other sovereign states. Kant seems to struggle with some fairly predictable problems in this respect. Most specifically, if other sovereign states are understood as necessary conditions for the autonomy of any particular state, those other states are just as liable to inhibit as to enable. The possibility of working out the proper relation between liberty and necessity within any sovereign state is always liable to be compromised by the necessities imposed by the collectivity of other states seeking their own freedoms within and under necessities. Indeed, the collectivity of other states may well come to have prior authority over the sovereignty of any particular state.

The pattern of interpretations of Kant in the theory of international relations is almost too predictably revealing in this respect, as if Kant makes an offer that cannot be refused, and then makes a contrary offer that cannot be refused either, leaving contrasting traditions of international relations theory clinging desperately to impossible choices that have been made with scant critical resistance. Choose "pluralism" or choose "solidarism," commit to "ethics" and so choose "solidarism," bolstering the choice with readings of a progressive history as "the expansion of international society" and speculations about the necessary if rocky road to a morally or legally defined cosmopolitanism. It is a familiar recipe, mastered by many very capable cooks. Nevertheless, there are clear difficulties in accepting either offer rather than in looking at the problem – or logic, or topology, or metaphysics, or instantiation of a discourse about origins and limits orchestrated through claims about the necessities and possibilities of a self-identical subject that can never be self-identical – that is driving Kant's specific formulations.

Thus, in some places, Kant does indeed seem to envisage a very strong role for the "international," a role that might even be extended, in some direction or another, to the "cosmopolitan." This view is especially signalled through references to the formation of a *civitas gentium*, variously translated as an international state, a universal state, or even a universal republic.[28] This is the reading of Kant preferred by supporters of a more significant role for international institutions with an explicitly supranational authority: the direction of extension is invariably up as well as forward. It thus opens the way for claims about the priority of international law over state law, the option later expressed in exemplary fashion by Hans Kelsen. It also opens a way for thinking about not only the subordination, but even the erasure of the sovereign state in favour of some higher authority. At a minimum, it allows for the system of states as the necessary but merely formal condition under which states might be recognized to be legitimate, to be sovereign, and thus as capable of autonomy. It also invites the possibility of an extension of such conditionality to include the much less formal specification of particular forms of government, population, culture, economy and religion necessary for recognition as a legitimate actor within the international. At a maximum, it opens the way to explicit attempts to escape from politics entirely in favour of a moral and legalistic universalism of autonomous subjects orchestrated from above, the direction in which many commentators, Habermas perhaps foremost among them, hope for a new cosmopolitanism to unfold.[29]

As one would expect of this most practised thinker of aporetic situations, however, Kant is distinctly unhappy about where the opening through which Habermas and so many others have forced their way might lead. The slippery slope is one that threatens not to send us cascading downwards, but to project

us upwards towards an authority, a "soulless despotism" that not only transcends the sovereign state, but might even transcend all earthly existence. The
point of the ambition for autonomy, after all, was to bring universality *within*
the modern subject, to affirm the possibilities of self-rule within and under the
law of the sovereign state, not of direct rule from somewhere much, much
further above. This was the point of making the *a priori* categories of knowledge a matter of human capacities, capacities for human judgement, rather
than of theological grace. This was also the point, it seems, of some of the
formulations of the problem pursued in the essay on "Perpetual Peace."[30]
While some of these formulations may admit the possibility that vertical
subordination might have been necessary within the state so as to get the
historical process under way, subordination becomes more obviously a problem
as the external conditions of possibility expressed by the system of states imply
movement along a line towards the cosmopolitan. The potential despotism of
a world republic is only part of a broader problem in this respect.

Despite the recent vogue for cosmopolitanism in the form now identified
with people such as Habermas, the general and, in many respects, more persuasive trend among recent interpreters of Kant's text has been to play down
the significance of references to any *civitas gentium* and to stress references
not only to more minimally international rather than supranational possibilities,[31] but even to distinctly statist rather than even minimally international
commitments.[32] The key references here are those to some kind of loose federation or union of sovereign states, or to an even looser federation of free
states.[33] The underlying force of such interpretations comes from the way they
seem to accord with Kant's general view that history works internally:
through and within the sovereign state itself, for example, rather than through
any coercive mechanisms above the sovereign state. This is the view that
seems to inform his reluctance to admit any right of rebellion predicated on
some "higher" law rather than working within the law that is necessary for an
eventual freedom,[34] as well as his resistance to policies of intervention.[35] It is
arguably the view that is expressed in his Doctrine of Right from 1797: "Any
action is right if it can coexist with everyone's freedom in accordance with a
universal moral law, or if on its maxim the freedom of choice of each can
coexist with everyone's freedom in accordance with a universal law."[36]

Kant's articulation of this view is certainly problematic. The ambition for
autonomy it expresses is always potentially close to solipsism. Neither individuals nor sovereign states can survive alone. Kant makes enough references to
a union or federation of states to suggest that he understands modern politics
to be state-systemic rather than merely statist in form. The potentially
autonomous subject needs both the sovereign state and the system of states to
provide the conditions of both principle and practice necessary for its potential to be achieved. Interpretations of Kant's claim that the civil constitution
of every state shall be republican that seek to translate him into a theorist of
modern liberal democracies may be attracted to a privileging of the sovereign
state, or even the individual subject over all other authorities, but they also

need to refer to the dynamics of a more encompassing order. The difficulty is to know what it means to refer to a more encompassing order: what it means to postulate an order that is external to, or superior to, the sovereign state that is supposed to be the ground of autonomy, of freedom within/under necessity within the particular ground on which universality might be brought into particular subjectivities. Even if Kant himself is understood to be articulating a regulative ideal of a world of autonomous subjects reconciling their particularity with universal reason inside, it is difficult to imagine that the collectivity of subjectivities would not constitute external conditions of possibility, or impossibility, in excess of the workings of the universalizing history at work within modern subjectivities.

In such a reading, in short, what is most instructive about Kant's account of the possibilities of modern political life is neither a defence of some future supranationality nor a defence of an order predicated on the sovereign state alone, but the way he seems to express an exemplary uncertainty about whether, as a condition of the possibility of any sovereign state, the system of sovereign states is to be located in a vertical plane above the sovereign state or in a horizontal plane of sovereign states. Crucially, so to speak, neither location seems possible. If horizontal (perhaps read in relation to Mercator's flat charts), it is difficult to see what the system of states might do either to assist or to constrain any particular state in its move to autonomy, unless it has some capacity or authority (whether as a constituted order or as an existentially disordered order) exceeding that of any particular state; in which case it is necessary to admit that there must be an unresolvable contradiction between the claim to state sovereignty and the claim to the necessities imposed by the system of states, or else to admit a clear, even if undecidable, prioritization of one over the other. If vertical, perhaps read in relation to Mercator's painstakingly constructed globes, it is difficult to see either how history can work its way through the sovereign state alone (in which case the ambition for autonomy is in some trouble), or how far up it is necessary to go in order to find the appropriate location for an authority that properly transcends the claims of the sovereign state (in which case questions arise about whether the status of universal reason is to be understood in terms of a transcendental theology or an immanent politics).[37]

Kant's political texts are certainly open to considerable interpretive contestation. Nevertheless, where most commentators with a specific interest in the status of the modern system of states tend to pick either a horizontal or a vertical interpretation of the place of "the international" in relation to the sovereign state, it would be more in keeping with Kant's own sensitivities to the contradictory character of any engagement with the dilemmas of human finitude to understand him as laying out a very difficult set of problems, in response to which neither of these options is satisfactory. To postulate an international that is outside the jurisdiction of the sovereign state in horizontal space is to countenance an international that is above the jurisdiction of the sovereign state in vertical space. To seek some account of the possibilities of human freedom within a sovereign state constituted in horizontal space that admits the necessity of an international order that is not only outside but above the sovereign state is to imagine that the difficulties of a political order conceived as a radical refusal of hierarchical forms of authority can only be resolved by an appeal to hierarchical forms of authority. As we know all too well, liberty and equality may be the regulative ambitions of a modern political order, but it has never been easy to see how it is possible to have both liberty and equality together at the same time and in the same place, although this remains a part of Hobbes' account of the political condition of modernity that all too many people would prefer to keep projecting onto some other time and some other place, in the manner that Hobbes himself has got away with for far too long.

Kant's texts do suggest various ways in which it might be possible to reconcile the apparently irreconcilable. Thus what I am calling the vertical aspiration for a *civitas gentium* might be understood as a regulative ideal that is not yet "the will of the nations,"[38] but which nevertheless offers the ideal ground on which the present might be judged: the ground that is immanent to the teleology enabling the necessary trajectory of modern freedom, but transcendent to the specific historical conditions that have been reached so far. Or it might be understood as the destination of a historical teleology that is actually in motion from the lesser option of a federation of states to the more ambitious option of a universal state: in motion largely as a consequence of the hidden hand of historical reason made manifest in the resort to war, helped partly by practices of "unsocial sociability" together with the contagious and educable desirability of the republican ideal that Kant thought was already becoming realized in some places, and partly by the generalized moral duty to act as if this teleology of freedom were inevitable, and thus as if humanity itself must be judged as an end in itself, the end to which all else is mere means;[39] in the succinct terms used by Karl-Otto Apel, as a "historical prognosis from the point of view of moral duty."[40] Or it might be understood as a more or less natural hierarchy from the political right expressed at the level of the sovereign state, at the bottom; international right at the level of the states system, in the middle; and cosmopolitan right at some level above, at the top.[41] Or it might be understood as an opportunity to increase the scale but reduce the number of sovereign states, so as to construct a new world order of superpowers in the manner canvassed in Schmitt's *Nomos of the Earth*.[42] Nevertheless, in all these possible formulations, whether appealing to vertical prioritization, temporal sequentialization, teleological necessity, or the establishment of international/cosmopolitan law as the ultimate external expression of human freedom, the central aspiration for autonomy working its way towards actualization within the sovereign state is severely compromised. Put into a hierarchical relation, the states system is likely simply to subsume the sovereignty of the state. Take the individual away from the state and make it the ultimate ground of cosmopolitan right, and anything we might recognize as a politics is dissolved through subordination to an ethics grounded in a presumed universal principle of reason, although precisely what or whose principle of reason this might be is presumably a very contentious political matter.

Alternatively, we might assume that history works entirely within particular subjectivities organized in a horizontal plane: that sovereign states are autarchic in their move to autonomy and that all relations of universality and particularity can be internalized both so as to avoid the consequences of a modern individualism as Hobbes described them, and to erase any contradictory relations with the claims of a states system through the simple denial of any systemic necessities enabling or inhibiting statist freedoms. In this way, a perpetual peace might be postulated as a different kind of regulative ideal, with history working its way entirely within a sovereign state, but only in terms of an account of autonomy that is indeed entirely solipsistic. Kant might then have a nice account of a perpetual peace, but he would not have a theory of international relations, or of politics. The very idea of a perpetual peace would imply not an inn-sign depicting a graveyard, but a place bereft of all signs of human habitation: not a Hobbesian world in which death is always imminent, but a world in which even birth is quite unthinkable, despite the birth of the modern subject of freedom that is being assumed. Or perhaps he would indeed have a theory of international relations, one generated by extrapolating from a solipsistic subjectivity to the kind of liberal nationalism and power politics celebrated by Weber, formalized by Schmitt, and canonized as political realism by the Carr and Morgenthau crowd: the theory of international relations as merely an effect of state action, not the condition of possibility of state action.

Some of these responses retain their attraction. They are attractive to those who would place ethics above politics as a way of providing a proper "ground" on which to give order to political contingency. They are attractive to radical individualists seeking to resist all claims about the enabling and constraining character of "society,"[43] as well as to those seeking some way of making legal claims about human rights,[44] while remaining deeply problematic for those who spend time thinking about what happens at the limits of the human body.[45] They are attractive to those who would draw discrete veils around the edges of a singular political community in order to speak about distributive justices, as well as to extreme nationalists and figures such as Schmitt, whose radically minimalist account of sovereignty as a capacity to decide exceptions within a specific state takes the ambition for autonomy precisely to the limit. They are attractive to those who think of regional integration in terms of scalar levels and bloc-formation. They are attractive to staunch supporters of a linear view of history as a developmental teleology, and thus to those who would articulate their violence-legitimating exceptionalisms not at the edges of the Schmittean state, but at the point in time distinguishing the mature and the immature, the modern point in time and space from which it has become possible to declare the sharpest of oppositions between the civilized and the barbarian. Many possibilities are enabled by plausibly Kantian attempts to reconcile the irreconcilable, not all of them as attractive as they have been made to seem in claims about the way he represents the apogee of modern ethical and political ambition. Nevertheless, it is difficult to read much of Kant without appreciating that he understood very well that all his attempts to reconcile the irreconcilable generated considerable difficulties. No one contemplating problems of human finitude, we might say, is going to feel entirely at ease with appeals to certainty, even if one has as much faith in the God-given (Protestant, and more specifically Pietist) eternities and geometrical accounts of reason that Kant absorbed from the culture of his time.

Kant's ambivalence is still very much with us. On the one hand, modernization has seemed to promise a universalization of the principle of state sovereignty and national self-determination working within a steadily expanding system of states; once, that is, the modern world has been distinguished from and valorized over all its others. The ambition for national self-determination now meets the ambition for a democratic peace; and both express the ambition for a modern subjectivity that is at once particular and universal, citizen and yet human, free and yet bound to a greater commonality under some rule of law. On the other, modernization has seemed to promise a universalization that would eventually overthrow or subsume all claims to state sovereignty, all contradictions between the claims of particular self-determination and the claims of a system of states that enables statist claims about national self-determination. Read as a linear trajectory from premodern diversities to modern universalities, narratives of modernization can inspire hopes for one world, for a single capitalist market, for a common humanity, for a more dialectical overcoming of all antagonisms that is more Hegelian than Hegel himself: for an End of History understood as the erasure of all differences of ideology, culture or political aspiration.[46] Read as an intensification of the contradictions between claims to universality and diversity expressed in the relation between the claims of state sovereignty and the claims of the system of states, however, modernization, the expansion of the capitalist market and talk of a common humanity can be read precisely as an assault on the great achievement of modern politics, on the great Kantian ideal of the principle of national freedoms operating within a common system enabling multiple national freedoms.

These two trajectories might be reconciled spatially: aspirations for state sovereignty and national self-determination in the South, and aspirations for something more universal for those in the North, with an integrating Europe as the leading light. Or they might be reconciled temporally: first state sovereignty and then something more universal. These are still such familiar discourses that we scarcely notice them, even if Cold War complacencies have long been disrupted, even forgotten. Yet neither reconciliation works to resolve competing claims of the sovereign state and system of sovereign states; merely, perhaps, to legitimize patterns of hegemony and inequality as a source of "order" within the system of states that are by no means all self-determining. The eventual solution is always located somewhere else, deferred, assigned to a process of bringing the world into modernity, or taking modernity further down the road to a universality that can only destroy the aspiration for universality within the particular that is our idealized hope for autonomy.

In the meantime, it can be made to seem, we have to live with the dilemmas that Kant identified: the dilemmas not of some international anarchy that the theorists of international relations need to keep themselves in business, but of a radical uncertainty about the double sources of authority expressed in relation to the sovereign state on the one hand, and the system of sovereign states on the other. Various forms of disorder are certainly characteristic of the states system, just as they are of the sovereign state. In both cases, disorder can take the form of hegemony and even tyranny quite as much as something approaching anarchy. Still, these are in principle secondary matters, thinkable only in relation to a modern political order that is radically split more or less on terms given by Kant's ambivalence; thinkable, that is, once political theory and international relations are split into two mutually exclusive discourses. We moderns aspire for freedom, for liberty, for autonomy, but only under conditions of necessity. For the most part, this aspiration has been worked out in terms of the necessities of state, of liberty under the rule of the sovereign law. Kant rightly understood that this statist aspiration is potentially at odds with the constraints liable to be imposed by other states caught up in the same dynamic. There can be no complete retreat into the particular sovereign state, for to contemplate the erasure of those other sovereign states or their subordination to some higher authority is to contemplate the end of the possibility of autonomy, of national self-determination, and the reversion to some version of *l'ancien régime*, to some sort of empire, to a politics of hierarchical subordination. Better, it has generally been thought, to work out an accommodation between the competing claims of state sovereignty and the claims of the system of states: an accommodation that occurs right at the border of the discourses of political theory and international relations, right at the limits that neither discourse is especially well prepared to engage.

This is, nevertheless, the accommodation that has become the official story about the way we live politically today, the accommodation that may be taken for granted as the condition of possibility for the distinction between two different analytical discourses. This accommodation is historically contingent, always potentially unstable, despite the degree to which it has been stabilized around the apparently natural borders of the territorial state. It is also an accommodation that is always haunted by a powerful sense that any other way of dealing with the contradiction between these competing claims must involve the shift to the vertical dimension that had such an appeal for Kant, but which he also knew to be unsustainable. Troubles on the cross of modernity articulated in horizontal space consistently invite the reconstruction of a cross in vertical space, of a line from below to above bisected not by the borders of territorial states, but by the line between immanent and transcendent authority, between earth and heaven, and by all those lines, or "levels," that can be erected somewhere in between.

In, out, up, down: repeat

We have been deluged with claims that much has changed since the days of the Cold War. Perhaps it has. I have especially echoed claims that something interesting is going on with respect to the boundaries, borders and limits within which we have come to expect the political life of modern subjectivities to be contained. Nevertheless, in most contexts sovereignty still appears to be largely synonymous with the sovereign state. It remains a term that is easy enough to take for granted, the fact of life that any textbook writer or states-man can simply assume so as to get on with seemingly more important things, even as the primary condition under which it might be possible to fulfil ambitions for freedom from hegemony and emancipation. The narratives that promise to take us on a journey away from the sovereign state, only to have us look longingly or fearfully at the state written on an even larger scale, remain alive and well, if only to remind us of what Europe, the United Nations or, the more recently influential term, global governance must or must not become. The ambivalence expressed in Kant's account of a federation or association of states that might either be the condition of possibility for republican freedoms, or the ground on which to develop higher forms of authority that might place limits on republican freedoms, is still our ambivalence, our double ambition both for self-determining republics (even "democracies") everywhere and for some way of avoiding the conflicts that seem to arise in a system of self-determining, sovereign but also democratic states in a system of sovereign states.

Framed in this way, only two options seem to be available to us: one imagined on a horizontal plane and one imagined on a vertical plane. These planes are imagined in the most abstract, but nevertheless regulative and constitutive, terms as a line directed out or a line directed up: lines hinged at a point of origin in the self-constituting modern subject that is itself imagined as a site of both secured liberties and regulated equalities enabled and enacted at the same place at the same time. This, at least, is one way of understanding what is at stake in Kant's often shaky and always ambivalent gamble on the enlightened potentials driving modern – enlightened – man.

One option is to keep negotiating and renegotiating forms of accommodation between the competing claims of state sovereignty and of the system of states that is the condition of possibility for the claim to state sovereignty. This option has come to mean a double injunction about the need for sover-eign states not to destroy the operation of the system of states that is their condition of possibility, on the one hand, and about the need for the system of states not to destroy the conditions under which the self-determination of sovereign states is possible, on the other. The key focus of the accommoda-tions that have been negotiated, in principle if not always in practice, has been the injunction not to intervene in the domestic affairs of other states. Hence the centrality of Article 2, paragraph 7 of the United Nations Charter com-bining an affirmation of the principle of domestic jurisdiction with an affir-mation of the requirements of systemic order: "Nothing contained in the present Charter shall authorize the United Nations to intervene in matters which are essentially within the domestic jurisdiction of any state or shall require the Members to submit such matters to settlement under the present Charter; but this principle shall not prejudice the application of enforcement measures under Chapter VII." This is parallelled within states by the accommodations that have been negotiated between the claims of security and the claims to liberty, claims expressed in constitutions, traditions of the rule of law, accounts of political/human rights, and so on. The aporia between the competing claims of state sovereignty (and thus the possibilities of liberty) and the demands of the system of states (and thus the necessities of security) is expressed in the line drawn at the boundaries of the sovereign state. These boundaries are drawn both in territorial space and in law. They express capacities for a sovereign exceptionalism enacted both in the name of the sovereign state and in the name of the system of sovereign states. These are the lines that allow us to know how to act politically because they tell us where we are politically: where we are, where we have come from, and where we might be going to.

While the inscription of this line in territorial space can be taken to affirm a sense of stability and permanence, its inscription in law more obviously affirms a radical instability and contingency. The great undecidability at the heart of modern political life plays out precisely where clear discriminations appear to have been made on the physical terrain of sovereign territoriality. Territorial space may have been naturalized as territorial place, as if place is somehow more natural than space, but the claims of sovereign law expressed as a limit in territorial space are always incomplete, contingent upon conditions of possibility exceeding their own capacity to decide exceptions, as Schmitt understood quite as well as Kant or Hobbes. Which has the greater – both prior and higher – authority, the sovereign state that might affirm its own freedom to the point of solipsism, affirm its own universality not only within its own particularity but also potentially within all particularities? Or the system of states that might affirm the freedom of all sovereign states as long as it is the right sort of freedom – the freedom that is compatible with the survival of the states system, or perhaps with a quasi-Kantian morality guiding the proper development of the states system as rather more than a system, or perhaps with the demands of specific states or groups of states capable of speaking on behalf of the states system, or perhaps with a need to ensure that the states system accommodates itself properly to the demands of particular forms of capitalist accumulation?

Answers to this question are undecidable in principle, although a capacity to accommodate demands arising from *both* the sovereign state and the system of sovereign states has been a necessary condition under which modern political life has been enabled in practice. It is no doubt the great ambition of modern political life that the question might finally be decided, that our split status as both citizens and humans, as both particularities and universalities, might finally be resolved one way or the other. Moreover, the apparently natural ground afforded by the inscription of territorial limits, the imaginary of island-states or self-absorbed nationalists, perhaps, no doubt offers an effective way of insisting that the question has indeed been resolved in the only way possible, given the impossibility of any final resolution that goes one way or the other. For any such final decision could promise only the erasure of modern political life, unless someone, perhaps a Kant reincarnate, can work out how to maintain modern forms of subjectivity while dispensing with those limits, boundaries, and capacities to exceptionalize that have enabled modern subjectivities to keep themselves to themselves, and to distinguish themselves from all others. The territorial boundaries of the modern sovereign state may mark the site of an accommodation between conflicting principles, but they do not mark any simple monopoly of authority emanating only from within, as the usual conflations of claims about state sovereignty and Weber's nationalist definition of the state would have us believe. Hobbes, Kant and Schmitt are all correct in their identification of sovereignty with origins and limits, but they also offer ample scope for thinking that sovereignty must involve much more than the centralized authority enabled by specific affirmations of origins and limits.

Some accommodation has indeed been achieved between competing and irreducible claims arising from a politics enabled by the modern sovereign state enabled by the modern system of sovereign states. We are all said to be multiple people/peoples of the singular United Nations. There must be no interventions into the domestic jurisdictions of sovereign states; but also no destroying the ordering (or civilizing) capacities of the system of states. Draw the line cleanly and authoritatively. Maximize international cooperation and minimize absolutist distinctions between friends and enemies. Maintain a reasonable scrutiny of the conditions under which the claims of liberty might be trumped by the claims of security in some state of emergency. Make sure that one's actions are humanitarian in principle, but also make sure that citizens stay more or less where they are supposed to be and obey the authorities that prevail where they are supposed to be. It is all familiar enough. We call it an international rather than a system of states, a historical construction rather than a natural condition, an achievement of at least a rudimentary form of liberty and equality rather than a mere struggle between powers. We have contrived to be both particular and universal, both citizen and member of an internationalized humanity, though only on the assumption that humanity is coextensive with those people and peoples who have been internationalized.

Moreover, although the principle of non-intervention in territorial space has a certain elegance and simplicity to it, the negotiations and accommodations associated with this principle have become extraordinarily complex. Diplomacies have been mobilized. Interventions have been made. Transgressions have sometimes risked destroying the structural formations of modern political life, and sometimes sustained those formations on slightly different terms. The interplay of domestic law and international law has become ever more difficult to reduce to clear-cut lines of territorial jurisdiction. Perhaps we have all indeed started to overcome the great modern rift between humans and citizens. Perhaps we need to appreciate what has been achieved through all the talk about some sort of integration, broader forms of community: the old North Atlantic Community, perhaps, or "Europe," or NAFTA and other sites of "regional integration." Others would say that, on the contrary, we need to appreciate what is at stake in all the talk about a loss of self-determination in the face of hegemonies and dominations of all kinds. Still others would wisely caution that terms like community or integration are likely to mask a much more convoluted delineation of boundaries, limits, hegemonies and disintegrations.

It is in this context that thinking about contemporary political life becomes so difficult, and confident appeals to linear histories and internationalist accommodations begin to wear so very thin. The antagonistic relation between demands for specifically modern forms of liberty, for self-determination, for autonomy in Kant's sense, and demands that we address the debilitating effects of the modern opposition between autonomous citizenships and some broader humanity, is no less troublesome just because the lines at the edge of the modern state mark sites of negotiated settlement rather than absolute distinction in the Schmittean/nationalist/realist manner. There may be good reason to celebrate the achievement in many places of institutions and practices capable of resisting any precipitous slide into sharp discriminations and essentialized friend–enemy relations; this may indeed be one of the lasting accomplishments of half a century of experimentation in Europe,[47] an experimentation often interpreted more broadly in relation to claims that whatever forms of violence we witness now do not arise from conventional wars between sovereign states.[48] Yet while these achievements may require some other understanding of the possible relationship between claims to citizenship and claims to humanity, and of the boundaries through which this relation is articulated, they do not, and cannot, lead to the collapse of one into the other, nor to the disappearance of authoritative discriminations between one and the other; cannot, that is, unless what is involved is merely a matter of constructing a larger state operating within the same system of states, or overcoming, or destroying, or transcending the world of modern politics enacted with the sovereign state and system of states.

I speak thus merely advisedly with some irony. There is clearly a lot at stake in suggestions that the relationship between claims to citizenship and claims to humanity, or between claims about freedoms and necessities within sovereign states and claims about freedoms and necessities within a system of sovereign states, or between what is taken to be normal and what is taken to be exceptional within and without the limits of the modern subject, the modern sovereign state and the modern system of sovereign states, is considerably more complex, and contested, than the conventional narratives suggest. There is clearly even more at stake in suggestions that the boundaries distinguishing and connecting the competing claims of sovereign states and the system of sovereign states must be overcome, destroyed or transcended.

Many of the great advantages of the formal claims of modern political life involved a certain clarity that came with sharp discriminations authorized in formal space. Subjectivities, properties, jurisdictions, representations, harmonies, rhythms, citizens, enemies and barbarians could all be distinguished, whether by rule or by decision, by brilliance or by routine. Many of these advantages came at tremendous cost. Exceptions were made. Enemies were designated. Wars were declared. Barbarians were colonized. Lines have been cut as well as drawn, drawn blood as well as abstract space, slashed partitions in time as well as on territory. The world has been excluded and then re-presented on terms given by the included.

Many of the advantages of modern discriminations may be disappearing, though discriminations are still authorized. Many of the grander narratives about contemporary structural and historical change (about "globalization," or "postmodernity," or a "war on terror") speak to the disappearance of these advantages. Many other grandiose narratives speak to the need to bring clear distinctions back in, with extraordinary military force if necessary. No doubt military force does have some capacity to enact sharp distinctions. Nevertheless, it remains entirely unclear that anyone, especially anyone employing crude military force, has a capacity to enact sharp distinctions in accordance with the maps of formal sovereignty within states enabled through the structuring capacities of a system of states, maps of what we know to be the condition under which we can imagine where and what modern political life might be. Perhaps the task can be taken up through new technologies of surveillance, biometric identification and all the other technologies being deployed in ambitions for a "homeland security"; or perhaps not.

So, no, attempting to reimagine the modern political imagination as a disappearance of boundaries is not an option. It is only one of many ways of pretending that our problems arise from a condition of diversity and fragmentation, not from a complex articulation of relations between unity and diversity, from contradictions between principles that cannot be read through the subject alone, the sovereign state alone, or the system of sovereign states alone. And yes, the way forward is very murky indeed. It is especially murky if one's lights are guided by the ambitions of a universalizing history that is already inscribed within a form of political life torn between the competing appeals of citizenship and humanity: appeals that already rest on a story about the origins of the modern world from which we have all come in, developed into modern subjects and subjectivities while struggling to look out towards those constitutive outsides from which we have already supposedly come in so as to become modern subjects.

It is in this apparently hopeless context that a second option, a move back to the vertical and the hierarchical, becomes so tempting. If it is no longer possible to be satisfied with Kant's sense that a federation or association of states (or what I have been calling a system of states, or even the international so fondly admired as the progressive ideology of all modern states) might enable the achievement of a modern and properly enlightened world of

mature subjectivities, then perhaps we should, after all, pursue Kant's spora-
dic comments about the need to constitute an authority that is more than a
federation or association, but is somehow above the authority of both the
sovereign state and the system of sovereign states. Modernity may have flattened the world just at the point when it was becoming clear that the world
was not flat, but many responses to the troubles experienced by forms of
political life orchestrated in a system of horizontal territorial spaces is, in
effect, to revert to images of hierarchy, to verticalization, to an overarching
universality, or empire, or an overarching moral order, or perhaps theocracy.
It seems hardly possible to articulate an ambition for a more progressive or
emancipatory politics without being drawn upwards. It is certainly impossible
to engage in a conversation about political life in Europe without hearing
constant references to a presumed hierarchy of levels. Many influential thinkers have taken their seats on the great bus of linear history, some on the
upper deck and some on the lower, invoking resources that were scarcely
imaginable to Kant himself, but all assuming that it will eventually take them
and us to where the air is cleaner and more cosmopolitan virtues might prevail.

That the alternative "where" that might provoke an alternative "what" of a
future politics is, for so many contemporary thinkers, simply "up," is really
quite striking. For "up" is an inherently worrying place to be in relation to
the claims of a modern political life envisaged on a flat horizontality. It is
worrying in that it provokes renewed concerns about the relation between
freedom and inequality, both within sovereign states (thus the concerns
expressed in categories of class or status, on the one hand, and in the uncertain relation between state sovereignty and popular sovereignty, on the other)
and within a system of sovereign states (hence especially the concerns
expressed in relation to great power hegemony, empires, and empire). Conversely, it is with reference to the possibility that the journey up might lead us
back to empire, in the singular, or to reason, in the singular, or to the legitimation of a singular empire through a singular reason, that we can understand much of the resistance to any claim about the need for greater
universality, and the consequent assumption that any resistance to any claims
to universality must entail another revival of a statist nationalism.

It is worrying, also, in that it provokes questions about what kind of limits
might be reached if we move vertically rather than horizontally: questions not
least about whether, in the process of trying to escape the aporias that modern
political life has constructed at the edges of the modern subject, the sovereign
state and the system of sovereign states, we are likely to re-encounter the
aporias once articulated at the boundaries of earth and heaven. It thus provokes questions also about how it is possible to project a discourse of exceptions enabled by a vertical aporia between a secular immanence and a
theological transcendence onto a horizontal plane at the edge of the state, or
the edge of the system of states, so as to legitimize and amplify a secular
violence with a theological violence; or the other way round. In both contexts
we are likely to become aware of the regulative force of the transcendent

perfection that lies just beyond the reach of an immanent politics, the transcendent perfection that mirrors the transcendent imperfection that lay just beyond the reach of Hobbes' attempt to identify a moment of founding. For the outside of the modern international may be identified not only in the horizontal spatiotemporality that enables an account of history as a process of becoming modern, but also in the vertical spatiotemporality of a higher morality that can guide us in our history to come. The standard stories about modernity may still tell us that we have successfully moved from theology to a purely secular rationality, but the very form of these stories about a secularizing modernization echoes specifically theological accounts of what it must mean to move from transcendence to immanence; and accounts of what it must mean to affirm alternatives to a specifically modern politics have by no means lost their desire to transcend a politics of immanence and transcendence.

There is no doubt that such aspirations are often expressed in perfectly coherent, indeed extraordinarily persuasive ways. They are perhaps especially persuasive when articulated not in terms of explicitly ethical considerations, but through an appeal to scale or to the treatment of problems at their appropriate *level*, the term that seems so innocent, yet which works with all the seductive power of a return to the theological/imperial universals considered, but resisted, by Hobbes and Kant alike. The sense of scale may be articulated so as to appeal to mathematical sympathies, whether merely functional or more ambitiously Platonist. Mathematics, after all, is often said to be the closest analogue to truth at work in the secular cultures of modernity, and if mathematics can be construed as an ascending order, then it must make sense to think of political life in an ascending order also. Alternatively, scale might be interpreted in qualitative rather than quantitative terms, whether pragmatically meritocratic, more ambitiously Aristotelian, or even more ambitiously Thomist. Where hierarchy once spelled trouble over the recalcitrance of empires, aristocracies and theocracies, such appeals to quantitative or qualitative scale have somehow come to suggest a way out of the troubles of a modern politics confronting the impossible antagonisms of its horizontal articulations.[49]

The most striking expression of what is at stake here can be found in the tripartite typology that informs almost every theoretical formulation to be found in the modern theory of international relations: the modern theory of relations between states in a states system that is sometimes understood in purely horizontal terms as having minimal authority over any particular state, and sometimes in more vertical terms as having some, but apparently never quite enough, authority over any particular state. Developed in the depths of Cold War certitudes and insecurities as a superficially reasonable typology that might organize what had already become an almost uncontrollable literature on the causes of wars as the crucial recurrent consequence of a statist politics enabled by a system of sovereign states,[50] this typology is a perfect expression of the codification of the modern subject expressed in the claim to state sovereignty; except that what is conceived internally as a construction in a flat horizontal territorial space is rendered vertically as a scale. To move out is to move up. The reverticalization of the world is rendered not as an aristocratic hierarchy of quality, but as a thoroughly secularized hierarchy of quantitative scale, of big and small, one bringing qualitative implications in its wake.

This so-called "levels of analysis" schema is scarcely challengeable as an expression of the ontological assumptions on which it is necessary to think about modern international relations. Anyone seeking to engage with modern theories of international relations confronts a discursive monolith, a founding myth enabling routinized displays of cliché after cliché ceasing only in death. Systems of states are big, individuals are small, and states are somewhere in between. Perfectly sensible, it might be said. Yet this hierarchical schematic is especially instructive when compared with the ways in which its primary categories are deployed in theories about politics within sovereign states. Modern theories about societies and politics within states have been obsessed with questions about how it is possible to sustain a reasonable accommodation, or balance, between claims about the free and equal modern subject that finally established itself against feudal cultures of subservience, and the tendencies towards inequalities, inequities and iniquities that survived feudalism or were generated by capitalism and industrialization. Liberals and socialists have fought among and between themselves about how best to reconcile these assumptions. In sharp but instructive contrast, the theory of international relations offers a typology in which the world of horizontal territorial spaces and individualized subjectivities is simply described as an apparently commonsensical hierarchy, with the universal though pluralistic system of states at the apex, the pluralistic and only potentially universal individual at the base, and the state in its proper place in the middle; always in the middle, in some respects a very odd place for a claimant to modern sovereignty to be, far from the beginning or end of things, far from the instantiation and limitation of sovereign authority, but precisely in a middle ground enabled by claims about the beginning and end of things. A discourse supposedly expressing the necessities of state sovereignty turns out to have no place for sovereignty, only for those spaces that sovereignty produces. The aporetic relation between the claims of state sovereignty and the sovereign claims of the system of states is summarily dismissed. International relations appears instead as a separate realm of action, constituted by states but, in a reversal of Kant, more or less autonomous from states. Nothing occurs at the border. The nasty politics of exceptionalism as a practice of sovereign activity is rendered instead as merely systemic behaviour, the effect of structural necessity alone.

As an expression of the inbred common sense of modern political discourse, this schema hides most of its ontological significance under a chaste appeal for analytical clarity and explanatory parsimony. Yet categories that manage to frame an account of the horizontal territorialities of the modern state as a hierarchical arrangement of inclusions and exclusions are neither modest nor simply analytical in their accomplishments, and parsimony often comes at the high cost of conceptual oversimplification and ideological conceit.

Freezing the contingent and horizontal relations between territorial states into a natural hierarchy, the levels of analysis schematic affirm the eternal legitimacy of the modern sovereign state. The dangerous line between inside and outside is turned into a series of apparently secure distinctions between above and below, big and small, universalizing and particularizing, strong and weak. A merely contingent point of transitions, transgressions, comings and goings is rendered as an ontological absolute. Political life is eviscerated and replaced by a liberal/modern metaphysics of scale that works as a ground of political necessity, and as an extreme idealization enabling claims to an extreme political realism. Schmitt is given a respectable face, dolled up in the powdered wigs of modern social science. Any Kelsenian sense of the sovereign determinations of the system of states is replaced with utilitarian models of rational action in some sort of market. Consequently, as a specifically modern reconciliation between the old theological categories of heaven and earth and the secular categories of here and there, or self and other, this classification is both aesthetically elegant and rhetorically persuasive. As a specifically *liberal* account of a world of individuals, states and anarchies, it renders all other political categories – of class, race, culture, gender, capitalism, modernity, and so on – entirely superfluous. What counts as politics is authorized through the drawing of nice tidy lines precisely in the place where the aporetic relationships between subjects, sovereignties and systems of sovereignties are enacted.

The brilliance of this move is not to be denied; nor its capacity radically to depoliticize the most intense sites, moments and practices of modern political life. Sovereignty can be erased as a problem and turned into a simple given amenable through logics of distribution and rational action. The Great Chain of Being, it seems, was not erased by the advent of modern spatial subjectivities. On the contrary, it has been reconstructed as an effect of modern spatial subjectivities. As in many other contexts, the theorists of international relations deserve credit for making explicit what the political theorists have usually assumed, but rarely spoken or even acknowledged. They deserve much less credit for affirming the assumptions of the political theorists as the way things are and must be, and for reproducing this radically depoliticized idealization of the world as the place in which the study of international relations must start.

Kant, it may be recalled, once famously referred to the starry heavens above and the moral law within,[51] although this is a phrase that rests uneasily with his adoption of a Newtonian conception of homogeneous, limitless space, with no place for Aristotelian essences or elements and no direction for heaven and earth. The temptation to move up in order to escape the contradictions of a political landscape laid out in territorial space remains enormously seductive even though our contemporary accounts of spatiotemporalities and directions are at odds with both a heaven above and a Newtonian/Kantian cosmology of spatial homogeneity. Fortunately or otherwise, however, the

starry heavens are not above in any sense that we can treat as either foundation or teleological destination: we may come across esoteric discussions of
aerospace law, strange debates among astronomers about whether Pluto is or
is not a planet, mad schemes for missile defence systems, scary stories about
atmospheric chemistry, and residual memories of the angelic hosts, but no
simple vertical understanding of the starry heavens above, except in the conviction that the problems of a horizontal politics *must* be solved by reverting
to the vertical. A mathematical sense of scale or various notions of qualitative
superiority and inferiority are nevertheless often sufficient to persuade us that
the only solution is to go up. This is what gives claims about globalization,
cosmopolitanism, and so on much of their appeal. It is all so very sensible,
and so very progressive. As a solution to the problems of a modern politics
articulated through limits extended horizontally, however, the attractions of
this particular metaphysics are not quite so obvious.

The problem of sovereignty is indeed a problem. It is a problem in the sense
that a broad range of trends have begun to force very basic questions about
authority and the authorization of authority onto many intensely practical
agendas. It is also a problem in the sense that spatiotemporally specific
accounts of what it means to pose questions about sovereignty, to articulate
answers to them, and to instantiate these answers in the myriad practices of
the modern state leave very little scope for thinking about sovereignty on any
other terms. It is nevertheless a problem that is increasingly difficult to pose or
answer in terms articulated by modern sovereignty in general, the modern
sovereign state in particular, or the various permutations through which the
spatiotemporal horizons expressed by the modern sovereign state have
become framed as the natural necessity of modern political life.

It is, it might be said, all a matter of perspective: not of those perspectives
that can be put in the plural as tactical grounds on which to advance relativistic claims about a world that cannot be known from any single ground, but
precisely of a specifically modern account of a line from subject to object,
knower to known, that is drawn as that which enables a modern perspective,
a modern objectivity, and a modern subjectivity. From the stance of the
modern subject we may gaze upon the object and render it as objective. From
the stance of a specifically Kantian subjectivity, we may gaze out or gaze up,
and be drawn, so to speak, in both cases, to question the very possibility of
ourselves as modern subjects. This is what leads us to both the promises and
tragedies of modern accounts of our humanity as subjectivity. Sometimes we
look out, or up, and think we see the world. Sometimes we look out, or up,
and see that we are radically cut adrift from the world.

It was by expressing such ambivalence that Kant had articulated a realm of
critical possibility, the possibility of human freedom enacted between the
limits of immanence and the limits of phenomenal knowledge, each limit
remaining an indication of what is beyond yet what is also constitutive of a
merely human capacity both to know and to become. In a dramatically different and yet recognizably Kantian era, Max Weber looked out and saw that

the world had indeed been brought into the modern, in ways that had set modern man even further adrift from all meaningful contact with any other world. He also looked up, saw all the perils of confusing an ethic of ultimate ends with an ethics of political responsibility, and affirmed the need for a new man, the new hero able to stand here and to do no other. From this radical-ized (Nietzscheanized but still recognizably Lutheran) Kantian stance, various lines cutting across the lines of perspective from man to world appeared in even starker light. One cuts between the claims of heavenly transcendence and earthly immanence, reaffirming old Machiavelli's brutal rupturing of a poli-tical ethics necessary for human freedom on earth and some other ethics guaranteed by Christian theology and affirmed by a motley assortment of popes and emperors. Another cuts between the claims of modernity and all other claims, affirming a linear even if tragic trajectory of internalization into modern subjectivity. Consequently, a further line was inscribed at the edge of the nation-state, the subject/object of ultimate value in relation to which Weber's new political hero could nevertheless stand, the line quickly affirmed by Schmitt's account of sovereignty as a capacity to make exceptions, the line that has been assumed but scarcely thought about since it was recast as the myth of origin, theory of history and claim to political necessity we have come to know as realism: the line affirmed in claims about sovereignty as a monopoly of power and authority and a capacity to decide the exception and deploy legitimate violence.

In these terms, the logics of subjectivity, nation, state, law and sovereignty can converge, the logic of the system of states that enables these particularistic logics can recede into a background blur, and no one need ask questions about the conditions under which the world has or has not been brought into the modern. Sovereignty is state sovereignty and state sovereignty simply is; although sovereignty is difficult, not to say impossible, to imagine as some-thing that simply is, and it is a matter of historical specificity that what we take modern subjects, nations, states and laws to be must be understood in large part in relation to what the specific forms of state sovereignty – forms that have no simple being – insist they must be.

Put this way, it is perhaps unsurprising that not many people have been keen to talk about sovereignty; inhibitions might be explained not only by the specificities of Cold War, but by a vague sense that to question sovereignty is to question the limits of modernity itself. Think about it too much, and the attempt to keep it under control as a thoroughly secularized concept amen-able to a mundane power politics must quickly fail, as many of those asso-ciated with Weberian and Schmittean accounts of how modernity works at its limits were quite aware. Put this way, also, it is unsurprising that when the erasure and ritualization of state sovereignty as an ungrounded ground of Cold War political life did eventually come under challenge among those interested in the workings of political principle, it did so in a way that insisted on the centrality of questions about "the mystical foundations of authority," to use the phrase popularized by Derrida's influential lecture on law.[52]

Indeed, now that the claim that sovereignty is in some trouble attracts an aura less of naive idealism than of pragmatic common sense, the more typical complaint about many contemporary discussions of sovereignty is not that they are the preserve of the dull and pedantic, but that they invoke forbidding and even dangerous theoretical, philosophical and even theological literatures; literatures of the kind I have tried to invoke rather gently and obliquely in discussing practices of discrimination, authorization and exceptionalism in the previous chapter, and by engaging in this chapter with some comments on the popularity of desires to escape from the aporetic frying pan of a politics arrayed in horizontal space into the aporetic fires of a politics aspiring to reach somewhere close to a transcendent infinity located somewhere above us.

Contemporary discussions of sovereignty are indeed now just as likely to invoke the philosophical eruptions of the 1960s popularly associated with Derrida, Foucault and Deleuze as they are F.H. Hinsley's conventional historical narrative from much the same era (though from a very different political and intellectual culture). While these more philosophically articulate literatures might be kept at bay in some places by rudimentary strategies of classification and caricature, there is little doubt that recent concerns with the linguistic turn, various (feminist, poststructuralist, postcolonial) suspicions of the modern subject, and so on, have played some small role in pushing claims about sovereignty out of its status as a privileged and boring technical matter into various arenas of contestation. Understood causally, this role of theoretical provocation is undoubtedly minor. Sovereignty has become increasingly contested as a concept primarily because many historical and structural trends have raised questions about sovereignty as a practice, and not only as a historically constituted and instituted practice of the modern system of states. Nevertheless, a considerable literature has now accumulated offering to make sense of its new status as a concept, a practice, or an institution that poses far more puzzles than it offers consoling answers: far more puzzles than can be controlled either through the clichéd debates between realists and idealists that once kept disciplinary expectations intact and the security analysts fixated on the violence of their idealized sovereign nation-states, or through more "progressive" appeals to a journey to somewhere above us. Kant's account of the regulative ideal, and regulative limits, of modern subjectivity rests upon judgements about time, space and identity that were always risky, to Kant's credit. The consequences of Kant's gamble on the necessary freedom enabling and sustaining modern subjectivity have now become more obviously disconcerting.

Most significantly, the easy and now almost natural equation between sovereignty and state sovereignty is beginning to unravel. To initiate analysis with state sovereignty, even if this involves, for example, replacing linear teleologies and simple tales of life before and after sovereign states with multidimensional, contested and contingent accounts of the beginnings of the modern states system, is precisely to avoid asking questions about how the relation between sovereignty and the concept/institution/practice of state sovereignty came to be established and how the relationship works.

Recent critical literatures move in many, often incompatible, directions. Nevertheless, it is at least possible to identify some key themes that begin to emerge, not always with great clarity, once claims about sovereignty and claims about state sovereignty are no longer treated as unproblematic synonyms. Indeed, the primary difficulty that arises when trying to make sense of the recent eruption of literatures in this context is less the need to unpack the consequences of conceptual conflation than the tendency for any such unpacking to expand to the point at which sovereignty becomes coextensive with modern politics as such. To interrogate modern accounts of sovereignty is to risk totalization; to risk expanding so as to encompass everything that Hobbes insisted must be accepted, so as to conclude that there can be no alternative to the options he so coolly lays out as the consequence of ambitions for both freedom and equality at the same place at the same time. This is no doubt the predictable fate of a principle that seeks to delineate an account of political possibility/necessity in relation to claims about human finitude in a culture so pervasively shaped through affirmations of a huge rift between man as subject and world as object. Points generate lines that flow off to infinity, until crossed at some point: some point in space enactable as the moment of always potential decision affirming the norms delineated up to that point. Points may mark the limit, the full stop, but they also risk internal expansion if one looks at them long enough: expansion to the circle, to the globe, to the world, to infinity; but only until boundaries, borders and limits are enacted, in one way or another.

6   Politics on the line

The geopolitics of judgement

First reprise: politicizations of sovereignty

The spatiotemporal rigidities of the Cold War eventually relaxed. Euphoria danced with nostalgia, at least until both were swept away by fresh worries about new wars, energy shortages, climatic transformations and economic failures. Claims about globalization seduced to the point of promiscuity, at least until new forms of exceptionalism disciplined all talk about apparently more hopeful possibilities into new accommodations with mass violence in the name of some ostensibly globalized, but in fact very localized but interconnected, forms of terror. Political practices and institutions nevertheless continued to exceed the expectations of individualized subjects, nation-states and the system of states. A bid for unipolarity ran into sand. Financial markets lost their magic. Other states made their presence felt. For some people, horizons brightened. Others saw very few reasons to be cheerful. Nothing stood still. Moreover, events seemed to evade any singular logic, whether structural or historical, although different readers will no doubt insist on the greater plausibility of some logics than of others, and may assign causal determinations far more readily than I think wise. In whatever ways the two decades following the fall of the Berlin Wall might come to be interpreted retrospectively, however, it has been difficult to ignore the degree to which grounds for political judgement have come to be regarded as worryingly insecure; though not so insecure as to preclude firm judgements that claims about security have been deployed more or less indiscriminately to justify scarcely credible acts of sovereign decision on the part of supposedly great, but utterly irresponsible, powers.

That is to say, contemporary conditions offer many grounds for thinking that sovereignty must be engaged as a problem, not a permanent or disappearing condition. Whether it has become any more of a problem than at any previous moment, or on what ground such comparisons might be made, remains unclear. It is nevertheless difficult to imagine any retrospective interpretation of recent events that does not pick up on widespread challenges to established principles of political judgement and the claim to sovereign authority through which political judgements are enacted. In any case, and no matter whether these challenges are ultimately judged to be serious or trivial, I would also say that it is far better in both scholarly and political terms to engage with sovereignty precisely as a problem, rather than to keep reproducing narratives about what sovereignty must be or must not be that are themselves produced by specific forms of sovereign authorization of grounds for judgement.

This is why I have pursued what might seem to be a fairly arcane quest through literatures about discrimination, authorization and the spatio-temporal boundaries, expressed both horizontally and vertically and as both origins and limits, of a modern political order organized within a system of sovereign states. If sovereignty is in some trouble, not least because political life does not always seem to be where it is supposed to be within the bounded authorities of a modern system of states, then this trouble will be expressed in relation to the practices through which modern forms of sovereignty were constituted as attempts to respond to pervasive difficulties in defining what the world is, or must be, how this world must be carved up, how the carve-up might become authoritative, and what must happen at the boundaries (borders and limits, spatial and temporal) of any authority that is thereby established. In this way, I have tried to avoid reproducing standard narratives about sovereignty that work as practices of the modern state so as to draw attention to some of the conditions under which such practices attempt to solve various problems of discrimination, authorization and delimitation by affirming a capacity to draw the line in accordance with a specific understanding of topological form: a form that enables a familiar conjunction between spatial extension across sovereign territories and the unfolding of a temporal teleology within spatialized forms of subjectivity. As should be clear from what I have said, however, attempts to avoid the standard narratives are not exactly guaranteed to have much success.

It is not that we have been suddenly thrown into some relativistic abyss, as much superficial and debilitating commentary about contemporary political life has sought to insist. Rather, we may have become slightly more aware of the historical and cultural contingency of the grounds on which modern grounds for political judgement were once established, and have had to be constantly reaffirmed and/or reinvented. It might be possible to argue that this supposed emancipation from the authority of tradition, or theology, or nature, was a mistake, but not to complain that the foundations of modern political life have somehow gone missing. The absence of any foundations beyond those constructed by modern political life itself has been precisely the ground on which modern subjects have been able to celebrate their presumed liberties, equalities and securities. It may also be that this famously groundless ground, and the presumptions about liberty, equality and security it enables, is in some trouble, but it is trouble that is unlikely to respond to assertions about relativism or the essential virtues of modern/liberal reason. There is no good scholarly reason to retreat to dogmatism in order to avoid critical interrogation of the conditions under which claims to reason and virtue, or claims about liberty, equality and security, might be sustained. It is certainly clear, more specifically, that no attempt to examine the conditions under which it might now be possible to speak about liberty, equality, security and other such principles in ways we (whoever this may be) might consider (through procedures that might be negotiated) appropriate (in some sense that might be agreed in the course of the negotiation) can avoid engaging with the limits of an internationalized order that can never sustain a claim to be a politics of the world.

Similarly, it is not that the logic of the system of states that eventually replaced, displaced or subordinated other logics of political/theological order has suddenly disappeared, as many contemporary literatures also claim; simply that we have become slightly more aware that the logic of a system of states is necessarily much more complex than it has been made to seem in the radically solipsistic nationalisms still informing many accounts of what it means to make claims to a theory of international relations, or indeed to a theory of politics. It is not necessary to invoke any especially fancy theorization to understand that dualistic accounts of the logic of friends and enemies is a profoundly misleading basis on which to examine the dynamics of modern political life, any more than it is to understand that practices of modern subjectivity cannot be captured through accounts of a radically solipsistic individualism of the kind that have become popular in some versions of modern liberal and economic ideology. No doubt some explanation for the popularity of radical solipsisms in the modern social sciences is called for. However, greater difficulties loom once the banality of dualistic readings of the logic of a system of states is understood and we try to come to terms with the practices through which apparently simple lines of discrimination between the internalities and externalities of modern subjectivities, whether individualistic, statist or systemic, work so as to produce very specific forms of subjectivity and objectivity.

This has sometimes been a central theme of classic accounts of what it means to speak about the sovereignty of the modern state, especially accounts in which apparently simple lines of discrimination work as sites of contradictory, mutually constitutive and self-constituting unity producing specific structures of norm and exception, in the sense expressed by Schmitt, or a present that produces a past that enables a present, as in the Hobbesian narrative about spatiotemporalities that must be at work in the assumption of a moment of social contract. As Hobbes already understood long before Schmitt, the sovereignty of the modern state – that mortal god – is located both within and outside the law it enacts. Similarly, the Schmittean exception affirms an externality in the very act of expressing limits to an internal norm. Such sources already suggest that there is no simple discrimination between internal and external, friend and enemy, national and international or before and after; rather, that the production of distinctions between internal and external and before and after are, literally, crucial to the procedures through which a specific understanding of the spatiotemporal conditions of modern subjectivity has been shaped within what appears to be the already achieved, normalized and centred space of the sovereign state. Whatever else one may think of such figures (and they are, of course, not the only ones who might be identified, simply two of the most difficult to dismiss from any list of authorities on the authorization of state sovereignty as the beginning and end of modern political authority), both Hobbes and Schmitt challenge the dualistic accounts of a sovereignty distributed on either side of a line of discrimination: accounts that silence all questions about the authorization of what counts as authority and about what happens at the spatiotemporal limits of sovereign authority.

The difference between the conventional dualism and the sort of duality, dialectic, self-production and aporia sometimes expressed by Hobbes and Schmitt might seem very minor in some respects, merely a subtle shift in what some might still regard as just a boundary; as, for all practical purposes, just a simple line of authorized discrimination. Moreover, neither Hobbes nor Schmitt seemed especially keen to dwell on the difference, being quite happy to affirm the naturalized ground whose production they had articulated so succinctly. Nevertheless, the implications of this difference are quite extensive.

It is in this context, for example, that we can understand many contemporary claims about universalism and enlightenment that ignore the very specific ways in which modern accounts of universality and enlightenment have been worked out in relation to the limits of modern subjectivity. Many commentators have played fast and loose with claims about the universality of modern subjectivity without acknowledging that modern subjectivity has been constructed as a claim about universality, and particularity, within very precise limits. What demands attention in this respect is neither the claim to universalism as such, nor the relativism often ascribed to anyone refusing to buy into such a claim, but the character of the limits within which such claims have been articulated. It might be possible to argue that, under specific historical conditions of modernization, the universality-within-particularity we call the modern subject (individual, statist or systemic) has become hegemonic as a cultural and political form, perhaps desirably so. Yet this is to make an argument not about universality as such, but about a specific political articulation of universality-within-particularity and particularity-within-universality that must necessarily generate huge problems at the point, or line or moment at which this articulation meets its external conditions of possibility – especially at which it claims to meet the world, and even more especially at which it claims to meet a world expressing possibilities for heterogeneity and differentiation as well as possibilities for some kind of planetary integrity.

It is at this point, or line, or moment that we must eventually remember the crucial difference between a modern politics orchestrated within a system of states and the logic of empire: the logic against which modernity is understood to have rebelled as the condition under which we now claim to be free, equal and secure subjects. It may be possible to urge the need for greater universality as the condition under which we might now imagine some other form of political imagination, or under which we might urge the need to universalize the modern universal/particular subject, but to pursue both, or even to assume that they are the same thing, can only lead to huge and very familiar problems at the limits of the world of modern subjects. To assert the universality of any particular value (like life, or freedom, or right, or justice) is immediately to express some kind of conditionality (like mortality, or necessity, or obligation, or law), and thus to invite some sort of limitation. To insist on the universality of a particular relation between universality and particularity within modern subjectivities is immediately to provoke suspicions about the imperial pretensions of a hegemonic culture, and about expectations for the eventual entry of all other cultures, even the world as such, into this particular subjectivity of universality-within-particularity. To insist that a modern political life orchestrated as a structure of universalities within particularities extended in territorial space, but enabling a temporal process of teleological perfectability within each particular space, offers the best way of accommodating demands for liberty, equality, security and, indeed, perpetual peace, is to entertain enormous hopes that the sites of aporetic contradiction where subjectivity meets subjectivity, and especially where sovereign states meet the sovereign system of sovereign states, can be resolved without too many disasters.

Considerable nonsense has undoubtedly been expressed in the name of political realism in the theory of international relations, especially as a way of excusing authoritarian practices and dogmatic accounts of national security, but amidst the nonsense it is possible to appreciate the force of its core demand that we pay attention to the possibility, and sometimes necessity, of violence at the edges of modern sovereign states: not only at the territorial borders of such states but also at the limits of (legal, cultural, ethical) principle within which modern subjectivities seek to reconcile, and secure, their liberties and equalities. If doctrines of political realism are understood to be deeply problematic, then they have to be problematized not in terms of their appeal to simplistic stories about human nature, national interests and so on, but in terms of their idealization of specific (statist, nationalist) forms of modern subjectivity, and of their willingness to address the consequences of the limits of modern subjectivity.

This is why I have long argued, against just about every attempt to develop a theory of international relations since at least the beginning of the Cold War, that it is such a mistake to initiate any analysis of modern politics with claims about political realism without first coming to terms with the idealizations of a specific repertoire of claims about the liberty, equality, security and self-determining capacities of modern subjects, whether individual or collective. This is also why the classic texts that are usually invoked to justify claims to a tradition of political realism, Machiavelli, Hobbes and Weber perhaps most especially, are so much more provocative than the contemporary literatures about international relations that remain content to examine only the presumed consequences of normative claims that go unexamined. Political realism is not the opposite of liberalism, to take a particularly influential recent conceit. It is, among other things, an expression of (diverse and contradictory) claims about what must happen when liberal universals, and liberal orchestrations of universals within particulars, reach their boundary conditions, the borders and limits at which exceptions must be declared in the name of a particular array of norms.

It is in this context, I have argued here, that Kant's troubled oscillation from limits expressed horizontally to limits expressed vertically offers such a powerful purchase on what is at stake in claims about political realism in the theory of international relations. If political realisms have come to work most insistently as engagements with the boundaries of modern liberalism, it should be little surprise to find that the thinker who has probably had the most to say about the boundaries of modernity (the boundaries that Weber reaffirms in a *machtpolitik* of liberal nationalism and Schmitt reaffirms in a defence of a much less agonistic form of nationalism) is Kant, precisely the thinker who has been most persistently cast as the exemplary alternative to all forms of political realism. This is certainly not to equate Kant with either Weber or Schmitt, or even to deny that Kant might offer resources for resisting their versions of liberal or illiberal nationalism, not least because Kant offers an account of aporetic limits that can be read as both national and international. Both figures nevertheless work within a recognizably Kantian account of what it means to affirm a political universe of potentially autonomous subjectivities enabled within finite limits. Consequently, it is by organizing my commentary around themes that find expression in Kant's multiple engagements with the limits of human finitude that I have tried to open out some of what is at stake in claims that modern forms of sovereignty are unsustainable, in many contexts and on many grounds.

I have especially tried to work with themes that stand out when sovereignty is understood not as the centralized form of political authority that is in its proper place once claims about state sovereignty are presumed to have been successful (the understanding expressed in Weber's idealized (though paradigmatically "realist") account of the nation state, the account that does much to enable Schmitt's specific formulation of a sovereign exceptionalism), but as a problem that requires some account of the beginning and ending of things, of origins and limits between which a centred claim to authority can be made to work as a naturalized middle ground. My guiding assumption in this respect has been that it is not very helpful to engage with the flood of literatures seeking to find alternatives to modern forms of sovereignty without developing some sense of the problems to which the sovereignty of modern states, organized within a system of sovereign states that is in some sense also sovereign, has come to be seen as the only possible answer. So, in working towards a conclusion, let me first consider in a little more detail what would be at stake in treating sovereignty as a problem, rather a condition that can be either confirmed or denied, and then say something about what might be involved in treating the boundaries, borders and limits of a politics affirmed by modern forms of sovereignty as particularly troubling sites of contemporary political life.

In the first instance, I want to insist that even if we remain committed to something like a Kantian understanding of where and what modern political life ought to be within the triple array of subject, sovereign state and system of sovereign states, the politics of boundaries, as both borders and limits, must become a far more troublesome affair than might be gathered from the way the disciplines of political analysis have themselves been constructed as expressions of such boundaries. In the second instance, however, I want to canvass some of what might be at stake if we become persuaded that the conventional narratives about boundaries, and about the forms of sovereignty that boundaries both express and enable, have become too elusive for either scholarly or practical comfort. In either case, and as with sovereignty, the most pressing analytical difficulties arise less from a need to understand the novelty of contemporary boundary conditions, important as this is, than the need to appreciate what is at stake in the specific idealizations of what boundaries must be that already work to overdetermine expectations of what novel forms of boundary condition, and thus of political possibilities and impossibilities, must be like.

Misterioso: being sovereign

Sovereignty has clearly become a pressing problem in many contexts: in relation to the relegitimation of markets as the primary source of political value, to the relegitimation of force deployed in the name of a security requiring mass murder and the curtailment of established liberties, and to the dawning recognition that the destructive effects of human activity on planetary eco-systems are going to be felt much, much sooner than almost anyone had expected, among others. From being the tacit ground on which Cold War scholarship could proceed without fear of disruption, sovereignty has quickly become a matter of great puzzlement: understood less as a brilliant solution to the most basic political problems posed by the construction of modern societies predicated on principles of liberty, equality and the universality-within-particularity and particularity-within-universality of modern forms of subjectivity than the site/moment at which these principles have been stretched quite literally to the limits. They have been stretched towards the limit as superpower hegemony threatened to shift from the horizontal logic of a system of states to the vertical logic of some singular imperium. They have been stretched towards the limit as sovereign declarations of exceptional conditions shift from the territorial edges of nation states to lines of spatio-temporal discrimination that elude conventional cartographies of here and there, or now and then. And they have been stretched towards the limit whenever appeals to humanity or the world as such have been deployed so as to claim that the established principles of modern political life within a system of states must be trumped by some other understanding of political authority.

At the same time, many literatures have sought to show that sovereignty has long been a more complex affair than Cold War stereotypes allowed.[1] Much of the critical force of such literatures has come from a widespread feeling that the term sovereignty has been used to bring far too many phenomena under an apparently singular name. Predictably, while it has become easier, even fashionable, to complain about conceptual conflation, the complaint also generates a sense of vertigo once the vast array of themes that might be explored, and the possible scholarly strategies available for such an exploration, become more familiar. Given the historical and structural transformations and conceptual manoeuvres that went into the production of modern forms of sovereignty expressing very specific accounts of the proper relation between singularity and multiplicity, and of the spatiotemporal form of the relation between singularity and multiplicity, this should not be surprising. Given what was at stake in the production of this specific form of sovereignty, it should be equally unsurprising that so many discussions of sovereignty work very hard to forestall intimations of vertigo.

Recent literatures focus especially on strategies for engaging with the general conditions under which modern claims about sovereignty have been enabled to *work* so successfully: to work, that is, as a complex historically, culturally and socially constituted array of practices rather than as the simple thing that such practices work so energetically to affirm.[2] The claim that state sovereignty is historically constituted and must be understood as an historically variable practice is especially uncontroversial, even if an appreciation of historical practices has done little to disperse deeply entrenched assumptions about structural, logical or topological continuity, for reasons that cannot be reduced to the specific demands of Cold War scholarship.

Sovereignty, as Hobbes already knew, is a very odd phenomenon, a claim to absolute power/authority that was itself arbitrary, thinkable only in some thought experiment of a timeless world capable of switching instantly from natural condition to abstract principle in the shake of a utilitarian/Protestant calculation; thinkable, that is, on the basis of a claim about what must have been at the beginning predicated on quite radical assumptions about what the modern, free and equal, desiring man had already become. Sovereignty, Hobbes knew better than most, can never be simply *there*. It has to be put into practice in order to identify the character, location and legitimacy of political authority, especially the authority to judge what is authoritative. Moreover, as architect of the artifice, Hobbes seems especially sensitive to the frailty of his achievement.

A name is, after all, only a name, and is subject to patterns of differentiation that have no necessary relation to the differentiation of whatever is named.[3] Nominalism requires some authority to make the name stick, to guarantee the correct interpretation in the face of impending Babel. In

Hobbes' constitutive narrative about the constitution of politics, the sovereignty of the state was itself supposed to be the authority that made all names stick while resting only on the dubious guarantees of contract; a contract, moreover, that required a scarcely credible convergence of reason and fear to save proto-bourgeois individuals from their nightmares of unregulated competition. Translating an abstract social calculus first into an account of a supposedly natural but paradigmatically modern condition, and then apparently back into abstract sovereign law, Hobbes portrayed the sovereign state as the solution to all troubles, theological, ontological and political; or at least as the primary solution that would in turn permit other solutions through government and law. It was nevertheless a nominalist solution, one rooted ultimately in the arbitrary character of all names, a solution that is quite at odds with all those attempts to use Hobbes' own name to affirm the brute realities of political life or to save the achievements of modernity from those contemporary nominalists who have given up completely on whoever wound the clockwork. As Hobbes saw well enough, and others soon saw even more clearly, what legalese can put together, legalese can quickly tear apart. Absolute sovereignty slides into legitimate revolution. Absolute authority has itself no absolute ground to stand on. What counts is the degree to which people can be persuaded to underwrite the sovereign power, can be persuaded by the proper curriculum, by the proper religion, by civic education. Hobbes may have been an archetypal nominalist in this respect, but he was certainly more prescient than most about the need for names to perform: to work so as to prevent slippages in definition, to guarantee the point beyond which certainties of knowledge might otherwise start moving out of control, might start especially to creep along the line heading for infinity, away from the measurably known, out to some world beyond the world that might be mapped within the coordinates of modern (geo)metrics.

Few would dispute that sovereignties are rarely as structurally, logically or topologically tight as their practices would have us believe. Sovereignties fall apart in the always potential contingency of everyday life. Even the most absolute sovereign authority has unintended consequences. What can go wrong often does. The unanticipated happens. Rationalities breed irrationalities. Lines take flight. Corruptions ensue. Times take their toll. Subjectivities perform themselves differently. Familiarity breeds contempt. Lives out-manoeuvre those who live them. Transgressions shift as well as sustain the norm. Variations on these well worn themes resound in many contemporary literatures.

Then other familiar themes return. What makes the performance of sovereignty credible if it has no essential or unchanging form? How can such a historically variable performance retain at least some family resemblance to the old accounts of sovereignty associated with Bodin, Hobbes and the Treaty of Westphalia? After pressing for greater sensitivities to sovereignty as a historical and contingent practice, suspicions recur that a great many sovereign performances seem to occur in a theatre that has seen versions of the play many times before. Questions about structure return to haunt assertions of historicity, and to enable opposing accounts of political life to masquerade as a singular tradition of political realism. In particular, the structural conditions of modernity as a historically specific obsession with historicity, or as a historical formation founded on the claims of a sovereign subjectivity, come to be suspected of enabling the performances that so many analysts prefer to insist cannot be reduced to the unchanging codes embodied in canonical texts and treaties. While sovereignties may work as genealogically constituted and reconstituted performances, their very performativity often seems to be enabled by the constitutive claim of modern forms of state sovereignty to be able to express a specific form of subjectivity, the subjectivity that is at once always potentially universal, but which always finds its home in a specific space, whether territory, institution or body.

Moreover, sovereignty has enabled a variety of institutions and practices through which to save the claim that all particularities can indeed be reconciled, that the regulative ideals of modern political life might be sustained despite all contingencies, and despite all confirmations of Fortuna's wiles and Murphy's Law. Claims about the formal equality of both individuals and states serve as a regulative and legitimizing principle despite obvious disparities of wealth and power. Federalisms, devolutions and regional organizations provide spaces in which the sharp edges of state sovereignty are dispersed across a gradient from centre to periphery. Spatially conceived distinctions between public and private spheres, or urban and rural jurisdictions, or the architectures of institutions and public spaces, make the transitions seem smooth and seamless. These solutions, it is said, are precisely spatial rather than historical, structural rather contingent.

Moreover, for all their apparent seamlessness within horizontal and territorial jurisdictions, spatialities are organized hierarchically. Private is subordinate to public, though in an age of global capital this is subject to interesting reversals. The global city is a contradiction in terms, or at least an experience that does very odd things to our understanding of local government. Social movements are supposed to be small events among the many small events that push interests upward to the great sovereign power. Subnational provinces/states are supposed to be clear about the hierarchical rules governing their allocation of national tax receipts: no foreign embassies, no armed forces, no pretence to national security. Inequalities have been recalibrated but not eliminated. The twin sirens at either end of this spatially organized hierarchy are clear enough. One can go down to the local, the regional, the small, the weak, the individual; or up to the EU, NAFTA or ASEAN, to the international/global, and eventually to the human. And in going up or down, in or out, contingency meets order, temporality meets spatiality. The puzzle of reconciling spatiality and temporality is already expressed through the historically specific structural reconciliation of spatiality and temporality affirmed in the practices of modern sovereignty. It is thus not difficult to see why one would not want to look too closely at what

Hobbes already knew to be a very strange beast indeed. Better to repeat the mantras about man, state and system of states, about the hierarchical organization of contradictions laid out horizontally, about the simple reality and necessity of a world we now imagine Hobbes imagining not so very long ago.

Nevertheless, even the limited range of literatures I have invoked so far suggests a need to look more carefully at the specific practices through which sovereignty has been enabled by the authorization of singular authorities: that is, in relation to processes in which the formulations systematized by Hobbes arrived late rather than started early; or at the specific practices through which the paradoxical character of sovereignty already expressed by Hobbes and delineated so sharply by Schmitt, whereby what is sovereign is final, what is final is sovereign, and the rule "lives off the exception," is largely (though never completely) obscured; or at the routines through which secular claims to sovereignty reproduce the authorizations of specific theological, linguistic and philosophical traditions that should have us digging among Homeric and Hebrew myths of origin, pondering Plato's brilliant aggregation of specific things under universal nouns, unravelling the early-modern accounts of a self-founding subjectivity informing Kant's politics of modern finitude, following the ways in which puzzles about origins are read into, or out of, more metaphysically defined puzzles of temporality and more prosaically messy practices of memory and forgetting, or collating counter-disciplinary accounts of how myths of creation generate specific discourses about creativity, change, evolution, revolution, eternal return and the emancipation of masters and slaves. There is more than enough scope to pursue claims about sovereignty into frustratingly elusive discussions about the origins of modern accounts of origins and the paradoxes of self-authorization under conditions of structural/ historical necessity, as well as to engage with their broad and contradictory resonances with the specific ontologies of space, time and subjectivity mobilized by the likes of Hobbes, Kant, Weber and Schmitt.[4]

Moreover, challenges to these practices also have to be understood in relation to the many different modalities in which different people and social practices now use and mobilize the resources enabled by claims to sovereignty in specific contexts. Modern accounts of sovereignty as a convergence upon a singular presence/present have long encouraged counter-narratives about the possibility of a singular alternative, the famous stories about Enlightenment and Counter-Enlightenment as well as about the need for sovereign authority to be seized by some other, more progressive Subject of History or about the future absence of sovereign authority that will eventually result from the unfolding of History. Grand narratives about practices of resistance and emancipation have been constructed in these terms,[5] terms that have come to seem like games played according to rules constituted by the most powerful, thereby ensuring that the less powerful are invariably disabled, co-opted, and easily tolerated. Some of what remains of "progressive" or "leftist" political aspiration still remains nostalgic for such narratives, with their heroic tales of the universal class, the common front and the potentially hegemonic counter-hegemony, even while people struggling to improve their lives under situations of duress might suspect that emancipation is likely to be a more elusive matter. Some analysts are drawn to unsettle received accounts of historical and philosophical/theological necessity. Others are drawn to examine much more precisely how peoples, movements and institutions are drawn to recast practices of sovereignty, often under experiences of quite immediate necessity. Questions about how sovereignty works, rather than simply is as the grand narratives say it is, are far from being the exclusive preserve of the theorists and intellectuals of political life.

Without venturing much further in any of these quite daunting scholarly directions, however, and without attempting to reproduce the precise philosophical reasoning that informs various critical literatures or the sharp differences they express, it is possible to distinguish four overlapping themes that have begun to be prised apart with increasing scholarly force in many recent literatures, and which I have sought to introduce less directly in the preceding analysis. Sovereignty, I will suggest first, can be understood as a problem, one that may or may not have universal resonance, but which certainly exceeds the simple equation of sovereignty with the accounts of modern state sovereignty. It is, second, a problem that has been posed in historically and culturally specific ways, as the usual stories about the shift from theological to secular authorities in early-modern Europe suggest most obviously. As such, and third, it has also received historically and culturally specific responses; the achievements of Bodin, Hobbes, Kant and so on are precisely achievements of people struggling to resolve massive historical and structural problems on the basis of profound intellectual and cultural innovations shaped by many determinate and indeterminate forces. Finally, these responses have found expression and embodiment in diverse claims of principle, institutionalized interests and forms of political practice. All call for much more extensive analysis than I can provide here. Nevertheless, to start with these four, it will be clear, is immediately to see the possibility of distinctions and classifications proliferating to an unmanageable level; the ease with which various scholarly literatures can nevertheless become entirely absorbed by very limited framings of what sovereignty involves; and how some of the ways in which we are encouraged to unravel the primary dimensions and tensions of modern politics innocently express the spatiotemporal discriminations authorized by the practices of modern sovereignty.[6]

Each of these themes offers almost unlimited scope for the kinds of detailed analysis that thrive in the contemporary division of intellectual labour. It is not difficult to imagine various readers asking why I do not say more about one category or another, or why some phenomena are included in one category rather than another, or why the sequence unfolds in a particular way. This is, indeed, the point of even such a limited exercise. What does come first? What does come last? What is therefore enabled in between? What enables the search for a sensible middle ground between entirely contingent extremes? How has a particular inscription of what counts as ground become a middle, a norm enabling contingent accounts of first and last to seem so necessary, as apparently natural as the lines, points, or moments at which contingent necessities affirm necessities and contingencies, securities and liberties, friends and enemies, moderns and their others?

In each case, it is difficult to look beyond the professionalized horizons that identify specific expressions of modern sovereignty, especially those that identify sovereignty with the sovereignty of modern states. In each case, also, it is often tempting to treat sovereignty as an achieved condition, as a thing, a reality that can and must be taken for granted; tempting, not least, because this is in large part what modern narratives about sovereignty have been so effective at affirming, thereby enabling powerful stories about the eternal presence or impending absence of the sovereign state and system of sovereign states that work so forcefully as a principle, institution and practice of presence and absence. Conversely, is it not difficult to imagine various ways in which it might be possible to work through the historical relation between, and mutual production of, several of the various expressions of modern state sovereignty I tentatively identify. Even to begin to examine the concept of sovereignty in such a crude and preliminary way is certainly sufficient to become increasingly puzzled by any claim about what sovereignty is. As a historical production, as a problem, and as a response to a problem that also generates subsequent problems, sovereignty is especially resistant to attempts to identify it as a thing, rather than as a highly variable practice that nevertheless works by generating its own appearance as a thing delimiting the spatiotemporal contexts in which things happen and also effacing any sense of its own production. Tricky stuff, sovereignty, as the metaphysicians will already insist, but also as the theorists of contemporary political practice are increasingly compelled to recognize once again.

To begin with, so to speak, sovereignty can be understood to be a problem, or rather a massive complexity of problems concerning the authorization of authority. Political theorists know this primarily as the problem of founding, the authorization of a discrimination between before and after that works as the ground on which to authorize all other discriminations. Others refer to myths of origin: to *Genesis* as genesis, to zero and nakedness, to noise before silence and silence before noise. "In the beginning was the word, and the word came with God, and the word was God."[7] This is a problem that is sometimes framed in a form of utopian speculation (Plato's *Republic* is perhaps the standard example, with Aristotle's teleology as our most familiar example of how origins are then enabled to proceed), sometimes as an urgently practical matter (as with Machiavelli and the republican tradition in general, as well as with constitutional theorists of all kinds), and sometimes as a more or less abstract puzzle featuring some kind of infinite regression or analytic of finitude that is solved by defining the limits enabling calculation, as with Hobbes' story of a supposed – both necessary and impossible – shift from a state of nature to a state of society and the resort to the foundational law of nature "by which man is forbidden to do that which is destructive of his life."[8]

It is in this sense that there is always a politics to the authorization of politics, an ultimately groundless ground, a resort to theology, or ontotheology, a demand for justification that cannot be finally justified.[9] It is in this sense that claims about the dangers of disappearing foundations in some postmodern world, or the insistence that we already have firm epistemological or methodological grounds on which to guarantee scholarly credibility in the analysis of sovereignty and its effects, seem so absurd. It is difficult to make much sense at all of what we call modern politics without coming to terms with the profound but never complete rejection of prepolitical foundations, whether of heavenly law, natural law or imperial law. This was the rejection that required the reframing of the problem of sovereignty on new, secular, terms, often with a lingering appeal to the God or Nature that had been put outside, like the cat or dog that nevertheless affirms a world of domesticity, but an appeal that had to be made in the face of intransigent separations, of radical dualisms, and of the eventually decisive prioritization of sovereign authority within and among modern states. Nakedness and silence are indeed very tricky matters, but attempts to associate disappearing foundations with some passing of modernity rather than with the very possibility of modernity are simply disingenuous; indeed quite outrageous. Perhaps some sovereign authority might be invoked to put a stop to it.

It is in relation to claims that sovereignty has to be understood as a problem that the critical literatures become most philosophically intense. They are forced to confront ways in which modern claims about sovereignty express ontological claims about being and becoming, being and non-being, and all the other apparently metaphysical or theological conceits that quickly drive most political actors, and analysts, to the nearest bar, or to dismiss arcane debates about "theory" as having nothing to do with "the real world." Yet there are always moments in political life – the state of emergency, the state of war, the demand for some shift in the supposed balance between liberty and security, the demand that the excluded accept the rules of inclusion before any claim to difference can be reconciled with any claim to a voice in the world – when claims about ultimate ontologies, about life and death, about being and belonging, become matters of immediate and dramatic policy. The enemy is evil, they may cry, while worrying little about the deeply problematic ontologies – or theologies – they enact and unleash. You must lay down your life for us, they will demand, while hoping that not too many people will call for long discussions about the grounds on which the boys from the boondocks are ordered to kill for the collective good. We were here first, they will assert, as claims to indigeneity, nationalist bloodlines, and the interpretation of religious and constitutional texts work their way through courts, schools, football grounds, military postures and the micro-cultures of the street and fast-food stall.

The problem of sovereignty is intensely difficult. It is not going to go away; unless, perhaps, in a very different understanding of a Kantian regulative ideal, we imagine a world with no origins, no limits, no discriminations enabled by accounts of origin and limit, and no authorizations authorized to discriminate. On the other hand, it may be that it is a problem that does not always have to be posed, or answered, in the same way. It may be that the kinds of discriminations, authorizations and exceptionalisms that are expressed in the canonical narratives about international relations are far more contingent than these narratives would have us believe. Hobbes and Schmitt may not be the last word on how we ought to be thinking about sovereignty as a problem, and the ontological resources on which they drew so as to understand what the problem involved may not be the only ones we might draw on now. Our possibilities may exceed the stories of possibility we have come to tell ourselves in relation to the sovereign claims of the modern state.

Given the improbable sustainability of an account of sovereignty grounded in the groundless ground of a story about the exceptional character of a modern world distinguished from all spatiotemporal others, and the even greater improbability that authoritative practices of discrimination in space and time will disappear so as to make all questions about politics, or indeed human existence, simply irrelevant, it seems most likely that other possibilities will take flight from contestations and negotiations among multiple claims about origins and limits. The world started neither in 1648, nor in the modern authorization of a discrimination between modernity and all its others, despite the way the totalizing spatiotemporalities of modern subjectivity tell us that this was indeed where we must look for the origins of contemporary possibilities and impossibilities. Accept Hobbes' assumptions in this respect, however, and while we might play out endless variations, no other harmonies or rhythms, no other timings or spacings, are possible.

Consequently, it is possible to distinguish a specifically modern framing of the problem of sovereignty. While there may be many resonances between the accounts of political founding articulated by Plato and Aristotle and those given by the political writers of early-modern Europe, the collapse of the authority structures of Christianity and the rise of modern capitalist society posed distinctive problems and opportunities. The Greek *polis* is not the modern state, and Thucydides' account of the Peloponnesian War does not translate automatically into a theory of international relations. The specific problem of founding new principalities that drives Machiavelli's *Prince*, of creating something new in the face of divine perfection, is not just any old problem of politics as usual, but one that tells us a lot about the recourse to ancient resources in order to instantiate recognizably modern accounts of what it means to found.[10] Again the broad historical context here is both vast and contested, but the prevailing narratives tell us about the broad conditions under which the subsumption of political authority under some kind of theological authority, mediated by popes, emperors and associated agents of hierarchical subordination, was challenged by an ambivalently secular claim to authority on the part of agents claiming to be the highest source of authority on earth. Hobbes is the key figure in the articulation of modern political thought precisely because he was so much more clear-eyed about the necessities and limits, but also ambiguities, of a politics cut adrift from transcendental authority of any kind. It is this clarity that reappears in Schmitt's account of sovereignty as a capacity to declare an exception, to declare limits that enable the norms that might be suspended. This is a capacity that is a political theology not in the sense of a return to God, but in the sense of having the same structure as the metaphysics of authority that God was once supposed to have been: a political theology fit for an age in which secularized people cannot return to a condition of enchantment; a political theology, perhaps, that might preserve a politics of modernity but at the cost of a profoundly disturbing assault upon the ambitions of a specifically modern liberalism.

Thus it is also possible to distinguish the modern framing of what it must mean to provide a plausible answer to the problem of sovereignty, a framing that refers not only to a vast historical canvas, but also to specific early-modern preoccupations with the infinity of space, especially as these preoccupations were articulated by the geometrical and neo-Platonist traditions of Galilean science.[11] This is the general story of the articulation of modern subjectivities, the construction of modern individuals as precisely divisibles rather than the political, or communal, creatures envisaged in Aristotelian traditions: the story of modern thought as a struggle with the limits of human finitude. This is the story that celebrates Descartes' foundational subjectivities and geometrical lines, Pascal's account of man caught mid-way between the finite and infinite, and Kant's account of human maturity as the potential presence of the universal moral law enacted within the lives of mature individuals living within mature republics.

Hence, to stay with the classic texts on sovereignty, the force of Hobbes' claims about the political necessity of affirming a post-Thomist metaphysics, his ridicule of a (philosophically) realist (or essentialist) account of language in favour of a radical nominalism, and his assertion of a specific account of space, time and subjectivity as the only possible, or at least only reasonable, ground on which to frame a story about reason, about freedom and necessity, about before and after, about life before politics and political life after the politics that enables a life of citizen-subjects. By far and away the most important part of the Hobbesian legacy for thinking about modern politics is his participation in the much broader construction of a modernity that understands itself as divided from, subsequent to, and having a potential that is much greater than, every possibility that it is not.

This participation is most evident in passages that can now seem entirely irrelevant to politics, in the passages about how the world must be carved up, must be understood, must be given voice. Tell everyone what it means to have authority, and to be the author of authority, and the task is almost over. Once this story is told, it can then be retold, and retold in terms already given by Hobbes' insistence that modern space, modern time, and modern identity must be the only ground on which to discuss political necessity and its possible freedoms. These terms necessitate a systematic erasure of other accounts of space, time, identity and political possibility, the erasure that is itself effaced in the story of an imagined shift from the state of nature to the state of political subjectivity. The conditions under which a Kant can articulate some sense of how to envisage a new world of mature modern subjects, and insist on a critical philosophy conscious of the need to examine the conditions of the possibility of enlightened knowledge, have then been set. The hard work of articulating the grounds on which a modern politics might be grounded has been done. Simplistic appropriations of Enlightenment may then proceed to imagine a universality of formal rationality and to envisage a world of (pluralist, Romantic) difference within a broader world of inclusions and exclusions enabled by a prior narrative of inclusions and exclusions.

Finally, it is possible to distinguish the expression of this specific way of responding to the problem of sovereignty under specific historical conditions in a broad range of specific sites. This is where the threat of proliferating categories can most easily run out of control and relations between categories become difficult to capture within the disciplinary strategies of modern scholarship. As a somewhat arbitrary, but also largely predictable, attempt to stem the multiplication, however, a dozen key expressions seem especially significant: perhaps because they may recall the arbitrary marking of hours on the conventional spatiotemporal image of the circle that expands from a point; perhaps because they may recall the twelve "rights of sovereignes" once enumerated by Hobbes himself;[12] and perhaps because intimations of both contingency and order are so crucial to the fixing of modern sovereignties on a grid of points and lines. In any case, all open up various ways of thinking about sovereignty as a problem that has been posed and in some sense resolved in powerful modern accounts of possibility and impossibility. Just a brief indication of some of the lines of analysis that might be opened up in this context offers at least a sense of what is involved when we simply assume that political life must occur within and between sovereign nation-states and that political life has always worked, and must continue to work, in the specifically twentieth-century conflation of the sovereign nation-state with the possibilities and limits of political life.

After midnight

First, we might examine the articulation of claims about sovereignty in relation to the modern state, an articulation once requiring the capacity to carry the enormous ontological responsibility of resolving grand puzzles about human finitude, of replacing the angels as markers of the margins (and thus centres) of temporal existence. Beginnings have been fixed, limits have been produced, monopolies of authority have been affirmed, in principle even if not always in practice, eventually even if not in the twinkling of some Hobbesian imagination. Sovereignty has been reshaped from multiple sources to become almost unthinkable in any other context. In the European versions of this process, at least, Hobbes can then take his retrospective place as the most crucial theorist of modern politics, while Schmitt can remind us of what is at stake in this account of beginnings and endings expressed at the limits of the sovereign state.

This articulation expresses a multiple resolution of the relation between universality and diversity, one articulated inside in relation to the individual subject, one articulated outside by the statist subject, and one worked out by a system of statist subjects aware of some other world beyond the bounds of modern reason. This resolution works as a distribution of potential freedoms in space and a teleology of potential freedoms in time, in both cases working towards the internalization of political possibility, the achievement of freedom *within* necessity *and* necessity *within* freedom. In this way we are brought to engage with characteristic attempts to derive definitions of sovereign authority and rights (and thus the legal status of any particular state as a legitimate actor in the system of states) from the claimed empirical attributes of any particular state, on the one hand, or from the willingness of other sovereign states to recognize the empirical attributes of any particular state as legitimately sovereign, on the other; and, in either the endogenous or exogenous case, of the constitutive effects of the legal rights to define upon all those empirical processes used to define what counts as a properly sovereign authority having rights.[13]

Second, we might engage with the problematic relation between the claim to state sovereignty and those other claims to authority that have been pushed outside but then brought inside under new conditions, reconstituted through a double process of exclusion from and subordination to the claims of the sovereign state. Thus secularization supposedly effected a separation between the transcendent authority claimed by the church and the secular authority claimed by the state, but while states claimed sovereign authority over church, the inscription of political authority was partly or even largely shaped by discourses of theological authority.[14] As regulative ideal or as practice of legitimation, as genealogical consequence or as metaphorical transference, as sociological effect or as ontotheological echo, claims to religious authority retain presence even as absence while working as absence, so as to affirm the presence of a sovereign state. The pattern varies, of course, especially as the specific traumas of secularization in Europe resonate less with the traumas of state formation elsewhere, but claims about a sharp distinction between state sovereignty and some other transcendent authority, understood in religious or perhaps mythical terms, are generally difficult to sustain. Schmitt's attempt to articulate a specifically political theology in secular terms, the characteristic attempts by statist authorities to appeal to the supplementary authority of sacred texts and institutions, and various attempts to subordinate secular political authority to some "higher" truth, all speak to the unsettled character of state sovereignty as a claim to the monopoly on authority in this respect.

Much the same can be said about those other sites that were explicitly excluded as a condition for a properly modern inclusion, the nature or humanity that lie outside the modern framing of subject and world, or subject and nature, or subject and citizen, but which can then be identified as the problematic other of the modern subject on terms given by the modern subject. To come into modernity, into the modern sovereign state, is to leave something out, a something to be experienced as loss or desire (as a mere phenomenon to be known only through categories brought by the knowing subject, in terms of Kantian epistemology, as the always unknowable other of the exotic in terms of the politics of alterity, as the never recoverable loss of enchantment in terms of Weberian discourses of modernization, as the unreachable guarantee of infinity, good or evil in terms of the workings of a politics of finitude), but always as a potential for some other authority. The presence and absence expressed by the modern sovereign state itself expresses the presence and absence of some other world. Opting for immanence, it might be said, does little to resolve a dualism of immanence and transcendence; though refusals of the dualism of immanence and transcendence that modern political life inherited and rescripted from specifically Christian traditions may well be a condition for any possibility of thinking about authority and the authorization of authority in some other way than is recorded in the standard stories of the emergence of the modern sovereign state.

Cities, too, were also gradually brought in and subordinated to a higher authority. Now cities are home to half of humanity. They energize forms of cosmopolitanism that are arguably much richer than those playing out narratives about the impending demise of the sovereign state. Many cities dwarf many states. Many express the greatest concentration of population and power within the states in which they are located. They are networked in ways that stimulate claims about the disappearance of boundaries, and they are often said to be the source of the most dynamic attempts to reimagine where and what political life might be.[15] Nevertheless, the prevailing traditions of political theory and theories of international relations still assume that cities are where and what they are supposed to be, at considerable cost, I would say, to their claims to scholarly credibility.

Third, we might engage with the problematic relation between the claim to state sovereignty and the authorities that have been cultivated largely within (even if pre-dating) the modern state, but that seek to expand their reach outside it. The claim to the universal and universalizing value of the capitalist market is especially significant in this respect. The juridical model of the sovereign state outlined by Hobbes was already caught up in processes pushing for what can reasonably be called the sovereign capacity of capital as the abstract value flowing from (and as Marx would later insist, subsequently working against) labour, so as generate, also paradoxically, the conversion of passions into the self-interest that generates apparently common interests.[16] As a story of founding, John Locke's cute narrative about the legitimacy of private property in a world that has been given to mankind in common may not have quite have the reach among political theorists of the story told by Hobbes, but in an age of powerful founding mythologies, it certainly ranks as among the most consequential.[17] Extremist accounts of the primacy of capital, and the self-constituting and self-regulating capacities of the margin (and its "derivatives") have not exactly had any less traumatic consequences than extremist accounts of the primacy of states and the self-constituting and self-regulating capacities of the exception. A lot of lines have been drawn in both cases.

Read as what has come to be called an international political economy, the claim to the sovereignty of market value may be understood as either subservient to, or hegemonic over, the claims of the sovereign state, depending on whether what we now call the political or the economic are understood to be determinate "in the last instance," as it was once said.[18] Read as what many insist is a globalizing political economy, the claim to market value, with all the productions, commodifications, discriminations, authorizations and exceptionalisms these entail, is more obviously antagonistic to – and might even be expected to result in the "withering away" of – the claims of the sovereign state. They are antagonistic most especially when, in claims about the explicitly globalizing character of contemporary economic life, both the sovereign state and the system of sovereign states are understood to be acting within a global economy, to be in a condition of immanence in relation to the transcendent authority of the market: an authority that might even be seen as having its own aura of divinity.

That it has proved to be almost impossible to imagine a political economy that does not lapse into a privileging of the political or the economic, and the valorization of the other as mere epiphenomenon, is an expression of the radical divergence between the two primary narratives about the source of ultimate value, of sovereign authority, that emerged from the collapse of feudal/theological authority in early-modern Europe. Yet while reconciliation of claims to a political sovereignty expressed in relations to a sovereign state and a sovereign people, and claims to a sovereignty of capital expressed through a logic of exchange in a competitive market, may have proved to be analytically troublesome, much of the history of the modern state centres on the way in which such a reconciliation has been achieved in practice. In this respect, narratives about mercantilism, the success of neo-Keynesian strategies of regulation, social-democratic understandings of collective welfare, and statist strategies of "development from above" all affirm the formal priority of a sovereignty understood in political terms, while allowing for suspicions that economy is a name for something that is at least as powerful and authoritative and just as capable of exercising sovereign decision over life and death as any sovereign state.

Nevertheless, that claims about the sovereignty of capital as a globalizing process find it so difficult to articulate any account of what it would mean to constitute a form of politics other than that predicated on the claims of sovereign states is an expression of the degree to which, for all that, the sovereignty of capital has been able to find some place within the state and states system, claims arising from the ownership of private property, the extraction of surplus value from people's labour, the conversion of all values into an abstract even if rationally universal price, and the capacity of some to accumulate wealth more easily than others, provides a very flimsy ground on which to articulate a plausible account of a desirable collective existence.[19] The shifts away from neo-Keynesian accommodations between state and market towards more forthright celebrations of a globalizing market that shaped so much political practice from the early 1970s to the retrenchments of 2008 may have expressed a profound reprioritization of sources of value and authority in this respect, but to the extent that they might have signalled some reinvigoration of political imagination, this was largely limited to the erosion of statist constraints on the automatic operation of market mechanisms understood as the primary origin, and limit, of political authority. Accounts of freedom in a capitalist market may well have shaped practices of sovereign authorization in economies that have, in turn, shaped the possibilities and limits of statist forms of politics, but they can hardly be said to have enabled any gripping alternative to accounts of political life that assume communities of individuals within states within a system of states.

Again, much the same can be said about other claims to authority that have emerged within the modern sovereign state, not least in relation to what is generally called civil society. Like capital, civil society was ultimately nurtured within statist authority, sometimes affirming specifically republican accounts of what a sovereign state should be, and sometimes struggling to draw a line between – set limits to – state sovereignty and popular sovereignty, public and private authority, and so on. As with capital, also, it is possible to entertain questions about temporal and authoritative priority, about which came first, which is ultimately more real or authentic, and which is, or ought to be, the site of political aspiration and authority now. Thus claims about the contemporary priority of the market in an era of globalization are now shadowed by similar claims about the necessity of establishing some kind of global civil society as the necessary condition of a new politics fit for an age in which sovereign states are disappearing, claims that similarly have difficulty engaging with questions about sovereign authority that statist accounts of civil society could assume were already settled. In this sense, the concept of global civil society can be read as a site of conceptual incoherence legitimizing liberal refusals to acknowledge the political limits of modern liberalism, though it may perhaps also be read as a site at which it might be possible to articulate some other understanding of political limits and collective authorization.[20]

Fourth, we might examine the articulation of the territorial extension of the sovereign territorial state, the convergence between *nomos* and space, law and land, authority and terrestrial jurisdiction: the space between beginning and end, and thus between a monopolistic centre and a spatiojuridical limit. In this context, we necessarily engage with the cross of modernity as it is articulated as if on a more or less flat horizontal space: both the line of separation of self/here and other/there, and the line of discrimination between self/here and other/there, *polis* and *polis*, norm and exception; but also the line of connection between self/here and other/there, this space and that space, the line that is at once the limit of one beginning and the beginning that must have another limit, another end, thereby producing a circle moving through a system of beginnings and endings that, as a space of horizontal territorialities, is usually assumed to have put an end to worlds written cyclically quite as much as they put an end to worlds written hierarchically. Some lines do go on a bit, even though linearity does not necessarily guarantee the shortest distance between points.

This articulation involved the delineation of geographical or geophysical place in terms of an abstract Euclidean space. It is analysed primarily in literatures in political geography and geopolitics,[21] but also in relation to the visual codes of modern representation in space and the parallels between the articulation of spatialized states and the articulation of spatialized accounts of private property. This articulation also involved what amounts to a novel form of global population control,[22] a systematic distribution of people in general to territorial spaces in particular, thereby generating tricky puzzles about how the spatialized elegance of the system of states was achieved in the face of competing forces,[23] why the universalizing claims of modern liberalism do not include the right to move anywhere,[24] as well as binary discourses about the limits of political possibility framed in terms of security and danger externally and citizenship and belonging internally, and thus the susceptibility of immigrants and refugees to practices of securitization and exceptionalism.[25] This capacity to fix space according to the cruciform coordinates of modernity enables both movement within space and the structuring of a time within space, a (paradigmatically Kantian) reworking of a classical teleology within the coordinates and containments of sovereign jurisdiction. But space is not always fixed so easily, although it is the spatial form of the modern sovereign state that encourages so much hope in our prevailing narratives of escape.[26] The boundaries imposed upon place in the name of an abstract space are as contingent as claims about those origins whose retrospectively imagined teleology is supposedly captured within an abstract space. The map is not the territory, though it does tell us what it must mean to think about territoriality. The territory is not the place, though accounts of territory do tell us how to understand the relation between place and place. The place is not the world, even though in knowing place rather than the map or territory we may be persuaded that we can finally touch the world as such. The form is not the substance, even though form itself may be read as substance. Nevertheless, the sovereignty of the modern state has come to work as a claim to territorial jurisdiction, and the relation between state sovereignty and the claims of the system of states is conventionally reconciled as an injunction not to undermine any other state's capacity to sustain its claim to such jurisdiction.

With sovereignty associated with the state, more or less dissociated from all competing claims to authority, and instantiated in the world by a claim to be situated on the world as territorial jurisdiction, as the convergence of limits in law and limits in a particular kind of space, we might move on to consider the relationship between claims to sovereignty and that so far strangely absent set

of creatures, human beings, people of flesh, blood and some sort of life. Many
might even start here, partly because modern state sovereignty is supposed to be
a popular sovereignty, in the sense that it expresses what eighteenth-century
writers were fond of calling the will of the people, and partly because accounts
of state sovereignty can also be told in terms of the constitution of a particular form of people, and persons, the modern subject in relation to whom
early-modern thinkers were able to imagine a people as individuals expressing
a collective will. Thus, *fifth*, we might examine the articulation of a deeply
problematic relationship between state sovereignty and individual subjectivity,
the relationship between and across the great fracture zone of the modern
domestic body-politic: the relationship between the modern self-constituting
subject aspiring to autonomy and the external conditions that enable, delimit
and always threaten this potential autonomy. In this context we are especially
presented with the framing of modern politics as a puzzle of relating the
macro-sovereignty of the state with the micro-sovereignty of individuals, a
puzzle resolved through practices of popular sovereignty understood as an
expression of collectivity, community, nationality, society, the body as well as
the will of the people, and so on, or as an expression of the particularity of
individuated bodies and the representation of the micro in the macro through
specific institutions of democracy.

This is the context in which the great success stories of modern politics are
usually celebrated: stories about the reconciliation of our claims to be both
free/autonomous individual/collective subjects, and yet also subject to the
ultimate authority of that sovereign that expresses our authentic (modern,
male, adult, human) subjectivity. Hobbesian traditions tell these stories as a
reconciliation through external imposition, as the civic freedoms possible for
modern subjects under the externally articulated though internally legitimized
laws of the sovereign state. Kantian traditions tell them more insistently as a
reconciliation through the internalization of reason within, through conscience, through the acknowledgement of the universal moral law by subjects
capable of subjectivity, capable of thinking for themselves while nevertheless
obeying and doing freely what they nevertheless have to do. Meanwhile,
Rousseauean traditions bring out the stark contradictions involved in any
claim that sovereignty involves the expression of some general will constituted,
or not, by individual subjects.

Although most of these success stories affirm the achievements of reconciliation, of the convergence of macro and micro, of external law and internal
conscience, of public solidarity and private autonomy and all the rest, the
possibility of radical rupture remains the always potential possibility. Go too
far in the direction of the micro, celebrate sovereign subjectivity, individual
conscience and self-interest, and politics dissolves in favour of various other
"values." Go too far in the direction of the macro, celebrate the sovereign
nation-state as the condition of possibility of sovereign subjectivities, and an
always potentially Schmittean nationalism beckons. Consequently, the claims
of modern political life are frequently expressed in terms of some sort of

balance, of some middle ground between the claims of state and subject, public and private, political and civil. Moreover, given that sovereignty and subjectivity can be reconciled only inside the sovereign state, questions about subjectivity tend to be of little interest to those concerned with political life external to the sovereign state, and arise only in relation to questions about how individual "personalities," or heroic "statesmen," or individual "ideas" or "perceptions" can sometimes "influence" the making of "foreign policy." Nevertheless, the practices of sovereign authority can always be made to work through drawing the line, demarcating the exception, defining the limit expressing the possibility of individual freedom under statist necessity, whether through juridical procedure or biopolitical resistance. In the meantime, forms of political life that do not quite fit into this particular (domestic) framing of micro and macro (towns and cities perhaps most obviously) are gradually squeezed out of contention.

The possibility of reconciling universality and particularity within the particular realm of the modern state is thereby affirmed, primarily in the name of the nation as the social and cultural form through which micro and macro are unified through a process of inclusion and exclusion, whether as an expression of something almost but never completely national or of something almost but never completely invented.[27] For however complex and bloody the historical sociology required to explain the rise of modern nationalism, its logic has followed impeccably in the traces of state sovereignty. The nation literally fills in the space made available by a sovereign territoriality, and affirms the unity of a singular people. Sometimes nations assume they have indeed attained the status of God's chosen people; sometimes they assert that they are precisely different from those nations that claim to be God's chosen people; and sometimes they are content to merely assert their specificity, their difference, their special cultural individuality in the great universal/particular family of nations. Moreover, once filling the space of sovereign territoriality, the dynamics of modern nationalism produce an account of history and temporality, of invented tradition, that fits into this space as well. Nationalistically intransigent readings of the implications of the early-modern trade-off between humanity and citizenship have often been treated simply as the barbaric voice of a reactionary militarism, and such intransigence undoubtedly still permits a barbaric militarism to thrive. It is also a blunt acknowledgement, the bad conscience of modern liberalism, that the great modern trade-off between humans and citizens, the constitution of the modern state as the territorial home in which citizens may indeed develop into properly human and properly rational beings, has distinct limits and enormous potential costs.

Both nationalist and internationalist readings of state sovereignty build upon assumptions about essentially homogeneous communities bounded in territorial space, whether as assertive nations or as rational autonomous republics/democracies. They depend upon a combination of dangerous affirmations, claims that the only possible subject of security is the nation/state guaranteeing citizenship, and excluded subjectivities, claims that all identities other than that of the universal man embodied in the principle, institution and practice of state sovereignty are literally rendered unspeakable in expressions of nationalist or statist solidarity.[28] Claims about danger set up our dominant narratives about the subject who is to be secured, the object of a security policy that is ostensibly pointed outwards. Excluded subjectivities provide our narratives about our freedom within and under necessity, our liberty under law, our democratic practices operating within the boundaries of dangerous affirmation. The exception enables the norm, the norm requires the exception; liberty and security thereby dance together though they are booked into the modern academy as stubbornly solo acts.

This is an entrenched theme of modern security analysis. Many of the concerns of modern political realism, for example, might be traced back to Max Weber's paradigmatic worries that the established privileges of the Junkers aristocrats, combined with the slow emergence of a middle class able to sustain a properly German nationalism, might open Germany to an unfortunate influx of Polish peasants from the east.[29] Conversely, much of the confidence of the political realists writing in the mid-twentieth century came from their observation that socialist aspirations for class struggle and cross-national solidarity had quickly melted in the face of the nationalist mobilizations of 1914. If massive solidarities among the working classes could not smash the solidarities of patriotic nationalisms, it seemed reasonable to conclude, no other articulation of identities and solidarities would be up to the task in any imaginable future.

Sixth, we might examine the articulation of a problematic relationship between the sovereignty of the singular state and the system of sovereign states that is the condition of possibility of any singular sovereign state: the relationship between and across the great fracture zone between the sovereign nation-state assumed by political theory and the fragmented system that is the focus of the theory of international relations. This is where I started posing questions about what it might mean to reimagine where and what politics must be, for despite all talk about the problematic status of modern accounts of individual subjectivity and nation-states, it is arguably in this context that the limits of a specific form of political possibility articulated within and beyond very specific limits have come to have the most sustained consideration in analyses of changing forms of global order.

In this context, we are confronted with the framing of modern politics as a puzzle of reconciling the micro-sovereignty of particular states with what might be called the macro-sovereignty of the states system, a macro-sovereignty that is sometimes said to express an even "higher" authority than the sovereignty of states because it is larger in scale and thus presumed to be more universal. Starting from the direction of the sovereign state, we can move through narratives about the primacy of a singular territorial authority, the idealization of the self-determining – autonomous, nationalist – singularity generating power-driven and self-interested foreign policies that, in turn, generate the security dilemmas and tragic anarchies celebrated as the realistic condition of the "international state of nature." Starting from the direction of the system of sovereign states, we can move through narratives about the primacy of the structural logic of a states system that might be condemned for its ordered disorder (the abstract idealization of modern freedom/equality as a pluralist anarchy), celebrated for its ordered disorder (the abstract idealization of modern freedom/anarchy as a pluralist internationalism), or tolerated for its impure and disorderly orders (the idealization of the "great" or hegemonic powers shouldering the responsibility of sustaining an international in the absence of the idealized freedom/equality assumed by the anarchical and international options).

Going up, there are limits to the "greatness" hegemonic powers can achieve before they render ideals of a free and equal anarchy/ international implausible and trigger fears of incipient empire. Going out, the limits of the claims of the sovereign state expressed as a capacity to decide exceptions to the norms expressed within eventually meet the limits of the claims of a system of sovereign states expressed as a capacity to decide exceptions to the norms of proper systemic behaviour. Somewhere between the limits of state sovereignty and system sovereignty, and within the limits of hegemonies that must not collapse into empire, the contradictions of a modern national/international politics have generated rules and diplomacies of systemic organization. These have been understood either as an expression of collectivity, community, internationality, international society, the body of we the people/peoples of the United Nations; or as an expression of the particularity of individuated bodies expressing and representing the micro in the macro through specific institutions of foreign policy and national defence. Yet such practices bring corollary uncertainties about whether state sovereignty affirms, not least, a principle of non-intervention within the domestic affairs of other states or, on the contrary, requires those who claim to speak for the international system to intervene so as to preserve international "order" against the disruptions of any particular ("revolutionary," "rogue," "failed," "imperial") state, or to "recognize" whether any specific state's claim to sovereignty is in fact legitimate.

These are the limits Kant already anticipated in his engagement with the limits of a finite subjectivity, and which were given sharp expression in the contrast between Schmittean claims about sovereignty as a capacity to decide exceptions in relation to the law of a specific state, and Kelsenian claims about the status of international law. They are expressed in the double legitimation of international violence as the condition under which modern politics might be brought to some order: to attain peace, prepare for war (the nationalist option); or to attain peace, pursue war against those who are not properly modern, or developed, or democratic, so as to ensure that the freedom/equality of international anarchy might eventually become the freedom/ equality of an international community or society, even if the process demands action by hegemons who are always in danger of courting empire. They have been expressed most recently in relation to the forms of sovereign exceptionalism deployed after 2001 by the US Bush administration in ways that highlight longstanding tensions between the supposedly exceptional character of the USA as a hegemonic/unilateral/universalizing presence within an international/multilateral order and the systemic necessities of that order: forms of exceptionalism that expose the fragility of so many apparently well meaning attempts to frame questions about human rights or a more global politics in relation to specifically American intellectual and cultural traditions.[30]

Narratives rooted in assumptions of a radical dualism – of a political theory split from a theory of international relations, of a cosmopolitan or global justice read as the grand alternative to the law of the sovereign state – have come to work very effectively so as to minimize sustained engagements with the contradictory and aporetic character of this double legitimation, encouraging the constant reproduction of a linear philosophy of history and discourses about the presence/absence of the sovereign state. Still, while such narratives encourage readings of many contemporary trends in terms of claims about the primacy of one over the other (humanitarian intervention over state sovereignty, international human rights over state law, demands for solidarity in a "war against terror" over the niceties of the rule of law and multilateral diplomacy, and so on), it remains necessary to understand many such trends as renegotiations and still more renegotiations of competing claims between one and the other.

This is what has been at stake in debates about intervention in Bosnia and Rwanda, about the invasion of Iraq, and about the status of international human rights and a great many international institutions and functional regimes, debates that seem unlikely to fade away, still less to find resolution on one side of the aporia or the other. It is what has been at stake in debates about the degree to which patterns of economic globalization generate new forms of cultural and political resistance grounded in demands for some kind of (statist, nationalist) autonomy, and thus about what state and nation, or indeed community and identity, might mean under contemporary conditions. It is central to the ways (whether understood in Hobbesian, Kantian or more updated Foucauldian terms) in which sovereign states have sought to construct populations as governable citizen-subjects in the name of freedom while the system of sovereign states has sought to construct acceptable statist subjects in the name of national self-determination, and thus to the many difficulties that arise from attempts to imagine some form of government, governance or governmentality that might be applied to a global order in which the constitutive contradictions of modern political life are assumed to have become irrelevant.

Where most analyses of modern sovereignty focus primarily on the antagonisms between popular sovereignty and state sovereignty, and between state sovereignty and the system of sovereign states, it is also necessary to consider, *seventh*, the articulation of practices deemed applicable to those times, places and subjectivities in which modern sovereignty is expressed only as an absence. These are the times, places and subjectivities that, theories of modernization insist, must be brought back in from their exclusions from a modernity expressed in the sovereign state and system of sovereign states, even though that state and system work only because modern sovereignty affirms the necessity of exclusion. As with Hobbes' narrative about spatio-temporal origins constructed from an assumed present, or Kant's aspiration for a perpetual peace enabled by a distinction between the mature and the immature, claims about state sovereignty and the system of sovereign states work because they affirm an absence that guarantees their assumed presence.

It is easy enough to conclude that this is scarcely of any contemporary relevance. Surely modernization and globalization have proceeded apace. Surely we are all one humanity. Surely there is no longer an outside to modernity. Surely it is no longer legitimate for colonial states to intervene in their colonies just because the colonies are not yet mature enough to determine their own fate. Surely something needs to be done to bring all the stragglers into modernity, whether by "empire lite" or resort to the "lesser evil." Such assumptions of insignificance are no doubt entirely persuasive as long as linear accounts of history, and the self-affirmation of modernity as distinct from all its others, are taken for granted. More likely, it is of considerable significance; significant, that is, in conceptual, empirical and ethical terms, and now perhaps especially in terms of uncertainties about where the boundaries of the modern world are to be located, and how those boundaries now work.

It is significant in conceptual terms because, while claims about the problems and possibilities inherent in what we now call the international are usually understood in relation to a spatially defined pattern of conflict or anarchy, they must be understood first in terms of a specific temporality, a theory of history, as a process of internalization, of subjectivization, as the process of bringing the world into the world of the modern while excluding all other worlds. Attempts to think about "change" in this context invariably deploy claims about temporality against claims about a dominant spatiality, whereas the international already expresses an account of a temporality that enables claims about a spatiality. To try to think about what it might mean to envisage change is presumably to challenge a specific articulation of spatio-temporal relations, and not least the account of a linear and internalizing history that is at work in the modern international. Consequently, there are serious conceptual problems involved in trying to find a way "outside" of a modern politics that has been constituted through an ambition to bring the world "inside", while largely refusing to acknowledge the logical impossibility of a pure theory of internalization, or the futility of modernity as a purely immanent challenge to theological dualities of immanence and transcendence.

It is significant in more empirical terms because so much of humanity might plausibly be said to be outside the modern inside/outside the international. The story of modern politics is a story of a pattern of inclusion and exclusion within a modern system of states, within the international. We are all the same, as humanity, but all different, as members of different national cultures: We the people/peoples of the United Nations. But this story of inclusion/exclusion, universality and particularity has been possible only as a consequence of differentiating the modern from the non-modern, First World from Third World, and authorizing that differentiation through an appeal to a teleology of a universalizing history. Some people, we know all too well, are treated as not properly modern, even as not properly human. Some authorities, we also know all too well, have been quite prepared to invoke the name of humanity in order to render some humans as entirely inhuman, beyond the remit of the Geneva Conventions, for example. In this context, we might think about, say, those indigenous peoples who are driven to seek sovereignty over territory, but are encouraged to seek the kind of sovereignty expressed by the modern state that works precisely as a demand for inclusion in a specifically modern system of inclusions/exclusions;[31] or about cultural, ethnic and other sorts of communities that are encouraged either to emulate the nation state as the only serious political expression of cultural politicization or to find some subordinate status within an acceptable pattern of statist nationalisms;[32] or about those who are effectively marginalized as mere objects of state power rather than as citizens of states by virtue of their poverty and irrelevance to modern capitalist forms of production, distribution and exchange;[33] or about those who are effectively marginalized as negations of the officially sanctioned ideal of modern citizen understood as the universally rational man.

Add up the populations that are claimed to live within the jurisdictions of the modern international, and the claim that the international gives expression to the whole of humanity has some credibility. This is, after all, how the official statistics are organized. Engage in any more sophisticated calculation of who precisely gets to participate in the world of the modern international, however, and the picture is anything but clear-cut. The usual story is that eventually we will all get there, all will be included, all made properly modern citizens: that modernity will eventually trickle down in economic terms even if Kantian aspirations for a world of morally autonomous subjectivities is assumed to be a bit pie-in-the-sky. This is the temporal promise of modernization as universal history, and the source of the difficulty of imagining "alternatives" at the "periphery" of a spatialized international order that nevertheless has some kind of "centre."[34] Yet any story of inclusion implies a story of exclusion, both stories hinging on the authorization of discriminations, of decisions about who should be in and who should be out, and under what conditions. The official stories all tell tales of inclusion. But official stories about the inclusions of the sovereign state and system of sovereign states systematically erase the complex patterns of exclusion that have enabled official stories of inclusion. Perhaps one would not expect them to do anything else, but then we might also insist that analyses of political life hardly count as scholarly if they simply take the official stories at their word.

It is significant in more ethical terms precisely because historical forms of, and assumptions about, exclusion work so as to constitute specific forms of inclusion. The constitution of modern subjects who aspire to a Kantian form of autonomy as a regulative ideal may well express the most inspiring ambition of modern political life, but it is an aspiration that works not only within the limits of states within a system of ostensibly free and equal states, but also as a claim to historical and moral superiority over those who have been excluded. At the statist limits of Kantian ambition we meet the Schmittean exception, but also the systemic capacity to make exceptions that might keep such exceptions in check. Legal provisions may be derogated or suspended within the rule of law, but the rule of law may itself be suspended through a decision of the sovereign power that acts both within and without the law; but thus engages with the law enacted in the name of the system of states, which may nevertheless collapse into a state of war. So much is so familiar. It is at the systemic limits of Kantian ambition, however, that we meet all the residual – and constitutive – discriminations marking modernity as a self-affirming but necessarily parochial way of being in, but not of being coextensive with, the world. It is in this context, for example, that we might understand the rhetorical articulation of the so-called war on terror through temporal claims about development and the need to bring the barbarians into a properly modern world, quite as much as through spatial claims about friends and enemies within a modern system of states.[35]

To think about the sovereign declaration of exceptions in these terms is to take us into a much broader conceptual arena than is captured by the established opposition between a Schmitt and a Kelsen, or their contemporary imitators. The problem of the origins and limits of modern political life in time, posed by Machiavelli, meets the problem of origin and limits of modern political life in space, posed by Hobbes, and the convergence poses enormous problems for attempts to work out a story about the temporal development of the modern subject within spatial limits of the kinds we find in the trajectory that takes us from Kant to Weber to contemporary concerns about "what comes after the modern subject." Contemporary claims about new forms of imperialism and empire or a simple shift to some globalized exceptionalism are entirely inadequate in this respect.[36]

All seven themes sketched so far could well be framed in relation to the genealogies of modern law, and many scholars have been content to think about sovereignty in purely legal terms: terms that I prefer to put *eighth* rather than first, even though everything I have said so far could indeed be framed in legal terms: beginning with the standard debates on the grounding of law in a time and space without ground except that which is somehow enacted as a grounding in time and space,[37] moving to struggles over the relationship between at least some minimal recognition of international law as an enabling condition of state law and jurisdictional independence within and under international law,[38] on to recent struggles to shift the advantage to claims about humanitarian intervention rather than to claims about sovereign self-determination,[39] on, further, to those contemporary accounts of international law that portray a complex web of relations and exceptions between sovereign states and international law and which see law itself more as a process than as a fixed line of discrimination,[40] and then on to the most recent expression of the always-present sense of crisis that pervades international law in its inability to stand up to great power brutalities and the use of force more generally.[41] In this context, sovereignty usually appears in the context of historical struggles between the claims of natural and positive law, or between the claims of positive law and the claims of some extra-legal conception of justice, or between the claims of power and the claims of authority, or between sovereignty as law and sovereignty as the competence to enact law. It is in relation to law, after all, that the paradoxical character of modern sovereignty is most especially apparent. Here we encounter the traditional concerns of political theories attempting to distinguish claims about legitimate authority from reductionist suspicions about power as an explanation of all claims to authority, or to insist that legitimate authority works as a specific form of power. Here we also encounter the articulation of the claim to state sovereignty in both domestic and international law and thus the generation of a problematic relation between constitutional and criminal law, between domestic and international jurisdiction, as well as the problematic legal status of claims about, say, humanitarian intervention, universal human rights, collective security, or global governance.[42]

Ninth, we might engage with the articulation of sovereignty in relation to specific state institutions as claimants to a monopoly of legitimate authority. This has involved the gradual institutional articulation of specific understandings of the proper relationship between power and authority as well as, for example, the distinction between that which is properly political and that which is merely civil, or social, or economic, or private. In this context, while Hobbes might be read as giving a maximalist account of the claims of state sovereignty, he might also be read as a minimalist account of state government. By contrast, much of the subsequent genealogy of the modern state might be read as a trend towards the maximalization of the statist institution and social forms, in ways that have enabled accounts of *machtpolitik*, the undifferentiated nation-state, and various modalities of authoritarian and totalitarian formations. This is the focus of what is most usually framed as theories of the modern state, whether through neo-Weberian attempts to explain the monopolization of power, neo-Marxist or mercantilist attempts to explain this monopolization as a more or less functional effect of prior economic forces, or simply as a variation on the theme that the state expresses and institutionalizes a natural, or democratically/nationally/socially achieved, convergence between state sovereignty and popular sovereignty. It is also the focus of contemporary bemusements about where the state stops and where statist forms of government morph into various forms of governmentality that elude easy categorization as public or private, political or economic/cultural, territorial or global.

From this direction, modern forms of sovereignty appear as an effect of various social productions, a consequence of the specific and often particularistic practices of power and governmentality explored by people like Michel

Foucault and Pierre Bourdieu, rather than of the ontopolitical dilemmas of founding and the paradoxical character of the groundless ground that takes us back to Hobbes, Kant and the self-production of modernity as a highly generalized historical formation. Nationalisms impinge, sometimes as invented traditions that play out the projection and negation of an idealized present that is already articulated by Hobbes' account of political founding, sometimes as expressions of contingent value that nevertheless provide ultimate ground in a Weberian politics of disenchantment, sometimes as myriad practices of inclusion and exclusion that work so hard to reduce political possibilities to communities and identities that can fit in among the horizontal grids of a system of sovereign states.[43] Sovereignty comes to life, so to speak, a life subject to examination less by philosophers, lawyers, quasi-theologians or political and international theorists than by sociologists, criminologists, and students of administrative regimes and institutionalized routines. And here, of course, we run headlong into questions about the relationship between the social and the political, questions that are at least as perplexing as those about the relation between the economic and the political.[44]

Tenth, we might distinguish a specific sort of social practice and engage with various technologies of sovereignty. Hobbes already recognized that his story had to be made persuasive, that the leap of fear and faith enabling his account of rational necessities demanded specific skills and techniques through which groundless authorizations might be made authoritative. Think the practices of representation familiar from any attempt to reconcile democracy with either state sovereignty or popular sovereignty. Think the practices of modern freedom analysed by Foucault in relation to forms of surveillance, disciplines of knowledge as power, regimes of truth, and the biopolitical shaping of populations. Think fingerprints, airports, the biometrical reduction of person to body, diplomacies, official secrets and bold-faced lies. Think the discipline of political science as an expression of the discriminations authorized by the sovereign claims of the modern state and system of states.

Speaking of authorizing practices, we might engage, *eleventh*, with the articulation of a multiplicity of other authorizing practices modelled on the claims of modern sovereignty. Such practices might be understood under such categories as culture, aesthetics, epistemology and scholarship. They might also be understood as practices of freedom, of the convergence of freedoms with necessities under specific conditions of authorization. In modern constructions of the world, to speak of authority of any kind, to envisage what it means to authorize laws, cultural codes, scholarly disciplines or methodological procedures, is to engage with at least some residual sense that authority is precisely a problem, and that modern forms of authorization resonate with (though emphatically do not simply reduce to) the forms of authority we associate with the sovereign state. After all, we do have our national and international standards, our approved curricula and our institutions of certification, our official histories and national statistics, our authorized authors, approved news media, and endless celebrations of "our" way of doing things here.

It is in this context that literatures in cultural and literary theory can claim to be concerned with questions about sovereignty quite as readily as those who believe political or international theorists should have a monopoly on the subject. Hobbes' concern with what counts as an authoritative reading of religious texts offers an obvious lesson to those tempted to make claims about realism of any kind. His assertion of what it means to avoid "absurdity" through the simple procedure of defining one's terms, here and now, offers an equally obvious lesson about many other constitutive moments of foundation in which origins are claimed in ways that erase the practices and histories that went into the production of those foundations. We might think about the de-authorization of what we can now only call nature and the authorization of property. Or the tropes of "discovery" under conditions of colonization. Or the giving of rights by the colonizer to the colonized, so as to give grounds for assertions against the colonizer, so as to efface any claim to a foundation that is prior to that given by the colonizer. Or the various procedures through which the sovereignty of any particular state is asserted as the unchallenge-able condition on which the claims of any other "nation" or "people" can be negotiated, whether in relation to "native title," "cultural rights," or the sovereignty of, say, the province/nation of Quebec in a Canada understood as one nation, two nations, many nations, or just a multicultural condition of aggregation and dispersal masquerading as a sovereign state. Or, of course, the procedures through which an academic discipline like international rela-tions works to affirm the necessity of specific claims about ontological, axio-logical and epistemological necessity while delegitimizing any interpretation of the conditions under which specific claims about necessity are treated as necessary,[45] and the ways in which the relation between practices of author-ization present in both claims to sovereignty and claims to epistemological credibility generate very difficult questions about the possibilities and limits of critique.[46]

Finally, *twelfth*, at darkest midnight, we might engage with the articulation of sovereignty in relation to claims about the necessity, legitimacy and limits of violence, about the violence legitimized by the declaration, under law, of a necessary exception or state of emergency, and the absence of violence under the rule of law enabled by the always possible declaration of the exception. The force of both Weberian accounts of the state as that which can success-fully claim a monopoly on the legitimate use of violence, and Schmittian accounts of sovereignty as a relation of an always potentially violent excep-tion, are easily ignored until expressed in claims about national security, the obligations of national citizenship, and the cool hypocrisy of liberal uni-versalisms that feign ignorance of the particularity of the territorial and legal spaces into which universality has supposedly been brought so as to enable the universalizing claims of modern sovereign subjectivities. In this context, after all, the mere incidence of violence is perhaps of little consequence. It is not exactly a rare event, but rather an all too common characteristic of supposedly peaceful and normalized societies. The conditions under which violence is taken to be legitimate is, however, as consequential as it is possible to be in modern political life. They speak not least to the need to understand the relation between sovereignty and boundaries, in terms not only of territorial borders, but also of the authorization of limits to authority and the practices through which violence is deemed acceptable or necessary.[47]

Many analysts (perhaps taking their cue from Marx and some others in the nineteenth century, Walter Benjamin and many others in the early twentieth century, or Giorgio Agamben, Michael Hardt and Antonio Negri more recently) have suggested that accounts of the constitutive violence of modern politics expressed at the territorial limits of the modern state hardly begin to give some purchase on the practices of contemporary violence, or the violence of contemporary political practices. Despite various simplistic claims that a state of exception has already become normalized across the face of the world,[48] contemporary cartographies of violence do seem to exceed the capacities of Weberian and Schmittean narratives. We nevertheless still confront familiar Machiavellian – and Kantian – questions about violence as a practice of freedom, as well as questions about how specific acts of violence are authorized, about the labelling/authorization of what counts as serious violence, about what kinds of violence come to be ascribed the status of terror, for example, or as political rather than economic violence, and about why we might act on the basis of worst-case scenarios rather than reasonable expectations of life in a risk society in framing claims about necessary violence in the name of security. And we confront – in ways that might be said to bring us full circle in a discussion of principles, institutions and practices that we have come to know through a specific spatiotemporal structuring of contradictions rather than of any circularities – with the violent inscription of origins and the authorization of discriminations that drive modern politics to its limits, its hypocrisies, and its characteristic attempts to negotiate accommodations between contradictory claims by authorizing lines of discrimination at specific sites of aporetic confrontation.

To start unpacking claims about sovereignty, then, is to engage with important fractures in the analysis of modern politics. Productive analyses of sovereignty are unlikely to come from any single scholarly perspective, least of all one that affirms the spatiotemporal discriminations affirmed by modern claims to sovereignty. They are more likely to pose questions about how various literatures have come to congeal around specific themes, as well as how claims about, say, the state and democracy, or international relations, comparative politics and the theory of the state might or might not be related. Generally speaking, the more one becomes preoccupied with any one of these specific expressions of the sovereignty of modern states, the less attention is paid to the relations among these different expressions; the specific conditions under which state sovereignty came to express a particular sort of response to more general questions about legitimate authority; the specific conditions under which questions about legitimate authority became a matter of urgency as a consequence of the gradual shift from religious hierarchies to secular territorialities, though in a manner that betrays a residual indebtedness to theological framing of questions about ultimate authority; and, most significantly, the way in which modern claims to state sovereignty express a series of profound questions, not an unproblematic reality established once and for all in 1648, in the texts of very clever philosophers, or in the unchanging forms of state institutions.

My categorizations and sequencing could have been different. Many questions are doubtless excluded. They could have started at any point, though the others would soon be implicated. It makes some sense to begin with the problem of beginnings, if only to show some of what is at stake once the problem of beginnings is erased in the normalization of disciplines, and the disciplining of normalizations. It also makes sense in that it might underline the degree to which to start with the literatures on any of these engagements with modern sovereignty is to be encouraged to stay within the terms set by that starting point. The most striking characteristic of contemporary debates about sovereignty, however, is that while they are happily obsessed with capacities to authorize discriminations at the spatial limit, they are very reluctant indeed to engage with the authorized discriminations that have enabled modern politics to work within very specific accounts of what must happen at the spatial limit. It may be possible to keep talking about the unfolding liberty of the modern subject that has been distinguished from the world, whether as nature or as other sorts of human beings; indeed, we have got this down to a fine art and are not going to give up our artistry very lightly. It may also be possible to talk about a politics that encompasses the world, of nature or of humanity as such; though we have embarrassingly little practice in doing so except in the cant that would offend Kant. The common denominator of all the entries into modern claims to sovereignty, however, is that it is certainly not possible to keep talking about both of these ambitions at once.

What is possible is to keep working within the logic of modern international order on the assumption that, at some point, it might be possible to perfect the relation between sovereign subjects living within sovereign states enabling and enabled by a system of sovereign states, with perfectability in each case being understood as an internalization of principles of universality-within-particularity and particularity-within-universality, and as necessarily creating serious problems at the limits where modern sovereignty expresses aporetic relations between sovereignties. And what is necessary in this context is not the impossible choice between nationalism and cosmopolitanism that disables so much contemporary debate about future possibilities, but the firm refusal of doctrinaire and irresponsible forms of both nationalism and cosmopolitanism that simply reproduce extremist accounts of political possibility and impossibility while pretending to be realistic, ethical and responsible. Knowing where political life is supposed to occur within the spaces of subjectivity within the modern international, we know both how to identify the most difficult sites of aporetic agonism/antagonism that still need to be engaged, and how to identify the antipolitical manoeuvres through which claims about contemporary politics work by systematically ignoring such sites.

It is in relation to this very conventional framing that so much contemporary political analysis seems to me to be blithely dogmatic and entirely unconcerned with the very specific conditions within and under which its claims to scholarly knowledge are enabled. Even if contemporary political life is to be found where the codes of a modern internationalized politics insist it must be found, there remains considerable scope for resistance to those practices and forms of scholarly analysis that work by refusing to engage either with the aporetic character of claims about modern sovereign authority, or with the constitutive exclusions that have enabled an always unstable array of inclusions and exclusions that permit us to think that we might, at some point, all attain some just and peaceful way of living our particularity-within-universality and universality-within-particularity. By all means celebrate the modern subject, the modern state or the modern system of states, but do not imagine that any of these might be celebrated in isolation, as expressions of either universality or particularity, or even as open to systematic analysis, without attention to the boundaries, borders and limits that both enable and disable relations between them; and do not imagine, especially, that such celebrations can ever find some easy way of speaking about, let alone arriving at, a politics that encompasses the world, or worlds, whose exclusion enables us to celebrate the modern subject, the modern state and the modern system of states. Even on these terms, sovereignty is a problem, and boundaries are a problem. Yet not everyone is convinced that we can afford to think about political life on the assumption that the modern subject, the sovereign state and the system of sovereign states express an entirely persuasive account of where and what we are as political beings, or that the world is as easily excluded as the codes of modern political life insist it, or they, must be.

To the ends of the earth

Second reprise: topologies, origins, limits

In all the great stories that must have been told about the origins of modern political life, man eventually abandons the cyclical rhythms of season, life and death, loses his grip on the certainties of transcendence, shifts from valuations of quality to measures of quantity, and falls to earth to find himself mapped upon it as both sovereign subject and subject of sovereign authority. The modern world thereby came to be appreciated for its orchestrations of flat spaces even as knowledge of its curvatures offered scope for other possibilities, other horizons, and other limits.

The stories that have since come to be inscribed so effectively in and through modern forms of sovereignty and subjectivity must have usurped or recast other stories, about gifts and sacrifice, exile and banishment, birth and submission: about, in Nancy's terms, some other "birth to presence."[49] Shaped as we have since become by modern refusals of all other such possibilities, we can imagine this modern man telling stories of his own self-foundation to his recently enlightened but still nervous self as the candlelight dims and the fires of modernization flare up, and out, and back. Although the voices of tradition have been sent upstairs, or to the garden shed, these stories express epic ambitions. They still work as myth, as instantiation of origin, as delineation of limitation.

The world, it is said, gradually came to be known by this modern subject even as it disappeared behind, or beneath, or beyond or before the world of known objectivities. New worlds appeared. Other worlds gave way, or became other than they were. Innovations were conceived. Brilliant masterpieces were enacted in sight, and then in sound, sometimes in principle and then in practice, sometimes in practice and then in principle. New discriminations were authorized. The world came to be included as the inclusive/exclusive spatiotemporal order of modernity even as it came to be excluded as the excluded/included spatiotemporal order enabling modern subjectivities and objectivities to explore a new world within. Modern man became the site of modern politics, a politics of intricate paradox and contradiction, of point, line and plane, of point, line and circle, of point, counterpoint and transgression, of individualized subjectivities discriminating among subjectivities, objectivities and alterities, of freedoms within and under necessities and necessities enabling freedoms within and beneath. Man fell to earth, but never quite reached it. He nevertheless had to invent the world anew, to invent the nature that seems to enable his very life and being yet from which he is permanently alienated, to invent a humanity that seems to enable his very being and life, yet from which he is permanently set adrift on his own freedoms within and under his newly invented understandings of necessity, and of law.

These stories have been narrated in many forms and rewritten many times, sometimes in ways that acknowledge the demands of scholarly scruple, but more often not. As comedy or tragedy, as pamphlet, tract or treatise, the written record offers traces and fragments that we now patch together to ensure that we know what must have been said about what must be done with such a strange creature. As a creature of many names (Cartesian man, Hobbesian man, Kantian man, modern man, liberal man, self-righteously sexist, colonial and solipsistic man), and with no guarantee that all these names identify any single manly creature, we can never be certain whether his identity names continuity or discontinuity, particularity or universality. Yet he is undoubtedly a creature who demands a name, the authorization of self that marks the spatiotemporal particularity of a self cut off from continuities and universalities of Being. Hierarchies may have collapsed, but another Fall unravelled secular hope from theological despair. Despite their variety, and despite all interpretive circularities, there seems to be some agreement that the stories that must have been told worked to affirm claims about a man who must become free yet must remain in chains, who can attain liberty only under conditions of necessity; a proper liberty, that is, under a proper account of necessity.

This is an agreement that at least allows us some understanding of how modernity came to express a revised repertoire of paradoxes and contradictions. As a specifically modern creature, as the abstract yet embodied singularity that speaks for the human, this man is supposed to both know his place in the world and to know himself to be a self by knowing where he is in the world. Justice as knowing one's place in a hierarchy has long given way to practices of knowing oneself in a horizontal space/place of extensivity. Yet knowing who and what he is by knowing where he is, this modern man also knows himself to be somehow elsewhere, as something other than he is. Knowing himself to be firmly ensconced as a citizen of a delimited space, he is vaguely aware that the space of modern political subjectivity has been cut adrift from the world to which he imagined himself as belonging, that his culture is somehow cut apart from his nature. Knowing himself to be a sovereign subject and subject of sovereignty, he knows himself to be himself because he is not the sovereign subject and subject of sovereignty somewhere else: that he is who he is because he is not someone other. Knowing himself to be a citizen, he thereby worries that he is not the man he thought he was, merely the citizen, the subject subjectivity who signs his name so as to affirm that he is only a modern man, the legal citizen of state, the being who is neither natural nor human, who celebrates his freedoms under law and laments both his disenchanted secularity and his alienation from other claimants to humanity. Knowing where he is, he simultaneously knows where and who he is not.

In retrospect, at least, such stories have been shaped by, and have helped to reshape, both questions about what it must mean to make a claim to sovereign authority, and the conditions under which it might be possible to articulate answers authorizing specific claims about what sovereign authority must become in a new world of modern freedoms and modern equalities. Not least, I have tended to stress, they provided very neat responses to claims about radical dualisms of earth and heaven, time and eternity, or finite and infinite, that had once been dealt with by a nice combination of faith and angels congregating just beyond the mundane orders of earthly existence. The claims of a continuous (Aristotelian, Thomist) hierarchy supposedly came into renewed tension with the claims of a more intransigent (Platonist, Augustinian) dualism. All the stereotypical moments of the rise of modernity – the Renaissance, the Reformation, the Scientific Revolution, nominalism, the modern subject, private property, the sovereign state, the system of sovereign states – involved an increasing primacy of dualism over hierarchical subordination. Consequently, these stereotypes have tended to stress the radical difference between the world of premodern hierarchies, essentialisms, natural laws and natural justice and the modern world of subjects, objects and sovereign authorities that have no ground beyond their own self-substantiation and self-representation.

For the early-modern European theorists confronting the universalizing pretensions of Christianity and empire, some account of what we have come to call citizenship within a specific sovereign community offered the basis for constructing an alternative account of political legitimacy that might dispense with God as the explicit source of earthly authority. It may well be that, in practice, the priority of citizenship over any claim to humanity was not always clear-cut. Dual allegiances to God and State, everyday assumptions that our specifically political identities are not so very different from our somehow more human identities, reconciliations of earthly and heavenly duties through notions of property, an ethical imperative or a realm of privacy freed from a realm of publicity, and so on, have all served to muddy the stark choice that accompanied the "huge outbreak of dualisms"[50] that shaped early European modernity. Yet if the choice was not always clear-cut, the implications of pushing the choice into clarity were well understood: allegiance to the secular sovereign has priority over allegiance to divinity; and the priority of a singular conception of citizenship requires a monolithic conception of political community and the eventual erasure of most diversities and identities into what James Tully has referred to as an "empire of uniformity;"[51] though this was, crucially, a uniformity that was at odds with principles of qualitatively differentiated hierarchy conventionally attributed to empire.[52]

In the rewriting of these stories that congeals in Hegel, we especially see the effects of readings of earlier stories about what it means to be the beneficiaries of Greek rationalism and Christian monotheism, inheritors of the great distinctions between a world of becoming and a world of Being, a world of many things and a world of single things, a world of immanence this side of eternity and a world of transcendence beyond. In this extraordinary reading of histories as History – of a singular history that works its way forward through the dialectic of singularity and particularity, of immanence and transcendence, of Kantian antinomies and future possibilities, of moving on by moving in and moving in by moving both on and up – we see the emerging problem of a universalizing story about the origin and movement of the world engaging with worlds other than the one from which it came in ways that express the effects not of any old singular system of singularities and universalities colliding with other forms of particularity and universality, but of a collision that expresses the inherent perfectability of all modern accounts of singularity and perfectability. This account of an emerging perfectability as a movement inwards so as to perfect the idealized universality/particularity of the modern subject – of man – simultaneously works as a movement outward, as a collision with others who are simultaneously understood as radically different, as always potentially enemies/barbarians, yet as always transcendentally the same – as always potentially human.

This move, from the eternalist stories of Hobbesian legalism to the historical, nationalist and biopolitical stories of absolute friends and enemies, haunted modern accounts of politics in the early decades of the twentieth

century, the era to which the institutionalization of the academic disciplines of
political analysis is usually traced. By then, the internalization of the world
could be taken for granted, more or less on terms given by Weber's reading of
the central internal contradictions of modernity as a rationalization that
intensifies irrationality: a contradiction that brings the problem of modern
subjectivity back to its early-modern status as a fallen but ungrounded creature, cut off from theological authority but not quite rooted in anything but
its own invention of a nature and a humanity from which it is nevertheless
authoritatively distinguished. Weber sought to rewrite the story of the possibility of modern subjectivity on new, but also familiar (again Lutheran),
terms: "here I stand, I can do no other," subsequently to be converted into
the familiar mantra of foreign policy, "this is in our national interest, we can
do no other." It was nevertheless a rewriting that was acutely aware that the
intensely existential man who struggles to keep up some ambition for political
responsibility is nevertheless responsible in a world of intensifying clashes
both with others in the game of international *machpolitik* but also of uncertain relations with other civilizations – with other traditions and other histories that may be, or perhaps may not be destined to follow the great road of
Hobbesian and Kantian reason and the inward trek towards a humanity that
can never reach beyond itself, not least to those whose inhumanity is the
ultimate guarantee of a modern story about the possibility of humanity. The
relation between Weber's portrayal of the fate of the modern subject or personality struggling to find meaning in an existential affirmation of self and
nation and his extraordinary engagements with all those other civilizations
that did not manage the "breakthrough" to modernity still remains instructive
in this respect.

It is in the broad context of such stories that explorers have long been
encouraged to go to the ends of the earth, as the saying goes. Quite where
these ends are to be found is unclear; unless navigation is delineated by two-
dimensional Mercator – in which case abrupt precipices over the edge are
always a possibility – or by three dimensional Mercator – in which case
intended destinations may be indeed be reached, on a continuum that has no
obvious end, in a cycle of inevitable repetitions, and without much need to
notice the choices and distortions enabling navigation as long as vision is
firmly focused on the inevitable route ahead. It is nonetheless a strange phrase
to use in relation to a spherical planet, only partly a telling holdover from
colonial eras used to framing the spatially and temporally distant as a straight
line out and back from some sovereign centre, even if that sovereign centre
was in agonistic relation with other sovereign centres imagining their own
distances from the ends of the earth.

Much of modern political life has taken the two-dimensional route, the one
wracked with nervousness about abrupt edges, the one laid out, in principle,
as an array of freedoms and equalities in horizontal territorialities: the one
mapped as points of intersection, as cruciforms and grids marking sites of
being from which this being, this individual subject that is precisely divisible,

may survey the world, negotiate its directions, its limits, its necessities, and its freedoms. Although the vistas may be a little densely textured, they are enabled by what is, in some respects, a very simple line, the very simplicity of which works to discourage too much worrying about the discriminations it enacts or the authorizations it enables. This is the line stretching from the modern subject out into the wider world beyond, out as far as the limits of the sovereign state, out further to the limits of the system of sovereign states, and out further still to the limits of the known world; the limits, that is, of the world that is known to the modern subject whose connection to the world is expressed positively by the hope that the line does indeed reach to the ends of the earth, and negatively by the lines by which it is itself intersected where modern subject meets the sovereign state, the sovereign state meets the system of sovereign states, and the system of sovereign states meets whatever it is that works as its constitutive outside: the ultimate but forgotten absence that enables an inner structuring of presences and absences.

These are all stories among stories. They are multiple, contestable and ret-rospective. They nevertheless carry enormous persuasive force. Their plausi-bility derives not least from their elegant expression of a broad range of problems that must have been solved in the articulation of political principle in early-modern Europe; must have been solved, that is, in order for us to have become what we think we are as modern political subjects and citizens living within the world of the modern international. Conversely, their implausibility derives from the extent to which their very elegance smacks of victor's history, translations of messy contingencies into the aesthetic beauties of modern self-determination, and, sometimes, the violence of attempts to naturalize their necessity in demands for action against those who will not be appropriately self-determined. Stories that tell us what must have been the case, given what has become the case, certainly ought to invite scepticism, even if we have absorbed them into our deepest desires and allowed the text-book writers to classify the world so elegantly in the modern trinity of man, state and system of states. The difficulty, of course, is that such stories are both plausible and implausible: implausible as history, but intensely plausible as our regulative account of what history must have been for us to have become what we are and for us to be able to imagine what we might become in any imaginable future.

Significant problems of historical interpretation are undoubtedly at stake in this choice of entry to the problems of contemporary political life. There are problems, not least, I have suggested, because a clear form of the modern system of states that is a condition of the very possibility of the sovereign state seems to have arrived considerably later than the sovereign state itself. This is undoubtedly to raise questions about the historical credibility of the sharp distinction that I have tended to draw between modern horizontalities and premodern verticalities. It will seem especially simplistic to those who rightly think that there is more to modern political life than the subject, the sovereign state and the modern system of states, though exactly how we might think that there is more to modern political life than the subject, the sovereign state and the modern system of states is not entirely clear.

No-one really believes that formalist claims to hierarchy are sufficient to explain the complexities of whatever political life is taken to have come before modernity. This would be a little silly, to say the least, just as silly as the assumption that everyone believed the earth to be flat until some crazy Europeans finally floated far enough away to find a world going round. Nevertheless, the effects of this narrative remain sufficiently pervasive to provide a conventionalized sense of what struggles to affirm modern accounts of authority must have been up against, given what we have come to be now: the need to challenge the universalizing claims of empire; the need to challenge the universalizing claims of transcendental theology; and the need to challenge the teleological essentialisms we now identify with such names as Aristotle and Aquinas and catch-phrases like the Great Chain of Being. Modernity, by contrast, is to be understood through its horizontal principles of organization. Expressed in relation to what we have come to call the international, modern political life articulates a radical critique of empire, of any overarching universal order except that of a system of states that expresses a paradigmatic account of the necessities and freedoms possible within a specific structuring of universality and particularity laid out on a flat horizontal grid and conceivable both as territoriality and as legal jurisdiction.

Expressed in relation to any specific part of this (always in principle, but not always in practice) international order, modern political life articulates a radical critique of the subordination of secular to sacred authority and a radical affirmation of principles of both freedom and equality. Again, no-one believes that formalist claims about a horizontal field of freedoms and equalities, or a decisive rupture with desires for transcendental or imperial authority, are sufficient to explain whatever we take modern political life to be. One would have to be not only a little crazy but entirely deluded to do so. Nevertheless, these claims affirm a set of regulative norms that no-one would be willing to exclude from accounts of what it means to engage in specifically modern forms of political life. If modern political life is not understood at least partly as a struggle to reconcile claims to liberty with claims to equality in the context of dynamics of modernization challenging the possibilities of equality and of spatiotemporal boundaries that put decisive limits on claims to liberty, then it is difficult to see what the famous canon of modern political theorists were up to, how any modern politician could find any kind of audience, or how the great doctrines of liberalism, socialism, nationalism and internationalism could have found any purchase in claims about reason, passion, identity, history, normativity or authority.

This narrative about the coming into being of modernity doubtless sends shivers down the spine of most self-respecting historians. It nevertheless affirms an almost unquestionable account of the origins and limits of modern political life; not one that might claim historical veracity, but one that does claim foundational necessity. Theorists of international relations have needed something like a Treaty of Westphalia as a more or less justifiable point of origin of a form of political life that can then be understood as an expression of a systematic structure of lines of inclusion and exclusion, organized both in space and in some kind of systemic, social or legal principle. Political theorists have needed something like Hobbes' story of the origins of the modern state that can be understood similarly as a systematic structure of lines of inclusion organized in space, society, institution and in law. One might occasionally invoke a more elaborately historical theory of the state, or of the states system, but for the most part the broad parameters of origin and limit will suffice. The way is then open for the usual duet of modern political spatiotemporalities: a regulative assumption of temporal progress internally and a regulative assumption of structural discontinuities in the system of states externally, with the hope that internal progress, the move towards autonomy, or more democratization, or whatever the current translation of progress as the realization of reason within free and equal subjects comes to be, will gradually drive the structures of the states system towards an external perfectability. Once this narrative becomes a standard operating principle, even if not a source of scholarly pride, then we can get a fairly clear idea of the way modernity will work when the going gets tough, when limits are broached and need to be resecured. Indeed we can get a fairly good sense also of what it means to invoke claims about security in relation to modern subjects subject to the authority and limits of the modern sovereign state and system of sovereign states.

The figures I have deployed in my engagement with this legacy – canonically codified but still potentially disruptive figures like Machiavelli, Hobbes, Kant, Weber and Schmitt, with Rousseau, Hegel, Marx, Nietzsche and a few others hovering somewhere in the shadows – express characteristically ambivalent responses to this new condition of novelty and continuity. Schmitt especially brings a momentary but intense focus to the ways in which absolute declarations of a yes and no must occur at the spatial and legal limits of a sovereign authority: a sovereign authority that is itself authorized through its capacity to make declarations of a yes and no, to decide exceptions to a norm that is sustained through a declaration of exceptions. While many people may complain about the circular reasoning, rejection of foundations, outbreaks of relativism, and legitimations of intolerable violence that this understanding of modern political life might bring, it is not an aberration. It is merely an expression of problems produced by the freedoms and equalities expressed in our strongest traditions of political ethics, and confirmed by the claim that we are, or must become, modern subjects acting as citizens of sovereign states within a system of sovereign states. The darker readings of this project of modernity that haunt such canonical texts – those of the supposedly more optimistic Kant quite as much as those of the overtly dismal Weber and Schmitt – find especially powerful expression in relation to claims about the system of states because it is in that context that the limits of modernity are most obviously engaged in grand claims about war and peace, on the one hand, and the bringing of the entire world into the structures of modernity, on the other. It is in this context that we see the most intense practices of authorized discriminations and the declaration of exceptions, but also the most intense elision of what is at stake in the aporetic structuring of modern political life through the reduction of profound problems to clichéd answers that work so very hard as affirmations of the necessary origins and limits of a particular account of our necessary origins and limits.

Faced with such stories, and such clichés, it is never entirely clear where one ought to situate the moment at which the sway of an intrinsically unstable hierarchical resolution of the proper relation between universality and particularity gave way to an also unstable modern insistence on a world of free and equal subjects. It has become conventional to say that, in political terms at least, things become clearer some time between Machiavelli and Hobbes. Machiavelli, reversing the Augustinian options, takes a stand for earth, or at least Florence, against heaven. Hobbes simply assumes that the world must conform to an abstract codification of free and equal individuals. What we see in both cases is not an assertion of the way things are, of the kind that have enabled half a century of textbook indoctrinations into the mysteries of international relations, but some quite profound struggles to rearticulate a problem of the proper relationship *between* universality and particularity. In general terms, we are then invited to engage with the familiar stories of a literally heroic attempt to find universality-within-particularity and particularity-within-universality. These are the stories of the presence and potential of the modern subject, the sovereign state and the system of sovereign states: stories, in a vertical plane, about the gradual capacity of the sovereign state and system of sovereign states to bring down all universalities from above and all particularities from below, so as to affirm monopolistic expressions of both universality and particularity within flat territorial jurisdictions; and stories, in a horizontal plane, about the gradual capacity of modern individualized subjects to bring universality within a particular, so that each particular might take its proper place within the universal, or rather, within the particular system of sovereign states that is the site at which we know how to speak of universality in political terms.

Despite an often intense awareness that many of the most difficult problems generated by this specific articulation of political possibility and impossibility occur at sites at which each moment of internalized universality-within-particularity and particularity-within-universality meets its constitutive outside, we have now become used to a very sharp division of scholarly labour in which constitutive outsides can be framed as merely marginal, merely exceptional, the province of the specialized hard men or those enamoured of some disappearing premodernity, some romantic world of nature or some unearthly brew of metaphysical speculation: the constitutive outsides as understood as the outer edge of a modern subjectivity within. With all the standard prejudices thereby confirmed, autonomous realms of always potential autonomy and a regulative ideal of always potential liberty and equality can be laid out for dissection, and for desire.

Abstracting the heroism of the modern individualized subject, we are easily seduced by the possibility that subject and world can be reconciled directly, that the individual citizen can become human, that the moral life within might be reconciled with a universal moral law expressing some more extensive world beyond. Abstracting the heroism of the modern sovereign state and all its national self-determinations, we are easily seduced by the possibility that we might move from particular to universal, from *polis* to *cosmopolis*, from pluralistic national interests to some common human interest. Abstracting the heroism of the system of sovereign states, we are easily seduced by the possibility that international relations might turn into a world politics, a politics of the entire world, even while knowing this to be an impossibility given both the founding rupture of the modern from the world, and the aporetic limits within which political life is enabled only within a universalizing particularity within a system of universalizing particularities that can never add up to any world as such. From the narrative stance offered by each heroic abstraction, each seduction seems perfectly reasonable, perfectly normal, sufficient to feed an obvious common sense that might trump any other common sense; but only until the limits of each heroic internalization of universality-within-particularity and particularity-within-universality kick in to affirm the necessary constraints upon modern accounts of liberty, equality and justice under sovereign law.

According to the stories that lead us down this analytical path, the new world of inclusions and exclusions that erupted some time between Machiavelli and Hobbes gradually expanded spatially or developed temporally until it filled all available space and must now be on the way to filling all available time. Such stories thereby affirm the spatiotemporality expressed as the modern international: the fulfilment, or the promise, of a new humanity, the world of modernity, of freedoms and obligations nevertheless predicated on the exclusion/inclusion of any other world. Despite all appearances, and some common sense, the international marks not the promise of a single world, one carrying all the potentialities of a modernizing universality, but the regulative rift between the world of modernity and all other worlds. To speak easily of the world, in the singular, or a world politics as a universality, or of globalization as the process that must finally drive us to such a fate, is to come up against the constitutive limits of a form of life that knows itself to be itself precisely because it has so brilliantly distinguished itself from the world so as to fulfil potential freedoms within a structure of sovereign authorizations that has no authorization beyond itself.

These are the stories celebrating the achievements, but also contradictions, scanned in my brief circular tour around horizons marked by discriminations, authorizations and delimitations expressed in and through the principles, practices and institutions of sovereign states enabling and enacted in the name both of a multiplicity of modern subjects and of a singular system of states – the singular multiplicity that can never quite turn into a politics of the world. In this reading, the terms international relations and world politics express the official possibilities before us both as synonym and as antonym. Between them, within the line distinguishing and affirming both their similarity and their difference, lie the claims of the modern subject, sovereign state and system of sovereign states to be able to resolve all contradictions between universality and particularity, similarity and difference, and spatiality and temporality on, within and across the lines marking their differentiation; or not. Played out through a simple logic of presence and absence, here today and gone tomorrow, pluralisms problematic and universalisms desirable, the doubled, tripled and quadrupled options of a modern political life grounded in the claims of state sovereignty express desires for a world beyond that can never be attained, merely postulated as a logic of desire that might regulate negotiations across all lines of aporetic instability.

For there can be no simple way out of a political order that is so tightly constructed as a system of ins and outs. There can be no simple way of transcending a logic of immanence and transcendence, no simple way of finding alternatives to a structure of norms and alternatives, no obvious way of escaping a politics of imprisonment and escape. Many thinkers have long insisted on this entirely elementary point. Many of them have nevertheless been brutally reinscribed into the familiar canon of potential escapees, reappropriated as prophets of transcendence and the grand ("ethical," "cosmopolitan," "postmodern") alternative, in ways that speak to the enormous persuasiveness of the stories we have been told about the necessities and possibilities of specifically modern forms of political necessity and possibility. Once reinscribed, it is always a simple matter to bring them under the appropriate disciplinary regime of a sovereign exceptionalism through which all claims to universality are contained within a universalizing particularity.

The nationalists and political realists always have such an easy time of it because they have only to mobilize some version of a Schmittean logic of exception as the norm we must simply take for granted. Their supposed realism works only as a reminder that we need to take care of the consequences of our ideals, whether as some luminous Kantian hope in the face of the necessities of human finitude, as some much darker Weberian sense of responsibility in the face of rationalized irrationality, or as the more usual self-righteousness about lines that must be drawn because, while we here are now more or less good modern liberals, they there are most certainly not, and need to be dealt with in order that we here might finally become what we already were to begin with. Moreover, if this is the logic that is always likely to trump all other ambitions *within* our cherished national communities, there is even less chance of a simple way out of a political order that is so tightly constructed as a system of multiple ins and outs organized so as to maintain a world of modern freedoms and equalities within normalized jurisdictions that may always threaten exception at the limit, but which must always meet other exceptions at the limit or else capitulate to some other, higher, authority that might bring us some other freedom and some other equality, but not of the kind that we have sustained in the ambition to be modern, self-determining subjects.

This is why the standard narratives about international relations tend to be so thoroughly depressing; though less depressing than those forms of liberal self-righteousness that are so willing to play out an exceptionalist politics while claiming some high ground of ethics, justice and cosmopolitan right. They are depressing not because they appeal so readily to some human propensity for evil, the predatory determinations of capitalism, or the meaningless iron cage of modernity expressing a desperate desire for meaning through a nationalist *machtpolitik*, but because they work to affirm a narrative about origins and limits enabling modern conceptions of subjectivity, citizenship and both individual and collective self-determination. Claims about political idealism and political realism, or about nationalism and cosmopolitanism, shaped by such narratives, are not opposites. There is, in this context, no simple choice between one and the other, and no possibility of moving from one to the other. They are co-productive, mutually constitutive, two sides of the same coin, as it is said: but they nevertheless work together very effectively by enabling a priority of one over the other so as to enable a politics that is always willing to authorize the most fateful discriminations over life and death.

In this respect, the degree to which it is Schmitt alone who has been resurrected under post-Cold War conditions as the exemplary figure in contemporary engagements with sovereignty tells us a lot about the continuing force of a merely statist logic of norm and exception, and about the continuing appeal of a specific form of theological imagination enabling both the conditions under which a secular modernity might be saved, even from liberalisms and democracies when necessary, and the apocalyptic dangers that justify the deployment of centralized authority at the spatial, social and legal limits of the modern sovereign state. One lesson that might still be learnt from Schmitt, however, is that resort to a statist politics of exception is by no means restricted to the fascistic forms of nationalism to which Schmitt himself was drawn, but is always the potential worst case scenario for any modern regime that thrives on worst case scenarios to sustain its legitimacy. Moreover, it is the presumption of worst cases, of extreme conditions, of the necessity for exceptions to any claim to universality, that has become the normalized condition under which the national and the international have been ripped apart in a scholarly division of labour that so easily speaks of justice in one and order in another, even while the bus promising to take us far away from the modern world of boundaries and limits keeps its mighty engines purring.

Despite the radically nationalist origins of much international relations theory, the modern sovereign state cannot be divorced from the system of sovereign states that is its necessary condition of possibility. The opposition between state law and international law, between Schmitt and Kelsen, to resort again to my risky shorthand of exemplary figures, begins to get at even tougher but entirely conventional problems, even though these have become so trivialized through loose claims about universalism and cosmopolitanism of the kind exemplified to the point of parody by so many otherwise very sophisticated thinkers. Together, Schmitt and Kelsen remind us that modern political life is both national and international, both universal and particular, expressing aporetic accounts of the location of ultimate authority that must always be negotiated. International law is no less constitutive of modern political life than is state law, despite the way it is always judged to be so flimsy when compared with the centralized legal authority of the sovereign state. Such judgements simply miss the point of the intense negotiation of the antagonisms at work at the intersection between state law and interstate law, antagonisms that always permit struggles over the superiority of one over the other in any particular situation, but cannot permit any general superiority of one over the other without affirming either the radical solipcism or the radically hierarchical subordination that Kant identified as the twin impossibilities of a politics that lays its bets on modern accounts of human freedom.

It is by reading the spatiotemporal articulation of modern politics through something like this account of how it must have been (rather than was) produced within a system of sovereign states that I have tried to understand some of what is at stake in claims about a potential move from an international politics to a politics that might encompass something we much too easily call "the world." In some ways, this is quite obviously a term that demands to be used very carefully, even with great trepidation. It is also, and again quite obviously, a term that we use without much thought at all, in grand defiance of many careful attempts, some of them celebrated as the core philosophical and scientific achievements of a specifically modern world, to show how any claim to a world as such must be inherently problematic.

As Kant himself most famously insisted, claims about the world attract multiple forms of dogmatism, against which it is necessary to pay careful attention to the conditions under which claims about the world come to be made, and to have authority. Even though the conditions under which, and the teleological assumptions through which, Kant sought to articulate the difference between dogma and critique may themselves be subject to extended dispute, it is in this sense that I have sought to examine some of the conditions under which it has become so easy to make claims about the world in ways that are widely assumed to offer solutions to problems arising from the structural logic of an internationalized system of states. While the ultimate force of my argument is directed against Kant, as well as against Hobbes before him and Schmitt, among others, after him, I have sought to cut through the muddied but hardened accretions of various disciplinary literatures so as to get at what is at stake in reiterated appeals to the world as a desirable solution to so many contemporary political problems, despite the force with which Hobbes, Kant and so many others have rightly insisted on the fragility of any claim about the world as such. In doing so, I have tried to get a grip on the profoundly contradictory and aporetic character of political formations that are more usually framed through formulaic dualisms inhibiting almost any critical engagement with modern practices of sovereignty. At the very least, I have suggested, any attempt to reimagine political possibilities and necessities now will have to take both the problem of sovereignty and the achievements of specifically modern forms of sovereignty far more seriously than is possible in scholarly disciplines governed by a normalized logic, cartography and theory of history affirming necessities and possibilities configured on one side of a line or the other.

I have especially suggested that proposals for a move from an international politics to a politics of the world expose much of the ground, or its absence, upon which the constitutive principles of modern political life have been constructed since the days of Hobbes and Kant, in ways that affirm profoundly contradictory forms of cliché, common sense and discursive ritual. One form rests upon a claim that the world has been, or will eventually be, brought into the spatiotemporal articulation of potentially sovereign subjectivities enabled within, and enabling, potentially sovereign states enabled within, and enabling, a potentially sovereign system of states. The other rests upon a recognition that the world has been excluded precisely as the condition under which modern politics has been articulated as a structuring of internalized subjectivities within states within a system of states.

For the most part, narratives of internalization prevail. Much of the authority of modern political practice is sustained by an assumption that the world has been, or is in the process of becoming, internalized within modern subjectivities, big and small. In principle, the system of states and all that it contains may then be taken to be coextensive with the world as such, and procedures may be envisaged for transforming such subjectivities into a more universal, cosmopolitan or global form of world politics. This pattern of internalization expresses a scale from small to large that is nevertheless ruptured where individuals meet states, states meet the system of states, and the system of states meets its external conditions of possibility in some world that is both rigorously excluded and constantly desired. These points of rupture give rise to the most difficult sites and moments of modern political life where and when claims about liberties, equalities and securities within converge with claims about the legitimacy of violence at the limit.

Part of the failure of much contemporary political analysis arises from the desire to treat these points of rupture as simple discriminations on a scale of established political orders, rather than as sites and moments of intense politicization and depoliticization through which these orders are established, sustained and delimited. This is what has happened in paradigmatic form through the construction of traditions of political theory and international relations theory, as if either they have nothing to do with each other, or it would be a simple matter to translate claims about political theory into claims about an international, or even world, politics. This is also what happens in many popular attempts to select either the particularized subject, or the particularized state, or the particularized system of states as the launching pad for the ride towards a universalizing future. An easy life of disciplinary virtue may be assured in either case, but neither the problem of sovereignty nor the achievements of specific modern forms of sovereignty are likely to be engaged, except to affirm patterns of presence and absence that can only affirm the standard narratives about what sovereignty must be.

In any case, the alternative form of common sense acknowledging the exclusionary character of modern forms of inclusion and exclusion can never be dismissed, not least because it expresses the conditions under which the prevailing narratives of internalization can be imagined at all. Whatever force there may be to claims about the need to think about our political possibilities and necessities in more global, cosmopolitan or universal terms, such claims will inevitably confront the constitutive limits of modern forms of politics affirming promises of inclusion, and of specific structures of inclusion and exclusion, that are ultimately predicated on the need to exclude the world so as to understand the possibility and necessity of a world of specifically modern political possibilities and necessities. This alternative will become especially insistent whenever the basic principles of modern subjectivity and self-determination are threatened: whenever inequalities, hegemonies or historical transformations promise to disperse a spatiotemporal array of modern subjectivities into something resembling the universal empires and principled inequalities explicitly, and often violently, repudiated by modern forms of liberty, equality, security, subjectivity, community and sovereign authority.

More specifically still, I have argued that the aporetic structuring of modern politics, expressed in the way accounts of an internationalized system of states and accounts of a potential politics of the world work as both synonym and antonym, is implicated in modern practices of sovereignty in ways that considerably exceed accounts of the sovereign state as a territorialized monopoly on legal authority and legitimate violence. I have especially sought to suggest not only that the distinction between them is much more complex than many powerful scholarly traditions have tended to assume, but that the forms of discrimination, authorization and exceptionalism expressed in this distinction are of considerable consequence for the ways in which much more specific boundaries, borders and limits sustain practices of sovereignty expressed within and between modern subjects, modern states and the modern system of states.

Consequently, I have suggested that any attempt to engage critically with claims about some other ways of acting politically than those affirming where and what political life must be within the modern subject, state and system of states must necessarily engage with the superficially absurd idea that there is an outside to the modern international: that there is a constitutive boundary between the political order articulated within an internationalized system of states and any possible claim to a world beyond, or at least to a world that might be understandable in the prevailing categories of modern political life.

The idea that there must be some outside to the modern international seems absurd, partly because it affirms the assumption that our potential and our future as human beings is precisely to come inside, to realize our being as subjects – as universals *within* particulars and particulars *within* universals – and partly because the structuring of the relation between subjects, states and system along a scale from small to large affirms the assumption that the international system of states is the most inclusive political articulation we can imagine, despite its flawed organization as a fragmented array of spatiotemporal inclusions and exclusions.

Much contemporary common sense is sustained by this sense of absurdity. Universalization can be assumed to be realizable both as a move towards the eventual autonomy of subjects, states and states-system, and as a move further along a scale from small to large. Not only is modern politics orchestrated as a systematic array of internalities and externalities expressed in a spatial or territorial form affirming a temporal or historical account of an exclusionary moment of founding permitting the realization of free and equal subjectivities within, but the dynamic through which this realization is assumed to be possible expresses hopes for further internalization, as subjectivization, and further externalization, as a shift along the scale of universalization that might eventually enable us to transcend the entire framework of internals and externals shaping the necessities and possibilities of modern politics.

The core problems I have been diagnosing in this way arise because any hopes pinned on an internalization of universality must presume a move away from something that is left out or left behind, and that any linear path from small to large, of the kind expressed in a scale from small to large encompassing individuals, states and states-system, must eventually fail to reach beyond the finite capacities of human existence and knowledge. Boundaries will be drawn in either case, and these boundaries will be expressed both as some kind of spatiotemporal bordering and as some kind of delimitation in (legal) principle. This is why I have sought to link Hobbes to the moment of founding, and to insist on Kant's acute awareness of the instabilities attending this logic of internalization and externalization, as well as to implicate both figures in contemporary debates about discrimination, authorization, exceptionalism, hierarchical solutions to contradictory relations between liberty and equality, the multidimensional problem of sovereignty, and the aporetic puzzles that must arise at the boundaries of modern political life even if one is convinced that the promises of modern subjectivity must still guide our understanding of any future political imagination. So much, in my view, for the still powerful intellectual universe in which Hobbes can represent an essentialized claim about reality, anarchy and necessity, and Kant can represent utopianized claims about peace, universality and possibility.

As Kant would put it, modern politics is a politics of finitude. It has become organized through the delimitation of finite sovereignties and subjectivities in an order that reproduces the aporetic limits of the modern system of states within its internal bounding of sovereignties and subjectivities. In this sense, the statist exception associated with Schmitt, and with the construction of a sharp distinction between political theory and international relations, tells us very little, for all that it disrupts many of the easy expectations of an enhanced pluralism or extended universalism expressed in so much contemporary political debate. The doubled exception where the state meets the system of states, where Schmitt meets Kelsen, where political theory meets the theory of international relations, tells us a great deal more. It demands engagement with the international conditions of modern political possibility and impossibility. It also demands scepticism about calls for a cosmopolitanism, humanitarianism or globalism that projects a quick switch from nationalist readings of a fragmented international to some kind of integrated order worthy of being called a world politics, and for much greater sensitivity towards the various ways in which claims about the cosmopolitan, the humanitarian and the global are already expressed within a fragmented international order in ways that are easily deployed in order to exclude many human beings, among other things. It is certainly not going to be very helpful to try to imagine other political possibilities without engaging with the extraordinarily elegant ways in which the desire for universality-within-particularity and particularity-within-universality is expressed within the modern international order, or with how this order expresses an immensely seductive account of what it means to desire liberty, equality and security, or both citizenship and humanity, even if there is reason to suggest that principles of liberty, equality, security, citizenship and humanity are all systematically undermined as well as sustained by the practices of this order.

Rather than offering a way of thinking about alternatives to modern political practices, claims about a structural or historical shift from international relations to a world politics offers only a way of understanding how so much modern politics works to affirm the spatiotemporal necessity of specific spatiotemporal forms of politics promising a world of liberties and equalities within the boundaries of modern subjects, modern states and the modern system of states. This is the promise of a condition that can be read positively as an affirmation of the universality-within-particularity and particularity-within-universality of modern subjectivities, big and small, but also negatively insofar as the promise is shadowed by imperfect relations between liberty and equality, by nationalist claims about the inevitability of war in defence of particularities, by imperial claims about the need to impose universal norms and orders, and by the multiple effects of the exclusions through which modern political life has been organized as a spatiotemporal order of inclusions and exclusions.

Consequently, by insisting on the continuing significance of both the synonym and the antonym, and thus on the patterns of both inclusion and exclusion that have enabled modern forms of political life to be articulated as the structure of inclusions and exclusions orchestrating relations between modern subjects, modern states and the modern system of states, I have sought to complicate the line distinguishing them not only so as to make it more difficult to assume that we might imagine some other form of politics simply by mapping out a linear road from the one condition to the other, but also to complicate various other lines that have become our regulative ideal of what it means to understand boundaries, understood especially as the convergence of territorial borders and legal limits that have come to define what it means to live within, and yet desire to escape, the spatiotemporal forms of modern political life.

Where so much supposedly progressive and emancipatory political analysis has been content to work within the patterns of desire for transcendence and necessary disappointment enabled by the distinction between an international politics and a politics of the world, I have sought to suggest that we might learn rather more by attending to the exemplary character of the distinction itself. It is a distinction that affirms the discriminations enabling the very idea of a specifically modern form of politics that might seek universality within its particularities and subjectivities. It enables us to think about modern forms of authority and authorization within boundaries understood as both territorial borders and legal/cultural limits. It expresses our ontotheological understanding of what it means to define and transgress a norm, to make an exception in the name of both necessity and freedom. It has itself become so normalized and naturalized that we can switch back and forth from synonym to antonym and even believe we are opting for radically different choices when we commit to claims about a political realism or a political idealism, as if one might possibly imagine one without the other. It even affords a formal common denominator among substantively diverse political doctrines, left, right, or somewhere in between. Driving so many accounts of what we ought to do about a politics of sovereign states, it works as a sovereign authorization of what it must mean to speak about modern sovereignty and its alternatives.

It has been in this sense that I have found the radically depoliticized character of Anglo-American theories of international relations to be such an interesting ground on which to think about the way so much contemporary political analysis works by affirming values predicated on a continuing commitment both to a politics of internalization and subjectivization and to a politics of externalization and escape. The categorial structure expressed by the theory of international relations may affirm a very powerful and elegant way of thinking about the possibilities of universality-within-particularity and particularity-within-universality, and the both positive and negative consequences produced by the structuring of these possibilities within boundaries that are always susceptible to aporetic antagonism, but they also affirm claims about universality that are produced through constitutive distinctions between the modern world and various other worlds, and claims about particularity and difference that are always subject to the regulative ideal of a very particular form of universality. This is not exactly a new problem. It may have been broached by a wide range of thinkers since at least the end of the nineteenth century, and even identified by some of the most canonical figures populating our most influential histories of political thought. Nevertheless, given the force of claims that we really should be thinking about a politics of the world, and at least equally important claims that we ought to be thinking about difference, heterogeneity, contingency and liberty in ways that are not contained within a logic of universality-within-particularity and particularity-within-universality, the theory of international relations offers an especially disturbing ground from which to engage the boundaries, borders and limits of a politics that aspires to the world but must always repudiate it, and aspires to diversity, heterogeneity, contingency and liberty but must always bring them in or keep them out. The theory of international relations may or may not have much to say about what happens within a political order structured as a series of inclusions and exclusions, but its most disturbing challenge to the contemporary political imagination is its affirmation of a prior array of inclusions and exclusions that enable us to think so clearly about universalities that are not universal and differences that must remain very much the same.

(Life is often hopeful) between the lines

It is tempting to conclude that the imagination of any other kind of political imagination must abandon accounts of boundaries as either here forever or about to disappear, and try to generate accounts of boundaries as much more complicated and problematic phenomena. Indeed, this conclusion is already expressed in my initial premises. I do expect our political futures to be characterized by practices of boundary formation that are much more diverse and elusive than is suggested by prevailing narratives about modern subjects, states, the system of states and the specifically modern forms of discrimination, authorization and exceptionalism these narratives both express and enable. Nevertheless, the grounds on which judgements might be made about novel forms of boundary formation remain unclear, largely because, I have been suggesting, so many attempts to think about contemporary boundaries have been overwhelmed by powerful narratives about their eternal presence or imminent absence articulated as a temporality of escape from, or eternal capture by, a spatialized political order of modern subjectivities.

It is certainly possible to draw upon many images of boundaries (like skin, tidal zones and other metaphors of ebb and flow) as multidimensional sites and moments, as guides to the many ways contemporary political boundaries absorb, excrete, sort, sieve or respond to danger. Many analysts (sociologists, anthropologists, novelists, journalists and many others) might help us think about richer palettes of shadings and shadows, of distributions, simultaneities, indistinctions and the temporal contingencies of spatial form, even while reminding us of the potential presence of some razor's edge. Historians might celebrate continuities, uncertainties and contingencies in order to subvert myths of foundation erected on a line drawn between modernity and all its others.[53] Topologists would want us to think about a less restricted repertoire of geometries, invite a richer formalization of spatiotemporal dispersions, and probably ask us to consider the potential implications of a Möbius ribbon that has no clear internality or externality.[54] To the extent that it has been possible to think about boundaries without reproducing pervasive accounts of presence and absence, many commentators seem to expect our collective political futures to experience a shift to a more diverse and complicated range of boundary practices. No big surprise, one might say.

Nevertheless, much of what I have said here has been intended to forestall any quick conclusion that our political futures will or should express a move from simple to complicated, even if it is likely that more technically precise notions of structural, topological and governmental complexity will increasingly inform the way we are able to imagine any other ways of acting politically. While I have no doubt that the imagination of any future politics will have to work through principles that will seem both more complicated, and in need of very precise empirical specification by comparison with the apparently elegant simplicities of scalar relations between subjects, states and system organized within clear spatiotemporal boundaries, I also think it a profound mistake to treat modern politics, and especially its practices of sovereignty and boundary formation, as the simplicity against which any possible future can be scripted as some form of complexity. On the contrary, the temptation to imagine any future politics as a complete switch from one condition to another – whether from international relations to world politics, from international relations to empire, from international relations to cosmopolis, from a modern international relations to a postmodern something else, or from international relations as the paradigm of crude simplifications of the necessities and possibilities of modern political life to something more suitably complex and multidimensional – is so strong that it is worth dwelling on the enormous complexity of what has come to be treated as the simplified, even simplistic, world from which we need to escape.

Consequently, rather than pretending that I have any especially clear view of what the boundaries of any future political order might be like, I would say that we need to appreciate what has already been at stake in the way modern politics, and most forms of political analysis, have so readily treated boundaries, borders and limits as mere lines distinguishing already established entities, especially as a ground from which to think about the boundaries of any future political order. This is why I have suggested that it is necessary to engage with a specific regulative ideal of what a boundary must be: the ideal, that is, of the straight, thin line that simply distinguishes here from there, them from us, and, less obviously but no less significantly, now from then. In what I have tended to treat as the exemplary case in early-modern European philosophy, science, and especially mathematics, the Galilean or Cartesian line drawn from man to world implies the line distinguishing man from world. It is in this context that I believe we must appreciate the force of Mercator's cartographic representations and the characteristic dilemmas of a modern subjectivity seeking to reach out to the world from which it has been liberated, while remaining at least vaguely aware of the limits of its own finitude: of the particularity of selves and collectivities of selves that can never quite realize ambitions for universality within. Thus, just as I have argued that the practices of modern sovereignty must be treated as a much more puzzling inheritance than might be guessed from the narratives of presence and absence such practices express and enable, it is necessary to insist on the already complex politics of boundaries expressing and enabling some of the most pervasive ambitions and achievements of modern life precisely because they have been normalized into regulative idealizations of past, present and future, as well as of the sovereign capacity to enact exceptions, or borders, or limits to any political norm.

This ideal of a straight, thin line expresses a specific topological form that we know most intimately from Euclidean definitions of points, lines and planes. It has long worked as a regulative ideal enabling a regulative ideal, and an authorization of a normalizing authority. It enables us to think about discrimination as the identification of already-constituted entities on either side of a line; to presume that space, territory and place are all contained within these lines while also generating suspicions that space is not only containable and knowable through its empirical expressions, but also transcendental and beyond the grasp of mere mortals; nevertheless to stop worrying about any worlds beyond the grounds of our apparently certain knowledge by defining the limit, the point at which we are able to draw the line between the finite and the infinite; to translate this presumed topology into a scalar line of temporal transition from one condition to another, or a revolutionary leap from one distinguishable condition to another; and, my most specific concern here, to assume that the modern internationalized system of states is actually or potentially coextensive with the world as such.

This latter assumption, I have especially tried to suggest, mobilizes all the narratives of capture and escape attending the creation and delimitation of potentially but never quite sovereign subjects, potentially but never quite sovereign states, and the potentially but never quite sovereign system of states: narratives that I have tried to mobilize in turn by running through some of the key moments at which variations on the theme of capture and escape work to affirm a specific idealization of boundaries as spatial sites and temporal moments, where very little happens. While I see no necessary reason to expect the topological inheritance of Euclidean points, lines and planes to remain persuasive, even as a regulative ideal let alone as a guide to empirical developments, nor any reason to expect boundaries, borders and limits to disappear from political life, I am persuaded that no significant political analysis of boundaries is now possible without an appreciation of the ways in which boundaries have long been sites and moments in which a great deal happens to produce the forms of political life that are subsequently treated as distinct entities distinguished by lines that do nothing at all.

So, keeping in mind the various directions from which I have sought to portray sovereignty as a problem exceeding the achievements of specific forms of sovereignty, let me close with a brief elaboration of five ways of thinking about boundaries that I have sought to highlight in the specific manner in which I have constructed my analysis. Again, the comments I make here are intended only as indications of many other analytical possibilities, all with extensive implications for how we might understand relations between practices of sovereignty and practices of bounding, bordering and the articulation of limits to any other political possibilities.

First, both the narrative of founding expressed by Hobbes in the seventeenth century, and the account of the relation of norm and exception formalized in a few minimalist but fateful phrases by Schmitt in the twentieth century, suggest a much more interesting array of mutually constitutive, contradictory and aporetic relationships, whether in terms of temporal origin or spatiotemporal delimitation. One key reason for engaging with paradigmatic theorists of sovereignty like Hobbes and Schmitt is that they do so much to disrupt as well as affirm assumptions of radical dualism guiding most popular accounts of modern sovereignty, and show how the appearance of radical dualism that is reproduced in claims about the eternal presence or imminent absence of sovereignty rest on practices for which terms like contradiction, mutual constitution and even aporia seem increasingly inadequate. Many forms of contemporary social, cultural and political analysis offer related accounts of the product that produces the producer, the after that produces the before, the creation that creates the creator, the effect that generates the cause, the order that produces the chaos, the other that produces the self, and the sovereignty that is both within and beyond the law. While identity may indeed be enacted time and time again on either side of a line, so that friend is forced to confront enemy and nation is required to confront nation across lines of sovereign discrimination, the sovereign capacity to decide exceptions to the norm that enables identity to be enacted on either side must always exceed any boundary, border or limit in order to authorize its capacity to authorize its own boundaries, borders, and limits.

Even though thinking about sovereignty in terms of contradictions, aporias and practices of founding where no foundations exist is at odds with most prevailing forms of commonsense, as well as with the expectations of many scholarly disciplines, it is entirely consistent with many conventional accounts of the dilemmas of modern subjectivity, those strange beings that know themselves to be subjects capable of knowing and being for ourselves precisely because they are in principle constitutively separated from any objective world outside themselves. Even though it might be argued that these dilemmas exceed the specific conditions of modern cultures, and might be framed differently in competing claims to modernity, it is fairly clear that the characteristic forms of freedom/alienation from the world that have been celebrated as such a great achievement of post-Renaissance societies have made it especially easy for modern political life to affirm both a Hobbesian account of a founding contract predicated on a historical narrative affirming the necessity and freedom of the modern world, and a Kantian aspiration for an internalized universal moral law that is always destined for imperfection. Here we are most certainly dealing not just with practices that are limited to the sovereignty of modern nation-states, but also with practices reaching into the creation myths and spatiotemporal trajectories expressed in theological, ontological and cultural traditions informing the practices of such states.

It is not just that the Treaty of Westphalia is a very dubious event with which to situate the origins of a modern international political order. It is obvious enough that Westphalia marks only one of many possibilities for thinking about the foundations of modern political life. Yet the search for *any* such origin will have profound implications for the way we think about limits, borders and boundaries. Begin in 1648 in particular, it might be said, and the route to a levels of analysis schematic in which the boundaries between individual subjects, nation-states and an international system are both assumed and erased is entirely predictable. As an expression of the normative topology of modern politics, and especially the ways in which antagonisms between both universality and particularity, and liberty and equality, have been resolved through a (Platonist and Aristotelian) hierarchy of scale that nevertheless effaces both the politics of origins and the politics of delimitation, the categorial scheme that has anchored the construction of Anglo-American theories of international relations for over half a century is undeniably brilliant in this respect. Begin with these categories, accept *these* assumptions, and there is no longer any need to think about anything other than the way modern political life is supposed to be.

Conversely, it is not just that Schmittean accounts of a sovereign exceptionalism offer a devastating retort to anyone presuming to speak of some liberal universalism or a politics of difference without limit, but that the demand for the delimitation of either universalizing or particularizing possibilities will both express and affirm a specific understanding of historical origins. There is little point in assuming that Schmitt can be understood only in the context of the 1920s and 1930s, important as I think that era was in shaping many of the contours of contemporary politics and political analysis, or that he can be dismissed as just another nasty character who associated with some other very nasty characters, although Schmitt's own legitimation of extraordinary violence is certainly intolerable. The account of sovereign limits he offered affirms a story about the origins and limits of a modern international order that is shared by many figures whom we tend to place on the side of the great and the good, not least the Kant who has become the default guide for most cosmopolitan critiques of sovereign delimitation.

With the Treaty of Westphalia and a Schmittean exceptionalism in place, and thus with the usual accounts of what it means to pursue a theory of international relations affirmed, a middle ground can be assumed and sovereignty can be located right at the centre of things as a monopoly over the deployment of legitimate violence within a specific spatialized territory. Again, Weber's reading of the modern state through the existential and nationalist decision demanded by processes of modernization and formal rationalization that undermine all grounds for the substantive justification of values is undoubtedly brilliant, not least because it struggles with both Kantian and Nietzschean accounts of origins and limits while constructing an account of the modernizing process from well within the presumptions of modernity. Nevertheless, while Weber's account of monopolistic power centred in a specific territory may offer a normalized ideal of what state sovereignty is supposed to be, in ways that have provided the still influential archetype for many claims to a political realism, it does so only by minimizing the way state sovereignty works to construct a centre between extremes; and, in the case of the highly nationalist state, to construct a centre that is itself capable of going to extremes.

Still, if even Hobbesian and Schmittean accounts of sovereignty, or indeed Weber's reading of the contradictions of modernization, raise questions about any sharp distinction between inner and outer in their accounts of origins and exceptions, there is reason to suspect that the relation between sovereignty and boundaries has never been accessible through a binary logic of presence and absence, here and there, or now and then. What may appear closed, whether as logic or historical/structural condition, invites other interpretations, not least of the practices through which appearances of closure are sustained. Hobbes, for example, might be read as a specifically English response to a specifically English revolution, but his authorization of authorities that might authorize takes us far beyond the spatiotemporality of one specific state in order to affirm the sovereignty of any particular state.

As Machiavelli would ardently insist, creation is a difficult art. Hobbes was very, very good at it, not only because he had a sophisticated sense of what was at stake in the structural upheavals and political interests expressed in the specific events of the English civil war, but also, and perhaps more significantly, because he had a similarly sharp sense of what was at stake in defining the possibilities of political life inside a finite order of calculation uncontaminated by the seductions of infinity. Creation has since become an especially difficult art for traditions that both celebrate their radical dynamism as modernizers, and yet cling to a myth of origins that must never change as the condition under which modern subjects can become what they are already supposed to be in an internationalized political order. It will be even more difficult for anyone who thinks that the regulative ideal of a line between one condition and another offers any useful way for thinking about an alternative to a structure of norms and alternatives, or for thinking about boundaries, borders and limits in ways that exceed the topological ideal of a line distinguishing old from new.

It matters whether we think about sovereignty in terms given by one specific account of what sovereignty must be, or seek to engage with the conditions under which that account has been enabled to claim where, when, what, why and how we are in the world and thus to imagine any other possibilities, or not. Many people find it daunting enough to come to terms with the enormous conceptual resources activated by people such as Hobbes in order to enable such a powerful account of the beginnings and endings of things, and to affirm such an extraordinary account of a middle ground that works both to shape geophysical ground and to produce groundless foundations. Yet the resources available to Hobbes and company are far removed from the way at least some people are now able to think about cosmologies, bodies, causalities and creations, even though probably very few of us have given much thought to how we might think about anything at all without succumbing to the dangerous attractions of an infinity beyond ourselves that shaped the imagination not only of Hobbes and his followers, but also many of those who have sought to resist Hobbesian conclusions.

Creation and delimitation is a very difficult art indeed, as so many canonical thinkers have recognized, but it is one in which anyone claiming to say anything about alternatives to modern accounts of the present and its alternatives will need to invest quite heavily. They will have to do so not least in relation to questions about the possibilities of critique, whether scholarly or more overtly political, given that our understanding of critical possibility since Kant has been enabled within a specific (Hobbesian) arena of sovereign authorization permitting a distinction between dogma and critique, but thus not permitting judgements about anything that is excluded in order to set up a struggle between dogmatism and critique.

There is clearly some incentive for established scholarly disciplines to hold onto the clichés that permit such questions to be cast as esoteric matters of concern only to theorists, philosophers, theologians or metaphysicians. Nevertheless, if challenges to established forms of sovereignty are as pressing as the volume of literature on these challenges seems to suggest, no matter how incoherently, these clichés will eventually have to give way to engagements with political principles that cannot simply assume the authorized discriminations expressed in claims about the boundaries of modern political possibility and impossibility. Like critique, political theory is not dispensable. Nevertheless, political theory cannot simply assume an essentializing distinction between internal and external expressions of a politics of subjects, states and system of states, or the narratives about the sovereign authorization of the sovereign authorities expressed in this distinction. Endless debates between nationalists and cosmopolitans are only symptoms of a much more serious problem in this respect, and no-one who feels comfortable within either of these categories can have much to say about the imagination of any other political possibilities and impossibilities.

Second, and consequently, the framing of modern political life within the regulative limits expressed in Hobbesian foundation myths and Schmittean exceptions affirms the prior framing of the three lines distinguishing man and nature, immanence and transcendence, and modern and premodern: lines that have been especially effective in showing how we must think about lines, and lines that have also been especially effective in effacing the practices through which these distinctions have come to have such enormous authority as grounds for authority. These three distinctions remain at the heart of contemporary political controversies, which nevertheless continue to be guided by the dualistic alternatives expressed in the regulative ambitions of a modern international order.

It is possible to respond to many contemporary ecological concerns by empowering state and interstate authorities to engage with dangers exceeding the standard conceptualizations of national security, but the response will also do much to heighten awareness of the stakes involved in the historical construction of a sharp distinction between man and nature. One can try to respond to patterns of poverty and mal-development by empowering sovereign authorities to bring the most disadvantaged into the modern world, but the attempt will also sharpen awareness of the stakes involved in bringing everyone into a modern capitalist order that works by promising freedom and equality among the excluded while simultaneously generating exclusions and inequalities, though not necessarily as a spatiotemporal hierarchy among developed and developing states. One can try to affirm secularization and enlightenment so as to avoid religious dogmatism, but suspicions will be confirmed not only that secularism is by no means free of dogma, but also that modern claims to secular immanence have been enabled by the very attempt to exclude transcendental or metaphysical possibilities, by ontotheologies and mysteries that enable much more than just religious commitments.

In all three contexts it is possible to identify many contemporary refusals, in principle and in practice, of the sharp line inviting us to become one thing or the other on either side so as to affirm nature or culture, tradition or modernity, religious transcendence or secular immanence, or to submit to discourses about enlightenment and romanticism, or relativism, or barbarism, or superstition that draw upon all three. Nevertheless, these distinctions remain very influential. They enable much of the disciplinary structure of contemporary political analysis. They will probably continue to inform the way we think about boundaries, borders and limits in many other contexts. Still, I would say that they are also clearly in considerable trouble, and it is difficult to see how any form of political practice that lays claim to some kind of progressive or emancipatory ambition can still take them for granted, rather than as sites of considerable uncertainty. The extent to which we might be able to think more creatively about boundaries, borders and limits certainly depends on our capacity to resist the lines the modern world has drawn to distinguish itself from these three versions of some other worlds beyond.

Third, and to become slightly (but only slightly) more specific, much of what is of interest about modern politics effectively works *within* lines rather than on either side of them. In the broadest terms, this is a major reason why I have sought to read Kant's account of modern political possibilities and impossibilities not in terms of the usual either/or, republican autonomy or supranational authority, but of a decisive uncertainty about which way to go in a world defined between the lines he draws between immanence and transcendence, on the one hand, and between the phenomena knowable to modern subjects and the noumena that are always beyond human knowledge, on the other: that is, within the line delimiting a normalized and normalizing modernity that must always be aware of the great unknowns lurking at either limit, and within the line marking the distinction between those who are willing to come within the world of modern delimitations and those who are not. With Kant, the framing of a temporal origin through a spatialized understanding of temporality sets up spatial limits that are always under assault temporally, but are nevertheless affirmed by the assault.

Well, no, this is hardly any more specific, let alone concrete, so why is this particular formulation so important in this context? It is, I would say, because it speaks to a politics that is out of line: out of line not only in the sense of a politics that is somehow both outside and inside that which is contained within a line; or in the sense of a politics that somehow deviates from the line that has been inscribed as appropriate; or even in the sense of a politics that has somehow run out of line and no longer has the resources to sustain its ambitions; but especially in the sense of a politics that has emerged from within a line. Topologies enable practices, and practices enable topologies, but the specific topology expressed as the sharp boundaries, borders and limits of modern political life within a sovereign system of sovereign states has been especially effective as a political practice that seems to do nothing more than distinguish already constituted forms of politics. I have sought to highlight several themes in this respect.

Thus I have argued that one of the primary implications of the framing of modern politics as an international order is that the complex negotiation between competing claims to universality and particularity is impossible to resolve by absorbing universality into particularity or particularity into universality without destroying the regulative ideal of a political order both of universalities within particularities and particularities within universalities that we know as the sovereign subject, the sovereign state and the sovereign system of states: the order in which sovereignty is never sovereign, and never contained within a singular boundary. What is of interest, therefore, is what happens where and when one boundary meets another, where, not least, the claims of sovereign states to domestic jurisdiction meet the claims of the sovereign system of states to collective order. Rather than one line distinguishing state from international levels of analysis, or a particular exception from a general exception, two lines – at the limits of the sovereign state and at the limits of a sovereign system of states – frame sites and moments of aporia and/or negotiation.

Many conventional forms of political analysis might claim to specialize in these worlds between lines that are nevertheless also conventionally reduced to a single line of absolute distinction. I have especially alluded to the tension between Schmitt and Kelsen as a way of highlighting the degree to which international law is constantly dismissed on radically nationalist grounds, rather than appreciated as a very complex array of often inconsistent accommodations among competing sovereignties. Analysts of foreign policy and diplomatic practice, and, indeed, many scholars attuned to the detailed historical or empirical record, might want to insist that they understand very well what it means to work between such lines. Analysts of the way modern cultures have distinguished themselves from nature, or theologies, or other cultures also might point to very large literatures exploring the ambiguities and shifting meanings at work in, say, constructions of the nation, cultural identity or gender as somehow both natural and invented. This understanding has nevertheless had remarkably little effect on disciplinary attachments to the single delineation of an either/or. These attachments have encouraged not only the radical nationalisms expressed in many claims about political realism, but also the normalization of an exceptionalist politics in the construction of academic disciplines, and a willingness by some currents of supposedly progressive political analysis to read all practices of bounding, bordering and delimitation as extreme versions of an essentializing exceptionalism. In this respect, the exemplary care with which Foucault approached the various manifestations of boundary/border/limit conditions in the practices of modern subjectivity, and the attentiveness with which he sought to locate these conditions in a much broader matrix of ontological, theological, sociological and historical traditions than is to be found in either Schmitt or Kelsen, stands in instructive contrast to nationalist versions of political realism, the reified categories of modern social science and contemporary notions of a generalized exceptionalism alike.

One especially striking example of how many political practices work by reducing all the tensions and contradictions expressed in a field arrayed between two boundaries to a practice organized on either side of a line that is assumed to be somewhere in between is the currently widespread use of metaphors of a balance between liberty and security within the modern state. This is a metaphor that has come to be used to legitimize many responses to supposedly novel forms of violence and terror. Whatever judgements might be made about the need for such responses, or about any specific renegotiation of what it might now mean to aspire to liberties and equalities under conditions of some necessity, this is a metaphor that works with impressive elegance to convert a politics expressed as a limit condition into a politics expressed as an uncontentious norm. In effect, it is a metaphor that works not only to enable specific policy responses to contemporary claims about danger and the ultimate primacy of security over liberty, but also to efface the constitutive antagonism between principles of state sovereignty and principles of popular sovereignty – the antagonism that is at the core of the most important historical struggles to construct modern liberal democratic societies within territorial borders and legal limits.

Concepts of balance have long provided appropriately slippery possibilities for propaganda, partly because they can be made to affirm either equilibrium or preponderance in a systemic balance of power and in strategies of nuclear deterrence. In more recent usage, they have been deployed so as to legitimize practices framed through a normalized distribution of values along a (bell) curve that eventually tapers off at the limit, or margin, or exception: the curve that has become the regulative ideal of a sovereign authority predicated on utilitarian accounts of market rationality. In this case, a balance might be located either somewhere near the top of a curve, within a normalized range, or very close to the extreme margin or site of exception, the point at which normal behaviour shifts to become a matter of, say, national security policy.

Mobilized as an affirmation of the priority of security over liberty, balance is imagined at the margin, the boundary, the exceptional moment that will ultimately secure the normalized condition within. Mobilized as a competition between competing but equal values, balance is imagined at the centre, the normalized middle ground that has already been secured for responsible political contestation.

Once liberty and security are defined as similar sorts of values competing in a normalized field of utilitarian calculation, they can be made to balance as if they are somewhere near the peak of a curve of rational judgement. If more security is necessary, we are constantly told, we will obviously have to give up some liberty. Very sensible, it might seem. Many attacks on democratic procedure and the rule of law have been legitimized in this way.[55] However, far from being similar sorts of values competing on a field of utilitarian calculation, the concepts of liberty and security that have been articulated within the modern sovereign state and system of states work precisely as an antagonism of norm and the limit, margin or exception to that norm: we are all at liberty except when limits are reached and exceptions are declared. It is in this sense that security has been understood to be the exemplary practice of state sovereignty, and thus as always working in the shadow of Hobbesian, Kantian, Schmittean or Weberian accounts of the sovereign decisionism necessary when norms reach their constitutive limit. Liberty, by contrast, has been understood to be the province of popular sovereignty, as working in relation to a civil society or community that takes responsibility for its own emancipatory possibilities, usually for both liberty and equality, even if under conditions set by the capacity of sovereign states.

In this sense, the widespread use of what has become a very seductive metaphor works not only to legitimize some very troubling – illiberal – assaults on many of the achievements of liberal democratic societies, but also to displace the entire burden of sovereign responsibility from the state to civil society. People must submit to a choice between two competing but similar values as a consequence of claims made by sovereign authorities whose responsibility for the exercise of sovereignty is thereby minimized. The crucial problem of the relation between popular sovereignty and state sovereignty, the problem to which all the achievements of democratic representation and the rule of law are counted as the most effective solutions we can imagine, is thereby reduced to a choice at a single point and moment. It makes all the difference possible in the world of modern politics whether that point and moment are constructed on a line that is imagined to be at the centre of a normalized politics, or one drawn at the boundary, border and limit at which a confirming exception to that norm is enacted. To frame the derogation of law as a matter of balance is to try to shift all matters of political responsibility onto the popular will rather than onto those charged with the most extreme matters of emergency and exception requiring the suspension of any popular will. It is hardly surprising that resistance to such moves has come from the highest reaches of legal jurisdiction, where responsibility for any derogation of law is rightly understood to rest not with popular choices between two competing values, but with the most demanding expressions of sovereign authority within a state.

It is in this context, moreover, that we now see potentially far-reaching attempts to reshape the most basic assumptions about human subjectivity that have enabled the claims about liberty that are supposed to be secured by the process of (re-)balancing. Advanced as practical or even simply technical responses to new forms of danger and risk, many contemporary security practices work not so as to secure the modern subject in whose name the need for security is invoked, but precisely to attack the principles enabling a politics of modern citizen-subjects.[56] Perhaps most significantly, where modern accounts of the citizenship enabling liberty, equality and security within specific limits affirm a politics that is somehow liberated from the determinations of natural law, and operationalized on the basis of political identities guaranteed by birth certificates and legal signatures within the jurisdiction of a sovereign law, claims about a need to rebalance the relation between liberty and security now sustain attempts to switch back to a more "natural" account of political identity through an array of biometric procedures that might finally identify and secure the real flesh-and-blood being of each person. This is certainly one way of dispensing with the niceties of Hobbes's nominalism, but it is an ambition that threatens to undermine not only particular liberties, but the very notion of a modern citizen that might have liberty precisely as a conscious and reasoning subject rather than as an essentialized object of some supposedly natural authenticity authorized somewhere beyond the bounds of political authority. Exceptionalisms that enable appeals to blood and belonging have a discouraging history, to say the least. Disarming metaphors of an apparently reasonable balance, and a reasonable middle ground, should not obscure the profound antagonisms of principle and practice at work within lines that reach from extreme to extreme; in this case, lines that work not only between the norms and limits of sovereign states, but also between the claims of humanity to be part of some natural world and the claims of modern citizens to define their liberties in some other way.

Attempted reductions of a field of possibilities to a single line domestically also have an external analogue, again driven by claims about the security of modern subjects that systematically efface the contradictory character of subjects requiring security. For it is in relation to claims about security that forms of inclusion and exclusion, organized within a system of sovereign states, are most easily framed through simple accounts of friends and enemies here and there, through existential accounts of same and other distinguished by a single line. This is the version of Schmitt found in Morgenthau's nationalist version of political realism, for example, but it is no less present in readings of difference and pluralism as minor variations within an international order the essential universality of which can be presumed by any state or analyst seeking to make claims about other states. In effect, the international is read either as a realm of radically different and irreconcilable "values" or "interests," as in Morgenthau's story, or as a comparative politics constructed on a ground of similarity that reduces difference to a competition among actors playing the same game with greater or fewer resources and skills, the version preferred by forms of social science that insist on mistaking a specific account of modern (or economic) rationality for politics.

Again, however, a single line of discrimination is precisely what cannot be assumed by any form of political life predicated on modern forms of subjectivity, which must work through accounts of a doubled rather than a singular other. Otherness is produced both by the subject that knows the other, and by the processes through which the subject is produced as a capacity to know others. Others may be known to us because of our constitutive capacity as modern subjects to know others on our own terms, but others may also be known to us as the kind of beings who were excluded as the condition under which we became modern subjects capable of knowing others in specific ways. The radically reified existentialism of Schmitt's friends and enemies may mark an extreme condition appropriate for a radically solipsistic and racist nationalism, but as such it can only affirm a dramatic dissolution of a political order predicated on an aporetic relation between statist and systemic forms of sovereignty, with each form potentially expressing a mutually constitutive rather than existential relation between norm and exception.

It is in this context that we might engage with many famous debates about how modern subjects might know their others: with, for example, debates about how cultures of modern science might understand cultures of witchcraft; or the capacity of statist discourses to switch very quickly from representations of other states as essentially the same as themselves to representations of radical difference that must be cast out from the acceptable community of states; or the otherness of the underdeveloped that lie outside the pattern of inside and outside established among those who have already been brought inside. Both academic debate and statist rhetoric may readily affirm rituals of radical dualism, but in the world of modern politics, relations between subjects and others will always have to be negotiated (by diplomats, by peacekeepers, by lawyers, by aid workers, by journalists, by practices of everyday life) between two lines (in topological terms) or between structured practices of intersubjectivity (in the terms used by more sociological, hermeneutic or phenomenological traditions).

Again, while this has been commonplace among multiple forms of analysis of modern subjectivities at least since the days of Kant, contemporary political discourse continues to reduce a complex field of political negotiation, structural antagonism, and sovereign authorization to a simple line of spatialized discrimination. Various equivalents of Schmitt's existentialist story about friends and enemies can then subdue any attempt to understand the practices of mutual production that produce extreme accounts of existential isolation and absolute antagonism. It seems unlikely, however, that any attempt to engage with such themes as the "conflict of civilizations," or intercultural relations, or the dynamics of mutual recognition in a system of

states, or the continuing effects of colonial relations, or the politics of indigeneity, or the relation of centres and margins can achieve very much without
some understanding of the interplay between doubled externalities at work in
practices of modern subjectivity.[57]

Despite all the attractions of reducing complex fields to a single line, whether internally or externally, many attempts to declare boundaries, borders
and limits obsolete are tempted by interim formulations of some kind of zone
through which internal might gradually flow into external and external might
flow into internal. There are indeed many reasons to be tempted. Various
metaphors of flow and movement have become necessary props for many
attempts to make sense of dynamic political, economic and cultural practices
that elude the metaphors of stasis and containment thriving among analysts
of the modern state and system of states. Yet claims about contemporary
transitions from containments to flows, as from spatialities to temporalities,
can easily be made to affirm a familiar scale running from a politics within
boundaries to one without them. The line may thicken. An intervening field
of play may become more visible, or audible, or sensible between its inner and
outer edges, but that field or zone is often read not as a site of complexities,
disaggregations, contradictions or even as a normal curve, but as a straight
diagonal from presence to absence, or small to big, or containment to flow, or
space to time. An opening to more interesting accounts of boundaries, borders and limits, especially accounts that seek to engage with the lives of
people (such as refugees) who might be understood as living within boundaries, or attempts to speak about more open fields of political possibility, is
thereby disciplined back into grand narratives in which presence opposes
absence, time opposes space, and readings of boundaries, borders and limits
as complicated zones of uncertain but potentially innovative political practices are reabsorbed back into stories about the future absence of boundaries,
borders and limits. The regulative ideal of a single line of authoritative discrimination is thus just as likely to inform claims about transformation as
claims about stasis in this respect. While concepts of zones and flows may
often be empirically appealing, part of the appeal lies in their scope for con-
flating territorial borders with legal limits and for reading both together
through a narrative about the simple presence or absence of a sovereign
authority. Zones and flows may indeed be indispensable concepts for understanding contemporary political life, but it is still easier to use them as a
way of forgetting about politics than to ascribe any meaning to politics in
such terms.

Fourth, all these preceding three groups of comments might be reformulated to stress their spatiotemporal expression in ways that respond to many
claims that the spatiotemporal character of contemporary politics has been
shifting fairly dramatically. Such claims often give rise to the grand general-
ization with which I began my commentary, to the effect that political life is
no longer where, or therefore what, it is supposed to be. Many of the emerging clichés of contemporary political analysis gather under the sign of the

spatiotemporal. Some refer to a shift from spatial forms maintaining order through time to patterns of movement, speed and acceleration that work through time to bring new relationalities, networks, movements of information and capital, places within circulations, and lines of flight destined for some apparatus of capture. Some refer to a shift from singularities of identity, subjectivity and nationality to multiple subjectivities, identities and citizenships. Some refer to a simultaneous move towards both local and global, as the modern subject, modern sovereign state and modern system of sovereign states lose their capacity to resolve all contradictions between universality and particularity within a spatiotemporal particularity. Some refer to the urban settings in which half of humanity now lives, even if this is to the studied disinterest of most conventional forms of political analysis. At least four very large, and by now quite familiar, patterns of analysis have been at play in the contemporary literature in this respect.

One pattern works from the observation that no matter how much we might be impressed by the dynamic and temporal quality of modernity as a culture of change, especially of changes driven by various forms of technological and capitalist forms of destruction and innovation, the primary forms through which modernity finds expression politically affirm claims about spatial continuity. Hobbesian architectures have trumped Machiavellian virtuosities. It may be, as I have insisted, that the appearance of continuity has been an effect of a great many temporal practices, especially of the practices of state/system sovereignty that have become our modern archetype of structural stasis, but the appearance of continuity and spatial order has been precisely the necessary ambition of a politics organized within a contradictory arrangement of sovereign states within a sovereign system of states. Many forms of futurology have been built upon a claim that the temporal dynamics of modernization must eventually overthrow the spatialized statics of states and states-system, and by forgetting that processes of modernization and structures of states and states-system express specific temporalities, and ways of accommodating competing spatiotemporalities, rather than any singular spatiality or temporality. Here two things seem reasonably clear.

On the one hand, the spatiotemporal articulation of many contemporary social, economic, cultural and technological dynamics seems to be significantly at odds with the expectations of political authority expressed in the spatiotemporal organization of sovereign states within a system of states. It is in this context that we might appreciate not only what is at stake in attempts to reconstruct some kind of state control over financial and other markets, but also a burgeoning web of international, transnational and non-governmental institutions and practices that far exceed the official codes of political cartography. Novel theories of complexity might be appropriate here, as may be less caricatured understandings of spatiotemporalities, but not the standard narratives that would have temporal processes undermining outmoded spatial forms.

On the other hand, however, the language of modern politics has tended to privilege an idealized spatiality as the ground on which to understand and control the mysteries of change and temporality. We have been comforted by the great trinity of universalizing teleologies, national histories, and calculated risk, but politics as an art of timing and contingency remains profoundly disruptive. The rage for determinacy that drives so many contemporary political practices, not least under the rubric of security, is unlikely to remove the need for the skills of political judgement and responsibility in the face of temporal contingencies that exceed the best laid plans of any risk manager or surveillance machine. Here it is perhaps useful to remember that Machiavelli once calmly praised princes who construct fortresses to secure themselves from the caprices of *fortuna* as well as those who refuse to do so (the judgement, for Machiavelli, depended on circumstances), but also firmly condemned princes who failed to understand, in either case, the profound interdependence of prince and people.[58] The republican city-state is doubtless implausible as a model for our collective futures, but the relationship between temporal contingency and political virtuosity explored by Machiavelli is clearly in need of more creative imagination than we now find in most contemporary narratives about danger and insecurity. Despite reifications of claims about a shared political realism, Machiavelli and Hobbes speak to very different accounts of the relationship between practices of politics under dangerous conditions. Neither sits comfortably with the accounts of this relationship that can be extracted from other canonical thinkers such as Clausewitz, Weber or Schmitt, whose accounts of the subject that is to be secured must be similarly suspect as guides to the ways we might think about this relationship now.

Another pattern works from the observation that the regulative ideal requiring that all political boundaries be, in effect, stacked on top of each other, to be viewed from above as mere lines on a map, is contrary to everything we know about the empirical practices of boundaries, whether understood as borders or as limits, and especially understood as both borders and limits. This ideal is not just a "territorial trap." It is an ambition that is crucial for the claims of a modern international political order to be able to construct a world of universality-within-particularity and particularity-within-universality. It would not take very much to show that this ideal has always been more effective in aspirational than in empirical terms. It is also a fair guess that while claims about globalization are unlikely to be persuasive in forms that imagine the erasure of boundaries, borders and limits in a move from pluralism to universalism, they are likely to be more persuasive in forms that imagine boundaries, borders and limits becoming further disaggregated, dislocated from territorial topographies, articulated in novel topological forms, laid out more obviously as zones and fields of practice, and increasingly susceptible to temporal quite as much as spatial accounts of what it means to authorize discriminations as boundaries, borders and limits. Under such conditions, moreover, it is quite likely that what once worked as a practice of internality might work instead as a practice of externality; the tendency for military forces to be used for internal security operations and for police forces to be used for international peacekeeping missions may be suggestive of broader, and perhaps quite profound, trends in this respect.[59]

Yet another pattern works with the regulative capacity very quickly to switch accounts of exceptions framed as temporal origin to accounts of exceptions framed as spatial limits; from limits regulated by temporal figures of the barbarian/primitive to limits regulated by spatial figures of the enemy/anarchy. This switching has long been a familiar characteristic of the discourses of war, and affirms some of the linkage between narratives of founding and narratives of delimitation expressed in modern practices of sovereign authority. Nevertheless, the intensity of this switching may have increased significantly over the past decade. Whether in the cultural codes shaped by the contemporary mass media, or in the rhetorical descant played out through claims about a global war on terror,[60] the capacity to construct modalities of alterity that can be given either temporal or spatial expression almost at will (and with scant regard for what scholarly communities might regard as knowledgeable histories or geographies) may suggest some broader shift in the way contemporary political practices mobilize assumptions about the spatiotemporalities of human existence.

A final pattern works with the canonical distinction between citizen and human, the distinction that has haunted modern political life since the formation of a modern statist and interstatist order out of the ruins of theological and imperial hierarchies in early-modern Europe. Contemporary debates about political identity (about class, race, ethnicity, gender, indigeneity, and so on) have complicated, but certainly not usurped, this framing of what it means to be a modern political subject. Not everyone has been willing to abandon claims that we are all human regardless of political citizenship. Conversely, not everyone has been willing to place claims to humanity above duties to citizenship. Reconciliation between these two aporetic identities shaping the modern political condition has been sought primarily through claims about the state as the necessary condition of security and autonomy enabling citizens to realize their humanity within and claims about the system of states as the collectivity of citizens that might eventually add up to some humanity. This is the spatial arrangement that may or may not permit, or at least enable, a regulative (Kantian) ideal of a historical/teleological process of enlightenment.

The vitality of this aporetic condition is readily gauged from many contemporary debates about human rights and humanitarian intervention. Many commentators remain content to play the predictable moves of citizen first or human first, thereby perpetuating the equally predictable oscillation from a nationalist political realism affirming the ethical priority of claims about citizenship to a cosmopolitan political idealism affirming a particular claim about what it means to be human under modern conditions. Still, many others are more inclined to insist, I suspect rightly, that spatiotemporal articulations of contemporary political identities considerably exceed this canonical cartography: that neither this particular understanding of citizenship nor this particular understanding of what it means to be human either exhausts the possibilities that might be desired, or makes sufficient sense of the empirical complexity of contemporary political orders marked, for example, by mobile populations with multiple citizenships confronting novel procedures for regulating immigration and controlling populations. If warranted, this is an insistence that may well provide the greatest challenge for anyone seeking to reimagine where, and therefore what, we take politics to be. Attempts to open up questions about political identity that fail to engage this challenge are likely to keep playing out a perpetual return to an idealized community-in-unity affirming the inescapability of some form of statist nationalism.

A move back up the scales of subordination has many attractions in this respect. Affirm the priority of either universality or particularity, and movement up or down the scalar order of being seems entirely logical. Nevertheless, Kant was ultimately right to be suspicious. Neither direction seems compatible with ambitions for a political order aspiring to achieve a condition of both universality-within-particularity and particularity-within-universality; compatible, that is with the regulative ideal of a modern understanding of autonomous subjectivities. Affirm the priority of universality, especially, and the ideal of a self-determination that has come to be expressed in the name of national citizenship must ultimately dissolve in favour of the regulative ideal of someone's concept of humanity: that is, of a concept conventionally associated with the threat of an imperium that has been the regulative negation of the promise of a politics of modern subjectivities. Hierarchies may indeed be possible, and even necessary, within this form of political order, but it is no more likely that principles of imperium will offer sustainable grounds for some other form of politics, than that principles of inequality can offer acceptable solutions to a politics of liberty and self-determination.

The meanings that might be given to concepts such as liberty, equality, security, citizenship, subjectivity, society, community, democracy, universality and particularity, as well as the relations between them, might all be up for contestation and renegotiation. Indeed, I think there can be very little doubt that this is the case, or that any of them can be rethought in isolation. There is, nevertheless, little point hoping that any of these terms can be rethought by requalifying them as somehow global or cosmopolitan in the sense prescribed by a revival of principles of hierarchical subordination. In any case, the desire for hierarchical subordination that pervades so much of the contemporary literature on contemporary political transformation betrays much the same fear of temporality and desire for a spatialized order as is already expressed in the modern state and system of states. Combine questions about how we might think about either similarities or differences in relation to claims about either citizenship or humanity without reaffirming the universality-within-particularity and particularity-within-universality of the modern subject, modern state and modern system of states with questions about what it might mean to think about a politics in time that does not relapse into a privileging of spatial order as the condition within which temporality might be controlled, and one can begin to get some sense of what might be involved in reimagining the modern political imagination. Narratives about a move from international relations to world politics may save a lot of work in this respect, but it is work that needs to be done, and done rather urgently.

Fifth, if the boundaries, borders and limits enacted by the structuring of modern subjects, sovereign states and system of sovereign states have worked to fix all claims to universality and diversity within a tightly articulated spatiotemporal framework of inclusions, exclusions and linear trajectories, we should expect not a shift from diversity to universality, or the other way around, but a rearticulation of relations of universality and particularity, of the spatiotemporalities of their ongoing rearticulation, and, more to the point, a more intense politicization and depoliticization (and thus politicization) of the authorization of discriminations between universality and particularity, and especially of the conditions under which what are taken to be acceptable forms of political life are suspended and violence is declared to be legitimate.

That is to say, to imagine the possibility of some way of imagining political life that does not relapse into some (idealized) version of the universality-within-particularity and particularity-within-universality expressed in the modern international system is to run into significant difficulties with ascribing meaning to the term politics itself. Some people may think this a sufficient reason to affirm the simple elegance of a modern internationalized political order, or to be nostalgic for the way this order was once supposed to have been, at least according to the essentializing accounts of the political that Schmitt expresses in extreme form. More likely, and as I have sought to suggest by leaving this term as open as possible, even at the cost of analytical precision, it is sufficient reason to resist reverting to essentialized accounts of the political, whether assuming a conventional account of a modern internationalized political order or suspecting that some quite profound transformations of this order are in process. I have played out two primary themes in this respect.

One arises from the difficulty of holding onto conceptions of *the* political that rest ultimately on conceptions of a firmly located political community, some distant heir to the classical *polis*, but grounded in specific claims about the priority of modern subjects, large and small, that can be simply distinguished from other firmly located political communities. Not the least concern arising from claims about globalization and cosmopolitanism, for example, has been that they have tended to renew suspicions about the desire to avoid politics by shifting as fast as possible into claims about ethics, market rationality, and/or a depoliticized administration of things. Indeed, some of the popularity of many claims about globalization might be explained precisely by the opportunity they have provided for reviving old attempts to treat politics as a mere epiphenomenon of a determinate economy, a subsystem or function of a broader social order, a mere mechanism for converting prior ethical principles into practice, or even something distastefully inferior to some higher cosmopolitan cultural tradition. Many disciplinary vultures have cast their eyes on the bits and pieces that might be picked up from theories of politics that no longer have a *polis* to talk about. Such ambitions may be misguided on many fronts, but it remains the case that not many of the concepts that give some more specific content to modern accounts of politics work very well unless framed in relation to a presumed spatial location containing a particular community among other communities.

The other is less obvious, but perhaps more important, and arises from the difficulty of sustaining claims about sovereignty in grand stories about a great founding and the increasingly obvious arbitrariness of the authorization of modern forms of sovereign authority. This is one of the key reasons why I have stressed the significance of the politics that produces a politics, the authorization of what it could possibly mean to affirm authority, that is played out in the early chapters of Hobbes' *Leviathan*. Many of the better known twentieth-century political analysts made their reputation by offering specific definitions of what politics must be in order to put the study of politics on some sort of systematic or quasi-scientific footing. Nietzsche doubtless would object that only something without a history can be defined, and that concepts of politics certainly do not have the status of the ahistorical. Hobbes might have smiled, shrugged or even winced at the naivety of any political analyst who might fail to understand the political stakes involved in defining what politics must be, or in thinking that sovereignty is a simple fact of life that must be taken as the foundational assumption of any modern political analysis.

One of the more elementary consequences of the practices of modern sovereignty as articulated by people like Hobbes is that any understanding of political life depends not on finding an acceptable definition, but on some analysis of the political practices through which definitions of the political come to be authorized. Hobbes may have hoped that the politics through which he produced a specific account of a politics would be quickly forgotten, and this is certainly the historical achievement expressed in many accounts of the political architecture he managed to shape. Since then, we have been confronted with questions about whether some practice is really political or merely something else, whether politics has lost its allure in favour of something else, or whether everything has been taken over by the political. Once *the* political is identified on either side of a line, whether a line distinguishing a politics of founding from a politics that is thereby founded, or a line distinguishing one site or moment of the political from another, essentialization quickly sets in and definitions perform as Hobbes would have expected. The problem of sovereignty is conjured away. Practices authorizing authority conveniently recede from the concerns of those who think they engage some already given real world. Accept the assumptions, define the point, decide the exception, but don't start asking questions about how assumptions and definitions are made and affirmed as grounds for subsequent authorities, not least as some middle ground that is home to some centralized authority or as the dangerous limits enabling claims about a middle ground.

Yet if lines of discrimination are not so simple or so secure, if the delimitation of the political is itself a political act, essentialization is not such an easy option; as Hobbes already knew, but as a broad range of contemporary analysts have had to work very hard to remind us. What must come to be of interest are the practices through which specific forms of politics are produced and made apparently unproblematic, but nevertheless subject to practices demonstrating how the apparently unproblematic works to enable or disable, to include or exclude, to authorize or de-authorize. These practices will occur on, or within, sites and moments of spatiotemporal bounding, not simply in those sites and moments produced through the act of authorizing discriminations between one condition and another. As practice, as response to and expression of spatiotemporal contingency rather than of a presumed spatiotemporal necessity, conceptions of *the* political must give way to practices through which anything is subject to politicization, any form of depoliticization must work as a practice of politicization, and many of the most fateful forms of politicization and depoliticization must occur in relation to the boundaries, borders and limits where and when most traditions of modern political analysis have preferred to assume that very little happens at all.

Just as accounts of modern rationality are far more productive when read in terms of the traditions of scepticism that appreciate the degree to which knowledge is a problem, rather than a dogma that can be deployed as a weapon under the banner of Enlightenment, so also modern accounts of political possibility and impossibility are better read in terms of the degree to which all universalizing claims are enabled within a particular, and very finely orchestrated, array of boundaries, borders and limits, and all particularizing claims are enabled within a particular, and equally finely orchestrated, array of claims to universality. The politicization and depoliticization of political possibilities and impossibilities, I have argued, is literally crucial for an understanding of what it means to speak of modern politics as an international politics. If it is the case that we can expect to be engaging with some as yet unpredictable rearticulation of the spatiotemporal conditions under which political lives are shaped, we should probably expect to be disappointed in traditions that try either to rediscover *the* political in some particular place, or to invent some other (depoliticized) version of the political somewhere in *the* world at large. The challenge, rather, is to imagine the potentials that might be created in a sustained politicization of the boundaries, borders and limits of modern political formations in ways that capitulate neither to a Schmittean exceptionalism nor to the self-righteous universalisms that must eventually drive us to accept some versions of a Schmittean exceptionalism as the condition under which we can affirm our self-righteous selves.

If hope lies in resistance to demands that we either escape from, or continue to submit to, a political order that is already constructed as a formalized practice of containment and escape, it lies also in a capacity to appreciate the contradictory character of that order and the cost of analytical procedures that presume a radical dualism as a ground of scholarly credibility; in a capacity to appreciate the cost of the constitutive exclusions that have enabled modern forms of politics to be constructed as an array of inclusions and exclusions enabling claims about the potential of modern subjectivity, but also dire warnings about the necessity of violence at the boundaries, borders and limits of such subjectivities; in a capacity to appreciate the constitutive intensity of political practices that are at work within boundaries, borders and limits at which it has become easy to assume that little of any consequence ever happens; in a capacity to appreciate the conditions enabling the formal structuring of modern politics as a specific articulation of spatiotemporal possibilities that might be subject to rearticulation; and in a capacity to appreciate what it might mean to resist demands for *the* political, or its eradication, while sustaining the possibility of politics.

Yes, still very abstract, it will be said; and altogether too many unanswered questions about ethics, rights, resistance, law, rights, security, liberty, equality, democracy and authority over life and death take flight from such openings to contingency. Still, better that they take flight from some understanding of a politics that has produced a specific array of contingent claims about the political than from any claim that we already know what politics must be because we know where it must be, and can thus presume that all the problems of modern politics can be solved – eventually, in principle – by perfecting an aporetic order that is always prone to fracture, or by shifting as fast as possible to a politics of the world that is necessarily beyond reach. In any case, abstractions – the concepts, the discriminations, the assumptions about the spatiotemporalities of politics and the politics of spatiotemporalities, the regulative ideals, the ontotheologies, the topologies, the authorizations of authority, the claims to sovereignty, the signatures and certificates, the declarations of limits, the presumptions of humanity – have had enormous potential to shape what we can and cannot be as both political and human beings. To engage with the constitutive capacities of such densely structured abstractions, and the contradictory principles and practices they express and enable, is perhaps also to enable and express other ways of becoming otherwise in worlds that do not end where we have learnt to draw the line with such elegance, and with such violence.

Notes

2 Political, international, theoretical

1 Readings of modernity of the kind I rely on here are notoriously contentious, not least when framed as a singular and universalizing formation. Most contemporary uses of the term are informed less by the concerns of historical specificity than by various accounts of an "era" or "culture" characterized by the turn from religious faith to a secular conception of rationality, and by the articulation of an ideal of an autonomous subject or individuality. Stories about the interplay of reason and subjectivity sustain most standard accounts of the Renaissance, Scientific Revolution, Reformation, Enlightenment, and so on, and became a primary concern of what emerged as the canonical tradition of modern philosophy from Descartes onwards, especially as this canon was encapsulated and reformulated by Kant and his successors. This story has long been contested, on many grounds, though much recent debate about Enlightenment, postmodernity, the death of God and the loss of foundations has tended to assume otherwise. It became especially problematic at the end of the nineteenth century, in ways that are perhaps best captured in Max Weber's analysis of the fate of the modern "personality" caught between a rationality of ultimate values and a rationality of instrumental modernization. I engage with all these themes in what follows, mainly with the two specific intentions of resisting the reduction of a rich and complex field of enquiry into a banal choice between universalism and relativism that guides much of the secondary literature, and, more specifically, of understanding the topological formalizations of a political order predicated on claims about a culture of modern subjectivities expressing claims to *both* universality and particularity made by individuals, states, and a system of states orchestrated on a scale reaching from the never quite infinitely small to the never quite infinitely large.

2 Thomas Hobbes, "The Introduction," *Leviathan* (1651), edited by Richard Tuck, Cambridge: Cambridge University Press, 1991, 11.

3 It will become apparent that I use terms like mutual constitution and contradiction fairly loosely, for reasons that should become clear; two in particular. On the one hand, I worry about the degree to which prevailing accounts of dialectics, associated especially with Hegel's vision of history but resting heavily on Aristotle's two-valued logic, assume that relations of antagonism can be resolved by privileging one half of a dualism so as to guarantee a temporal (teleological or historical) move towards a presumed universality. On the other hand, while I argue for greater attention to both practices of mutual production and logics of contradiction in the analysis of sovereignty and boundary conditions, I also argue that the analysis of both sovereignty and boundaries requires scepticism towards practices and logics

capable of essentializing identities and conditions on either side of a dualism. It is in this context, especially, that I think it important to distinguish between still provocative accounts of the relationship between norm and exception found in various literatures on sovereignty, and the accounts of friend–enemy relations informing popular claims about the consequences of state sovereignty found in various traditions of political realism in Anglo-American theories of international relations. Nevertheless, my own sense of what is at stake here has been shaped less by technical literatures on sovereignties or logics than by texts such as François Hartog *The Mirror of Herodotus: The Representation of the Other in the Writing of History*, translated by Janet Lloyd, Chicago: University of Chicago Press, 1988; Amitav Ghosh, *The Shadow Lines*, Delhi: Ravi Dayal Publisher, 1988; and Ashis Nandy, *The Intimate Enemy: Loss and Recovery of Self Under Colonialism*, Delhi: Oxford University Press, 1983.

4 For an argument to this effect, see R.B.J. Walker, *Inside/Outside: International Relations as Political Theory*, Cambridge: Cambridge University Press, 1993. This analysis, which sketches some of the ground for the argument developed here, focuses primarily on a claim that the key categories of the Anglo-American theory of international relations, like the key categories of liberal political theory, are derived from an idealized account of sovereign statehood, and can thus be understood as an effect of a spatiotemporal absence made possible by the spatiotemporal presence celebrated by liberal political theory. The profoundly influential discourses we have come to know as political theory and international relations theory are both kept in motion by the systematic exclusion of their most important conditions of possibility from critical analysis.

To summarize: the theory of international relations must be situated as a practice *of* modern sovereign states before it can be understood as a sequence of claims *about* the practices of modern states. As a practice of the modern sovereign state, it necessarily reifies and constantly reaffirms a specifically modern account of space, time and identity. This reification is constantly played out in a debate between "political realists" and "political idealists" that uncritically reproduces a (paradigmatically Hobbesian) logic of desire and impossibility. Consequently, any analysis that takes these categories for granted, whether in the name of political necessity, normative ambition or of empirical social science, must necessarily tell us much more about the practices legitimized by this idealization of the modern state than about any phenomena in some supposedly real or empirical world. Refusing to problematize its own constitutive assumptions and instead insisting on both their reality and inevitability, the theory of international relations has been constantly reproduced as a sequence of supposedly "great debates" about appropriate "method" (whether or not scholars should adopt the methodology of natural science); the place of "values" (whether scholars are or should be value-free and whether or not normative theory has an essential place in their work); the status of "foundations" (whether or not there are sufficiently firm grounds on which scholars might affirm their claims about features of the events and processes they study); the future of the state; and the possibilities of historical/structural change, all of which work to affirm a modern logic of sovereign desire and impossibility as the only legitimate ground for both scholarship and political practice.

For complementary analyses placing greater emphasis on the productive effects of specific forms of subjectivity, see the essays of Richard K. Ashley, especially "Living on Borderlines: Man, Poststructuralism and War," in James Der Derian and Michael Shapiro, eds, *International/Intertextual Relations: Boundaries of Knowledge and Practice in World Politics*, Lexington: Lexington Books, 1988, 259–321; and Richard K. Ashley and R.B.J. Walker, "Reading Dissidence/Writing the Discipline: Crisis and the Question of Sovereignty in International Studies," *International Studies Quarterly*, 34, September 1990, 367–416. For a sustained reading of similar material through a more explicitly genealogical account of the relation between sovereignty and knowledge, see Jens Bartelson, *A Genealogy of Sovereignty*, Cambridge: Cambridge University Press, 1995. For an important recent analysis of contemporary attempts to make sense of sovereignty which, like much of my own work, seeks to disentangle the analysis of sovereignty from historically specific (modern, liberal) accounts of what it *must* be, see Raia Prokhovnik, *Sovereignties: Contemporary Theory and Practice*, Basingstoke: Palgrave Macmillan, 2007.

5 For helpful introductions to the various ways in which debates about modernity and subjectivity have been constructed, see, for example, Anthony Cascardi, *The Subject of Modernity*, Cambridge: Cambridge University Press, 1992; J.B. Schneewind, *The Invention of Autonomy: A History of Modern Moral Philosophy*, Cambridge: Cambridge University Press, 1998; Harvie Ferguson, *Modernity and Subjectivity: Body, Soul, Spirit*, Charlottesville: University Press of Virginia, 2000; Timothy J. Reiss, *The Discourse of Modernism*, Ithaca: Cornell University Press, 1982; Louis Dupré, *Passages to Modernity: An Essay in the Hermeneutics of Nature and Culture* New Haven: Yale University Press, 1993; Robert B. Pippin, *Modernism as a Philosophical Problem*, Oxford: Blackwell, 1991, 2nd edn 1999: Alain Touraine, *Critique of Modernity*, translated by David Macey, Oxford: Blackwell, 1995; Niklas Luhmann, *Observations on Modernity*, translated by William Whobrey, Stanford: Stanford University Press, 1998; and David Kolb, *The Critique of Pure Modernity: Hegel, Heidegger and After*, Chicago: University of Chicago Press, 1986.

My own reading of the philosophical framing of such debates has been shaped by five sources, each of which, while more or less problematic on both philosophical and historical grounds, has served as a reminder that modernity has to be understood as a problem before it can be approached either as history or as cultural formation. These are: Ernst Cassirer, *Individual and Cosmos in Renaissance Philosophy* (1927) translated by M. Domandi, New York: Harper and Row, 1963, and Cassirer's subsequent journeys around the multiple universes of neo-Kantianism; Gaston Bachelard, *Le Nouvel Esprit scientifique* (1934), Paris: Presses Universitaires de France, 1973, and Bachelard's subsequent shift to the languages of aesthetics, especially in *The Poetics of Space* (1957), translated by Maria Jolas, Boston: Beacon Press, 1969; Michel Foucault's early texts, especially *History of Madness* (1961/72), edited by Jean Khalfa, translated by Jonathan Murphy and Jean Khalfa, Abingdon: Routledge, 2006; and *The Order of Things* (1966), New York: Random House, 1970; many texts by Gilles Deleuze, especially *Difference and Repetition* (1968), translated by Paul Patton, New York: Columbia University Press, 1994; and the extensive literature on the history of science from Galileo to Newton, especially as this literature has sometimes struggled to escape the stranglehold of neo-Kantianism, and even more especially as it has been concerned with the genealogy of concepts of space and time that were eventually expressed in Kant's critical philosophy.

6 To privilege the identification of modernity with the challenges posed by the emergence of a system of states in post-Renaissance Europe is especially to resist the more familiar sense of modernity as a singular historical, cultural or philosophical achievement that finds little meaningful expression until much later: in relation to Enlightenment, Romanticism, Revolutionary France, capitalist/industrial society, and so on. What interests me here, however, is the conditions under which questions about politics came to be asked in what now appear (anachronistically) to be characteristically modern form, not the substantive ways in which such questions were answered. Machiavelli, for example, was not a modern in any clearly recognizable sense that one might attribute to Descartes, Hobbes or Kant. In posing questions about the possibility of founding a political community on

something other than the eternal laws of heaven and empire, however, and thus posing further questions about, for example, the relation between political ethics and religious or private ethics, Machiavelli articulated concerns about freedom, power and authority that are recognizable to more or less every thinker in what is generally taken to be the modern political canon. Weber's resolutely modern distinction between an ethics of absolute ends and an ethics of responsibility, for example, is recognizably Machiavellian in this sense.

In the same way, the structural form of the modern states system, with its multiple arrangements of inclusion *and* exclusion, universality *and* particularity, provided the crucial context in which the more familiar concerns of modern thought and culture could be domesticated, so to speak. The intellectual history of modernity has been written largely in narrowly domestic and national terms, even if sometimes comparatively, and has been especially informed by judgements about eighteenth-century enlightenments. Predictably, much of the contemporary "postcolonial" critique of such histories has sought to expose the structuring of exclusions on a global scale that generated a legacy of ethnocentric universals. The secular modernities expressed in, say, the 1648 Treaty of Westphalia and similar moments of "origin," this critique can be read as suggesting, must be contextualized in relation to other possible ways of reading world histories, and thus to various logics of colonialism and empire rather than of a states system. In a similar spirit, my identification of modernity with the emergence of the states system in early-modern Europe is intended both as a shorthand reminder of the parochialisms embedded in many more familiar accounts of what modernity must be, and a suggestion that the inclusions/exclusions expressed in the European states system, with its own constitutive exclusions, provide a neglected dimension of debates about modernity that, partly as a consequence, remain either resolutely Eurocentric or determined to resist European/Western hegemony, with both options encouraging essentializing accounts of modernity and its others.

7 A large, though very uneven, literature has begun to accumulate in this context. For a sustained argument for the importance of an explicitly international political theory, see Kimberly Hutchings, *International Political Theory*, London: Sage, 1999. For a thoughtful general survey of the interplay of political theory and the theory of international relations from a (broadly Hegelian) perspective that nevertheless reproduces rather than questions the inclusionary/exclusionary discourses of the modern state, see David Boucher, *Political Theories of International Relations*, Oxford: Oxford University Press, 1998. For an important collection of essays on classic texts, see Beate Jahn, ed., *Classical Theory in International Relations*, Cambridge: Cambridge University Press, 2006. For recent attempts to develop an innovative history of international thought, see Edward Keene, *International Thought: An Historical Introduction*, Cambridge: Polity Press, 2005; and Torbjorn L. Knutson, *A History of International Relations Theory*, Manchester: Manchester University Press, 2nd edn 1997. For helpful introductions to the accumulating secondary and tertiary literatures, most of which simply seek to apply canonical political theorists to international relations in ways that I find very problematic, see Chris Brown, *Sovereignty, Rights and Justice: International Political Theory Today*, Cambridge: Polity Press, 2002; and especially Nicholas J. Rengger, *International Relations, Political Theory and the Problem of Order: Beyond International Relations Theory?*, London: Routledge, 2000. For a compendium of extracts from a fairly motley assortment of thinkers who have had something to say about "the international," see Chris Brown, Terry Nardin and Nicholas Rengger, *International Relations in Political Thought*, Cambridge: Cambridge University Press, 2002.

8 Among the vast range of literature that has accumulated since the 1970s, especially since claims about globalization became commonplace in the 1990s and claims about empire proliferated after 2001, I think of such divergent forms of analysis as

those developed by David Held, Anthony McGrew, David Goldblatt and Jonathan Perraton, *Global Transformations: Politics, Economic and Culture*, Cambridge: Polity Press, 1999; David Held, Danielle Archibuchi and M. Kohler, eds, *Re-Imagining Political Community*, Cambridge: Polity Press, 1998; David Held and Anthony McGrew, eds, *The Global Transformations Reader*, Cambridge: Polity Press, 2003; Jan Aart Scholte, *Globalization: A Critical Introduction*, London: Macmillan, 2000; Pheng Cheah and Bruce Robbins, eds, *Cosmopolitics: Thinking and Feeling Beyond the Nation*, Minneapolis: University of Minnesota Press, 1998; Andrew Linklater, *The Transformation of Political Community: Ethical Foundations for the Post-Westphalian Era*, Cambridge: Polity Press, 1998; Mary Kaldor, *Global Civil Society: An Answer to War*, Cambridge: Polity Press, 2003; John Keene, *Global Civil Society*, Cambridge: Cambridge University Press, 2003; Ulrich Beck, *Power in the Global Age: A New Global Political Economy*, translated by Kathleen Cross, Cambridge: Polity Press, 2005; Beck, *Cosmopolitan Vision*, translated by Ciaran Cronin, Cambridge: Polity Press, 2006; Simon Caney, *Justice Beyond Borders: A Global Political Theory*, Oxford: Oxford University Press, 2006; Michael Hardt and Antonio Negri, *Empire*, Cambridge, MA: Harvard University Press, 2000; as well as many burgeoning literatures on global or human security, democracy, rights, and so on. I especially appreciate the many interventions on this theme by Richard Falk, partly because of the boldness of vision he brings to his analyses, but even more so because of his sensitivity to the uneven contexts in which vision might be enabled or crushed.

Some of these texts are often very suggestive substantively and pose provocative and important questions, even if, as I argue here, they do so in ways that tend to affirm a range of answers that remain well within a modern statist understanding of political possibility. I would especially wish to distinguish them from the economistic innocence about political life found in once-influential texts such as Kenichi Ohmae, *The Borderless World: Power and Strategy in the Interlinked Economy*, London: Collins, 1990; Thomas L. Friedman, *The Lexus and the Olive Tree*, New York: Farrar, Strauss and Giroux, 2000; and, a title that is especially instructive for my purposes here, Friedman's *The World is Flat: A Brief History of the Twenty-First Century*, New York: Farrar, Straus and Giroux, 2005.

9 Affirmations of the continuing presence of the state were once made mainly in terms of claims about military security, generally through an affirmation of one version or another of a claim about "political realism." They have increasingly become framed in relation to accounts of the nation-state as the only viable resistance to a globalizing market economy, partly in ways that hark back to mercantilist objections to claims about free trade and Keynesian traditions of political economy, but primarily on the basis of the kind of nationalism that made such an impact on European accounts of the sovereign state in the early decades of the twentieth century. See, for example, Paul Hirst and Graeme Thompson, *Globalization in Question: The International Economy and the Possibilities of Governance*, Cambridge: Polity Press, 1996; Linda Weiss, *The Myth of the Powerless State: Governing the Economy in a Global Era*, Cambridge: Polity Press, 1998; Alan Scott, ed., *The Limits of Globalization: Cases and Arguments*, London: Routledge, 1997; Samy Cohen, *The Resilience of the State: Democracy and the Challenge of Globalization*, translated by Jonathan Derrick, London: Hurst, 2006; Pierre Manent, *A World Beyond Politics: A Defense of the Nation-State*, translated by Marc Lepain, Princeton: Princeton University Press, 2006; Chantal Mouffe, *On the Political*, London: Routledge, 2005; and Jean L. Cohen, "Whose Sovereignty? Empire versus International Law," *Ethics and International Affairs* 18:3, 2004, 1–24. For an exemplary echo of the way many Cold War era discussions of state sovereignty took the form of claims about what might be called the essential invariance of the logic of a system of sovereign states under conditions of historical transformation,

see Robert Jackson, "Sovereignty and its Presuppositions: Before 9/11 and After," *Political Studies*, 55, 2007, 297–317.

Again, such texts are often suggestive, especially in drawing attention to forms of state power that are often underappreciated just because, in some respects, states are no longer what they were supposed to have been, and, as with Mouffe and Cohen, in drawing attention to the tension between claims to an international and claims to a singular empire, that is part of my concern here. Nevertheless, the temptation to fall back into mercantilist, social-democratic or more bluntly nationalist traditions, that place such enormous hopes on the state as the agent that might heroically maintain an autonomous space for political action in a world of modernization and a globalizing capitalism, offers an all too seductive and, in my view, naive response to those literatures claiming that the state is somehow obsolete. Especially perplexing is the tendency to fall back upon accounts of the nation-state associated with Max Weber and Carl Schmitt in the era immediately following the First World War, the tendency expressed in an exemplary manner in Paul Hirst, *War and Power in the Twenty-First Century*, Cambridge: Polity Press, 2001. As I will argue, Weber and Schmitt express much of what is at stake in claims about the modern sovereign state under nationalist conditions, especially conditions marked by uncertainties about the status of modern accounts of subjectivity and subjectivities. Their readings of the fate and limits of the modern subject enable much of the undoubted force of claims about political realism when deployed against claims about globalization, cosmopolitanism and so on. Nevertheless, just like the literatures on globalization and cosmopolitanism, contemporary literatures that fall back on formulations expressed with such clarity and vividness by Weber and Schmitt both underplay the specificity of modern constructions of sovereignty, and pay little attention to the relationship between claims to state sovereignty and the system of states that enables any particular claim to state sovereignty.

10 As just one telling example, while there are extensive literatures both on boundaries understood as geographical frontiers and borders and on limits of legal and theoretical principle, there are very few attempts to examine both at once, despite signs of theoretical innovation in both geography and law; an exception is Nicholas Blomley, *Law, Space and the Geographies of Power*, New York: Guilford Press, 1994. Part of the burden of my argument here is to suggest that, in the specific context of international relations, this is at least partly because traditions of geopolitics have been drawn to fairly simplistic accounts of power rather than to spatiotemporal articulations of authority and authorizations of spatiotemporal boundaries. While I certainly think that students of international relations need to pay a lot more attention to the politics of law, claims about a normative or historical shift from national law to international or cosmopolitan law need to be treated with considerable suspicion.

11 E.H. Carr, *The Twenty Years' Crisis, 1919–39*, London: Macmillan, 1939, revised edn 1946; and Hans J. Morgenthau, *Politics Among Nations*, Chicago: University of Chicago Press, 1948. It is possible, and important, to read these two texts in relation to the more sophisticated and politically charged engagements with the (largely early twentieth-century German) histories and intellectual traditions from which they arise. It is also possible to read, and to some extent excuse, them as attempts to inform policy communities under specific (mid-twentieth-century British and American) historical conditions rather than as serious scholarly texts: as suggested, for example, by Charles Jones, *E.H. Carr and International Relations: A Duty to Lie*, Cambridge: Cambridge University Press, 1998. They nevertheless remain quite extraordinary sites through which to understand how some appreciation of the antagonisms expressed in European theories of modernity, state and international law came to be converted back into crudely dualistic choices between

politics and ethics and political realism and political idealism, and how such choices came to be inscribed as the constitutive foundations of a discipline that could so easily exorcise any serious engagement with its own historical or conceptual conditions of possibility.

Versions of Weber and Schmitt are especially visible in the nationalist rendition of friend–enemy relations that animates so much of Morgenthau's text, while Marx, Weber and Karl Mannheim's sociology of knowledge meet awkwardly in the muddled accounts of ideology and interests offered by Carr. In both cases, this does permit a limited degree of creative re-reading, and certainly warrants greater attention to a complex intellectual history. Nevertheless, much of the subsequent character of Anglo-American theories of international relations has been shaped by the conceptual conflations and overdetermining dualisms popularized by such texts. The specific reception of these texts was itself shaped by the supposed demands of Cold War and the revival of positivistic conceptions of social science, in ways that might still profit from the critical attentions of theories of the state, power and knowledge that Carr and Morgenthau, along with Raymond Aron, John Herz and many others, at least understood to be of critical significance.

Some important contextualization of the specifically German intellectual context here is to be found in the classic study by Friedrich Meinecke, *Cosmopolitanism and the National State* (1907), translated by Robert B. Kimber, Princeton: Princeton University Press, 1963.

12 They are, however, still reproduced in many introductory texts shaping the analysis of international relations, a field that has come to thrive on an especially rich, indeed completely indigestible, smörgåsbord of "isms" "paradigms" and "perspectives" that serve both to "introduce" the objects and methods of study and to render them almost impervious to critical analysis. Most derive from and ultimately reify three primary and mutually constitutive distinctions, all usually framed as sharp dualisms: between political realism and political idealism, between some kind of pre-social ontological realism and what is now called constructivism, and between state and state system. These are elaborated so as to identify a potential middle ground between dualistic extremes (the so-called Grotian tradition of the so-called English School of international relations theory); to redescribe difficult problems under less disconcerting labels (as when liberalism and realism are claimed to be discrete rather than mutually constitutive traditions); to affirm commonalities between sharply opposed positions (as with the historicist and nationalist tendencies of "classical realism" and the structuralist, internationalist and largely utilitarian forms of "neo-realism"); to convert practices of mutual constitution into reified alternatives (as with both liberalism and realism and state and states system); and to render complex sites of contestation over ontological and epistemological questions into ready-packaged "positions" that can be chosen by the careful student consumer (so that a sharply delimited range of claimed objectivisms can be squared with admissions of some kind of relativism). The overall effect is that international relations has tended to be taught less as a site of historically constituted problems than a naturally given reality subject to a decisionistic or consumerist choice among competing points of view; much as Cold War textbooks on political theory were once constructed as a choice among competing political ideologies, only some of which were supposed to be taken seriously by any right-thinking reader.

13 The allusion is to David Lowenthal, *The Past is a Foreign Country*, Cambridge: Cambridge University Press, 1985, and is also made by Barry Hindess in his reflections on related themes, to which I am much indebted; see Hindess, "The Past is Another Culture," *International Political Sociology*, 1:4, 2007, 325–38. Lowenthal's title itself alludes to the famous first line of a novel, *The Go-Between*, by L.P. Hartley, London: Penguin, 1953: "The past is a foreign country; they do

things differently there." It expresses the highly problematic assumption, which I engage in various ways, that temporal and spatial tropes are easily convertible into each other, not least so as to enable the developmental view of history that enables the spatial narratives of modern theories of the sovereign state and system of sovereign states, and the spatial narratives that in turn produce developmentalist accounts of temporality. See also Johannes Fabien, *Time and the Other*, New York: Columbia University Press, 1983, which develops an anthropological critique of modern temporalities that parallels many of my own concerns.

14 For literatures with a specific interest in theories of international relations, but with a much broader reach in this respect, see especially Friedrich V. Kratochwil, "Of Systems, Boundaries and Territoriality: An Inquiry into the Formation of the State System," *World Politics*, 39:1, October 1986, 27–52; Kratochwil, "The Politics of Place and Origin: An Inquiry into the Changing Boundaries of Representation, Citizenship, and Legitimacy," in Michi Ebata and Beverly Neufeld, eds, *Confronting the Political in International Relations*, Basingstoke: Macmillan, 2000, 185–211; Michael Shapiro and Hayward Alker, eds, *Challenging Boundaries*, Minneapolis: University of Minnesota Press, 1996; Mathias Albert, David Jacobson and Yosef Lapid, eds, *Identities, Borders, Orders: Rethinking International Relations Theory*, Boulder: Lynne Rienner, 2001; Noel Parker, ed., *The Geopolitics of Europe's Identity: Centers, Boundaries and Margins*, New York: Palgrave Macmillan, 2008; Didier Bigo and Elspeth Guild, eds, *Controlling Frontiers: Free Movement Into and Within Europe*, Aldershot: Ashgate, 2005; Anastassia Tsoukala "Boundary-Creating Processes and the Social Construction of Threat," *Alternatives: Global, Local, Political*, 33:2, 2008. 137–52; Eiki Berg and Henk van Houtum, eds, *Routing Borders Between Territories, Discourses and Practices*, Aldershot: Ashgate, 2003; Hastings Donnan and Thomas M. Wilson, *Borders: Frontiers of Identity, Nation and State*, Oxford: Berg, 1999; Mary L. Dudziak and Leti Volpp, eds, *Legal Borderlands: Law and the Construction of American Borders*, Baltimore: Johns Hopkins University Press, 2006; Heather N. Nicol and Ian Townsend-Gault, eds, *Holding the Line: Borders in a Global World*, Vancouver: UBC Press, 2004; Michael Loriaux, *European Union and the Deconstruction of the Rhineland Frontier*, Cambridge: Cambridge University Press, 2008; Thomas Diez, "The Paradox of Europe's Borders," *Comparative European Politics*, 4, 2006, 235–52; Roxanne Lynn Doty, "States of Exception on the Mexico–US Border: Security 'Decisions' and US Border Controls," *International Political Sociology*, 1:2, June 2007, 113–37; and Nick Vaughan-Williams, *Border Politics: The Limits of Sovereign Power*, Edinburgh: University of Edinburgh Press, 2009.

See also, among many other texts, Malcolm Anderson, *Frontiers: Territory and State Formation in the Modern World*, Cambridge: Polity Press, 1996; John Agnew and Stuart Corbridge, *Mastering Space: Hegemony, Territory and International Political Economy*, London: Routledge, 1995; Geroid O'Tuathail, *Critical Geopolitics: The Politics of Writing Global Space*, Minneapolis: University of Minnesota Press, 1998; David Newman, "The Lines that Continue to Separate Us: Borders in Our 'Borderless' World," *Progress in Human Geography*, 30:2, 2006; Nicholas Blomley "Law, Property, and the Geography of Violence: The Frontier, the Survey and the Grid," *Annals of the Association of American Geographers*, 93:1, 2003, 121–41; Emmanuel Brunet-Jailly, "Theorizing Borders: An Interdisciplinary Perspective" *Geopolitics*, 10, 2005, 633–49; Christopher K. Ansell and Guiseppe di Palma, *Restructuring Territoriality: Europe and the United States Compared*, Cambridge: Cambridge University Press, 2004; and David Miller and Sohail Hashmi, eds, *Boundaries and Justice: Diverse Ethical Perspectives*, Princeton: Princeton University Press, 2001.

For classic geographical texts that remain interesting in part because of the way they express an historically interesting mix of worries about German traditions of *geopolitik* and opportunities for framing the modernizing capacities of newly decolonized states, see Ladis K.D. Kristof, "The Nature of Frontiers and Boundaries," *Annals* of the Association of American Geographers, 49, 1959, 269–82; Stephen B. Jones, "Boundary Concepts in the Setting of Place and Time," *Annals of the Association of American Geographers*, 49, 1959, 241–55; and J.R.V. Prescott, *The Geography of Frontiers and Boundaries*, London: Hutchinson, 1965.

15 Among many trajectories of complication in this respect, see Maurice Merleau-Ponty, *The Visible and the Invisible* (1964), translated by Alphonso Lingis, Evanston, IL: Northwestern University Press, 1968; M.C. Dillon, *Mereleau Ponty's Ontology*, 2nd edn, Evanston, IL: Northwestern University Press, 1997; Renaud Barbaras, *Desire and Distance: Introduction to a Phenomenology of Perception*, translated by Paul B. Milan, Stanford: Stanford University Press, 2006; Jacques Derrida, *On Touching – Jean-Luc Nancy*, translated by Christine Irizarry, Stanford: Stanford University Press, 2005; Margrit Shildrick, *Leaky Bodies and Boundaries: Feminism. Postmodernism and (Bio)ethics*, London: Routledge, 1997; Irvin C. Schick, *The Erotic Margin: Sexuality and Spatiality in Alterist Discourse*, New York: Verso, 1999; and Ritu Menon and Kamla Bhasin, eds, *Borders and Boundaries: Women in India's Partition*, New Delhi: Kali for Women, 1998.

16 See, among many others, Donald M. Lowe, *History of Bourgeois Perception*, Chicago: University of Chicago Press, 1982; David Michael Levin, *The Opening of Vision: Nihilism and the Postmodern Situation*, London: Routledge, 1988; Levin, ed., *Modernity and the Hegemony of Vision*, Berkeley: University of California Press, 1993; Levin, ed., *Sites of Vision: The Discursive Construction of Sight in the History of Philosophy*, Cambridge: MIT Press, 1999; William McNeill, *The Glance of the Edge: Heidegger, Aristotle and the Ends of Theory*, Albany: State University of New York Press, 1999; Gary Shapiro, *Archeologies of Vision: Foucault and Nietzsche on Seeing and Saying*, Chicago: University of Chicago Press, 2003; Susan Buck-Morse, *The Dialectic of Seeing: Walter Benjamin and the Arcades Project*, Cambridge, MA: MIT Press, 1989; and Richard Rorty, *Philosophy and the Mirror of Nature*, Princeton: Princeton University Press, 1979.

17 I think here of the richly suggestive literatures arising from many sociological and geographical traditions that nonetheless struggle to show how their analyses challenge established claims about power and authority, in ways that express long-standing differences between sociology and political theory. See, for example, Manuel Castells, *The Rise of Network Society*, Oxford: Blackwell, 1997; John Urry, *Global Complexity*, Cambridge: Polity Press, 2003; Arjun Appadurai, *Modernity at Large: Cultural Dimensions of Globalization*, Minneapolis: University of Minnesota Press, 1998; and Saskia Sassen, *Territory, Authority, Rights: From Medieval to Global Assemblages*, Princeton: Princeton University Press, 2006.

18 Much of the influential literature on the future of the state continues to confuse claims about the continuing institutional capacity of states with claims about the continuing ability of states to monopolize all claims to legitimate authority, as well as the capacity to mediate all relations of universality and particularity within convergent spatiotemporal and legal limits. Analyses of the modern state are susceptible to the same clichés of presence and absence as are boundaries, primarily because these clichés express the spatiotemporal claims of foundation and limitation through which modern states were once constituted under specific spatiotemporal conditions. I see little reason to discount the significance of states, but also no reason to interpret this significance through modern statist accounts of foundation, continuity, limitation or spatiotemporal transformation. I develop this argument primarily in relation to claims about state sovereignty, but I hope the implications for any analysis of the state framed as a matter of continuing presence or imminent absence is clear enough. In this respect, the difficulty posed by so much of the literature on the theory of international relations is not that it

overemphasizes the significance of the state, but that it is so easily drawn to superficial accounts of what states are and what they do.

19 As will become obvious, the characterizations of historical context I invoke at various points work mainly as simplifying caricatures, in ways that seek to clarify the degree to which modern accounts of political life, and of international relations in particular, rest heavily but also uneasily on a specific array of caricatured histories. They are intended less as the kind of history recommended not least by contemporary historians of political thought than as a response to the limits of a modern history that frames its own origins in a way that must produce our familiar stories of a transition from premodern to modern. This is the modern history understood as an affirmation of novelty, an affirmation that, as Nietzsche claimed, results in neurotic obsession with an unchanging novelty or a threatening obsolescence: an obsession that makes historical change more or less unthinkable.

As Constantin Fasolt puts it in the conclusion of an intense, incisive and to my mind crucial engagement with this problem, to which I will return: "So long as politics continues to rely on sovereignty and citizens exercise their right to self-determination, there needs to be some medieval period in the past from which they have progressed. ... Chronologies may vary. But the tripartite pattern of true ancient origins, corrupt medieval intermission, and modern emergence to sovereign self determination is built into history itself – not, to repeat, because that is what happened, but because it is a transcendental category of the historical imagination, a necessary condition for the very possibility of thinking about the past as history and living now." Fasolt, *The Limits of History*, Chicago: University of Chicago Press, 2004, 228. Cf. Reinhart Koselleck, *Critique and Crisis: Enlightenment and the Pathogenesis of Modern Society*, Cambridge, MA: MIT Press, 1988; and Koselleck, *Futures Past: On the Semantics of Historical Time*, translated by Keith Tribe, Cambridge, MA: MIT Press, 1985. For an especially useful account of the fixation with origins that characterizes so much of the work of seventeenth- and eighteenth-century thinkers, especially Descartes, Vico and Kant, see Catherine Labio, *Origins and the Enlightenment: Aesthetic Epistemology from Descartes to Kant*, Ithaca: Cornell University Press, 2004. Much of the historiographical context here can be understood in relation to much broader resistance to conventional stories about the emergence of modern "man," not least those shaped by Jacob Burckhardt's account of a Renaissance ideal that never managed to fit any known individual.

It is in this general spirit that I work here mainly with a sketch of what, according to its own reification of space and time, the history of modern state sovereignty *must* have been. It is this account that has played such a crucial part in the production of canonical routines and caricatured texts that remain so difficult to avoid in even the most historically sensitive scholarship, and which informs the practices of modern sovereignty with which I am specifically concerned. Similarly, my reading of historical texts is concerned less to contrast received caricatures with more historically contextualized interpretations than to show how these caricatures work to sustain banal and depoliticizing answers to questions that remain provocative. Given this stance, it is probably worth noting that I am generally persuaded of the need to privilege a (post-Machiavellian, post-Nietzschean) sense of historicity, contingency and genealogy in the history of modern political thought; indeed such a need has informed my earlier work and continues to inform my sense of future possibilities. I am equally persuaded, however, of the need to come to terms with the practices through which historical contingencies are given retrospective order through hegemonic practices of interpretation. Many histories of philosophy, for example, are still inclined to struggle within the dualistic Kantian categories through which philosophy was framed by post-Kantians both as a convenient history and as a specific account of what counts as a legitimate philosophical problem. In my view, the claims of modern state sovereignty, at least as these have come to work in contemporary political practice, have been similarly effective in reifying temporal contingencies into spatial necessities, with Kant again playing a crucial role in the process. While historically minded scholarship may have worked valiantly, even if not always successfully, to overcome the methodological sin of anachronism, the broad structuring of the disciplines of modern scholarship is still authorized largely by the spatiotemporal discriminations that affirm the internal/ external account of political possibility affirmed by the claim to state sovereignty. This is why almost all the significant recent literature on state sovereignty begins from the insistence that, as a practice that subsumes all spatiotemporal contingencies into claims about necessity, state sovereignty must itself be understood as a spatiotemporally contingent practice.

20 Carl Schmitt, *Political Theology: Four Chapters on the Concept of Sovereignty* (1922/34), translated by Charles Schwab, Cambridge, MA: MIT Press, 1985.

21 René Descartes, *Descartes: Philosophical Writings*, edited and translated by G.E.M. Anscombe and Peter Geach, London: Nelson, 1964; and Galileo Galilei, *Dialogues and Mathematical Demonstrations Concerning Two New Sciences* (1638), translated by Henry Crew and Alfonso De Salvio, New York: Macmillan, 1914.

 The significance of Galileo's reformulation of the distinction between primary and secondary qualities as a moment in the shift from classical to Cartesian ontologies is often greatly underappreciated; to the extent that the distinction is noted at all, it is more usually in the context of John Locke's later woolly empiricism. For a brief but sharp discussion see E.A. Burtt, *The Metaphysical Foundations of Modern Science* (1924, revised 1932), New York: Doubleday, 1954, 83ff. Once the objective world of primary qualities is distinguished from the subjective world of secondary qualities (in a reworking of a complex Aristotelian inheritance), the way is open for the gap in between to be framed as a straight Euclidean line, one that is both static, thereby encouraging the development of epistemology as a knowledge of regularities rather than transformations, and understandable as a desirable but impossible move from finitude to infinity. This has had profound implications for the way in which the problem of knowledge has been posed in modern philosophy, not least in relation to Kant's treatment of the categories of space and time as *a priori* conditions of knowing. Much of the historical background to the spatiotemporal articulation of modern politics also can be usefully read in relation to this achievement. Read in terms of a line of relation between subject and object as well as a line separating subject and object, even these paradigmatically dualistic renditions of modern thought suggest a more complex array of possibilities in the way distinctions have been made and authorized in the modern world. Much of my thinking about modern forms of distinction and authorization has been informed especially by engagement with Galileo's framing of the problems of modern epistemology in these terms, and especially by the way Kant recasts this legacy in his framing of the puzzles of human finitude.

22 Immanuel Kant, *Critique of Pure Reason* (1781), translated and edited by Paul Guyer and Allen W. Wood, Cambridge: Cambridge University Press, 1998, a text, I will gradually insist, that cannot be ignored in any attempt to make sense of Kant's framing of the aporetic character of modern political possibility and impossibility.

23 Among many treatments of this theme, see Cassirer, *Individual and Cosmos in Renaissance Philosophy*; Burtt, *The Metaphysical Foundations of Modern Science*; Dupré, *Passage to Modernity*; Reiss, *The Discourse of Modernism*; Gerd Buchdahl, *Metaphysics and the Philosophy of Science: The Classical Origins, Descartes to Kant*, Oxford: Blackwell, 1969; Stephen Gaukroger, *The Emergence of a Scientific Culture: Science and the Shaping of Modernity*, 1210–1685, Oxford: Clarendon Press, 2006; Arthur C. Danto, *Connections to the World*, Berkeley: University of California Press, 1989; and, even more broadly, Pierre Hadot, *The Veil of Isis: An*

Essay on the History of the Idea of Nature (2004), translated by Michael Chase, Cambridge, MA: Harvard University Press, 2006. Much of the literature on comparative philosophy also attests to the privileged status of epistemology in modern "Western" philosophical traditions that has developed as a consequence; my own thinking on such comparisons, which inform some of the specific framing of the problem of a "world politics" that drives this book, is much indebted to formative conversations with E.A. Burtt, Bin-Ky Tan, Alastair M. Taylor, Joseph Needham, Ashis Nandy, Dhirubhai Sheth and Kevin Frost, among many others.

24 Kant, "What is Enlightenment?" in H.S. Reiss, ed., *Kant: Political Writings*, 2nd edn, Cambridge: Cambridge University Press, 1991, 54–60. This is probably the most accessible source in English of Kant's political writings, but for alternative translations of some texts, see Immanuel Kant, *Practical Philosophy*, translated and edited by Mary J. Gregor, Cambridge: Cambridge University Press, 1996, in which "What is Enlightenment?" is at 11–22.

25 Kant, "Idea for a Universal History with a Cosmopolitan Purpose," in Reiss, ed., *Kant: Political Writings*, 41–53.

26 Kant, "Perpetual Peace: A Philosophical Sketch," in Reiss, ed., *Kant: Political Writings*, 93–130; cf. Kant, "Toward perpetual peace," in *Kant: Practical Philosophy*, 311–52.

27 The now largely forgotten proliferation of neo-Kantianisms in the late-nineteenth century remains an important background against which to engage with many more recent debates about scientific and socio-scientific clams to knowledge; see, for example, Thomas E. Willey, *Back to Kant: The Revival of Kantianism in German Social and Historical Thought, 1860–1914*, Detroit: Wayne State University Press, 1978. For an insightful mapping of this legacy that affirms much of my own sense of its significance for contemporary debates, see Edward Skidelsky, *Ernst Cassirer: The Last Philosopher of Culture*, Princeton: Princeton University Press, 2008.

28 See Martin Wight, *Systems of States*, edited by Hedley Bull, Leicester: Leicester University Press, 1978, which remains an under-appreciated text despite Wight's celebrated place in the formation of the supposedly "English School" of international relations.

29 Max Weber, "Politics as a Vocation," (1919) in *Max Weber: The Vocation Lectures*, translated by Rodney Livingstone, edited by David Owen and Tracy B. Strong, Indianapolis: Hackett, 2004, 32–94. For a generalized discussion of Weber's significance for theories of international relations, see R.B.J. Walker, "Violence, Modernity, Silence: From Max Weber to International Relations Theory," in G. Michael Dillon and David Campbell, eds, *The Political Subject of Violence*, Manchester University Press, 1993, 137–60.

The interpretation of Weber is notoriously contested. My own reading has been shaped especially by Karl Lowith, *Max Weber and Karl Marx* (1932), London: Routledge, 1993; Wolfgang J. Mommsen, *Max Weber and German Politics, 1890–1920* (1959), translated by Michael S. Sternberg, Chicago: University of Chicago Press, 1984; Wilhelm Hennis, *Max Weber: Essays in Reconstruction*, translated by Keith Tribe, London: Allen & Unwin, 1988; Harvey Goldman, *Max Weber and Thomas Mann: Calling and Shaping of the Self*, Berkeley: University of California Press 1988; and various studies by Kari Palonen, including "Max Weber's Reconceptualization of Freedom," *Political Theory*, 27:4, 1999, 523–44; Palonen, "Was Max Weber a 'Nationalist'? A Study in the Rhetoric of Conceptual Change," *Max Weber Studies*, 1, 2000, and Pertti Ahonen and Kari Palonen, eds, *Dis-Embalming Max Weber*, Jyväskylä: SoPhi, 1999. Helpful contextualization is developed in Duncan Kelly, *The State of the Political: Conceptions of Politics and the State in the Thought of Max Weber, Carl Schmitt and Franz Neumann*, Oxford: Oxford University Press for the British Academy, 2003; and J.W. Burrow, *The*

Crisis of Reason: European Thought, 1848–1914, New Haven: Yale University Press, 2000.

30 For helpful recent discussions of this venerable theme, one that will be taken up in various ways in the present analysis, see Peter Fitzpatrick, *Modernism and the Grounds of Law*, Cambridge: Cambridge University Press, 2001; William Rasch, *Sovereignty and its Discontents: On the Primacy of Conflict and the Structure of the Political*, London: Birkbeck Law Press, 2004; and Costas Douzinas and Adam Geary, *Critical Jurisprudence: The Political Philosophy of Justice*, Oxford: Hart, 2005. Much of the recent literature on this theme has been preoccupied with the trials and tribulations of modern philosophy after the so-called "linguistic turn." Some broader perspective is provided by reflecting on, say, Plato's narrative strategies when founding the ideal of the just city in *The Republic*, on anthropological accounts of the social origins and consequences of myths of origin, on Freud's meditations on Moses and the origins of monotheism, or, as I will tend to stress here while keeping these other possibilities in mind, Hobbes' authorization of the authorization of sovereign authority in his *Leviathan*.

31 Frank R. Ankerschmit, *Aesthetic Politics: Political Philosophy Beyond Fact and Value*, Stanford: Stanford University Press, 1996, 65. Many recent rhetorical claims about a supposedly global war on terror, a war that is, in principle, everywhere, reproduce the same (in my view flawed) logic.

32 Useful introductions to this general theme include Edward S. Casey, *The Fate of Place: A Philosophical History*, Berkeley: University of California Press, 1997; Yi-Fu Tuan, *Space and Place: The Perspective of Experience*, Minneapolis: University of Minnesota Press, 1977; Matt Sparke, *In the Space of Theory: Postfoundational Geographies of the Nation-State*, Minneapolis: University of Minnesota Press, 2005; and Doreen Massey, *For Space*, London: Sage, 2005. Massey's observation that "both the romance of the bounded place and the romance of free flow" hinder engagement with "the necessary negotiations of real politics" (p. 174) especially resonates with my concerns here, though I would prefer to resist the rhetorical resort to terms like "necessary" and "real" in thinking about contemporary spatiotemporalities; I would especially prefer to resist them in relation to still popular claims that place is somehow more real and less politically constructed than abstract conceptions of space. Cf. Ernst Cassirer, "Mythic, Aesthetic and Theoretical Space," translated by D.P. Verene and L.H. Foster, *Man and World*, 2:1, 1969, 3–17; and David Harvey, "Space as a Keyword," in Harvey, *Spaces of Global Capitalism: Towards a Theory of Uneven Development*, London: Verso, 2006, 117–48.

33 See, for example, Sheldon Wolin's *Politics and Vision: Continuity and Innovation in Western Political Thought*, Boston: Little, Brown, 1960; extended edn Princeton University Press, 2005, which remains a stimulating guide on this theme, as on many others, despite both its tendency to reify a canonical tradition of political theory and its resolutely domestic gaze. See also the now neglected writings of Cornelius Castoriadis, especially *The Imaginary Institution of Society* translated by Kathleen Blamey, Cambridge: Polity Press, 1987; and *World in Fragments: Writings on Politics, Society, Psychoanalysis, and the Imagination*, edited and translated by David Ames Curtis, Stanford: Stanford University Press, 1997.

My use of the term political imagination is indebted to both Wolin and Castoriadis, though I have resisted explicit engagement here with the difficult theoretical and philosophical issues these two very different but still stimulating writers run into in their attempts to challenge contemporary assumptions about the limits of the modern political imagination, let alone with questions about subjectivity and agency that are provoked by their use of the term "imagination". Much of what remains interesting in specifically American forms of political theory seems to me to have been enabled in one way or another by Wolin's interventions. Castoriadis' double concern with political and ontological traditions is more closely related to my own way of posing questions about political possibility, and perhaps marks a more European sensibility in this respect. I hope it will become clear, however, that my present argument is concerned with the limits of modern forms of political theorization in both their (Anglo-) American and European variations, and that the absence of "the international" from even the most suggestive political theory texts, like those of Wolin and Castoriadis, ought to be a matter of much broader concern.

34 Doubts about the former assumption have been sharpened through formulations given by texts like Bruno Latour, *We Have Never Been Modern*, translated by Catherine Porter, Cambridge, MA: Harvard University Press, 1993; doubts about the latter assumption resonate through just about every text of contemporary social, cultural and political theory. My own intention here is to underline the degree to which the certainties and uncertainties attending both assumptions ought to be understood in relation to the potentials and limits of an international politics.

35 Claims about the "postmodern" have especially come to offer a way of celebrating one half of a dualism – difference, pluralism, language, temporality, relativism – so as to reaffirm specifically modern framings of dualistic options, rather than the critical appreciations of the conditions under which these dualisms work that have been attempted in those texts that have nevertheless been appropriated into some postmodern canon. The same general tendency is at work in attempts to conflate modernity with clearly universal and grounded conditions of Enlightenment (against which mere relativism may be identified by those who claim to be enlightened) rather than with the traditions of both scepticism and critical possibility that I take to be the more conventional, and more persuasive, expressions of what is at stake in claims about a specifically modern understanding of philosophy and culture. Both tendencies have led to a widespread banalization of debate about theoretical and methodological principles in the analysis of international relations, and drive the current vogue for "isms" and "perspectives."

36 I have refrained from packing the text with commentaries on the many debates that might be invoked by reference to claims about grounding, preferring to leave the implications of this metaphor as open as possible. While there has been a recent vogue for claims about "foundations" in this respect, I hope it is clear that in my usage the metaphor speaks to the *problem* of sovereign authorization on the one hand and the relation between topography (or territory) and topology (or the properties of continuity and limit in geometrical form), on the other, as well as to my broader concern with what it might now mean to speak about "the world" in political terms.

37 I use the term diagnostic in the sense affirmed by David Levi Strauss: "I like the word *diagnostic* because it accurately puts the analysis in medical pathological terms and religious terms at the same time. It means 'to distinguish, make distinctions'; literally 'to know apart or between' (reading between the lines). ... " Strauss, "Reading Desert Storm: Rethinking Resistance," in his *Between Dog and Wolf: Essays on Art and Politics in the Twilight of the Millennium*, Brooklyn, NY: Autonomedia, 1999, 97–103, at 97. The term may also suggest an interest in Foucauldian accounts of a biopolitics, though this is not a tradition on which I draw very much here except as an interesting way of thinking about practices of nationalism.

38 These comments should not be interpreted as a sign of opposition in principle to demands for rigorous research in the analysis of political life; on the contrary. I am simply unimpressed by the way demands for causal or empirical rigour so often serve to legitimize the deployment of simplistic and often profoundly ideological categories as the necessary starting point for research. As I note briefly at various points, the methodological pluralism that has been widely sustained against mid-

twentieth-century claims about the possibility of a single ("logical positivist") model of scholarly enquiry has been undermined all too frequently by fairly dogmatic disciplinary orthodoxies that require sociological and institutional rather than philosophical understanding. The availability of a manageable or acceptable concept has often been more important than consideration of what that concept might express, or what makes it manageable or acceptable as a starting point or site of delimitation. Claims to knowledge express conceptual limits, quite as much as expectations of yet another white swan offer logically risky grounds for claims about the universe of swans. Moreover, framings of limits in matters of claims to knowledge have much in common with our framing of limits in political terms. In this context, Abraham Kaplan's crisply Kantian warning that "the appropriate conceptualization of the problem prefigures its solution" remains all too pertinent; see Kaplan, *The Conduct of Inquiry*, San Francisco: Chandler Publishing, 1964, 53.

Despite many problems, the broad debates once stimulated by the shared neo-Kantianisms of Karl Popper and T.S. Kuhn remain significant in this context; for sharp accounts see Steve Fuller, *Kuhn vs Popper*, Cambridge: Icon Books, 2003; and Peter Galison and David J. Stump, eds, *The Disunity of Science: Boundaries, Contexts, and Power*, Stanford University Press, 1999. For a salutary discussion of the causality problem in international relations in particular, see Hidemi Suganami, *On the Causes of War*, Oxford: Clarendon Press, 1996. The undeniable need for much greater sociological attention to the disciplinary practices of international relations as an institutionalized form of scholarship has been pressed especially by Steve Smith; see, for example, Smith, "Alternative and Critical Perspectives," in Michael Brecher and Frank P. Harvey, eds *Millennial Reflections on International Studies*, Ann Arbor: University of Michigan Press, 2002, 195–208; see also Ole Waever, "The Sociology of a Not So International Discipline: American and European Developments in International Relations," *International Organization*, 52, 1998, 687–727.

39 I might note that were I concerned with causal and explanatory theory rather than with principles of authority, authorization, judgement and jurisdiction, I would not pay so much attention to forms of international relations theory that have been severed from historical analyses of production, consumption, distribution and exchange under specifically capitalist conditions, nor with those from which theories of the modern capitalist state have been largely evacuated. In these respects I am broadly in sympathy with the ambitions of at least some forms of international/global political economy, as well as an international/global political sociology, while also suspecting that the term "political" still requires more intensive interrogation whenever it precedes the terms "economy" or "society", and that the tendency to shift much too rapidly from an international to some world or some global is no less problematic in such contexts than in the more conventional Anglo-American theories of international relations.

40 It will be apparent that much of my argument is articulated against what we have come to know as a Platonist inheritance in particular, and that I tend to frame Aristotelian ambitions as a consolidation rather than a critique of this inheritance. I do not doubt that both figures can still be engaged in productive ways, not least because Plato especially is such an elusive figure. A reclamation of Aristotle certainly animates a wide range of thoughtful and, up to a point, instructive contemporary attempts, by the likes of Charles Taylor, Alasdair MacIntyre and Sheldon Wolin, to challenge the hegemony of utilitarian, rationalist and other ahistorical and non-interpretive forms of social science. Similarly, in the theory of international relations, the important attempts by people such as Nicholas Onuf and Friedrich Kratochwil to work through some of the problems that concern me here rest on a much more positive response to Aristotle than I have yet been able to muster, though it would not be difficult to trace some of the categories I use

back to Aristotelian sources. See especially Nicholas Greenwood Onuf, *Worlds of Our Making*, Columbia: University of South Carolina Press, 1989; and Friedrich Kratochwil, *Rules, Norms and Decisions: On the Conditions of Practical Legal Reasoning in International Relations and Domestic Affairs*, Cambridge: Cambridge University Press, 1989.

This broadly Aristotelian heritage certainly enables a lot more work to be done than the thin empiricism that has subsequently adopted the constructivist label as a convenient way of forestalling awkward questions about human practices of self-making and the relation of language and world. At issue here is not whether political life is constructed or not, but the conditions under which we, as constituted subjects, might understand the processes through which we have been constituted; the writings of Giambattista Vico remain relevant in this respect. The modern political imagination remains deeply indebted to an (imagined) opposition between Plato and Aristotle (and thus between being and becoming, form and cause, and all the rest), not least through Kant's framing of the problem of human freedom in ways that combine a Platonist understanding of form with an Aristotelian account of teleology. Nevertheless, one of the crucial implications of contemporary claims that political life does not always occur where it is supposed to occur is that conventional readings of an opposition between these two figures in relation to an assumed *polis* must be destined for some significant destabilization.

It remains quite striking that recourse to "the Greeks" in the theory of international relations generally involves reference to Thucydides as an historian or moralist rather than to the standard Platonist or Aristotelian sources of our traditions of political theory. Perhaps Sophocles or, better, Herodotus might provide a better starting point, if only to suggest that it is precisely the starting point that needs to be placed in question. Nevertheless, a few international relations scholars have risked engagement with the idea that "the Greeks" may have other things to offer in this and many other contexts; see, for example, Michael Dillon, *Politics of Security*, London: Routledge, 1996; and Costas Constantinou, "The Beautiful Nation: Reflections on the Aesthetics of Hellenism," *Alternatives: Global, Local, Political*, 31:1, 2006, 53–75.

41 Read as history, what we call the international came to be named (by Jeremy Bentham) only in the very late eighteenth century. It may make sense to use it as an explanatory category only since the nineteenth century. Read as structure, however, the international is invariably traced back much further, to the mid-seventeenth century at least, and even to various premodern formations: thus Thucydides. Despite their limitations as history, structuralist readings rightly insist that the modern state emerged only under external conditions of possibility, even if these conditions are misleadingly identified as international. It is because the emergence of particular states necessarily implied, in principle, something like a system of particular states, that it has become conventional to read paradigmatic theorists of a domestic politics as if they were paradigmatic theorists of international relations, Machiavelli and Hobbes most pervasively, and in many ways most perversely.

Nevertheless, whether read historically or structurally, most analyses of the modern international have been shaped by an overwhelming sense of the teleological necessity of the system of states that must eventually provide the conditions under which the modern state might be enabled and perfected. This teleology might be read into the Treaty of Westphalia of 1648, understood as something like a founding constitution of the modern international; or into the ambivalences articulated in Kant's essay on *Perpetual Peace*, understood as the paradigmatic statement of what it means to think about the international in relation to modern subjectivities; or into contemporary attempts to insist on the need for properly democratic states as legitimate members of a properly international community.

This teleology has effectively resolved what otherwise appears to be the paradoxical coexistence of an international that was, in principle, already in action, enabling the emergence of the state in the early-modern period and, in practice, identifiable as a systematized structure only some two centuries later. As my analysis here seeks to affirm, many contemporary difficulties express uncertainties as to whether this teleology, reworked from Aristotle by Kant, remains either sustainable or desirable.

42 The affirmation is most explicit in theories of international relations, and is expressed with exemplary clarity in Kenneth Waltz, *Man, the State and War*, New York: University of Columbia Press, 1956, although the even less nuanced methodological formulation advanced by J. David Singer may have had even greater influence; see Singer, "The Levels of Analysis Problem in International Relations," *World Politics*, 14:1, 1961, 77–92. It has been central to many debates about, for example, what it means to engage in the analysis of "foreign policy" or to bring "comparative politics" into conjunction with "international relations." The extraordinary reach of Waltz's text as an explicit or tacit starting point for thinking about international relations over the past 50 years derives less from its substantive content, which is mixed at best, than from its cool reification of the categories of subject, state, and system of states as a structural hierarchy rendering relationships between these three categories, and thus some of the most basic contradictions animating modern political life, more or less invisible. Whereas most so-called mainstream theories of international relations, especially those working with ahistorical or structural forms of social science, tend to engage with their material as if this set of categories offers the only possible starting point, it is one that would seem deeply problematic not only to various contemporary critical traditions but also to a broad range of texts that have been absorbed retroactively into the canonical literatures of the discipline and deployed in this text.

It is in this sense that my primary engagements with international relations theory concern neither methodological commitments nor specific accounts of political realism or instrumental reason, and so on, which are quite secondary and derivative matters, but the relations, and constitutive limits, that are systematically erased in conventional accounts of "man," "state" and "the international." While this erasure is especially explicit in theories of international relations, in ways that make Waltz's text such an interesting example of the way normative claims about modern political life have been able to masquerade as claims to political realism, it is implicit in many if not most other forms of modern political analysis. By the same token, my argument is directed equally against the very possibility of what has come to be called a critical theory of international relations, on the grounds that any analysis that reifies the international in such a way has not the least hope of being critical. At the same time, any analysis that ignores the problems and limits of "the international" is in deep trouble. Hence my attempt to subvert much of what now counts as the theory of international relations in the forms enabled by the levels of analysis schemata and related conceits, while also seeking to affirm the importance of the problems expressed by the international articulations of modern politics. For my specific purposes here, Waltz's tripartite schematic is interesting less as a constitutive text in the theory of international relations than as an exemplary rendition of a constitutive contradiction between horizontal and vertical accounts of modern political organization and authority more generally: as an elegant expression of the tacit cartography of the most pervasive forms of political analysis in the second half of the twentieth century.

43 Here I refer to another of the primary but underappreciated contradictions of modern politics, especially as modern claims about politics are expressed in claims about the international: while state sovereignty may be, among other possibilities, a claim to a monopoly of legitimate authority within a particular territory, state sovereignty cannot be the highest claim to authority in modern political life given

that a sovereign state could be neither thinkable nor achievable without some kind of system sustaining the plurality of sovereign states. As I will insist, while both the relative claims of system and state, and the status of claims to universality expressed in the systemic conditions of possibility of the sovereign state, offer grounds for endless dispute, simple dichotomies between systemic and statist determinations have tended to overwhelm almost any appreciation of dialectics and contradictions in this context.

Perhaps the most common tendency in this respect has been to admit the formal but not empirical force of this contradiction on the grounds that states often act in a radically solipsistic – hyper-nationalist – manner, thereby justifying both a radical dualism of state and system and an account of the system as a radical anarchy. This manoeuvre involves both treating an exception as the norm and ignoring the mutually constitutive relation between norm and exception, and thus a pretence that drawing a simple line between claims to state sovereignty and the claims of the system of sovereign states is sufficient to hide all the hard work involved in any relationship between norm and exception. This, I will suggest, is one source of the endless search for categories that might fill a middle ground between norm and exception.

Formulated briefly and with little regard for variations in historical formulation, but in terms that I seek to clarify as my analysis moves along, the "principle" which even sovereign states are supposed to respect embodies at least four negatives: no relapse from a system of states into the kind of universal empire that would undermine the very possibility of modern self-determinations (the source, for example, of multiple anxieties about the unilateralism of recent US administrations as well as of claims about the need for collective security against those who threaten the survival of the states system); no religious wars (and thus, for example, the claim that the passions of ultimate ends must not get in the way of a rational pursuit of interests); no meddling in the affairs of other sovereign jurisdictions (as in the claim to non-intervention, at least up to the point at which systemic survival is threatened); and no barbarians (only those who are judged to be responsibly modern can be recognized as legitimate participants in the world expressed in the states system, so various kinds of special status for decolonizing, developing and rogue states). This "principle" is often invoked, perversely, under a claim about an "international anarchy," but only by adding at least two positives: all states must be autonomous; and all states must be equal – the liberal ideal expressed embryonically in Hobbes' account of individuals in a state of nature, though not of states in a state of war. These positives must be read, in turn, in relation to some specific claims about the conditions under which we might take principles of freedom and equality as constitutive assumptions about political possibility, especially, I would say, that temporalities must be organized within spatial forms. In this way we may identify some of what is at stake in claims that any theory of international relations must begin on the premises of a mixed bag of ontological possibilities that have been codified as political realism. These premises have little to do with scholarly claims to any particular reality, but a lot to do with a multiply contestable claim about where the analysis of political life ought to start, where it must end, and on what normative assumptions.

44 For an incisive critique of attempts to develop a critical analysis of the limits of the sovereign state, including those by Ashley, Bartelson and myself cited above, see Jens Bartelson, *The Critique of The State*, Cambridge: Cambridge University Press, 2001; and Bartelson "Second Natures: Is the State Identical with Itself," *European Journal of International Relations*, 4:3, 1998, 295–326.

Bartelson is right to suggest that much of the critical literature has been unable to imagine alternatives to the state because our basic political concepts are so heavily conditioned by the state. Nevertheless, I would want to resist the all-or-nothing character of Bartelson's conclusions by insisting, first, that there is no point in developing a critique of the state that is not simultaneously a critique of the states system and its limits (so that the dangers of circular reasoning and political pessimism are more difficult and pressing than even Bartelson allows); but also, second, that the forms of circular reasoning and political pessimism that are so characteristic of most critiques of the state and states system rest upon assumptions that may be constantly reproduced in practice but ought to have very little status as serious scholarship, whatever their status in the construction of modern scholarly disciplines. The first point explains why, even though I have indeed formulated some of my work in terms of a critique of the state and its continuing grip on the contemporary political imagination, this has only been part of a broader project seeking to make sense of the contradictory relation between universalizing claims about a world politics and the particular claims of modern or Western reason. The second point explains why I think it so important to understand the political effects of intellectual practices. Both points sustain my conviction that it is the international rather than the state that is in need of sustained critical interrogation, and indeed that the reason why so much of the literature on international relations has been so banal is precisely that the stakes are so high and that the questions that need to be opened up have such immense reach, and not only because this literature has been associated with specific hegemonic states.

45 Jean-Luc Nancy, "War, Right, Sovereignty – Techne," (1991) in Nancy, *Being Singular Plural*, translated by Anne E. O'Byrne and Robert D. Richardson, Stanford: Stanford University Press, 2000, 101–43, at 141–42. See also Nancy, *The Sense of the World* (1993), translated by Jeffrey S. Librett, Minneapolis: University of Minnesota Press, 1997. One of Nancy's most recent books, *The Creation of the World, or Globalization* (2002), translated by François Raffoul and David Pettigrew, Albany: SUNY Press, 2007, touches on many of the questions that have provoked my own analysis, although I became aware of it only after my text was essentially complete. I especially appreciate Nancy's way of contrasting some future "creation" of "the world" with contemporary forms of globalization, his treatment of many paradoxes arising from claims about the world as such, and his sense of the need to reimagine possibilities of political creativity without falling back on (mono)theological accounts of creation.

46 In my view, three speculative questions asked by Hans Lindahl invite positive responses: "For could it be that sovereignty is the name of a *problem*, far more than its solution? If so, would attempts to move 'beyond' sovereignty unwittingly reintroduce the problem in another guise? Might not calls to proscribe the word 'sovereignty' from our legal and political vocabulary simply conceal the problem it names, thereby failing to deal with it?" Lindahl, "Sovereignty and Representation in the European Union," in Neil Walker, ed., *Sovereignty in Transition: Essays in European Law*, Oxford: Hart, 2003, 87–114. Lindahl's analysis usefully examines sovereignty in terms of the contingency of the unity of political community under modernity, and rightly stresses the role of a politics of representation in constituting such unity, especially in Europe. Affirming Lindahl's suspicions, my own concern here is directed more to the contingency of a relation between unity and diversity in the structuring of a modern international order more generally.

47 I use the word "critical" here in a broad sense to encompass literatures that various textbook commentaries have carved into the familiar "isms": postmodernism, poststructuralism, constructivism, Critical Theory, feminism, postcolonialism, and so on. The discipline of international relations has been especially susceptible to such carve-ups, to the point that much of its literature has abandoned any sense of philosophical or logical integrity, but the problem is pervasive across many other disciplines. Quite apart from the awkward disjunction between the easy resort to classifications of theoretical traditions explicitly concerned with the dangers of

taking at face value historically and culturally embedded systems of discrimination and authorization, such commentaries tend to underestimate the problems that generate specific intellectual traditions and overestimate the coherence of "perspectives" that might be deployed in order to examine some supposedly common reality. "Critique" at least has the merit of expressing the indispensable, though never easy, distinction, associated in modern thought with Kant, between dogmatism and those claims to knowledge which rest on some interrogation of their (social, economic, ontological, epistemological) conditions of possibility. It also has the merit of stressing commonalities among the many forms of critical analysis that, in the Anglo-American academic disciplines at least, have been converted into textbook-friendly but intellectually vacuous and pedagogically debilitating doctrines organized so as to minimize any sense of the problems to which specific literatures have sought to respond, as well as irresponsibly to maximize associations with negativity and relativism. Even so, serious difficulties with this concept are already signalled by the different versions offered by Kant himself, by Hegel's commentary on Kant's ahistoricism, and by Foucault's commentary on Kant's assumption of a juridical model of sovereign authority.

For a brief discussion of the relationship between sovereignty and critique in international relations theory, see R.B.J. Walker, "Alternative, Critical, Political," in Michael Brecher and Frank Harvey, eds, *Millennium Reflections on International Studies*, Ann Arbor: University of Michigan Press, 2002, 258–70. For an account of critique as a "concept with a history," see Willi Goetschel, *Constituting Critique: Kant's Writing as Critical Praxis*, translated by Eric Schwab, Durham, NC: Duke University Press, 1994. For a useful engagement with contemporary attempts to resist Kant's juridical account of critique, see Andrew Cutrofello, *Discipline and Critique: Kant, Poststructuralism and the Problem of Resistance*, Albany: SUNY Press, 1994.

48 Jean-Luc Nancy, "The Jurisdiction of the Hegelian Monarch," (1982) in Nancy, *The Birth to Presence*, Stanford: Stanford University Press, 1993, 110–42, at 142.

3 The politics of escape

1 The most common move in the early Cold War era was to affirm something like a Weberian account of power politics, dismiss the states system as weak by comparison with state power, and then conclude that *either* the state *or* the system driven entirely by individualized state interests is all that requires attention. This move is expressed especially in dismissive treatments of international law, as in the discussion of sovereignty in Morgenthau's *Politics Among Nations*. A more subtle move occurs in texts like Hedley Bull's *The Anarchical Society*, London: Macmillan, 1977, in which a foundational distinction between and valorization of order over justice is superimposed onto an analysis that is, in many respects, highly sensitive to the complex, multidimensional and even contradictory structuring of the system of states as an historical practice. Both moves encouraged the erasure of the problem of sovereign authority from the scholarly agenda and its replacement with nationalist accounts of the state, on the one hand, and utilitarian accounts of systemic logic, on the other.

Affirmations of a more complementary relation between the sovereign state and the system of sovereign states are not hard to find. For example, much of James N. Rosenau's useful commentary on global governance works with a concept of a continuum between state and system; see especially Rosenau, *The United Nations in a Turbulent World*, Boulder: Lynne Rienner, 1992; and Rosenau, *Along the Domestic–Foreign Frontier: Exploring Governance in a Turbulent World*, Cambridge: Cambridge University Press, 1997. While I understand how notions of a continuum might be useful in thinking about changing patterns of governance, engagement with claims about sovereign authority demand an appreciation of the profoundly contradictory and ultimately aporetic rather than continuous character of this relation. It is not hard to appreciate the force of either the radical dualism of Cold War *machtpolitik* or ideas about a continuum expressed by scholars like Rosenau, but my analysis here seeks to engage with the construction of a contradictory relation that already enables and reproduces claims about both nationalist monism and continuities of interdependence.

2 Nicolo Machiavelli, *The Prince*, Quentin Skinner and Russell Price, eds, Cambridge: Cambridge University Press, 1988. I take it for granted that whatever other disagreements are to be found in the vast interpretive literature, most scholarly conventions agree that Machiavelli articulates the need to engage competing accounts of ethical life rather than a crude opposition between ethics and politics. For a sketch of my own sense of Machiavelli's significance in this respect, especially in relation to competing accounts of a politics of temporality, see Walker, *Inside/ Outside*, 26 ff.

3 See the claims about the unity of religion, natural law, European identity or modernity as the broad condition under which the system of states developed in such texts as Martin Wight, *Systems of States;* and E.B.F. Midgley, *The Natural Law Tradition and the Theory of International Relations*, London: Elek Books, 1975.

4 In classical rhetoric, the term *aporia* signalled a technique for putting a claim in doubt by arguing both sides of the argument. In the perhaps now classical traditions of (Derridean) deconstruction, it signalled the impasse at which a text undermines its own rhetorical form and thus deconstructs itself. Here I draw perhaps rather vaguely on both, and perhaps on even earlier associations with some demon of difficulty, but with the fairly limited intention of referring to the undecidable character of competing claims to sovereignty expressed by the modern subject, state and system of states.

5 More complex accounts of the emergence of international relations as a scholarly field have begun to appear in the recent literature, shaped especially by Brian C. Schmitt, *The Political Discourse of Anarchy: A Disciplinary History of International Relations*, Albany: SUNY Press, 1998.

6 James C. Scott, *Seeing Like a State: How Certain Schemes to Improve the Human Condition Have Failed*, New Haven: Yale University Press, 1998.

7 Chinua Achebe, *Things Fall Apart* (1958), Oxford: Heinemann, 1986. Cf. William Butler Yeats' poem "The Second Coming," written in 1921, an era that is especially resonant with many contemporary debates about sovereignty.

8 Hobbes, *Leviathan*, Chapter 1, 14. For influential readings of the continuity of Hobbes' analysis with that of Aristotelian and Christian natural law traditions, as well as with Stoicism, see Michael Oakeshott, "Introduction," in Thomas Hobbes, *Leviathan*, Oxford: Basil Blackwell, 1957, vii–lxvi; and Howard Warrender, *The Political Philosophy of Hobbes*, Oxford: Clarendon, 1957. The once standard characterization of the broader "history of ideas" here is Arthur O. Lovejoy, *The Great Chain of Being*, New York: Harper, 1960.

9 In this respect, Hobbes is the great forgotten figure of modern political thought, someone who could himself be turned into both the founding father of a radically secular utilitarianism (to stay alive, obey the secular sovereign) and the keeper of a minimalist tradition of deontological ethics (to fulfil a religious duty to stay alive, obey the sovereign). Whatever Hobbes' own intentions, the degree to which the great foundation myth of modern political life might be told in either radically secular or religious terms offered many advantages. It is this more ambivalent, even if un-Hobbesian, Hobbes who resonates with many attempts to legitimize the accumulation of private property, the wonders of a capitalist market, the claims of an enlightened reason, the demands of a universal ethics, and the legitimacy of the

sovereignty of so many modern states by an appeal to an always mysterious transcendental status of some kind. Conversely, however, and despite the constant attempts to return to Kant as the high point of a modern ethical tradition, or to the supposedly kinder and gentler worlds of Locke, Smith or Bentham, it is the clear-eyed Hobbes who looms out of the fog of contemporary debates about ethics to insist that the modern compromise between political ethics and some other ethics rests on claims about a radically secular and political foundation that has no foundation outside itself even if, as I suggest later, he has to invent an apparent outside so as to tell a story about how our founding authorizations came to be.

Claims about the lingering, or even prior, role of theology in Hobbes' apparently radical secularism have played an important role in scholarly literature on Hobbes' theory of obligation. On the whole, Skinner seems right to resist the claims made by A.E. Taylor, F.C. Hood, Howard Warrender and other defenders of a deontological interpretation, and to resist them both in terms of textual evidence and in relation to an historical context that makes this claim "incredible." Nevertheless, these claims have surely been enabled by a broader struggle to reconcile the rationality of modern utilitarianism with a rationality rooted in some kind of Christian metaphysics (not only the interpretation of a duty to obey as the practical way of fulfilling a prior duty to God to stay alive but also the resort to geometry as, effectively, the language both of creation and of secular reason). Hobbes himself may or may not be an exception to the more general tendency simply to assume a reconciliation between secular and sacred, but the general trend has carried enormous historical weight, not least in those practices through which modern sovereignties work to naturalize their authority to authorize.

For Skinner's influential commentary on this problem, see his "The Context of Hobbes' Theory of Political Obligation," in Quentin Skinner, *Visions of Politics, III, Hobbes and Civil Science*, Cambridge: Cambridge University Press, 2002, 264–86. For very different recent attempts to resist claims about a simple dualism of politics and theology in ways that rightly seek to resist the characteristic legitimation strategies of modernity, see William Connolly, *Why I am not a Secularist*, Minneapolis: University of Minnesota Press, 1999; Stephen Toulmin, *Cosmopolis: The Hidden Agenda of Modernity*, Chicago: University of Chicago Press, 1992; and John Gray, *Black Mass: Apocalyptic Religion and the Death of Utopia*, London: Allen Lane, 2007. For a suggestive reading of Hobbes less in relation to Christian theological traditions than as a challenge to the very different cosmologies that had found expression in various republican traditions, see Skinner, *Hobbes and Republican Liberty*, Cambridge: Cambridge University Press, 2008.

10 A presumed opposition between Hobbes and Kant has become one of the most effective strategies enabling the primary discursive manoeuvres structuring modern theories of international relations. Their names are assigned to competing traditions, often with someone like Hugo Grotius assigned as a sensible middle ground, as in the specific categorizations popularized by Martin Wight; see, for example, Martin Wight, *International Theory: The Three Traditions*, Gabriele Wight and Brian Porter, eds, Leicester: Leicester University Press for the Royal Institute of International Affairs, 1991; Herbert Butterfield and Martin Wight, eds, *Diplomatic Investigations*, London: George Allen & Unwin, 1966; as well as Bull, *The Anarchical Society*.

The opposition builds on a variety of ways in which Kant does indeed offer a sharp critique of some of Hobbes' claims, in the manner recently expressed with great clarity in Howard Williams, *Kant's Critique of Hobbes*, Cardiff: University of Wales Press, 2003. Still, Kant's critique of Hobbes (as well as his appreciation of Locke) can be read largely as a refinement and elaboration of concepts of, say, liberty and equality, and as part of a broader struggle to reconcile state sovereignty with popular sovereignty, that is ultimately grounded in a similar affirmation of the freedom/necessity of modern subjectivities. They arguably share quite as much as they dispute, and what they share is now probably of considerably greater importance than their disagreements. There is no doubt a great gulf between the celebration of freedom under the necessities expressed by the sovereign state and the celebration of freedom under the necessities of an enlightened and subjectivized conscience, or between a writer impressed by the spatial ontologies of Galileo and a writer impressed by the spatial ontologies of Newton; but this is not a gulf that warrants the conversion of a conventional (and heavily caricatured) story celebrating the elaboration of liberal principles into the polarized choices available for thinking about contemporary possibilities. The unfortunate fate of poor Grotius, as of the so-called English School of International Relations that has partly ordained itself in his name, has been to have become yet another hopelessly muddled middle ground between impossible extremes.

Much better, I would say, to read Hobbes and Kant against themselves, to see how they each both open up and shut down options in relation to questions that somehow persist, though not in the form or under conditions that could be assumed in their times. Others might well protest so much concern with such canonical figures, though it is difficult to see how we might understand the way problems of sovereignty, subjectivity and limits have been posed for modern politics without engaging them in some way.

11 As Hobbes insists at an early and, in my view, crucial moment in his argument, "Whatsoever we imagine, is Finite. Therefore there is no idea, or conception of anything we call Infinite. ... No man therefore can conceive any thing, but he must conceive it in some place; and imbued with some determinate magnitude; and which may be divided into parts; nor that any thing is all in this place, and all in another place at the same time; nor that two, or more things can be in one, and the same place at once: For none of these things ever have, or can be incident to Sense; but are absurd speeches, taken upon credit (without any signification at all,) from deceived Philosophers, or deceiving Schoolmen." Hobbes, *Leviathan*, Chapter 3, 24. Cf. Euclid, *The Elements*, translated by Thomas L. Heath, Santa Fé, NM.: Green Lion Press, 2002, especially Euclid's definition, at the beginning of Book 1, of the point ("that which has no part"), the line ("breadthless length"), the extremities of a line ("points") and a straight line ("a line which lies evenly with the points on itself"). In both cases, claims about certain knowledge rest upon the brilliant strategy of simply defining the points marking "the extremity of anything" (Euclid's definition of a boundary) within which calculation is possible, the strategy that nevertheless generates many familiar puzzles (especially about concepts of space, truth and universality) involving the relationship between claims enabled within defined limits and whatever might lie beyond such limits, as well as many mathematical strategies, like the infinitesimal numbers introduced by Leibnitz, for responding to them.

Helpful accounts of the implications of claims about infinity for the construction of modern understandings of the world and its limits include Dan Pedoe, *Geometry and the Liberal Arts*, London: Penguin, 1976; Paolo Zellini, *A Brief History of Infinity* (1980), translated by David Marsh, London: Penguin, 2005; Richard Morris, *Achilles in the Quantum Universe*, New York: Henry Holt, 1997; Eli Maor, *To Infinity and Beyond: A Cultural History of the Infinite*, Princeton: Princeton University Press, 1991; Jacques Taminiaux, *Dialectic and Difference: Finitude in Modern Thought*, Atlantic Highlands, NJ: Humanities Press, International, 1985; Gilles Deleuze and Félix Guattari, *A Thousand Plateaus: Capitalism and Schizophrenia* (1980), translated by Brian Massumi, Minneapolis: University of Minnesota Press, 1987; Quentin Meillassoux, *After Finitude: An Essay on the Necessity of Contingency*, London: Continuum, 2008; and Michel Serres, *Les Origins de la Géométrie*, Paris: Flammarian, 1993.

12 Just as much is to be gained by focusing on the similarities rather than a stylized opposition between Hobbes and Kant, so much is also to be gained by shifting Machiavelli and Hobbes out of the undifferentiated category of political realism. Neither may be saints, perhaps to their credit, and both may mark crucial moments in the elaboration of modern concepts of liberty, but it requires either a really impressive degree of interpretive oafishness, or a powerful need to produce very sharp oppositions between claims to universality and claims to diversity, in order to produce the conflated identities that still shape contemporary accounts of the international.

13 A theme popularized especially by Paul Virilio, *Speed and Politics: An Essay on Dromology*, New York: Semiotext(e), 1986. See also Virilio, *The Virilio Reader*, James Der Derian, ed., Oxford: Blackwell, 1998.

14 I am thinking here especially of a wide range of readings of modernity that privilege the dynamics of capitalist industrialization more or less in the spirit of Marx; as in the voluminous and always interesting work of Fredric Jameson and David Harvey.

15 Fasolt, *The Limits of History*, Chicago: University of Chicago Press, 2004.

16 Fasolt's explicit concern is with Hermann Conring of Saxony (1606–81), but his primary target is the familiar problem of anachronism in the history of political thought, a problem that Fasolt, contrary, for example, to those pursuing recently flourishing forms of historical contextualization, seems to think inevitable. Resistance to Fasolt's analysis of the limits of history as a mode of knowing is developed in a thoughtful commentary by Ian Hunter, "The State of History and the Empire of Metaphysics," *History and Theory*, 44, May 2005, 289–303 (though Hunter aims his critique at positions he ascribes to Edmund Husserl rather than to earlier forms of neo-Kantianism, which would, I think, be more telling of the stakes involved). Hunter's own analysis of early modern struggles over rival accounts of Enlightenment also offers many points of entry into the broader historiographical controversies involved here; see Hunter, *Rival Enlightenments: Civil and Metaphysical Philosophy in Early Modern Germany*, Cambridge: Cambridge University Press, 2001. My own sense is that Fasolt's analysis, and the kind of reaction to it expressed by Hunter, is crucial not only for the epistemological claims of historical knowledge but even more so for what it means to speak about the limits of the modern state and system of states, in that it raises questions about the relationship between the difficult work that is enacted at the spatial limits of the state and system of states, and the work that has been done to enact a history of the origins of modern political life within the state and system of states. In either case, what can appear to be merely a thin line obscures a much more complex process, and it probably matters a good deal whether one is examining the inner or outer edge of such a line, from which direction, and through one kind of logic rather than another.

　　Modern histories can, and I would say must, be read in many ways, but especially in ways that are sensitive to accounts of origins and limits that enable historians to articulate their narratives on the basis of assumptions about temporality and temporalities. Hence the significance, not least for thinkers like Jacques Derrida and Michel Foucault, of Husserl's attempts to think about the origins of geometry, or Martin Heidegger's concern with modernity's capacity to conceal its own origins, as well as the provocative force of attempts by writers like Gilles Deleuze to counter Cartesian accounts of the founding of modernity on geometrical lines through reference to Leibnizian, Spinozian, Nietzschean and Bergsonian alternatives.

17 On the multiplicity of ontological and especially spatiotemporal commitments expressed in the claim to political realism, see Walker, *Inside/Outside*, especially chapters 3 and 4.

For some sense of how diverse and even contradictory commitments still come to be packaged up under this wonderfully capacious label, see Jack Donnelly, *Realism and International Relations*, Cambridge: Cambridge University Press, 2000. For a fairly persuasive sense of how many of these commitments might be understood as multiple expressions of a tragic view of politics, one that is sharply at odds with much that is now called political realism, see Richard Ned Lebow, *The Tragic Vision of Politics: Ethics, Interests and Orders*, Cambridge: Cambridge University Press, 2003. For a reading of realism as an expression of attempts to convert traditional rules of European diplomacy into American social science, see Stefano Guzzini, *Realism in International Relations and International Political Economy*, London: Routledge, 1998. For examples of recent attempts to simultaneously recover and complicate claims about political realism as a singular tradition, see Michael C. Williams, *The Realist Tradition and the Limits of International Relations*, Cambridge: Cambridge University Press, 2005; and Sean Molloy, *The Hidden History of Realism: A Genealogy of Power Politics*, Basingstoke: Palgrave Macmillan, 2006.

Despite the value of trying to recover some of the "normative" vision and Weberian understanding of political responsibility that was buried in the Cold War stereotypes, as, for example, Williams seeks to do, there is little point in doing so without a clear sense of how political realism is ultimately enabled by (and unintelligible except in relation to) prior "idealist" claims about the primacy of modern subjectivity, a primacy that must force a concern not with ethics, norms or political responsibility as such, but with ethics, normativity and political responsibility at the limit. To begin to think about international relations as if the mish-mash of propositions that are so often sold under this label is indeed "the dominant theory of international relations," or that it is somehow opposed to rather than a constitutive part of liberal, nationalist or other aspirations is, in my view, to give up any claim to either scholarly credibility or critical possibility.

18 All three cases have been taken to affirm some of the most radical dualisms of modern political thought, and yet each retains a profound sense of the dangers and perhaps impossibilities of radical dualisms. It is this ambivalence, and what in very broad terms I would call their (often extremely reluctant) willingness to engage with contingencies and contradictions in political life, that I try to mobilize here.

19 Claude Lefort, *Democracy and Political Theory*, Minneapolis: University of Minnesota Press, 1988; and Norberto Bobbio, *Democracy and Dictatorship: The Nature and Limits of State Power*, translated by Peter Kennealy, Cambridge: Polity Press, 1989, remain useful introductions to increasingly forgotten but no less relevant literatures on this theme.

20 Helpful recent discussions include Ankersmit, *Aesthetic Politics*; Wendy Brown, *Politics out of History*, Princeton: Princeton University Press, 2001; and Marjorie Garber, Beatrice Hanssen and Rebecca L. Walkowitz, eds, *The Turn to Ethics*, New York: Routledge, 2000.

21 Exemplars of recently influential styles of analysis include Ernesto Laclau, *Emancipation(s)*, London: Verso, 1996; Judith Butler, Ernesto Laclau and Slovoj Zizek, *Contingency, Hegemony, Universality*, London and New York: Verso, 2000; Jacques Rancière, *Disagreement: Politics and Philosophy* translated by Julie Rose, Minneapolis: University of Minnesota Press, 1999; William E. Connolly, *Pluralism*, Durham, NC: Duke University Press, 2005; Connolly, *Identity\ Difference: Democratic Negotiations of Political Paradox*, Ithaca: Cornell University Press, 1991; Warren Magnusson, *The Search for Political Space*, Toronto: University of Toronto Press, 1996; Hent de Vries and Samuel Weber, eds, *Violence, Identity and Self Determination*, Stanford: Stanford University Press, 1997; David Ingram, ed., *The Political*, Oxford: Blackwell, 2002; and Kari Palonen and R.B.J. Walker, eds, "Politics Revisited," Special Issue of *Alternatives: Global, Local, Political*, 28, 2003.

22 R.B.J. Walker, "The Subject of Security," in Keith Krause and Michael C. Williams, eds, *Critical Security Studies: Concepts and Cases*, Minneapolis: University of Minnesota Press, 1997, 61–81.

23 On the one hand, for example, many versions of globalization theory extend and complicate claims about the loss of politics to a market rationality while, on the other hand, many claims about empire and an indiscriminate or even generalized exceptionalism in the "war on terror" extend and complicate claims about an excess of politics in some new authoritarian form.

24 For an especially rich analysis in this respect, one that has shaped many of the formulations I adopt here, see Ashley, "Living on Border Lines." Cf. Jacques Derrida, "Living On: Borderlines," translated by James Hulbert, in Harold Bloom *et al.*, *Deconstruction and Criticism*, New York: Seabury Press, 1989. For a still useful overview of the specifically Derridean engagement with the constitutive outside that has informed much recent analysis of boundaries and limits, see Rudolph Gasché, *The Tain of the Mirror: Derrida and the Philosophy of Reflection*, Cambridge, MA: Harvard University Press, 1986.

25 For an extensive account of the practice of drawing lines as, literally, defining modern cultural practices, see Patrick Maynard, *Drawing Distinctions: The Varieties of Graphic Expression*, Ithaca: Cornell University Press, 2005.

26 Helpful discussions of this general theme in various contexts are developed in Elizabeth Grosz, ed., *Becomings: Explorations in Time, Memory, and Futures*, Ithaca: Cornell University Press, 1999; John Bender and David E. Wellbery, eds, *Chronotypes: The Construction of Time*, Stanford: Stanford University Press, 1991; Luhman, *Observations on Modernity*; and Kari Palonen, *The Struggle with Time: A Conceptual History of "Politics" as an Activity*, Hamburg: LIT Verlag, 2006.

27 Which is not to say that attempts to speak of humanity as such are easy even in terms that tend to shy away from politics. See, for example, Emmanuel Levinas, *Totality and Infinity: An Essay on Exteriority* (1961), translated by Alphonso Lingis, Pittsburg: Duquesne University Press, 1969; Tzvetan Todorov, *Life in Common: An Essay in General Anthropology* (1995) translated by Katherine Golsan and Lucy Golsan, Lincoln: University of Nebraska Press, 2001; Raimond Gaita, *A Common Humanity: Thinking About Love and Truth and Justice*, London: Routledge, 2000; and Peter Singer, *One World: The Ethics of Globalization*, New Haven: Yale University Press, 2002.

28 At a minimum, the terms international system and system of states generally refer to the structural relations among the plurality of more or less autonomous statist political communities that emerged in early modern Europe and became the regulative norm after the formal decolonizations of the twentieth century. Brief but helpful discussions include Maurice Keens-Soper, "The Practice of a States System," in Michael Donelan, ed., *The Reason of States*, London: George Allen & Unwin, 1978, 25–44; Martin Wight, *Systems of States*; Richard Rosecrance, *Action and Reaction in World Politics: International Systems in Perspective*, Boston: Little, Brown, 1963; Ernst B. Haas, "The Balance of Power: Prescription, Concept, or Propaganda," *World Politics*, 5(4), July 1953, 442–77; and Richard Little, *The Balance of Power in International Relations: Metaphors, Myths and Models*, Cambridge: Cambridge University Press, 2007.

Most of what now counts as a mainstream of theories about the structure of this system consists of a heterogeneous array of hypotheses, models and logics (invoking various claims about utilitarian reason, institutional dynamics, structure–agency, power–knowledge, ideology–interest, and so on) that are familiar from other fields of social and political analysis. Especially strong influences have recently come from micro-economics rather than the metaphors drawn from classical mechanics and biology that were more familiar in earlier literatures. These theories express a broad range of by no means trivial analytical difficulties, generating the core literatures and debates of international relations theory in the process. Some arise from automatic conflations of state and nation that enable a rapid slide from accounts of sovereignty associated with a seventeenth-century Hobbesian legalist nominalism to accounts of sovereignty associated with Schmitt's early twentieth-century nationalist decisionism. Some relate to analytical distinctions between system and subsystem. Some concern relations between structural determination and political agency, often in ways that conflate claims about systemic determinism with claims about an ontological or epistemological realism, thereby enabling a systematic marginalization of historical practices of objectification. Some relate to very different understandings of what it means to engage in a theory of systems and the most appropriate ontological and analogical languages for doing so. The most pervasive difficulties, however, remain those arising from the relation between state sovereignty and the system of sovereign states, a problem that is often simply brushed aside in much of this literature. This largely explains why much of the prevailing literature is so concerned with the conditionalities of structural order and disorder, why it is so hypersensitive to the demands of causal explanation, and why it is so naive about questions of political principle; it is this combination that has made Waltz's *Theory of International Politics* such a paradigmatic text for many international relations scholars, sometimes as an ideal of rigorous explanation and sometimes as an exemplary trivialization of political analysis. For an earlier expression of similar tendencies, see Morton Kaplan, *System and Process in International Politics*, New York: John Wiley, 1957.

Some tendencies towards trivialization are successfully resisted in Barry Buzan, Charles Jones and Richard Little, eds, *The Logic of Anarchy: Neorealism to Structural Realism*, New York: Columbia University Press, 1993, which develops a judicious elaboration and defence of Waltzian structuralism while nevertheless affirming the "levels of analysis" schematic that I believe to be crucial to the way various puzzles they examine (involving relations of structure and agency, structural spatialization and historical contingency, and vertical and horizontal (or distributional) forms of structural articulation) have been framed as irresolvable antagonisms. See also Buzan and Little, *International Systems in World History: Remaking the Study of International Relations*, Oxford: Oxford University Press, 2000, which rightly insists on a more historical approach to the analysis of state systems, but offers an alternative that shifts uneasily between a (sometimes Whiggish, sometimes paternalistic, sometimes tragic) progressivism, a kind of storehouse of examples that might have interested Machiavelli, and a rather positivistic reduction of history to a set of ahistorical hypotheses about structures susceptible to transformation. In addition to a very strong, indeed enabling commitment to an account of levels of analysis on a "spatial scale (small to large, individual to system)" (441), Buzan and Little reduce the opposition between structure and history to one between structure and action, thereby avoiding questions about spatiotemporally specific forms of spatiotemporality that I take to be crucial for the structuring of modern forms of states system.

29 The notion that the system of states must be understood as a rule-governed practice has perhaps been developed with greatest theoretical sophistication by scholars grounded in the political analysis of international law, as with Kratochwil, *Rules, Norms and Decisions* and Onuf, *World of Our Making*. Useful contextualizations of the legal background are provided by Martti Koskenniemi, *The Gentle Civilizer of Nations: The Rise and Fall of International Law, 1870–1960*, Cambridge: Cambridge University Press, 2002, and Anthony Clark Arend, *Legal Rules and International Society*, Oxford: Oxford University Press, 1999, although the distinguishing quality of this literature also lies in its impressive historical and philosophical erudition more generally.

This literature has had to struggle against extreme nationalist dismissals of the relevance of international law as merely a realm of ideas without a centralized capacity for enforcement: one of the ways in which claims about political realism have worked to affirm very specific normative claims, especially in relation to accounts of a specifically American national interest or national security. Contrary to radical nationalists, or even those who play out their nationalist realism through neo-Weberian accounts of responsibility, the long-established literature on the emergence of such rules historically has a much stronger claim on what it might mean to have a tradition of international relations theory, one in which international law has an indispensable role. In this context, it would not be so easy to draw the usual sharp contrast between political realism and accounts of the supposedly novel development of various "international regimes" that have built on specifically utilitarian accounts of cooperation under conditions of competition such as the accounts of international interdependence popularized by Robert O. Keohane and Joseph Nye, *Power and Interdependence*, Boston: Little, Brown, 1977; and Robert Axelrod, *The Evolution of Cooperation*, New York: Basic Books, 1984; or such a sharp contrast with the considerably richer concept of hegemony developed by Antonio Gramsci that has been used to examine the way rule-governed practices are especially shaped by the "great powers" and/or the demands of capital, as in the work of Stephen Gill, *Gramsci, Historical Materialism and International Relations*, Cambridge: Cambridge University Press, 1993.

Much the same might be said about recent appeals to "constructivism" in the analysis of international relations. Many recent contributions to this genre draw on a variety of sociological theories to explain the production of collective norms, often in ways that say more about the consequences of the systematic exclusion of social theory from Anglo-American political science than about how social theory might now work in contexts in which statist understandings of a society are profoundly problematic. Alexander Wendt, *Social Theory of International Politics*, Cambridge: Cambridge University Press, 1999, is the most ambitious text here, though its ambitions are sharply constrained by disconcerting leaps into very murky claims about epistemological and political principle. In many respects, "constructivism" has come to name research aspirations for which many of the standard concerns of classical social theory have had to be reinvented within a discipline that has worked very hard to keep sociology and the social at bay, in ways that parallel the marginalization of international law. Among the consequences have been a recourse to epiphenomenal or "superstructuralist" accounts of language, culture and identity, slides from a concern with "idealist" accounts of norms to "idealist" philosophies of history understood as the realization of a liberal teleology, and rhetorical appeals to the need for an empirical research programme as a way of evading questions about the relation between knowledge and power. Pertinent commentary in this respect is developed by George Marcus in his "Foreword" to Jutta Weldes, Mark Laffey, Hugh Gusterson and Raymond Duvall, *Cultures of Insecurity: States, Communities and the Production of Danger*, Minneapolis: University of Minnesota Press, 1999, vii–xvi. See also the commentaries developed in Maja Zehfuss, *Constructivism in International Relations: The Politics of Reality*, Cambridge: Cambridge University Press, 2002; and Stefano Guzzini and Anna Leander, eds, *Constructivism and International Relations: Alexander Wendt and His Critics*, London: Routledge, 2006.

30 The notion of an international society is especially associated with the English School of international relations theory. Its most influential text is Bull, *The Anarchical Society*. Especially important elaborations include Paul Keal, *Unspoken Rules and Superpower Dominance*, London: Macmillan, 1983; and Ian Clark, *Legitimacy in International Society*, Oxford: Oxford University Press, 2005. Important commentaries include Andrew Linklater and Hidemi Suganami, *The*

English School of International Relations: A Contemporary Reassessment, Cambridge: Cambridge University Press, 2006; and Edward Keene, *Beyond the Anarchical Society: Grotius, Colonialism and Order in World Politics*, Cambridge: Cambridge University Press, 2002. It is also perhaps worth recalling one text, among others, that has for some reason been excluded from membership in what has in any case become a curiously defined English School, but which develops similar themes without reliance on contentious traditions of historiography and in ways that highlight tensions between structural ontologies and political action: John Burton, *Systems, States, Diplomacy and Rules*, Cambridge: Cambridge University Press, 1969. For better or worse, much of my own understanding of what counts as a political theory of international relations was initially shaped by the competing and inadequate languages deployed by Bull and Burton; I remain indebted to both for shaping my decision to move in very different directions. Similar difficulties have been posed more recently in relation to the work of Niklas Luhmann; see Mathias Albert and Lena Hilkermeier, eds, *Observing International Relations: Niklas Luhman and World Politics*, London: Routledge, 2004. The text with which the early literature of the English School ought to be compared, however, is Carl Schmitt's nostalgic elegy for the pre-twentieth-century European order, *The Nomos of the Earth in the International Law of the Jus Publicum Europaeum* (1950/1974), translated by Gary L. Ulmen, New York: Telos, 2003.

31 Despite the popularity of claims about anarchy, it would be difficult to find any credible theorist of international relations willing to affirm a claim that international relations expresses the kind of freedom and equality implied by quasi-Hobbesian notions of an international anarchy, at least not until every state has equal access to weapons of mass destruction; although references to anarchy are commonly used to embed such a claim without overt justification precisely so as to justify an extreme case. On the contrary, international order, it is generally assumed, derives in large part from the fact of inequality, of the "responsibility" of the "great powers" and the "stability," even "universality," generated by "hegemons."

In this respect, two sorts of problem arise. First, and most familiar, there is the problem of reconciling the responsibility of hegemonic states with the principle of international equality, as when the UN Security Council is assumed to have prior authority over the UN General Assembly. Second, there is the problem, canvassed especially in relation to the radical behaviour of recent US administrations, of identifying the conditions under which the hegemony that is said to be necessary for international order might mutate into a hegemony that undermines the very principles of international order: that shows signs of mutating into empire, in the singular, rather than just the plural and competing empires that have long been understood to be compatible with the maintenance of international order.

For a brief analysis of the tension between equality and inequality domestically and internationally, see Walker, "International/Inequality," in Mustapha Kamal Pasha and Craig N. Murphy, eds, *International Relations and the New Inequality*, Oxford: Blackwell, 2002, 7–24. For an important historical analysis of the interplay between claims to sovereign authority, claims to hegemonic inequality, and claims about the limits of legitimate participation in the system of states, see Gerry Simpson, *Great Powers and Outlaw States*, Cambridge: Cambridge University Press, 2004. For a more explicitly legalistic reading, see Benedict Kingsbury, "Sovereignty and Inequality," in Andrew Hurrell and Ngaire Woods, eds, *Inequality, Globalization, and World Politics*, Oxford: Oxford University Press, 1999, 66–94.

32 To take just one example from the specific literatures that I engage at various points, the distinction between the "merely" systemic and more elaborately societal accounts of inter-state order, or what the English School often refer to as "pluralism" and "solidarism," offers an especially seductive way of thinking about change and temporality as a progressive move from the former to the latter. In this

context, the problem is already inherent in the way Wight and Bull set up this distinction so as to invite speculation about a more sensible middle ground, rather than by insisting that the system of states works both through the operation of more or less routinized practices and the delineation of limits to those practices – in ways that are not so unfamiliar from the history of modern states. Reifying some of the usual perspectives or isms (in this case named after Hobbes, Grotius and Kant), this tradition predictably has been drawn to move back and forth along the spatial terrain from norm to limit, to keep postulating a progressivist account of escape to some other political order, and, unsurprisingly, to keep coming up against the contradictions of a modern political order expressing both the necessity and possibility of escape. Invocations of a Grotian middle ground in this context perform much the same function as invocations of a sensible middle ground between liberty and security within states: the function, that is, of deflecting attention from the contradictory character of modern political life and from questions about authority, and sovereignty, that necessarily arise when norms are suspended in favour of exceptional conditions. While I am sympathetic to the more societal narratives affirmed by many texts of the English School, the constitutive distinction between pluralism and solidarism has been a profound mistake.

The continuing effect of this set of moves within this particular literature can be traced in the latter part of Linklater and Suganami, *The English School of International Relations*, which expresses Linklater's distinctive attempt to combine elements of English School thinking with the quasi-Kantian legalism associated with Jürgen Habermas in a way that runs into serious logical problems. I take up the broadly Kantian challenges at stake here later in my present analysis, but for commentary on the limits of Linklater's specific reading of a progressivist international politics see R.B.J. Walker, "The Hierarchicalization of Political Community," (part of a Forum on Andrew Linklater), *Review of International Studies*, 25:1, January 1999, pp.151–56; and Walker, "Citizenship and the Modern Subject," in Kimberly Hutchings and Roland Dannreuther, eds, *Cosmopolitan Citizenship*, London: Macmillan, 1999, 171–200. See also Beate Jahn, "One Step Forward, Two Steps Back: Critical Theory as the Latest Edition of Liberal Idealism," *Millennium: Journal of International Studies*, 27:3, 1998, 613–41.

33 For an extended discussion of this point, see Bartelson, *Critique of the State*.

34 I think here especially of the ways in which the sense of temporal contingency to be found in Machiavelli was largely erased in favour of more spatially organized accounts of the relations between freedom and necessity found in Hobbes, and the reshaping of this relation as a process of linear and teleological History found in the later texts of Kant and in much of Hegel; but also of various ways in which a quasi-Machiavellian sense of contingency and an attempt to read Kant and Hegel without assuming linear teleologies have become key themes permeating much contemporary political thought. See, for example, Sakari Hanninen, "The Eternal Return of Politics," *Alternatives: Global, Local, Political*, 28:2, 2003, Jean-Luc Nancy, *Hegel: The Restlessness of the Negative*, translated by Jason Smith and Steven Miller, Minneapolis: University of Minnesota Press, 2002; and Palonen, *The Struggle with Time*.

I also think of the way in which political readings of modernity have been over-determined by Leo Strauss's account of both Machiavelli and Hobbes as "moderns" in the sense that they mark a shift from the "classical" idealism (of both Athens and Jerusalem) capable of giving universal answers to questions of right, wrong and social order to an age of "historicism" or "realism" (or nihilism, relativism and contingency). Much of the difficulty of contemporary political theory derives from the extent to which this framing of freedom and contingency against an assumed natural and unhistorical necessity is able to subvert any sense of the historical contingency of the framing of the problem of necessity and contingency.

For an especially sharp discussion of the Straussian legacy in this respect, see Miguel E. Vatter, "The Machiavellian Legacy: Origins and Outcomes of the Conflict Between Politics and Morality in Modernity," Florence: European University Institute Working Paper, SPS No 2, 1999; see also Vatter, *Between Form and Event: Machiavelli's Theory of Political Freedom*, Dordrecht: Kluwer, 2000. I share the increasingly widespread view that the recovery of Machiavelli from Straussian accounts of modernity is one of the most important sites of contemporary political critique.

For lucid general accounts of how claims about temporality and change have been expressed in modern social and political thought, see, for example, Wolin, *Politics and Vision*; John Gunnell, *Political Philosophy and Time*, Middletown, CT: Wesleyan University Press, 1968; Geoffrey Hawthorn, *Enlightenment and Despair: A History of Social Theory*, Cambridge: Cambridge University Press, 2nd edn,1987; and Alex Callinicos, *Social Theory: A Historical Introduction*, Cambridge: Polity Press, 1999. More generally, see Frank E. Manuel, *Shapes of Philosophical History*, London: George Allen & Unwin, 1965; Maurice Mandelbaum, *History, Man and Reason: A Study in Nineteenth Century Thought*, Baltimore: The Johns Hopkins Press, 1971; David Gross, *The Past in Ruins: Tradition and the Critique of Modernity*, Amherst: University of Massachusetts Press, 1992; Michael Allen Gillespie, *Hegel, Heidegger and the Ground of History*, Chicago: University of Chicago Press, 1984; and Fredric Jameson, *The Seeds of Time*, New York: Columbia University Press, 1994. For a rich account of the Greek and medieval philosophies of temporality, paradox and origin that remain in play in many contemporary debates see Richard Sorabji, *Time, Creation, and the Continuum: Theories in Antiquity and the Early Middle Ages*, Ithaca: Cornell University Press, 1983.

35 Weber, "Politics as Vocation."

36 It is quite striking that the text of the UN Charter is so rarely treated as an interesting site for political theory despite the ways in which it expresses paradigmatic principles of modern sovereignty (in Article 2, Paragraph 7, for example, and the power-balancing arrangements enabled under Articles 51–54), principles of necessary inequalities in the practices of international order (expressed in the tension between the General Assembly and the Security Council, for example, and the collective security scheme envisaged in Article 43), and intimations of institutional novelty (in Articles 99–101 concerning the office of the Secretary General, for example, as well as in the space that has subsequently been carved out by the Specialized Agencies). The legacies of colonialism expressed in this text are also worth some reflection. As a text that expresses many of the crucial contradictions of modern politics, especially as these were being negotiated in the midst of a global war, it remains more interesting than it has been made to seem in the largely functionalist and institutionalist narratives that have organized the subsequent analysis of "international organization," a term that has come to both express and elide tensions between a system of states and some kind of hierarchical order. The use I make of a distinction between horizontal and vertical conceptions of modern politics is partly a response to the contradictions expressed in this text.

37 For the classic attempt to insist that the tension (understood, I think fatally, as a simple dualism rather than an aporetic double) between claims to citizenship and claims to humanity poses the key problems of any theory of international relations (understood, I also think fatally, as an autonomous scholarly discipline), see Andrew Linklater, *Men and Citizens in the Theory of International Relations*, London: Macmillan, 1982, 2nd edn 1990.

38 Among many other examples, this ambivalence has enabled the discursive alliance between multilateralist and unilateralist claims about the priority of "humanitarian intervention" over the principle of non-intervention in the domestic affairs of sovereign states since the mid-1990s. The tensions expressed in the competing yet

synergistic logics informing these claims became increasingly apparent after the US declaration of the need for "pre-emptive intervention" in Iraq in 2002–03, and especially in the differing yet ultimately convergent legitimations of mass violence in the name of "ethics" expressed in US President Bush's overtly imperial unilateralism and UK Prime Minister Blair's more nuanced but nonetheless imperial multilateralism. I take up this theme in R.B.J. Walker, "War, Terror, Judgement," in Bulent Gokay and R.B.J. Walker, eds, *September 11, 2001: War, Terror and Judgement*, London: Frank Cass, 2003, 62–83.

39 I think here especially of Marx's treatment of the massive practices expressed in the line marking a transition from labour to exchange as sites of value in the first three chapters of the first volume of *Capital*; and J.S. Mill's meditation on the impossible line between public and private in *On Liberty*; both texts offering much richer sites for thinking politically than the standardized Marxisms and liberalisms into which they have been subsumed.

40 For an accessible and suggestive biography, see Nicholas Crane, *Mercator: The Man Who Mapped the World*, London: Weidenfeld & Nicholson, 2002. Mercator is interesting not only for the technical mathematical achievements of the projection that organized accurate navigation along parallels of latitude and longitude (at the expense of the spatial distortions that have since come to seem so natural), or for the degree to which he was caught up in broader currents of religious struggle, scientific imagination and the European "discovery" of the world, but also because of his theological obsessions with beginnings and endings, and the incongruity between his own experience of border crossings and multiple locations and the modern borders that have come to imitate the fixed lines and grids that enabled him to spatialize place so effectively. Crane depicts Mercator as recognizing that it is "a small step from locative sentimentality to territorial bigotry" (321), a step that has indeed had enormous consequences for the subsequent organization of modern politics. For a defence of Mercator's achievements and a critique of some of the more familiar complaints about the way some parts of the world are made to seem bigger and others smaller on his maps, see Mark Monmonier, *Rhumb Lines and Map Wars: A Social History of the Mercator Projection*, Chicago: University of Chicago Press, 2004. More generally, see John P. Snyder, *Flattening the Earth: Two Thousand Years of Map Projections*, Chicago: University of Chicago Press, 1993; and Christian Jacob, *The Sovereign Map: Theoretical Approaches in Cartography Throughout History*, Edward H. Dahl, ed., translated by Tom Conley, Chicago: University of Chicago Press, 2006.

41 Hence, to take only one example, the efforts of the historical approach to the history of political thought to overcome the anachronistic projection of the modern state as the context in which the entire history of political thought can be framed. See, most notably, Quentin Skinner's still indispensable *The Foundations of Modern Political Thought*, two volumes, Cambridge: Cambridge University Press, 1978, though both the unironic reference to "foundations" and the lack of interest in an emerging states system are instructive once again; Skinner, *Visions of Politics*, three volumes, Cambridge: Cambridge University Press, 2002; and Skinner, "The State," in T. Ball, J. Farr and R. Hanson, eds, *Political Innovation and Conceptual Change*, Cambridge: Cambridge University Press, 1989, 89–131. See also the interesting interpretation of Skinner's achievement from a position that draws on Reinhart Koselleck's understanding of conceptual history in Kari Palonen, *Quentin Skinner: History, Politics, Rhetoric*, Cambridge: Polity Press, 2003.

More generally, see Ernst H. Kantorowicz, *The King's Two Bodies: A Study in Medieval Political Theology*, Princeton: Princeton University Press, 1957; J.H. Burns, with the assistance of Mark Goldie, ed., *The Cambridge History of Political Thought, 1450–1700*, Cambridge: Cambridge University Press, 1991; J.G.A. Pocock, *The Machiavellian Moment: Florentine Political Thought and the Atlantic*

Republican Tradition, Princeton: Princeton University Press, 1975; Maurizio Viroli, *From Politics to Reason of State: The Acquisition and Transformation of the Language of Politics, 1250–1600*, Cambridge: Cambridge University Press, 1992; Richard Flathman, *Thomas Hobbes: Skepticism, Individuality and Chastened Politics*, Newbury Park: Sage, 1993; and Richard Tuck, *Philosophy and Government, 1572–1651*, Cambridge: Cambridge University Press, 1993.

42 .A shift towards various philosophies of (especially spatiotemporal) relationality have been widely canvassed since the early twentieth century, usually with at least one ear open to the implications of post-Einsteinian physics and post-cubist aesthetics on the one hand, and various echoes of earlier writers such as Leibniz and Spinoza on the other. Many attempts made in the 1960s and early 1970s to think about the dynamic structuring of the modern states system as a form of self-organizing or cybernetic system, as a network of mutually constitutive relations, expressed similar insights. These were rapidly eclipsed by the reduction of systems theory to a series of metaphors rooted in images of the containerized (and thus "black-boxable") state or the utilitarian rationality of a market economy subject to "inputs" and "outputs," or to a good old-fashioned mechanical balance of power. Theoretical discussions of relationality and self-organizing systems now tend to be raised under such rubrics as "chaos theory," though it remains to be seen how far these discussions have a capacity to enable a sharper sense of the spatiotemporal contingency of political life. For a suggestive commentary in this respect, see Arkady Plotnitsky, *Complementarity: Anti-Epistemology After Bohr and Derrida*, Durham, NC: Duke University Press, 1994.

43 See especially Weber, "The Profession and Vocation of Politics," a text that, among other things, manages both to offer a paradigmatically modern account of where and what political life is about, and simultaneously to problematize the very possibility of politics under modern conditions.

44 For suggestive commentaries on this theme, see, for example, Hartog, *The Mirror of Herodotus*; Jacques Derrida, *Politics of Friendship*, translated by George Collins, London and New York: Verso, 1997; and Simon Critchley, *Ethics–Politics–Subjectivity*, London: Verso, 1999.

45 The classic text here remains Alexandre Koyré, *From the Closed World to the Infinite Universe*, Baltimore: The Johns Hopkins Press, 1957.

46 See, among many, M.M. Goldsmith, *Hobbes' Science of Politics*, New York: Columbia University Press, 1966; and Gunnell, *Political Philosophy and Time*.

47 Carl von Clausewitz, *On War* (1832), translated by Michael Howard and Peter Paret, Princeton: Princeton University Press, 1984.

48 Partha Chatterjee, *Nationalism and the Colonial World: A Coopted Discourse*, London: Zed Books, 1986; Ashis Nandy, *The Illegitimacy of Nationalism*, Delhi: Oxford University Press, 1994.

49 I use this simple formulation as a way of connecting my explicit concern with the need to reimagine a political life informed by the inside/outside structure of the modern state and states system, and my implicit concern with a variety of attempts to engage with the difficulty of "thinking otherwise" in more explicitly philosophical terms. Here I might mention traditions that seek to think about the need for openness towards the completely other (Emmanuel Levinas); or to engage with the unnamably different beyond the already (gendered) constitution of the same and the different (Luce Irigaray); or the "excessive" rather than the functionally useful (George Bataille); or the trace always left by the repressed or excluded outside on the inside that seeks to claim the sharpest of borders (Jacques Derrida); or the actions, events and movements that force an inside to recognize and engage with the outside, the unthought, that both enables and resists it (Gilles Deleuze); or the specific genealogies and practices through which modern conceptions of subjectivity have been enabled and limited by the unthought (Michel Foucault); or the

struggles by all such thinkers to resist the Aristotelian/Hegelian logic of identity and contradiction that works so powerfully to reaffirm a simple distinction between inside and outside.

50 Symptomatically, perhaps the least noticed but most important commonality marked by the popular inscription of figures such as Habermas and Foucault as definers of the primary debates in late twentieth-century European political theory was the degree to which questions about international relations made only a late appearance in their work: in relation to the relevance of a highly modified form of Kantian ethics in a more "cosmopolitan" Europe/world in the case of Habermas; and in relation to the role of violence and war in the constitution of modern subjectivities in the case of Foucault.

   While Habermas belatedly sought to think about the possibilities of a quasi-Kantian conception of cosmopolitanism, he did so in a way that simply ignored the problem of the international, opting instead for the usual shift from *polis* to cosmopolis that, as I argue here, reproduces the ethnocentric and statist logic expressed as a discourse of presence and absence on the one hand and the subsumption of politics into ethics on the other. Foucault, on the other hand, had a much better grasp on the question of the limits within which this logic works, especially in his two remarkable series of lectures, *"Society must be Defended:" Lectures at the Collège de France, 1975–1976*, translated by David Macey, New York: Picador, 2003; and *Security, Territory, Population: Lectures at the Collège de France, 1977–1978*, translated by Graham Burchill, Basingstoke: Palgrave, 2007; for commentary see especially Didier Bigo, "Security: A Field Left Fallow," in Andrew Neal and Michael Dillon, eds, *Foucault on Politics, Security and War*, Basingstoke: Palgrave, 2008, 93–114; and Andrew Neal, *Exceptionalism and the Politics of Counter-Terrorism: Liberty, Security and the War on Terror*, London: Routledge, 2009. Nevertheless, he also remained disturbingly ethnocentric in many respects, even though his writings remain one of the key sites through which contemporary social and political theory has begun to engage with sovereignty as a problem, rather than as just one expression of a pluralism that must be overcome through someone's universalism; for commentary, see Vivienne Jabri, "Michel Foucault's Analytics of War: The Social, the International, the Racial," *International Political Sociology*, 1:1, March 2007, 67–82.

51 John Rawls, *A Theory of Justice*, Oxford: Oxford University Press, 1972. Rawls' text has been widely, and in some respects rightly, championed as an invigorating challenge to the many complacencies of mid-twentieth century Anglo-American political theory, but also brought many complacencies of its own. Glen Newey's claim that "liberal political philosophers aim at the supersession of the ostensible subject matter of their discipline – that is, they aim at a post-political order," (2) seems to me to capture Rawls' participation in a broader trend in this respect; see Newey, *After Politics: The Rejection of Politics in Contemporary Liberal Political Philosophy*, Basingstoke: Palgrave, 2001. Newey's analysis speaks both to the widespread tendency in the Anglo-American world to treat politics merely as a form of applied ethics or the legal enforcement of established moral standards, and also to a failure to question the form of political community that most forms of liberalism simply assume, whether in its individualistic or more "communitarian" versions. A similarly paradigmatic example is Ronald Dworkin, *Sovereign Virtue: The Theory and Practice of Equality*, Cambridge, MA: Harvard University Press, 2000, but the problem exceeds the myopias of any specific author.

   For my purposes here, the post-political character of this kind of liberal political theory becomes especially problematic when projected onto an international arena, as if the limits of a modern political community must be simply taken for granted in relation to any specific community but systematically ignored through the application of ethics to relations among communities. In this sense, post-politics

works as a form of political irresponsibility, as a dogmatic practice that is dramatically at odds with the claims to openness, pluralism and freedom that liberal
political theory has sought to affirm. The substitution of applied ethics and certain
kinds of law for politics is also characteristic of literatures on contemporary forms
of cosmopolitanism that seek to challenge the kind of internationalism that Rawls
takes for granted, even in his later work. A particularly instructive example of the
tangles into which many political philosophers have been led as a consequence is
Thomas Nagel, "The Problem of Global Justice," *Philosophy and Public Affairs*,
33:2, 2005, 113–47.

Liberalism, it should also be noted immediately, is not the only problematic
tradition in this respect. Many of the primary critiques of modern liberalism –
those rooted in accounts of a socialist or nationalist community, for example, or in
the nostalgia for the *polis* associated with followers of Leo Strauss – share a similar
and perhaps even more troubling taste for veils. It should also be noted that liberalism draws upon a much richer array of resources than one might suspect from its
narrowly Rawlsian versions.

52 Andrew Vincent, *The Nature of Political Theory*, Oxford: Oxford University Press,
2004. Other symptomatic discussions of the limits of much contemporary political
theory that speak to my concerns here include Jacques Rancière, *On the Shores of
Politics*, translated by Liz Heron, London: Verso, 1995; Etienne Balibar, *Politics
and the Other Scene*, translated by Christine Jones, James Swenson and Chris
Turner, London: Verso, 2002; John Gray, *Endgames: Questions in Late Modern
Political Thought*, Cambridge: Polity Press, 1997; Paul W. Kahn, *Putting Liberalism in its Place*, Princeton: Princeton University Press, 2005; George Kateb, *Patriotism and Other Mistakes*, New Haven: Yale University Press, 2006; Raymond
Geuss, *History and Illusion in Politics*, Cambridge: Cambridge University Press,
2001; Andrew Gamble, *Politics and Fate*, Cambridge: Polity Press, 2000; and
Mouffe, *On the Political*.

53 This was perhaps the most important and still underappreciated point advanced in
Hedley Bull's complaint about the universalizing methodological pretensions emanating from American political science departments in the 1960s; for the complaint, and various responses to it, see Klaus Knorr and James N. Rosenau, eds,
Contending Approaches to International Politics, Princeton: Princeton University
Press, 1969. For Bull, the kind of ontological dualism expressed in Martin Wight's
influential essay "Why is there no International Theory?" (in Butterfield and
Wight, eds, *Diplomatic Investigations*) implied an epistemological dualism, making
the generalizing methods associated with social science inappropriate for the more
contingent realm of international relations. Most of the ensuing debate quickly
became obsessed with debates about epistemology in general, and then became
mired in dubious characterizations of knowledge derived either from English historiography or various attempts to either resuscitate (in the name of behavioural-
ism) or repudiate (in order to avoid the perceived liberalism of political science) the
mouldering beast of logical positivism: for a useful account of the counter-
enlightenment character of Morgenthau's version of political realism in this
respect, see Nicolas Guilhot, "The Realist Gambit: Postwar American Political
Science and The Birth of IR Theory," *International Political Sociology*, 2:4, 2008,
pp. 281–304. Consequently, the force of Bull's attempt to pose epistemological
questions in terms of prior ontological concerns rapidly dissipated.

The consequence of what was sometimes feted as a second "great debate"
(though better understood as a set of skirmishes in a broader struggle between
political realism and political idealism) has been that questions about method in
international relations theory have been posed almost entirely in terms that assume
a ground of similarity and comparability, not a ground of problematic relations
between similarity and difference. In specifically disciplinary terms, this has meant

that questions about method have been dominated either by traditions of comparative politics or by the analysis of a specific (generally US) state. The radical dualism expressed by Bull and Wight may be unsustainable, but so too is the radical monism assumed by traditions of comparative and American political analysis. The same tendency simply to affirm a ground of similarity is at work in the imposition of ontologies of rational action onto an international system, an imposition that is invariably justified on grounds of method with little attention to either the scholarly or the political stakes of the ontological imposition. It is at work also in the framing of a supposed science of international relations in purely structuralist terms, with the consequence that attention to the possibilities of change (the possibility of the end of the Cold War, most notoriously) has become a lost art. The core problems that are at the heart of international relations, questions precisely about the relations between universality and particularity, between state sovereignty and the system of sovereign states, and between what counts as norm and what counts as exception, are all thereby muted.

54 The exemplary discussion is Peter B. Evans, Dietrich Rueschemeyer and Theda Scocpol, eds, *Bringing the State Back In*, Cambridge: Cambridge University Press, 1985.

55 Christine Helliwell and Barry Hindess, "The 'Empire of Uniformity' and the Government of Subject Peoples," *Cultural Values*, 6:1/2, 2002, 139–52; Gerd Baumann, *The Multicultural Riddle: Rethinking National, Ethnic and Religious Identities*, London: Routledge, 1999; R.B.J. Walker, "Multiculturalism and Leaking Boundaries," in Dieter Haselbach, ed., *Multiculturalism in a World of Leaking Boundaries*, Munster: LIT Verlag, 1998, 309–22.

56 Gilles Deleuze, "Nietzsche," (1965) in Deleuze, *Pure Immanence: Essays on a Life*, translated by Anne Boyman, New York: Zone Books, 2001, 71.

57 The background literature here is enormous. Expressions of traditions that have informed my thinking include Pierre Duhem, *Medieval Cosmology: Theories of Infinity, Place, Time, Void and the Plurality of Worlds* (an abridged edition of Duhem's extraordinary multi-volume *Le systèm du monde. Histoire des doctrines cosmologiques de Platon à Copernic*), edited and translated by Roger Ariew, Chicago: University of Chicago Press, 1985; Koyré, *From the Closed World to the Infinite Universe*; Max Jammer, *Concepts of Space: The History of Theories of Space in Physics*, 2nd edn, Cambridge, MA: Harvard University Press, 1969; Edmund Husserl, *The Crisis of European Science and Transcendental Phenomenology: An Introduction to Phenomenological Philosophy*, translated by David Carr, Evanston, IL: Northwestern University Press, 1970; Cassirer, *The Individual and Cosmos in Renaissance Philosophy*; Gaston Bachelard, *The Poetics of Space*; Claudia Brodsky Lacour, *Lines of Thought: Discourse, Architectonics, and the Origins of Modern Philosophy*, Durham, NC: Duke University Press, 1996; Karsten Harries, *Infinity and Perspective*, Cambridge, MA: MIT Press, 2001; Edward S. Casey, *The Fate of Place*; Edward S. Casey, *Getting Back into Place: Toward a Renewed Understanding of the Place World*, Bloomington: Indiana University Press, 1993; Yi-Fu Tuan, *Space and Place*; Henri Lefebre, *The Production of Space*, translated by Donald Nicholson-Smith, Oxford: Blackwell, 1991; Robert David Sack, *Conceptions of Space in Social Thought: A Geographic Perspective*, London: Macmillan, 1980; Mike Crang and Nigel Thrift, eds, *Thinking Space*, London: Routledge, 2000; and Paul Adams *et al.*, eds, *Textures of Place: Exploring Humanist Geographies*, Minneapolis: University of Minnesota Press, 2001.

For a brief but suggestive essay that poses questions about the politics of space that come close to my specific concerns here, see J. Peter Euben, "The Polis, Globalization, and the Politics of Place," in Aryeh Botwinick and William E. Connolly, eds, *Democracy and Vision: Sheldon Wolin and the Vicissitudes of the Political*, Princeton: Princeton University Press, 2001, 256–89. For an important recent attempt to think about what it might mean to develop a more imaginative and more politically critical geography, especially in relation to the problems of alterity and exceptionalism, see Derek Gregory, *The Colonial Present*, Oxford: Blackwell, 2004.

4 Sovereignties, origins, limits

1 For a discussion that has quietly percolated into many familiar debates about scientific explanation, see Gaston Bachelard, *The Philosophy of No* (1940) translated by G.C. Waterstone, New York: Orion Press, 1969.
2 Bartelson, *Genealogy of Sovereignty*; Walker, *Inside/Outside*.
3 Among many ways of engaging this theme, see Jean-Pierre Vernant, *The Origins of Greek Thought* (1962), Ithaca: Cornell University Press, 1982; René Girard, *Violence and the Sacred* (1972) translated by Patrick Gregory, Baltimore: Johns Hopkins University Press, 1977; Georges Bataille, *Visions of Excess: Selected Writings 1927–1939*, translated by A. Stockl, Minneapolis: University of Minnesota Press, 1985; Giorgio Agamben, *Homo Sacer: Sovereign Power and Bare Life*, translated by Daniel Heller-Roazen, Stanford: Stanford University Press, 1998; Lesek Kolakowski, *Metaphysical Horror*, revised edn, London: Penguin, 2001; Paul W. Kahn, *Sacred Violence: Torture, Terror, and Sovereignty*, Ann Arbor: University of Michigan Press, 2008; Thomas Blom Hansen and Finn Stepputat, eds, *Sovereign Bodies: Citizens, Migrants and States in the Postcolonial World*, Princeton: Princeton University Press, 2005; and Veena Das and Deborah Poole, eds, *Anthropology in the Margins of the State*, Santa Fé: School of American Research Press, 2004.
4 Jean Bodin, *On Sovereignty: Four Chapters from Six Books of the Commonwealth*, translated by Julian H. Franklin, Cambridge: Cambridge University Press, 1992; and Hobbes, *Leviathan*.
5 Skinner, *The Foundations of Modern Political Thought*; Kantorowicz, *The King's Two Bodies*; Otto Gierke, *Political Theories of the Middle Age*, translated by F.W. Maitland, Cambridge: Cambridge University Press, 1900; J.N. Figgis, *Studies in the History of Political Thought from Gerson to Grotius*, Cambridge: Cambridge University Press, 2nd edn 1916; M.J. Wilks, *The Problem of Sovereignty in the Later Middle Ages*, Cambridge: Cambridge University Press,1963; and Ken MacMillan, *Sovereignty and Possession in the English New World: The Legal Foundations of Empire, 1576–1640*, Cambridge: Cambridge University Press, 2006.
6 See F.H. Hinsley, *Sovereignty*, London: C.A. Watts, 1966, which has long stood as a standard historical narrative; and the selections collected in W.J. Stankiewicz, ed., *In Defence of Sovereignty* New York: Oxford University Press, 1969.
7 As I hope will become clear in the following chapter, it is precisely because Kant's framing of the problem of international relations rests on his prior delineation, in his *Critique of Pure Reason*, of the limits of human finitude understood in relation to both temporal immanence and phenomenal experience, that he is to be understood not as the theorist of either national autonomy or some kind of cosmopolitanism, the two familiar stereotypes, but precisely as a theorist of the aporetic character of a politics organized within the modern subject, the modern sovereign state and the modern system of states: the theorist, in my view, of the impossibility of international relations. The present chapter, however, is inspired more by the way Hobbes sets out a politics of authoritative discriminations that has shaped Kant's reading of modern politics as necessarily international, even if international politics is necessarily impossible.
8 See the discussion in David Armitage, "Hobbes and the Foundations of Modern International Thought," in Annabel Brett and James Tully, with Holly Hamilton-

Bleakley, eds, *Rethinking the Foundations of Modern Political Thought*, Cambridge: Cambridge University Press, 2006, 219–35. See also Brian Schmidt, *The Political Discourse of Anarchy*.

9 Fasolt, *The Limits of History*. Cf. Ranajit Guha, *History at the Limits of World-History*, New York: Columbia University Press, 2002; and Walter Mignolo, *The Darker Side of the Renaissance: Literacy, Territoriality and Colonization*, Ann Arbor: University of Michigan Press, 1995.

10 For helpful discussion of this vast theme, see Georg von Wright, *Explanation and Understanding*, Ithaca: Cornell University Press, 1971. See also Ernst Cassirer, *The Logic of the Cultural Sciences* (1940), translated by S.G. Lofts, New Haven: Yale University Press, 2000; T.K. Seung, *Structuralism and Hermeneutics*, New York: Columbia University Press, 1982; and Leszek Kolakowski, *The Alienation of Reason*, translated by Norbert Guterman, New York: Doubleday, 1968. For some sense of how this theme has filtered into now routinized debates about the dualistic structure of modern social science (echoing much more extensive narratives about "the human" and its conditions of possibility in the process), see Charles Taylor, "Interpretation and the Sciences of Man," *Review of Metaphysics*, 25, 1971, 3–51; Anthony Giddens; *The Constitution of Society*, Cambridge: Polity Press, 1984; and Martin Hollis and Steve Smith, *Explaining and Understanding International Relations*, Oxford: Oxford University Press, 1990.

11 Discussions of the practices of classification have been a staple of many forms of contemporary social and political analysis, often provoked by the diverse texts of Jacques Derrida and Michel Foucault, but also by logics of scientific explanation. In addition to such now standard sources, see Hartog, *The Mirror of Herodotus*; Jack Goody, *The Domestication of the Savage Mind*, Cambridge University Press, 1977; Georges Canguilhem, *The Normal and the Pathological* (1966) translated by Carolyn R. Fawcett and Robert S. Cohen, New York: Zone Books, 1991; R.G. Collingwood, *An Essay on Method* (1933), Bristol: Thoemmes Press, 1995; Pierre Bourdieu, *Distinction: A Social Critique of the Judgement of Taste* (1979), Cambridge, MA: Harvard University Press, 1984; Kirstie McClure, "The Issue of Foundations: Scientized Politics, Politicized Science, and Feminist Critical Practice," in Judith Butler and Joan Scott, eds, *Feminists Theorize the Political*, London: Routledge, 1992, 341–68; Judith Butler, *Gender Trouble*, New York: Routledge, 1990; Donna Haraway, *Primate Visions: Gender, Race and Nature in the World of Modern Science*, London: Verso, 1992; Zygmunt Bauman, *Modernity and Ambivalence*, Cambridge: Polity Press, 1991; and Friedrich A. Kittler, *Discourse Networks* 1800/1900, translated by Michael Metteer with Chris Cullens, Stanford: Stanford University Press, 1990. For a surprisingly rare general history of classification, see David Knight, *Ordering the World: A History of Classifying*, London: Burnett Books with André Deutsch, 1981.

Instructively, the most influential explicit discussions of classification in the modern social sciences have occurred in anthropology, especially in relation to the early writings of Durkheim and Mauss; see Emile Durkheim and Marcel Mauss, *Primitive Classification* (1903) translated and edited by Rodney Needham, Chicago: University of Chicago Press: 1963; Emile Durkheim, *The Division of Labor in Society* (1893) translated by George Simpson, New York: Free Press, 1947; and N.J. Allen, *Categories and Classifications: Maussian Reflections on the Social*, Oxford: Berghahn, 2000.

12 It is always useful to compare the classification strategies formalized in Aristotle's *Politics*, and their articulation in temporal cycles of idealization and corruption, with the tendency of contemporary texts on comparative politics to privilege both a territorial spatiality and a developmentalist teleology.

For a still resonant analysis of the broad classification strategies of Cold War social science, see Carl E. Pletch, "The Three Worlds, or the Division of Socio-Scientific

Labor, Circa 1950–75," *Comparative Studies in Society and History*, 23:4, October 1981, 565–90. For a powerful contemporary discussion see Michael J. Shapiro, *Methods and Nations: Cultural Governance and the Indigenous Subject*, London: Routledge, 2004, which converges with my present analysis at many points.

13 Among many classic texts, and trajectories of analysis, that might be invoked here, see Norbert Elias, *The Civilizing Process*, revised edn, London: Blackwell, 2000; Michel Foucault, *History of Madness*; Michel de Certeau, *The Practices of Everyday Life*, Berkeley: University of California Press, 1984; Yi-Fu Tuan, *Segmented Worlds and Self: Group Life and Individual Consciousness*, Minneapolis: University of Minnesota Press, 1982; Georges Gurvitch, *The Social Frameworks of Knowledge* (1966) translated by Margaret Thompson and Kenneth A. Thompson, Oxford: Blackwell, 1971; Edward Said, *Orientalism*, New York: 1978; and Henry Louis Gates, Jr, ed., *"Race," Writing and Difference*, Chicago: University of Chicago Press, 1985.

14 John Locke, *Second Treatise of Government*, in Locke, *Two Treatises of Government* (1690), edited by Peter Laslett, Cambridge: Cambridge University Press, 2nd edn 1967; Chapter 5; and Karl Marx, *Capital, Volume 1, A Critique of Political Economy* (1867), translated by Ben Fowkes, London: Pelican, 1976, chapters 1–3. See also David Harvey, "The Spatial Fix: Hegel, Von Thunen and Marx," *Antipode*, 13:3, 1981, 1–12. In the specific context of international relations theory, see especially Kurt Burch, *"Property" and the Making of the International System*, Boulder: Lynne Rienner, 1998.

15 My thinking about such themes has been shaped through participation in various collective projects over several decades, such as Randolph B. Persaud and R.B.J. Walker, eds, "Race in International Relations," Special Issue of *Alternatives: Global, Local, Political*, 26:4, October–December 2001; and Sankaran Krishna and R.B.J. Walker, eds, "Partition," Special Issue of *Alternatives: Global, Local, Political*, 27:2, 2002.

16 Martin Heidegger, *Being and Time* (1927), translated by John Macquarrie and Edward Robinson, New York: Harper and Row, 1962. Cf. Aristotle, *Metaphysics*, especially VI and VII. For a useful comparison of Heidegger and Hegel in terms of their engagement with the "origins" of philosophy, especially in relation to Heraclitus, see Denis J. Schmidt, *The Ubiquity of the Finite: Hegel, Heidegger and the Entitlements of Philosophy*, Cambridge, MA: MIT Press, 1988. It is also worth recalling in this context that the Greek term *arche* might be translated both as "origin" and as "to rule over."

17 Usually in a manner that is traced especially to Ludwig Wittgenstein, *Tractacus Logico-Philosophicus* (1921), London: Routledge, 1961.

18 Hence the broad resonance of Jacques Derrida's rigorous and precise procedure of "deconstruction," as well as of the notion of an undecidable proposition derived from Kurt Gödel's mathematics. See especially Derrida, *Dissemination*, translated by Barbara Johnson, Chicago: University of Chicago Press, 1981.

19 See for example, the recent sociological literatures on governmentality informed by some of the work of Michel Foucault: Jacques Donzelot, *The Policing of Families* translated by R. Hurley, New York: Pantheon, 1979; Graham Burchell, Colin Gordon and Peter Miller, eds, *The Foucault Effect: Studies in Governmentality*, London: Harvester, 1991; Nikolas Rose, *Powers of Freedom: Reframing Political Thought*, Cambridge: Cambridge University Press, 1999; Mitchell Dean, *Governmentality: Power and Rule in Modern Society*, London: Sage, 1999; Mitchell Dean, *Critical and Effective Histories: Foucault's Methods and Historical Sociology*, London: Routledge, 1994; and Andrew Barry, *Political Machines: Governing a Technological Society*, London: Athlone, 2001.

20 This formulation is intentionally open to both Weberian and Foucauldian interpretations. For a recent contribution to Weberian accounts of power see Gianfranco

Poggi, *Forms of Power*, Cambridge: Polity, 2001. For a critical reading of the potentials of Foucauldian innovations, see Barry Hindess, *Discourses of Power: From Hobbes to Foucault*, Oxford: Blackwell, 1996.

21 Carl Schmitt, *Political Theology*.

22 For a subtle discussion, see Quentin Skinner, "Hobbes and the Purely Artificial Person of the State," in Skinner, *Visions of Politics III: Hobbes and Civil Science*, Cambridge: Cambridge University Press, 2002, 177–208. On Hobbes' "epoch-making" treatment of the consequent problem of political representation, see Skinner, "Hobbes on Persons, Authors and Representatives," in Patricia Springborg, ed., *The Cambridge Companion to Hobbes's Leviathan*, Cambridge: Cambridge University Press, 2007, 157–80.

23 See especially Hobbes, *Leviathan*, chapters 1–9. For a sharp reading of the ways in which the discriminations effected in these early chapters play out in relation to (indigenous) contexts in which challenges to the hegemony of modernist categories are central to the possibility of another politics, of other sovereignties and other modernities, see Karena Shaw, *Indigeneity and Political Theory: Sovereignty and the Limits of the Political*, London: Routledge, 2008. For a reading of the specifically Ciceronian discursive context in which Hobbes sought to render his own position persuasive, see Quentin Skinner, *Reason and Rhetoric in the Philosophy of Hobbes*, Cambridge: Cambridge University Press, 1996, especially 294 ff; and Skinner, *Visions of Politics III*, 87–141, and *passim*. Cf. David Johnson, *The Rhetoric of Leviathan*, Cambridge: Cambridge University Press, 1986; and Ted H. Miller, "The Uniqueness of *Leviathan*: Authorizing Poets, Philosophers and Sovereigns," in Tom Sorell and Luc Foisneau, eds, *"Leviathan" After 350 Years*, Oxford: Oxford University Press, 2004, 75–103.

Skinner's general claim that inattention to Hobbes' rhetorical strategies has resulted in a massive oversimplification of Hobbes' views seems to me to be incontrovertible, though I am not persuaded that one needs to be quite so finely attuned to historical context to come to this conclusion; a careful reading of Hobbes' explicit discussion of language in the early chapters of *Leviathan* provides a useful corrective to most of the caricatures currently in circulation. In general terms, however, Skinner's attempt to defamiliarize this most caricatured of canonical thinkers is very effective. My own reading of Hobbes is more narrowly shaped by my sense of the brilliance, and much broader resonance, of his response to challenges to prevailing cosmological and ontological traditions posed by various forms of scepticism, nominalism and neo-Platonism in general and by the formal character of Galilean mechanics and mathematics in particular.

It may be worth noting that the main alternative to my focus on Hobbes as the key text on modern sovereignty usually involves the late sixteenth-century counterpoint between Jean Bodin's account of the need for a unitary secular authority in the face of wars of religious authority and the subsequent articulation of something like a popular sovereignty by Althusius; an alternative that offers both the advantage and the disadvantage of not having to engage with the brilliance and rigor of Hobbes' struggles with the very possibility of a politics of modern subjectivities and authorizations.

24 Hobbes, *Leviathan*, final paragraph of chapter 13, 90; I take up this theme more extensively below.

It is worth emphasizing the importance of the appropriation of only a few very specific themes from Hobbes in the formulation of accounts of state sovereignty in the theory of international relations. The references are invariably to chapters 11 and 13 of *Leviathan*, in which Hobbes works out an account of the structural conflicts that must arise in a world of free and equal individuals driven by desire after desire. In this context, sovereignty is read in relation to the structural necessities of a state of nature understood as a paradigmatic account of the "security dilemma," which can then be read in turn through modern theories of rational economic decisions. Against this reading, it is sometimes, but only sometimes, noticed that Hobbes explicitly denies, towards the end of chapter 13, that the state of war between states is directly analogous to a state of nature among equal (and equally vulnerable) individuals. War, he briefly observes, is good for states. This is a denial that might allow Hobbes to be included as a theorist of a wide range of positions that have developed in response to claims about an "international anarchy," for it is a denial that minimizes the importance of the equality that drives competition among individuals and thus opens up a role for great power hegemony or "the society of states" as practices of international order. Attempts to save Hobbes from crude caricature exercise a now considerable literature; for a particularly subtle discussion, see Noel Malcolm, "Hobbes's Theory of International Relations," in Malcolm, *Aspects of Hobbes*, Oxford: Clarendon, 2002, 432–56. For an attempt to situate Hobbes in a broader story of the development of "the international," see Richard Tuck, *The Rights of War and Peace: Political Thought and the International Order from Grotius to Kant*, Oxford: Oxford University Press, 1999.

25 Schmitt, *Political Theology*. For more extensive commentary both on Schmitt and on the recent revival of interest in a thinker who, despite the few logically elegant sentences on which I focus here, is unusually difficult to identify with any single political stance, and who was engaged in questions about politics that have many contemporary resonances, see Gopal Balakrishnan, *The Enemy: An Intellectual Portrait of Carl Schmitt*, London: Verso, 2000; William E. Scheuerman, *Between the Norm and the Exception: The Frankfurt School and the Rule of Law*, Cambridge, MA: MIT Press, 1994; David Dyzenhaus, ed., *Law as Politics: Carl Schmitt's Critique of Liberalism*, Durham, NC: Duke University Press, 1998; John P. McCormick, *Carl Schmitt's Critique of Liberalism: Against Politics as Technology*, Cambridge: Cambridge University Press, 1996; Andrew Norris, "Carl Schmitt's Political Metaphysics: On the Secularization of 'the Outermost Sphere'," *Theory and Event*, 4:1, 2000; and Sergei Prozorov, "X/Xs: Toward a General Theory of the Exception," *Alternatives: Global, Local, Political*, 30:1, 2005, 81–111. For a reading of Schmitt that has been especially helpful in clarifying my own sense of his contemporary relevance, but also in alerting me to the critical potential of some of his later writings, see Grigoris Ananiadis, "Carl Schmitt on Kosovo: Or Taking War Seriously," in Dusan Bjelic and Obrad Savic, eds, *The Balkans as a Metaphor: Between Globalization and Fragmentation*, Cambridge, MA: MIT Press, 2002, 117–62.

26 See especially Jacques Derrida, "Force of Law: The 'Mystical Foundations of Authority'," in Derrida, *Acts of Religion*, New York: Routledge, 2002, 228–98. See also Giorgio Agamben, *Means Without End: Notes on Politics*, Minneapolis: University of Minnesota Press, 2000; Agamben, *Homo Sacer*; and Agamben, *State of Exception*, Chicago: University of Chicago Press, 2005.

27 Weber, "The Profession and Vocation of Politics." See especially Hennis, *Max Weber: Essays in Reconstruction*.

28 Gyorgy Lukacs, *History and Class Consciousness: Studies in Marxist Dialectics* (1923), translated by Rodney Livingstone, Cambridge, MA: MIT Press, 1971.

29 Walter Benjamin, "Critique of Violence" (1921) in *Walter Benjamin: Selected Writings, Volume 1, 1913–1926*, edited by Marcus Bullock and Michael Jennings, Cambridge, MA: Harvard University Press, 1996, 236–52.

30 Georges Sorel, *Reflections on Violence* (1908), edited by Jeremy Jennings, Cambridge: Cambridge University Press, 1999.

31 Schmitt, *The Concept of the Political* (1932), translated with an Introduction by George Schwab and New Foreword by Tracy Strong, Chicago: University of Chicago Press, 1996.

32 Schmitt, *Political Theology*, 15. Cf. Hobbes, *Leviathan*, Chapter 18 and *passim*. The formulation has a wider resonance: see, for example, Ludwig Wittgenstein, *Tractacus Logico-Philosophicus*, 3.

33 Foucault distinguishes between juridical or Hobbesian accounts of sovereignty as a capacity to make decisions and what he calls biopower, understood as a positive, enabling, life-administering power to control, manage and optimize social forces that are always necessarily resisting while constituting this enabling power. This capacity might be thought of as consistent with both a Kantian move to enable and constitute mature autonomous subjectivities, and a nationalist capacity to generate collective national subjects and mobilize populations, not least so that the preparation for war works to constitute and discipline – secure – societies. See, among others, Foucault, *History of Sexuality*, Vol. 1; Foucault, "Society Must be Defended;" and Foucault, "Security, Territory, Population."

34 Much is missed when debates about science and social science move so quickly from figures such as Hume, Kant and Comte straight to figures such as Carl Hempel and the mid-twentieth-century literature on scientific explanation, without dwelling on the degree to which movements like the Vienna Circle and philosophies of logical positivism sought to enact some sort of restoration after an era in which philosophies of knowledge had proliferated in response to collapse of the transcendental guarantees of Kantian and Newtonian reason – to cut another long story very short. For a helpful introduction to this material, see Kolakowski, *The Alienation of Reason*, especially chapter 8: "Logical Empiricism: A Scientistic Defense of Threatened Civilization," 169ff.

35 Exemplified by the rescripting of Weber's tragic and multiply ambivalent reading of the process of modernization as an intensifying contradiction between rationality and irrationality into a straightforward celebration of rational progress, with Weber himself being converted into a proponent of a value free social science as if he were a particularly naive remnant of an old English empiricism.

36 Leo Strauss, *Natural Right and History*, Chicago: University of Chicago Press, 1965; and Strauss, "Notes on Schmitt's *Concept of the Political*," in Heinrich Meier, *Carl Schmitt and Leo Strauss: The Hidden Dialogue*, translated by J. Harvey Lomax, Chicago: University of Chicago Press, 1995. For useful discussion here, see Robert House, "From Legitimacy to Dictatorship and Back Again: Leo Strauss's Critique of the Anti-Liberalism of Carl Schmitt," in Dyzenhuis, 56–91. For an account of some contemporary reverberations, see Anne Norton, *Leo Strauss and the Politics of American Empire*, New Haven: Yale University Press, 2004.

37 William E. Scheuerman, "The Unholy Alliance of Carl Schmitt and Friedrick A. Hayek," *Constellations*, 4:2, 1997, 172–88. Scheuerman goes as far as to suggest that a comparison of Schmitt and Hayek offers an interesting way of thinking about a broader "elective affinity" between free-market economics and authoritarian politics.

38 For a recent attempt to insist on the contemporary significance of this relation, see Hidemi Suganami, "Understanding Sovereignty Through Kelsen/Schmitt," *Review of International Studies*, 33, 2007, 511–30. While Suganami's reasoning works through a more analytical idiom, his analysis affirms my own sense that, as he puts it in his final sentence, "Kelsenian and Schmittean conceptions are linked by the underlying practice of sovereignty, which appears inescapably to be intertwined with the *possibility* of arbitrary violence – although how it produces its concrete manifestations could not be understood without a detailed historical and sociological analysis."

39 In a late formulation: "Sovereignty in the sense of supreme authority can be nothing but the quality of a legal order. Therefore the problem of the sovereignty of the state is the problem of the sovereignty of the national legal order in its relation to the international legal order." Hans Kelsen, "Sovereignty and International

Law," *Georgetown Law Journal*, 48:4, Summer 1960, 627–40. Cf. Kelsen, *Pure Theory of Law*, translated by Max Knight, Berkeley: University of California Press, 1970. For helpful recent commentary, see Lars Vinx, *Hans Kelsen's Pure Theory of Law: Legality and Legitimacy*, Oxford: Oxford University Press, 2007. Kelsen's position is especially interesting for its formulation of what I have been calling the *aporetic* relation between state sovereignty and the system of sovereign states as a matter of complete indifference to "the science of law": as a matter of indecision rather than of the decision that is central for Schmitt. Quite apart from their specific historical context and relations, Kelsen is also of more general interest as an expression of what is effectively a vertical construal of international law that offers such a clear contrast with Schmitt's explicitly horizontal (yet ultimately also vertical) understanding of state law.

40 See especially Chantal Mouffe, ed., *The Challenge of Carl Schmitt*, London: Verso, 1999. Mouffe rightly sees the need "to think both with and against Schmitt" as a site in which it might be possible to devise, in Mouffe's terms, "ways in which antagonism can be transformed into agonism" and "to envisage a democratic form of commonality which makes room for conflictual pluralism" (p. 5). The key difficulty that remains only sketchily addressed in Mouffe's formulation, as in many if not most other contemporary forms of radically pluralistic democratic theory, however, is precisely the form of commonality that might enable and sustain a conflictual or agonal pluralism; that is, the problem of international relations that both guarantees and threatens the modern form of political community. Here Mouffe seems to follow Schmitt's later work outlining a world of pluralistic or multipolar blocs, deploying a critique of cosmopolitanism and unilateralism in order to return to something like a system of states, but on a different scale, a conceptual move that I find deeply problematic.

41 The resonance can be made to seem especially strong in the writings of Hans J. Morgenthau. For useful discussions see Hans-Karl Pichler, "The Godfathers of 'Truth': Max Weber and Carl Schmitt in Morgenthau's Theory of Power Politics," *Review of International Studies*, 24:2, April 1998, 185–200; Tarak Barkawi, "Strategy as a Vocation," Weber, Morgenthau and Modern Strategic Studies, *Review of International Studies*, 24:2, April 1998, 159–84; Koskeniemi, *The Gentle Civilizer of Nations*, especially 413 ff.; William Scheuerman, *Carl Schmitt: The End of Law*, Lanham, MD: Rowman and Littlefield, 1999; and Scheuerman, "Carl Schmitt and Hans Morgenthau: Realism and Beyond," in Michael C. Williams, ed., *Realism Reconsidered: The Legacy of Hans J. Morgenthau in International Relations*, Oxford: Oxford University Press, 2007, 62–92.

42 Walker, *Inside/Outside*, Chapter 7; Walker, *The Subject of Security*; Campbell, *Writing Security*; Jef Huysmans, *The Politics of Insecurity: Fear, Migration and Asylum in the EU*, London: Routledge, 2006; Foucault, *"Society Must Be Defended."*

43 For example, Michael Ignatieff, *The Lesser Evil: Political Ethics in an Age of Terror*, London: Penguin, 2004, which manages to effect a Schmittean judgement about norms and exceptions while studiously avoiding all hard questions about sovereignty, let alone responsibility, by affirming an especially forthright brand of liberal imperialism. See also Ignatieff, *Empire Lite: Nation Building in Bosnia, Kosovo, Afghanistan*, New York: Vintage, 2003. For helpful commentary on the "(neo)liberal" backdrop to the "neoconservative" ideologies informing recent US administrations, see Tony Smith, *A Pact With the Devil: Washington's Bid for World Supremacy and the Betrayal of the American Promise*, New York: Routledge, 2007. For recent texts that stand in sharp contrast with Ignatieff from within much more critically aware liberal engagements with ethical dilemmas posed by contemporary claims about globalisms and universalities, see Iris Marion Young, *Global Challenges: War, Self-Determination and Responsibility*, Cambridge: Polity, 2007; and Axel Honneth, *Disrespect: The Normative Foundations of Critical*

Theory, Cambridge: Polity, 2007. For an instructive comparison of Ignatieff with J. A. Hobson, a prominent liberal in an earlier age, see David Long, "Liberalism, Imperialism, and Empire," *Studies in Political Economy*, 78, Autumn 2006, 201–23. Many texts that have responded to the sloppy self-righteousness exemplified by Ignatieff are also seriously problematic. For example, Michael Howard's classic, *War and the Liberal Conscience*, Oxford: Oxford University Press, 1977, is undermined by both a fairly indiscriminate understanding of what counts as liberalism, and only a vague specification of the Clausewitzian and Schmittean accounts of sovereignty that seem to inform his analysis. Alan Gilbert, *Must Global Politics Constrain Democracy? Great-Power Realism, Democratic Peace and Internationalism*, Princeton: Princeton University Press, 1999, while rightly motivated by corruptions of American democracy over the course of the Vietnam war, simply takes the boundary between domestic and international relations as a given while simultaneously assuming the erasure of these boundaries as a ground for critique.

The text that has opened up much greater awareness of what is at stake in this respect in the Anglo-American theory of international relations is Campbell, *Writing Security;* along with some, but certainly not all, elements of what has come to be called "critical security studies."

44 As with Will Kymlicka, *Multicultural Citizenship: A Liberal Theory of Minority Rights*, Oxford: Oxford University Press, 1995; and, more explicitly, Kymlicka, *Politics in the Vernacular: Nationalism, Multiculturalism, and Citizenship*, Oxford: Oxford University Press, 2001.

That Kymlicka can so easily affirm forms of liberal nationalism in the context of contemporary Canadian political life is really quite startling; the Canadian case especially affirms that pluralisms, or indeed polities, are not easily so contained within either nationalisms or ethnicities. Many Canadian political theorists may indeed be thinking about forms of political pluralism in increasingly interesting ways, especially in relation to challenges posed by claims to indigeneity, but the Weberian and Schmittean inheritances that Kymlicka seems to have absorbed from Ernst Gellner's robustly monolithic modernism provides a far greater challenge than he seems to recognize. This is, in part, why I so appreciate the much greater attentiveness to both the aporetic and international character of contemporary American political life driving William Connolly's readings of democratic possibilities, even though these readings also respond primarily to a specific national context; see especially Connolly, *Identity\Difference: Democratic Negotiations of Political Paradox*, Ithaca: Cornell University of Minnesota Press, 1991; Connolly, *The Ethos of Pluralization*, Minneapolis: University of Minnesota Press, 1995; and Connolly, *Pluralism*, Durham: Duke University Press, 2005.

45 Thus it is not uncommon to find commentators worrying that few other disciplines look to the discipline of international relations for explicit inspiration, even in an era in which "the international" or "the global" is so obviously challenging the received theoretical traditions of so many fields of scholarship. For a complaint to this effect, see Barry Buzan and Richard Little, "Why International Relations has failed as an intellectual project and what to do about it," *Millennium: Journal of International Studies*, 30:1, 2001, 19–39. Much of their critique is well taken. Nevertheless, I think it a fundamental mistake to expect the discipline of international relations to measure up to the standards of more "normal" disciplines. In many respects, the sophistication of this discipline lies precisely in its lack of sophistication, in its capacity to mobilize caricatures and clichés that no other discipline would take seriously, but which nevertheless helps to enable the reproduction of a specific structure of scholarly disciplines.

46 Clausewitz, *On War*.

47 Giorgio Agamben, *Homo Sacer*, 7.

48 Agamben's analysis seems to work through an opposition between a particularistic form of exceptionalism of the kind articulated by Schmitt and the more generalized exceptionalism expressed in Walter Benjamin's more apocalyptic (and, in my view, even more disturbing) comments on history, revolution and divine violence; his detailed analysis of the Schmitt–Benjamin relation in *State of Exception* is especially illuminating. However (and leaving aside the enormous conceptual difficulties involved in postulating a condition of "bare life," the absurdity of Agamben's use of this concept as a metaphor for contemporary practices of internment and exclusion, and the degree to which quasi-theological legitimations of violence surface among many supposedly progressive thinkers quite as easily as among Schmittean "realists"), neither option seems to me to get at either the specifically international context in which Schmitt's position ought to be situated, nor the much more complex contemporary situation in which exceptions are undoubtedly made, but in terms that are neither simply particularistic nor general. Agamben has done much to reopen debates about exceptionalism and the relevant conceptual genealogy, but also to close down analysis of its contemporary implications. For a discussion of some of the conceptual context here, see R.B.J. Walker, "l'International, l'imperial, l'exceptionnel," *Cultures et Conflits*, 58, Ete 2005, 13–51. For a broad range of research seeking to understand the much more complex social and legal patterns of exceptionalism that may be identified in contemporary European responses to claims about the need to reorder the relationship between liberty and security in response to terrorist violence, see the website of the CHALLENGE research project at www.libertysecurity.org.
49 The exclusion of foreigners and many other non-citizens is often noted, but the other exclusions may be more consequential. See Plato, *The Republic*, translated by Allan Bloom, New York: Basic Books, 1968, Book 1, 328b–331d, with its theatrical banishment of Cephalus, sometimes taken to be just an apolitical businessman, but perhaps more interestingly read as an expression of the traditional authority of the elders and oral culture, before the serious discussion of founding the just city even begins; and the comments about music and poetics in Books III and X. Comparison with the first two chapters of Hobbes' *Leviathan* is instructive. Both texts offer exemplary accounts of how to instantiate a founding inclusion/exclusion so as to enable a discourse about specific forms of inclusion and exclusion.
50 It is also worth remembering that the very ideal of the peaceful *polis* we have inherited from Athens was itself enabled by what Nicole Loraux has called a "founding forgetting" of, an active practice of amnesty towards, prior divisions in the life in that particular city; see Nicole Loraux, *The Divided City: On Meaning and Forgetting in Ancient Athens*, New York: Zone Books, 2002, 43.
51 See especially the classic analysis in Girard, *Violence and the Sacred*.
52 For especially suggestive analyses that are sensitive both to the interplay of philosophical, aesthetic and strategic practices in modern (American) cultural life and to the limits of modern claims about international relations, see various texts by Michael J. Shapiro, especially *Violent Cartographies: Mapping Cultures of War*, Minneapolis: University of Minnesota Press, 1997; *Cinematic Political Thought: Narrating Race, Nation and Gender*, Edinburgh: University of Edinburgh Press, 1999; *Cinematic Geopolitics*, London: Routledge, 2008; as well as *Methods and Nations*.
53 In contemporary social theory, the concept of a network society has been especially popularized by Manuel Castels; see especially *The Rise of the Network Society*, Oxford: Blackwell, 1996. See also Michael Burawoy *et al.*, *Global Ethnography: Forces, Connections and Imaginations in a Postmodern World*, Berkeley: University of California Press, 2000.
    In an earlier text, and with similar ideas in mind, I once tried to distinguish between two contrasting conceptions of "world order" that were already emerging

in the ambitions and practices of many social movements at the end of the Cold War era: one rooted in various forms of universalizing humanism that threatened to reproduce statist patterns of inclusion and exclusion on a global scale, and one articulated in more relational terms, a "politics of connections" as I called them. See Walker, *One World, Many Worlds*, Boulder: Lynne Rienner, 1988; and the companion volume, Saul H. Mendlovitz and R.B.J. Walker, eds, *Towards a Just World Peace: Perspectives from Social Movements*, London: Butterworths, 1987. While *One World, Many Worlds* was sometimes interpreted as a romantic cele-bration of the potentials of "critical social movements," it was intended more as a critique of many such movements, especially those that understood their critical potential in either statist or globalist terms, rather than in relation to changing patterns of inclusion/exclusion that are not easily mapped as either statist or global. The relation between critique and the practices of social movements still seems to me to be a site of difficult questions rather than of easy claims about "emancipa-tion," "resistance," and so on. However, subsequent trends and literatures have only reinforced my view that the need to articulate a politics of connections of some kind has become an emerging commonsense in many different contexts, though this seems to me to be a commonsense that is in need of more sustained empirical research as well as conceptual imagination. Distinctions between critical and other movements remain very tricky, as do distinctions between new and more conventional forms of movement; I re-engage tangentially with some of these pro-blems in "Social Movements/World Politics," *Millennium: Journal of International Studies*, 23:3, Winter 1994, 669–700; and Walker, "They Seek it Here, They Seek it There: Looking for Politics in Clayoquot Sound," in Karena Shaw and Warren Magnusson, eds, *A Political Space: Reading the Global Through Clayoquot Sound*, Minneapolis: University of Minnesota Press, 2003, 237–62.

54 Henri Bergson, *The Two Sources of Morality and Religion*, New York: Henry Holt, 1935, 296. See also, for example, Arthur O. Lovejoy, *Revolt Against Dualism*, La Salle, Illinois: Open Court Publishing, 1930; Alfred North Whitehead, *Science and the Modern World*, Cambridge: Cambridge University Press, 1926; and George Herbert Mead, *The Philosophy of the Act*, Chicago: University of Chicago Press, 1938. These three texts, among many, might serve as a reminder in some quarters that at least some of the lines of critical enquiry associated with Paris in the 1960s have been active for a long time, and not only among the "continental" philosophers.

55 The failure of attempts by logical positivists such as Rudolph Carnap and Carl Hempel, and Neo-Kantians such as Karl Popper, to sustain a plausible demarca-tion principle distinguishing science from its unscientific others, perhaps the key moment in the twentieth century attempt to privilege science as the foundational moment of modern knowledge, remains instructive. Quite apart from the failure in principle, the very attempt to distinguish "science" as a privileged discourse has come to seem simply uninteresting, a forgotten aspect of Cold War ideology. However, the question of what counts as an interesting question, a sustainable assumption, or, in Karl Popper's terms, as open to rational criticism, remains important, and I am not convinced that the conservative sociology of science that has taken its cue from Thomas Kuhn is especially persuasive in this respect.

56 Rorty, *Philosophy and the Mirror of Nature*.

57 Jean-François Lyotard, *The Postmodern Condition: A Report on Knowledge*, translated by Geoff Bennington and Brian Masumi, Minneapolis: University of Minnesota Press, 1984.

58 See Andrew Vincent, *The Nature of Political Theory*.

59 Heidegger, *Being and Time*.

60 For recent critical commentary, see Benno Teschke, *The Myth of 1648: Class, Geopolitics and the Making of Modern International Relations*, London, Verso, 2003; Andreas Ossiander, "Sovereignty, International Relations, and the

Westphalian Myth," *International Organization*, 55, 2001, 251–88; and Prokhovnik, *Sovereignties*.

61 For a succinct but effective reading of the Treaty of Westphalia in these terms, see Ian Hunter, "Westphalia and the Desacralization of Politics," in Barry Hindess and Margaret Jolly, eds, *Thinking Peace, Making Peace*, Occasional Paper 1/2001, Canberra: Academy of the Social Sciences in Australia, 2001, 36–44. For an interesting comparison with interpretations of the shift from Ming and Qing dynasties in China in "1644," see Jonathan Hay, "The Suspension of Dynastic Time," in John Hay, ed., *Boundaries in China*, London: Reaktion Books, 1994, 171–97.

62 Cf. Max Weber, *The Protestant Ethic and the Spirit of Capitalism* (1904–5), translated by Talcott Parsons, New York: Scribners, 1930.

63 Hedley Bull and Adam Watson, eds, *The Expansion of International Society*, Oxford: Clarendon Press, 1984. See also Wight, *Systems of States*; Adam Watson, *The Evolution of International Society*, London: Routledge, 1992; Gerrit Gong, *The Standard of Civilization in International Relations*, Oxford: Oxford University Press, 1984; Robert Jackson, *Quasi-states: Sovereignty, International Relations and the Third World*, Cambridge: Cambridge University Press, 1990; and James Mayall, *Nationalism and International Society*, Cambridge: Cambridge University Press, 1990. See also Bertrand Badie, *The Imported State: The Westernization of the Political Order*, translated by Claudia Royal, Stanford: Stanford University Press, 2000. Some comparative perspective on this literature is provided by Jacinta O'Hagan, *Conceptualizing the West in International Relations*, Basingstoke: Palgrave, 2002; and Martti Koskenniemi, *The Gentle Civilizer of Nations: The Rise and Fall of International Law, 1870–1960*, Cambridge: Cambridge University Press, 2001, especially 98ff;

64 For an appreciation in these terms, see Roger Epp, "The English School on the Frontiers of International Society," in Tim Dunne *et al.*, ed., *The Eighty Years Crisis: International Relations 1919–1999*, Cambridge: Cambridge University Press, 1998, 47–63.

65 Bull and Watson, eds, *The Expansion of International Society*, 7.

66 Bull and Watson, eds, *The Expansion of International Society*, 7–8.

67 Bull and Watson, eds, *The Expansion of International Society*, 435.

68 This is, for example, the impression encouraged by Linklater and Suganami, *The English School of International Relations*, which offers an excellent updated account of the antagonism between spatial and temporal commitments that animates the work of Wight, Bull and others who have been appropriated into this "school." Nevertheless, a commitment to a progressive history within the parameters of an internationalized modernity is, in some respects, even stronger here than in Bull and Wight, especially in the second half of the book and building on Linklater's distinctive commitments in this respect. The reading of Kant offered in this text, while more persuasive than the versions offered by Wight and Bull, remains a telling indicator of the way in which he is so often read as an innocent interrogator of the aporias of modernity: as the proto-Critical theorist who is strangely unaware of the demands of critique, and who is especially innocent of the problems posed by a politics of human finitude in an age still haunted by transcendental authority and by its own exclusion from an infinite universe.

69 Cf. Bull, *The Anarchical Society*.

70 Hedley Bull, "The Emergence of a Universal International Society," in Bull and Watson, eds, *The Expansion of International Society*, 117–26. See also what is in some ways Bull's most interesting text, "Justice in International Relations: The 1983–84 Hagey Lectures," Waterloo, Ontario: University of Waterloo Publications Distribution Service, 1984.

71 W.W. Rostow, *The Stages of Economic Growth: A Non-Communist Manifesto*, Cambridge: Cambridge University Press, 1960. Linklater and Suganami

understandably prefer to invoke Norbert Elias, *The History of Manners: The Civilizing Process*, Vol. 1, Oxford: Blackwell, 1978.

72 Edward Keene's very useful commentary on this literature is critical of its tendency to focus on a one-sided, European, account of international order, thereby omitting the order of "hierarchical institutions through which colonial and imperial powers transmitted the supposed benefits of their civilization to the rest of the world." Keene, *Beyond the Anarchical Society*, xi. For Keene, the classical international order was dualistic, characterized by processes of "toleration" in the spatial order achieved among Europeans and temporal processes of "civilization" elsewhere, and he rightly seeks to provide some broader context to the conservative parochialisms of the prevailing literature on the society of states. Given the twentieth-century process of decolonization and European struggles against fascism, Keene also argues that "this division of the world into two patterns of political and legal order has collapsed, to be replaced by a single global order," one in which the two "fundamentally different purposes of international order" have now become more seriously in contradiction.

I think there is much to be said for this analysis, but, as my argument here suggests, I see neither such a radical dualism between the purposes of "toleration" and "civilization" (but rather two complementary moments in the formation of a modern subjectivity that works as a co-constitution of self and other) nor an historical move to a single contemporary global order organized on the basis of contradictions between these two purposes (though this is one way of understanding how discursive oppositions between, say, domestic jurisdiction and humanitarian intervention or self-determination and properly democratic administration are now articulated). Keene's account of history involves a shift from "two worlds" to "one world," whereas I prefer to stress the multiple and changing articulation of identity/difference relations within the modern states system and the always doubled form of the "outside" of the modern subject that is enabled within the modern states system. I certainly agree with Keene that without some broader historical contextualization of parochial European accounts of international order, we are in danger of repeating demands for new thinking that have been recurring for at least a century, but my own sense is that a larger part of the problem here is the continuing force of various accounts of what history must have been given prevailing assumptions about what the future of the modern subject must continue to be.

73 Even at the time when *The Expansion of International Society* was written, one might have expected a rather more sustained engagement with the kinds of histories stimulated by, say Fernand Braudel or Immanuel Wallerstein.

For a collection of essays from the same era that offers a range of rather different views of what is at stake in the parochial origins of universalizing accounts of international relations, see R.B.J. Walker, ed., *Culture, Ideology and World Order*, Boulder: Westview, 1984. For some sense of how these concerns have been taken up at the intersection of world history and postcolonial theory, see, for example, Guha, *History at the Limits of World-History*; Walter D. Mignolo, *Local Histories/ Global Designs: Coloniality, Subaltern Knowledges and Border Thinking*, Princeton: Princeton University Press, 2000; André Gunder Frank, *Re-Orient: Global Economy in the Asian Age*, Berkeley: University of California Press, 1998; and especially Dipesh Chakrabarty, *Provincializing Europe: Post Colonial Thought and Historical Difference*, Princeton: Princeton University Press, 2000.

In the more specific context of international relations theory, see, as illustrative of an increasingly broad range of literatures, Siba N'Zatioula Grovogui, *Sovereigns, Quasi Sovereigns, and Africans*, Minneapolis: University of Minnesota Press, 1996; Grovogui, *Beyond Anarchy and Institutions: Memories of International Order and Institutions*, London: Palgrave, 2006; Sankaran Krishna, *Postcolonial Insecurities: India, Sri Lanka and the Question of Nationhood*, Minneapolis: University of

Minnesota Press, 1999; Sankaran Krishna, *Globalization and Postcolonialism: Hegemony and Resistance in the Twenty-first Century* (Lanham, MD: Rowman and Littlefield, 2009). Karena Shaw, "Indigeneity and the International," *Millennium: Journal of International Studies*, 31:1, 2002, 55–81; Paul Keal, *European Conquest and the Rights of Indigenous Peoples: The Moral Backwardness of International Society*, Cambridge: University of Cambridge Press, 2003; Mark Salter, *Barbarians and Civilization in International Relations*, London: Zed Books, 2002; David Blaney and Naeem Inayatullah, *International Relations and the Problem of Difference*, New York: Routledge, 2004; David Long and Brian C. Schmidt, eds, *Imperialism and Internationalism in the Discipline of International Relations*, Albany: State University of New York Press, 2005; Roxanne Doty, *Imperial Encounters*, Minneapolis: University of Minnesota Press, 1996; Philip Darby, *The Fiction of Imperialism: Reading Between International Relations and Postcolonialism*, London: Cassell, 1998; Anthony J. Paolini, *Navigating Modernity: Postcolonialism, Identity and International Relations*, edited by Anthony Elliot and Anthony Moran, Boulder: Lynne Rienner, 1999; Beate Jahn, "Kant, Mill and Illiberal Legacies in International Affairs," *International Organization*, 59:1, 2005, 95–125; Alex Maroya, "Rethinking the Nation-State from the Frontier," *Millennium: Journal of International Studies*, 32:2, 2003, 267–92; and Brett Bowden, "In the name of Progress and Peace: The Standard of Civilization and the Universalizing Project," *Alternatives: Global, Local, Political*, 29:1, 2004, 43–68.

More generally, and among many, see Fabian, *Time and the Other*; Adam Kuper, *The Reinvention of Primitive Society: Transformations of a Myth* (1988), London: Routledge, 2005; Edward Said, *Culture and Imperialism*, New York: Alfred A. Knopf, 1993; Partha Chatterjee, *Nationalist Thought and the Colonial World*; Achille Mbembe, *On the Postcolony*, Berkeley: University of California Press, 2001; Arturo Escobar, *Encountering Development: The Making and Unmaking of the Third World*, Princeton: Princeton University Press, 1995; Timothy Mitchell, *Colonizing Egypt*, 2nd edn, Berkeley: University of California Press, 1991; Timothy Mitchell, ed., *Questions of Modernity*, Minneapolis: University of Minnesota Press, 2000; Gayatri C. Spivak, *A Critique of Postcolonial Reason: Toward a History of the Vanishing Present*, Cambridge, MA: Harvard University Press, 1999; Spivak, "Can the Subaltern Speak?" in Patrick Williams and Laura Chrisman, eds, *Colonial Discourse and Post-Colonial Theory*, New York: Columbia University Press, 1992, 66–111; Mahmood Mamdani, *Citizen and Subject*, Princeton: Princeton University Press, 1996; and Jonathan Xavier Inda and Renato Rosaldo, eds, *The Anthropology of Globalization: A Reader*, Oxford: Blackwell, 2002.

74 Immanuel Wallerstein, *The Modern World System*, three volumes, New York: Academic Press, 1974–89; Fernand Braudel, *Civilization and Capitalism, 15th–18th Century*, three volumes, New York: Collins, 1985.

75 Ashis Nandy *et al.*, *Barbaric Others: A Manifesto on Western Racism*, London: Pluto Press, 1993.

76 Todorov, *The Conquest of America*.

77 Kevin Frost, *Revisioning Enlightenment: A Critique of Classical Orientation*, PhD dissertation, La Trobe University, Melbourne, 2001.

78 Clausewitz, *On War*.

79 Foucault, *Society Must Be Defended*.

80 Some of these, especially problems posed by accounts of nature as a God-given perfection and the effects of early anthropological narratives, are discussed by Kinch Hoekstra, "Hobbes on the Natural Condition of Mankind," in Springborg, ed., *The Cambridge Companion to Hobbes's Leviathan*, 109–27. See also two other very interesting essays in the same volume, Horst Bredekamp, "Thomas Hobbes's Visual Strategies," 29–60, and the work referenced there on Hobbes's

understanding of optics; and Johan Tralau, "Leviathan, the Best of Myth: Medusa, Dionysos, and the Riddle of Hobbes's Sovereign Monster," 61–81.

81 This radicalism may also be read as an accommodation with Aristotelian, Stoic and theological traditions rather than a straightforward repudiation of them; I am intentionally oversimplifying a longer story about the genealogies of modern individualism.

82 For an attempt to read the significance of parallels between modern accounts of nature and contemporary claims about security that are enabled by Hobbesian assumptions, see Walker, "On the Protection of Nature and the Nature of Protection," in Jef Huysmans, Andrew Dobson and Raia Prokhovnik, eds, *The Politics of Protection*, London: Routledge, 2006, 189–202.

83 The concept of a state of nature has a complex history. For a detailed account of the "hesitations, uncertainties and alterations" in Hobbes' usage, see François Tricaud, "Hobbes's Conception of the State of Nature from 1640 to 1651: Evolution and Ambiguities," in G.A.J. Rogers and Alan Ryan, eds, *Perspectives on Thomas Hobbes*, 107–24. Tricaud's claim that in *Leviathan* the concept appears "as a scientific diagram, in which only a few really essential forces are taken into consideration" (122) accords with my own sense of the text, although I am not convinced that these really essential forces can be reduced to substantive claims about fear of death and appetite for such goods as are generally desired. Helpful entries into large literatures on the use of this concept are Andrzej Rapaczynski, *Nature and Politics: Liberalism in the Philosophies of Hobbes, Locke and Rousseau*, Ithaca: Cornall University Press, 1987; and Beate Jahn, *The Cultural Construction of International Relations: The Invention of the State of Nature*, Basingstoke: Palgrave, 2000.

84 Hobbes, *Leviathan*, chapter 13, 89–90.

85 Hobbes, *Leviathan*, 13.

86 Hobbes, *Leviathan*, chapter 14.

87 Hobbes, *Leviathan*, chapter 13, final paragraph.

88 Schmitt, *Political Theology*, 15.

89 And one that draws attention to some of the paradoxical character of Hobbes's reasoning more generally. For a useful if diffuse discussion, see Matthew H. Kramer, *Hobbes and the Paradoxes of Political Origins*, Basingstoke: Macmillan, 1997.

Many other crucial moves are expressed in Hobbes' account of a magical moment of collective decision. It is in effect the point at which Hobbes allows a radical contingency to occur so that there may be a minimum of contingency elsewhere (in sharp contrast with, say, Machiavelli, for whom politics is largely a matter of living with and responding to contingency and temporality). It is echoed in the motif of the temporal moment of decision marking a boundary that reappears in Schmitt's exception at the spatial boundaries of the nation-state. A multitude of specific and highly consequential trends, like the shift from natural rights to political rights, from natural law to positive law, from the sins of usury to the virtue of interest, from contingency as fortune to contingency as statistical probability, and so on might be inserted into the mere moment/point of spatiotemporal transformation from there to here and then to now. Most significantly, however, it offers what remains our paradigmatic expression of the specific relation between the paradox of founding and the articulation of specifically modern relations of spatiotemporality.

Hobbes is not the only interesting site for exploration of such themes; the most obvious parallel/contrast is with Jean-Jacques Rousseau. For very useful commentary in this respect, see Jean Starobinski, *Jean-Jacques Rousseau: Transparency and Obstruction*, translated by Arthur Goldhammer (1971), Chicago: University of Chicago Press, 1988, especially the 1962 essay "Rousseau and the Search for Origins," 271–80; as well as commentaries such as Derrida's "Force of Law"; Bonnie

Honig, "Declarations of Independence: Arendt and Derrida on the Problem of Founding a Republic," *American Political Science Review*, 85:1, March 1991, 97–113; and Paul Ricoeur, "The Political Paradox," in *History and Truth*, translated by Charles A. Kelbley, Evanston, IL: Northwestern University Press, 1965, 247–70.

90 I develop this theme in R.B.J. Walker, "The Doubled Outsides of the Modern International."

91 Samuel Huntington, *The Conflict of Civilizations and the Remaking of World Order*, New York: Simon and Schuster, 1996.

5 Split finitudes, seductive heirarchies

1 See, for example, Hinsley, *Sovereignty*; Stankiewicz, ed., *In Defence of Sovereignty*; Alan James, *Sovereign Statehood*, London: Allen and Unwin, 1986; and Robert Jackson, ed., *Sovereignty at the Millennium*, Oxford: Blackwell, with the Political Studies Association, 1999. For more recent comprehensive discussions, see Christopher W. Morris, *An Essay on the Modern State*, Cambridge: Cambridge University Press, 1998; Hideaki Shinoda, *Re-Examining Sovereignty: From Classical Theory to the Golden Age*, London: Macmillan and New York: St Martin's Press, 2000; Neil Walker, ed., *Sovereignty in Transition*; and especially Prokkhovnik, *Sovereignties*.

2 For an important exception, see Koskenniemi, *The Gentle Civilizer of Nations*.

3 Among many, see Alfred Cobban, *The Nation State and National Self-Determination* (1945), New York: Crowell, revised edn, 1970; Anthony Cassese, *Self-Determination of Peoples*, Cambridge: Cambridge University Press, 1995; Nazila Ghanea and Alexandra Xanthaki, eds, *Minorities, Peoples and Self-Determination: Essays in Honour of Patrick Thornberry*, Leiden: Martinus Nijhoff, 2005.

4 Jürgen Habermas, "Modernity: An Unfinished Project" (1980), in Seyla Benhabib and Maurizio Passerin d'Entreves, eds, *Habermas and the Unfinished Project of Modernity: Critical Essays on the Philosophical Discourse of Modernity*, Cambridge, MA: MIT Press, 1997; and Habermas, *The Philosophical Discourse of Modernity: Twelve Lectures*, translated by F. Lawrence, Cambridge: Cambridge University Press, 1987.

5 The shifting judgements about the significance of nuclear weapons offered by John Herz remain suggestive; see Herz, *International Politics in the Atomic Age*, New York: Columbia University Press, 1959; and Herz, "The Territorial State Revisited: Reflections on the Future of the Nation State," *Polity*, 1:1, 1968, 11–34.

6 David Easton, *The Political System: An Inquiry into the State of Political Science*, New York: Knopf, 1953; Peter Laslett, ed., *Philosophy, Politics and Society*, first series, Oxford: Blackwell, 1956. For an exemplary codification of what has been achieved by the expulsion of politics from political philosophy, see Robert E. Goodin and Philip Pettit, eds, *Companion to Contemporary Political Philosophy*, Oxford: Blackwell, 1993. For brief but appropriate commentary, see Vincent, *The Nature of Political Theory*, 91ff.

7 Paul Ricoeur, "The Teleological and Deontological Structures of Action: Aristotle and/or Kant?" in A. Phillips Griffiths, ed., *Contemporary French Philosophy*, Cambridge: Cambridge University Press, 1987, 99–112.

8 For one of the very few attempts to come to terms with this rather basic methodological problem in contemporary political theory see James Tully, "The Kantian Idea of Europe: Critical and Cosmopolitan Perspectives," in Anthony Pagden, ed., *The Idea of Europe: From Antiquity to the European Union*, Cambridge: Cambridge University Press, 2002, 331–58. See also some of the essays in Hindess and Walker, eds, *The Cost of Kant*.

9 For a powerful reading of how such narratives work in relation both to claims about territory and about terror, a reading that intersects with the argument I seek to develop here, see Barry Hindess, "Terrortory," *Alternatives: Global, Local, Political*, 31:3, July–September 2006, 243–58.

10 Kant, *Critique of Pure Reason*. Many recent attempts to read Kant's major philosophical texts politically have followed Karl Jaspers, Hannah Arendt and Hans Saner in emphasizing Kant's *Critique of Judgement*; see Jaspers, *Kant*, edited by Hannah Arendt, translated by Ralph Mannheim, New York: Harcourt Brace, 1962; Hans Saner, *Kant's Political Thought: Its Origins and Development* (1967), translated by E.B. Ashton, Chicago: University of Chicago Press, 1973, which is the commentary from which I began to take my own bearings on Kant's politics (after prior interest in the epistemological role of Newtonian accounts of space and time in his account of the constitutive categories of experience); and Hannah Arendt, *Lectures on Kant's Political Philosophy*, edited by Ronald Beiner, Chicago: University of Chicago Press, 1982. This general line of influence is readily visible, to a greater or lesser degree, in the few sustained engagements with Kant's later writings by theorists of international relations; see especially Jens Bartelson, "The Trial of Judgement: A Note on Kant and the Paradoxes of Internationalism," *International Studies Quarterly*, 39, 1995, 255–79; and Mark F.N. Franke, *Global Limits: Immanuel Kant, International Relations and Critique of World Politics*, Albany: SUNY Press, 2001. My own comments here also build on this interpretive move, but also on a prior sense that Kant's framing of the problem of human finitude in the first Critique remains central to the way he engages with the origins, possibilities and limits of human freedom in the later writings. Let me stress, however, that I am not seeking to engage in the highly technical universe of Kant interpretation, merely to highlight some symptomatic peculiarities in the use of Kant in literatures on international relations over the past 50 years or so.

11 Hence, in my view, the importance of various attempts to think about "world order" under Cold War conditions in which it was almost impossible to think about international relations in any kind of critical spirit; for an appreciation in these terms see "World Order and the Reconstitution of Political Life," in Richard Falk, Robert Johansen and Samuel Kim, eds, *The Constitutional Foundations of World Peace*, Albany: SUNY Press, 1993, 191–209.

12 For detailed readings of some of the ontological and political conceits expressed in this process, see Ashley and Walker, "Reading Dissidence/Writing the Discipline."

13 Kant, "Perpetual Peace," Second Definitive Article, in *Kant: Political Writings*, 100; or "a federalism of free states," Kant, *Practical Philosophy*, 325.

14 The most instructive texts for thinking about the United Nations as an expression of the constitutive limits of modern political life perhaps remain the two paradigmatic texts from the 1960s by Inis J. Claude, Jr: *Power and International Relations*, New York: Random House, 1962; and *Swords into Plowshares*, New York: Random House, 1956.

15 Jürgen Habermas, "Kant's Idea of Perpetual Peace, with the Benefit of Two Hundred Years' Hindsight," in James Bohman and Mathias Lutz-Bachmann, eds, *Perpetual Peace: Essays on Kant's Cosmopolitan Ideal*, Cambridge, MA: MIT Press, 1997, 113–53, at 128.

16 As with the once influential formulations of Grenville Clark and Louis B. Sohn, *World Peace Through World Law*, Cambridge, MA: Harvard University Press, 1958.

17 Kant, "Perpetual Peace," in *Kant: Political Writings*, 105. Compare with Kant, "Idea for a Universal History with a Cosmopolitan Purpose," in *Kant: Political Writings*, 41–53.

18 Dianne Morgan, *Kant Trouble: The Obscurities of the Enlightened*, London: Routledge, 2000. See also Peter D. Fenves, *Late Kant: Towards Another Law of the Earth*, New York: Routledge, 2003.

19 Kant, *Critique of Pure Reason.*
20 This tendency is noted in Katrin Flikschuh, *Kant and Modern Political Philosophy*, Cambridge: Cambridge University Press, 2000.
21 See the careful reading of such literatures in Franke, *Global Limits*; and Franke, "Returning to Kant as a Critique of International Relations." in Hindess and Walker, eds, *The Cost of Kant*. See also the account of the history of interpretations of "Perpetual Peace" in Eric S. Easley, *The War Over "Perpetual Peace*," New York: Palgrave Macmillan, 2004. While rather too schematic, and with any reference to other Kantian texts ruthlessly excised, Easley's loosely Mannheimian sociology of knowledge offers a clear account of the way selective references to specific parts of the text have enabled interpretations favourable to what I am here calling horizontal and vertical accounts of the place of the states system in relation to the sovereign state.
22 Generally speaking, Kant's writings from the 1780s, like the "Idea for a Universal History," defend an ideal of a federation of states with strong coercive authority, while those from the 1790s, like "Theory and Practice" and "Perpetual Peace," shifted towards an idealized league without coercive powers but with the added element of (a very minimal) cosmopolitan right of entry for refugees in peril, and so on. Kant's reading of the dynamics leading to the French Revolution may have been significant in this shift, but the conceptual problem is more pervasive, leading to the central interpretive disputes about whether "Perpetual Peace" itself defends a coercive federation or non-coercive league of states.
23 As Bartelson has put it: "most versions of modern internationalism have quite uncritically assumed that the modern subject and the sovereign state can and will remain identical with themselves in the course of internationalist transformation, an assumption that helps to explain why modern internationalism has remained insensitive to the historicity of both. The modern subject and the sovereign state have occupied a privileged position in the proposed *solutions* to the problem of internationalism, not where they rightly belong, that is, as integral parts of the *problem* itself. In this respect, the problem of internationalism is also a problem of the limits of modernity." Bartelson, "The Trial of Judgement," 275.
24 "*Enlightenment is man's emergence from his self-incurred immaturity. Immaturity* is the inability to use one's own understanding without the guidance of another. ... The motto of enlightenment is therefore: ... Have courage to use your *own* understanding." Kant, "An Answer to the Question: 'What is Enlightenment?'," in *Kant: Political Writings*, 54–60, at 54 (italics in the original).
25 Helpful discussions include Paul Guyer, *Kant on Freedom, Law and Happiness*, Cambridge: Cambridge University Press, 2000; and Martti Koskienniemi, "Kant and International Law," in Hindess and Walker, eds, *The Cost of Kant*.
26 Although much contemporary critical analysis can be understood as a re-engagement with Kant's achievement in this respect, much of its force has been dissipated in superficial generalizations about postmodernity and so on, especially those celebrating figures such as Habermas as the true heirs of Kant in contemporary political thought. This is, to put it mildly, a judgement that rests on a very narrow account of what Kant was up to. To take a particularly instructive example, arguably one of the most important meditations on (and sociohistorical reworking of) Kant's narrative of founding is Michel Foucault's *History of Madness* (1961/1972), edited by Jean Khalfa, translated by Jonathan Murphy and Jean Khalfa, London: Routledge, 2006, although much of Derrida's work might also be understood in this context. For readings of Foucault's engagement with this aspect of Kant, and the traditions of phenomenology it enabled, see Beatrice Han, *Foucault's Critical Project: Between the Transcendental and the Historical* (1998), translated by Edward Pile, Stanford: Stanford University Press, 2002; Han, "Foucault and Heidegger on Kant and Finitude," in Alan Milchman and Alan Rosenberg, eds,

Foucault and Heidegger: Critical Encounters, Minneapolis: University of Minnesota Press, 2003, 127–62; Laura Hengehold, *The Body Problematic: Political Imagination in Kant and Foucault*, University Park: The Pennsylvania State University Press, 2007; Kevin Thompson, "Historicity and Transcendentality: Foucault, Cavailles, and the Phenomenology of the Concept," *History and Theory*, 47:1, February 2008, 1–18; and, less directly, Michel Serres, "The Geometry of the Incommunicable: Madness," translated by Felicia McCarren, in Arnold I. Davidson, ed., *Foucault and His Interlocutors*, Chicago: University of Chicago Press, 1997, 36–56.

27 Pauline Kleingeld's succinct but selective formulation offers a regulative ideal of a regulative ideal in this respect: for Kant, "true peace is possible only when states are organized internally according to 'republican' principles, when they are organized externally into a voluntary league that promotes peace, and when they respect the human rights not only of their own citizens but also of foreigners. He regards these three main requirements as intrinsically connected and argues that they can be successfully met only jointly." Pauline Kleingeld, "Kant's Theory of Peace," in Paul Guyer, ed., *Kant and Modern Philosophy*, Cambridge: Cambridge University Press, 2006, 477–504, at 477.

28 For example, in "On the Common Saying: 'This May be True in Theory, but it does not Apply in Practice,'" in Kant, *Political Writings*, 61–92.

29 Habermas is perhaps the contemporary thinker who has worked most industriously to read Kant as a prescription for a reverticalization of modern life. See Habermas, "Kant's Idea of Perpetual Peace, with the Benefit of Two Hundred Years' Hindsight," at 147 and 148. For commentary, see William Rasch, "A Just War? Or just a War? Schmitt vs Habermas," Chapter 2 of Rasch, *Sovereignty and its Discontents*, 49–63; and Thomas Mertens, "Cosmopolitanism and Citizenship: Kant Against Habermas," *European Journal of Philosophy*, 4, 1996, 328–47.

Habermas' more recent summary of his relation to Kant gives an exemplary account of how Kant's rigorous even if ambivalent analysis can be subverted in favour of something far more dogmatic; see Jürgen Habermas, "The Kantian Project and the Divided West," Part 4 of Habermas, *The Divided West*, edited and translated by Ciaran Cronin, Cambridge: Polity, 2006, 113–93. In very short order, this text frames the politics of states as a problem of pluralism (to which the solution must be universalism), reduces political realism to power politics (to which an ethics must provide the necessary corrective), turns American unilateralism into a matter of liberal moralism (thereby finessing the problematic relationship between universality, hegemony and empire), and appropriates international law as the vehicle carrying all the promises of cosmopolitan teleology (thereby assuming that the *aporetic* relation between state law and international law must be resolved in favour of the latter). Given this beginning, it is not surprising that the rest of the text works to avoid, or as Habermas prefers, improve upon Kant's analysis. Habermas is right to be critical of the radical assault on modern political principles mounted by an American administration that has violated many of the most important principles of international order; and right also in his resistance not only to Schmitt's essentialistic politics of friend and enemy, but also to Schmitt's later moves up the scale from sovereign states to continent-sized blocs. Despite his apparent intentions, however, the central tension between sovereign states and the system of states that begins to emerge with considerable clarity in Kant's later writings is simply evaded, except insofar as a particular statist understanding of what counts as a constitutional order is projected onto the system of states as a higher authority. Whatever might be said about the details of Habermas' interpretation of Kant in this context, it is certainly difficult to see how any useful engagement with his legacy can be predicted upon the clichéd readings of a statist pluralism, power, ethics and hegemony that Habermas deploys without shame yet which immediately disable any meaningful engagement with the internationalized systemic order within which relations between plurality and universality have already been established, albeit in the unstable manner that Kant, unlike Habermas, already grasped fairly well.

30 Kant, "Perpetual Peace," especially at 102. Cf "The Metaphysics of Morals," at 171ff.

31 The reigning orthodoxy in international relations in this respect has especially been shaped by Hinsley, *Power and the Pursuit of Peace*; W.B. Gallie, *Philosophers of Peace and War*, Cambridge: Cambridge University Press, 1978; and Kenneth W. Waltz, "Kant, Liberalism and War," *American Political Science Review*, 56, 1962, 331–40. More recent discussions include Pauline Kleingold, "Approaching Perpetual Peace: Kant's Defence of a League of States and his Ideal of a World Federation," *European Journal of Philosophy*, 12:3, 2004, 304–25.

32 This is the move recently exemplified in theories about a democratic peace popularized especially by Michael Doyle. See especially Doyle, "Kant, Liberal Legacies, and Foreign Affairs," *Philosophy and Public Affairs*, 12, 1983, 205–35 and 325–53; and Doyle, *Ways of War and Peace: Realism, Liberalism, and Socialism*, New York: Norton, 1997. It is a move that is especially indebted to the first definitive article of "Perpetual Peace," that "the civil constitution of state shall be republican," although the slippage from republics to democracies is hardly a minor matter, not least in the formulation of claims that might be tested against some historical record, to claims about the relationship between liberty and democracy, and to judgements about what is to count as a democracy. See, among many others, Patrick Riley, *Kant's Political Philosophy*, Rowman and Littlefield,1982; John Macmillan, "Immanuel Kant and the Democratic Peace," in Beate Jahn, ed., *Classical Theory in International Relations*, Cambridge: Cambridge University Press, 2006, 52–73; and Bruce Buchan, "Explaining War and Peace: Kant and Liberal International Relations Theory," *Alternatives: Global, Local, Political*, 27:4, 2002, 407–28. In relation to my argument here, see also the claim made by Douglas M. Gibler, in his "Bordering on Peace: Democracy, Territorial Issues, and Conflict," *International Studies Quarterly*, 51:3, September 2007, 509–32, at 509, that democracy and peace are both symptoms rather than causes of the removal of territorial issues between neighbours, and that "after controlling for the presence of stable borders, joint democracy exercises no pacifying effect on conflict behavior from 1946 to 1999."

33 Among many formulations: "This federation does not aim to acquire any power like that of a state, but merely to preserve and secure the *freedom* of the state itself, along with that of the other confederated states, although this does not mean that they need to submit to public laws and to a coercive power which enforces them, as do men in a state of nature." Kant, "Perpetual Peace," in Kant, *Political Writings*, 104.

34 On rebellion as the "most punishable crime," the prohibition of which must be "absolute," see Kant, "On the Common Saying: 'This May be True in Theory, but it does not Apply in Practice,'" in Kant, *Political Writings*, 81.

35 "Perpetual Peace," 118.

36 Kant, "Metaphysics of Morals: Part 1, Metaphysical first principles of the doctrine of right," in Kant, *Practical Philosophy*, at 387; cf. *Kant: Political Writings*, 133. While I stress here the way this formulation plays out in relation to the structures of an interstate order, it also plays out in Kant's struggles with the tension between his critique of European imperialism and his commitment to a universalist conception of humanity or cosmopolitan right. In both contexts, the crucial difficulties arise not from any simple Kantian universalism of the kind made popular by some contemporary claims about cosmopolitanism but the limits within which Kant's celebration of freedom and human diversity is sustained. Cosmopolitanism in this sense names a site of profound antagonisms, not an easy perch from which to survey "the world" and its possibilities.

37 As the editors of a collection of reflections on Kant's account of a Perpetual Peace were driven to conclude, "Escaping the dilemmas of despotism and fragmentation remains the most difficult institutional challenge of a cosmopolitan order; showing how the public use of reason permits both unity and difference is a task that the Kantian conception of reason has yet to solve." James Bohman and Mathias Lutz-Bachmann, eds, *Perpetual Peace*, 18. Indeed.

38 Kant, "Perpetual Peace,"105.

39 In this sense, Kant's shift from the hierarchical view expressed in "The Idea for a Universal History" of 1784 to the horizontal view expressed in the "Perpetual Peace" of 1795 can be read as a failure of nerve. Nerve can be restored by appealing to the tentative and pragmatic quality of Kant's view of History; see, for example, Elizabeth Ellis, *Kant's Politics: Provisional Theory for an Uncertain World*, New Haven: Yale University Press, 2005. Bolder readings can envisage something closer to a sequence of stages: as in, for example, Georg Cavallar, *Kant and the Theory and Practice of International Right*, Cardiff: University of Wales Press, 1999.

   In this respect, the crucial complement to "Perpetual Peace" is "Idea for a Universal History with a Cosmopolitan Purpose," in *Kant: Political Writings*, 41–53. See also "Conjectures on the Beginnings of Human History," in *Kant: Political Writings*, 221–34; Kant, *Anthropology from a Pragmatic Point of View*, translated by Victor Lyle Dowdell (Carbondale: Southern Illinois University Press, 1978).

40 Karl-Otto Apel, "Kant's 'Towards Perpetual Peace' as Historical Prognosis from the Point of View of Moral Duty," in Bohman and Lutz-Bachmann, eds, *Perpetual Peace*, 79–110.

41 For a sustained reading of Kant's texts that is both highly attentive both to Kant's ambivalences and to continuities between the "philosophical" and "political" texts, and yet concludes with a clear affirmation of hierarchy, see Otfried Hoffe, *Kant's Cosmopolitan Theory of Law and Peace*, translated by Alexandra Newton, Cambridge: Cambridge University Press, 2006: "Kant's moderate political cosmopolitanism is more precisely both a complementary and subsidiary cosmopolitanism" (201).

42 Schmitt, *The Nomos of the Earth*.

43 Thus much the same problem that troubles Kant's account of the autonomy of sovereign states in relation to the status of the system of states haunts Kantian engagements with concepts of the autonomous subjectivity of individuals in relation to the social processes that make that subjectivity possible. Such engagements are usually forced to draw the line between individual and society through an appeal to a distinction between the rational, mature and thus in principle autonomous subject and a dependent immaturity: the line drawn not only as a temporal distinction at a certain age, but also as a qualitative distinction between certain kinds of subjectivities framed through categories of gender, race or class.

44 Cecilia Lynch, "Kant, the Republican Peace, and Moral Guidance"; Fernando R. Tesón, "The Kantian Theory of International Law," *Columbia Law Review* 92:1, January 1992, 53–102.

45 And who thus try to understand the body as the site at which the problem of immanence and transcendence might be rethought, rather than as a site of immanence counterposed to the transcendence of ideas and so on. See especially Merleau-Ponty, *The Visible and the Invisible*, which develops a critique of the radical scepticism arising from either immanent or transcendental accounts of bodily existence in ways that speak to the broader pattern I address here. On the broader significance of Merleau-Ponty's account of this problem, see Dillon, *Merleau-Ponty's Ontology*. On the broadly Heideggerian problematization of the relation between claims about the end of metaphysics and the possibilities of thinking beyond metaphysics as a limit, see John Sallis, *Delimitations: Phenomenology and*

the End of Metaphysics, 2nd expanded edn, Bloomington, Indiana: Indiana University Press, 1995; and Mark C. Taylor, *Altarity*, University of Chicago Press, 1987.

46 Thus the broad resonance of Daniel Bell's Cold War account of *The End of Ideology*, Glencoe, IL: Free Press, 1960, and Francis Fukayama's apologia for a universalizing liberalism in *The End of History and the Last Man*, New York: Free Press, 1992.

47 Of the many texts celebrating the achievements and potentials of "Europe," I would single out the important essays by Étienne Balibar collected in his *We, The People of Europe? Reflections on Transnational Citizenship*, translated by James Swenson, Princeton: Princeton University Press, 2004, a text that has shaped some of my own formulations of what it means to engage with sovereignties and borders. It nevertheless remains an intensely Eurocentric text, and its primary engagement with sovereignty understandably remains focused on the possibilities of a popular sovereignty in relation to one particular site of (transnational) identities. The problem is not simply that there are other places in the world, but that Europe has long been articulated globally and the world has been articulated within Europe in ways that ought to place all claims about a Europe, a world or any we-the-people under serious suspicion.

More generally, the degree to which so many political analyses of "Europe" have been constructed on the basis of an opposition between a horizontal ground of intergovernmental relations and a hierarchical structure of "levels" offers an especially instructive example of the way in which claims about political novelty manage to force many dynamic phenomena into very conventional categories of analysis. Many of the problems of such literatures might be traceable to the reduction of politics to various kinds of utilitarianism or functionalism (associated especially with David Mitrany) and neofunctionalism (as developed by Ernst B. Haas and others) in ways that are perhaps relevant for contemporary claims about a "democratic deficit" and even a constitutional crisis in Europe. Nevertheless, many of the conceptual difficulties at play in this context express highly contestable assumptions about Europe as a spatiotemporal formation that seem to force any intimation of political transformation into the search for "higher levels."

For an analysis that seeks to link the problem of ethnocentricism to the resort to a politics of levels, see R.B.J. Walker, "Europe is Not Where it is Supposed to Be," in Morten Kelstrup and Michael Williams, eds, *International Relations and the Politics of European Integration*, London: Routledge, 2000, 14–32.

48 See, for example, Andrew Mack *et al.*, *The Human Security Report*, Oxford: Oxford University Press, 2005.

49 For an interesting range of contemporary discussions on this theme, see Mark A. Wrathall, ed., *Religion After Metaphysics*, Cambridge: Cambridge University Press, 2003. Charles Taylor's essay in this volume offers an especially telling example of an explicit distinction between the "horizontal" or "closed world structures" of modernity and the "vertical" or "transcendent" which (for Taylor unfortunately) find "no place" in the horizontal. See Taylor, "Closed World Structures," pp. 47–68.

Much is undoubtedly at stake in contemporary attempts to rethink the "secularization thesis," and "the death of God," and perhaps especially in attempts to appreciate the degree to which the framing of modern politics is indebted to specifically Christian accounts of immanence/transcendence, whether genealogically or metaphorically, and not least in relation to the accounts of sovereignty expressed by thinkers such as Hobbes, Kant and Schmitt. Nevertheless, here I am concerned primarily just to draw attention to the continuing force of spatiotemporal metaphors that lead so many sophisticated theorists of modernity, and not only those with explicitly religious commitments, such as Taylor, to think that the way forwards is to climb upwards. Problems arising from claims about the place or non-place of explicit religious commitments in modern political life do not exhaust the problems arising from the way in which specific religious commitments encourage specific ontological commitments, not least in relation to claims about higher and lower and the vast metaphorical fields through which hierarchical articulations of value express specific monotheistic accounts of immanence and transcendence.

50 Waltz, *Man, the State and War*. For useful commentaries on related problems arising from claims about scale in geographical analysis, see James McCarthy, "Scale, Sovereignty, and Strategy in Environmental Governance," *Antipode*, 2005, 731–53; and Engin Isin, "City.State: Critique of Scalar Thought," *Citizenship Studies*, 11:2, 2007, 211–28. For a reading of the levels of analysis typology as an expression of specific concepts of scale, spatiality, and what I call, following Pierre-Maxim Schuhl, the Theme of Gulliver, see Walker, *Inside/Outside*, 125ff.

51 See the conclusion of Kant, *Critique of Practical Reason* (1788).

52 Derrida, "Mystical Foundations of Authority."

6 Politics on the line

1 See, especially, Prokhovnik, *Sovereignties*.

2 That sovereignty *works* rather than simply *is* has become the common conclusion affirmed by a broad range of otherwise diverging literatures. See, among others, Alan James, *Sovereign Statehood*; Krasner, *Sovereignty: Organized Hypocrisy*; Janice E. Thomson, *Mercenaries, Pirates and Sovereigns*, Princeton: Princeton University Press, 1994; Hendryk Spruyt, *The Sovereign State and its Competitors*, Princeton: Princeton University Press, 1994; Sohail H. Hashmi, ed., *State Sovereignty: Change and Persistence in International Relations*, Pennsylvania State University Press, 1997; Thomas J. Biersteker and Cynthia Weber, eds, *State Sovereignty as Social Construct*, Cambridge: Cambridge University Press, 1996; Nicholas Greenwood Onuf, *The Republican Legacy in International Thought*, Cambridge: Cambridge University Press, 1998, 111 ff.; Daniel Philpott, *Revolutions in Sovereignty: How Ideas Shaped Modern International Relations*, Princeton: Princeton University Press, 2001; Bartelson, *A Genealogy of Sovereignty*; Cynthia Weber, *Simulating Sovereignty*, Cambridge: Cambridge University Press, 1995; Richard K. Ashley, "Untying the Sovereign State: A Double Reading of the Anarchy Problematique," *Millennium: Journal of International Studies*, 17, 1988, 227–62; John Ruggie, "Territoriality and Beyond: Problematizing Modernity in International Relations," *International Organization*, 47, Winter 1993, 139–64; and Walker, *Inside/Outside*.

3 This is one of the key themes developed in Ferdinand de Saussure's *Course in General Linguistics*, translated by Wade Baskin, New York: McGraw Hill, 1966, and subsequently radicalized by many "poststructuralist" thinkers. Despite such associations, the preoccupation of so much contemporary theory with various forms of nominalism is certainly not a radical departure from problems Hobbes might have understood quite well. On the related phrase, "the map is not the territory," see Alfred Korzybski, *Science and Sanity: An Introduction to Non-Aristotelian Systems and General Semantics*, New York: Institute of General Semantics, 1933. It is also worth noting the very different but no less suggestive context in which the liberating potentials of the politics of naming were expressed in the early decades of the twentieth century, in Marcel Duchamp's exemplary (1917) account of his "ready-mades," objects understood to be art because they were chosen by the artist and given a new titles constituting new objects. These and many other similar moves informed influential twentieth-century accounts of what it means to be culturally and intellectually innovative, but in some respects they can be read as attempts to recover the enabling potentials of a politics of nominalism in the face of many insistent practices of reification and essentialization.

4 Especially fertile lines of enquiry are suggested by Michel Serres, *Genesis* (1982), translated by Genevieve James and James Nielson, Ann Arbor: University of Michigan Press, 1995; George Steiner, *Grammars of Creation*, London: Faber and Faber, 2001; Gunnell, *Political Philosophy and Time;* Sorabji, *Time, Creation and the Continuum*; and Duhem, *Medieval Cosmology*.

Many strands of contemporary critical theory have been animated by questions about the origins of modern reason understood as unchanging topological form, especially as these questions were posed in the reading of modernity articulated by Edmund Husserl, "The Origin of Geometry" (1936), in Husserl, *The Crisis of European Sciences and Transcendental Phenomenology*, Evanston: Northwestern University Press, 1970, 353–78. See, especially, Jacques Derrida, *Edmund Husserl's Origin of Geometry: An Introduction* (1962), translated by John P. Leavey, Jr, Lincoln: University of Nebraska Press, 1989; Derrida, *The Problem of Genesis in Husserl's Philosophy*, (1990) translated by Marion Hobson, Chicago: University of Chicago Press, 2003; Paola Maratti, *Genesis and Trace: Derrida Reading Husserl and Heidegger*, Stanford: Stanford University Press, 2005; and Foucault, *History of Madness*.

Related themes animate the work of many contemporary writers concerned with the relation between politics and ontology, especially insofar as it might be possible to avoid prevailing narratives about origin through appeals to ontologies of difference, multiplicity, production, pure immanence, becoming, and so on. Quite apart from the merits of any specific ontology, however, the relation between ontology and politics is clearly at the heart of questions about sovereignty as the authorization of sovereign authority I seek to canvass here.

5 In the context of the early 1920s, which I have been stressing through references to figures such as Weber, Schmitt and Benjamin, the most telling texts are probably V. I. Lenin, *State and Revolution* (1918), New York: International Publishers, 1932; and Gyorgy Lukacs, *History and Class Consciousness*.

6 One of the most influential recent discussions of sovereignty in international relations takes a few very tentative steps towards disaggregating different concepts of sovereignty, but still clings tenaciously to the conventional narrative. See Stephen D. Krasner, *Sovereignty: Organized Hypocrisy*, Princeton: Princeton University Press, 1999. Krasner has been more aware than many writers of the simplistic character of the standard accounts of state sovereignty, and offers significant challenges to Cold War accounts of sovereignty as a monolithic entity, especially by showing how the practices of sovereignty as an institution are capable of contradictory functions. Nevertheless, Krasner's attempted disaggregation is predicated not only on a sharp division between internal and external, but also on a sharp division between what he calls authority and control. Most strikingly, his analysis is expressed in a tone of surprise that a practice that works through a claim to solve contradictions should generate a politics of systematic hypocrisy. Moreover, he claims to be able to read the consequences of such hypocrisy less in relation to the contradictions of the states system or to a politics of spatiotemporal contingency than to a metaphorical field derived from utilitarian accounts of rational action. Fortunately or unfortunately, the practices of sovereignty are perhaps the last place in which serious analysis can be content with a rationalist account of human action. Such accounts may well illuminate practices governed by some kinds of norm, but practices involving a capacity to decide exceptions to such norms pose a considerable challenge in this respect. Indeed, while Krasner's narratives say quite a bit about the actions of some actors, they say surprisingly little about the practices of sovereignty. Like so much of the conventional literature on sovereignty and international relations, it is almost touchingly naive about what it means to make a claim to authority, what it takes to make such a claim work, and how such a claim works in relation to specific forms of power and to constitutive contradictions between sovereign state and system of sovereign states.

 7 John I.1.
 8 Hobbes, *Leviathan*, chapter 14.
 9 Hence the broad resonance of Derrida's term *différance* so as to speak about a spatialization of time and a temporalization of space in ways other than those given by modern narratives about origins and foundations affirmed by the distinction between space and time.
10 Machiavelli, *The Prince*, especially Chapters 1 and 6.
11 Koyré, *From the Closed World to the Infinite Universe*; Jammer, *Concepts of Space*; Harries, *Infinity and Perspective*; and Lacour, *Lines of Thought*.
12 Hobbes, *Leviathan*, chapter 18.
13 Disputes about whether sovereign authority is derived internally from the attributes of statehood – an organized government, a clearly defined authority, independence from external control, and so on – or externally from "recognition" by the broader international community, pervades the classical literatures of international law. While extensive, however, these literatures are characterized by remarkably little systematic analysis of the tricky slide from empirical condition to legal authority, and still less of the constitutive effects of this slide. Various contemporary cases – Bosnia-Herzegovina, Chechnia, Palestine, as well as various claims about "rogue states" – pose obvious problems in this context, but perhaps the most far-reaching discussions have involved the status of state sovereignty in post-colonial contexts. See, for example, Robert H. Jackson, *Quasi-States*; and the critique of Jackson in Grovogui, *Sovereigns, Quasi Sovereigns, and Africans*.
14 Competing versions of the "secularization thesis" have obviously been central to many forms of social theory, but in relation to practices of sovereignty important entries into substantial literatures include Carl Schmitt, *Political Theology*; Karl Lowith, *Meaning in History*, Chicago: University of Chicago Press, 1949; Hans Blumenberg, *The Legitimacy of the Modern Age* (1966), Cambridge, MA: MIT Press, 1983; and Claude Lefort, "The Permanence of the Theologico-Political," in Lefort, *Democracy and Political Theory*, Cambridge: Polity, 1988, 213–55. For useful commentary on continuities and discontinuities between theological traditions and modern forms of secular sovereignty see Govert Buijis, "'*Que les Latins appellent maiestatem*': An Exploration into the Theological Background of the Concept of Sovereignty," In Neil Walker, ed., *Sovereignty in Transition*, 229–57.
15 There are, of course, many attempts to assess the significance of cities for contemporary political life in terms of both their scale and structural form, but also as the source of a metaphorical field that avoids some of the conceits expressed in statist and internationalist categories, and as a site for thinking about practices of democratization; see especially Magnusson, *The Search for Political Space*; and Engin Isin, ed., *Democracy, Citizenship and the Global City*, London: Routledge, 2000.
16 Though considerably exaggerated with respect to Hobbes especially, C.B. Macpherson's *The Political Theory of Possessive Individualism*, Oxford: Oxford University Press, 1962, remains significant in this respect; as do the stories told in Albert Hirshman, *The Passions and the Interests*, Princeton: Princeton University Press, 1977; and Ian Hacking, *The Emergence of Probability*, 2nd edn, Cambridge: Cambridge University Press, 2006.
17 John Locke, *Second Treatise of Government*, chapter 5.
18 Christopher Chase-Dunn, "Interstate System and Capitalist World Economy: One Logic or Two?" *International Studies Quarterly*, 25:1, March 1981, 19–42.
19 One of the attractions of "rational choice theory" and other version of utilitarian calculation that have been popular in the analysis of international systems is that they permit an apparent translation from claims to value affirmed by sovereign states and claims to value affirmed by capitalist markets, and thus the elision of almost everything that is at stake in the historical struggle between these two sources of ultimate value.

20 The concept of global civil society has been used to express a great diversity of claims, usually grounded in strong normative aspirations and rich sociological descriptions, but not so well attuned to questions about political principle. I have tried to engage some of the limits of this concept in various places, beginning with "Social Movements/World Politics," and generally arguing that the rich empirical material encompassed by this concept has been overinterpreted through assumptions about the sovereign state and/or through claims about an historical shift to "world politics" that I seek to put in question here. See also the discussion in Mustapha Kamal Pasha and David Blaney, "Elusive Paradise: The Promise and Peril of Global Civil Society," *Alternatives*, 23, 1998, 417–50.

21 The classic discussion is John A. Agnew, "The Territorial Trap: The Geographical Assumptions of International Relations Theory," *Review of International Political Economy*, 1, 1994, 53–80. In a more recent discussion Agnew argues strongly that "sovereignty is neither inherently territorial nor is it exclusively organized on a state-by-state basis," argues for a concept of "effective sovereignty," and distinguishes four "'sovereignty regimes' that result from distinctive combinations of central state authority (legitimate despotic power) on the one hand, and degree of political territoriality (the administration of infrastructural power) on the other." See Agnew, "Sovereignty Regimes: Territoriality and State Authority in Contemporary World Politics," *Annals of the Association of American Geographers*, 95:2, 2005, 437–61; see also Agnew, "No Borders, No Nations: Making Greece in Macedonia," *Annals of the Association of American Geographers*, 97:2, 2007, 398–422. The recent work of many other geographers is also helpful in this context; see for example Stuart Elden, "Terror and Territory," *Antipode* 39:5, 2007, 821–45; and Harmut Behr, "Deterritorialization and the Transformation of Statehood: The Paradox of Globalization," *Geopolitics*, 13, 2008, 259–382.

  While I find Agnew's analysis to be very suggestive and often empirically persuasive, my own reading of the problem seeks to resist both the traditional reading of sovereignty as centralized authority that still informs his analysis, and any claim about "effective sovereignty" that plays down the force of the authorization of authority problem and thus the regulative ideal of the sovereignty–territory relation expressed in the standard narratives and the topologies that inform these ideals.

22 To borrow a formulation from Barry Hindess; see Hindess, "Divide and Rule: The International Character of Modern Citizenship," *European Journal of Social Theory*, 1:1, 1998, 57–70; and Hindess, "Divide and Govern: Governmental Aspects of the Modern States System," in Richard Ericson and Nico Stehr, eds, *Governing Modern Societies*, Toronto: University of Toronto Press, 2000, 118–40.

23 Raymond Aron, *Peace and War: A Theory of International Relations*, translated by Richard Howard and Annette Baker Fox, New York: Praeger, 1967; Spruyt, *The Nations State and its Competitors*; Thompson, *Mercenaries, Pirates and Sovereigns*; Charles Tilly, *Coercion, Capital, and European States, AD 990–1992*, Cambridge, MA: Blackwell, 1992; Gianfranco Poggi, *The Development of the Modern State: A Sociological Introduction*, Stanford: Stanford University Press, 1978; and Turan Kayaoglu, "The Extension of Westphalian Sovereignty: State Building and the Abolition of Extraterritoriality," *International Studies Quarterly*, 51:3, 2007, 649–75.

24 For a synoptic discussion, see Phillip Cole, *Philosophers of Exclusion: Political Theory and Immigration*, Edinburgh: Edinburgh University Press, 2000. Among many other discussions, see Suzanne McGrath Dale, "The Flying Dutchman Dichotomy: The International Right to Leave v. The Sovereign Right to Exclude," *Dickenson Journal of International Law*, 9:2, 1991, 359–85; Bonnie Honig, *Democracy and the Foreigner*, Princeton: Princeton University Press, 2001; and Peter Nyers, *Rethinking Refugees: Beyond States of Emergency*, London: Routledge, 2006.

25 Didier Bigo, "Security and Immigration: Towards a Governmentality of Unease," *Alternatives/Cultures et Conflits*, 27, 2002, 63–92; Didier Bigo and Anastasia

Tsoukala, eds, *Terror, Insecurity and Liberty: Illiberal Practices of Liberal Regimes After 9/11*, London: Routledge, 2008; and Huysmans, *The Politics of Insecurity.*

26 The geographer Yi-Fu Tuan has taken up this thematic from a more phenomenological direction in his *Escapism*, Baltimore: Johns Hopkins University Press, 1998. For a more Heideggerian analysis, see Emmanuel Levinas, *On Escape* (1982), translated by Bettina Bergo, Stanford: Stanford University Press, 2003.

27 Thus the now often exemplary contrast drawn between Ernst Gellner, for whom nationalism invents nations where they scarcely existed, and Anthony Smith, for whom it is possible to trace at least the enabling roots of nations in prior "ethnies." See Gellner, *Nations and Nationalism*, Oxford; Blackwell, 1983; Smith, *The Ethnic Origins of Nations*, Oxford: Blackwell, 1986; and Smith, *Nationalism and Modernism*, London: Routledge, 1998.

28 Hence, symptomatically, the extraordinary difficulty of engaging with categories of culture and gender in the theory of international relations in ways that do not simply reproduce the constitutive assumptions of the theory that these concepts are often intended to challenge. "Culture" and "gender" are both included as constitutive assumptions about modern politics and then framed as "secondary," "marginal" and so on. This is a theme I have explored in several contexts, including "World Politics and Western Reason: Universalism, Pluralism, Hegemony," *Alternatives*, 7:2, 1981, reprinted in Walker, ed., *Culture, Ideology, World Order*, Boulder: Westview, 1984, 192–216; "The Concept of Culture in the Theory of International Relations," in John Chay, ed., *Culture and International Relations*, New York: Praeger, 1990, 3–17; and "Gender and Critique in the Theory of International Relations," in V. Spike Peterson, ed., *Gendered States: Feminist (Re) Visions of International Relations Theory*, Boulder: Lynne Rienner, 1992, 179–202. Similarly, the key difficulty posed by claims about the need for more environmentally engaged forms of political theory and practice is less the way in which "the environment" or "nature" has been ignored or excluded than the way it has been included in ways that simultaneously enable modern politics and depoliticize this enabling.

29 Max Weber, "The National State and Economic Policy," (Weber's Inaugural Address at the University of Freiburg, 1895), in *Weber's Political Writings.*

30 See, for example, the essays collected in Michael Ignatieff, ed., *American Exceptionalism and Human Rights*, Princeton: Princeton University Press, 2005. This volume contains interesting analyses of the multiple causalities at work within the USA in this respect, especially in relation to its historical traditions of constitutional law. There are also occasional, but only occasional, glimpses of how the logic of a sovereign exceptionalism deployable in relation to the constitution of an autonomous nation-state within a system of states intersects with the logic of an exceptionalism that works as a resistance to the demands of a system of states on grounds either of a radical cultural difference that exceeds the bounds of systemic pluralism (usually expressed as the "isolationalist" impulse) or of claims to a singular empire (recently expressed as the "unilateralist" impulse). Ignatieff's own influential writings express some of the most egregious examples of a failure to work through these two logics with any degree of scholarly seriousness, in ways that have come to legitimize claims about the necessities of a specifically American version of the liberal imperialism and imperialist liberalism once associated with European colonialisms. Other forthright attempts to equate international mechanisms for the promotion of human rights with imperialist conceptions of American policy are not difficult to find; for an influential example, see Anne-Marie Slaughter, *A New World Order*, Princeton: Princeton University Press, 2004.

31 See, for example, Joanne Barker, ed., *Sovereignty Matters: Locations of Contestation and Possibility in Indigenous Struggles for Self-Determination*, Lincoln: University of Nebraska Press, 2005; Cf. Shaw, *Indigeneity and Political Theory.*

32 Partha Chatterjee, *Nationalist Thought and the Colonial World*.
33 Recent contributions to a large literature, much of it concerned to contest hegemonic accounts of "development," include Arjun Appadurai, *Fear of Small Numbers: An Essay on the Geography of Anger*, Durham: Duke University Press, 2006; and Partha Chatterjee, *The Politics of the Governed: Reflections on Popular Politics in Most of the World*, New York: Columbia University Press, 2004.
34 This theme is explored in R.B.J. Walker, Joao Nogueira and Nizar Messari, eds, *Displacing the International*.
35 It is in this context that a contrast may be drawn between the understanding of modernization informing Weberian accounts of the internal dynamics of modernizing states within a system of states, and the understanding of modernization informing contemporary claims about the need to bring all states within a modern international order. The same underlying teleological narrative is at work in both cases, but legitimations of the "war against terror" are notable for their invocation more of neocolonial narratives about the expansion of international society and the inevitability of modernity as a civilizational form than of the competitive dynamics of modernizing states in an international system. For an attempt to suggest that Weber is as relevant for thinking about the legitimation of violence in the name of the war on terror as for the legitimation of nationalist *machtpolitik*, not least in relation to Weber's insistence on a politics of responsibility in the face of a modernizing rationality that generates characteristic forms of irrationality and decisionism, see Walker, "War, Terror, Judgement."
36 I have developed this argument in R.B.J. Walker, "L'International, l'imperial, l'exceptionnel."
37 Fitzpatrick, *Modernism and the Grounds of Law*.
38 This theme receives some treatment in most of the standard texts on the history of international law, a field that has become a rather esoteric specialization cut off from contemporary political analysis more generally, thereby sustaining the tendency for international relations theory to assume a radical nationalism as its necessary point of origin.
39 For a succinct overview see the essays by Henry Shue, Nicholas J. Wheeler and Jennifer M. Welsh in Jennifer M. Welsh, ed., *Humanitarian Intervention and International Relations*, Oxford: Oxford University Press, 2004. For an influential statement of much conventional wisdom in this context, see International Commission on Intervention and State Sovereignty, *The Responsibility to Protect: Report of the International Commission on Intervention and State Sovereignty*, Ottawa: International Development Research Centre, 2001. For contrasting evaluations, see Ramesh Thakur, "In Defence of The Responsibility to Protect," *International Journal of Human Rights*, 7:3, 2003; Daniel Warner, "Responsibility to Protect and the Limits of Imagination," *International Journal of Human Rights*, 7:3, 2003; Warner, "The Responsibility to Protect and Irresponsible, Cynical Engagement," *Millennium: Journal of International Studies*, 32:1, 2003, 109–21; and B.K. Greener, "Liberalism and the Use of Force: Core Themes and Conceptual Tensions," *Alternatives: Global, Local, Political*, 32:3, 2007, 295–318. For a more sustained discussion, see Anne Orford, *Reading Humanitarian Intervention: Human Rights and the Use of Force in International Law*, Cambridge: Cambridge University Press, 2003.
40 Koskenniemi, *From Apology to Utopia*; Cf. Robert M. Unger, *Law in Modern Society: Toward a Criticism of Social Theory*, New York: Free Press, 1976.
41 Provocative discussions include Hilary Charlesworth, "International Law: A Discipline in Crisis," *Modern Law Review*, 65:3, 2002, 377–92; Anne Orford, "The Destiny of International Law," *Leiden Journal of International Law*, 17, 2004, 441–76.
42 Among many, see Ingrid Detter De Lupis, *International Law and the Independent State*, Aldershot: Gower, 1975/1987; Johan D. Vander Vyver, "Sovereignty and

Human Rights in Constitutional and International Law," *Emory International Law Review*, 5, 1991, 321–443.

43 .One of the key achievements of Hobbes' story about a shift from a state of nature to a political society has been to help shape a conflation of the two modes of alterity framed as civilization/barbarism, on the one hand, and friend/enemy on the other. A related conflation is effected by the primary tropes of modern nationalism. This is especially clear in accounts of nationalism as both a necessary consequence and invention of industrialization (an account launched with some subtlety by Max Weber, turned into a no-holds-barred structural determinism by Ernst Gellner, and expressed in all those simple conflations of the term "state" with "nation-state"). In this context, the problem of sovereign "founding" is expressed both in debates about whether nations are "natural" or "cultural" formations and about the degree to which the "invention of tradition" mimics Hobbes' narrative about the projection of a present ideal back to a point of origin. The classic texts in this respect are Gellner, *Nations and Nationalism*; and Benedict Anderson, *Imagined Communities*, London: Verso, 1983. Not surprisingly, various postcolonial writers have noticed that, in effect, a logic of colonization has been superimposed on the logic of the modern system of states, thereby encouraging resistance to colonization through various appeals to the statist nationalism that work as a "co-opted discourse" involving "intimate enemies." See Chatterjee, *Nationalism and the Colonial World*; and Nandy, *The Intimate Enemy*.

44 Didier Bigo and R.B.J. Walker, "International, Political, Sociology," *International Political Sociology*, 1:1, March 2007, 1–6; Bigo and Walker, "Political Sociology and the Problem of the International," *Millennium: Journal of International Studies*, 2006, 725–40.

45 As Richard Ashley has been especially incisive in demonstrating, while the academic discipline of international relations has been explicitly framed as an attempt to understand sovereignty and its consequences, it also works precisely as a sovereignty practice and needs to be examined as such if its claims to knowledge about sovereignty are to be taken seriously. Hence Ashley's concern, which I share, though in a less micropolitical register, with the strategies and tactics used to discipline dissent and ensure self-regulation: with threats of dismissal; strategies of seduction; invitations to engage in dissent within acceptable limits; repeated claims about an acceptable "mainstream"; practices of normalization and exceptionalism enacted in a discipline concerned with norms and exceptions; practices of war within a discipline concerned with war; practices seeking to stabilize an array of stabilities and instabilities in a discipline concerned to understand the unstable relation between stability and instability, or space and time; and practices affirming practices of inclusion that permit specific accounts of inclusion/exclusion within a discipline concerned with the consequences of a specific inclusion/exclusion understood as the only way of being in a world that can never know that which is excluded as the condition under which inclusion works as inclusion/exclusion. Confirming the analysis, however, it is only very rarely that Ashley's work is identified as an engagement with many of the exemplary practices of modern sovereignty, being consigned instead to a category of poststructuralism that is somehow intent on undermining all foundations rather than critically engaged with the conditions under which contingent foundations have been affirmed as inevitable.

46 Bartelson, *Genealogies of Sovereignty*; Bartelson, *Critique of the State*.

47 For a recent discussion that speaks both to the political theologies that I have invoked at various points and to contemporary debates about terror and torture, see Kahn, *Sacred Violence*.

48 Benjamin, "Theses on the Philosophy of History"; Agamben, *Homo Sacer*; Hardt and Negri, *Empire*.

49 Nancy, *The Birth to Presence*.

50 This phrase comes from R.G. Collingwood, *The Idea of Nature*, Oxford: Clarendon Press, 1945, at p. 100.

51 James Tully, *Strange Multiplicity: Constitutionalism in an Age of Diversity*, Cambridge: Cambridge University Press, 1995, especially pp. 58–98.

52 The reconciliation between the homogeneous spaces of modernity and hierarchical forms of subordination was effected in large part by a colonial or developmental understanding of the relation between advanced and less advanced cultures, a theme taken up in the commentary on Tully developed in Helliwell and Hindess, "The 'Empire of Uniformity' and the Government of Subject Peoples."

53 For just two recent examples, see Anthony Pagden, *Worlds at War: The 2500-Year Struggle Between East and West*, Oxford: Oxford University Press, 2008; and David Levering Lewis, *God's Crucible: Islam and the Making of Europe, 570–1215*, New York, W.W. Norton, 2008.

54 Didier Bigo, "Internal and External Security(ies): The Möbius Ribbon," in Albert, Jacobson and Lapid, eds, *Identities, Borders and Orders*, 93–136; Didier Bigo and R.B.J. Walker, "Political Sociology and the Problem of the International,"; Giorgio Agamben, *Means Without End*; and Slavoj Žižek. *The Parallax View*, Cambridge, MA: MIT Press, 2006.

55 For a forthright attempt to read liberty and security as common values on a normal curve of rationality, see Eric Posner and Adrian Vermeule, *Terror in the Balance: Security, Liberty, and the Courts*, Oxford: Oxford University Press, 2007. Among many useful attempts to resist the effects of the metaphor of balance in this context, see Jeremy Waldren, "Security and Liberty: The Image of Balance," *The Journal of Political Philosophy*, 11:2, 2003, 191–210; Lucia Zedner, "Securing Liberty in the Face of Terror: Reflections from Criminal Justice," *Journal of Law and Society*, 32:4, December 2005, 507–33; and Mark Neocleous, "Security, Liberty and the Myth of Balance: Towards a Critique of Security Politics," *Contemporary Political Theory*, 6:2, May 2007, 131–49.

56 For detailed analyses of the many practices that have been enacted in the name of a balance between liberty and security, yet which point to an emerging field of governance and governmentality that is sharply at odds with at least liberal democratic accounts of these concepts and the relation between them, see Didier Bigo, Serio Carrera, Elspeth Guild and R.B.J. Walker, "The Changing Landscape of European Liberty and Security. The Mid-Term Report of the CHALLENGE Project," *International Social Science Journal*, 59(192), 283–308, as well as the many documents stored on the CHALLENGE website at www.libertysecurity.org.

57 For an extended discussion, see R.B.J. Walker, "The Doubled Outsides of the Modern International."

58 Machiavelli, *The Prince*, chapter 20.

59 For analyses of how boundaries often work as a relay in which sovereignty oscillates between domestic and foreign, see Elspeth Guild, *Security and Migration in the 21st Century* (Cambridge: Polity, 2009); Philippe Bonditti, *L'antiterrorisme aux Etats-Unis (1946–2007): Une analyse foucauldienne de la transformation de l'exercice de la souverainete et l'art de gouverner*, doctoral thesis, Sciences-Po, Paris, November 2008; James Der Derian, *Virtuous War: Mapping the Military–Industrial–Media–Entertainment Network*, Boulder: Westview, 2001; and Heriberto Cairo, "The Duty of the Benevolent Master: From Sovereignty to Suzerainty and the Biopolitics of Intervention," *Alternatives: Global, Local, Political*, 31:3, 285–311. See also various literatures on, for example, the projection of domestic/criminal law to sites under foreign military action; on states exercising powers through occupation or invitation; on the spaces and times of transit and migration; on *maquilidora* production complexes; on new practices and technologies of boundary-making/affirmation; and on multiple forms of deterritorialization.

60 It is arguable that the force of contemporary uses of terms such as terror and terrorism derives not only from memories of historical experience, but also from the way they now enable a co-articulation of spatial tropes about enemies and temporal tropes about barbarians; much of it also arguably comes from the way they enable a co-articulation of internal accounts of policing and external accounts of military action. That is, they are terms that work in part because they have the capacity to mobilize and shape forms of political practice that do not depend on clear distinctions between either space and time or internal and external. Articulated as a universal or global, they now signal a politics of neither (inter)statist nor general exceptions, but a symptomatic capacity to authorize discriminations in ways that elude the predictable cartographies of modern politics.

Bibliography

Achebe, Chinua, *Things Fall Apart* (1958), Oxford: Heinemann, 1986.

Adams, Paul *et al.*, eds, *Textures of Place: Exploring Humanist Geographies*, Minneapolis: University of Minnesota Press, 2001.

Agamben, Giorgio, *Means Without End: Notes on Politics* (1996), translated by Vincenzo Binetti and Cesarino, Minneapolis: University of Minnesota Press, 2000.

—— *Homo Sacer: Sovereign Power and Bare Life*, translated by Daniel Heller-Roazen, Stanford: Stanford University Press, 1998.

—— *State of Exception*, Chicago: University of Chicago Press, 2005.

Agnew, John A., "The Territorial Trap: The Geographical Assumptions of International Relations Theory," *Review of International Political Economy*, 1:1, 1994, 53–80.

—— "Sovereignty Regimes: Territoriality and State Authority in Contemporary World Politics," *Annals of the Association of American Geographers*, 95:2, 2005, 437–61.

—— "No Borders, No Nations: Making Greece in Macedonia," *Annals of the Association of American Geographers*, 97:2, 2007, 398–422.

—— and Stuart Corbridge, *Mastering Space: Hegemony, Territory and International Political Economy*, London: Routledge, 1995.

Ahonen, Pertti and Kari Palonen, eds, *Dis-Embalming Max Weber*, Jyväskylä: SoPhi, 1999.

Albert, Mathias and Lena Hilkermeier, eds, *Observing International Relations: Niklas Luhman and World Politics*, London: Routledge, 2004.

Albert, Mathias, David Jacobson and Yosef Lapid, eds, *Identities, Borders, Orders: Rethinking International Relations Theory*, Boulder: Lynne Rienner, 2001.

Allen, N.J., *Categories and Classifications: Maussian Reflections on the Social*, Oxford: Berghahn, 2000.

Ananiadis, Grigoris, "Carl Schmitt on Kosovo: Or Taking War Seriously," in Dusan Bjelic and Obrad Savic, eds, *The Balkans as a Metaphor: Between Globalization and Fragmentation*, Cambridge, MA: MIT Press, 2002,117–62.

Anderson, Benedict, *Imagined Communities*, London: Verso, 1983.

Anderson, Malcolm, *Frontiers: Territory and State Formation in the Modern World*, Cambridge: Polity Press, 1996.

Ankerschmit, Frank R., *Aesthetic Politics: Political Philosophy Beyond Fact and Value*, Stanford: Stanford University Press, 1996.

Ansell, Christopher K. and Guiseppe di Palma, *Restructuring Teritoriality: Europe and the United States Compared*, Cambridge: Cambridge University Press, 2004.

Apel, Karl-Otto, "Kant's 'Towards Perpetual Peace' as Historical Prognosis from the Point of View of Moral Duty," in James Bohman and Mathias Lutz-Bachmann, eds, *Perpetual Peace: Essays on Kant's Cosmopolitan Ideal*, Cambridge, MA: MIT Press, 1997, 79–110.

Aron, Raymond, *Peace and War: A Theory of International Relations*, translated by Richard Howard and Annette Baker Fox, New York: Praeger, 1967.

Appadurai, Arjun, *Modernity at Large: Cultural Dimensions of Globalization*, Minneapolis: University of Minnesota Press, 1998.

—— *Fear of Small Numbers: An Essay on the Geography of Anger*, Durham: Duke University Press, 2006.

Arend, Anthony Clark, *Legal Rules and International Society*, Oxford: Oxford University Press, 1999.

Arendt, Hannah, *Lectures on Kant's Political Philosophy*, edited by Ronald Beiner, Chicago: University of Chicago Press, 1982.

Armitage, David, "Hobbes and the Foundations of Modern International Thought," in Annabel Brett and James Tully, with Holly Hamilton-Bleakley, eds, *Rethinking the Foundations of Modern Political Thought*, Cambridge: Cambridge University Press, 2006, 219–35.

Ashley, Richard K., "Living on Borderlines: Man, Poststructuralism and War," in James Der Derian and Michael Shapiro, eds, *International/Intertextual Relations: Boundaries of Knowledge and Practice in World Politics*, Lexington: Lexington Books, 1988, 259–321.

——, "Untying the Sovereign State: A Double Reading of the Anarchy Problematique," *Millennium: Journal of International Studies*, 17, 1988, 227–62.

—— and R.B.J. Walker, "Reading Dissidence/Writing the Discipline: Crisis and the Question of Sovereignty in International Studies," *International Studies Quarterly*, 34, September 1990, 367–416.

Axelrod, Robert, *The Evolution of Cooperation*, New York: Basic Books, 1984.

Bachelard, Gaston, *Le Nouvel Esprit scientifique* (1934), Paris: Presses Universitaires de France, 1973.

—— *The Philosophy of No* (1940), translated by G.C. Waterstone, New York: Orion Press, 1969.

—— *The Poetics of Space* (1957), translated by Maria Jolas, Boston: Beacon Press, 1969.

Badie, Bertrand, *The Imported State: The Westernization of the Political Order*, translated by Claudia Royal, Stanford: Stanford University Press, 2000.

Balakrishnan, Gopal, *The Enemy: An Intellectual Portrait of Carl Schmitt*, London: Verso, 2000.

Balibar, Etienne, *Politics and the Other Scene*, translated by Christine Jones, James Swenson and Chris Turner, London: Verso, 2002.

—— *We, The People of Europe? Reflections on Transnational Citizenship*, translated by James Swenson, Princeton: Princeton University Press, 2004.

Barbaras, Renaud, *Desire and Distance: Introduction to a Phenomenology of Perception*, translated by Paul B. Milan, Stanford: Stanford University Press, 2006.

Barkawi, Tarak, "'Strategy as a Vocation', Weber, Morgenthau and Modern Strategic Studies," *Review of International Studies*, 24:2, April 1998.

Barker, Joanne, ed., *Sovereignty Matters: Locations of Contestation and Possibility in Indigenous Struggles for Self-Determination*, Lincoln: University of Nebraska Press, 2005.

Barnes, Jonathan, ed., *The Complete Works of Aristotle*, Princeton: Princeton University Press, 1984.

Barry, Andrew, *Political Machines: Governing a Technological Society*, London: Athlone, 2001.

Bartelson, Jens, *A Genealogy of Sovereignty*, Cambridge: Cambridge University Press, 1995.

——, "The Trial of Judgement: A Note on Kant and the Paradoxes of Internationalism," *International Studies Quarterly*, 39, 1995, 255–79

—— "Second Natures: Is the State Identical with Itself?" *European Journal of International Relations*, 4:3, 1998, 295–326.

—— *The Critique of The State*, Cambridge: Cambridge University Press, 2001.

Bataille, Georges, *Visions of Excess: Selected Writings 1927–1939*, translated by A. Stockl Minneapolis: University of Minnesota Press, 1985.

Bauman, Zygmunt, *Modernity and Ambivalence*, Cambridge: Polity Press, 1991.

Baumann, Gerd, *The Multicultural Riddle: Rethinking National, Ethnic and Religious Identities*, London: Routledge, 1999.

Beck, Ulrich, *Power in the Global Age: A New Global Political Economy*, translated by Kathleen Cross, Cambridge: Polity Press, 2005.

—— *Cosmopolitan Vision*, translated by Ciaran Cronin, Cambridge: Polity Press, 2006.

Behr, Harmut, "Deterritorialization and the Transformation of Statehood: The Paradox of Globalization," *Geopolitics*, 13, 2008, 259–382.

Bell, David, *The End of Ideology*, Glencoe, IL: Free Press, 1960.

Bender, John and David E. Wellbery, eds, *Chronotypes: The Construction of Time*, Stanford: Stanford University Press, 1991.

Benjamin, Walter, "Critique of Violence" (1921), in *Walter Benjamin: Selected Writings, Volume 1, 1913–1926*, edited by Marcus Bullock and Michael Jennings, Cambridge, MA: Harvard University Press, 1996, 236–52.

Berg, Eiki and Henk van Houtum, eds, *Routing Borders Between Territories, Discourses and Practices*, Aldershot: Ashgate, 2003.

Bergson, Henri, *The Two Sources of Morality and Religion*, New York: Henry Holt, 1935.

Biersteker, Thomas J. and Cynthia Weber, eds, *State Sovereignty as Social Construct*, Cambridge: Cambridge University Press, 1996.

Bigo, Didier "Internal and External Securit(y)ies: The Möbius Ribbon," in Mathias Albert, David Jacobson and Yosef Lapid, eds, *Identities, Borders and Orders*, Minneapolis: University of Minnesota Press, 2001, 93–136.

—— "Security and Immigration: Towards a Governmentality of Unease," *Alternatives/Cultures et Conflits*, 27, 2002, 63–92;

—— "International, Political, Sociology," *International Political Sociology*, 1:1, March 2007, 1–6.

—— "Security: A Field Left Fallow," in Andrew Neal and Michael Dillon, eds, *Foucault on Politics, Security and War*, Basingstoke: Palgrave, 2008, 93–114.

—— and Elspeth Guild, eds, *Controlling Frontiers: Free Movement Into and Within Europe*, Aldershot: Ashgate, 2005.

—— and Anastasia Tsoukala, eds, *Terror, Insecurity and Liberty: Illiberal Practices of Liberal Regimes After 9/11*, London: Routledge, 2008.

—— and R.B.J. Walker, "Political Sociology and the Problem of the International," *Millennium: Journal of International Studies*, 2006, 725–40.

—— Sergio Carrera, Elspeth Guild and R.B.J. Walker, "The Changing Landscape of European Liberty and Security: The Mid-Term Report of the CHALLENGE Project," *International Social Science Journal*, 59(192) 283–308.

Blaney, David and Naeem Inayatullah, *International Relations and the Problem of Difference*, New York: Routledge, 2004.

Blomley, Nicholas, *Law, Space and the Geographies of Power*, New York: Guilford Press, 1994.

—— "Law, Property and the Geography of Violence: The Frontier, the Survey and the Grid," *Annals* of *the Association of American Geographers* 93:1, 2003, 121–41

Blumenberg, Hans, *The Legitimacy of the Modern Age* (1966), Cambridge, MA: MIT Press, 1983.

Bobbio, Norberto, *Democracy and Dictatorship: The Nature and Limits of State Power*, translated by Peter Kennealy, Cambridge: Polity Press, 1989.

Bodin, Jean, *On Sovereignty: Four Chapters from Six Books of the Commonwealth* (1576), translated by Julian H. Franklin, Cambridge: Cambridge University Press, 1992.

Bohman, James and Mathias Lutz-Bachmann, eds, *Perpetual Peace: Essays on Kant's Cosmopolitan Ideal* Cambridge, MA: MIT Press, 1997.

Bonditti, Philippe, *L'antiterrorisme aux Etats-Unis 1946–2007: Une analyse fou-cauldienne de la transformation de l'exercice de la souverainete at l'art de gouverner,* Doctoral thesis, Sciences-Po, Paris, November 2008.

Boucher, David, *Political Theories of International Relations*, Oxford: Oxford University Press, 1998.

Bourdieu, Pierre, *Distinction: A Social Critique of the Judgement of Taste* (1979), Cambridge, MA: Harvard University Press, 1984.

Braudel, Fernand, *Civilization and Capitalism, 15th–18th Century*, three volumes, New York: Collins, 1985.

Bredekamp, Horst, "Thomas Hobbes's Visual Strategies," in Patricia Springborg, ed., *The Cambridge Companion to Hobbes's Leviathan*, Cambridge: Cambridge University Press, 2007, 29–60

Bowden, Brett, "In the name of Progress and Peace: The Standard of Civilization and the Universalizing Project," *Alternatives: Global, Local, Political*, 29:1, Jan–Feb 2004, 43–68.

Brodsky Lacour, Claudia, *Lines of Thought: Discourse, Architectonics, and the Origins of Modern Philosophy*, Durham, NC: Duke University Press, 1996.

Brown, Chris, *Sovereignty, Rights and Justice: International Political Theory Today*, Cambridge: Polity Press, 2002.

—— Terry Nardin and Nicholas Rengger, *International Relations in Political Thought*, Cambridge: Cambridge University Press, 2002.

Brown, Wendy, *Politics out of History*, Princeton: Princeton University Press, 2001.

Brunet-Jailly, Emmanuel, "Theorizing Borders: An Interdisciplinary Perspective," *Geopolitics* 10, 2005, 633–49.

Buchan, Bruce "Explaining War and Peace: Kant and Liberal International Relations Theory," *Alternatives: Global, Local, Political*, 27:4, 2002, 407–28.

Buchdahl, Gerd, *Metaphysics and the Philosophy of Science: The Classical Origins, Descartes to Kant*, Oxford: Blackwell, 1969.

Buck-Morse, Susan, *The Dialectic of Seeing: Walter Benjamin and the Arcades Project*, Cambridge, MA: MIT Press, 1989.

Buijis, Govert, "'Que les Latins appellent maiestatem': An Exploration into the Theological Background of the Concept of Sovereignty," in Neil Walker, ed., *Sovereignty in Transition: Essays in European Law*, Oxford: Hart, 2003, 229–57.

Bull, Hedley, *The Anarchical Society*, London: Macmillan, 1977.

—— "The Emergence of a Universal International Society," in Hedley Bull and Adam Watson, eds, *The Expansion of International Society*, Oxford: Clarendon Press, 1984, 117–26.

—— "Justice in International Relations: The 1983–84 Hagey Lectures," Waterloo, Ontario: University of Waterloo Publications Distribution Service, 1984.

—— and Adam Watson, eds, *The Expansion of International Society*, Oxford: Clarendon Press, 1984.

Burawoy, Michael *et al.*, *Global Ethnography: Forces, Connections and Imaginations in a Postmodern World*, Berkeley: University of California Press, 2000.

Burch, Kurt, *"Property" and the Making of the International System*, Boulder: Lynne Rienner, 1998.

Burchell, Graham, Colin Gordon and Peter Miller, eds, *The Foucault Effect: Studies in Governmentality*, London: Harvester, 1991.

Burns, J.H., with the assistance of Mark Goldie, ed., *The Cambridge History of Political Thought, 1450–1700*, Cambridge: Cambridge University Press, 1991.

Burrow, J.W. *The Crisis of Reason: European Thought, 1848–1914*, New Haven: Yale University Press, 2000.

Burton, John, *Systems, States, Diplomacy and Rules*, Cambridge: Cambridge University Press, 1969.

Burtt, E.A., *The Metaphysical Foundations of Modern Science* (1924, revised 1932), New York: Doubleday, 1954.

Butler, Judith, *Gender Trouble*, New York: Routledge, 1990.

—— Ernesto Laclau and Slovoj Zizek, *Contingency, Hegemony, Universality*, London and New York: Verso, 2000.

Butterfield, Herbert and Martin Wight, eds, *Diplomatic Investigations*, London: George Allen and Unwin, 1966.

Buzan, Barry, "Why International Relations has failed as an intellectual project and what to do about it," *Millennium: Journal of International Studies*, 301, 2001, 19–39.

Buzan, Barry and Richard Little, *International Systems in World History: Remaking the Study of International Relations*, Oxford: Oxford University Press, 2000.

Buzan, Barry, Charles Jones and Richard Little, eds, *The Logic of Anarchy: Neorealism to Structural Realism*, New York: Columbia University Press, 1993.

Cairo, Heriberto, "The Duty of the Benevolent Master: From Sovereignty to Suzerainty and the Biopolitics of Intervention," *Alternatives: Global, Local, Political*, 31:3, 2006, 285–311.

Callinicos, Alex, *Social Theory: A Historical Introduction*, Cambridge: Polity Press, 1999.

Caney, Simon, *Justice Beyond Borders: A Global Political Theory*, Oxford: Oxford University Press, 2006.

Canguilhem, Georges, *The Normal and the Pathological* (1966), translated by Carolyn R. Fawcett and Robert S. Cohen, New York: Zone Books, 1991.

Carr, E.H., *The Twenty Years' Crisis, 1919–39*, London: Macmillan, 1939, revised edn 1946.

Cascardi, Anthony, *The Subject of Modernity*, Cambridge: Cambridge University Press, 1992.

Casey, Edward S., *Getting Back into Place: Toward a Renewed Understanding of the Place World*, Bloomington: Indiana University Press, 1993.

—— *The Fate of Place: A Philosophical History*, Berkeley: University of California Press, 1997.

Cassese, Anthony, *Self-Determination of Peoples*, Cambridge: Cambridge University Press, 1995.

Cassirer, Ernst, *Individual and Cosmos in Renaissance Philosophy* (1927), translated by M. Domandi New York: Harper and Row, 1963.

—— *The Logic of the Cultural Sciences* (1940), translated by S.G. Lofts, New Haven: Yale University Press, 2000.

—— "Mythic, Aesthetic and Theoretical Space," translated by D.P. Verene and L.H. Foster, *Man and World*, 2:1, 1969, 3–17.

Castells, Manuel, *The Rise of Network Society*, Oxford: Blackwell, 1996.

Castoriadis, Cornelius, *The Imaginary Institution of Society*, translated by Kathleen Blamey, Cambridge: Polity Press, 1987.

—— *World in Fragments: Writings on Politics, Society, Psychoanalysis, and the Imagination*, edited and translated by David Ames Curtis, Stanford: Stanford University Press, 1997.

Cavallar, Georg, *Kant and the Theory and Practice of International Right*, Cardiff: University of Wales Press, 1999.

Chakrabarty, Dipesh, *Provincializing Europe: Post Colonial Thought and Historical Difference*, Princeton: Princeton University Press, 2000.

Charlesworth, Hilary, "International Law: A Discipline in Crisis," *Modern Law Review*, 65:3, 2002, 377–92;

Chase-Dunn, Christopher, "Interstate System and Capitalist World Economy: One Logic or Two?" *International Studies Quarterly*, 25:1, March 1981, 19–42.

Chatterjee, Partha, *Nationalism and the Colonial World: A Co-opted Discourse*, London: Zed Books, 1986.

—— *The Politics of the Governed: Reflections on Popular Politics in Most of the World*, New York: Columbia University Press, 2004.

Cheah, Pheng and Bruce Robbins, eds, *Cosmopolitics: Thinking and Feeling Beyond the Nation*, Minneapolis: University of Minnesota Press, 1998.

Clark, Grenville and Louis B. Sohn, *World Peace Through World Law*, Cambridge, MA: Harvard University Press, 1958.

Clark, Ian, *Legitimacy in International Society*, Oxford: Oxford University Press, 2005.

Claude Jr, Inis J., *Swords into Ploughshares*, New York: Random House, 1956.

—— *Power and International Relations*, New York: Random House, 1962.

von Clausewitz, Carl, *On War* (1832), translated by Michael Howard and Peter Paret, Princeton: Princeton University Press, 1984.

Cobban, Alfred, *The Nation State and National Self-Determination* (1945), New York: Crowell, revised edn, 1970.

Cohen, Jean L., "Whose Sovereignty? Empire Versus International Law," *Ethics and International Affairs* 18:3, 2004, 1–24.

Cohen, Samy, *The Resilience of the State: Democracy and the Challenge of Globalization*, translated by Jonathan Derrick, London: Hurst, 2006.

Cole, Phillip, *Philosophers of Exclusion: Political Theory and Immigration*, Edinburgh: Edinburgh University Press, 2000.

Collingwood, R.G., *An Essay on Method* (1933), Bristol: Thoemmes Press, 1995.

—— *The Idea of Nature*, Oxford: Clarendon Press, 1945.

Connolly, William E., *Identity\Difference: Democratic Negotiations of Political Paradox*, Ithaca: Cornell University Press, 1991.

—— *The Ethos of Pluralization*, Minneapolis: University of Minnesota Press, 1995.

—— *Why I am not a Secularist*, Minneapolis: University of Minnesota Press, 1999.

—— *Pluralism*, Durham, NC: Duke University Press, 2005.

Constantinou, Costas, "The Beautiful Nation: Reflections on the Aesthetics of Hellenism," *Alternatives: Global, Local, Political*, 31:1, 2006, 53–75.

Crane, Nicholas, *Mercator: The Man Who Mapped the World*, London: Weidenfeld and Nicholson, 2002.

Crang, Mike and Nigel Thrift, eds, *Thinking Space*, London: Routledge, 2000.

Critchley, Simon, *Ethics–Politics–Subjectivity*, London: Verso, 1999.

Cutrofello, Andrew, *Discipline and Critique: Kant, Poststructuralism and the Problem of Resistance*, Albany: SUNY Press, 1994.

Dale, Suzanne McGrath, "The Flying Dutchman Dichotomy: The International Right to Leave v. The Sovereign Right to Exclude," *Dickenson Journal of International Law*, 9:2, Spring 1991, 359–85.

Danto, Arthur C., *Connections to the World*, Berkeley: University of California Press, 1989.

Darby, Philip, *The Fiction of Imperialism: Reading Between International Relations and Postcolonialism*, London: Cassell, 1998.

Das, Veena and Deborah Poole, eds, *Anthropology in the Margins of the State*, Santa Fé: School of American Research Press, 2004.

Dean, Mitchell, *Critical and Effective Histories: Foucault's Methods and Historical Sociology*, London: Routledge, 1994.

—— *Governmentality: Power and Rule in Modern Society*, London: Sage, 1999.

Deleuze, Gilles, *Difference and Repetition* (1968), translated by Paul Patton, New York: Columbia University Press, 1994.

—— *Pure Immanence: Essays on a Life*, translated by Anne Boyman, New York: Zone Books, 2001.

—— and Félix Guattari, *A Thousand Plateaus: Capitalism and Schizophrenia* (1980), translated by Brian Massumi, Minneapolis: University of Minnesota Press, 1987.

De Certeau, Michel, *The Practices of Everyday Life*, Berkeley: University of California Press, 1984.

De Lupis, Ingrid Detter, *International Law and the Independent State*, Aldershot: Gower, 1975/1987.

Der Derian, James, *Virtuous War: Mapping the Military–Industrial–Media–Entertainment Network*, Boulder: Westview, 2001.

Derrida, Jacques, *Edmund Husserl's Origin of Geometry: An Introduction* (1962), translated by John P. Leavey Jr, Lincoln: University of Nebraska Press, 1989.

—— *Dissemination*, translated by Barbara Johnson, Chicago: University of Chicago Press, 1981.

—— "Living On: Borderlines," translated by James Hulbert, in Harold Bloom *et al.*, *Deconstruction and Criticism*, New York: Seabury Press, 1989.

—— *The Problem of Genesis in Husserl's Philosophy* (1990), translated by Marion Hobson, Chicago: University of Chicago Press, 2003.

—— *Politics of Friendship*, translated by George Collins, London and New York: Verso, 1997.

—— "Force of Law: The 'Mystical Foundations of Authority'," in Jacques Derrida, *Acts of Religion*, New York: Routledge, 2002, 228–98.

—— *On Touching – Jean-Luc Nancy*, translated by Christine Irizarry Stanford: Stanford University Press, 2005.

Descartes, René, *Descartes: Philosophical Writings*, edited and translated by G.E.M. Anscombe and Peter Geach, London: Nelson, 1964.

De Saussure, Ferdinand, *Course in General Linguistics*, translated by Wade Baskin, New York: McGraw Hill, 1966.

De Vries, Hent and Samuel Weber, eds, *Violence, Identity and Self Determination*, Stanford: Stanford University Press, 1997

Diez, Thomas, "The Paradox of Europe's Borders," *Comparative European Politics*, 4, 2006, 235–52.

Dillon, M.C., *Merleau Ponty's Ontology*, 2nd edn, Evanston, IL: Northwestern University Press, 1997.

Dillon, Michael, *Politics of Security*, London: Routledge, 1996.

Donnelly, Jack, *Realism and International Relations*, Cambridge: Cambridge University Press, 2000.

Donzelot, Jacques, *The Policing of Families*, translated by R. Hurley, New York: Pantheon, 1979.

Doty, Roxanne, *Imperial Encounters*, Minneapolis: University of Minnesota Press, 1996.

—— "States of Exception on the Mexico–US Border: Security 'Decisions' and US Border Controls," *International Political Sociology*, 1:2, June 2007, 113–37.

Donnan, Hastings and Thomas M. Wilson, *Borders: Frontiers of Identity, Nation and State*, Oxford: Berg, 1999.

Douzinas, Costas and Adam Geary, *Critical Jurisprudence: The Political Philosophy of Justice*, Oxford: Hart, 2005.

Doyle, Michael, "Kant, Liberal Legacies and Foreign Affairs," *Philosophy and Public Affairs*, 12, 1983, 205–35 and 325–53.

—— *Ways of War and Peace: Realism, Liberalism, and Socialism*, New York: Norton, 1997.

Dudziak, Mary L. and Leti Volpp, eds, *Legal Borderlands: Law and the Construction of American Borders*, Baltimore: Johns Hopkins University Press, 2006.

Duhem, Pierre, *Medieval Cosmology: Theories of Infinity, Place, Time, Void and the Plurality of Worlds*, edited and translated by Roger Ariew, Chicago: University of Chicago Press, 1985.

Dupré, Louis, *Passages to Modernity: An Essay in the Hermeneutics of Nature and Culture*, New Haven: Yale University Press, 1993.

Durkheim, Emile, *The Division of Labor in Society* (1893), translated by George Simpson New York: Free Press, 1947.

—— and Marcel Mauss, *Primitive Classification* (1903), translated and edited by Rodney Needham, Chicago: University of Chicago Press, 1963.

Dworkin, Ronald, *Sovereign Virtue: The Theory and Practice of Equality*, Cambridge, MA: Harvard University Press, 2000.

Dyzenhaus, David, ed., *Law as Politics: Carl Schmitt's Critique of Liberalism*, Durham, NC: Duke University Press, 1998.

Easley, Eric S., *The War Over "Perpetual Peace,"* New York: Palgrave Macmillan, 2004.

Easton, David, *The Political System: An Inquiry into the State of Political Science*, New York: Knopf, 1953.

Elden, Stuart, "Terror and Territory," *Antipode* 39:5, 2007. 821–45.

Elias, Norbert, *The Civilizing Process* 1978, revised edn, London: Blackwell, 2000.

Ellis, Elizabeth, *Kant's Politics: Provisional Theory for an Uncertain World*, New Haven: Yale University Press, 2005.

Epp, Roger, "The English School on the Frontiers of International Society," in Tim Dunne *et al.*, ed., *The Eighty Years Crisis: International Relations 1919–1999*, Cambridge: Cambridge University Press, 1998, 47–63.

Escobar, Arturo, *Encountering Development: The Making and Unmaking of the Third World*, Princeton: Princeton University Press, 1995.

Euben, J. Peter, "The Polis, Globalization and the Politics of Place," in Aryeh Botwinick and William E. Connolly, eds, *Democracy and Vision: Sheldon Wolin and the Vicissitudes of the Political*, Princeton: Princeton University Press, 2001, 256–89.

Evans, Peter B., Dietrich Rueschemeyer and Theda Scocpol, eds, *Bringing the State Back In*, Cambridge: Cambridge University Press, 1985.

Euclid, *The Elements*, translated by Thomas L. Heath, Santa Fé, NM: Green Lion Press, 2002.

Fabien, Johannes, *Time and the Other*, New York: Columbia University Press, 1983.

Fasolt, Constantin, *The Limits of History*, Chicago: University of Chicago Press, 2004.

Fenves, Peter D., *Late Kant: Towards Another Law of the Earth*, New York: Routledge, 2003.

Ferguson, Harvie, *Modernity and Subjectivity: Body, Soul, Spirit*, Charlottesville: University Press of Virginia, 2000.

Fitzpatrick, Peter, *Modernism and the Grounds of Law*, Cambridge: Cambridge University Press, 2001.

Flathman, Richard, *Thomas Hobbes: Skepticism, Individuality and Chastened Politics*, Newbury Park: Sage, 1993.

Figgis, J.N., *Studies in the History of Political Thought from Gerson to Grotius*, Cambridge: Cambridge University Press, 2nd edn, 1916.

Flikschuh, Katrin, *Kant and Modern Political Philosophy*, Cambridge: Cambridge University Press, 2000.

Foucault, Michel, *History of Madness* (1961/72), edited by Jean Khalfa, translated by Jonathan Murphy and Jean Khalfa, Abingdon: Routledge, 2006.

—— *The Order of Things* (1966), New York: Random House, 1970.

——, *Society must be Defended: Lectures at the Collège de France, 1975–1976*, translated by David Macey, New York: Picador, 2003.

—— *Security, Territory, Population: Lectures at the Collège de France, 1977–1978*, translated by Graham Burchill, Basingstoke: Palgrave, 2007.

Frank, André Gunder, *Re-Orient: Global Economy in the Asian Age*, Berkeley: University of California Press, 1998.

Franke, Mark F.N., *Global Limits: Immanuel Kant, International Relations and Critique of World Politics*, Albany: SUNY Press, 2001.

Friedman, Thomas L., *The Lexus and the Olive Tree*, New York: Farrar, Strauss and Giroux, 2000.

—— *The World is Flat: A Brief History of the Twenty-First Century*, New York: Farrar, Straus and Giroux, 2005.

Frost, Kevin, *Revisioning Enlightenment: A Critique of Classical Orientation*, doctoral dissertation, La Trobe University, Melbourne, 2001.

Fukayama, Francis, *The End of History and the Last Man*, New York: Free Press,1992.

Fuller, Steve, *Kuhn vs Popper*, Cambridge: Icon Books, 2003.

Gaita, Raimond, *A Common Humanity: Thinking About Love and Truth and Justice*, London: Routledge, 2000.

Galilei, Galileo, *Dialogues and Mathematical Demonstrations Concerning Two New Sciences* (1638), translated by Henry Crew and Alfonso De Salvio, New York: Macmillan, 1914.

Galison, Peter and David J. Stump, eds, *The Disunity of Science: Boundaries, Contexts, and Power*, Stanford: Stanford University Press, 1999.

Gallie, W.B., *Philosophers of Peace and War*, Cambridge: Cambridge University Press, 1978.

Gamble, Andrew, *Politics and Fate*, Cambridge: Polity Press, 2000.

Garber, Marjorie, Beatrice Hanssen and Rebecca L. Walkowitz, eds, *The Turn to Ethics*, New York: Routledge, 2000.

Gasché, Rudolph, *The Tain of the Mirror: Derrida and the Philosophy of Reflection*, Cambridge: Harvard University Press, 1986.

Gates Jr, Henry Louis, ed., *"Race," Writing and Difference*, Chicago: University of Chicago Press, 1985.

Gellner, Ernst, *Nations and Nationalism*, Oxford; Blackwell, 1983.

Geuss, Raymond, *History and Illusion in Politics*, Cambridge: Cambridge University Press, 2001.

Ghanea, Nazila and Alexandra Xanthaki, eds, *Minorities, Peoples and Self-Determination: Essays in Honour of Patrick Thornberry*, Leiden: Martinus Nijhoff, 2005.

Ghosh, Amitav, *The Shadow Lines*, Delhi: Ravi Dayal Publisher, 1988.

Gibler, Douglas M., "Bordering on Peace: Democracy, Territorial Issues and Conflict, *International Studies Quarterly*, 51:3, September 2007, 509–32.

Giddens, Anthony, *The Constitution of Society*, Cambridge: Polity Press, 1984.

Gierke, Otto, *Political Theories of the Middle Age*, translated by F.W. Maitland, Cambridge: Cambridge University Press, 1900.

Gilbert, Alan, *Must Global Politics Constrain Democracy? Great-Power Realism, Democratic Peace and Internationalism*, Princeton: Princeton University Press, 1999.

Gill, Stephen, *Gramsci, Historical Materialism and International Relations*, Cambridge: Cambridge University Press, 1993.

Gillespie, Michael Allen, *Hegel, Heidegger and the Ground of History*, Chicago: University of Chicago Press, 1984.

Girard, René, *Violence and the Sacred* (1972), translated by Patrick Gregory, Baltimore: Johns Hopkins University Press, 1977.

Goetschel, Willi, *Constituting Critique: Kant's Writing as Critical Praxis*, translated by Eric Schwab Durham, NC: Duke University Press, 1994.

Goldman, Harvey, *Max Weber and Thomas Mann: Calling and Shaping of the Self*, Berkeley: University of California Press, 1988.

Goldsmith, M.M., *Hobbes' Science of Politics*, New York: Columbia University Press, 1966.

Gong, Gerrit, *The Standard of Civilization in International Relations*, Oxford: Oxford University Press, 1984.

Goodin, Robert E. and Philip Pettit, eds, *Companion to Contemporary Political Philosophy*, Oxford: Blackwell, 1993.

Goody, Jack, *The Domestication of the Savage Mind*, Cambridge: Cambridge University Press, 1977.

Gray, John, *Endgames: Questions in Late Modern Political Thought*, Cambridge: Polity Press, 1997

—— *Black Mass: Apocalyptic Religion and the Death of Utopia*, London: Allen Lane, 2007.

Gregory, Derek, *The Colonial Present*, Oxford: Blackwell, 2004.

Greener, B.K., "Liberalism and the Use of Force: Core Themes and Conceptual Tensions," *Alternatives: Global, Local, Political*, 32:3, 2007, 295–318.

Gross, David, *The Past in Ruins: Tradition and the Critique of Modernity*, Amherst: University of Massachusetts Press, 1992.

Grosz, Elizabeth, ed. *Becomings: Explorations in Time, Memory, and Futures*, Ithaca: Cornell University Press, 1999.

Grovogui, Siba N'Zatioula, *Sovereigns, Quasi Sovereigns, and Africans*, Minneapolis: University of Minnesota Press, 1996.

——, *Beyond Anarchy and Institutions: Memories of International Order and Institutions* London: Palgrave, 2006.

Guha, Ranajit, *History at the Limits of World-History*, New York: Columbia University Press, 2002.

Guild, Elspeth, *Security and Migration in the 21st Century*, Cambridge: Polity Press, 2009.

Guilhot, Nicolas, "The Realist Gambit: Postwar American Political Science and The Birth of IR Theory," *International Political Sociology*, 2:4, 2008, 281–304.

Gunnell, John, *Political Philosophy and Time*, Middletown, CT: Wesleyan University Press, 1968.

Gurvitch, Georges, *The Social Frameworks of Knowledge* (1966), translated by Margaret Thompson and Kenneth A. Thompson, Oxford: Blackwell, 1971.

Guyer, Paul, *Kant on Freedom, Law and Happiness*, Cambridge: Cambridge University Press, 2000.

Guzzini, Stefano, *Realism in International Relations and International Political Economy*, London: Routledge, 1998.

Guzzini, Stefano and Anna Leander, eds, *Constructivism and International Relations: Alexander Wendt and His Critics* London: Routledge, 2006.

Haas, Ernst B., "The Balance of Power: Prescription, Concept, or Propaganda," *World Politics*, 54, July 1953, 442–77.

Habermas, Jürgen, "Modernity: An Unfinished Project" (1980), in Seyla Benhabib and Maurizio Passerin d'Entreves, eds, *Habermas and the Unfinished Project of Modernity: Critical Essays on the Philosophical Discourse of Modernity*, Cambridge, MA: MIT Press, 1997.

—— *The Philosophical Discourse of Modernity: Twelve Lectures*, translated by F. Lawrence, Cambridge: Cambridge University Press, 1987.

—— "Kant's Idea of Perpetual Peace, with the Benefit of Two Hundred Years' Hindsight," in James Bohman and Mathias Lutz-Bachmann, eds, *Perpetual Peace: Essays on Kant's Cosmopolitan Ideal*, Cambridge, MA: MIT Press, 1997.

—— "The Kantian Project and the Divided West," Part 4 of Habermas, *The Divided West*, edited and translated by Ciaran Cronin, Cambridge: Polity Press, 2006, 113–93.

Hacking, Ian, *The Emergence of Probability*, 2nd edn, Cambridge: Cambridge University Press, 2006.

Hadot, Pierre, *The Veil of Isis: An Essay on the History of the Idea of Nature*, 2004, translated by Michael Chase, Cambridge, MA: Harvard University Press, 2006.

Han, Beatrice, *Foucault's Critical Project: Between the Transcendental and the Historical* (1998), translated by Edward Pile, Stanford: Stanford University Press, 2002.

—— "Foucault and Heidegger on Kant and Finitude," in Alan Milchman and Alan Rosenberg, eds, *Foucault and Heidegger: Critical Encounters*, Minneapolis: University of Minnesota Press, 2003, 127–62.

Hanninen, Sakari, "The Eternal Return of Politics," *Alternatives: Global, Local, Political*, 28:2, 2003, 287.

Hansen, Thomas Blom and Finn Stepputat, eds, *Sovereign Bodies: Citizens, Migrants and States in the Postcolonial World*, Princeton: Princeton University Press, 2005.

Haraway, Donna, *Primate Visions: Gender, Race and Nature in the World of Modern Science*, London: Verso, 1992.

Hardt, Michael and Antonio Negri, *Empire*, Cambridge, MA: Harvard University Press, 2000.

Harries, Karsten, *Infinity and Perspective*, Cambridge, MA: MIT Press, 2001.

Hartog, François, *The Mirror of Herodotus: The Representation of the Other in the Writing of History*, translated by Janet Lloyd, Chicago: University of Chicago Press, 1988.

Harvey, David, "The Spatial Fix: Hegel, Von Thunen and Marx," *Antipode*, 13:3, 1981, 1–12.

—— "Space as a Keyword," in Harvey, *Spaces of Global Capitalism: Towards a Theory of Uneven Development*, London: Verso, 2006, 117–48.

Hashmi, Sohail H., ed., *State Sovereignty: Change and Persistence in International Relations*, Philadelphia: Pennsylvania State University Press, 1997.

Hawthorn, Geoffrey, *Enlightenment and Despair: A History of Social Theory*, Cambridge: Cambridge University Press, 2nd edn, 1987.

Hay, Jonathan, "The Suspension of Dynastic Time," in John Hay, ed., *Boundaries in China*, London: Reaktion Books, 1994, 171–97.

Heidegger, Martin, *Being and Time* (1927), translated by John Macquarrie and Edward Robinson, New York: Harper and Row, 1962.

Held, David and Anthony McGrew, eds, *The Global Transformations Reader*, Cambridge: Polity Press, 2003.

Held, David, Danielle Archibuchi and M. Kohler, eds, *Re-Imagining Political Community*, Cambridge: Polity Press, 1998.

Held, David, Anthony McGrew, David Goldblatt and Jonathan Perraton, *Global Transformations: Politics, Economic and Culture*, Cambridge: Polity Press, 1999.

Helliwell, Christine and Barry Hindess, "The 'Empire of Uniformity' and the Government of Subject Peoples," *Cultural Values*, 6:1/2, 2002, 139–52.

Hengehold, Laura, *The Body Problematic: Political Imagination in Kant and Foucault*, University Park: Pennsylvania State University Press, 2007.

Hennis, Wilhelm, *Max Weber: Essays in Reconstruction*, translated by Keith Tribe London: Allen and Unwin, 1988.

Herz, John, *International Politics in the Atomic Age*, New York: Columbia University Press, 1959.

—— "The Territorial State Revisited: Reflections on the Future of the Nation State," *Polity*, 1:1, 1968, 11–34.

Hindess, Barry, *Discourses of Power: From Hobbes to Foucault*, Oxford: Blackwell, 1996.

—— "Divide and Rule: The International Character of Modern Citizenship," *European Journal of Social Theory*, 1:1, 1998, 57–70.

—— "Divide and Govern: Governmental Aspects of the Modern States System," in Richard Ericson and Nico Stehr, eds, *Governing Modern Societies*, Toronto: University of Toronto Press, 2000, 118–40.

—— "Terrortory," *Alternatives: Global, Local, Political*, 31:3, July–Sep, 2006, 243–58.

——, "The Past is Another Culture," *International Political Sociology*, 1:4, 2007, 325–38.

—— and R.B.J. Walker, eds, *The Cost of Kant*, London: Routledge, 2009.

Hinsley, F.H., *Sovereignty*, London: C.A. Watts, 1966.

Hirshman, Albert, *The Passions and the Interests*, Princeton: Princeton University Press, 1977.

Hirst, Paul, *War and Power in the Twenty-First Century*, Cambridge: Polity Press, 2001.

—— and Graeme Thompson, *Globalization in Question: The International Economy and the Possibilities of Governance*, Cambridge: Polity Press, 1996.

Hobbes, Thomas, *Leviathan* (1651), edited by Richard Tuck, Cambridge: Cambridge University Press, 1991.

Hoekstra, Kinch, "Hobbes on the Natural Condition of Mankind," in Patricia Springborg, ed., *The Cambridge Companion to Hobbes's Leviathan*, Cambridge: Cambridge University Press, 2007, 109–27.

Hoffe, Otfried, *Kant's Cosmopolitan Theory of Law and Peace*, translated by Alexandra Newton, Cambridge: Cambridge University Press, 2006.

Hollis, Martin and Steve Smith, *Explaining and Understanding International Relations*, Oxford: Oxford University Press, 1990.

Honig, Bonnie, "Declarations of Independence: Arendt and Derrida on the Problem of Founding a Republic," *American Political Science Review*, 85:1, March 1991, 97–113.

—— *Democracy and the Foreigner* Princeton: Princeton University Press, 2001.

Honneth, Axel, *Disrespect: The Normative Foundations of Critical Theory*, Cambridge: Polity Press, 2007.

House, Robert, "From Legitimacy to Dictatorship and Back Again: Leo Strauss's Critique of the Anti-Liberalism of Carl Schmitt," in David Dyzenhuis, ed., *Law as Politics: Carl Schmitt's Critique of Liberalism*, Durham, NC: Duke University Press, 1998, 56–91.

Howard, Michael, *War and the Liberal Conscience*, Oxford: Oxford University Press, 1977.

Hunter, Ian, *Rival Enlightenments: Civil and Metaphysical Philosophy in Early Modern Germany*, Cambridge: Cambridge University Press, 2001.

—— "Westphalia and the Desacralization of Politics," in Barry Hindess and Margaret Jolly, eds, *Thinking Peace, Making Peace*, Occasional Paper 1/2001, Canberra: Academy of the Social Sciences in Australia, 2001, 36–44.

—— "The State of History and the Empire of Metaphysics," *History and Theory*, 44, May 2005, 289–303.

Huntington, Samuel, *The Conflict of Civilizations and the Remaking of World Order*, New York: Simon and Schuster, 1996.

Husserl, Edmund, *The Crisis of European Science and Transcendental Phenomenology: An Introduction to Phenomenological Philosophy*, translated by David Carr, Evanston, IL: Northwestern University Press, 1970.

Huysmans, Jef, *The Politics of Insecurity: Fear, Migration and Asylum in the EU*, London: Routledge, 2006.

Ignatieff, Michael, *Empire Lite: Nation Building in Bosnia, Kosovo, Afghanistan*, New York: Vintage, 2003.

—— *The Lesser Evil: Political Ethics in an Age of Terror*, London: Penguin, 2004.

——, ed., *American Exceptionalism and Human Rights*, Princeton: Princeton University Press, 2005.

Inda, Jonathan Xavier and Renato Rosaldo, eds, *The Anthropology of Globalization: A Reader*, Oxford: Blackwell, 2002.

Ingram, David, ed., *The Political*, Oxford: Blackwell, 2002.

International Commission on Intervention and State Sovereignty, *The Responsibility to Protect: Report of the International Commission on Intervention and State Sovereignty*, Ottawa: International Development Research Centre, 2001.

Isin, Engin, ed., *Democracy, Citizenship and the Global City*, London: Routledge, 2000.

——, "City.State: Critique of Scalar Thought," *Citizenship Studies*, 11:2, 2007, 211–28.

Hutchings, Kimberly, *International Political Theory*, London: Sage, 1999.

Jabri, Vivienne, "Michel Foucault's Analytics of War: The Social, the International, the Racial," *International Political Sociology*, 1:1, March 2007, 67–82.

——, *War and the Transformation of Global Politics*, Basingstoke: Palgrave Macmillan, 2007.

Jackson, Robert, *Quasi-states: Sovereignty, International Relations and the Third World*, Cambridge: Cambridge University Press, 1990.

—— ed., *Sovereignty at the Millennium*, Oxford: Blackwell, with the Political Studies Association, 1999.

Jacob, Christian, *The Sovereign Map: Theoretical Approaches in Cartography Throughout History*, translated by Tom Conley, edited by Edward H. Dahl, Chicago: University of Chicago Press, 2006.

Jahn, Beate, "One Step Forward, Two Steps Back: Critical Theory as the Latest Edition of Liberal Idealism," *Millennium: Journal of International Studies*, 27:3, 1998, 613–41.

—— *The Cultural Construction of International Relations: The Invention of the State of Nature*, Basingstoke: Palgrave, 2000.

—— "Kant, Mill and Illiberal Legacies in International Affairs," *International Organization*, 59:1, 2005, 95–125.

—— ed., *Classical Theory in International Relations*, Cambridge: Cambridge University Press, 2006.

James, Alan, *Sovereign Statehood*, London: Allen and Unwin, 1986.

Jameson, Fredric, *The Seeds of Time*, New York: Columbia University Press, 1994.

Jammer, Max, *Concepts of Space: The History of Theories of Space in Physics*, 2nd edn, Cambridge, MA: Harvard University Press, 1969.

Jaspers, Karl, *Kant*, edited by Hannah Arendt, translated by Ralph Mannheim, New York: Harcourt Brace, 1962.

Johnson, David, *The Rhetoric of Leviathan*, Cambridge: Cambridge University Press, 1986.

Jones, Charles, *E. H. Carr and International Relations: A Duty to Lie*, Cambridge: Cambridge University Press, 1998.

Jones, Stephen B., "Boundary Concepts in the Setting of Place and Time," *Annals of the Association of American Geographers*, 49, 1959, 241–55.

Kaldor, Mary, *Global Civil Society: An Answer to War*, Cambridge: Polity Press, 2003.

Kahn, Paul W., *Putting Liberalism in its Place*, Princeton: Princeton University Press, 2005.

—— *Sacred Violence: Torture, Terror, and Sovereignty*, Ann Arbor: University of Michigan Press, 2008.

Kateb, George, *Patriotism and Other Mistakes*, New Haven: Yale University Press, 2006.

Kant, Immanuel, *Critique of Pure Reason* (1781), translated and edited by Paul Guyer and Allen W. Wood, Cambridge: Cambridge University Press, 1998.

—— *Anthropology from a Pragmatic Point of View*, translated by Victor Lyle Dowdell, Carbondale: Southern Illinois University Press, 1978.

—— *Kant: Political Writings*, 2nd edn, Cambridge: Cambridge University Press, 1991.

—— *Practical Philosophy*, translated and edited by Mary J. Gregor, Cambridge: Cambridge University Press, 1996.

Kantorowicz, Ernst H. *The King's Two Bodies: A Study in Medieval Political Theology*, Princeton: Princeton University Press, 1957.

Kaplan, Morton, *System and Process in International Politics*, New York: John Wiley, 1957.

Kayaoglu, Turan, "The Extension of Westphalian Sovereignty: State Building and the Abolition of Extraterritoriality," *International Studies Quarterly*, 51:3, 2007, 649–75.

Keal, Paul, *Unspoken Rules and Superpower Dominance*, London: Macmillan, 1983.

——, *European Conquest and the Rights of Indigenous Peoples: The Moral Backwardness of International Society*, Cambridge: University of Cambridge Press, 2003.

Keene, Edward, *Beyond the Anarchical Society: Grotius, Colonialism and Order in World Politics*, Cambridge: Cambridge University Press, 2002.

—— *International Thought: An Historical Introduction*, Cambridge: Polity Press, 2005.

Keene, John, *Global Civil Society*, Cambridge: Cambridge University Press, 2003.

Keens-Soper, Maurice, "The Practice of a States System," in Michael Donelan, ed., *The Reason of States*, London: George Allen and Unwin, 1978, 25–44.

Kelly, Duncan, *The State of the Political: Conceptions of Politics and the State in the Thought of Max Weber, Carl Schmitt and Franz Neumann*, Oxford: Oxford University Press for the British Academy, 2003.

Kelsen, Hans, "Sovereignty and International Law," *Georgetown Law Journal*, 48:4, Summer 1960, 627–40.

—— *Pure Theory of Law*, translated by Max Knight, Berkeley: University of California Press, 1970.

Keohane, Robert O. and Joseph Nye, *Power and Interdependence*, Boston: Little, Brown, 1977.

Kingsbury, Benedict, "Sovereignty and Inequality," in Andrew Hurrell and Ngaire Woods, eds, *Inequality, Globalization, and World Politics*, Oxford: Oxford University Press, 1999, 66–94.

Kittler, Friedrich A., *Discourse Networks, 1800/1900*, translated by Michael Metteer with Chris Cullens, Stanford: Stanford University Press, 1990.

Kleingeld, Pauline, "Approaching Perpetual Peace: Kant's Defence of a League of States and his Ideal of a World Federation," *European Journal of Philosophy*, 12:3, 2004, 304–25.

—— "Kant's Theory of Peace," in Paul Guyer, ed., *Kant and Modern Philosophy*, Cambridge: Cambridge University Press, 2006, 477–504, at 477.

Knight, David, *Ordering the World: A History of Classifying*, London: Burnett Books with André Deutsch, 1981.

Knorr, Klaus and James N. Rosenau, eds, *Contending Approaches to International Politics*, Princeton: Princeton University Press, 1969.

Knutson, Torbjorn L., *A History of International Relations Theory*, Manchester: Manchester University Press, 2nd edn, 1997.

Kolakowski, Leszek, *The Alienation of Reason*, translated by Norbert Guterman, New York: Doubleday, 1968.

—— *Metaphysical Horror*, revised edn, London: Penguin, 2001.

Kolb, David, *The Critique of Pure Modernity: Hegel, Heidegger and After*, Chicago: University of Chicago Press, 1986.

Korzybski, Alfred, *Science and Sanity: An Introduction to Non-Aristotelian Systems and General Semantics*, New York: Institute of General Semantics, 1933.

Koselleck, Reinhart, *Futures Past: On the Semantics of Historical Time*, translated by Keith Tribe, Cambridge, MA: MIT Press, 1985.

—— *Critique and Crisis: Enlightenment and the Pathogenesis of Modern Society*, Cambridge, MA: MIT Press, 1988.

Koskenniemi, Martti, *The Gentle Civilizer of Nations: The Rise and Fall of International Law, 1870–1960*, Cambridge: Cambridge University Press, 2001.

—— "Kant and International Law," in Barry Hindess and R.B.J. Walker, eds, *The Cost of Kant*, London: Routledge, forthcoming.

Koyré, Alexandre, *From the Closed World to the Infinite Universe*, Baltimore: Johns Hopkins University Press, 1957.

Kramer, Matthew H., *Hobbes and the Paradoxes of Political Origins*, Basingstoke: Macmillan, 1997.

Krasner, Stephen D., *Sovereignty: Organized Hypocrisy*, Princeton: Princeton University Press, 1999.

Kratochwil, Friedrich V., "Of Systems, Boundaries and Territoriality: An Inquiry into the Formation of the State System," *World Politics*, 39:1, 1986, 27–52.

—— *Rules, Norms and Decisions: On the Conditions of Practical Legal Reasoning in International Relations and Domestic Affairs*, Cambridge: Cambridge University Press, 1989.

—— "The Politics of Place and Origin: An Inquiry into the Changing Boundaries of Representation, Citizenship and Legitimacy," in Michi Ebata and Beverly Neufeld, eds, *Confronting the Political in International Relations*, Basingstoke: Macmillan, 2000, 185–211.

Krishna, Sankaran, *Postcolonial Insecurities: India, Sri Lanka and the Question of Nationhood*, Minneapolis: University of Minnesota Press, 1999.

—— and R.B.J. Walker, eds, "Partition," Special Issue of *Alternatives: Global, Local, Political* 27:2, 2002.

—— *Globalization and postcolonialism: Hegemony and Resistance in the Twenty-first Century*, Lanham, MD: Rowman and Littlefield, 2009.

Kristof, Ladis K.D., "The Nature of Frontiers and Boundaries," *Annals of the Association of American Geographers*, 49, 1959, 269–82.

Kuper, Adam, *The Reinvention of Primitive Society: Transformations of a Myth* (1988), London: Routledge, 2005.

Kymlicka, Will, *Multicultural Citizenship: A Liberal Theory of Minority Rights*, Oxford: Oxford University Press, 1995.

—— *Politics in the Vernacular: Nationalism, Multiculturalism, and Citizenship*, Oxford: Oxford University Press, 2001.

Labio, Catherine, *Origins and the Enlightenment: Aesthetic Epistemology from Descartes to Kant*, Ithaca: Cornell University Press, 2004.

Laclau, Ernesto, *Emancipations*, London: Verso, 1996.

Laslett, Peter, ed., *Philosophy, Politics and Society*, first series, Oxford: Blackwell, 1956.

Latour, Bruno, *We Have Never Been Modern*, translated by Catherine Porter, Cambridge, MA: Harvard University Press, 1993.

Lebow, Richard Ned, *The Tragic Vision of Politics: Ethics, Interests and Orders*, Cambridge: Cambridge University Press, 2003.

Lefebvre, Henri, *The Production of Space*, translated by Donald Nicholson-Smith, Oxford: Blackwell, 1991.

Lefort, Claude, *Democracy and Political Theory*, Minneapolis: University of Minnesota Press, 1988.

Lenin, V.I., *State and Revolution* (1918), New York: International Publishers, 1932.

Levin, David Michael, *The Opening of Vision: Nihilism and the Postmodern Situation*, London: Routledge, 1988.

—— ed., *Modernity and the Hegemony of Vision*, Berkeley: University of California Press, 1993.

—— ed., *Sites of Vision: The Discursive Construction of Sight in the History of Philosophy*, Cambridge: MIT Press, 1999.

Levinas, Emmanuel, *Totality and Infinity: An Essay on Exteriority* (1961), translated by Alphonso Lingis, Pittsburg: Duquesne University Press, 1969.

—— *On Escape* 1982, translated by Bettina Bergo, Stanford: Stanford University Press, 2003.

Lewis, David Levering, *God's Crucible: Islam and the Making of Europe, 570–1215*, New York, W. W. Norton, 2008.

Lindahl, Hans, "Sovereignty and Representation in the European Union," in Neil Walker, ed., *Sovereignty in Transition: Essays in European Law*, Oxford: Hart, 2003, 87–114.

Linklater, Andrew, *Men and Citizens in the Theory of International Relations*, London: Macmillan, 1982, 2nd edn, 1990.

—— *The Transformation of Political Community: Ethical Foundations for the Post-Westphalian Era*, Cambridge: Polity Press, 1998.

—— and Hidemi Suganami, *The English School of International Relations: A Contemporary Reassessment*, Cambridge: Cambridge University Press, 2006.

Little, Richard, *The Balance of Power in International Relations: Metaphors, Myths and Models*, Cambridge: Cambridge University Press, 2007.

Locke, John, *Second Treatise of Government*, in Locke, *Two Treatises of Government* (1690), edited by Peter Laslett, Cambridge: Cambridge University Press, 2nd edn, 1967.

Long, David, "Liberalism, Imperialism and Empire," *Studies in Political Economy*, 78, Autumn 2006, 201–23.

—— and Brian C. Schmidt, eds, *Imperialism and Internationalism in the Discipline of International Relations*, Albany: State University of New York Press, 2005.

Loraux, Nicole, *The Divided City: On Meaning and Forgetting in Ancient Athens*, New York: Zone Books, 2002.

Loriaux, Michael, *European Union and the Deconstruction of the Rhineland Frontier*, Cambridge: Cambridge University Press, 2008.

Lovejoy, Arthur O., *Revolt Against Dualism*, La Salle, IL: Open Court Publishing, 1930.

—— *The Great Chain of Being*, New York: Harper, 1960.

Lowe, Donald M., *History of Bourgeois Perception*, Chicago: University of Chicago Press, 1982.

Lowenthal, David, *The Past is a Foreign Country*, Cambridge: Cambridge University Press, 1985.

Löwith, Karl, *Max Weber and Karl Marx* (1932), London: Routledge, 1993.

—— *Meaning in History*, Chicago: University of Chicago Press, 1949.

Lukacs, Gyorgy, *History and Class Consciousness: Studies in Marxist Dialectics* (1923), translated by Rodney Livingstone, Cambridge, MA: MIT Press, 1971.

Luhmann, Niklas, *Observations on Modernity*, translated by William Whobrey, Stanford: Stanford University Press, 1998.

Lynch, Cecilia, "Kant, the Republican Peace and Moral Guidance," *Ethics and International Affairs*, 8, 1994, 39–58.

Lyotard, Jean-François, *The Postmodern Condition: A Report on Knowledge*, translated by Geoff Bennington and Brian Masumi, Minneapolis: University of Minnesota Press, 1984.

McCarthy, James, "Scale, Sovereignty and Strategy in Environmental Governance," *Antipode*, 2005, 731–53.

McClure, Kirstie, "The Issue of Foundations: Scientized Politics, Politicized Science and Feminist Critical Practice," in Judith Butler and Joan Scott, eds, *Feminists Theorize the Political*, London: Routledge, 1992, 341–68.

McCormick, John P., *Carl Schmitt's Critique of Liberalism: Against Politics as Technology*, Cambridge: Cambridge University Press, 1996.

Machiavelli, Nicolo, *The Prince*, edited by Quentin Skinner and Russell Price, Cambridge: Cambridge University Press, 1988.

Mack, Andrew *et al.*, *The Human Security Report*, Oxford: Oxford University Press, 2005.

MacMillan, Ken, *Sovereignty and Possession in the English New World: The Legal Foundations of Empire, 1576–1640*, Cambridge: Cambridge University Press, 2006.

Macmillan, John, "Immanuel Kant and the Democratic Peace," in Beate Jahn, ed., *Classical Theory in International Relations*, Cambridge: Cambridge University Press, 2006, 52–73.

McNeil, William, *The Glance of the Edge: Heidegger, Aristotle and the Ends of Theory*, Albany: State University of New York Press, 1999.

Macpherson, C.B., *The Political Theory of Possessive Individualism*, Oxford: Oxford University Press, 1962.

Magnusson, Warren, *The Search for Political Space*, Toronto: University of Toronto Press, 1996.

Malcolm, Noel, "Hobbes's Theory of International Relations," in Malcolm, *Aspects of Hobbes*, Oxford: Clarendon, 2002, 432–56.

Mamdani, Mahmood, *Citizen and Subject*, Princeton: Princeton University Press, 1996.

Mandelbaum, Maurice, *History, Man and Reason: A Study in Nineteenth Century Thought*, Baltimore: Johns Hopkins University Press, 1971.

Manent, Pierre, *A World Beyond Politics? A Defense of the Nation-State*, translated by Marc Lepain, Princeton: Princeton University Press, 2006.

Manuel, Frank E., *Shapes of Philosophical History*, London: George Allen and Unwin, 1965.

Maor, Eli, *To Infinity and Beyond: A Cultural History of the Infinite*, Princeton: Princeton University Press, 1991.

Maratti, Paolo, *Genesis and Trace: Derrida Reading Husserl and Heidegger*, Stanford: Stanford University Press, 2005.

Marcus, George, "Foreword," to Jutta Weldes, Mark Laffey, Hugh Gusterson and Raymond Duvall, eds, *Cultures of Insecurity: States, Communities and the Production of Danger*, Minneapolis: University of Minnesota Press, 1999, vii–xvi.

Maroya, Alex, "Rethinking the Nation-State from the Frontier," *Millennium: Journal of International Studies*, 32:2, 2003, 267–92.

Marx, Karl, *Capital, Volume 1, A Critique of Political Economy* (1867), translated by Ben Fowkes, London: Pelican, 1976.

Massey, Doreen, *For Space*, London: Sage, 2005.

Mayall, James, *Nationalism and International Society*, Cambridge: Cambridge University Press, 1990.

Maynard, Patrick, *Drawing Distinctions: The Varieties of Graphic Expression*, Ithaca: Cornell University Press, 2005.

Mbembe, Achille, *On the Postcolony*, Berkeley: University of California Press, 2001.

Mead, George Herbert, *The Philosophy of the Act*, Chicago: University of Chicago Press, 1938.

Meier, Heinrich, *Carl Schmitt and Leo Strauss: The Hidden Dialogue*, translated by J. Harvey Lomax, Chicago: University of Chicago Press, 1995.

Meillassoux, Quentin, *After Finitude: An Essay on the Necessity of Contingency*, London: Continuum, 2008.

Meinecke, Friedrich, *Cosmopolitanism and the National State* (1907), translated by Robert B. Kimber, Princeton: Princeton University Press, 1963.

Mendlovitz, Saul H. and R.B.J. Walker, eds, *Towards a Just World Peace: Perspectives from Social Movements*, London: Butterworths, 1987.

Menon, Ritu and Kamla Bhasin, eds, *Borders and Boundaries: Women in India's Partition*, New Delhi: Kali for Women, 1998.

Merleau Ponty, Maurice, *The Visible and the Invisible* (1964), edited by Claude Lefort, translated by Alphonso Lingis, Evanston: Northwestern University Press, 1968.

Mertens, Thomas, "Cosmopolitanism and Citizenship: Kant Against Habermas," *European Journal of Philosophy*, 4, 1996, 328–47.

Midgley, E.B.F., *The Natural Law Tradition and the Theory of International Relations*, London: Elek Books, 1975.

Mignolo, Walter, *The Darker Side of the Renaissance: Literacy, Territoriality and Colonization*, Ann Arbor: University of Michigan Press, 1995.

—— *Local Histories/Global Designs: Coloniality, Subaltern Knowledges and Border Thinking*, Princeton: Princeton University Press, 2000.

Miller, David and Sohail Hashmi, eds, *Boundaries and Justice: Diverse Ethical Perspectives*, Princeton: Princeton University Press, 2001.

Miller, Ted H., "The Uniqueness of *Leviathan*: Authorizing Poets, Philosophers and Sovereigns," in Tom Sorell and Luc Foisneau, eds, *"Leviathan" After 350 Years*, Oxford: Oxford University Press, 2004, 75–103.

Mitchell, Timothy, *Colonizing Egypt*, 2nd edn, Berkeley: University of California Press, 1991.

—— ed., *Questions of Modernity*, Minneapolis: University of Minnesota Press, 2000.

Molloy, Sean, *The Hidden History of Realism: A Genealogy of Power Politics*, Basingstoke: Palgrave Macmillan, 2006.

Mommsen, Wolfgang J., *Max Weber and German Politics, 1890–1920* (1959), translated by Michael S. Sternberg, Chicago: University of Chicago Press, 1984.

Monmomier, Mark, *Rhumb Lines and Map Wars: A Social History of the Mercator Projection*, Chicago: University of Chicago Press, 2004.

Morgan, Dianne, *Kant Trouble: The Obscurities of the Enlightened*, London: Routledge, 2000.

Morgenthau, Hans J., *Politics Among Nations*, Chicago: University of Chicago Press, 1948.

Morris, Christopher W., *An Essay on the Modern State*, Cambridge: Cambridge University Press, 1998.

Morris, Richard, *Achilles in the Quantum Universe*, New York: Henry Holt, 1997.

Mouffe, Chantal, ed., *The Challenge of Carl Schmitt*, London: Verso, 1999.

—— *On the Political*, London: Routledge, 2005.

Nagel, Thomas, "The Problem of Global Justice," *Philosophy and Public Affairs*, 33:2, 2005, 113–47.

Nancy, Jean-Luc, *The Birth to Presence*, Stanford: Stanford University Press, 1993.

—— *The Sense of the World* (1993), translated by Jeffrey S. Librett, Minneapolis: University of Minnesota Press, 1997.

—— *Being Singular Plural* (1996), translated by Anne E. O'Byrne and Robert D. Richardson, Stanford: Stanford University Press, 2000.

—— *Hegel: The Restlessness of the Negative* (1997), translated by Jason Smith and Steven Miller, Minneapolis: University of Minnesota Press, 2002.

—— *The Creation of the World, or Globalization* (2002), translated by Francois Raffoul and David Pettigrew, Albany: SUNY Press, 2007.

Nandy, Ashis, *The Intimate Enemy: Loss and Recovery of Self Under Colonialism* Delhi: Oxford University Press, 1983.

—— *The Illegitimacy of Nationalism*, Delhi: Oxford University Press, 1994.

—— Ziauddin Sardar and Merryl Wyn Davies, *Barbaric Others: A Manifesto on Western Racism*, London: Pluto Press, 1993.

Neal, Andrew, *Exceptionalism and the Politics of Counter-Terrorism: Liberty, Security and the War on Terror*, London: Routledge, 2009.

Neocleous, Mark, "Security, Liberty and the Myth of Balance: Towards a Critique of Security Politics," *Contemporary Political Theory*, 6:2, 2007, 131–49.

Newman, David, "The Lines that Continue to Separate Us: Borders in Our 'Borderless' World," *Progress in Human Geography*, 30:2, 2006, 143–61.

Nicol, Heather N. and Ian Townsend-Gault, eds, *Holding the Line: Borders in a Global World*, Vancouver: UBC Press, 2004.

Norris, Andrew, "Carl Schmitt's Political Metaphysics: On the Secularization of 'the Outermost Sphere'," *Theory and Event*, 4:1, 2000, 27pp.

Norton, Anne, *Leo Strauss and the Politics of American Empire*, New Haven: Yale University Press, 2004.

Nyers, Peter, *Rethinking Refugees: Beyond States of Emergency*, London: Routledge, 2006.

Oakeshott, Michael, "Introduction," in Thomas Hobbes, *Leviathan*, Oxford: Basil Blackwell, 1957.

O'Hagen, Jacinta, *Conceptualizing the West in International Relations*, Basingstoke: Palgrave, 2002.

Ohmae, Kenichi, *The Borderless World: Power and Strategy in the Interlinked Economy*, London: Collins, 1990.

Onuf, Nicholas Greenwood, *Worlds of Our Making*, Columbia: University of South Carolina Press, 1989.

—— *The Republican Legacy in International Thought*, Cambridge: Cambridge University Press, 1998.

Orford, Anne, *Reading Humanitarian Intervention: Human Rights and the Use of Force in International Law*, Cambridge: Cambridge University Press, 2003.

—— "The Destiny of International Law," *Leiden Journal of International Law*, 17, 2004, 441–76.

Ossiander, Andreas, "Sovereignty, International Relations and the Westphalian Myth," *International Organization*, 55, 2001, 251–88.

O'Tuathail, Geroid, *Critical Geopolitics: The Politics of Writing Global Space*, Minneapolis: University of Minnesota Press, 1998.

Pagden, Anthony, *Worlds at War: The 2500-Year Struggle Between East and West*, Oxford: Oxford University Press, 2008.

Palonen, Kari, "Max Weber's Reconceptualization of Freedom," *Political Theory*, 27:4, 1999, 523–44.

—— "Was Max Weber a 'Nationalist'? A Study in the Rhetoric of Conceptual Change," *Max Weber Studies*, 1:2, May 2001, 196–214.

—— *Quentin Skinner: History, Politics, Rhetoric* Cambridge: Polity Press, 2003.

—— *The Struggle with Time: A Conceptual History of "Politics" as an Activity*, Hamburg: LIT Verlag, 2006.

Palonen, Kari and R.B.J. Walker, eds, "Politics Revisited," Special Issue of *Alternatives: Global, Local, Political*, 28, 2003.

Paolini, Anthony J., *Navigating Modernity: Postcolonialism, Identity and International Relations*, edited by Anthony Elliot and Anthony Moran, Boulder: Lynne Rienner, 1999.

Parker, Noel, ed., *The Geopolitics of Europe's Identity: Centers, Boundaries and Margins*, London: Palgrave Macmillan, 2008.

—— and David Blaney, "Elusive Paradise: The Promise and Peril of Global Civil Society," *Alternatives*, 23, 1998, 417–50.

Pedoe, Dan, *Geometry and the Liberal Arts*, London: Penguin, 1976.

Persaud, Randolph B. and R.B.J. Walker, eds, "Race in International Relations," Special Issue of *Alternatives: Global, Local, Political* 26:4, Oct–Dec 2001.

Philpott, Daniel, *Revolutions in Sovereignty: How Ideas Shaped Modern International Relations*, Princeton: Princeton University Press, 2001.

Pichler, Hans-Karl, "The Godfathers of 'Truth': Max Weber and Carl Schmitt in Morgenthau's Theory of Power Politics," *Review of International Studies*, 24:2, April 1998, 185–200.

Pippin, Robert B., *Modernism as a Philosophical Problem*, Oxford: Blackwell, 1991, 2nd edn, 1999.

Plato, *The Republic*, translated by Allan Bloom, New York: Basic Books, 1968.

Pletch, Carl E., "The Three Worlds, or the Division of Socio-Scientific Labor, Circa 1950–75," *Comparative Studies in Society and History*, 23:4, October 1981, 565–90.

Plotnitsky, Arkady, *Complementarity: Anti-Epistemology After Bohr and Derrida*, Durham, NC: Duke University Press, 1994.

Pocock, J.G.A., *The Machiavellian Moment: Florentine Political Thought and the Atlantic Republican Tradition*, Princeton: Princeton University Press, 1975.

Poggi, Gianfranco, *The Development of the Modern State: A Sociological Introduction*, Stanford: Stanford University Press, 1978.

—— *Forms of Power* Cambridge: Polity Press, 2001.

Posner, Eric and Adrian Vermeule, *Terror in the Balance: Security, Liberty, and the Courts*, Oxford: Oxford University Press, 2007.

Prescott, J.R.V., *The Geography of Frontiers and Boundaries*, London: Hutchinson, 1965.

Prokhovnik, Raia, *Sovereignties: Contemporary Theory and Practice*, Basingstoke: Palgrave Macmillan, 2007.

Prozorov, Sergei, "X/Xs: Toward a General Theory of the Exception," *Alternatives: Global, Local, Political*, 30:1, 2005, 81–111.

Rancière, Jacques, *On the Shores of Politics*, translated by Liz Heron, London: Verso, 1995.

—— *Disagreement: Politics and Philosophy*, translated by Julie Rose, Minneapolis: University of Minnesota Press, 1999.

Rapaczynski, Andrzej, *Nature and Politics: Liberalism in the Philosophies of Hobbes, Locke and Rousseau*, Ithaca: Cornell University Press, 1987.

Rasch, William, *Sovereignty and its Discontents: On the Primacy of Conflict and the Structure of the Political*, London: Birkbeck Law Press, 2004.

Rawls, John, *A Theory of Justice*, Oxford: Oxford University Press, 1972.

Reiss, Timothy J., *The Discourse of Modernism*, Ithaca: Cornell University Press, 1982.

Rengger, Nicholas J., *International Relations, Political Theory and the Problem of Order: Beyond International Relations Theory?* London: Routledge, 2000.

Ricoeur, Paul, "The Political Paradox, in *History and Truth*," translated by Charles A Kelbley, Evanston IL, Northwestern University Press, 1965, 247–70.

—— "The Teleological and Deontological Structures of Action: Aristotle and/or Kant?" in A. Phillips Griffiths, ed., *Contemporary French Philosophy*, Cambridge: Cambridge University Press, 1987, 99–112.

Riley, Patrick, *Kant's Political Philosophy*, Rowman and Littlefield,1982.

Rorty, Richard, *Philosophy and the Mirror of Nature*, Princeton: Princeton University Press, 1979.

Rose, Nikolas, *Powers of Freedom: Reframing Political Thought*, Cambridge: Cambridge University Press, 1999.

Rosecrance, Richard, *Action and Reaction in World Politics: International Systems in Perspective*, Boston: Little Brown, 1963.

Rosenau, James, N., *The United Nations in a Turbulent World*, Boulder: Lynne Rienner, 1992.

—— *Along the Domestic–Foreign Frontier: Exploring Governance in a Turbulent World*, Cambridge: Cambridge University Press, 1997.

Rostow, W.W., *The Stages of Economic Growth: A Non-Communist Manifesto*, Cambridge: Cambridge University Press,1960.

Ruggie, John G., "Territoriality and Beyond: Problematizing Modernity in International Relations," *International Organization*, 47,Winter 1993, 139–64.

Sack, Robert David, *Conceptions of Space in Social Thought: A Geographic Perspective*, London: Macmillan, 1980.

Saïd, Edward, *Orientalism*, New York: Pantheon, 1978.

—— *Culture and Imperialism*, New York: Alfred A. Knopf, 1993.

Sallis, John, *Delimitations: Phenomenology and the End of Metaphysics*, 2nd expanded edn, Bloomington, IN: Indiana University Press, 1995.

Salter, Mark, *Barbarians and Civilization in International Relations*, London: Zed Books, 2002.

Saner, Hans, *Kant's Political Thought: Its Origins and Development* (1967), translated by E.B. Ashton, Chicago: University of Chicago Press, 1973.

Sassen, Saskia, *Territory, Authority, Rights: From Medieval to Global Assemblages*, Princeton: Princeton University Press, 2006.

Scheuerman, William E., *Between the Norm and the Exception: The Frankfurt School and the Rule of Law*, Cambridge, MA: MIT Press, 1994.

—— "The Unholy Alliance of Carl Schmitt and Friedrick A. Hayek," *Constellations*, 4:2, 1997, 172–88.

—— *Carl Schmitt: The End of Law*, Lanham, MD: Rowman and Littlefield, 1999.

—— Carl Schmitt and Hans Morgenthau: "Realism and Beyond," in Michael C. Williams, ed., *Realism Reconsidered: The Legacy of Hans J. Morgenthau in International Relations*, Oxford: Oxford University Press, 2007, 62–92.

Schick, Irvin C., *The Erotic Margin: Sexuality and Spatiality in Alterist Discourse*, New York: Verso, 1999.

Schmidt, Denis J., *The Ubiquity of the Finite: Hegel, Heidegger and the Entitlements of Philosophy*, Cambridge, MA: MIT Press, 1988.

Schmitt, Brian C., *The Political Discourse of Anarchy: A Disciplinary History of International Relations*, Albany: SUNY Press, 1998.

Schmitt, Carl, *Political Theology: Four Chapters on the Concept of Sovereignty* (1922/34), translated by Charles Schwab, Cambridge, MA: MIT Press, 1985.

—— *The Concept of the Political* (1932) translated with an Introduction by George Schwab and new Foreword by Tracy Strong, Chicago: University of Chicago Press, 1996.

—— *The Nomos of the Earth in the International Law of the Jus Publicum Europaeum* (1950/1974), translated by Gary L. Ulmen, New York: Telos, 2003.

Schneewind, J.B., *The Invention of Autonomy: A History of Modern Moral Philosophy*, Cambridge: Cambridge University Press, 1998.

Scholte, Jan Aart, *Globalization: A Critical Introduction*, London: Macmillan, 2000.

Scott, Alan, ed., *The Limits of Globalization: Cases and Arguments*, London: Routledge, 1997.

Scott, James C., *Seeing Like a State: How Certain Schemes to Improve the Human Condition Have Failed*, New Haven: Yale University Press, 1998.

Serres, Michel, *Genesis* (1982) translated by Genevieve James and James Nielson, Ann Arbor: University of Michigan Press, 1995.

—— *Les Origins de la Géométrie*, Paris Flammarian, 1993.

—— "The Geometry of the Incommunicable: Madness," translated by Felicia McCarren, in Arnold I. Davidson, ed., *Foucault and His Interlocutors*, Chicago: University of Chicago Press, 1997, 36–56.

Seung, T.K., *Structuralism and Hermeneutics*, New York: Columbia University Press, 1982.

Shapiro, Gary, *Archeologies of Vision: Foucault and Nietzsche on Seeing and Saying*, Chicago: University of Chicago Press, 2003.

Shapiro, Michael J., *Violent Cartographies: Mapping Cultures of War*, Minneapolis: University of Minnesota Press, 1997.

—— *Cinematic Political Thought: Narrating Race, Nation and Gender*, Edinburgh: University of Edinburgh Press, 1999.

—— *Methods and Nations: Cultural Governance and the Indigenous Subject*, New York: Routledge, 2004.

—— *Cinematic Geopolitics*, London: Routledge, 2008

—— and Hayward Alker, eds, *Challenging Boundaries*, Minneapolis: University of Minnesota Press, 1996.

Shaw, Karena, "Indigeneity and the International," *Millennium: Journal of International Studies*, 31:1, 2002, 55–81.

—— *Indigeneity and Political Theory: Sovereignty and the Limits of the Political*, London: Routledge, 2008.

Shildrick, Margrit, *Leaky Bodies and Boundaries: Feminism, Postmodernism and Bio Ethics*, London: Routledge, 1997.

Shinoda, Hideaki, *Re-Examining Sovereignty: From Classical Theory to the Golden Age*, London: Macmillan and New York: St Martin's Press, 2000.

Simpson, Gerry, *Great Powers and Outlaw States*, Cambridge: Cambridge University Press, 2004.

Singer, J. David, "The Levels of Analysis Problem in International Relations," *World Politics*, 14:1, 1961, 77–92.

Singer, Peter, *One World: The Ethics of Globalization*, New Haven: Yale University Press, 2002.

Skidelsky, Edward, *Ernst Cassirer: The Last Philosopher of Culture*, Princeton: Princeton University Press, 2008.

Skinner, Quentin, *The Foundations of Modern Political Thought*, two volumes, Cambridge: Cambridge University Press, 1978,

—— "The State," in T. Ball, J. Farr and R. Hanson, eds, *Political Innovation and Conceptual Change* Cambridge: Cambridge University Press, 1989, 89–131.

—— *Reason and Rhetoric in the Philosophy of Hobbes*, Cambridge: Cambridge University Press, 1996.

—— *Visions of Politics, III, Hobbes and Civil Science*, Cambridge: Cambridge University Press, 2002.

—— "Hobbes on Persons, Authors and Representatives," in Patricia Springborg, ed., *The Cambridge Companion to Hobbes's Leviathan*, Cambridge: Cambridge University Press, 2007, 157–80.

—— *Hobbes and Republican Liberty*, Cambridge: Cambridge University Press, 2008.

Slaughter, Anne-Marie, *A New World Order*, Princeton: Princeton University Press, 2004.

Smith, Anthony, *The Ethnic Origins of Nations*, Oxford: Blackwell, 1986.

—— *Nationalism and Modernism*, London: Routledge, 1998.

Smith, Tony, *A Pact With the Devil: Washington's Bid for World Supremacy and the Betrayal of the American Promise*, New York: Routledge, 2007.

Smith, Steve, "Alternative and Critical Perspectives," in Michael Brecher and Frank P. Harvey, eds, *Millennial Reflections on International Studies*, Ann Arbor: University of Michigan Press, 2002, 195–208.

Snyder, John P., *Flattening the Earth: Two Thousand Years of Map Projections*, Chicago: University of Chicago Press, 1993.

Sorabji, Richard, *Time, Creation, and the Continuum: Theories in Antiquity and the Early Middle Ages*, Ithaca: Cornell University Press, 1983.

Sorel, Georges, *Reflections on Violence* (1908), edited by Jeremy Jennings, Cambridge: Cambridge University Press, 1999.

Sparke, Matt, *In the Space of Theory: Postfoundational Geographies of the Nation-State*, Minneapolis: University of Minnesota Press, 2005.

Spivak, Gayatri C., *A Critique of Postcolonial Reason: Toward a History of the Vanishing Present*, Cambridge, MA: Harvard University Press, 1999.

—— "Can the Subaltern Speak?" in Patrick Williams and Laura Chrisman, eds, *Colonial Discourse and Post-Colonial Theory*, New York: Columbia University Press, 1992, 66–111.

Spruyt, Hendryk, *The Sovereign State and its Competitors*, Princeton: Princeton University Press, 1994.

Starobinski, Jean, *Jean-Jacques Rousseau: Transparency and Obstruction*, translated by Arthur Goldhammer, 1971, Chicago: University of Chicago Press, 1988.

Stankiewicz, W.J., ed., *In Defence of Sovereignty*, New York: Oxford University Press, 1969.

Steiner, George, *Grammars of Creation*, London: Faber and Faber, 2001.

Strauss, David Levi, "Reading Desert Storm: Rethinking Resistance," in his *Between Dog and Wolf: Essays on Art and Politics in the Twilight of the Millennium*, Brooklyn, NY: Autonomedia, 1999, 97–103.

Strauss, Leo, *Natural Right and History*, Chicago: University of Chicago Press, 1965.

Suganami, Hidemi, *On the Causes of War*, Oxford: Clarendon Press, 1996.

—— "Understanding Sovereignty Through Kelsen/Schmitt," *Review of International Studies*, 33, 2007, 511–30.

Taminiaux, Jacques, *Dialectic and Difference: Finitude in Modern Thought*, Atlantic Highlands, NJ: Humanities Press, 1985.

Taylor, Charles, "Interpretation and the Sciences of Man," *Review of Metaphysics*, 25, 1971, 3–51.

Taylor, Mark C., *Altarity*, University of Chicago Press, 1987.

Teschke, Benno, *The Myth of 1648: Class, Geopolitics and the Making of Modern International Relations*, London, Verso, 2003.

Tesón, Fernando R., "The Kantian Theory of International Law," *Columbia Law Review* 92:1, 1992, 53–102.

Thakur, Ramesh, "In Defence of The Responsibility to Protect," *International Journal of Human Rights*, 7:3, 2003.

Thomson, Janice E., *Mercenaries, Pirates and Sovereigns*, Princeton: Princeton University Press, 1994.

Thompson, Kevin, "Historicity and Transcendentality: Foucault, Cavailles and the Phenomenology of the Concept," *History and Theory*, 47:1, 2008, 1–18.

Tilly, Charles, *Coercion, Capital, and European States, AD. 990–1992*, Cambridge, MA: Blackwell, 1992.

Todorov, Tzvetan, *Life in Common: An Essay in General Anthropology* (1995), translated by Katherine Golsan and Lucy Golsan, Lincoln: University of Nebraska Press, 2001.

Toulmin, Stephen, *Cosmopolis: The Hidden Agenda of Modernity*, Chicago: University of Chicago Press, 1992.

Touraine, Alain, *Critique of Modernity*, translated by David Macey, Oxford: Blackwell, 1995.

Tralau, Johan, "Leviathan, the Best of Myth: Medusa, Dionysos and the Riddle of Hobbes's Sovereign Monster," in Patricia Springborg, ed., *The Cambridge Companion to Hobbes's Leviathan*, Cambridge: Cambridge University Press, 2007, 61–81.

Tricaud, François, "Hobbes's Conception of the State of Nature from 1640 to 1651: Evolution and Ambiguities," in G.A.J. Rogers and Alan Ryan, eds, *Perspectives on Thomas Hobbes*, Oxford: Clarendon Press, 1988, 107–24.

Tsoukala, Anastassia, "Boundary-Creating Processes and the Social Construction of Threat," *Alternatives: Global, Local, Political*, 33:2, 2008, 137–52.

Tuan, Yi-Fu, *Space and Place: The Perspective of Experience*, Minneapolis: University of Minnesota Press, 1977.

—— *Segmented Worlds and Self: Group Life and Individual Consciousness*, Minneapolis: University of Minnesota Press, 1982.

—— *Escapism*, Baltimore: Johns Hopkins University Press, 1998.

Tuck, Richard, *Philosophy and Government, 1572–1651*, Cambridge: Cambridge University Press, 1993.

—— *The Rights of War and Peace: Political Thought and the International Order from Grotius to Kant*, Oxford: Oxford University Press, 1999.

Tully, James, *Strange Multiplicity: Constitutionalism in an Age of Diversity*, Cambridge: Cambridge University Press, 1995.

—— "The Kantian Idea of Europe: Critical and Cosmopolitan Perspectives," in Anthony Pagden, ed., *The Idea of Europe: From Antiquity to the European Union*, Cambridge: Cambridge University Press, 2002, 331–58.

Unger, Robert M., *Law in Modern Society: Toward a Criticism of Social Theory*, New York: Free Press, 1976.

United Nations, *Charter of the United Nations and Statute of the International Court of Justice*, New York: United Nations, 1985, www.un.org/aboutun/charter

Urry, John, *Global Complexity*, Cambridge: Polity Press, 2003.

Vatter, Miguel E., "The Machiavellian Legacy: Origins and Outcomes of the Conflict Between Politics and Morality in Modernity," Working Paper, SPS No. 2, Florence: European University Institute, 1999.

—— *Between Form and Event: Machiavelli's Theory of Political Freedom*, Dordrecht: Kluwer, 2000.

Vaughan-Williams, Nick, *Border Politics: The Limits of Sovereign Power*, Edinburgh: University of Edinburgh Press, 2009.

Vernant, Jean-Pierre, *The Origins of Greek Thought* (1962), Ithaca: Cornell University Press, 1982.

Vincent, Andrew, *The Nature of Political Theory*, Oxford: Oxford University Press, 2004.

Vinx, Lars, *Hans Kelsen's Pure Theory of Law: Legality and Legitimacy*, Oxford: Oxford University Press, 2007.

Viroli, Maurizio, *From Politics to Reason of State: The Acquisition and Transformation of the Language of Politics, 1250–1600*, Cambridge: Cambridge University Press, 1992.

Virilio, Paul, *Speed and Politics: An Essay on Dromology*, New York: Semiotexte, 1986.

—— *The Virilio Reader*, edited by James Der Derian, Oxford: Blackwell, 1998

Vander Vyver, Johan D., "Sovereignty and Human Rights in Constitutional and International Law," *Emory International Law Review*, 5, 1991, 321–443.

Von Wright, Georg H., *Explanation and Understanding*, Ithaca: Cornell University Press, 1971.

Waever, Ole, "The Sociology of a Not So International Discipline: American and European Developments in International Relations," *International Organization*, 52, 1998, 687–727.

Waldren, Jeremy, "Security and Liberty: The Image of Balance," *Journal of Political Philosophy*, 11:2, 2003, 191–210.

Walker, Neil, ed., *Sovereignty in Transition: Essays in European Law*, Oxford: Hart, 2003, 87–114.

Walker, R.B.J., "World Politics and Western Reason: Universalism, Pluralism, Hegemony," *Alternatives*, 7:2, 1981.

—— ed., *Culture, Ideology and World Order*, Boulder: Westview, 1984.

—— *One World, Many Worlds* Boulder: Lynne Rienner, 1988.

—— "The Concept of Culture in the Theory of International Relations," in John Chay, ed., *Culture and International Relations*, New York: Praeger, 1990, 3–17

—— "Gender and Critique in the Theory of International Relations," in V. Spike Peterson, ed., *Gendered States: Feminist ReVisions of International Relations Theory*, Boulder: Lynne Rienner, 1992, 179–202.

—— *Inside/Outside: International Relations as Political Theory*, Cambridge: Cambridge University Press, 1993.

—— "Violence, Modernity, Silence: From Max Weber to International Relations Theory," in G. Michael Dillon and David Campbell, eds, *The Political Subject of Violence*, Manchester: Manchester University Press, 1993, 137–60.

—— "World Order and the Reconstitution of Political Life," in Richard Falk, Robert Johansen and Samuel Kim, eds, *The Constitutional Foundations of World Peace*, Albany: SUNY Press, 1993, 191–209.

—— "Social Movements/World Politics," *Millennium: Journal of International Studies*, 23:3, Winter 1994, 669–700.

—— "The Subject of Security," in Keith Krause and Michael C. Williams, eds, *Critical Security Studies: Concepts and Cases*, Minneapolis: University of Minnesota Press, 1997, 61–81.

—— "Multiculturalism and Leaking Boundaries," in Dieter Haselbach, ed., *Multiculturalism in a World of Leaking Boundaries*, Münster: LIT Verlag, 1998, 309–22.

—— "The Hierarchicalization of Political Community," *Review of International Studies*, 25:1, 1999, 151–56.

—— "Citizenship and the Modern Subject," in Kimberly Hutchings and Roland Dannreuther, eds, *Cosmopolitan Citizenship*, London: Macmillan, 1999, 171–200.

—— "Europe is Not Where it is Supposed to Be," in Morten Kelstrup and Michael Williams, ed., *International Relations and the Politics of European Integration*, London: Routledge, 2000, 14–32.

—— "Alternative, Critical, Political," in Michael Brecher and Frank Harvey, eds, *Millennium Reflections on International Studies*, Ann Arbor: University of Michigan Press, 2002, 258–70.

—— "International/Inequality," in Mustapha Kamal Pasha and Craig N. Murphy, eds, *International Relations and the New Inequality*, Oxford: Blackwell, 2002, 7–24.

—— "War, Terror, Judgement," in Bulent Gokay and R.B.J. Walker, eds, *September 11, 2001: War, Terror and Judgement*, London: Frank Cass, 2003, 62–83.

—— "They Seek it Here, They Seek it There: Looking for Politics in Clayoquot Sound," in Karena Shaw and Warren Magnusson, eds, *A Political Space: Reading the Global Through Clayoquot Sound*, Minneapolis: University of Minnesota Press, 2003, 237–62.

—— "L'International, l'imperial, l'exceptionnel," *Cultures et Conflits*, 58, Été 2005, 13–51.

—— "On the Protection of Nature and the Nature of Protection," in Jef Huysmans, Andrew Dobson and Raia Prokhovnik, eds, *The Politics of Protection*, London: Routledge, 2006, 189–202.

—— "The Doubled Outsides of the Modern International," in R.B.J. Walker, João Nogueira and Nizar Messari, eds, *Displacing the International: Essays on the Legacy of Peripheral Politics*, London: Routledge, forthcoming 2009.

Wallerstein, Immanuel, *The Modern World System*, three volumes, New York: Academic Press, 1974–89.

Waltz, Kenneth W., *Man, the State and War*, New York: University of Columbia Press, 1956.

——, "Kant, Liberalism and War," *American Political Science Review*, 56, 1962, 331–40.

Warner, Daniel, "Responsibility to Protect and the Limits of Imagination," *International Journal of Human Rights*, 7:3, 2003.

—— "The Responsibility to Protect and Irresponsible, Cynical Engagement," *Millennium: Journal of International Studies*, 32:1, 2003, 109–21.

Warrender, Howard, *The Political Philosophy of Hobbes*, Oxford: Clarendon, 1957.

Watson, Adam, *The Evolution of International Society*, London: Routledge, 1992.

Weber, Cynthia, *Simulating Sovereignty*, Cambridge: Cambridge University Press, 1995.

Weber, Max, "The National State and Economic Policy," (1895) in *Weber's Political Writings*, edited by Peter Lassman and Ronald Speirs, Cambridge: Cambridge University Press, 1994, 1–28.

—— "Politics as a Vocation," (1919), in *Max Weber: The Vocation Lectures*, translated by Rodney Livingstone, edited by David Owen and Tracy B. Strong, Indianapolis: Hackett, 2004, 32–94.

—— *The Protestant Ethic and the Spirit of Capitalism* (1904–05), translated by Talcott Parsons, New York: Scribners, 1930.

Welsh, Jennifer M., ed., *Humanitarian Intervention and International Relations*, Oxford: Oxford University Press, 2004.

Weiss, Linda, *The Myth of the Powerless State: Governing the Economy in a Global Era*, Cambridge: Polity Press, 1998.

Wendt, Alexander, *Social Theory of International Politics*, Cambridge: Cambridge University Press, 1999.

Whitehead, Alfred North, *Science and the Modern World*, Cambridge: Cambridge University Press, 1926.

Wight, Martin, *Systems of States*, edited by Hedley Bull, Leicester: Leicester University Press, 1978.

—— *International Theory: The Three Traditions*, edited by Gabriele Wight and Brian Porter, Leicester: Leicester University Press for the Royal Institute of International Affairs, 1991.

Wilks, M.J., *The Problem of Sovereignty in the Later Middle Ages*, Cambridge: Cambridge University Press, 1963.

Willey, Thomas E., *Back to Kant: The Revival of Kantianism in German Social and Historical Thought, 1860–1914*, Detroit: Wayne State University Press, 1978.

Williams, Howard, *Kant's Critique of Hobbes*, Cardiff: University of Wales Press, 2003.

Williams, Michael C., *The Realist Tradition and the Limits of International Relations*, Cambridge: Cambridge University Press, 2005.

Wittgenstein, Ludwig, *Tractacus Logico-Philosophicus* (1921), London: Routledge, 1961.

Wolin, Sheldon, *Politics and Vision: Continuity and Innovation in Western Political Thought*, Boston: Little Brown, 1960; extended edn, Princeton: Princeton University Press, 2005.

Wrathall, Mark A., ed., *Religion after Metaphysics*, Cambridge: Cambridge University Press, 2003.

Young, Iris Marion, *Global Challenges: War, Self-Determination and Responsibility*, Cambridge: Polity Press, 2007.

Zedner, Lucia, "Securing Liberty in the Face of Terror: Reflections from Criminal Justice," *Journal of Law and Society*, 32:4, December 2005, 507–33.

Zehfuss, Maja, *Constructivism in International Relations: The Politics of Reality*, Cambridge: Cambridge University Press, 2002.

Zellini, Paolo, *A Brief History of Infinity* (1980), translated by David Marsh, London: Penguin, 2005.

Žižek, Slavoj, *The Parallax View*, Cambridge, MA: MIT Press, 2006.

Index